THE NEW DIRECT MARKETING

How to Implement A Profit-Driven Database Marketing Strategy

Second Edition

David Shepard Associates, Inc.

With Individual Contributions by
Rajeev Batra, Ph.D.
Andrew Deutch
George Orme
Bruce Ratner, Ph.D.
Dhiraj Sharma, Ph.D.
David Shepard

IRWIN
Professional Publishing

Burr Ridge, Illinois
New York, New York

IRWIN
Concerned About Our Environment
In recognition of the fact that our company is a large end-user of fragile yet replenishable resources, we at IRWIN can assure you that every effort is made to meet or exceed Environmental Protection Agency (EPA) recommendations and requirements for a "greener" workplace.
To preserve these natural assets, a number of environmental policies, both companywide and department-specific, have been implemented. From the use of 50% recycled paper in our textbooks to the printing of promotional materials with recycled stock and soy inks to our office paper recycling program, we are committed to reducing waste and replacing environmentally unsafe products with safer alternatives.

Editor-in-chief: Jeffrey A. Krames
Project editor: Rita McMullen
Production manager: Laurie Kersch
Designer: Mercedes Santos
Art manager: Kim Meriwether
Compositor: Wm. C. Brown Communications, Inc.
Typeface: 11/13 Palatino
Printer: The Maple-Vail Book Manufacturing Group

Library of Congress Cataloging-in-Publication Data

The New direct marketing: how to implement a profit-driven database marketing strategy/David Shepard Associates, Inc.; with individual contributions by Rajeev Batra . . . [et al.].—2nd ed.
p. cm.
Includes index.
ISBN 1-55623-809-6
1. Direct marketing—Data processing. 2. Data base marketing. 3. Data base management. 4. Direct marketing—Statistical methods. I. Batra, Rajeev. II. David Shepard Associates.
HF5415. 126.N48 1995
658.8′4—dc20 94-1235

Printed in the United States of America
1 2 3 4 5 6 7 8 9 0 MP 1 0 9 8 7 6 5 4

Preface

In the preface to the first edition of *The New Direct Marketing* we commented on the number of books that had already been published on the subject of direct and database marketing and wondered aloud if the world really needed another one. Of course, we then immediately attempted to justify our existence by arguing that *our* text would treat the more difficult aspects of database marketing—database systems, statistical modeling, and database economics—in more detail than that found in any other book written on the subject of database marketing, and we promised we would do so in a language that nonprogrammers and nonstatisticians could understand.

Well, apparently we kept all our promises. The first edition has been a huge success and we are particularly proud of the fact that *The New Direct Marketing* is widely used in both graduate and undergraduate courses in direct marketing as well as by practitioners in the United States, Europe, Asia, and South America.

Nevertheless, a second edition was required for a number of reasons. First, database technology has advanced considerably in just three short years. Our first edition focused attention on mainframe-based database systems. This second edition covers not only mainframe systems, but client-server systems and PC systems as well. Readers of the first edition will find the chapters on database systems to be either entirely new or substantially revised to reflect the changes that have taken place in this area.

Second, we have three more years of practical modeling experience under our collective belt that we want to share with our readers. This experience is reflected primarily in chapters 15, 16, and 19. Chapter 15 goes into more depth with regard to EDA (exploratory data analysis) and extends the discussion of principal components as a useful tool for data reduction, particularly the reduction of census data for use in response models. It also introduces the topic of product affinity analysis. In Chapter 16 we have attempted to provide the reader with an introduction to the subject of neural networks. The use of neural network algothrims as an alternative to the more traditional regression-based techniques is a hot topic in direct marketing today. Our treatment of the subject is intended to first explain how neural networks work and then compare the results of a neural network solution to the results of a regression solution. In Chapter 19 we share tips for handling the many real-life data processing and management issues you will surely encounter as you attempt to implement your models in a rapidly changing business environment.

Third, the vendor section of the book has been completely updated and enlarged with the latest materials available from both data and software suppliers. This feature of the book has proved to be of exceptional value to new direct marketers who need to understand the range of data and services available to them today.

Fortunately, many of the chapters on statistics and economics did not require revision, so they appear essentially as they did in the first edition.

Finally, we would like to remind our readers that this text is a joint product of its six authors: George Orme, who wrote the opening chapter positioning database marketing in today's integrated marketing environment; Andrew Deutch and Dhiraj Sharma, who wrote the chapters on data and database management systems; Bruce Ratner, who wrote the chapters on statistics, predictive modeling, EDA, and neural nets; Rajeev Batra, who wrote the chapter on classical segmentation; and David Shepard, who wrote the chapters on economics and the role of modeling in a database environment.

Again, a special thanks to our clients—you know who you are—who have lived with us through these last three years as we have jointly tried to expand the boundaries of database marketing applications.

DSA

Contents

Chapter 1

An Overview of the New Direct Marketing

INTRODUCTION

The marketing evolution that began in the mid-1980s is still going. We continue to see companies shift from a strictly *product*-driven marketing emphasis to a much more *customer*-driven emphasis.

We continue to see marketing change its primary concentration from identifying and exploiting opportunistic product "gaps" to a process that goes well beyond mere product advantages, focusing on target audiences, individual customer preferences, consumer demographics, and lifestyles.

We continue to see more and more marketers strive to improve marketing performance by targeting products and services to particular market niches.

We continue to see more emphasis on customer service and customer loyalty programs as ways to strengthen and sustain customer relationships in today's crowded and highly competitive marketplace.

Essentially, we continue to see more and more companies de-massifying their marketing efforts in an attempt to more effectively and efficiently achieve their sales and profit goals.

Back in 1989 in our first edition, we included the following excerpt from Stan Rapp and Tom Collins's book *Maxi-Marketing* because it provided an excellent summary of the new direction that was emerging.[1]

> Every established norm in advertising and promotion is being transformed . . . We are living through the shift from selling virtually everyone the same thing a generation ago to fulfilling the individual needs and tastes of better-educated consumers by supplying them with customized products and services. The shift [is] from "get a sale now at any cost" to building and managing customer databases that track the lifetime value of your relationship with each customer. As the cost of accumulating and accessing data drops, the ability to talk directly to your prospects and customers—and to build one-to-one relationships with them—will continue to grow.

Today, what Rapp and Collins observed has progressed in just a few short years to the point where general business media periodically publish stories about the ways "successful companies are using detailed knowledge of their customers to help them spot sales opportunities."[2]

---

[1]S Rapp and T Collins, *Maxi-Marketing* (New York: McGraw-Hill, 1987).

[2]"Smart Selling . . . How Companies Are Winning Over Today's Tougher Customers," *Business Week*, August 3, 1992, p. 46.

In one particular cover story *Business Week* noted that among the keys to better selling (and marketing) is

> focusing the entire company on its customers [and forging] Electronic Links [that] use computerized marketing and distribution technology to track relationships with customers, make sure the right products get to the right stores at the right times, and make order-taking easy. It all adds up to high-tech *intimacy*. (Italics added.)

Not surprisingly, to properly manage such intimacy and truly take advantage of opportunities in this new age of marketing, marketers will have to understand both the methodology and the economics of database marketing.

In some cases, this means marketers will have to learn what data about their customers is important for analysis and decision making and what is not. They will also need to expand their knowledge of how a database works, including what is involved in storing, accessing, manipulating, and analyzing data and ultimately turning it into valuable, strategic information.

It also means they will have to apply new thinking, embrace new marketing methods, and focus on the strategic implications of using database marketing in today's fragmented and complex marketplace.

That is why we have written this book. Our purpose is not to add to what has already been written regarding the changing marketplace or the database marketing evolution, but to provide a practical guide on how to profitably use database technology and new, innovative direct marketing methods to become smarter, more efficient, and more effective marketers.

As such, it is a handbook for direct marketing companies and users of direct marketing methods.

It is important to note that direct marketing used to be something only direct marketing or direct mail companies did. However, as name and address files were expanded to include huge amounts of marketing information and as companies began to see the potential marketing benefits that would result from building databases of customers and prospects, the scope and technical complexity of the tasks required to implement marketing programs increased dramatically. Consequently, the term ***database marketing*** became a more accurate description of the processes involved, and it has become synonymous with the term ***direct marketing*** among both traditional and nontraditional practitioners.

Yet for many people, the word *database* has a very strong data processing connotation. In fact, although it is true that advanced computer systems, including database management software and powerful computer hardware, are required to implement the most sophisticated database marketing programs, we intentionally chose not to title this book *Database Marketing* in order to emphasize the broader nature of the new direct marketing. Data processing resources are only one part of the new direct marketing equation that, when all parts are working together, can dramatically improve the marketing effectiveness of both traditional and nontraditional direct marketing practitioners.

In this first chapter we define the new direct marketing and discuss its five key components. We also highlight ways in which different types of marketers apply the new direct marketing and provide a framework for using it to develop marketing strategies and programs.

In Chapter 2, we discuss how to gather and use both primary and secondary data to identify customer and prospect profiles.

In Chapters 3 through 9 we outline the key considerations and criteria that must be evaluated to select the best combination of hardware and software for any given situation. We also discuss how to select a database management system and how to decide whether the entire database marketing process should be done in-house or with a combination of internal and external resources.

In Chapters 10 through 15 we discuss the statistical techniques used to analyze data, create and profile market segments, and predict outcomes such as response rates and sales. We also provide sufficiently detailed explanations of the processes, including modeling performance standards, to help marketers not only appreciate the power of the techniques, but also become much better users and buyers of statistical services.

In Chapters 11 through 19, we look at the economics of the new direct marketing and discuss the financial implications of these new methods as they pertain to both traditional and nontraditional direct marketing principles and practices.

Now we need to define exactly what the new direct marketing is and how companies are using it to enhance their marketing effectiveness.

THE NEW DIRECT MARKETING: WHAT IS IT?

The new direct marketing is an information-driven marketing process, managed by database technology, that enables marketers to develop, test, implement, measure, and appropriately modify customized marketing programs and strategies.

To implement the new direct marketing you need to know how to

- Identify and gather relevant data about customers and prospects.
- Use database technology to transform raw data into powerful and accessible marketing information.
- Apply statistical techniques to customer and prospect databases to analyze behavior, isolate relatively homogeneous market segments, and score and rank individuals in terms of their probability of behaving in a variety of predictable ways (responding, buying, returning, paying, staying or leaving, and so on).
- Evaluate the economics of gathering, manipulating, and analyzing data and capitalize on the economics of developing and implementing data-driven marketing programs.
- Creatively act on the marketing opportunities that emerge from these processes to develop individual customer relationships and to build business.

Given the above elements, the new direct marketing is much broader in scope than what has been regarded traditionally as either direct marketing or database marketing.

In the past, direct marketing has been distinguishable from other marketing disciplines because of its emphasis on initiating a direct relationship between a buyer and a seller, a relationship that until recently centered primarily on the exchange of goods and services. Such a relationship, although often beginning with efforts across various channels of communication and media (i.e., TV, direct mail, print, and so on) was almost always fulfilled through only one ***direct*** channel of distribution (i.e., mail order). As such it did not involve any intermediary.

However, in today's marketing environment, with rising costs, crowded supermarket and retail shelves, and overstuffed mailboxes, smart marketers are not just using the new direct marketing to efficiently consummate a sale, they are also using it to build store traffic and identify the most efficient ways to generate leads and sales across multiple communication and distribution channels.

For these types of marketers exchanging information is becoming almost as important as exchanging goods and services. As a result these marketers are implementing programs to develop information about individuals. In some cases, they are establishing ongoing dialogue with customers that go well beyond acknowledging a customer relationship or nurturing customer loyalty. Such dialogues make use of in-package surveys, special questionnaires, opinion polls, and annual tracking studies, as well as point of sale (POS) programs that automatically reward buyers with discounts and special offers while electronically recording what they are purchasing.

Significantly, such dialogues facilitate gathering information of value to both consumers and marketers. For consumers, these dialogues not only provide a mechanism to register preferences regarding merchandise and method of purchase, but also allow them to help mold new products and services based on their interests, lifestyles, and purchase patterns. Additionally, these dialogues enable consumers to continually make known their perceptions and attitudes about a company's products and services. Thus, they offer consumers the chance to play a more active, ongoing role in the buyer-seller relationship and help create a stronger affinity between consumers and companies. For marketers, these dialogues produce more timely and accurate information about usage and buying habits. For example, they enable companies to track individual usage behavior and identify individual purchase habits so marketers can account for a specific product's or brand's share of a consumer's total category purchases.

Consequently, marketers are able to use the information to develop *customized* marketing strategies and programs for *individuals* or small groups of customers and no longer have to settle for one single solution or program to best fit their complex marketing situations.

In addition to capturing information, the new direct marketing also enables marketers to use it more easily. Until now, customer data and product data were usually only "linked" after countless hours of analysis and extrapolation. Even the most sophisticated marketers had a tough time matching product sales and individual customer performance. But now, using the new direct marketing, marketers can first marry product sales and data concerning individual customer attributes and characteristics and then, using statistical techniques such as those discussed in Chapters 10 through 15, develop ways to quantify market size and market demand for products or services.

Significantly, companies that are able to marry such individual customer information on an ongoing basis can more accurately and quickly evaluate opportunities and precisely identify who is buying what, how often, and why. More importantly, they can connect this information to which elements within the market mix are most likely to motivate consumers to switch or stay with a given brand.

Strategically, then, the new direct marketing is based on the premise that not all customers are alike and that by gathering, maintaining, and analyzing detailed information about customers and prospects, marketers can identify key market segments and optimize the process of planning, pricing, promoting, and consummating an exchange between sellers and buyers that satisfies both individual and organizational objectives.

APPLICATIONS AND ADVANTAGES

Lead Grading

One advantage of the new direct marketing is that it allows marketers to know more about various types of customers and prospects and to "grade" prospects by determining, as Lester Wunderman says, if a prospect is willing to buy, able to buy, and ready to buy your goods or services.

A good example of this practice is the way some automotive manufacturers encourage prospects to qualify themselves during the initial stages of the information exchange process. These automotive advertisers often ask prospects to indicate when they are planning to purchase so the sellers can gauge prospects' readiness to buy. They also ask what the consumer is currently driving and how long they have been driving it so the sellers can develop a consideration set—the competitive makes and models the consumer is also likely to be considering aside from the company's particular model(s). Then these advertisers use this information to develop a superior competitive position that not only highlights the benefits of their own makes and models, but also is customized to the prospect's needs and wants.

It is important to note that oftentimes the information companies capture is not only used to grade leads, but also can be used later to reactive leads and target follow-up promotions. In Chapter 2, we describe in greater detail how financial services firms have found that the more they learn about customers and prospects, the better able they are to trigger programs that promote appropriate products to selected audiences at the most opportune times.

Customized Targeting at the Right Time

Another way the new direct marketing can help marketers is by enabling them to reach consumers with the right product and the right offer at the right time.

Negative option book and record clubs illustrate this point well. As a *Wall Street Journal* article explains, some clubs no longer send the same set of options to all members. Instead, as Markus Wilhelm of Doubleday Book Club noted, "Segmentation is the wave of the future."[3] Today both Book-of-the-Month Club and Doubleday customize offers based on a member's previous selections and purchases as well as demographic and lifestyle information captured through previous communications.

Two outcomes are resulting from such customization. First, the clubs are seeing a reduction in attrition because members receive selections better suited to their tastes and interests. Second, members are buying more books.

---

[3]"For The Nation's Troubled Book Clubs, Main Selections of This Year is Change," *The Wall Street Journal*, July 25, 1992, Section B, p. 1.

Thus, customizing by treating different types of members differently not only helps minimize the expense of sending offers that are not appropriate for certain customers or prospects, but also helps enhance the company's relationship because it encourages the customer to feel that "this company understands me and knows what I like, what I am interested in."

New Information and Past Results Help Formulate New Strategies

The new direct marketing is more than just using a marketing database to selectively target offers to customers and prospects; it allows marketers to continually incorporate new information and results back into the database.

Marketers record each response in the database so they can develop future strategies and executions using the collective results of previous efforts. This means companies can allocate marketing resources based on current, up-to-date results that include a comprehensive performance history for each customer.

Consequently, marketers are able to develop highly targeted customer acquisition and marketing retention programs and, more importantly, profitably customize the sequence and flow of marketing communications.

Using the new direct marketing, leading catalogers have found that they can regulate the number of times they promote to a customer. By selectively targeting, they can also *customize* which version of the catalog a customer receives, the complete catalog or a smaller special interest catalog. As a result, they have been able to help offset continually rising costs and maximize profits.

Information Can Drive New Programs and Fuel New Revenue Sources

The new direct marketing can also be used by enterprising third-party marketers to bring together companies and customers.

American Express, for example, created a program that used a bill insert promotion to let cardmembers know that buying a new car has "never been easier" because they could use their American Express cards to charge their down payments. The insert then listed over 25 import and domestic manufacturers where the card would be honored.

The cardmembers were asked to indicate which vehicles they would like to know more about so American Express could arrange for *information* and literature to be sent from the manufacturer. Over 100,000 responses were generated.

Aside from demonstrating how the card can produce qualified leads for automotive manufacturers, this effort also enabled American Express to use the information to identify the characteristics of cardmembers who were interested in certain types of cars. Using statistical modeling, they were able to create profiles of who responded for each type of car and then segment their entire file accordingly.

As a result, American Express can now develop cooperative marketing programs with key manufacturers to help them target promotions to American Express cardmembers who will most likely respond and to provide special incentives to charge the down payment for their new purchase on the American Express card.

This is an excellent example of how using the new direct marketing can help everyone win. Consumers win because they can conveniently choose which cars they want to know more about. The automotive manufacturers win because they receive qualified leads. American Express wins because card usage expands when the number of places that honor the card and the number of ways cardmembers can use the card increase.

Information Can Foster New Services and Generate Repeat Orders

Another way companies are using the new direct marketing is to develop special "services" to help make it easy for customers to buy more, more often.

For example, some catalog companies now assign customers a unique customer ID number so each time they call or place an order customer service representatives can easily and quickly access the customer's record and avoid asking for the same information over and over again.

Not only can marketers use their promotion history and information about products purchased to customize cross-selling opportunities, but also they can use previous purchases as the basis for offering customers a new service, as some gift catalogers have. A leading food cataloger, a well-known fruit cataloger, and a Maine holiday wreath company all send last year's gift list, including the special message associated with each gift, to customers to help them conveniently send the same gifts the following year. For many consumers the receipt of last year's list reminds them to place their order again, and they oftentimes add new names before the revised list is sent back.

Thus, with one well-targeted and service-oriented promotion effort, these companies capture more business and differentiate themselves from other competitors in their category.

Ongoing Communication Efforts Can Increase Customer Loyalty

For many companies another major advantage of the new direct marketing is that it offers the ability to establish a two-way communication with the consumer through a variety of channels. As noted earlier, the purpose of such communication is not only to generate a sale, but also to manage a relationship and develop greater customer allegiance and brand loyalty.

Engendering customer loyalty has become vital to many companies. Good customers are too valuable and too hard to find for companies to risk losing one by being passive, indifferent, or indistinguishable from the competition.

Bob Stone, in his classic book *Successful Direct Marketing,* points out that the heart of building and maintaining customer loyalty is *customized persuasion.*[4] Based on the premise that all customers are not created equal—approximately 80 percent of all repeat business for goods and services comes from 20 percent of a customer base—proponents of customer loyalty programs target specific marketing efforts to the most fertile 20 percent of their database.

It is interesting to note, from an historical perspective, that although book clubs such as Book-of-the-Month Club and the Literary Guild have been offering dividend or bonus points as a means of rewarding purchases for as long as anyone can remember, airlines were among the first nontraditional direct marketers to recognize the opportunity to provide rewards to help retain the loyalty of selected customers. They realized

---

[4]B Stone, *Successful Direct Marketing,* 4th ed. (Chicago: NTC Publishing Group, 1988).

that the more a customer purchases their product and the greater the rewards, the greater the incentive for these customers to keep purchasing their product. As a result, airline frequent flyer programs have become the standard in terms of such customer loyalty programs.

And, of course, hotels that are dependent on frequent travelers and repeat business have also initiated similar reward programs.

Other categories of business have also adapted programs for frequent customers. Telecommunications companies such as MCI, AT&T, and Sprint all offer incentives to stimulate usage. In some cases, they also offer special discounts on merchandise for points accrued because of the amount of service used over a given period of time.

Financial service companies have also used rewards to differentiate their credit cards from the pack. Citicorp's Citi-Dollars and the Discover Card's annual percentage rebate on purchases are but two examples.

More recently, some marketers have expanded the scope of their reward programs by forming alliances with other programs. One such program offered by American Airlines and Citibank VISA enables members not only to earn points for each mile flown, but also to earn miles for every dollar a member spends with a special *American Advantage VISA card.* In addition, members also can earn bonus miles for flying certain routes, staying in certain hotels, or renting from certain car rental companies.

Not surprisingly, American Express responded to this joint effort with an alliance of its own, *Membership Miles.* In this program American Express cardmembers not only earn miles for every dollar they spend with the American Express card and bonus miles when they stay at certain hotels, eat at certain restaurants, or rent from certain car rental companies, but, in addition, they can ***combine*** miles earned using the card with miles earned from a *choice* of different airline frequent flyer programs, including Delta, Northwest, Continental, and Southwest.

Significantly, these marketers are learning that, aside from constantly keeping in touch with their members, one of the keys to success is targeting promotions and bonus offers based on previous purchases, buying patterns, and the member's stated preferences. Just as with book clubs' negative option selections that we noted earlier, the customer wants to be recognized as an individual and treated accordingly.

In the future, it will be the companies that can gather, store, and use such information to their competitive advantage by developing new strategies and carefully targeted programs that will benefit the most from the new direct marketing.

Moreover, these companies will develop an ongoing dialogue with their customers and prospects because they know that every contact is an opportunity for an exchange of information and that although a particular effort might not produce a sale itself, the cumulative effect of such communications definitely has an impact on consumer attitudes and loyalty. Thus, managing the communications mix and developing different customer contact strategies for different types of customers has become an important element in the new direct marketing.

SUMMARY

Over the years, regardless of whether marketers operated in a direct marketing environment or the mass marketing arena, one of their major responsibilities has been to develop strategies utilizing products or services that offer the best opportunity of achieving a company's overall business goals.

Today, in an information marketing environment, marketers can execute this responsibility with more precision than ever before. Marketers are analyzing more relevant and timely customer-level information. They are correlating customer-level data with traditional measure of off-the-shelf purchases. They are creating ongoing customer dialogues to funnel relevant information to the marketing database. They are enhancing their databases with survey, demographic, psychographic, and lifestyle data. They are using highly sophisticated mathematical segmentation and predictive models. They are identifying who is buying what, and how often. They are measuring which elements within the marketing mix motivate consumers to make a purchase decision to switch or stay with a given brand. In short, today's information-driven marketers have all the tools necessary to develop new products and new marketing strategies in ways unheard of just a few years ago.

It is important to note, however, that although marketers have access to more powerful tools and more information than ever before, growing consumer sensitivities regarding the misuse of such information seriously threaten future practices.

Consequently, although it seemed just a few years ago that the new direct marketing would only improve sales as more companies came to understand the power of the marketing database in an information-driven economy, today database marketers must find a way to decelerate the growing perception that their activities invade people's "right to privacy" if they are going to be truly successful in the 1990s.

Chapter 2

Sources of Marketing Data

The new direct marketing requires vast amounts of data from a variety of sources: internally developed customer data and externally acquired geodemographic, attitudinal, lifestyle, financial, and survey data. All these data sources are critical elements of the new direct marketing. Data makes it possible to identify the characteristics associated with our best, worst, and marginal customers. Data provides the basis for segmenting customers into relatively homogeneous groups with similar characteristics, attitudes, or needs. Data is the key to all predictive models. Data is essential to identifying people on prospect files and on rented lists with characteristics similar to those of our best customers.

TRANSACTION-DRIVEN CUSTOMER AND PROSPECT DATA

Customer performance data, which includes all sales and promotion activity that has occurred as a result of the customer's relationship with a company, is, of course, the most important data that direct marketers have about their customers. Examples of this type of data are shown in Figure 6–4 in Chapter 6.

Customer Performance Data

Direct marketers have consistently found that customer performance data, obtained directly from *transaction* records, is the most relevant data when it comes to building reliable predictive models. Key performance measures such as recency, frequency, and monetary value data are no less important in the new direct marketing than they were in classical or traditional direct marketing. But in the new direct marketing these data elements are combined in new ways with additional data sources that enable direct marketers to be more efficient and more profitable.

Chapters 2 through 9 should be read together. Chapter 2 discusses data, what it is, and how it is gathered and organized. Chapters 3 through 9 focus on how customer data gets into the marketing database, how it is used in the modeling process, how model scores are used to select customers and prospects from the database, and how the database is used to analyze promotion results. Remember, the marketing data base itself is a tool—it is the engine that makes the new direct marketing possible. But data is the fuel that provides the marketing database with its power.

Although performance data is the most important type of data we have about customers, it is not available in equal measure for all customers. The database will have a much richer data history for older customers than for new customers. Accordingly, many direct marketers find it advantageous to calculate new data elements that make it easier to compare all their customers without regard to the length of time that customers have been on the file. Typically, these data elements include such measures as total number and value of purchases divided by months on file. Chapter 6 describes these data elements in greater detail.

Prospect Data

Prospects—those people to whom we have promoted in the past but who have not yet purchased from us—have no performance data at all, other than a history of the promotions we have sent.

Interestingly, creating a *promotion history* for prospects has been a relatively recent development primarily undertaken by major mailers. To achieve their information objectives while complying with the ethical guidelines about including outside *rented* names in such a promotion history, marketers have negotiated "multiple-usage" rights to these names and made it clear their intent is to maintain a record of how many times prospects receive which promotions. Not surprisingly, these firms have found it extremely valuable to use such information to more effectively target their mailings.

Other marketers, such as publishers, have found that the cost of maintaining such a history can exceed the resulting gain in marketing effectiveness. More specifically, for a magazine publisher that sends millions of direct mail pieces as part of annual or seasonal promotion efforts to which the only meaningful response would be the purchase of a subscription, there is no meaningful gradation of responses—the prospect either responds or not. For these marketers, creating a promotion history would be cost prohibitive.

Other types of direct marketing situations, such as lead generation, cross-selling, and most back-end marketing activities, in which marketers are developing and managing a relationship, often have numerous levels of communication with prospects during the conversion process. For these activities it is critical to track who has received which communications and when.

In Chapter 1, we mentioned how automobile companies use information exchanges with customers and prospects to grade leads and customize communications accordingly. Now consider the case of a financial services firm that is generating leads for a variety of investment programs. Some leads or prospects who are actually interested in the programs offered may not be able to invest their funds immediately. In this situation, the financial services marketer may have to make a considerable investment—in both time and money—to nurture the relationship before the prospect can be converted into a customer. The dialogue between the financial services firm and the prospect may begin as the result of direct mail; direct response media such as print, broadcast, or free standing insert (FSI); or word of mouth passed along by satisfied customers. Once the dialogue has been established, the marketer can use the promotional process to nurture the relationship with the prospect. If used strategically, this dialogue may include gathering data about the prospect through surveys that will contribute to conversion at a later date. For example, during the relationship-building or "courtship" process, the marketer may learn through surveys that the prospect has a child who will enter college in two years. The marketer can instruct the database to contact the prospect with an appropriate message at that time.

Additionally, the marketer may use the promotional dialogue to learn about the prospect's savings and investment goals so promotions for the right products can be sent to the right prospects at the right time.

In packaged goods businesses, a customer may initiate a similar dialogue by responding via an in-store display, a rebate coupon, in-pack or on-pack surveys, or direct response media opportunities. Once the customer has responded, the manufacturer can use the information to develop programs intended to nurture customer loyalty and maintain or increase share.

Thus, in applying the new direct marketing, all information is potentially important, not just the types of data previously associated only with postacquisition customer performance. Hence, data gathering is an ongoing process, which oftentimes begins prior to a purchase, and we must pay careful attention to how we communicate to customers and prospects, when we communicate with them, and what data we attempt to capture at each stage of the relationship-building process.

DIRECTLY SUPPLIED AND EXTERNALLY ACQUIRED DATA

In addition to data from transactions, two other sources of data are critically important to the new direct marketing:

1. Data that is provided directly by individuals (customers, prospects, and even nonprospects) about themselves.
2. Data about customers and prospects that is purchased from third-party sources.

For the purposes of this book, we have divided purchased data into four main types—demographic, attitudinal, lifestyle, and financial. Although social scientists use a number of complex taxonomies to classify data by type and therefore may disagree with the classification used in this text, we find that marketers generally consider it appropriate for working purposes. One reason for our use of this classification is that it describes the types of data that can be purchased commercially and appended to customer and prospect files. Therefore, we consider our taxonomy of purchased data practical and workable for marketers. Appendix B includes listings of the data elements that appear in a number of the major commercially available databases. Certainly other databases exist and you can consult the Direct Marketing Association for a more complete census of data suppliers. However, the listings provided give a very good idea of the data overlay sources and the enhancement data available.

DIRECTLY SUPPLIED DATA

Directly supplied data consists of data obtained directly from customers, prospects, or suspects.[1] It is generally captured from lead-generation questionnaires, customer surveys, interviews, focus groups, or other direct interactions with individuals. The use of directly supplied data has increased dramatically over the past few years, and with the advent of bar code scanners, home shopping, interactive television, and other

[1]Suspects are people who marketers think may be interested in products but who are not yet being actively promoted.

electronic media, the number of channels through which data can be collected directly from customers and prospects will increase exponentially.

Directly supplied data consist of three major types:

- ***Demographic*** data such as age, income, education level, marital status, sex or gender, home ownership, and so on.
- ***Attitudinal*** data showing attitudes about products, including desired features, unmet needs, and psychographic barriers to purchase, as well as attitudes concerning lifestyles, social and personal values, opinions, and the like.
- ***Behavioral*** data such as purchase and buying habits, brand preferences, and product and brand usage.

In the past, this type of data was often the province of market research, and marketers used it primarily to provide direction for programs that addressed large groups of customers and prospects. Market research used demographic and behavioral data to get a better "fix" on the characteristics of a market segment and attitudinal data to provide a sense of which issues were important to various groups of customers and therefore should be emphasized in promotional materials.

Market researchers use directly supplied data to identify new product opportunities or new segments within the marketplace. This is usually done by sending product research surveys to a representative sample of customers or prospects to determine what products and services they are interested in but do not currently purchase from the firm sending the questionnaire.

Although the data gathered by market research surveys has always been valuable for the strategic direction and product development guidance it provides, in the past it has had certain limitations for database marketing. That is, although market researchers for a financial services firm could tell their marketing counterparts that 20 percent of the company's prospects were males between 40 and 45 years old who earn between $50,000 and $75,000 and are interested in investing in mutual funds, they were unable to identify the specific individuals who comprised the 20 percent. So although the information about the firm's prospects was important because it described a fairly large segment within the file, it did not provide an opportunity for promotion because the individuals whose characteristics matched the desired profile could not be identified by name.

More recently, however, as improved database technology enables companies to capture and manipulate large amounts of individual-level data cost effectively, the value of surveys has expanded beyond market research and has become an increasingly important component of the mainstream marketing process.

Perhaps a more important reason for this trend is the recognition that nontargeted mailings are becoming increasingly expensive and hence strategies to decrease the cost per order are essential. Marketers in a wide variety of businesses who collect data about customers and prospects, at the individual level can include this data as a central component of the market segmentation process.

Collecting and Using Directly Supplied Data Via Surveys

There is an old Vaudeville routine in which one character makes a series of requests of another. Each request is increasingly unreasonable. When the other character finally says no, and states that the request is unreasonable, the first character shrugs his shoulders, turns to the audience and says, "It doesn't hurt to ask."

Many companies, perhaps fearing a negative reaction by customers and prospects, are reluctant to ask the questions that are most important for improving their business and their customer service. In adhering to ethical and legal standards when asking questions of their customers and prospects and taking care to ask those questions in inoffensive ways, many companies fail to ask the questions they really care most about. Companies that do ask the critical questions are often surprised to learn just how willing customers and prospects are to provide information about themselves. This is especially true when the surveys are viewed as part of a plan to improve customer service.

Thus, the goal for companies that use surveys should be to capture relevant information about customers and prospects that will help increase sales and profitability while positioning the requests as being of primary benefit to the audience. As such the survey should be developed from the *customer perspective* and should be perceived as nonintrusive and adding value to the relationship. It is also important to assure customers and prospects that their responses will be confidential and will not be used for purposes other than those stated.

Data Requested Differ by Industry

Financial services marketers. Financial services marketers typically want to know the customer or prospect's

- Age
- Income
- Home owner status
- Home value
- Household composition
- Occupation
- Employment status

Major life stage changes, such as retirement, job changes, buying a new home, or children entering or finishing college, may require or create different financial services needs.

In addition, financial services marketers may wish to know attitudinal and behavioral information, such as what other financial services products the customer or prospect owns, how satisfied she is with those products, and her intention to buy other products over the next 12 months.

For investment product marketers it is particularly valuable to know

- If the customer or prospect owns fixed-term investment instruments (such as CDs).
- When the instruments will mature.
- The level of funds they will release.
- The investment objectives the customer or prospect has for such funds.

Each of these pieces of information can help companies define which promotions for which products are most appropriate to the interests and needs of the target audience.

Examples of questions asked by financial services marketers. Attitudinal information, such as the amount of risk an investor is willing to take and information about investment objectives, such as sheltering income from taxes or producing guaranteed monthly income, is critically important if targeted marketing efforts are to be successful for financial services marketers. Therefore, they tend to ask attitudinal questions like these:

- How do you feel about investing through the mail?
- What is your tolerance for risk?
- How do you decide to make a particular investment?
- How do you keep informed?
- What is your opinion about banks, stockbrokers, insurance agents?

Financial services marketers also use behavioral questions to get at decisions that have actually been made, such as these:

- Are you currently invested in stocks, bonds, mutual funds, real estate?
- Do you use a stockbroker or investment adviser or subscribe to financial newsletters?

And, of course, demographic questions elicit information about age, income, occupation, wealth, and so forth.

Negative option businesses. Many negative option businesses, such as book or record clubs, have traditionally treated all their customers the same once the customers became "members" of the club. That is, they sent announcements with the same frequency and used promotional materials that were identical or nearly identical, differing only in the cover or lead selection offered.

However, as we mentioned in Chapter 1, companies such as the Doubleday Book and Record Club and the Book-of-the-Month Club are beginning to take advantage of today's desktop publishing and database software technology to vary the promotion frequency, enclosure materials, or catalogs based on customers' stated interests, prior purchase behavior, returns, credit level, and so on.

This type of customization and selective fulfillment, driven by information in the marketing database, can include modifying the basic offer from *negative option* to *positive option.* (In negative option clubs, main selections are automatically sent unless members return an advance announcement card requesting that the selection not be sent. In positive option programs, members must specifically order merchandise and there are no automatic shipments.) These changes can result in significant profit improvements by reducing the clubs' cost of promotion and increasing the average value and total number of customer orders through increased customer satisfaction.

Moreover, customization can be applied not only to the products included in the company's own promotion materials, but also to the *ride along* or *co-op* promotions that may be included in statements or in the promotion envelopes themselves.

Examples of questions asked by book clubs. For book clubs the survey questions are, of course, quite different than those asked for a financial services marketer. The key information to support such a data-driven program for book clubs would be reading interests, reading habits and preferences, and current and previous book club memberships. Much of this information can be obtained as part of the initial enrollment form or as part of a brief welcome survey questionnaire sent to new members. A book club survey would include questions such as these:

- How many books do you typically purchase in a year?
- How many of these are general fiction and how many are nonfiction?
- In which special categories do you normally purchase?
- Do you enjoy the convenience of the negative option program?
- Would you prefer to be enrolled in a positive option program?

The relevant behavior questions for a book club would include these:

- How many books did you buy last year in a book store?
- Have you previously been a member of a book club?
- If you were previously a member of a book club, what was your primary reason for leaving the club?

The demographic questions for a book club would be similar to those mentioned for financial services marketers, except that they would probably include the highest education level attained.

Using Survey Data: A Case History

Through market research, a direct marketer of insurance products found that the single most important data element for its business was the age of the prospect. If the prospect's age were known, the insurance company could target its promotions and generally send the right *first offer.* A prospect's response to the initial offer began a dialogue in which the company was able to learn about other insurance products the customer owned. With this information the company was able to be more successful in its cross-selling efforts.

To develop a reliable source of age data the company had spent a considerable amount of money and several years testing age data from a number of data vendors. But these efforts were disappointing for several reasons:

- Some age data was estimated rather than actual.
- Coverage was limited to only a portion of the file, because the match rate between the prospect file and the external file was often as low as 50 percent.
- The cost of age data was relatively high when applied to a large number of leads.

Because the insurance company mailed promotions to its entire prospect file *four times per year,* managers decided to include a short survey, with an initial communication that asked prospects their date of birth, what other insurance products they owned (from a limited list), and their level of satisfaction with these products.

The result of including a survey as part of its prospect communications enabled the insurance company to accomplish three goals:

- **Better targeting.** Product promotions could be targeted more appropriately because age, product ownership, and product satisfaction information was acquired directly from prospects.
- **Better mailing efficiencies.** Promotion expenses could be better managed because prospects who did not respond to the survey could now be mailed a different type of offer or could be excluded from further promotion efforts.
- **Reduced dependence on less accurate data sources.** The company avoided relying on purchased data that was both expensive and often inaccurate.

Additional Uses of Survey Results

Another way marketers can use survey results is to exclude prospects who do not respond at all from any future mailings based on the assumption that prospects who are unwilling to respond to a brief survey are unlikely to respond to a product promotion.

Additionally, of course, as noted earlier, marketers can use survey information to better target and regulate who they *should* contact, with what message, and how often.

Using a questionnaire to gather primary data about the target audience is valuable for another reason. Some companies have found that although models may tell us something about a prospect's willingness and ability to purchase based on similarities between the prospects' personal and financial characteristics and those of current customers, models are unlikely to have access to data about the readiness of prospects to purchase. So although predictive models based on internally available data can reduce the target audience and models that include appended data can further improve the base models, the economics of the promotion still may not work because information about readiness to purchase is often unavailable unless marketers have already been in direct communication with customers and prospects. This is where the survey data can be very valuable.

One way of capturing the necessary information is to shift from one-step to two-step promotions in which the first step is an inexpensive, simplified attitude and behavior survey. This approach captures data that helps marketers understand the readiness and willingness of customers to purchase and can also improve the economics of the promotion by limiting the number of expensive pieces that will ultimately be mailed. See Chapters 16 through 19 for examples comparing the economics of one-step versus two-step promotions.

Another benefit of using a questionnaire as the first step in a two-step process is that some of the people who respond but do not initially convert may provide other valuable information about themselves that will help the marketer in future efforts. The marketer can capture this information in the database and instruct the system to mail a promotion piece when the prospect will be ready to purchase or at a "magic moment."

Magic moment marketing, a well-established technique in the insurance industry, is the concept of mailing a life insurance upgrade or cross-sell promotion to policyholders on their birthdays or at a preset number of days prior to policy renewal. The policyholder's birth date and effective dates of coverage are maintained in the database, and the database is instructed to "wake up" and send a certain promotional piece at a preset number of days prior to the event. This is but one example of how an information-oriented communication with customers and prospects can yield valuable results that may extend beyond the promotion at hand.

Although this section describes situations in which modeling alone may be unable to improve conversion performance to the point where it is economically viable, in many situations modeling alone *is* sufficient and the addition of primary data, from an economic perspective, is not necessary. However, as marketing efforts become more and more personalized and marketers attempt to establish and maintain true one-to-one relationships with their customers, including primary data or data directly supplied by the customer or prospect will become increasingly common.

Using Survey Data to Assign Customers and Prospects to Segments

The assumption underlying all segmentation analyses is that a single customer or prospect file consists of a small number of relatively homogeneous market segments and that each market segment consists of individuals whose attitudes toward a company's products or services are similar to others within the same segment but different from those in the other segments. Presumably, if you knew to which segment an individual belonged and the average attitude of that segment toward your product or service, you would market to the individuals within that segment differently than you would market to individuals within other segments. The issues, then, are to (1) confirm that the segments exist, (2) determine the attitudes and characteristics of each segment, and (3) figure out a cost-effective way to assign all individuals on your customer or prospect database to the correct segment.

Once the responses to the survey are received, statistical techniques (see Chapter 15, "Segmentation Analysis," for more information on the techniques themselves) are used to assign all responders to a small number (three to six) of relatively homogeneous segments. If attitude questions are the principal basis for the segmentation, as is frequently the case, then members of each segment have attitudes toward the subject in question that are similar to others within the same segment and dissimilar to those in other segments.

The tradition in segmentation studies is to assign a name to each segment that represents the predominant attitude of the group toward the product or service offered. For example, in financial services analysis, you will likely find such groups as the new-money risk takers, the new-money schizophrenics, and the old-money or hard-pressed savers. As you can tell from this naming scheme, each group's attitude toward investing has been combined with the group's ability to invest to provide a more meaningful description of the group.

As stated earlier, general marketers have used this kind of segmentation study for years to gain insights into the composition and needs of individual market segments. However, for this information to be truly useful for direct marketers, we need a cost-effective technique for assigning all customers or all prospects to the appropriate segments.

Sending a full-blown segmentation survey to everyone on a multimillion-name database is often not cost-effective.

Direct marketers can assign customers or prospects to the appropriate segment in at least two ways. The first method involves analyzing all the questions asked in the survey to discover a relatively small number of questions that do a very good job of assigning individuals to segments. It is not unusual to discover that the answers to 6 to 10 questions can result in nearly the same assignment (70 to 80 percent correct assignment) as the full-blown questionnaire. If this were the case, then it could be cost-effective to send an abbreviated form of the complete survey to a much larger universe of names.

Of course, even sending an abbreviated survey to a large number of names can be very expensive. Therefore, before executing this approach attempt to determine if you can accurately predict segment membership by correlating known customer data with survey data in a model that assigns a probability of segment membership to each individual on the database. The exact procedure entails building some form of regression model in which segment membership is the variable to be predicted, and customer data and any available overlay data comprise the independent predictor variables. (You will find material about regression models and other statistical techniques in Chapters 10 through 15.)

In practice, some combination of both methods might work best. For example, suppose a segmentation study discovered four segments within the customer database, with one segment being particularly important. Let's further assume that a mathematical model that predicted membership in this particular segment was strong but certainly not 100 percent accurate. In this case, an abbreviated survey might be mailed to all customers with a higher than average probability of membership in this key segment. The survey would enable the marketer to gather more data about a key market segment without the expense of mailing to everyone on the database. An additional step that some companies take is to develop models that predict survey response based on prior survey mailings. These models can further limit the selection of survey recipients to those names that are predicted to respond to the survey.

Response rates to surveys depend on the strength of the relationship between the company and its customers and may vary from less than 10 percent to better than 50 percent. Some companies, to improve response rate to surveys, include premiums ranging from extra chances in sweepstakes, to price discounts, to cash. The expected response rate is critical to the design of the survey. In general, most segmentation studies require at least 3,000 to 5,000 responses. If the survey response rate is 50 percent, this means sending out 10,000 or so surveys. On the other hand, if the expected response rate is in the vicinity of 10 percent, then a much larger number of questionnaires must be mailed, and the issue of nonresponse bias becomes important. That is, if only 10 percent of the individuals who receive the survey complete it, how representative can these 10 percent be of the entire universe of customers or prospects? The answer is probably not very representative, and care must be taken to insure the reliability of results. One way marketers sometimes evaluate the reliability of results in situations such as these is to use a telemarketing survey to confirm answers to key questions.

DATA PURCHASED FROM THIRD-PARTY SOURCES

Although directly captured data provide unique information about people's attitudes, expectations, and personal behavior, direct data are not always available to marketers at the initial stages of a targeting process. In many cases, purchasing data from secondary sources can be a cost-effective way of enhancing the strength of models.

As stated above, *secondary data* is defined as data acquired from third-party sources rather than provided by the individuals themselves. This includes data from U.S. census sources as well as commercially developed databases.

Demographic, attitudinal, lifestyle, and financial data are available to varying degrees at both the geographical level and the individual level. Geographical data is based on various levels of small-area geography including census tracts, ZIP codes, ZIP+4, block groups, and postal carrier routes.

A question that is always asked is whether to operate at the ZIP code or census tract block group level when using geo-demographic data. Obviously, ZIP code data is readily available and easy to use. The use of block group data requires "geo-coding" a file to associate each address in it with a block group, census tract, or both. Generally, this process costs a few dollars per thousand and adds some time to the data-appending process.

On the surface, it would appear that the smaller geographic unit would offer superior predictive precision. However, because there is considerable error between either unit's average income, age, or educational level and the true values belonging to individuals within either the ZIP code or the block group, the practical consequence of using the block group over the ZIP code might not be as great as you would expect.

Whether to use the ZIP code or block group also depends on the task at hand. If you were renting a small number of names (50,000 to 100,000) and their incomes had to be greater than, say, $100,000, then we would probably recommend using block group data. On the other hand, if you were renting a million or more names or simply overlaying a database for profiling purposes, ZIP code data may be satisfactory. The recommended approach is to pose the specific question to the vendor and perhaps test both methods to see which works best for your application.

Table 2–1 shows the approximate number of each standard geographical unit in the United States at which demographic data are available.

Geography-Based Demographic Data

Geography-based demographic data is produced through a series of statistical calculations applied to U.S. census data. It is sold under a number of product names by various companies such as Donnelley (ClusterPlus), Claritas (PRIZM), National Decision Systems (MICROVISION), and others. Appendix B contains descriptions of the major clustering products.

The statistical techniques used to produce geography-based demographic data vary according to the type of data being analyzed. Data elements are generally either categorical or continuous. Categorical data elements describe *one-dimensional conditions* such as the customer's state of residence, sex, or occupation. Customers live in only one state at a time, are either male or female, and generally have a single occupation. In each of these cases, the customer or prospect can have only one value for

TABLE 2–1

Unit	*Number of Units*	*Approximate Number of Households per Unit*
Residential ZIP codes	36,000	2,400
Carrier routes	210,000	400
Block groups	250,000	340

each condition. Because these types of data elements assign customers or prospects to *categories* they are referred to as *categorical variables.* Categorical variables are analyzed using a special set of statistical techniques, including cross-tabulations and frequency distributions.

Other data elements, such as age and income, are not limited to categorical values. Because these data elements can have *any* values, they are referred to as *continuous.* These data elements are analyzed using different statistical techniques such as averages (means), ranges (minimum, maximum), and so on.

The U.S. Census Bureau captures both categorical and continuous data elements at the census tract, block group, and enumeration district levels. Commercial data vendors make this same data available at postal boundary levels, which makes it easier and more convenient for direct mail marketers to use the data. Census Bureau Data are broken down by ZIP codes (both five-digit and the nine-digit ZIP+4) and sometimes at the postal carrier route level to develop profiles for small-area geographical units.

Once statistical measures are calculated for each block group, other techniques, notably factor and cluster analysis, are applied to the data to "cluster" block groups with similar characteristics into neighborhood "types." These neighborhood types have similar profiles in terms of average home value, average income, family size, home type, occupation, age, presence of children, and so on.

Geo-demographic data vendors support the notion that "birds of a feather flock together," which assumes that individuals will, for the most part, reflect the characteristics of the neighborhoods in which they live. Neighborhoods with common demographic characteristics may be geographically contiguous or may be located throughout the country. In numerous case studies, marketers have been able to project the purchase behavior of customers to prospects who live in similar geographical clusters in different cities.

Although the "birds of a feather" theory may be true in some respects, such as home value, it may not be true for other characteristics. One reason for disparities is that in a typical suburban neighborhood, other than a new development, immediate neighbors may have bought their homes at different times. Depending on when the home was purchased, the purchase price may vary dramatically. In suburbs of large cities, for example, a four-bedroom house may have cost $30,000 in the 1950s, $60,000 in the 1960s, $120,000 in the 1970s, $360,000 in the 1980s and $300,000 in the 1990s. So current home value alone may not be as precise an indicator of income, net worth, and lifestyle as we might imagine.

TABLE 2–2
Neighborhood Comparison

Neighbor	*Age*	*Marital Status*	*Home Value (in thousands)*	*Household Income (in thousands)*	*Number of Persons in Household*
Allen	75	Married	$300	$400	2
Baker	86	Widowed	300	11	1
Corcoran	38	Married	300	149	4
Doyle	59	Married	300	52	6
Everett	38	Married	300	85	5
Freeman	50	Married	300	65	5
Average	58			$123	

Table 2–2 shows the individual-level demographic characteristics of six neighbors in a typical suburban neighborhood, all of whom have homes of similar value.

As you can see, the ages, incomes, and family sizes of each neighbor are dramatically different. Census data would be based on averages, but the ages of only two neighbors are close to the average age and the income of only one neighbor is close to the average income. Similarly, the life stage and lifestyle of each of the neighbors are different, and importantly, the differences are not likely to be picked up by geography-based data.

Another point to consider about geo-demographic data is that neighborhoods change and data gets old quickly. Areas that are undergoing transition—in whatever direction—may be missed and false assumptions about neighborhoods might be made. In many urban areas, gentrification, or the influx of young, relatively upscale professionals, into old, sometimes run-down areas, has changed the characteristics of many neighborhoods.

Young, two-career families have, in many cases, traded proximity to work—and shorter commutes—for the space and comfort traditionally associated with suburban living. Townhouse developments or renovation of existing brownstones and inner-city apartments have lured many relatively wealthy people into areas that were previously economically disadvantaged.

Although the impact of these trends may be well known locally, a national marketer may not be aware of them for a number of key markets and may therefore invest inappropriately in a direct marketing campaign for one of two reasons:

1. A marketer may forgo promoting to people in a certain neighborhood because out-of-date geo-demographic data may not accurately report the neighborhood's ascendancy. In this case, an uninformed marketer may give up a good opportunity.
2. A marketer may be up-to-date on changes that are in progress but may inadvertently market to holdovers from the neighborhood's previous status rather than to the newly arrived group. In this case, by targeting to the wrong people in an area, the marketer may spend promotional dollars on people who are unlikely to respond. This situation can be improved through the use of additional screens, such as change-of-address date, often involving combining data from a variety of sources.

Despite the obvious limitations of geo-demographic data—it is based on average conditions that may in fact not be representative of any of the individuals in a given neighborhood—companies that have not previously applied any external data to their customer and prospect files may find it quite helpful. Using geo-demographic data may be especially cost-effective for companies that market to individuals who live in *contiguous neighborhoods* rather than to individual households that are more geographically dispersed.

In some industries, geo-demographic data may be a very cost-effective means of describing neighborhoods. A cable television multisystem operator (MSO) used Claritas's PRIZM data to find out how similar the neighborhoods in a new franchise were to neighborhoods in which the MSO had previously had successful marketing campaigns for premium services. The MSO tested marketing programs similar to successful ones used in different cities in neighborhoods that were similar in terms of their PRIZM cluster types. The results in the new market were very highly correlated with the results in the original city and the test significantly outpulled the control. In this situation, the MSO successfully used geo-demographic look-alikes at the neighborhood level.

National Databases as Sources of Data for File Enhancement

Many direct marketers find that they have insufficient data about their customers to make strategic marketing decisions. To develop customer profiles and hopefully be able to segment their files, additional data concerning age, income, wealth, home value, automobile ownership, presence of children, mail-order responsiveness, and so on may be very helpful.

In this case, compiled lists are very useful, primarily because of their nearly total coverage of U.S. households. Match rates between house files and compiled lists typically are in the range of 45 to 65 percent, and among home owners or mail-responsive individuals they are frequently higher.[2]

Attitudinal data. Attitudinal data from third-party data sources usually does not involve a customer's or prospect's attitudes about particular products or services, but rather deals with people's opinions, mores, and perceptions about such diverse subjects as lifestyle, personal values, politics, religion, and other societal issues.

Marketers tend to use attitudinal data when they are planning to launch a campaign or introduce new products into communities where they do not have previous experience. The cable television industry makes extensive use of attitudinal data when deciding whether it should promote pay services that feature R-rated or PG-rated movies. HBO responded to the attitudes of its audience, as well as age and lifestyle characteristics, when it introduced the Cinemax service. Market research showed that a large number of households throughout the country, based on age, education, and moral and religious background, objected to the

[2]Note that an overall match rate of 45 to 65 percent does not mean that all matching names have values for all data elements. On individual data elements, match rates are typically much lower, often in the range of 5 to 10 percent.

level of sex, violence, and adult language used in many R-rated films. In response to the attitudes expressed in the market research and the projections of potential viewership among people with similar attitudes, HBO launched Cinemax, which, unlike the more mainstream HBO, offered movies that contained little or no sex, violence, or adult language.

Geography-based attitudinal data. As in the case of demographic data, attitudinal data can be developed internally through surveys or purchased at the geographic level. To use geography-based attitudinal data for its own customer file a marketer would purchase data, such as PRIZM or ClusterPlus, that has been linked to the VALS 2 Segmentation System[3] and overlay it onto the customer file or a representative sample if the file is very large. The marketer could then statistically analyze the relationship between people who live in areas where certain types of customer behavior are dominant and the associated VALS categories of those people.[4] The marketer may find that the best customers tend to come from the actualizer and achievers categories. If this were the case, then the marketer would want to promote its products to more people in those categories by looking for clusters that had a disproportionately high percentage of people classified as actualizers and achievers.

Lifestyle data. The commercial development of lifestyle data grew out of a recognition that geo-demographic data often could not sufficiently describe differences in personal interests and leisure time activities to satisfy the informational requirements of marketers.

A number of geo-demographic data vendors have added value to their databases by combining their geo-demographic clusters with market research data. Claritas, for example, combined its geo-demographic cluster data with Simmons market research data. The resulting product enables client companies to link general buyer behavior characteristics that Claritas captured on a neighborhood basis with the actual purchase performance of their customers.

Other data vendors have similarly combined their geo-demographic files with data from Simmons, VALS, MRI, and other sources to add power to their data. Donnelley's Affluence Model provides a means of predicting the affluence of individual households. This product works alone or in combination with Donnelley's CONQUEST desktop market analysis tool or with ClusterPlus, which is Donnelley's neighborhood segmentation system.

By combining geo-demographic data with purchase behavior and other consumer data, marketers increase the odds that they are placing their

---

[3]VALS 2 is a revision of VALS, an acronym for *Values and Lifestyles,* produced by SRI International. It offers marketers a classification of customers and markets based on psychographic characteristics. In its revised version VALS 2 uses two fundamental dimensions, *self-orientation* and *consumer resources,* to provide a framework for how and why consumers are motivated to purchase products and services. The VALS 2 topology defines three self-orientations—principle, status, and action—according to a consumer's physical, demographic, and material means to act upon them. As a result, VALS 2 categorizes consumers into such groupings as actualizers, fulfilled, believers, achievers, strivers, experiencers, makers, and strugglers. Consumers are assigned to VALS categories based on their answers to a 30-question survey. Each geo-demographic cluster group is associated with a distribution of the VALS categories.

[4]N. J. Olson, K. Ricke, and P. Weisenberger, "Using VALS to Target Market through Package Segmentation," *Journal of Direct Marketing Research* 1, no. 2 (Spring/Summer 1987).

advertisements in print or electronic media that they know have significant reach among people whose characteristics match the profile of their current customers.

In direct mail, the same approach can help identify prospects based on a combination of their neighborhood type and their buyer behavior characteristics. Appendix B lists a number of other vendors that have combined their geo-demographic databases with market research data.

Vendors of lifestyle data approach the capture and management of behavioral information in a different way. One of the most innovative companies in this field is National Demographics and Lifestyles: The Lifestyle Selector (NDL), which was established in the 1970s and has subsequently been acquired by R. L. Polk.

NDL compiles its data in a unique and fascinating way. The company provides highly automated warranty card processing services to manufacturers, distributors, and retailers. The manufacturer attaches warranty cards to its products and a second card that contains a demographic and lifestyle questionnaire, which are then sent to NDL for processing. NDL then provides the warranty information to the manufacturers in machine readable form, along with lifestyle data about the purchasers of their own products, and NDL adds the lifestyle data it has captured to its own proprietary database. Appendix B describes the data captured by NDL.

NDL then uses the demographic and lifestyle data in a number of ways. It offers a data-appending and list-profiling service for list owners to help them understand the lifestyle characteristics of their own customers beyond what they may have known or inferred based on product purchases and the original list sources. Once a list profile has been developed, list owners can rent from NDL additional names of people whose lifestyle characteristics are similar to those of their current customers.

Marketers also can send rented lists, with the approval of list owners, to NDL for screening, selecting only those names that have the desired sets of lifestyle characteristics or those that have the highest scores according to predictive models.[5] NDL's research staff can develop these models for a marketer, or the marketer can develop the models internally, depending on staff capabilities and cost. The downside to this approach is that appending data and scoring rented lists can rapidly become an expensive proposition.

A third approach is for marketers to take the lifestyle profile NDL developed for their house lists and apply it to their prospect files, again, on a categorical or a statistical modeling basis. In the categorical approach, the marketer would use cross-tabulation to select prospects who fall into the same categories as currently successful customers. Using statistical modeling, the marketer would apply these characteristics to the prospect file so that promotions would be sent only to those prospects who had the highest scores based on degree of similarity with lifestyle characteristics (and most likely, with other internally available data such as list source and geography).

---

[5]The ethical issues of screening rented lists are well covered in the Direct Marketing Association List Practices Information Task Force's *List Practices Handbook* (New York; Direct Marketing Association, 1988), which we urge you to consult.

Marketers could use the NDL lifestyle profile in a fourth way, as a guideline for sources of other rented names. If, for example, a company's best customers all had indicated an interest in tennis, golf, and camping, a marketer might increase its rental of lists oriented to those interests.

Financial data. Financial data providers are list compilers of a special type. Unlike the Polks, Donnelleys, and Metromails of the industry, who obtain their data from a variety of sources, financial data providers all get their data through service bureaus that they either own or for whom they perform clearinghouse services.

Among the largest providers of financial data are TRW Target Marketing Services and Trans Union. Both companies have access to data about credit card purchases, installment loans, applications for credit, and payment history for a very high percentage of credit-using households in the United States. The type and extent of financial data available from each of these companies change frequently, so marketers interested in using financial data should independently contact representatives of each firm for detailed information.

Taking the geo-demographic data concept of "birds of a feather" a step further, financial data can help further differentiate members of a potential market based on their actual financial performance. Marketers can send their house lists to either of the vendors listed above, as they would to any of the providers of other types of secondary data, and the vendor will produce a financial profile of customers on the file. For example, marketers may learn that their best customers tend to have these characteristics:

- More than six revolving credit accounts.
- At least four bank cards.
- Average revolving credit balances in excess of $500.
- Very few payments that are more than 30 days late.
- At least two department store credit cards.

The service would provide this information as averages or indexes for groups of people, not at the individual consumer level.

Armed with this information, marketers could send their prospect lists to financial data vendors to identify prospects whose financial characteristics are similar to those of their customers—promotions would be sent to those people but less frequently or not at all to people whose characteristics differed. Additionally, marketers might rent the names of people whose financial characteristics are similar to those of their best customers.

Some marketers have worked with financial data vendors to develop models that predict how well names on the financial data files are expected to perform as customers of their businesses. Then, names from rented lists can be compared to the scored file to screen out names that are unlikely to perform well and either promote them differently or not at all.

This approach enables marketers to avoid mailing to people who are unlikely to be interested in, or unlikely to pay for, their products. By the same token, it can help marketers to find the "needles in the haystack"—those prospects who actually have the financial means and track record to be good prospects for certain products but who live in neighborhoods that models based on geo-demographic data alone might exclude from promotion.

To make data more accessible to marketers while remaining within the ethical and legal standards that govern the use of individual specific data, some vendors of financial data have developed clusters and financial lifestyle overlays that are similar in concept to the neighborhood and lifestyle clusters developed by vendors of other types of secondary data. These overlays can be appended to a company's customer or prospect file, and the company can then either develop its own scoring models or simply use the overlays as categorical selection criteria.

Demographic data. Several companies, including R L Polk, Donnelley, Metromail, Neodata, Infobase, and others, have compiled household lists of names and addresses and a great deal of individual-specific data for the vast majority of U.S. households. Each of the major vendors of individual-specific data compiles its lists in a slightly different way.

The R L Polk Company compiles its lists from a number of public record sources, but most notably from state motor vehicle registration information. At present, Polk provides direct marketers with motor vehicle registration data for 33 states. At one time more states participated, but recent concerns and legislation concerning privacy have curtailed access to information in some states. This data consists of the make, model, and year of automobiles individuals currently own and previously owned. It also indicates the value of individual autos and total value of autos by household.

R L Polk adds a number of other primary data elements, as well as computed data elements such as income, to the base file. In many cases, imputed income is based on a combination of the individual's age, home value, occupation, automobile ownership and ownership pattern, neighborhood type, and other factors. Some computed individual or household level data is essentially a geo-demographic average of block group data.

Most recently, Polk Direct introduced a new segmentation product called ***Niches.*** Using all the data available in Polk's national database, the company classified all households as belonging to one of 26 Niches. For marketers requiring further discrimination, each household also belongs to one of 108 ***SuperNiches*** (TM). Using this scheme marketers can rent names identified by a predefined segmentation plan and be confident that all the names they rent fall into the segment they're targeting.

Whereas R L Polk originally compiled its data from state motor vehicle registration departments and from its own city directory business, Donnelley Marketing and Metromail originally compiled their data through their telephone directory and city directory businesses. Over the years, each of these companies has expanded its sources to include additional public record agencies, private list compilers, list owners who use their facilities for other computer processing, and new primary name acquisition businesses (e.g., Donnelley's Carol Wright).

Although many of the variables included in data of this type are similar to geo-demographic data in content, they differ in one critical aspect: all data are specific to named individuals rather than to a set of geography-based summaries. That is, if the individual-specific age data says that John Smith of 123 Elm street, Anytown, USA, is 37 years old, you can rest assured that the specific John Smith in question is 37 years old. It does not mean that he lives in a block group or ZIP code in which the average age is 37, although this might also be the case.

In the case of some variables, for example, presence of children, implicit data may be used. And in cases where the specific age of an individual is not known, age may be stated in terms of the range that is most probable based on a number of other variables that are known with certainty. For example, if it is known that a household includes children under five, it will be inferred that the children's mother is not older than 45 and that the father is not older than 50. Although there will certainly be cases in which this inference is inaccurate, for the majority of cases it will be reasonably close when combined with known data elements.

How to Obtain Enhancement Data

To obtain enhancement data contact the companies listed in Appendix B or, as suggested previously, contact the Direct Marketing Association to obtain a complete list of recommended member organizations in the field. As in the case of service bureaus and software vendors we discuss later, it is always a good idea to ask the vendors for references and to spend the time required to learn from other companies' experiences prior to committing your own firm's resources.

National Databases as Sources of Names

Marketers use national databases in several ways. One way is simply to use the national database as a source of names. The marketer would specify characteristics of people that are desirable for a particular promotion. The national database company's account executive would then work with the programming staff to produce a customized selection of names from the firm's national database file.

Although national databases that include individual-specific data may be a valuable source of names, many marketers find that names from rented lists belonging to mail-order businesses outperform names selected from national databases. In most cases, this is because the source of the rented list indicates two important factors:

1. People whose names are on the list are direct mail responsive.
2. The content of the magazine or the nature of the catalog or other business that is the source of the list may provide clues about the person's interests.

However, there are notable examples of marketers finding great success using national databases as sources of names. In one case an atuomobile company (Company A) was planning a campaign with the objective of stealing market share from its principal competitor (Company B). Company A developed an expensive mailing package and sent it to owners of Company B's cars who were at the stage of the car ownership cycle during which people begin to contemplate the purchase of their next car. Using R L Polk data to determine car ownership and the stage of the ownership cycle, Company A customized the direct mail package to include the name, address, and telephone number of the most conveniently located Company A dealer. This approach enabled Company A to target its offer to the desired segment, support its dealer network, and provide potential customers with the added convenience of local dealer information.

In another case, an automobile company (Company C) planned to launch a customer reacquisition program by targeting owners of selected cars who had previously owned a Company C product. Company C selected names of owners of selected makes and models from the R L Polk file, matched this list against its own file of former customers, and rolled out a campaign that combined reacquisition with model upgrade strategies.

The Polk file was extremely valuable as a source of names to Company A and Company C in these examples specifically because the file contained automobile data. But numerous examples can be cited of applications that are not primarily related to automobiles and that use national databases quite differently.

Using Acquired Data to Predict Segment Membership

Professional journals have reported a number of innovative marketing programs that rely on gathering, analyzing, and manipulating data. One example involves the use of survey simulators to predict direct marketing response. This approach used surveys to gather data about the characteristics of individuals within the target audience and to link these characteristics to the rate and manner in which people indicated they would respond to a promotion. Green and Moore theorized that people with similar individual characteristics would have similar attitudes and that by "quantifying" a dry run of a promotion, which linked attitudinal data to data about individual characteristics, the results of a promotion rollout could be predicted.[6] By using survey data in this manner prior to mailing, Green and Moore were able to help their clients focus promotion dollars on the campaigns that had the greatest potential for success based on the characteristics of the target audience.

This example is notable because it employed research concepts as part of the mainstream marketing process that would normally be limited to market research. This approach was a cost-effective way to reduce the size of the target audience to those people who were most likely to respond.

---

[6] M E Green and E Moore, "Using Survey Simulators to Predict Direct Mail Response," *Journal of Direct Marketing Research* 1, no. 2 (Spring/Summer 1987).

Chapter 3

Buzzwords

A WORD ABOUT BUZZWORDS[1]

In the first edition of *The New Direct Marketing,* we provided nontechnical readers with easy-to-understand translations of technical terms they were likely to encounter in discussions with their own Management Information Systems (MIS) groups and with vendors.

We have greatly expanded the technology sections of *The New Direct Marketing* in this edition to reflect new developments in computer hardware and software technology during the past three years and the extent to which these changes have impacted the price performance of database management system (DBMS) applications.

Inevitably, expanding the information about technology has led to including many new terms that may be unfamiliar. Accordingly, we have added additional buzzwords to help you understand these important developments.

Like the classification of data types that we developed in Chapter 2, the definitions of technical terms here are likely to differ from the orthodox definitions of academics and data processing industry leaders. However, as in the case of data, we have attempted to use practical definitions that will help marketers understand the technical terms they are likely to encounter in making decisions about database management system (DBMS) products they will use as part of the new direct marketing.

We recommend that readers who are unfamiliar with technical terminology read through all the buzzwords prior to reading Chapters 4 through 19. Within these chapters, footnotes that refer readers to the appropriate buzzwords accompany the first appearance of each technical term.

BUZZWORD 1: GENERATIONS OF LANGUAGES

In the world of mainframe computing, there are currently four "generations" of languages. First-generation languages speak directly to the computer in machine language.

If you would like to see what machine language looks like, the next time your PC is at the C prompt (C:\>), type TYPE COMMAND.COM. The resulting gibberish of odd lines and happy faces will be meaningless to you. Fortunately, it is meaningful to your computer.

[1]*Buzzwords* are technical terms commonly used by data processing MIS professionals and computer hardware and software vendors. We have assembled and defined buzzwords in terms that nontechnicians will readily understand.

These languages are actually combinations of 1s and 0s that the computer reads directly as positive and negative pulses of electricity. Although machine language is extremely difficult for mortals to understand, it is actually the most efficient way for computers to process instructions.

Second-generation languages such as Assembler are a step closer to languages that humans can understand than are machine languages. They are "machine-like" in the words and syntax they employ but not quite as great a stretch for programmers as writing in machine language. There are actually some relics from the 1960s who can still write programs in Assembler and, in fact, more programs in use today than you might expect are written in Assembler. It is an extremely efficient language for very large, data-intense programs because it can be compiled into machine language and made to run very efficiently.

Third-generation, procedural languages like COBOL and FORTRAN were invented to make life easier for programmers and, in fact, they do. One reason is that programming routines are built into these languages so programmers can write in a kind of shorthand, knowing that the COMMAND level instructions in COBOL will perform fairly complex functions for them.

Third-generation languages are translated or *compiled*[2] into machine language, but because they are even further removed from the simple 1s and 0s that the computer requires than are second-generation languages, a price is paid in processing efficiency. So although third-generation languages help improve the productivity of programmers, they actually lower the productivity of computers. Based on the decreasing cost of computer processing and the increasing cost of programmers, however, this trade-off in efficiencies is one that most companies are prepared to make.

Fourth-generation languages (4GLs) like FOCUS, NATURAL, USER LANGUAGE, IDEAL, or SQL use very simple "verbs" and syntax, and they can be used both by programmers and end users. The apparent simplicity of the 4GLs provides a great deal of power to programmers or nonprogramming end users, but at a great price. Because they are written at such a high level, they can be incredibly inefficient for computers to process.

An apocryphal story holds that several of the fourth-generation languages were developed, and are secretly owned, by manufacturers of hardware because the inefficiencies inherent in fourth-generation languages make it necessary for companies to buy larger, more expensive computers. Fourth-generation languages are available for DBMS products that we refer to in this book. However, many of the DBMS products themselves are written in Assembler to increase processing efficiency.

---

[2]*Compilers* are computer programs that translate computer programs written in languages like Assembler, PL-1, COBOL, FORTRAN, or C into machine language, a series of 1s and 0s that computers can read directly. The results of a compiled program can be read only by computers.

Procedural Languages

Assembler is more machine-like in its appearance than more familiar languages like COBOL or FORTRAN. In Assembler a program that added two data fields together would look like the following:[3]

```
Load fld 1, R1
Load fld 2, R2
Add R1, R2, R3
Save R3, fld 3
```

Procedural languages like COBOL or FORTRAN provide detailed, line-by-line instructions to programs. A procedural language would include commands within programs like these:

```
GO TO LINE 24
ADD THE QUANTITY SHOWN IN FIELD X TO THE QUANTITY IN
FIELD Y
STORE THE SUM IN FIELD Z
THEN GO TO LINE 30
```

A fourth-generation language would use English-like prose to accomplish the same purpose, and would include commands like this:

```
FIELD Z = FIELD X + FIELD Y
```

BUZZWORD 2: SQL

SQL is an abbreviation for Structured Query Language, the American National Standards Institute (ANSI)[4] accepted standard language for relational database technology. Although the name may initially seem as intimidating as all the other unfamiliar acronyms of computer technology, the language itself is fairly simple in concept. SQL (pronounced SE-QUEL by true techies) consists of a very small number of verbs. Because it is a high-level language (fourth generation), each of these verbs packs a lot of power. See the example of SQL code that follows.

Suppose we had a relational database table called CUSTOMER that contained the following data elements: customer number; customer name; address including city, state, and ZIP code; purchase amount; number of purchases; and number of promotions. An extract of this database follows.

If we wanted to create a file of customers who were from Texas and had purchase amounts in excess of $60, we could write the following program in SQL:

```
CREATE VIEW TEXASBUYERS (CUST#, STATE, PURCHASE$)
AS SELECT CUSTOMER.CUST# , CUSTOMER.STATE,CUSTOMER.PURCHASE$
FROM CUSTOMER WHERE STATE = 'TX' AND PURCHASE$ > 60;4
```

Although the language may seem a bit foreign, consider how few verbs were required to produce the desired view of the data. CREATE VIEW TEXASBUYERS tells the database to create a new table called TEXASBUYERS. The items in parentheses (CUST#, STATE, PURCHASE$) are

[3]Where R1,R2, and R3 denote internal machine registers 1, 2, and 3, respectively.

[4]SQL and most 4 GLs will accept symbols (e.g.,>) or abbreviation (e.g., GT). Both are shown in this text.

Customer Table

Customer Number	State	Purchase Amount	Number of Purchases	Source Code	Number of Promotions
1347	TX	$ 54	6	04	07
0259	NY	126	10	03	15
3268	AR	27	5	01	06
2139	TX	95	4	02	07
0134	NJ	182	12	04	12
0865	AR	315	17	02	06
0932	TX	191	9	04	11
1136	OK	88	8	03	15
2437	MT	113	12	04	09
4521	LA	43	6	08	07

the elements we wish to include in the new table. The SELECT statement tells us which data elements we wish to extract from the existing table called CUSTOMER. The two WHERE statements, STATE = `TX' and PURCHASE$ GT 60, specify the conditions that must be met by any records that are to be included in our new table.

Once this table is created, any number of analyses can be conducted.

BUZZWORD 3: FLAT FILES AND VSAM FILE STRUCTURES

To understand the differences in file structures, think of spreadsheet programs. In the spreadsheet, the rows are records and the columns are fields. The spreadsheet is a file. A flat file doesn't contain any additional intelligence of organization beyond the record level. To know the range and average amounts of purchases contained in the file, a marketer would have to perform some data processing operations.

With a spreadsheet a marketer could specify the range and the system could calculate the minimum, maximum, or average levels for any field. Additionally, the file could be sorted in ascending or descending sequence for a primary and secondary sort field. If a marketer using a spreadsheet wanted to know the range and average purchase level of customers who live in Texas, a simple approach would be to sort the file by state as the primary key and then by purchase amount as the secondary key. It would then be relatively simple to calculate the range and average purchase levels for the Texans.

In many ways, spreadsheets function like simple database management systems. If only the mainframe world were as conceptually simple! Unfortunately for marketers, many of whom are extremely facile with spreadsheet products, the data processing complexities of direct marketing require either mainframe systems that, for the most part, are nowhere near as user friendly as end users would like or the use of separate platforms for decision support functions.

In a mainframe environment, a file like the spreadsheet file described above would be considered a flat file because there is no hierarchy of organization that would make it easier for the end users to get the information faster. To answer a question such as we posed earlier (i.e., "How many Texans had purchases greater than $60?"), it would be necessary to search every record in the file sequentially to be certain we had not left out any Texans.

To make life a little simpler IBM developed a product called VSAM, which is an acronym for Virtual System Access Method. This product enables programmers to establish indexes or keys by which specified fields can be accessed more readily. For example, if STATE were an indexed field in a VSAM file, it would be much easier to answer the Texas query. When the query was entered, the program would use the VSAM file structure to lock in on the STATE field, and within the STATE field it would examine only the Texans.

VSAM enables programmers to establish indexes on a number of different fields at the same time. Thus, if we knew in advance all the fields we would like to be able to reach through indexes and rarely made any changes to this design, we could develop a very efficient application using VSAM file structures rather than the more complex and expensive database management system products.

However, most end users do not know what their requirements will be in the future, and marketers especially must acknowledge that their data requirements are going to change continually over time. Therefore, the functional requirements of marketers rather than a technical limitation of VSAM make DBMS technology essential for the new direct marketing.

BUZZWORD 4: INDEXES[5]

How Indexes Are Used

Indexes in data processing are very much like the indexes readers are familiar with that appear in books. In books, the index indicates the page on which a particular subject, name, or term appears. In database systems, indexes "point" the programs to the desired data and provide an efficient means of getting there without having to read the intervening records.

One of the most important elements, and one of the major differences between the various commercially available database management system products, is the way in which indexes are structured.

If, for example, we want to easily locate all the people who live in the state of Massachusetts, we would build an index by state. Then, rather than searching sequentially through all our customer records, which might be arranged in customer ID or alphabetical sequence, our search would begin by going to the state index, locating the record numbers of all customers whose entry in the state index is MA, creating a temporary file of those records, and then posing whatever further queries we have about those customers to this Massachusetts-only subset of the file. Reducing the file to include only the relevant set of records makes subsequent processing much more efficient.

Indexes become even more important to ease of access and good performance when we formulate complex queries that require data from a

[5]Two types of indexes are referred to in this text. At times the term is used to describe calculated values for categorical variables. In the present context, the term is used to describe a means of representing locations of data values in records. Readers who wish to know more about the subject of indexes and related technical subjects are referred to CJ Date, *An Introduction to Database Systems,* vol. I, 4th ed. (Reading, MA: Addison-Wesley, 1986).

number of different tables or files.[6] If the data fields in question have been indexed, we may be able to answer the query entirely by consulting indexes rather than by reading actual records.

For example, suppose that we want to know the number of people who live in New York, Massachusetts, and Connecticut who purchased products 123, 456, or 789. If address and purchase information were maintained in separate tables, this query could be processed by reading the state index and the product index, selecting the records of only those people who live in the three states indicated, and then selecting the records of only those people who purchased products 123, 456, or 789. The two extracted index files would then be joined on the customer ID field, and the resulting set would provide the desired answer.

If we knew that this type of query would be asked frequently, we would probably design the application so both data elements appear in the same table. This would improve response time because the join would be eliminated.

One of the most challenging issues for database designers is determining which fields in a table should be indexed and how tables in the database should be related. If the database is to successfully support marketing, marketers must provide the system's designers with a great deal of guidance and direction concerning which queries are most important and which data elements are related to each other. The resulting database design optimizes the data capture, storage, and manipulation requirements to achieve the maximum benefit for marketing.

Let's return to our question of how many Texans in the file had total purchase amounts in excess of $60 to see how it could be answered using indexes. To get this information, we would identify Texans within the state index and then do an index search for purchase amount. We would then create a "found set" within the index of records that met the desired conditions. Tables 3–1 through 3–5 show how this works.

Table 3–1 repeats the customer table that illustrated Buzzword 2. In Table 3–2, the original file has been indexed by customer number within state.

If a query were made to find the number of Texans who had total purchases in excess of $60, the database would search the index of the state file until it found the Texans, then perform all further processing within the found set of Texans. (See Table 3–3.)

Because we are only interested in knowing the range and average purchase levels for Texans (for this specific query) the found set would include only the relevant pieces of data. (See Table 3–4.)

Although we did not specifically request the customer number, it will normally be carried to maintain our link to the actual customer and purchase tables.

The result of the query, based on the found set, would be the count of Texans on the file who have purchases in excess of $60, which equals two. (See Table 3–5.)

Although it may appear, in this example, that the database worked very hard to answer a simple question, consider how well this approach would work with multiple conditions and very large files.

---

[6]We use the terms *tables* and *files* interchangeably.

TABLE 3–1
Flat File

Customer Number	*State*	*Purchase Amount*	*Number of Purchases*	*Source Code*	*Number of Promotions*
1347	TX	$ 54	6	04	07
0259	NY	126	10	03	15
3268	AR	27	5	01	06
2139	TX	95	4	02	07
0134	NJ	182	12	04	12
0865	AR	315	17	02	06
0932	TX	191	9	04	11
1136	OK	88	8	03	15
2437	MT	113	12	04	09
4521	LA	43	6	08	07

TABLE 3–2
A File Indexed by Customer Number within State

Customer Number	*State*	*Purchase Amount*	*Number of Purchases*	*Source Code*	*Number of Promotions*
0865	AR	$315	17	02	06
3268	AR	27	5	01	06
4521	LA	43	6	08	07
2437	MT	113	12	04	09
0134	NJ	182	12	04	12
0259	NY	126	10	03	15
1136	OK	88	8	03	15
0932	TX	191	9	04	11
1347	TX	54	6	04	07
2139	TX	95	4	02	07

TABLE 3–3
The Found Set of Texans

Customer Number	*State*	*Purchase Amount*	*Number of Purchases*	*Source Code*	*Number of Promotions*
0932	TX	$191	9	04	11
1347	TX	54	6	04	07
2139	TX	95	4	02	07

TABLE 3–4
The Reduced Found Set of Texans

Customer Number	*State*	*Purchase Amount*
0932	TX	$191
1347	TX	54
2139	TX	95

TABLE 3–5
The Found Set of Texans Who Have Purchases in Excess of $60

Customer Number	*State*	*Purchase Amount*
0932	TX	$191
2139	TX	95

BUZZWORD 5: PRODUCTIVITY TOOLS

Developers of database management systems have long realized that if their products are to be truly successful, they have to put the power of sophisticated data processing in the hands of end users who are not data processing professionals. This goal becomes more difficult if the end users have no knowledge of programming whatsoever.

An initial response was to provide *menus,* that is, tables of processes that could be selected by positioning the cursor over the item or by keying the first letter of the word and hitting the enter key. Users of PC spreadsheet programs will be very familiar with this concept.

More recently, software and hardware developers have offered *mouse* devices as an alternative and often easier means of selecting menu items. Mouse devices are small machines that control a target-like cross-hair image, arrow, or I-Bar on the screen. The end user moves the mouse over a flat surface until the indicator is positioned over the desired menu item and then presses a button on the mouse. This process selects the menu item in exactly the same way that cursor movement or keying the first letter of the desired item would. Some software products include icons, which are visual representations of the functions offered on the menu. The user positions the mouse over the desired icon and clicks a mouse button to make the selection.

BUZZWORD 6: LOGICAL AND PHYSICAL DESIGN

According to CJ Date,[7] the conceptual or logical database design consists of identifying the entities of interest to the enterprise and the information recorded about those entities. In other words, each firm must decide which of the data elements contained in its various applications will be contained in the database and define the relationships between those data elements. Generally, this is the job of the database administrator (DBA), but it is done in conjunction with the user sponsors.

The *physical design of the database,* again according to Date, is the definition of the storage structure and associated mapping of the system. In other words, the physical design of the database consists of determining which data elements should be contained in which tables, and how the tables are related to each other by primary and secondary key fields.

Key fields are the data elements that appear in more than one table and serve as a link, both logical and physical, between tables.

By *logical design,* we mean the data elements that will be included in the database and the way the elements in the data tables relate to each other. As part of the physical design, the system designer groups the data

[7]CJ Date, *An Introduction to Database Systems,* vol. 1, 4th ed. (Reading, MA: Addison-Wesley, 1986).

elements that seem to logically belong together into physical tables so elements that are likely to be involved in the same queries are included in the same tables. This grouping improves response time for queries by reducing the number of table joins[8], the number of inputs and outputs (I/Os)[9] and the amount of seek time[10] that the system must spend in bringing together the data elements required to answer the query.

Physical design also refers to the size of files. The placement of data on physical devices (generally, direct access storage devices, or DASD) is considered "tuning" and is not technically part of the physical design of the system. However, it is sometimes included under this definition anyway because the database administrator (DBA) and system designers are responsible for tuning the application to run as efficiently as possible. Proper placement of data helps reduce the time that will be required to get data from DASD into the computer's main memory. So you can see that response time is affected both by the logical and physical design of the system as well as by the placement of data and other tuning issues.

BUZZWORD 7: CPU

The central processing unit (CPU) is the heart of the computer—this is where the work gets done. In a PC, the CPU is defined in terms of the RAM (random access memory) and the processing speed. For example, a 486/33 machine with two MB of RAM refers to a PC that has an 80486 chip with a processing speed of 33 megahertz and two megabytes of core memory that the computer can use for processing. In a mainframe environment, RAM is referred to as core memory or internal memory, and processing speed is generally quoted in a measurement called MIPS (millions of instructions per second).

Channel

Channels are the electronic paths used to get data into and out of the CPU. If data cannot efficiently get into and out of the CPU, processing will slow down. This is like having a car with a very large engine capacity that has a clogged fuel line. Although the engine could make the car go very fast, it is unable to do this processing if it cannot get the fuel it needs.

Channel capacity and channel contention are major concerns to the system designers responsible for the processing efficiency.

Channel Contention

If the physical storage of data on DASD is not efficient, then channel contention will develop in mainframe systems. Channel contention is analogous to a clogged highway or artery in which too many blocks of data are

---

[8]*Table joins* are the means that relational databases use to bring together data stored in different tables. The tables are "joined" using a common field in much the same way that third-generation systems merge files using a common data element.

[9]Inputs and outputs (I/Os) are the number of times that data must be brought from disk drives into the computer's main memory and the number of times that data that is already in the computer's main memory must be stored on disks. Channel contention is directly proportional to the number of I/Os, and busy channels can delay processing in the same way that traffic jams can occur on highways during rush hour.

[10]*Seek time* is the time required for the system to find the right file and data needed to answer the query. See Buzzword 7 for a detailed description of seek time.

attempting to get through a constrained space. In data processing, the result is that one block of data must wait until the passageway is clear, and end users experience delays in response time.

A PC environment, other than a network environment, generally includes only one disk drive and one channel. Seek time in a PC environment is reduced by storing files in directories or subdirectories to minimize the number of files that must be searched prior to loading data. In a mainframe environment, where there are multiple disk drives and multiple channels, efficiency is increased by physically designing systems so data elements that are likely to be used in the same queries are distributed across multiple DASD units and channels. This distribution reduces channel contention, that is, the number of data requests that are attempting to get through an individual channel at the same time.

Direct Access Storage Device (DASD)

Disk drives (direct access storage devices, or DASD) are the most common form of external memory, or data storage, in on-line computing environments. Companies use disk drives to store data that they know they will need frequently. Programs issue commands or *calls* that tell the system which data files are needed for the process in question. The CPU then sends a message over the channel to find the data that the program needs. A PC environment generally has only one disk drive and one channel over which data enters and leaves the CPU.

Seek Time

When the program requests data the command goes through the channel to the disk drive(s) to find it. The time required for the request to find the right data and bring it back to the CPU is referred to as *seek time* because the program is seeking the data. System designers attempt to design systems initially to minimize time. However, as a system is used and more and more data is stored, the initial efficiencies of physical data storage tend to erode, and a conscious effort must be made to reposition data to produce greater efficiencies of operation. This function, called *tuning,* is generally the responsibility of the database administrator.

BUZZWORD 8: SUMMARY FILES

Summary files are files that have been created by extracting and summarizing data from one or more tables in the database. Their purpose is to provide quicker response time by grouping data that we know in advance will be important and will be accessed frequently.

A typical case where summary files would benefit system performance would be a situation where a number of different tables must be joined to bring together data for queries or reports. If, for example, we always want to know the counts of products purchased by state and source of purchaser, we would probably want to create a summary file to speed up this process. A fully "normalized" database would maintain data about customers and products purchased in separate tables.

Normalization

Normalization means that each piece of data appears only once, minimizing if not eliminating data redundancy. In a relational database environment, data is normalized as much as possible. One of the functions of the DBMS product itself is to "navigate" through different tables to find the required data.

However, to gain processing efficiency, it may be desirable to *denormalize* the data design to some extent by maintaining selected data elements in more than one table. Although this practice violates the relational model, it is a compromise many companies are willing to make to improve performance.

BUZZWORD 9: TYPES OF DATABASE PRODUCTS

Hierarchical

The oldest and fastest (in certain circumstances) type of DBMS products are hierarchical. These products establish a series of defined paths (not unlike the VSAM description), and data access and processing are very fast. Hierarchical systems are commonly used for banking, airline reservations, and other applications that require very high-speed processing and rarely change the paths of data storage or retrieval.

Inverted File

Inverted files are like hierarchical database structures except that they work from the bottom up rather than from the top down. This enables programmers to design systems that will allow access to virtually any field within the system from any other point. Creating indexes that link key fields enhances high-speed access from point to point. Examples of inverted file systems are Model 204, Adabas, and Computer Associates' Datacom/DB. Inverted file systems are very commonly used for direct marketing applications because their combination of processing speed and flexibility is well suited to this environment.

Relational

Relational systems are essentially collections of relatively simple tables from which the user combines and extracts information in a virtually unlimited number of ways. These are the most flexible of all database management systems, but some performance has been sacrificed to provide their flexibility and, as a result, they are generally not as fast as inverted file or hierarchical systems. In practice, direct marketers tend to use file applications that are relational in concept and relational applications that are structured like inverted files to achieve the most effective compromise between flexibility and performance.

Multiple Specialized Platforms

An emerging trend is the use of multiple platforms, each designed for a special purpose, to optimize both the performance requirements of operations support systems and the flexibility and performance requirements of decision support systems. This trend is described in more detail in later chapters.

Chapter 4

Why Companies Are Building Database Marketing Systems

In the preceding chapters we presented reasons why both traditional and nontraditional direct marketers are concluding that they need more information about their customers to market more effectively. Whereas traditional computer systems have been adequate for supporting transaction-oriented, single-event-driven businesses, marketers now require greater access to information about their customers and a clear understanding of the total relationship that exists between the customer and the company. Because existing systems do not provide this information, new systems, *database marketing systems,* are being developed that do meet today's need for marketing information.

DATABASE MARKETING SYSTEMS

Existing, transaction-based systems do not provide adequate information about customers and prospects for at least two reasons:

1. Transaction data captured in the course of normal business is not sufficient to answer the firm's marketing questions. In other words, even though important data might come into the firm, it is lost.
2. Data is not lost, but the form in which the data is currently captured and maintained makes it inaccessible to marketers.

In the former case, it is unlikely that the database approach will be able to solve the company's information problems because the data needed is simply not captured. To capture different or additional information, existing systems would have to be modified. If the changes required are extensive enough, the systems might even have to be redesigned. Redesign can be a very expensive proposition for companies that are in a third-generation systems environment because changes to programs and file structures—such as adding or deleting data fields—take a great deal of time and expense.[1]

[1]Most business systems in use today are written in *third-generation* procedural languages such as COBOL and use either flat files or VSAM file structures to store data. In typical third-generation environments, access to information about customers is limited to the data structures and paths that we have defined in advance. So, if we *knew* that we were always going to examine performance by state of residence or by the individual's original list source, we could design the application to provide us with this data very quickly. However, if our selection criteria were to change, major modifications to programs, reports, inquiry screens, file structures, libraries, and other aspects of the system would be required. In a third-generation environment, these changes require programmer intervention, which is both time-consuming and expensive.

Companies whose access to data is limited by the format in which data is captured and stored, rather than by the data that is captured, have more options. Database marketing applications can be designed to accept data from the company's numerous transaction-based systems and consolidate the data into a customer-oriented marketing database.

SCOPE OF THE MARKETING DATABASE APPLICATION

Most firms create the marketing database as an independent application and use it primarily as an analytical and promotional tool that consolidates, maintains, and analyzes data originally captured through multiple business systems such as fulfillment, order entry, inventory, accounts receivable, and so on.

An alternative to this approach is to convert existing business systems, generally supported by third-generation technology, to a database platform, and to fulfill Marketing database needs directly as a by-product of the underlying database structure. This integrated approach is very expensive and it is not recommended unless there are other reasons for converting existing systems to a database structure. This option is discussed later in the chapter.

An advantage of limiting the scope of the marketing database to analysis, reporting, and promotion is that it is much simpler to develop and maintain, requiring less time and fewer resources, and does not disrupt the firm's other existing systems. In many companies existing systems run very efficiently, and it is questionable whether a fourth-generation version of the applications would offer improved performance.

An additional advantage of limiting the marketing database scope is that the analysis and promotion applications are less critical to the firm as a whole in the sense that disrupting their availability will not bring the company's business to a halt in the same way as would a disruption of the order entry system. Even if the marketing database had to be reloaded and recreated from backup files, the company could continue to operate.

The Marketing Database as an Analysis and Promotion Tool Only

If the marketing database is used only for analysis and promotion, its functions are limited to inquiries, analysis and reporting, and name selection for mailings based on data currently available in existing transaction-driven operating systems. Naturally, the level of detail currently captured in the transaction systems and loaded to the database limits the extent of analysis because you cannot analyze data you don't have (more on this subject later).

If the process of selecting names for promotion is done outside the marketing database but response attribution is to be tracked by the marketing database, you must provide for capturing and consolidating promotion history and response information in the marketing database.

Fully Integrated Database System

A fully integrated database system fully combines the company's business, decision support, and marketing systems into what would appear to be a single integrated database application. In fact, these systems are usually developed as a series of applications, each of which is designed to perform a specific set of functions and each of which is separately optimized to take maximum advantage of processing efficiency and system performance.

As compared to using the database for analysis and promotion only, the fully integrated application approach assumes you will replace several applications as part of the process of developing a marketing database. And, although the ideal approach for some companies may be to ultimately develop a totally integrated operational and marketing database system, everyone involved should realize that this cannot happen overnight. Marketers, especially, should be aware that it is not uncommon for companies to assign project priorities so the first phase of the conversion deals with the most critical business systems, and the marketing database application is often assigned a relatively low priority.

Other Reasons for Choosing a DBMS Environment

Even if a company's existing systems are performing satisfactorily, the company may still wish to migrate to a DBMS environment for productivity reasons, albeit at the expense of processing and storage efficiencies. The main advantage of converting to a fourth-generation, database environment is the reduction in time required to develop and modify applications. This advantage should be carefully weighed against the efficiencies mentioned above before undertaking the conversion project.

In general, initial application development is considerably faster (at least 40 to 60 percent) using fourth-generation language tools in a database environment than in a conventional third-generation environment. Subsequent modifications to applications are at least three times faster in a fourth-generation database environment. Despite these benefits, we are not suggesting that efficient, smoothly functioning transaction-driven operating systems be thrown out and replaced merely because they are based on third-generation technology.

Many firms have had considerable success in maintaining existing transaction systems and developing interfaces from these applications to the marketing database. As long as the required data is available in a timely manner and the existing systems are part of the firm's strategic technology plan, there may be no reason to replace an existing transaction system. After all, if it isn't broken, there may be no reason to fix it.

Chapter 5

What Do You Want the Database to Do?

KEY ISSUES TO CONSIDER BEFORE COMMITTING TO A DATABASE STRATEGY

Before you begin the database design and development process there should be agreement on the applications the database is expected to support or, stated as simply as possible, *what it is that you want the database to help you do.* This phase of the database development process is concerned with identifying your *business needs and the functional requirements* to meet them.

In theory business needs and functional requirements could be developed independently and sequentially, with one team of marketing personnel defining the business needs and a second team of management information system (MIS) professionals developing the functional requirements. In this framework, business needs are essentially marketing's desires, and the functional requirements are MIS's translation of those desires into a specific plan for accomplishing marketing's needs. This plan or functional requirements document will include the following:

- A listing and detailed description of each of the individual business files to be brought into the database process.
- A statement and description of the data to be retained from individual files.
- A plan describing how the records from individual files will be linked together.
- A plan for consolidating individual customers into households.
- A plan defining how often the database will be updated.
- A definition of what new data values will be created during the update process.
- A description of how the database will be accessed by the marketing department.
- A statement of how quickly database queries need to be answered.
- Descriptions of how the database will perform the operations included in the business needs analysis such as these, among others:
  - Response analysis.
  - Profiling.
  - Scoring.
  - Selecting names for promotions.
  - Reporting.

As we stated above, in theory, business needs and functional requirements could be developed sequentially, but in practice it makes much more sense for a team of marketing and MIS professionals to work together from the very start of the project to develop the business needs document, with the MIS team then doing the bulk of the work required to complete the more technical functional requirements portion of the project. One reason for recommending this team approach to the development of a marketing database is that some of the things marketing might want the database to do might not be possible without major and costly changes to one or more of the supporting business systems. MIS personnel, who should be familiar with all the supporting business systems, are in a position to point out these situations right away. This joint approach minimizes false starts and disappointments later on in the project and allows a reasonably defined marketing database to be completed quickly.

Many readers may find the notion of marketing and MIS people working closely together to agree on anything strange. But cooperation can and must be achieved if the marketing database project is to succeed in a reasonable time frame and at a reasonable cost. One reason for the continuing conflict between MIS personnel and marketing staff is that their objectives are frequently in conflict. Whereas the marketing group typically wants immediate access to all data and data relationships, the MIS group is responsible for delivering systems that can be updated within existing production windows[1] and provide satisfactory on-line response time.

One of the goals of this chapter is to give both marketing and MIS professionals an appreciation of each others' concerns about the implications of the requirements imposed by the database project. Marketing people, to whom this book is principally addressed, should be particularly alert to the problem of imposing requirements that cannot be met without incurring major expenditures. No marketing professional wants to be in the position of explaining why a seemingly simple request has escalated into a million dollar (or more) project that could require converting the company's operating systems from VM to MVS, especially since the marketing person has probably never heard of either and doesn't care to.

BUSINESS NEEDS AND FUNCTIONAL REQUIREMENTS

A marketing database should, at a very minimum, be able to perform several basic marketing functions:

- Answering ad hoc questions (queries) about the characteristics and behavior of customers or prospects.
- Selecting names for future promotions based on ad hoc criteria, marketing events, or name scoring models.
- Tracking promotion results and profiling responders and nonresponders.

We will address each of these subjects individually, starting with ad hoc queries.

Queries

As we stated above, one of the most important issues to address when designing a marketing database is to define the kinds of questions the database must be able to answer. The more specific the marketing group can be when defining business needs and functional requirements the better because the answers to these questions will help MIS define the logical and physical design of the system.[2] In our experience developing sample

[1]*Production windows* are the time slots during which computer systems perform updates, produce off-line reports, transmit and receive data from other systems, and perform other maintenance activities.

[2]The terms *logical design* and *physical design* are defined in the discussion of Buzzword 6.

queries offers the best way (if not the only way) for marketing and technical people to effectively communicate with each other about exactly what data *will* or *will not* be in the database and what data will be immediately accessible or not.

In effect the marketing person is saying, *this is what I want to know, and this is how quickly I need an answer.* And the technical people are saying, *we can or cannot answer this question given the data that we all agreed to keep,* or *we can answer this question but not immediately given the way we have agreed to design the database.*

Only after a good number of truly painstaking sessions will both sides finally understand what is expected of the database application and what is possible. This kind of information is very difficult to absorb from flowchart presentations, and marketing people are well advised to avoid signing off on functional requirements until this question and answer process has been completed.

To give you a better idea of the kinds of questions that should be raised in these question and answer sessions we have posed a set of typical database questions. For the purpose of this discussion queries have been divided into two types:

1. Type I: Queries that can be answered directly and fully using the marketing database.
2. Type II: More complex queries that require additional analysis beyond what the database has been designed to provide. In this case, the database would be expected to provide *support,* for example, producing files that could readily be downloaded to other computing environments such as Statistical Analysis System (SAS) or a PC-based spreadsheet.

Type I queries: examples

1. Calculate the response rate to Promotion X.
2. Compare the profiles of customers who responded to Promotion X to nonresponders and determine whether there are any differences between these profiles that *appear* to be significant.
3. Count the number of current purchasers of Product A who are also purchasers of Product B.
4. How many purchasers of Product A come from the following states and have household incomes between $25,000 and $35,000?
5. Does there appear to be a regional variation in response to promotions for Product X?
6. Count the number of customers who are purchasers of Product A, who have not purchased Product B, and have not been promoted for *any* products within the past 12 months, 6 months, 3 months, and so on.
7. What is the age distribution of purchasers of Product A?
8. How many current purchasers of Product A have purchased at least one other product?
9. What is the distribution by age and sex by state of responders to Promotion X?
10. How many former customers of Business A are active customers of Business B?
11. How many current customers make multiple purchases?
12. How many current customers have upgraded their product ownership?

13. Identify customers who have *never* received a cross-sell promotion.
14. What is the average credit balance for customers who have outstanding credit balances?
15. Develop profiles of customers by
    a. Product category
    b. State
    c. Source media
    d. Demographic cluster type
16. Develop counts of customers who meet criteria for particular product offers.
17. Select, based on predictive models, those customers who are most likely to be responsive to new product offers.
18. How do different customer segments react to different copy?
19. Are customers who once bought through telemarketing more likely to buy again through telemarketing?
20. Flag grandparents and any possible information on the grandchild.
21. What was the customer's original purchase channel (phone, mail, charge, direct, walk-in)?

Type II queries: examples

1. Are cross-sell and direct mail promotions optimally coordinated?
2. Can coordination be improved to avoid same-product mailings to *recent* conversions?
3. How many same-product mailings, on average, are required prior to conversion?
4. Based on modeling results, how many promotions for the same product are warranted for given customers?
5. Could the existing calendar-driven sequence of promotions be replaced by a more targeted sequence, and if so, what would be some variations in sequence and packaging?
6. Can calendar-driven promotion sequence be integrated with event-driven promotions?
7. Can targeted promotion frequencies be implemented based on cost per account criteria?
8. What is the optimum level of multibuying to avoid overloading "good" customers?
9. Is there a point in time at which it can be determined that customers will never respond?
10. Does length of residence have any impact on response?
11. How long should historical, inactive records that have not been updated be kept?
12. Can customer profiles from one file be matched to profiles of other files?

Selecting Names for Future Promotions

Ad hoc selections. Marketers can use the marketing database to select names for promotions in a variety of ways. Name selections can be the result of an ad hoc query, as discussed above. In this situation the database will tell you how many names meet a particular criterion and those names can be flagged (split for testing if appropriate), coded, and selected for a particular promotion. Of course, the database will keep track of the entire process so you can analyze responses after the promotion is complete.

Event-driven promotions. Another way to use the database for promotions is to have the update process identify particular events that trigger a promotion. For example, the update can check the customer's birthdate and, if it is within a specified time limit, say 30 days, select the name to receive a mailing. Or, the purchase of a particular product or service may prompt a promotion for another related product and so on. Event-driven promotions (or *if, then* promotions) can and should be a major source of mailings or telephone contacts in a database environment.

Scoring models. A third and important type of database-drive promotion results from scoring models. One of the most important tasks of the database is to facilitate the creation of statistical models and the subsequent implementation of model results. The first part of this process is to make the selection of names for statistical analysis easier.

Companies that perform statistical analysis in-house may use any of several platforms, including mainframes, PCs, or workstations, for modeling. If the work is to be done in the same environment where the data resides, the task of the database is to extract a file that contains the desired number of names and the specified data elements and produce an output file in the form that the statistical analysis product requires.[3]

Selecting Names Based on Model Scores

After a model has been built, the database must be able to implement its results by executing scoring equations, storing scores, and providing a facility for selecting customers, based on their scores, for specific direct marketing programs. This process includes these elements:

- Incorporating the model equations into the language used by the database system.[4]
- Executing the scoring equation within the database so all records that meet the conditions specified for the sample group will be scored using the scoring equation. (See Chapters 10 through 15, which discuss statistical analysis and modeling.)
- Storing the scores produced by the scoring equation in the database.
- Sorting the file in descending sequence by score.
- Dividing the file into a number of equal-sized groups (frequently 10 groups or deciles).
- Assigning customer records to their appropriate deciles, based on their scores.
- Storing the decile score for each customer record along with its raw score, the name of the model, and the date on which the model was run.
- Providing a facility for selecting names based on the decile, or raw score, which was assigned by the scoring model.

---

[3]If the analysis is to be done on a separate platform and the file is relatively small, the file may be electronically transferred using the company's standard interconnection protocols. For PC to workstation, or mainframe to workstation transfers, you would generally use Transmission Control Protocol/Internet Protocol (TCP/IP)-based file transfer programs. For mainframe to PC transfers, companies generally use IRMA, PCOX or similar communications products. If the analysis file is larger or if the analysis work is going to be done using third-party computer facilities, the analysis file is generally stored on magnetic tape.

[4]In some cases, COBOL or FORTRAN may be used for more complex mathematical functions if the database system's fourth-generation language does not support mathematical functions efficiently.

Tracking Promotion Results and Profiling

The third critical database function is tracking promotion results and profiling. In this regard the database should be capable of producing reports that show this information for any promotion or combination of promotions:

- The number of pieces mailed (or calls made) and the number of responses broken down by key code or test cell identifier and by decile or some other measure related to scoring.
- Profiles of responders.

Profiles are most easily accomplished by the creation *on demand* of simple tables. For example, the simplest kind of table has only one dimension, such as response rate by state, response by gender, response by PRIZM code, or response by any other variable in the database. A more complicated, but still easy-to-read table might include two variables, say state and gender, so you could see the response rate for each state and gender combination. More complicated three- or four-way tables (at this point they are called cross-tabs) are certainly possible, but they are much more difficult to read.

Another and perhaps more actionable use of profiling is to accomplish these tasks:

- Score a file according to a scoring model.
- Sort the file into deciles or some other convenient grouping.
- Profile all deciles using demographic data, lifestyle data, or both.
- Then compare the profiles of the most responsive segments of the file to the profiles of the least responsive.

If significant differences are found between responsive and unresponsive segments, then there may be reason to believe that different creative approaches might be more effective for the low-performing deciles than the current control, which is probably being mailed to the entire file.

Still another variation on profiling is to use the database to discover product affinities. If, for example, you found that persons who bought Product A also tended to buy Product B, then you might mail a Product B promotion to all Product A owners, of course suppressing those that already owned Product B.

USER-FRIENDLY ENVIRONMENTS

The marketing database should provide a user-friendly environment in which marketers can perform all the functions discussed above without requiring programming intervention by data processing professionals.

Since the advent of the personal computer in the early 1980s, marketers who have little or no programming experience have become used to performing analytical tasks independently of their company's data processing professionals. Many PC users are now familiar with microcomputer tools such as spreadsheets, databases, and graphics programs and have become used to working with menus, icons, pop-up screens, point-and-click mouse devices, guided modes of operation, and on-line help screens that assist them in performing complex data analysis tasks.

Because of the power of these tools, many PC users are entirely unaware that to perform the desired tasks the PC-based products are actually writing complex computer programs in the background. Consequently, although all fourth-generation database products include an attractive and *relatively* user-friendly query facility, or front end, users are frequently disappointed in the time it takes to answer what the colorful menus suggest are relatively simple questions. Therefore, to keep user and management expectations in perspective, companies should approve both the screens that will be used to submit queries and the response times associated with queries of differing complexity using prototype versions of applications prior to committing to a final database design.

An attractive feature of many database products is that queries can be saved and reused, or modified to suit the needs of other end users. Queries that are used on an ongoing basis can be stored and "secured" by limiting access to authorized users. The alterations can often be made in English or natural language terms, or by returning to menu screens and modifying existing queries using menus and point-and-click techniques.

Some state-of-the-art systems combine the power of mainframe or workstation processing with the ease of use of PCs—end users can simply indicate the functions they wish to perform without being aware of which tasks are being performed on the mainframe or workstation and which on the PC.

In a well-designed marketing database, end users can gain access to data about customers, products, promotions, catalogs, transactions, or other data in a virtually unlimited number of ways simply by using menu screens or by selecting previously generated reports or queries. Regularly occurring reports such as daily response to promotions can be set up to provide each end user with an individual report that supports his unique information needs.

These highly individual reporting capabilities are referred to as *views* of the data. Although end users often think only in terms of their own desktop device providing the information they seek, it is actually the database engine that makes this limitless variety of views possible.

TURNAROUND TIME

In the process of defining functional requirements turnaround times for various types of functions become particularly important. That is, which functions must be performed in seconds, which in minutes, and which ones overnight?

It is a natural tendency for marketers to request that all information, in any combination, be available immediately at all times. The relative importance of various queries should be weighed, however, because system performance does not come free of charge, and quick response time often requires an increased investment in computer hardware.

Improving response time generally means increasing the number of Direct Access Storage Device (DASD) units, increasing channel capacity, and most often, increasing Central Processing Unit (CPU) capacity (similar to adding memory cards to a PC), both in terms of processing power and memory. This can become expensive very quickly, so you should instead take a selective approach, based on priorities.

Generally speaking, marketers will want to get quick responses to simple queries, for example, the number of people from source X who purchased more than four units within the past six months. A query of this type should generally be available within 30 to 60 seconds.

The importance of quick turnaround for simple queries is that marketers will formulate new questions based on the answers they receive, and maximum productivity is achieved if response time is quick enough to maintain the marketer's train of thought. Although turnaround time of minutes, rather than hours or days, for simple queries may seem rapid today, many studies of interactive productivity have shown that when computer response time exceeds 20 seconds, an end user's mind begins to wander and she may begin doing desk work, returning telephone calls, or initiating other activities that distract her from the set of queries at hand.

In an inverted file database structure[5] such as Model 204, Datacom/DB, or ADABAS, queries that involve quick counts, as in the example above, are typically handled within a few seconds, even on databases containing several million records through the use of indexes.[6] Complex, ad hoc queries are likely to take much longer to produce. This is especially true if multiple database tables have to be joined together to produce the desired information and/or if access to non-indexed data is required.

Here, the trade-off becomes frequency of queries versus system performance. If the query will be asked frequently it may be appropriate to develop tables that contain all the required data elements and pay the price in additional data storage and update time. If the query will be asked infrequently, overnight response using the table structure already in existence may be adequate. Standard management reports are likely to continue to be produced on an overnight, weekly, or even monthly basis.

To improve the response time for complex queries, some companies design their database marketing applications to contain all the data elements required to answer the queries in a single table, or at most, a small number of tables. Unfortunately, structuring a database in this way generally results in increased update time for the marketing database. For fully integrated database marketing applications, the problem may be even worse because large records contained in single tables can constrain response time for processing transactions. This is one of the reasons that some companies create separate databases for marketing analysis and operations.

Some companies with very large customer databases are moving toward using representative sample databases for analysis. They can use these files to perform analysis efficiently while providing statistically significant estimates of the actual distributions of records on the customer file. Once the selection criteria have been defined using the sample database, less time-sensitive processes can execute programs against the full database to select the actual records for promotion.

To better understand the impact that their information requests will have on the cost and performance of their database marketing applications, marketers should work together with their MIS groups to determine whether the importance of certain queries and the frequency with which they are made justify the costs. Systems personnel may be able to

---

[5]See Buzzword 9 for definitions of types of database products.

[6]See Buzzword 4 for description of indexes.

suggest alternative means of delivering the required information that would have less of an impact on system performance and data storage costs.

In fact, the more that marketers know about how the technology works and the issues that their MIS professionals must resolve in designing an application, the more control they can exercise over the quality and functionality of the marketing database system. In recognition of this fact, many vendors of DBMS software, as well as universities and professional associations, offer courses in DBMS technology that are oriented to end users.

The functional requirements issues raised in this chapter have a major impact on how the database will be created and updated and on the hardware and software tools used to build and support the database. These subjects will be addressed in the following chapters.

Chapter 6

Creating and Updating the Database

A FRAMEWORK FOR IMPLEMENTING A DATABASE PROJECT

In Chapter 5 we discussed the process of creating a detailed business needs and functional requirements document for a marketing database. Both in theory and in practice this process can be completed prior to a thorough review and evaluation of the data elements currently included in each of the individual files expected to be brought into the database. However, it is often more practical to begin by identifying the data in the individual business files from which the database will be created and maintained. In broad outline form the process could proceed as follows:

1. Decide whether the database will be created and maintained at an outside service bureau or developed internally. For the purpose of this discussion let's assume that we will be using an outside service bureau and that internal data processing departments will be sending files to the service bureau to update the database.
2. Have the database team (a concept suggested in Chapter 5) develop a preliminary list of the business needs the database will be expected to support.
3. Identify the individual business and promotional files to be included in the database.
4. Review the data elements contained in each contributing file.
5. Select from each file only the data elements you wish to bring into the database.
6. On a file-by-file basis define the data elements you might wish to create by comparing end-of-period updates. You can develop cumulative statistics (if only period data exists) or period statistics (if only cumulative data exists).
7. Decide where the data processing work defined above (extracting individual data elements and creating new data elements) is to be done—at one (or more) of the internal data-processing departments or at the service bureau.
8. Decide which, if any, *data enhancement files* will be brought into the database.
9. Decide on a methodology for consolidating information about individual customers.
10. Decide on a methodology for consolidating customers into households.
11. Develop a preliminary database design.
12. Decide how frequently the database will be updated.
13. Determine whether the update process will require updating existing records *within the database,* whether database records will periodically be replaced, or whether the optimal approach for your company will be a combination of both update methods.

14. Go back to the preliminary list of business needs and determine if the available data, the consolidation plan, and the database design is capable of meeting the business needs.
15. Revise elements of the plan as necessary.

WILL THE DATABASE BE CREATED AND MAINTAINED IN-HOUSE OR AT AN OUTSIDE SERVICE BUREAU?

Should the entire database marketing process be done in-house, or should a combination of internal and external resources be considered?

There are three principal reasons why some companies prefer to do the entire job of developing a marketing database in-house: (1) cost, (2) control, and (3) customization.

Cost. There is always a perception that it is less expensive to develop applications in-house because the programmers on staff are part of a fixed cost budget. This assumption must be validated, however, based on the existing workload of the in-house staff; whether they are fully occupied supporting other projects; and, if so, the incremental cost of additional programmers required for the database marketing project. All these factors must be compared to the cost of using external resources.

Control. For many companies control is a more important consideration than cost. The customer list is the lifeblood of most direct marketing companies. Any use of external facilities must, by definition, create additional risk of exposure for the integrity and confidentiality of a company's data. To maintain control of critical data while using external resources companies must first assess the risk and then manage that risk through procedural and contractual measures in conjunction with the external service provider.

Customization. Customization is one of the most important reasons to consider doing the project in-house. No matter how committed an external service provider is to the company's project, no one understands a firm's data as well as the people who work with it every day. Consequently, a system developed by an external service provider might not provide the same level of customized screens, menus, and reporting capabilities that an internally developed application would offer.

External Vendors

There are two principal reasons to consider using external resources when developing a marketing database: (1) experience and facilities and (2) speed.

Experience and facilities. If the company does not have a DBMS product in-house or if it uses a different DBMS product for the marketing database, time (and therefore money) must be invested in getting the MIS staff up to speed on the product before any application development work can begin.

Meanwhile, the application development process will remain stalled until the marketing group and the MIS group have developed a functional requirements document, discussed design issues, and in many cases, reinvented the wheel a few times before the MIS group is ready to get down to serious application development work. While all this preparatory work is going on, the marketing group *still* will not have the access it requires to data, and it will continue to make decisions based on the same quality of information that was available before the application development process began.

One of the most important benefits an external service provider can offer a company at this point in its application development process is the experience and the facilities that enable marketers to load their current data into a database format, get immediate access to their data so they can make better marketing decisions, and give them a chance to develop some hands-on experience with database technology. This hands-on experience will have direct benefits when it comes to defining the functional requirements of their own applications.

Speed. Marketers often cannot wait until the application is completed internally to make their critical marketing decisions. By using external facilities the database marketing application can be available for use much sooner. Therefore, marketing decisions can be made in a timely manner, based on much better information; as a result, higher quality decisions are likely.

A Combined Approach

The database decision doesn't have to be either in-house or an outside service bureau. Many companies find that the most successful approach is to use external services for those functions that are most efficiently done externally, while concentrating their development activities on internal resources. For example, although most companies may be able to define the *rules* for matching and householding, few are as experienced as service bureaus at performing these operations.

Therefore, for some companies, it is actually more efficient to use external services for the full range of database marketing services at first, and, at a later date, to bring the application in-house. This is generally true both for licensed versions of a vendor's preexisting database marketing application and for totally customized solutions that have been developed for client companies by vendors. Most vendors will assist client companies in making the transition to maintaining the database in-house and will often continue to provide services such as National Change of Address (NCOA), lettershop, or creative services.

The important point to remember is that using external services and internal resources are not mutually exclusive approaches. The specific mix of services depends on the company, its available resources, and the development timetable.

WHAT DATA IS NEEDED TO PERFORM THE REQUIRED FUNCTIONS?

The database team should develop a preliminary list of business needs, as discussed in detail in Chapter 5. The next step is defining the data elements that will be needed to perform the required functions, a three-step process:

1. Identify the business and promotional files that should be included in the database.
2. Review the data elements contained in each contributing file.
3. Select from each file only the data elements you wish to bring into the database.

Identify the Files to Be Included in the Database

Several constraints affect selecting files for inclusion. Although some marketers would like to include all the data that ever existed about all customers back to the beginning of time, this approach will not be practical, affordable, or even necessarily valuable from an informational perspective.

Issues to consider include these:

- Some files may not be available because of company policy decisions, interdivisional politics, or logistical difficulty. Files that are too hard to get can either be replaced with others or simply excluded from the initial database. If the project team finds that the available files do not offer adequate information to justify the database, then corporate commitment and sponsorship of the project need to be revisited.
- How much promotion history is available? If two to three years of history may be available, how much of it is still relevant? Most companies find that one year of detailed data and two to three years of summary data are adequate for building a promotion history. If less data is available, then it will be more difficult to differentiate customers based on their promotion histories. More emphasis would therefore have to be placed on current promotions.
- What level of transaction data is available? Some companies maintain their transaction data as period statistics, such as sales this month, returns this month, and so on. Other companies maintain their data as current, cumulative snapshots in the customer file, such as sales to date, returns to date, and so on. How the data is captured may determine if preprocessing activities of one type or another are required (more on this subject later in this chapter).

So the first step in the process is to identify the files to be included in the database based on their availability and their information content.

Review the Data Elements Contained in Each Contributing File

Once the desired subset of available files has been identified, a thorough review of the data elements contained in each file must be conducted. This process will require detailed reviews of each data element with the data processing or end user personnel who are most familiar with each file to determine the precise meaning of each data element. Adequate time must be allocated for this process, which may take anywhere from one day to a few weeks—there are no shortcuts.

Select the Data Elements that Are Needed from Each File

Two sets of data elements are likely to be identified during the review of data elements:

1. Those data elements that clearly need to be included.
2. Additional data elements that are not as clearly necessary but that the team feels uncomfortable about leaving out without further review.

Actually, both sets of data elements should be included. Marketers will learn more about the individual data elements as they use the database, and some of the "extra" elements that were initially included will prove to be valuable. They will find that others, as well as some of the "certain" choices, are of little value. Generally, it makes sense to revisit the selection of data elements after about a year of using the database, as the value of each data element becomes clearer, and to modify the database loader programs accordingly.

DEFINE DATA ELEMENTS THAT MUST BE CREATED DURING UPDATES

Earlier in this chapter, we described two ways in which customer files may be kept, as cumulative statistics or as period statistics.

If customer records are kept as *cumulative statistics,* such as sales-to-date, purchases-to-date, and so on, then it will be desirable to calculate *period statistics* during each update cycle. Similarly, if customer records are kept as *period statistics,* then it may be necessary to calculate *cumulative statistics* during the update process. Most companies' transaction files contain a small number of cumulative statistic fields and a larger number of period statistic fields. We will discuss *how* these statistics are calculated later in this chapter.

HOW WILL DATA GET INTO THE MARKETING DATABASE?

Once we have identified the data elements that are to be included in the marketing database the next step in the process is to determine *how* the data elements will get there. This process can be accomplished in three ways, each of which has different cost and processing implications:

1. **Data extraction by data providers.** The desired data elements can be extracted from existing files by a series of programs written and maintained by the data providers. This approach helps minimize the volume of data that must be processed during the initial load and subsequent updates and can reduce the time required and costs associated with these processes. The disadvantage to this approach is that, over time, the data elements to be included in the marketing database are likely to change, and each change in data elements will require corresponding changes not only to the database loader programs, but also to the data extraction programs.
2. **Data extraction including creation of summary calculated data.** In addition to the processes described for the first option, this variation includes calculating summary data fields such as the total sales per customer during the period across all business units, the average purchases to date, and so on. This approach shares all the advantages and disadvantages of the prior process and adds the complexity of performing calculations on data elements during the extraction process.
3. **Providing complete, unextracted copies of existing files to database loader.** Complete, unextracted copies of all existing files can be provided to the database loader, and the database loader can sort out which records to include and exclude. This is the simplest approach for the data providers, but it involves the greatest amount of work and cost for the database loaders. One advantage that it offers is that over time, as the data elements to be included in the database change, it may be simpler and more cost-effective to modify only the database loader rather than modifying both the database loader and the extract programs.

Each of these approaches has cost, time, and organizational implications depending on whether the processing work is to be performed in-house or at a service bureau. Although the choices for each company will vary according to such factors as the complexity of the database application, size of the database, number of internal file sources, and availability of internal resources, there is no free lunch for anyone on this issue.

In-House Processing Implications

One of the objectives for most companies in developing a marketing database application is to bring together *all* the information known about customers throughout their relationship with the company. This often requires bringing together files from a number of different business units or profit centers, each of which has its own agenda and priorities.

In companies with a small number of data sources, the internal MIS management would have to provide extracts of data on an ongoing basis. Depending on the workload of the MIS group and the priorities of other projects, high-level sponsorship for the data needs of the marketing database may be required to get the programming projects and subsequent processing work approved.

In companies where the data sources are from more than one division, it may be necessary to negotiate arrangements with multiple divisions, first to provide data at all, and second to gain cooperation for providing data on an ongoing basis. In some cases, divisions will incur personnel or processing costs for performing data extractions that may have to be paid for either by the database project or through some other internal cost transfer mechanism. These issues often need to be resolved at a fairly high level within companies *before* long-term commitments for the support of the database application can be made.

Service Bureau Processing Implications

If a service bureau is to perform the data extraction and other preprocessing activities, companies should consider how the service bureau charges and how these charges will impact the costs of the project. For example, if a large number of records will be preprocessed during each update cycle, the service bureau cost could be significant, particularly if the service bureau charges based on the number of records passed. Companies may wish to consider performing some or all of the preprocessing work internally and then sending the files to the service bureau in these cases:

1. The service bureau's charges for preprocessing files exceed an acceptable level.
2. Adequate and affordable processing services are available in-house.

Although service bureaus offer "painless processing," avoiding any of the political issues associated with internal processing, their services are not free, and the costs may be prohibitive over the duration of the project. Considerations will vary from company to company, but the issues are constant. Each company must evaluate its options and select the approach that is most appropriate based on cost and convenience.

DECIDE WHICH, IF ANY, DATA ENHANCEMENT FILES WILL BE USED

Several companies are in the business of selling enhancement data that they have either compiled themselves or that they offer on behalf of other data vendor companies. Chapter 2 described the data elements available for enhancement as secondary data that is purchased from external sources. Secondary data is available on a license basis directly to customer companies or through the major service bureaus. In Chapter 2 we described what the data elements are, and in later chapters we describe how you can use these enhancement data elements for modeling or profiling as part of the new direct marketing.

As part of the process of building a database, companies must decide which, if any, of the enhancement data variables they will include in their databases so the database design and the database loader programs can accommodate this data.

FIGURE 6–1

	Table I Customer Data	*Table II Purchase Data*	
Data Elements	Customer ID Name Address Demographic Data	Customer ID Purchase Date Catalog Number Product Code Item Code	*Repeating Records*

CONSOLIDATING RECORDS

A difficult, time-consuming, and often expensive step in the database loading process is record consolidation. Many firms capture customer records in transaction-oriented systems, and multiple records for individuals and households may exist on the file. Before these records are loaded into the database, duplicates must be identified and in some cases "scrubbed" (a process described later in this chapter), so the marketer will have the clearest idea possible of how many customers there are and what their relationships may be to each other.

In a single-product company, if unique customer IDs or match codes are used in the fulfillment system, it is likely that only one record will exist for each customer. However, many companies, particularly in financial services, may have a number of different relationships with a single customer. If the firm's data processing systems are account-based rather than customer-based, it is very likely that the company will be unaware of the total relationship it has with a customer and that each product group will be unaware of the customer's relationships with other parts of the firm.

As part of the initial consolidation process, companies may choose to build a cross-reference file that links all account numbers associated with a given customer using a unique customer ID. The customer ID should be unique and *not* based on the customer's name and address because these may change over time, making it more difficult to maintain data integrity within the database.

As shown in Figure 6–1, customer ID is a keyed field, meaning that it is one of the fields used to link a number of different tables together.

Duplicate Identification

To consolidate records at the customer level, a duplicate identification process must be executed prior to loading names into the database to identify which records belong to the same customer. Most often, duplicate identification processes are based on names and addresses. More sophisticated duplicate identification software products use a number of algorithms to predict the probability of two records belonging to the same person. Users can set the criteria to be tighter or looser, as required by the marketing application, and the algorithms within the program will suggest which customers are duplicates and which are unique.

Although the software used to perform duplicate identification is the same as that used to *eliminate* duplicates when preparing mailings from multiple internal sources or from rented lists, the intent of the process is entirely different when building a customer or prospect database. Here the goal is to capture *all the information* related to each customer or prospect and to consolidate data that would otherwise be fragmented across a number of different records into a single and complete picture of that individual's relationship with the company.

The matching algorithms can be set either loosely or tightly depending on how critical an exact match must be for the company's application. For example, companies that are interested in mailing into *households* rather than to specific individuals within those households may be satisfied if the last name and the address match exactly. In some cases, if they are certain that an address is not a multiple dwelling, they will be satisfied with an address match alone.

Address Standardization

Address standardization software such as LPC's *Finalist* or Group 1's *Code-l Plus* can deal with transposed street addresses and incorrect street names. For example, is *123 Oak Street, 132 Oak Street,* or *132 Oat Street* correct? By comparing these addresses to national databases and by using the *Delivery Sequence File* (DSF), marketers can automatically determine if

- The ZIP code matches the city and state portions of the address.
- The ZIP code (or corrected ZIP code) contains an Oak Street, an Oat Street, or both.
- The street numbers along the street in question lie within the bounds of the ZIP code.
- The street number is a valid address.
- The address is a business or residence and whether a residence is a single family or multi-family dwelling unit.

Matching Issues

It is not unusual to find variations in the spelling of an individual name within a company's files. One company found the names Robert Smith, Bob Smith, R. Smith, and Robt Smythe all listed at the same address. We may assume that these are the same individual, but it is possible that these are records of a father and son; a grandfather, father, and son; or possibly unrelated individuals. You can set parameters for the matching software to consider these versions of a name as a single name or to retain them as multiple individuals, depending on the requirements of the mailer.

Once all these issues have been addressed, *all iterations of the address* contained in the files can be corrected and the matching process can be completed efficiently.

Often companies that have multiple business files store name and address data in different formats in each file. In this situation, duplicate identification software must be flexible enough to *parse*[1] through the elements of a name and, in some cases, to determine what comprises the first name, last name, middle name or initial, title, suffix, or other elements. Many service bureaus and some large companies have developed dictionaries of first names, last names, titles, and suffixes to use as a reference during this process.

The duplicate identification (or merge/purge process—we use the terms interchangeably) may be equally important for prospect files, since these may contain a history of prior inquiries and related promotions to prospects. For many companies, the number of previous inquiries that a

---

[1]*Parsing* is a computer process in which data elements are read one position at a time and compared to tables to determine whether the data is valid, and if so, what it means.

FIGURE 6–2

City Federal ITF
Anthony Smith Julia Smith JTTNT IRA
123 Elm Street
Anytown, USA

FIGURE 6–3

Anthony and Julia Smith
123 Elm Street
Anytown, USA

prospect has made is a very strong predictor of eventual conversion. Prior inquiry information about products other than those currently owned by customers may also be available. If so, this data may provide additional guidance for how to market in a cross-selling campaign.

Scrubbing

For financial services companies registration information may be imbedded in the customer record as part of the name and address, as shown in Figure 6–2. In this example, we begin an examination of account information for Anthony and Julia Smith, who have a number of different relationships with City Federal Bank.

In Figure 6–2, we see that City Federal is the trustee for a trust fund account owned by Anthony and Julia Smith as joint tenants. Before we could match this customer record against a customer record like that shown in Figure 6–3, we would first have to strip out registration information unrelated to name and address.

In a specialized application of parsing and dictionary use, scrubbing software would recognize that City Federal, ITF, and JTTNT are all terms that are not names or addresses of individuals. It would strip out this data and prepare a new record that could be matched much more readily using merge/purge software. In addition, scrubbing software interprets and retains the *meaning* of registration data so that its information value is not lost.

Householding

Identifying which customers are actually members of the same household can be a complicated process. Two scenarios follow—one typical householding process based on names and addresses and one that represents more complex and, in the new direct marketing, more common situations.

Householding based on names and addresses. Once the file is scrubbed, we must take some additional steps to accurately and efficiently market to households. Suppose that Anthony Smith also had an IRA and that the mortgage for the home where he and his wife reside is in Julia's name alone. To understand the full extent of the Smith's relationships with City Federal, as well as their household relationship, the bank would have to go through all the steps we described.

First, the software would perform the household match using an algorithm that matched the Smiths by ZIP code, last name, and street address.

The first name comparison would show that Anthony and Julia were two different people. Joint account information would further establish the relationship between the two; however, we would have to obtain the fact that they are married to each other either from other account information or from external sources, or we would infer it based on the sex and age of each individual.

Understanding the relationships between customers in a household may be essential to a company's marketing efforts because inappropriate copy or artwork may have a negative impact on response. Accordingly, companies must be careful about making assumptions concerning relationships within households and may wish to maintain scores that represent levels of certainty about relationships. These scores in turn could be used to determine how deeply into a file a certain promotion should be mailed.

Let's say that City Federal identified Julia and Anthony Smith's relationship as husband and wife based on specific data contained in their trust records. In this case, the value (or confidence level) that Anthony and Julia are married could be set at 100 percent. But suppose that this specific data were not available. Based on other information, Anthony and Julia's ages were known to be 55 and 53 respectively, and a match of their first names against a dictionary showed that they were male and female respectively. In this situation, City Federal could not be certain that Anthony and Julia were not brother and sister, or even cousins.

If we knew children were in the household, we might have further reason to infer that the Smiths are a conventional family, but even this set of relationships would not provide the same level of certainty as would documentation *within the account.* Therefore, a promotion that featured a conventional family situation and product set might or might not be appropriate. And as many direct marketers have found, promotions with inappropriate or inaccurate personalization can underperform nonpersonalized promotions.

Identifying more complex relationships between customers. Some companies may wish to use householding techniques to identify more complex relationships between customers. Consider a company that has insurance products, retail sales, catalog sales, and house credit cards that may be used for purchases in each of these product lines. To illustrate the complexity of customer relationships, we can describe four situations—Type I, Type II, Type III, and Type IV households. These classifications are not meant to be exhaustive, but rather they are intended to illustrate the kinds of decisions marketers must face when formulating rules to define households.

1. **Type I households.** Type I households are the basic case described above in which customers who have the same last name and who live at the same address constitute a household. In addition to these characteristics, they may in addition have credit card account numbers or insurance policy numbers in common.

2. **Type II households.** Type II households consist of individuals who have different last names, live at the same address, and have credit card account numbers or insurance policy numbers in common. These households

may consist of married couples in which the wife has kept her maiden name, parent-child situations in which the parent is responsible for the child's financial obligations or the reverse, or sets of unmarried individuals whose relationships are sufficiently permanent for them to have established shared financial obligations.

3. Type III households. Type III households consist of individuals who have common account numbers or policy numbers, live at *different* addresses, and may or may not have a common last name. Type III household structures would be typical for parents who have financial responsibility for dependent children who may be away at school or who at least maintain a separate residence, or of individuals who have financial responsibility for dependent parents who maintain a separate residence.

4. Type IV households. Type IV households consist of individuals who live at the same address, have different last names, and do not have account numbers or policy numbers in common. These households would be typical of roommates who share a dwelling, but do not share financial responsibilities.

Each of these household types represents a different marketing opportunity, and marketers could apply the information captured during the data consolidation process to select different groups of customers for different types of promotions.

As part of the data consolidation process the company could obtain counts of the total number of relationships with each customer or related group of customers. Subtotals of the number of relationships could also be calculated by product category. For example, marketers might wish to know the total number of insurance policies for an individual customer or household. This calculation could be based on the number of policies owned by individuals who comprise each of the household types described above.

Similarly, credit card account numbers used for retail or catalog purchases could be linked, either within a single residence or across multiple residences. The number of relationships at the customer or household level may be used in combination with information about individual customer purchases and promotion history to develop statistical models that predict response to promotion efforts.

DEVELOP A PRELIMINARY DATABASE DESIGN

Once a company's data had been consolidated at the individual and household level, the next step in the process would be to populate a marketing database with this data. This requires that a preliminary database design has been developed by data processing professionals, either within the company or at the service bureau if the marketing database application is being developed externally. Figure 6–4 contains a series of tables that together comprise a preliminary database design for a catalog company. Although the specific data elements would vary for different types of companies, this example will help you understand the types of tables that a marketing database likely includes and the organization of data elements within each table.

Figure 6–5 illustrates data that would be stored in summary form in a typical marketing database after the summary fields had been created either during the data-extraction or the data-loading process.

FIGURE 6–4
Data Tables

Customer Table	*Repeat Purchase Table*	*Item Table*	*Catalog Promo Table*	*Print/FSI Promo Table*	*Broadcast Promo Table*	*Catalog Source Table*
			Key Fields			
Customer ID	Customer ID	Item Code	Catalog Number Item Code	Key Code	Key Code	Catalog Number Key Code Offer Code
			Nonrecurring Fields			
Name Address Match Code Prior Name Prior Address Individual Demographic Data Original Source Code Date of First Purchase	Purchase IDs Actual Catalog Number Attributed Catalog Number Purchase Date Purchase Amount Payment Mode Ordering Mode	Item Cost Subject Code Product Code Description	Date Mailed Quantity Mailed Item Price Percent of Page Page Number and Position Key Code Offer Code Test Code Production Costs Fixed Variable Total Cost Description	Ad Code Release Date Media Cost Circulation Offer Code Production Costs Fixed Variable Total Cost	Ad Code On Air Date Air Time 800 Phone Number Production Costs Fixed Variable Total Cost Description	Duplication Rate versus House File Quantity Ordered Quantity Mailed Costs Broker ID Creative Code Test Code

Print/FSI Source Table	*Medium Table*	*Offer Code Table*	*Deciles Table*	*Model Table*	*Purchase Item Table*
		Key Fields			
Key Code Offer Code	Medium Code Key Code	Offer Code Catalog Number	Customer ID Model Code	Model Code	Item Code Purchase ID
		Nonrecurring Fields			
Circulation Creative Code Test Code Description Costs	Major Media Code(s) Description	Description	Model Score Date of Scoring Decile Code	Model Name Model Description	

Customer Table

Data Element	*Description*
	Key Fields
Customer ID	A unique customer identification code that, once assigned, will always remain associated with that customer. This is used to link the customer table with a number of other tables in the database and to help identify repeat customers who may have been archived from the system because of inactivity.
	Nonrecurring Fields
Name	Customer's current name.
Address	Customer's current address.
Match Code	A match code based on the customer's current name and address. This code makes customers who are already on the database easily identifiable when new orders or inquiries are received. Match codes are associated with the unique customer ID.
Prior Name	Some marketers like to carry at least one prior name on the database.
Prior Address	Similarly, some marketers like to carry one or two prior addresses on the file for ease of identifying customers who have moved.
Individual Level Demographic Data	Through modeling, many marketers have found that demographic data, for example, individual age, income, lifestyle, home value, and so on is useful in predicting response to a particular promotion and lifetime value of customers. A number of fields are usually made available for storing this data in the customer table, even though the specific data elements that will fill these fields may not be known at the time the database is created.
Original Source Code	This field links individual customers with their original source. Although it would also be possible to link customers by source via the purchase table, there are many instances in which it is desirable to determine the number or the characteristics of customers who come from a particular source without having to sort through their purchase behavior. Also, since the original source code will not change, it makes sense to maintain this as one of the static fields in the customer table.
Date of First Purchase	Although the purchase table will capture dates of all future purchases, the date of first purchase defines a class of purchasers, and is therefore often maintained separately.

Repeat Purchase Table

Data Element	Description
	Key Fields
Customer ID	The unique customer ID is the link between purchases made and the customers who made them.
	Purchase Data Elements that Recur with Each Purchase or Return Transaction
Purchase ID	The purchase ID identifies individual purchase or return transactions so detailed information about purchases could be obtained if desired.
Actual Catalog Number	The catalog number (catalog) that the customer bought from.
Attributed Catalog Number	In situations where the actual catalog number is unknown, an attributed catalog number is calculated, usually based on the most recent catalog that contained the purchased item that was mailed to the customer prior to ordering.
Purchase Date	For all subsequent purchases, the date of the purchase is maintained in the purchase table.
Purchase Amount	For each purchase, the purchase amount is maintained.
Payment Mode	An indicator is often maintained to show whether a purchase was made using cash or a credit card. This data may be important in the future when selecting customers for certain promotions.
Ordering Mode	An indicator is maintained to show whether an order was placed by mail or by telephone.

Item Table

Data Element	Description
	Key Fields
Item Code	This field links the item table with other tables, including purchase, product, and catalog, and through them with customers.
	Nonrecurring Fields
Item Cost	The cost of an item to the cataloger.
Subject Code	The subject with which each item in the table is associated.
Product Code	The product type with which each item is associated.
Description	A free-form description of the item.

Catalog Promotion Table

Data Element	*Description*
	Key Fields
Catalog Number	Each catalog has a unique identification number.
Item Code(s)	Item code field links specific items purchased to the catalog from which they were purchased. Because prices and costs of items may vary depending on quantities ordered or special promotions, each combination of catalog code with item code is able to support unique prices and costs. This data is carried in detail in the item table.
	Nonrecurring Fields
Date Mailed	Each catalog has a unique value for date mailed, which will be maintained in the database.
Quantity Mailed	The mailing quantity of each catalog is maintained for subsequent analysis.
Item Price	The standard (or default) price for an item. This may change for special offers or for certain catalogs. The combination of item code and catalog code is linked with a unique price.
Percent of Page	Indicates the percent of page in a catalog given to a specific item.
Page Number and Position	Indicates the page of the catalog on which the item appeared and the position of the item on the page.
Key Code	Links catalog number to specific mailing source(s).
Offer Code(s)	Provision for unique codes to describe the offers being conducted in a specific catalog.
Test Code(s)	Provision for unique codes to describe the offers being conducted in a specific catalog.
Costs	Costs associated with mailing.
Production Costs	For each catalog mailing, costs, including list rental, postage, and detailed production, are maintained so that return on promotion can subsequently be calculated.
Fixed Costs	
Color Separations	
Type	
Mechanicals	
Creative	
Variable Costs	
Printing	
Lettershop	
Lists	
Postage	
Return Postage	
Total Costs	Total of all fixed and variable costs associated with production and distribution of catalog.
Descriptive Data	
Number of Pages	The number of pages in the catalog is maintained.
Free-Form Description	Free-form text describes the seasonality, theme, coloration, or other relevant data about the department.

Print/FSI Promotion Table

Data Element	*Description*
	Key Fields
Key Code	Links to other tables.
	Nonrecurring Fields
Ad Code	Unique ID for each ad.
Release Date	The date on which the periodical issue will be released.
Media Cost	Cost per page for print, cost of production, and distribution for FSIs.
Circulation	Circulation of periodical or guaranteed distribution volume for FSIs.
Offer Code	As in direct mail, specific offers can be tested in other media.
Production Costs Fixed Color Separations Type Mechanicals Photography Creative Variable Costs Printing Media	Cost associated with print or FSI promotions. For each promotion, costs include production, creative, and other fixed costs, as well as variable costs such as printing and distribution.
Response Cost	Inbound coupon or telephone response cost.
Lettershop Postage Return Postage	
Total Costs	Total of production, response, and media expenses.

Broadcast Promotion Table

Data Element	*Description*
	Key Fields
Key Code	Links to other tables.
	Nonrecurring Fields
Ad Code	Unique ID for each ad.
On-Air Date	Date on which promotion airs.
Air Time	Media cost for airtime used.
800 Phone Number	In-bound response costs.
Production Costs	
Fixed	Costs of developing broadcast promotion including creative, talent, studio expenses, and so on.
Variable	Airtime, response expenses, and so on.
Total Costs	Total of production, airtime, and response expenses.
Description	Free-form description of ad content.

Catalog Source Table

Data Element	*Description*
	Key Fields
Catalog Number	Unique catalog ID that source is being used for.
Key Code	Specific use of a particular medium, for example, the *New York Times*, November 9 issue.
Offer Code	
	Nonrecurring Fields
Duplication Rate versus House File	Many direct marketers have found that the density of the duplication rate between the house file and an external source is predictive of response the next time that the source is used for promotion.
Quantity Ordered	Number of names considered for promotion from a source.
Quantity Mailed	Net number of names mailed after merge, purge, suppression, and so on.
Costs	List rental.
Broker ID	Unique identifier for each list or media broker.
Creative Code(s)	Different creative packages are constantly being tested. This code links sources with the specific creative packages they are being mailed.
Test Code(s)	Within an offer or creative package, a variety of tests may be used in each mailing. The source table captures a code that identifies the specific test people are being subjected to.

Print/FSI Source Tables

Data Element	*Description*
	Key Fields
Key Code(s)	This unique identifier links the source table with the print/FSI promotion table so the cataloger will know which sources received which promotions.
Offer Code(s)	A unique identifier that links specific offers with the sources to which the offers were mailed.
	Nonrecurring Fields
Circulation	For print sources, this is the number of guaranteed names that have direct visual access to an ad. Response is calculated against the circulation number in much the same way that response rate is calculated against quantity mailed for direct mail promotions.
Creative Code(s)	Different creative packages are constantly being tested. This code links sources with the specific creative packages they are being mailed.
Test Code(s)	Within an offer or creative package, a variety of tests may be used in each mailing. The source table captures a code that will identify the specific test people are being subjected to.
Free-Form Description	Free-form text that identifies the list source in detail.
Costs	Costs in relevant units, for example, per page, black and white versus color versus four-color bleed.

Medium Table

Data Element	Description
	Key Fields
Medium Code(s)	Specific periodical or newspaper, for example, the *New York Times, Time.*
Key Code(s)	Specific use of a medium for a particular promotion or subset of a promotion.
	Nonrecurring Fields
Major Media Code(s)	Indicates whether medium is a rented list, broadcast, space, and so on, and for space, the type of medium, for example, magazine, newspaper.
Description	Free-form description of medium.

Offer Table

Data Element	Description
	Key Fields
Offer Code(s)	Identifies a specific offer that may include discounts, special premiums, and so on.
Catalog Number	Ties specific offers to specific department numbers.
	Nonrecurring Fields
Description	Free-form description of offer.

Deciles Table

Data Element	Description
	Key Fields
Customer ID	Provides link to customer table and customer data.
Model Code	Unique code for each scoring model.
	Nonrecurring Fields
Model Score	Score produced by model.
Date of Scoring	Date model was used to score names in customer table.
Decile Code	Indicates the decile that customers or prospects are assigned to by the various models.

Model Table

Data Element	Description
	Key Fields
Model Code	Unique code for each scoring model. Link to decile table.
	Nonrecurring Fields
Model Name	Name of each scoring model.
Model Description	Free-form description of each scoring model.

Purchase Item Table

Data Element	Description
	Key Fields
Item Code	Links purchases to the items purchased. There may be several items purchased in one transaction.
Purchase ID	Links to repeat purchase table so that data about purchase transactions can be related to items purchased.

FIGURE 6–5
Examples of Summary Information

By Customer
- Total purchases
- Total orders
- Total mailings
- Product frequency (how many times a product code ordered)
- Subject frequency (how many times a subject code ordered)

By Source
- Key code (specific mailings)
- Total sales
- Total costs
- Profit calculations:
  1. CPM
  2. CPO
  3. Average sales
  4. Sales per thousand pieces mailed
  5. Profit per thousand pieces mailed
  6. Average lifetime value for customers

By Department
- Total sales
- Total costs
- Profitability measures:
  1. CPM
  2. CPO
  3. Average sales
  4. Sales per thousand pieces mailed
  5. Profit per thousand pieces mailed
  6. Average lifetime value for customers

By Item
- Item number
- Total sales
- Total usages (departments)

FREQUENCY OF UPDATE OR REPLACEMENT

The frequency of update or table replacement is generally driven as much by operational processing windows as by marketing's information needs. Both replacement and updating are time-consuming processes. The frequency of updating or replacement determines how well the database represents the actual customer master file. If promotional decisions (for example, who should be mailed what) are based largely on buyer behavior, most marketers will want information to be as current as possible to avoid excluding active customers from promotion.

Updates need not be more frequent than the decision-making interval requires. If, for example, a company makes two mailings a year, it may only be necessary to update the file sufficiently in advance of the two mailings to provide the data required for name selection. As long as the intervening months' files are stored so they will be accessible for update processing, the company can put off processing the information until it is actually required for decision making.

Although less frequent updating may make financial sense, particularly in situations where a company's marketing database is maintained at a service bureau, many companies opt to update more frequently to support ongoing analysis and reporting between mailing cycles.

A nightly update schedule that includes the following information is typical for many companies:

- Purchase and return data for current customers, including total sales, by
  - department
  - item/SKU
  - product type.
- Customer data, including new customers and customer change-of-address data.
- Performance by list source during a campaign.

Other companies update the following information less frequently, often quarterly:

- Address correction from external sources.
- Assignment of customers to product groups.
- External demographic data about customers.
- Performance index by demographic or ZIP cluster.

Creating Separate Databases for Marketing to Avoid Conflicts

Many companies have a priority conflict between analytical users of data, such as marketers, and operational or production users of data, such as customer service or data processing operations. In general, if a company has only one system to support both analysis and operations and if the two functions are being operated simultaneously, conflicts in processing priority are inevitable. This is one of several reasons that a number of direct marketing companies create separate databases for each function. Then, each application can be separately tuned to operate at optimal efficiency. Performance may be further enhanced by decoupling the operations support and decision support functions and operating them on separate hardware and software platforms, each of which has been optimized to support the requirements of its application. These configuration issues are discussed in detail in Chapter 8.

From a data standpoint, the separation of functions requires maintaining separate files of data for operations and for decision support, which requires spending more money for data storage, either in the mainframe, workstation, or PC environment, depending on the configuration selected. However, data storage is relatively inexpensive.

For example, the space required to store 2 million records, each containing 1,000 bytes (characters) of data in a mainframe environment, ranges from about $1,000 to $1,500 per month.[2] Even with the additional space required to store indexes for the files, the cost would be less than $2,000 per month. Marketers should evaluate the additional cost of data storage required to support its database marketing applications in the same way that they evaluate all other business investments. That is, the incremental value of the data, in terms of increased profitability to the company, must outweigh the incremental cost of data storage.[3] Marketers should be able to calculate the increased revenues or savings that would occur based on the decisions they would be able to make if the additional data were available.

The potential disadvantage of maintaining separate data for operations and decision support is that marketers will not have up-to-the-minute, or real-time, data in their file. Marketing's data will be accurate only through the time that the marketing database was last updated. Many companies update key files daily, twice a day, or in some cases, on a real-time basis. However, some data pertaining to customers, list sources, items, or departments does not change on a daily basis except when new records are added.

Purchase or return transaction data, on the other hand, may change several times during the course of a day. A large-sized catalog company, for example, could have anywhere from 50,000 to 100,000 customer transactions per day. Although these transactions are extremely important to the company's business, marketers rarely require real-time transactions. For calculation of trends, distribution by list source, or the comparative performance of items or product type, real-time data is not necessary.

Level of Detail of Data

Data may be brought into the database at the detailed transaction level or at some level of summarization. If the data does not enter the database at the detailed transaction level, then marketers will not be able to analyze relationships in the database at this level of detail.

Although it is only logical that data can't be viewed at a lower level than it exists in the system, many MIS professionals have experienced the frustration of trying to explain this fact to their marketing colleagues six months after the database project is completed. This is one more reason why the dialogue between the marketing and MIS members of the database team referred to earlier in this chapter is so essential.

Although it may be desirable to have data available at the lowest possible level of detail, cost and operational considerations must be weighed. Detailed transaction-level data, in virtually all cases, requires more data storage, higher processing costs,[4] and a longer update processing window than would be required for summary data.

---

[2]In a workstation or PC environment, data storage can be purchased for as little as $1,000 to $2,500 per gigabyte.

[3] Data storage costs have been falling rapidly as improvements in technology have increased the density at which data can be stored. When we were writing the second edition of *The New Direct Marketing,* AT&T Bell Labs announced the development of a fiber-optic technology that supports data storage at a density of 45 gigabytes per inch. This is 200 to 300 times greater than existing technologies support. By the time you read this note, the technology may be available commercially.

[4]If the company uses a service bureau or a charge-back algorithm for computer usage, these will be real costs. If there is no charge for internal data processing, there would not be a direct service cost associated with increased processing.

WILL THE DATABASE BE UPDATED OR REPLACED?

Will data actually be updated, that is modified, in the database or will the system replace the current database tables with more current snapshots of customer data? If the update is performed within the database, then more complex programming is required so the application can actually find previous records, then perform adds, changes, and deletes to existing tables.

Alternatively, if the update is done in the transaction system and the database tables are to be replaced by fresh information, it may be necessary to modify existing transaction systems so data at the detailed level will be available to the database. The extent of the modifications will depend on the level of detail the transaction system currently maintains. For example, if a customer had $100 in sales from six purchases at the time of the last update and $160 in sales resulting from nine purchases in the current update, what was the value of each purchase during this period? Were there three equal purchases of $20? Were there two purchases at $10 and one at $40? The answers to these questions may determine the type of promotion the marketer wishes to send. If detailed transaction level data is not made available to the database, then the opportunity to differentiate customers at this level may be lost.

If the *replacement* approach is used, the database may be required to maintain a history of prior snapshots of the files. In this case, pseudotransactions may be calculated based on the difference in values between current snapshots and prior snapshots of selected variables. Then, in addition to replacing prior values, counter-oriented fields showing the activity during the current month may be populated using the values produced by the pseudotransactions. Many companies combine the replenishment and update approaches, updating frequently changing fields, such as sales, each month using detailed transaction records and less frequently changing fields, such as customer demographics, periodically.

In companies that wish to maintain historical data in their marketing databases, marketers must decide these issues:

- How much historical data is to be maintained.
- What level of detail to maintain.
- For how long a period the data is to be retained.

Many companies work with a rolling 24- or 36-month view of their data.

RETURN TO BUSINESS NEEDS AND DETERMINE ADEQUACY OF PLAN FOR MEETING NEEDS

Prior to proceeding with the database project, the project team should reconvene to evaluate how well the data elements that have been incorporated into the preliminary database design and the functional capabilities designed for the database meet the original business needs. Typically, as projects progress, decisions are made based on such issues as data availability, cost and complexity of processing, cost of data storage, and anticipated costs of development and implementation that cause changes in original specifications. In more than a few cases final applications were significantly different from the original business requirements, and in too many cases, they failed to meet the original business requirements entirely.

For these reasons, a thorough review should be performed *prior* to beginning the implementation phase of the project to insure that the database marketing application, as planned, meets the business requirements as stated.

If, during this review process the database team determines that in light of information discovered during the project, the company's business needs have actually *changed* and the database application will have to perform somewhat different functions from those originally anticipated, three actions are available to companies:

1. If the changes are relatively minor, then the design should be revisited to incorporate those changes and then proceed.
2. If the changes are major and consist primarily of additions to the original set of functions, then the original project can proceed as planned and the enhancements can be added as part of the next version of the application.
3. If the changes are major and are a significant departure from the original business requirements, then the project should be stopped and the entire process, beginning with business needs assessment, should begin again.

By maintaining continuity of team members from the marketing and data processing groups throughout the project, the original business needs and the resulting database design should be a close fit. However, some companies have found that projects can take on a life of their own with the result that the differences between the system design and the original requirements comes as a complete surprise even to those who have participated throughout the process. The step-by-step approach in this chapter should minimize the likelihood of that occurring.

Chapter 7

Hardware and Software Issues

DEVELOPMENTS IN TECHNOLOGY

When we were researching and writing the first edition of *The New Direct Marketing,* we limited our descriptions of database technology to mainframe-based products. In the four years since, a virtual technological revolution has occurred; new hardware and software platforms have been introduced and the price performance of the tools available to direct marketers has dramatically improved.

Three years ago, database management system (DBMS) solutions were necessarily compromises between high-speed transaction processing and the flexibility required by marketers for analysis and decision support. As is often the case, compromise solutions were ultimately satisfying to neither group. Operations groups found that transactions could not be processed as quickly as they could in traditional third-generation systems using flat files with VSAM keys; marketers found that the turnaround time for routine queries was unacceptably slow.

The technological improvements and price performance advances of the past four years have made this compromise unnecessary and have made it possible to decouple the systems that support operations and the systems that support decisions, thereby reflecting the fundamental functional differences of each corporate group. That is, in the same way that operations and marketing analysis functions tend to be performed by different personnel or departments within companies, the computer systems that support each group can also be separated. To the extent that these systems share data, the integration of data can be accomplished by *communication* between systems rather than through structural integration as in the past.

In one sense, the separation of systems across multiple platforms is revolutionary. In another sense, it merely reflects the way in which people work together within companies. When marketing people need to obtain information from operational staff, they hold meetings, send memoranda, or make telephone calls. In much the same way, marketing professionals can *extract* selected data from operational support systems and load it into decision-support systems where they can access and analyze it. In many cases, the results of their analyses are passed back to the operational support systems as files for implementation by fulfillment or other systems, thereby closing the loop.

The way in which these new technologies work and the numerous ways in which they may be deployed to support the new direct marketing are described in detail in this chapter and in Chapters 8 and 9.

THE IMPACT OF WORKSTATIONS

One of the most important changes of the past few years has been the dramatic improvement in workstation price performance. Workstations offer not only superior price performance, but also increased flexibility and connectivity than do mainframe processing environments. As costs continue to drop, the financial advantages of workstation technology will become even more compelling.

In this chapter and the following two chapters we will describe

- Why companies are using workstation technology to separate their decision-support systems from their operating support systems.
- How workstation technology works.
- How multiplatform environments may be configured to achieve maximum flexibility and performance at minimum cost.

Many firms that are considering database marketing systems already have mainframe computing environments, but increasing numbers of companies are developing database marketing systems in midframe, workstation, microcomputer, or specialized database computing environments.

A number of software vendors have products that can be operated in any of these environments, whereas others are limited to only one or two. We discuss software issues later in this chapter and list software products for each of the computing environments in Appendix B.

Although the *functional* requirements of the marketing group will primarily drive the selection of a database management system (DBMS) product to be used as the core software for the marketing database, a number of very important technical issues concerning hardware, configuration, data communications, and software must be addressed as part of the selection process, and the company's MIS management should be actively involved in addressing them.

Although the platform selection process should logically flow from business needs to functional requirements to selection of core DBMS software to selection of hardware, this approach may not be practical for some companies. Most firms must operate within the constraints of their existing hardware environments, the guidelines of their future technology plans, or both. Because hardware may be the initial constraining factor, we will describe the key issues associated with each class of hardware first.

HARDWARE ISSUES

The mainframe computer hardware environment at most companies is either IBM or non-IBM.

Mainframe Computers

IBM has about a 60 percent share of mainframe installations, with the balance going to Unisys, the larger Wang systems, IBM plug-compatibles (e.g., Amdahl, Hitachi, etc.), and clusters of midframe computers (e.g., Digital Equipment). For the purposes of this discussion, we will focus on the IBM mainframe environment and separately discuss the midframe computers, whether configured in clusters or as stand-alone machines.

Although the IBM (and plug-compatible) machines are among the largest computers available for most commercial applications, their capacity is not limitless. Memory and processing power can be added on but incremental growth for mainframe computers is relatively expensive. MIS management, like any other corporate management, attempts to scale the available capacity of computer resources to the known and anticipated resource level required. Unless major growth is expected in the immediate future, few MIS directors would want to incur the expense of significant excess computer capacity.

Typical data centers achieve optimal system performance when 65 to 75 percent of available CPU capacity is being consumed. At this level of use, applications get the processing power they need to provide generally acceptable response time for on-line transactions while sufficient capacity remains available to support the requirements of background transactions and the operating system.

A key hardware issue facing most companies today is downsizing. Improvements in price performance and flexibility of midframes, workstations, and microcomputers have led many companies to consider taking at least some of their applications off the mainframe. There are many reasons for this trend, including lower cost for incremental hardware growth; lower cost for application development, maintenance, and operation; lower costs for data storage; and greater flexibility in application use.

Among the key hardware issues to consider therefore, are these:

1. Is the firm's current hardware environment mainframe only or does it include other platforms?
2. Is the firm's technology plan restricted to mainframe processing or are other platforms either designated or under consideration?
3. Can the firm's existing hardware communicate with additional platforms such as midframes, workstations, or PC networks?

The answers to these questions may limit the list of DBMS software products that can be considered.

Midframe Computers

Increasing numbers of companies are finding midframe computers to be a cost-effective alternative to mainframe computer systems. This is especially true for companies that configure several midframe computers into clusters that can easily rival or exceed the capacity of mainframe computers at a lower total cost. In addition, mainframe computers can be configured to redirect work to other parts of the cluster if one CPU in the cluster goes down. In this situation, companies may attempt to continue operating all their applications at a degraded performance level or, alternatively, shutting down less critical applications so the most critical applications can operate at their normal levels. This is one reason that midframe clusters have been adopted by a number of companies for whom continuous uptime is a critical issue. Companies in fields as diverse as financial services and publishing have based their technology strategies on midframe clusters.

Another reason that this approach has increased in popularity is that the cost of incremental growth is often considerably less than comparable growth in a mainframe computing environment. If additional processing requirements develop, the firm can simply add an additional CPU to the cluster, thereby increasing CPU processing power and memory.

A third reason for recent growth in this segment is that midframe computers are often thought of as departmental machines. Because each unit is relatively inexpensive and can support a number of users ranging from fewer than 8 to more than 100, depending on the size of the cluster, the purchase price of midframe computers is often within the annual computing budget of a single large department, rather than requiring a capital investment that would necessitate corporate approval and would normally go through the MIS department. In decentralized companies, this factor alone may drive the hardware acquisition decision.

For some companies, developing a marketing database in a standalone, midframe computer environment may make far greater economic sense than expanding the mainframe computer environment solely to support the new application. The final hardware decision for the database marketing application will be a function of the existing hardware environment, available capacity within the existing environment, and whether alternative platforms are part of the company's strategic direction. These factors are different for each company.

Companies that are considering midframe computers as part of their database marketing application should be familiar with such vendors as Digital Equipment (DEC), which is by far the leader in this segment; Data General; Hewlett-Packardt (HP); Stratus; Perkin-Elmer; Prime; and Wang. IBM's AS/400 computers serve a dual role:

1. They provide an unbounded migration and growth path for IBM's Series 3 computers (Systems 34, 36, and 38).
2. They can be a cost-effective solution for companies that are either bringing computer processing in-house for the first time or for companies that are downsizing from mainframe computers. AS/400 systems include an integrated DBMS platform as part of their operating systems.

Key issues for midframe environments include these:

1. Is there an existing DBMS product in place, and if so, can it support the functional requirements of the database marketing application?
2. If not, does the existing midframe environment support other DBMS products that *do* support the functional requirements?
3. Can the existing midframe environment be expanded cost-effectively if necessary to support the database marketing application?
4. If the existing environment *cannot* be expanded cost-effectively, *or* if DBMS products that will support the company's functional requirements will not operate in the existing hardware environment, other hardware must be brought in to support the DBMS product selected.
5. If another hardware platform were brought in, can data be extracted from existing applications and loaded into the new hardware environment as electronic file transfers, or must a tape transfer approach be used?

Workstations

The word *workstation* is used to denote a wide variety of computer systems, ranging from a single-user, single-display workstation to multiuser network servers. All these workstations are built using the recent vintage central processing units (CPUs) called reduced instruction set computer (RISC) chips, which provide very high performance for modest prices. Almost all of them, with a few exceptions, run the Unix or Unix-like operating systems. In addition, they can all be networked with each other and with mainframes and minis. Such computers are offered by SUN Microsystems, IBM, HP, DEC, and others.

In addition to providing good price-performance ratios, these computers offer flexibility, ease of software programming, comprehensive facilities for system administration, and elaborate tools for implementing user-friendly interfaces. They can be networked among themselves and with mainframes or minis for rapid data transfer. Thus, a company's operations data could continue to reside on existing mainframe(s), mini(s), or both. From time to time, selected parts of this data could be sent down to one or more workstations configured and programmed to perform decision-support functions (analysis, name selection, etc.). The addition of a workstation computer would not disrupt the existing computer system(s) and would enable the marketing department to carry out analysis without affecting daily operations.

A caveat in this context is that in addition to acquiring the workstation computer, a company needs access to qualified systems administration personnel to perform routine software maintenance and backups on the Unix operating system. Such personnel could be hired or subcontracted on a part-time basis, or in-house personnel could be trained in Unix through courses offered by the vendors and several third parties.

Due to ease of incorporation and networking, these computers are expected to be used in decision support work in the immediate future. As the new technology gets more established and gains wider acceptance, it should begin to make headway into the operations side also. Chapter 9 gives additional details on workstations and client-server configurations.

Microcomputers

Microcomputer processing power and storage capacity continue to increase at a dramatic rate. The advent of microcomputer networks has increased potential processing power and storage capacity by such an extent that large networks easily rival the power of midframe computers and begin to approach the power of small mainframe configurations as well. Equally important is the flexibility that microcomputer networks provide end users in terms of file sharing and the use of common, professionally managed applications.

Compared to stand-alone microcomputer environments, which were the only option a few years ago and remain the predominant configuration for microcomputers, networks now provide many companies with full-function computer applications at a fraction of the cost for comparable applications operating in mainframe or even midframe configurations.

Although microcomputers and microcomputer networks today offer companies a much wider range of hardware choices for their marketing databases, the issues of cost, technical support, data integrity, updating, and system management have become increasingly complicated.

The major players in the microcomputer marketplace—IBM, Apple, Compaq, Toshiba, Zenith, Dell, and so on—have become household words. All the major microcomputer products being used for database applications are IBM compatible, including the newer products from Apple. As a result of its acquisition of NCR, AT&T has once again become a major player in the microcomputer market.

Companies also are becoming more familiar with networking products and the companies that make them, such as Novell, Pyramid, Banyan, Ethernet, and the like.

Regardless of which hardware decision companies make, they should keep one thought in mind when evaluating database management systems to support their database marketing applications: *All database management systems require a great deal of computer capacity.* This should not be surprising, especially when you consider all the work they do. Remember that the ease of use, menu-driven screens, pop-up windows, and all the other tools that enable marketing end users to directly access information about their customers, without having to rely on the intervention of data processing professionals, require greater processing power and data storage. As in all resource allocation considerations, there is no such thing as a free lunch. All the productivity and user-friendly features that we want in a database management system can only be made available by including large numbers of very complicated computer programs as part of the packages.

The trade-off for increased access to data and increased productivity on the part of end users is the increased cost of CPU hardware and, often, of data storage as well. Companies must evaluate the additional benefits to the firm as a result of increased end-user productivity in the context of increased computer hardware expenses and in terms of the firm's strategic technology plan.

For marketing-driven firms, this evaluation usually comes out on the side of the database management system. In any event, marketing and MIS management must be prepared to discuss the issues of the company's strategic technology plan, function, flexibility, and cost in the context of overall benefit to the firm.

The key issue concerning microcomputers is that many users still think of microcomputers as stand-alone PCs rather than computer environments that can support complex, often critical applications. As a result, many companies fail to provide adequate support for PC applications because they don't realize that microcomputers and networks must be supported by the same level of data processing professionals that support companies' other computer applications. Companies that anticipate developing database marketing applications using microcomputer environments must be aware of these points:

- The role of the database administrator (DBA) is just as critical in this environment as in any other.
- Data integrity must be maintained. Therefore the ability to alter codes, data, or both must be strictly limited and enforced.
- Data security is increasingly important. Many companies programmatically limit the data that can be downloaded or use diskless PCs to reduce the risk of data theft or loss.

SOFTWARE ISSUES

Existing Database Management System Software

Some companies may already have a database management system in place. If this is the case, then the marketing group and the MIS group should first consider whether the company's existing systems can support the additional functional requirements that the marketing group has defined for the database marketing application. To the extent possible, it is preferable to use resources that are in place to reduce the initial cost of developing a marketing database and apply programming skills that have already been developed on other projects.

Types of DBMS Products

DBMS products fall into three general categories:

1. Hierarchical
2. Inverted file
3. Relational

Appendix B contains a listing and description of database management system products by type.

Hierarchical systems. The first DBMS products, for example, IBM's IMS, used a hierarchical structure. Hierarchical databases are designed for efficiency in high-volume transaction environments. Although they are much more flexible than non-DBMS systems, their structure can often limit the flexibility required for the types of ad hoc queries that marketing end users typically require.

Hierarchical systems were designed primarily to support limited analytical flexibility while providing support for high-volume transaction applications. As a result, many companies use hierarchical DBMS products to support customer service, airline or hotel reservation, or financial applications. Although these DBMS products offer greater analytical and reporting flexibility than traditional third-generation systems, they are not designed to support the multiplicity of views or the ad hoc query requirements of today's database marketing applications.

IBM's DB2 and SQL/DS products, along with Computer Associates' IDMS/R, were developed partly to bridge the gap between today's requirements and the hierarchical DBMS products that are ideal for large-volume transaction environments. A number of utility programs have been developed that make it relatively easy to load data from hierarchical systems to relational database environments.

So, although existing hierarchical DBMS products themselves may not be ideal for database marketing applications, companies that are already using them for order entry, customer service, or other transaction-oriented applications may find that their hierarchical systems, when used in combination with other DBMS products, provide a great deal of the information required for marketing.

Inverted file systems. If the company's existing database has an inverted file structure, for example, Computer Associates' Datacom/DB, Computer Corporation of America's Model 204, or Software A.G.'s Adabas, the marketing group would find these software products especially well suited for database marketing applications. In fact, a number of major direct marketing companies, including Scudder Stevens & Clark, RL Polk, Metromail, and Kraft General Foods (for its original marketing database), have database marketing applications that are based on these software products.

One major difference between these products is that CCA's Model 204 and Computer Associates' Datacom/DB are designed to run exclusively in IBM or IBM-compatible environments, whereas Adabas is designed to run on IBM, DEC, and a variety of other vendors' hardware. Companies that do not currently have IBM environments should be cognizant of this fact when they evaluate products.

Inverted file systems are popular for direct marketing applications because they are very good at providing quick counts of records that meet specified conditions. To produce quick counts, inverted file systems can create indexed versions of the data stored in their files. If queries can be answered by index-only processing, that is, not actually reading raw data records, they can produce counts for databases of several million records in a matter of a few minutes at most. In many cases, the database can return query responses in seconds.

To take full advantage of the power of index-only processing, marketers must be very conscious of which variables are important enough to be indexed and which data relationships should be predefined. Although marketers have a natural tendency to create indexes for every variable field, this approach will result in significantly slower updates and data loads. Whereas, the indexing approach is satisfactory for simple counts, it tends to be slow if additional conditions are added in the analysis process; for example, reports comparing year-to-date performance this year with corresponding numbers for previous years for a specified set of product codes.

Developing a true understanding of the trade-offs involved in designing the database to be efficient for both processing and updating requires years of experience. That is one reason many firms hire consulting systems analysts and designers who have several years of hands-on experience with the database product they selected. Consulting expertise during the early stages of the database design process can save literally years of development time and processing headaches.

Relational systems. Relational technology is based on the premise that data redundancy should be minimized and that the most logical arrangement of data within a database is in a series of tables that can be logically joined by key fields.

From a logical standpoint, this arrangement of data makes a great deal of sense. From a practical standpoint, however, logical joins, if done on a dynamic basis (that is, while the application is operating on-line and while end users are waiting for results), have proven to be an inefficient way to link data for the types of queries that are typical for direct marketers.

As a result, relational databases used for the kinds of quick counts described above tend to be designed to look like inverted files. If quick counts are a requirement, relational databases are generally structured as one large file in which virtually all fields are indexed.

In some cases, summary files that already contain counts known to be important may be produced as part of the regular production process so key pieces of information for the firm are prepared in advance. The query process can then function more like a "look-up table" and avoid actually counting records.

Although the ability to perform quick counts is not an essential function for all database users, it is particularly important to direct marketers. For this reason, you would expect the number of direct marketing users whose systems are based on relational database systems to be small. However, this is not actually the case.

Relational database technology has been used for database marketing for several reasons. One is that the way in which relational databases are structured, using a process called *normalizing,* is very similar to the way in which marketers visualize their data. Relational technology organizes data elements into logical tables and links them by common data elements. Figure 6–1 in Chapter 6 is an example of this process.

The utility and dictionary functions available within relational database product families make it relatively easy to extract the desired data elements from the numerous, often fragmented, files in which they are currently captured, and to load the data elements into logical groupings that are more appropriate for the kinds of questions marketers tend to ask. Once the data has been loaded into the relational table format, all the queries and reports that marketers require can be produced readily.

Another reason for using a relational database is that IBM, which controls about 60 percent of the mainframe computing marketplace in the United States, has made the strategic decision to support relational technology. To stimulate usage of its relational products, IBM has placed its DB2 and SQL/DS products in thousands of data centers that are committed to the IBM product line.

Because the cost of database management system software is relatively high and technical support staff are expensive, it is only natural that companies with a database management system in-house would want to develop new applications using whatever system is in place.

One of the criticisms of DB2 has been that it is difficult for end users who are not data processing professionals to use. For that reason, a number of products have been developed to bridge the gap between the kinds of menu-driven, PC-based screens that end users are comfortable with and the database management system itself.

Some user-interface products, for example, Natural/SQL, are add-ons to the product lines of other mainframe DBMS products—in this case, Software A.G.'s Adabas. Oracle also has a number of user-friendly tools that can readily be used in conjunction with DB2 or with its own line of DBMS products. Because the Oracle database product itself is written in SQL,[1] any programs written using its products will, by definition, be compatible with an SQL product environment like DB2's.

Metaphor, an independently developed product that has been acquired by IBM, can be operated on IBM PS2 platforms and can be used as a user-friendly bridge to IBM's DB2, SQL/DS, or OS/2 databases.

Metaphor's screens consist of a series of menus and icons that resemble Apple's MacIntosh, Microsoft's Windows, or other products that are the staples of the point-and-click approach to end-user computing. All these products tend to lower the resistance that computerphobes have toward using technology.

Metaphor enables end users to have access to data that may be stored in a number of different tables and to perform very complex data analysis tasks without requiring any knowledge of programming or systems. All

---

[1]SQL is the abbreviation for Structured Query Language, which is the American National Standards Institute (ANSI) standard language that underlies all relational database management systems. (See Buzzword 2 in Chapter 3.)

end users need to do is point the Metaphor mouse at the appropriate icons on the screen and click. Once a listing of the available database files is displayed, end users can select the desired files by pointing and clicking the mouse. A display of the fields contained within the table is readily available, and end users can select fields from within tables, combine these with fields selected from other tables, and dynamically create the database needed to solve the marketing questions they have in mind.

Another relational product that has had considerable success in the last few years is *Oracle,* a relational database developed and marketed by the Oracle Corporation. Oracle's success has come about for two primary reasons:

1. It is an exceptionally good relational database product.
2. Oracle is committed to platform independence (see the definition that follows).

From its inception as a company, Oracle has been committed to the concept of platform independence. That is, Oracle's products are developed so they can be used on virtually any computer hardware and with virtually any operating system. It is one of the very few products that can be used on the full range of IBM mainframe machines, the full line of DEC midframes, and virtually any IBM-compatible microcomputer.

This flexibility is ideal for companies that use DEC or other midframe equipment as departmental machines because programs can be written in any of the environments and then be run in any of the other environments without changing a single line of program code.

If properly designed, relational database systems can be very well suited for the requirements of database marketing, and in some cases, if the marketing database is to be linked with other applications that the company is running, it may be cost-effective for firms to go with a single-vendor, single-DBMS strategy. Again, a company's strategic technology plan is a very important component of the DBMS selection process.

Products for the Unix environment. As stated earlier in this text, Unix-based workstation products are becoming increasingly important platforms for database marketing. A number of high-performance database management system (DBMS) products have been developed for this environment, including *Sybase, Informix, Ingres,* and the Unix-based version of *Oracle.*

Direct marketers can think of these platforms as consisting of two distinct parts: the core DBMS and application development tools.

The core DBMS in all these products functions as a data repository that allows data manipulations using the SQL language. These cores support on-line transactions and provide a variety of locking features for implementing concurrent updates from simultaneous users. In addition, they can also perform functions related to rollback and recovery. In short, they provide all the facilities needed to build *mission-critical* applications that must be reliable and crash-resistant.

In addition to the core DBMS, the above-mentioned products also provide programming tools to build applications that can be used by the end users and data administrators. These tools can support full-screen applications on a variety of access terminals ranging from plain ASCII terminals to dial-up PCs. They can also support batch and command-line operations intended for data administrators. In almost all cases, the core data can be accessed outside the *relational-paradigm* using a conventional (third-generation) language, for example, COBOL, Pascal, or C, in combination with SQL. Such a combination is called *embedded SQL.* Report generators are another kind of access tool which are provided by the vendors and various third parties. Some report generators are based upon fourth-generation report-writing languages, whereas others are screen based and provide an interactive interface.

To summarize, the set of facilities available for data storage and manipulation and for building applications provide a rich environment suitable for building software applications even for the most demanding needs.

Customized Applications for Direct Marketing

A number of DBMS manufacturers have ventured into the realm of application development, generally in specific industries. Oracle, for example, has developed a number of applications for financial services users. IBM's DBMS software has been used as the core of a number of database-oriented applications, including payroll and personnel systems. Vendors have developed versions of their products with DB2 as the core database system. It is likely that this pattern will continue into the future as more and more database-oriented applications are developed.

MarketPulse is a generic database marketing system developed by Computer Corporation of America. (CCA is the company that developed Model 204, mentioned earlier in the discussion of inverted file systems.)

Other customized applications for direct marketing. Other applications that were developed to serve the direct marketing industry include *MarketVision,* developed by ACS, *Private Eye* and *Navigator,* developed by Cross-Z, *Customer Insight,* developed by Customer Insight Company, *OKRA,* and *Fast-Count DBMS* which was developed by Megaplex Software and is marketed through DSA. These products take advantage of the improved price performance of PC and client-server platforms to provide increased end-user access, flexibility and processing speed. The advantages of these non-mainframe hardware platforms and configuration options for their use are described in Chapters 8 and 9.

SUMMARY

This discussion was intended to show how marketers can use database management system technology to support the information needs of marketing and to help both marketers and MIS professionals understand the issues they must address to ensure successful implementations of marketing database applications.

We mentioned a small number of vendors' products as representative examples of current trends in DBMS technology. For a more complete listing and description of the products offered by a number of different vendors, please see the product directory in Appendix B.

Chapter 8

Impact of New Computer Technology on Business

DATA PROCESSING TECHNOLOGIES

In Chapter 7, we stated that database management system software decisions were, until recently, compromises between the operational and decision support users within companies, and that technology constraints had precluded many companies from using technology in ways that suited their business requirements. In this chapter, we will describe how recent trends in hardware and software technology have made it possible to design and implement systems that more appropriately reflect the information environments of the new direct marketing.

COMPUTER APPLICATIONS IN BUSINESS

Since the advent of the personal computer in the early 1980s the nature of computer applications in business has changed, and today's technology has further accelerated the rate of change. Prior to the personal computer, most business applications were *transaction* oriented, including such functions as payroll, accounts payable, accounts receivable, general ledger, inventory management, order entry, and shipping. Because computers in those days were primarily thought of as *counting* machines, counting functions predominated in their use. Periodic, scheduled reports were produced, generally as printouts, and business analysts, including marketers, used the available *hard-copy* reports for decision making. Reports were rarely modified because the modification process was time consuming and expensive.

When the personal computer arrived on the scene, many analysts and executives began to use spreadsheets and basic database products on their PCs to perform analytical tasks that exceeded the capability or flexibility of existing mainframe applications, particularly for reporting and for asking all the *what-if* questions that are the lifeblood of marketing users and the bane of data processing managers.

In the early years, many companies' data processing professionals viewed PCs as novelties and did not develop or support applications for them. As a result, many analytical users would *rekey* data that had appeared in mainframe-produced reports so the data could be viewed or analyzed in different ways. Leading-edge companies, at this time, were those that downloaded mainframe-produced data to PC environments to avoid at least the rekeying aspect of the operation. In a technological sense, downloading eliminated the need for marketers to carry around heavy printouts and hunch over keyboards to rekey data, enabling them to walk upright and emerge from the role of secondary data entry clerks to that of decision makers.

Although most companies have evolved beyond this prehistoric stage of information management, even functions such as downloading to more user-friendly platforms have not yet become universal. This chapter shows how some companies are using today's technology to accomplish the decision-making processes of database marketing cost-effectively *without* disrupting or degrading day-to-day operations.

Operating Support Systems for Day-to-Day Processing

Most companies can divide their information processing functions into two categories: day-to-day operations and decision making. Day-to-day operations include all the transaction-oriented processes that were the initial thrust of business computing, including customer transactions such as orders, invoices, and statements; accounting transactions such as payroll, accounts payable, accounts receivable; and batch jobs including posting transactions and producing preprogrammed reports.

Because these functions support day-to-day operations, we refer to them as operational support system (OSS) technology. The repetitive, predictable, machine-resource intensive nature of OSS applications make them well suited to mainframe computing environments. Although a great deal of work is required to make them operate smoothly, they are often referred to as *production* jobs and are perceived as background activities that somehow happen automatically.

Operations managers frequently lament that OSS jobs are only noticed when something goes wrong and are rarely appreciated when everything works as expected. They are the utility applications of most companies that we expect to function with certainty—lights going on when we flip a switch or a dial tone sounding when we raise a telephone handset. Most data centers use software products that schedule which jobs will run at which time and in which sequence and that identify which jobs have prerequisite jobs that must be successfully completed before others can be initiated.

The on-line aspects of these applications, such as data entry, customer service, and production management, generally use software products such as CICS[1] to manage transaction sessions and tune computer systems to provide maximum operating efficiency for these transaction-oriented on-line functions during business hours. After business hours, many data centers change their computers' internal software configurations to provide maximum operating efficiency for batch jobs, including transaction posting, updates, backups, and so on.

As more and more information is captured through business transactions and more and more reporting is required within companies and by regulatory agencies, transaction windows become tighter and tighter and most companies find themselves chronically in need of additional processing cycles. In mainframe processing environments, additional processing cycles are expensive, and because of the way machines are configured, companies must often take steps larger than immediately required for each increment.

In addition to processing windows, data center managers are always cognizant of their requirements for direct access storage device (DASD) space. As more and more transactions shift from tape storage to disk storage, the number of disk drives in most data centers increases dramatically.

---

[1]CICS is IBM's on-line teleprocessing monitor.

Some large data centers have so many acres of floor space dedicated to disk drives that they refer to this section of their machine room floor as the *DASD farm.* Like processing power, DASD is expensive in the mainframe environment. Although manufacturers somewhat alleviated the problem by increasing the capacity of each DASD unit so that today three times the amount of data can be stored in the same footprint[2] required for single-density DASD units a few years ago, the cost of DASD units for mainframe computers is still relatively high.[3]

Because of the hefty additional data processing and data storage costs that must be incurred to support ad hoc processing and because the traditional OSS world is so predictable in its schedules, inputs, outputs, and resource consumption, data center managers are loathe to support decision-support system (DSS) activities in the same computing environment. During business hours ad hoc DSS requirements, which are often intensive users of computer resources, can disrupt on-line customer service and data entry functions because they divert some of the computer's power away from these tasks.

DSS applications can further contend for limited computer space if they require data that is also being sought by on-line OSS applications. Contention between these disparate types of applications can result in processing delays that keep customers on the telephone longer and in productivity decreases for both OSS and DSS users within the company. Many direct marketing companies are able to measure the costs of these delays in terms of increased toll call charges and abandoned calls that could not be serviced because customer service personnel were not available to handle the calls in a timely manner.

Decision-Support Systems

Unlike operating support systems, decision-support systems (DSS) are used to analyze customer data. Marketers can use them to gain insights into customer performance, identify promotable or nonpromotable segments within the customer and prospect files, detect trends in product purchasing or particularly successful types of promotions, and so on. Marketing analysts use this data to make informed resource allocation decisions for advertising and promotion expenses, product development, and name selection for future promotional efforts.

In addition, marketers (and most upper management) find it more effective to communicate their findings and recommendations using graphical and tabular representations of data rather than the raw data that traditionally result from preprogrammed reports.

Need for flexibility and quick response. The *what-if* types of analyses that marketers use require flexibility in the way questions are posed and in the way data can be accessed and also quick response so interaction with the company's data will be as close to conversational as possible. Studies have shown that with delays of more than 20 seconds from

---

[2]*Footprint* is defined as the amount of floor space occupied by a computer hardware device, such as a CPU, tape drive, or DASD unit.

[3] Lease costs are approximately $1,500 to $2,000 per unit per month for 7.5 GB of data storage (based on triple density 3380 DASD units, and assuming a 36-month lease).

the time the enter key has been pressed until the response appears on the computer monitor analysts initiate other activities, such as returning telephone calls. By the time the analyst returns to the analysis task, his train of thought has been broken and his productivity reduced.

DSS technology. DSS technology, like OSS technology, may be mainframe based. However, unlike OSS technology, DSS technology requires custom programs for analysis and reports. In addition, in the mainframe environment DSS activities may degrade response time for critical activities such as customer service. Mainframe systems, with few exceptions, are not as flexible as other platforms, particularly when it comes to presentation tools such as graphics and analysis tools such as spreadsheets. In fact, the more of these tools available in the mainframe environment, the worse will be the performance for other mainframe applications. As we discussed, marketers will not tolerate slow response time.

Wish List

So if we could develop a wish list of the information management functions required for the new direct marketing, what would we include?

Certainly we would want to include modular growth, so we could add inexpensive modules for additional processing capacity and upgrade the functions of existing modules. We would want to have an adequate number of data processing cycles and adequate data storage for both the OSS and the DSS environments, but we would want to acquire these at lower costs than currently available in the mainframe environment. To avoid the data contention and resource contention issues we discussed, we would ideally want to have separate computers for the OSS and the DSS functions tuned to optimally support the needs of each environment. Separate platforms must, however, be able to communicate with each other, readily exchanging data through data extraction and electronic file transfer for downloads and uploads. In addition, we would want the DSS computing environment to have flexible tools for analysis and presentation.

SALIENT TRENDS IN TECHNOLOGY

So how do we get there from here? We begin by examining the salient trends in technology and then determining how these can best be applied to support the new direct marketing.

Improvements in Price Performance

For the past decade, there have been yearly improvements in price performance in every aspect of data processing and of 25 to 35 percent in the price performance of mainframe computers. In other words, the same level of data processing costs 25 to 35 percent less each year, or in each year companies can gain 25 to 35 percent improved performance for the same price. During the same period, comparable rates of improvement in price performance have not occurred in any other industry. If comparable improvements in price performance had occurred in the automobile industry during the same period, an automobile that cost $20,000 in 1982 would today cost less than $1,200.[4]

[4]Assuming annual price improvements of 25 percent.

Many economists and historians compare this rate of improvement in price performance to the economic changes associated with the Industrial Revolution. Whereas the Industrial Revolution dramatically reduced costs by shifting production from manual to mechanical means, the Information Revolution is extending the computational and analytical abilities of today's workers to levels previously unimaginable.

And that's just the beginning of the story. Price performance for microcomputers is improving at eight times the rate of mainframes and that for RISC [5] technology is improving at four times the rate of microcomputers.

The net effect of these improvements is evident from advertising in trade and general interest publications for workstation computers with 57 MIPS[6] of processing power for approximately $7,000.[7] Data storage, which can be prohibitively expensive for mainframe computing environments, now can be *purchased* for $1,000 to $2,500 per gigabyte.[8] Functionality has also been improved. In March, 1994, IBM announced a *Laptop* RISC computer for $12,000.

These costs demonstrate the dramatic improvements in the price performance of individual computing devices. But earlier we discussed using multiple platforms to support the new direct marketing. What opportunities do the trends in technology offer for multiple platform environments?

MULTIPLE CPUs

Multiple platforms, with separate computing platforms for each functional group within a company, require multiple CPUs. To work together effectively, these multiple CPUs must be able to communicate efficiently and effectively using standard, inexpensive communications and data processing links. This is conceptually no different from people who work in different departments being able to exchange information by telephone. As in the case of telephones, particularly those attached to PBXs,[9] computers can communicate with each other through *networks.*

Computer networks, like telephone networks, are hard-wired physical circuits that support communications between and among the computer devices attached to them. Chapter 9 describes in detail the different types of computer networks currently in use, the speeds at which they can transfer data, the protocols they use, the functions they can perform, and their cost. For purposes of this discussion, be aware that computer networks exist and that they are a critical component of getting computers to communicate with each other.

---

[5]RISC is an acronym for Reduced Instruction Set Chips, the technology used in workstation platforms.

[6]MIPS is an acronym for millions of instructions per second, a commonly used measure of computer processing power.

[7]As of mid-1994. This figure will change by the time you read this book; either the cost will drop, the number of MIPS will increase, or both.

[8]A gigabyte is equal to 1 billion bytes, roughly 600 thousand pages of text, or 500 copies of *War and Peace.*

[9]A private branch exchange (PBX) is an internal telephone switch that enables people using telephones attached to the same network to call from extension to extension without using external telephone lines.

OPEN-SYSTEMS ARCHITECTURE

A very important trend in computer technology during the past few years has been the evolution and adoption of open-systems architectural standards. In the not too distant past, computer operating systems were different for each manufacturer's set of products. For example, IBM had its DOS, MVS, and CMS operating environments that IBM computers and some compatibles, notably Amdahl and Hitachi, could use. Digital Equipment (DEC) had different operating systems, which did not communicate directly with IBM's. Data General had still another set.

In the Unix world, there were three different Unix operating systems, Berkeley Unix, AT&T Unix (now Novell), and SCO Unix. IBM's entry into Unix-based products produced the AIX environment, still another version of Unix. The mainframe-based operating systems tended to be proprietary, whereas the Unix-based products tended to be more similar. Manufacturers liked proprietary environments because they helped justify higher profit margins for their products. In addition, closed or proprietary environments encouraged many companies to use software products from a single vendor or a very limited set of vendors because vendors would naturally make every effort to ensure that their own suite of products would work together in a customer's data center. Customers in multiple vendor environments, by contrast, tended to experience problems with each manufacturer's technical support team if their software products did not work together smoothly.

However, because of a recognition of computing requirements in the marketplace and a desire to be part of any future configurations, computer hardware manufacturers have more or less agreed upon open-systems architecture, which allows many manufacturers' products to work cooperatively in their customers' data centers. This development was critical for businesses to consider using workstations in their computing environments because these devices all use Unix-based operating systems.

Standard Interfaces

Open systems require a standard set of interfaces between operating systems, DBMS products, communications protocols, and graphical user interfaces (GUIs).[10]

It is not enough, however, just to *have* open systems. Companies must have well-defined and published interfaces so software developers know exactly how their software will work in each environment and how data communications will flow from one platform to another within the same configuration or between configurations.

Standard interfaces make it possible for software developers to produce applications that can be operated in a number of different operating system environments. Standard interfaces make it possible for companies to use applications on a number of different computer platforms,

---

[10]Graphical user interfaces, or GUIs, are software products that provide users with "user friendly" screens. These products include tools like mouses and screen images in the form of icons. Apple's MacIntosh, Microsoft's Windows and IBM's OS2 are examples of GUI environments.

generally without having to modify their applications. The applications are, therefore, *independent* of the platforms on which they are being operated, hence the term *platform independent.*

The advantages of using platform-independent applications are numerous. They enable companies to use their computer applications on one computer platform and, when they have outgrown the capacity of that platform, to seamlessly move the application to another, larger platform, whether or not the new platform is manufactured by the same manufacturer as the former device.

In addition, companies may wish to simultaneously operate the same application on numerous platforms if, for example, a number of different business units all use the same set of applications. A single applications maintenance team can then support all versions of the application, regardless of differences in the platforms on which the application is being operated, because the application itself is platform independent.

Many DBMS products, for example Oracle, Informix, Sybase, and Ingres, are also platform independent. All these DBMS products can be operated in any Unix-based environment, on any manufacturer's computers, and several can be operated in *non-Unix* environments as well, for example in PC-DOS or even in mainframe environments.

Platform independence becomes critically important when applications that use GUI tools on PCs are linked to DBMS products on individual PCs or on PC networks and subsequently to DBMS products on workstations or mainframe computers that are connected using local area networks (LANs). In this type of environment, it is essential that all components within the configuration work smoothly together and that they work in precisely the way they are expected to work together each and every time.

Chapter 9

Configurations to Support Business Needs

BUSINESS NEEDS AND TRENDS IN COMPUTER TECHNOLOGY

In Chapter 8 we developed a wish list of computer-related business needs to support daily operations and decision-support work. Because daily operations can be predefined and thus preprogrammed, whereas decision-support operations are more spontaneous, the needs of the two types of applications are quite different from each other. Decision-support requirements are not always satisfactorily met by conventional computer technology, which includes the use of mainframes, minis, or both connected to *dumb* terminals that are designed to efficiently support preprogrammed rather than decision-support applications.

The three major trends in computer technology that were discussed in the previous chapter, namely, improvements in the price-performance ratio, availability of local and wide-area networking, and the evolution of open-systems architecture, support both types of business needs efficiently by utilizing *client-server configurations.* In this chapter, we present a brief, nontechnical overview of client-server technology, explain its salient benefits, and discuss several configurations that businesses can use to meet the needs in the wish list we developed in the previous chapter.

CLIENT-SERVER TECHNOLOGY

As its name indicates, client-server technology consists of clients and servers whose roles are very similar to those encountered in everyday business: clients make certain requests and the servers carry out those requests. The main difference, of course, is that the clients and servers are both computers, albeit of different sizes and capacities. In addition, because the clients and servers cannot communicate using the communication media used by human beings, they exchange requests and responses over a computer network that forms the backbone of any client-server configuration (see Figure 9–1). Thus, not only are the clients and servers computers, but also they must be equipped with appropriate communication hardware and software.

Typically, end users interact with their respective client computers (or client stations) to *compose* work requests. A work request, for example, may be to examine a customer record, to perform an analysis or a name selection step, or to make a report. The client computer transforms that request into a message that the server computer can understand and sends it to the server over the network.

The server analyzes the message to identify the requesting client and the work requested. It then carries out the request and communicates the results back to the requesting client by sending a message the client can understand. The server sends the response message over the same

FIGURE 9–1
Client-Server Technology: What Is It?

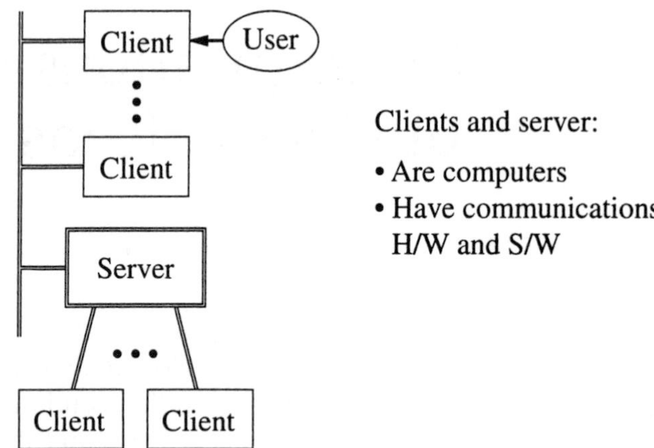

network on which it received the request. The client computer, upon receiving the response message, extracts the results from it and displays them on the screen for the end user.

As shown in Figure 9–1, the simplest client-server configuration must have at least one server; it may, however, have several client computers. The networking hardware and software is set up to allow all clients to communicate with the server and vice-versa. The clients may not be able to communicate with each other—that type of communication is not necessary for client-server interactions.

As the above example indicates, the client computer's primary responsibility is to support end-user interactions and to provide a user-friendly human interface. This may involve screen painting, echoing keyboard input, displaying results, supporting point-and-click actions using the mouse, and so on. While these operations are going on, the server on the network is not disturbed at all. The server is contacted (and therefore interrupted) only when a request has been fully formed and requires server action.

The primary responsibility of the server is to receive requests from all the clients on the network and carry out those requests as fast as possible, without worrying about how the work request was composed and how the results will be displayed on the screen.

Due to the nature of the work load, clients are generally small, single-user computers, whereas servers are much more powerful computers that can support multiple clients. In addition, depending upon the type of user interaction, clients, servers, or both could be specialized for different users' needs (more on specialization later in this chapter).

BENEFITS OF CLIENT-SERVER CONFIGURATIONS

The primary benefit of using client-server configurations is a good price-performance ratio. Because the clients and servers use an open-systems approach, you can mix and match different vendors' products to design the most suitable configuration for a given set of needs. The competition between the products that can fulfill any role in the system tends to drive the quality up and prices down. In contrast, as Figure 9–2 shows, the proprietary mainframes and minis have vendor-specific hardware and

FIGURE 9–2
Client-Server Technology: Different from Mainframes and Minis

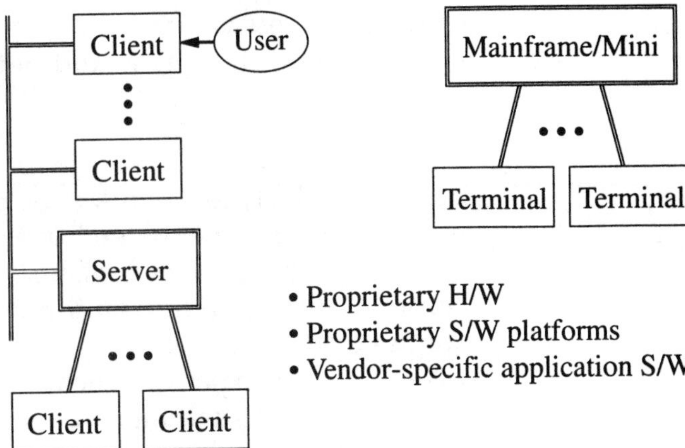
Client
User
Client
Server
Client
Client
Mainframe/Mini
Terminal
Terminal
• Proprietary H/W
• Proprietary S/W platforms
• Vendor-specific application S/W

FIGURE 9–3
Client-Server Technology: Division of Labor

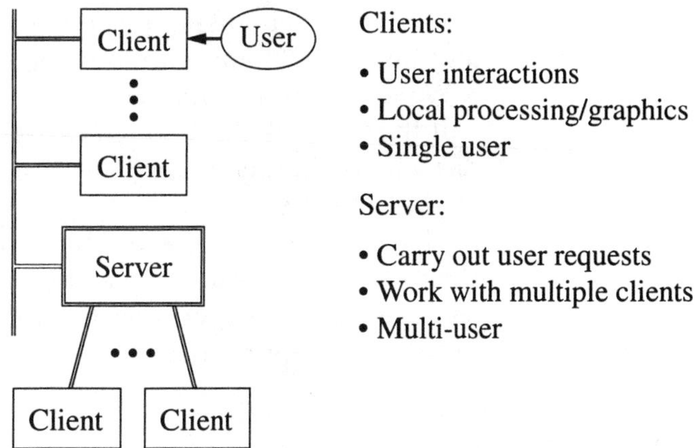
Client
User
Client
Server
Client
Client
Clients:
• User interactions
• Local processing/graphics
• Single user
Server:
• Carry out user requests
• Work with multiple clients
• Multi-user

software, which tend to be more expensive and less flexible than the equivalent products in the open-systems marketplace.

Another factor that improves the price-performance ratio of client-server configurations is division of labor between the clients and the server (see Figure 9–3). The clients are small, inexpensive computers largely responsible for the human interface and are deployed one per user. On the other hand, the servers are more expensive shared computers assigned the responsibility of carrying out client requests. Servers are not interrupted for human interface, and thus they can perform their own tasks more efficiently. Such a division of labor is not easily achieved by mainframes and minis because the main computers also provide human interface, which slows down their performance of back-end tasks.

In addition to providing attractive price-performance ratios, the client-server configurations provide flexibility and incremental growth. We can match client computers to the human-interface needs of their end users. We can also connect multiple servers on the networks that are specialized for different classes of requests. If we need more computing power, we can add more servers of the same type. If we need more storage capacity, we can add more disk drives to any server. In contrast to conventional mainframe configurations, these changes would all be incremental and would not necessitate major upgrades of the overall system. If managed properly, these changes would not create major disruptions in service either.

DIFFERENT KINDS OF CLIENTS

Based upon the type of work to be performed by the end users, the client computers could be of several types. These different types of client computers offer different local disk storage, type of display (text, graphics, high-resolution graphics), and type of operating system (single-user or multitasking).

A relatively inexpensive client computer may be a DOS PC with small, low-capacity disks and human-interface tools for text applications. Such a configuration would be adequate for data entry applications.

If the end users require a graphical interface for their work, the client PC would need to be equipped with a faster processor, additional disk storage, and a *Windows*-based front end for human interface.

For more elaborate applications, the client computer could be a multitasking Unix station with local disk storage, high-resolution display, and X-Windows human interface.

If the network has enough capacity, the clients may not have any local disk at all—all their storage requirements could be served by shared disks on the network.

These different types of client computers could coexist in the same client-server configuration, as long as the networking aspects of the system are well managed and the requests from the client computers are routed to the appropriate servers.

DIFFERENT KINDS OF SERVERS

Just as client computers can be of different types, so can the servers. Different types of servers satisfy specialized requests that they are specially equipped to carry out. Figure 9–4 shows three different types of servers.

The database server should have fast disk drives and a large amount of disk capacity. In addition, it should have enough main memory (RAM) to satisfy several simultaneous requests and a database management system to store and manage data. All the data-related requests, for example, retrieving customer records, would be routed to this server.

The file server's needs are similar to those of the data server, except the file server may not need as much disk capacity and those disks may not have to be as fast. It would be used to store files shared by different end users. Thus, all requests related to retrieving shared files, such as word processing files, would be routed to this server.

The communication server, on the other hand, should be equipped with specialized communication equipment to connect to computers outside the client-server cluster. The communication server shown in Figure 9–4 can connect to a mainframe over a dial-up or T-1 line. Specialized communication servers are available to connect from one local-area network to another, from a local-area network to a wide-area network, or from one wide-area network to another.

FIGURE 9–4
Client-Server Technology: Different Kinds of Servers

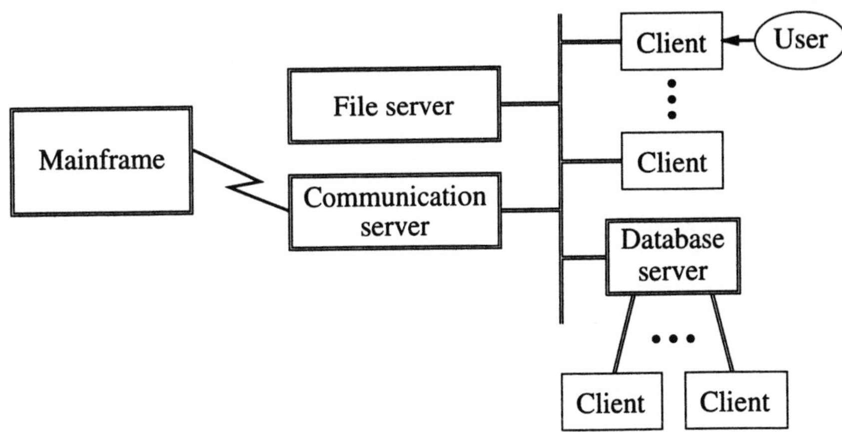

DIFFERENT TYPES OF NETWORKS

In the discussion above, we talked about the client computers and servers exchanging messages over a network. In open-systems architecture, the network, just like the clients and servers we just described, can also be of several different types. All that matters is that it is able to transmit all the required messages at a satisfactory rate of speed so the clients do not have to wait too long for a response.

If all the computers in a client-server configuration resided in a single building, for example, within a campus environment in which buildings are less than a mile apart, they could be connected using a local-area network such as Ethernet or Token Ring. The information-carrying capacity of such networks can range from 10 to 100 megabits per second, and the networks can easily connect hundreds of computers in one cluster.

If, on the other hand, the computers to be connected are spread apart over distances of more than one mile, they would have to use a wide-area network. Such networks usually carry less information than local-area networks—they can carry as much as 10 kilobits to 1 megabit of information per second. They may be configured using leased telephone lines, T-1 lines, or even fiber optic links.

EXAMPLES

So far, we have discussed the availability of a variety of affordable computer and communication hardware available from a variety of vendors. We thus have the building blocks we can use to configure client-server systems to meet most requirements. These building blocks can be used in endless ways to create practical solutions to business needs. In the following section, we present three examples of increasing complexity to illustrate the flexibility of the building blocks.

Happy Combination of Old and New Technologies

The first example, shown in Figure 9–5, assumes that the day-to-day operations are already being supported by a mainframe (or a mini). That system, although perennially in need of more computing cycles and disk space, does help run the business satisfactorily.

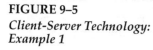

FIGURE 9–5
Client-Server Technology: Example 1

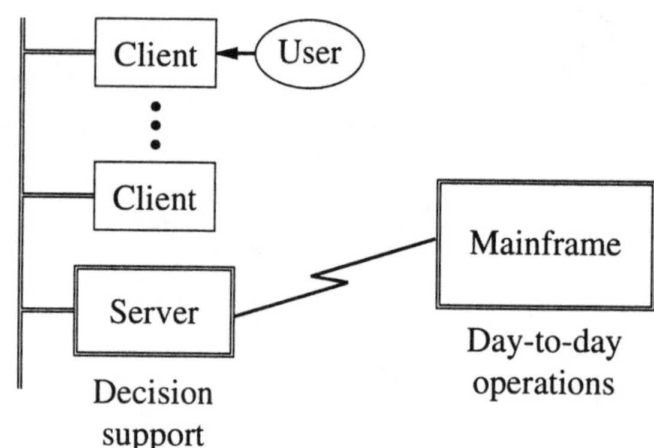

The mainframe, however, is not adequate for decision-support work, which would put an additional burden on its already stretched resources and demand a level of flexibility that the mainframe is not designed to handle. In addition, the decision-support work would interfere with the production windows of the *next* batch run.

To provide decision-support capabilities, we add a bit of new technology on the left in the form of a simple client-server cluster with one server. This new technology will happily coexist with the old technology and will communicate with the latter using either a dedicated line or a wide-area link depicted by the jagged line in the figure.

From time to time, selected data will be extracted from the mainframe database(s) and sent down to the decision-support server over the communication link. That data will be stored on the server in a form that allows the end users (for example, marketing analysts) to perform analysis, name selection, and similar tasks. After a marketing campaign has been fully *defined* in the decision-support environment, predefined data sets will be created and uploaded to the mainframe where they will be acted upon by the operations software. Responses to the marketing campaign thus created will flow to the decision-support server as part of future data downloads from the mainframe.

The primary benefit of this configuration is that it does not call for major changes to the mainframe side, but it still manages to provide much-needed flexibility at an affordable price.

All New Technology

The second example, shown in Figure 9–6, portrays a configuration in which the daily operations are also performed by a server on the network. This server can communicate with decision-support servers right over the network—the link to the mainframe is not needed anymore. The operations server is connected to several data entry terminals using point-to-point lines or a wide-area network.

The primary benefits of this configuration are modular growth and high-speed connection between the operations and decision-support servers. As the need for computing power expands on either side, additional servers can be added on the network incrementally. Because these additional servers will be able to exchange data over the network, they will be seamlessly integrated with the existing set of servers.

FIGURE 9–6
Client-Server Technology: Example 2

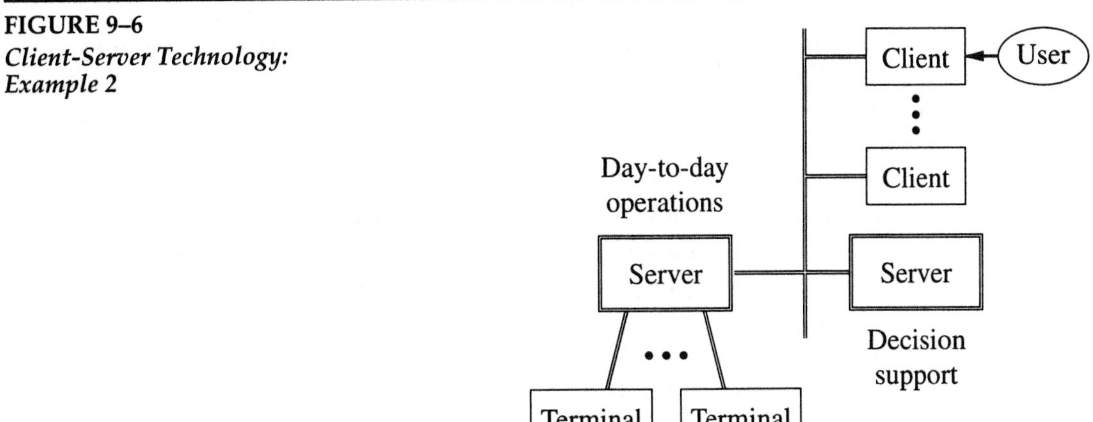

FIGURE 9–7
Client-Server Technology: Example 3

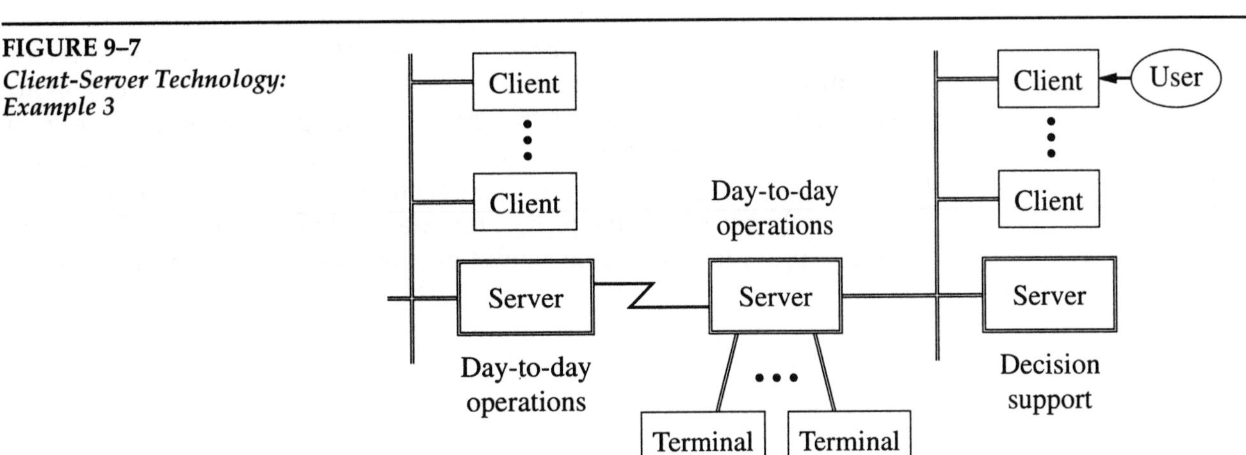

Multilocation Installation Using All New Technology

Our last example builds on the previous one to support a remote office location. The remote office has a client-server cluster of its own shown on the left in Figure 9–7. The server there supports the daily operations of the remote office and is connected with the central server by a wide-area link. Thus, the remote server could exchange information with the central operations server to provide users on either side of the wide-area link an up-to-date view of the operations data.

The decision-support server is not at all affected by adding the remote server. It continues to exchange information with the central operations server that is located on the same local-area network.

REVISITING THE WISH LIST AND OUTLINING FUTURE STEPS

As illustrated by the three examples we just discussed, the use of new technology has made it possible for us to achieve most of the items on our wish list for decision-support work. We can provide different computing systems to support the daily operations and decision-support work. We can supply ample computing power for decision-support work to provide adequate response time, without interfering with daily operations. Lastly, we can achieve affordable incremental growth in computing power and disk space.

The use of new technology, however, is only one component of a complete solution to business needs. The deployment of new kinds of systems creates challenges for personnel because the new systems have very different programming and administration requirements from traditional systems.

The old systems were mostly batch oriented, whereas the new ones are more interactive. They involve the use of new operating systems (e.g., Unix operating system) and are heavily dependent on communication software for exchanging information with other computers.

All this implies that computer support personnel have to be retrained in the care and feeding of the new kinds of systems on several fronts, including new operating systems, networks, application software, database management systems, and programming languages. Such training is readily available from the vendors themselves or even from independent training organizations.

In addition to the training issue, the use of new technology involves thinking about computer systems in a different way, most notably, recognizing modularity and incremental growth. We need to think about small, powerful computers that can be interconnected to accomplish bigger tasks. We also need to think of specialized computer systems for selected tasks. As planners and decision makers embrace this new thinking, businesses would be better able to harness the newly evolved computer technology to provide cost-effective solutions for their ever-expanding needs.

Chapter 10

The Basics of Statistical Analysis

THE PROCESS OF DATA ANALYSIS

Data analysis is a process. It starts with observations of an event, a behavior, or an outcome that are first encoded into data (called variables), then analyzed, and eventually turned into information. (See Figure 10–1.)

EXAMPLE 1

An example will illustrate the process.

Let's consider a catalog marketer who sells woodworking tools and supplies. Catalogs are mailed four times a year to all customers. The company has 1 million names on its customer file (database). For each customer on the database, there is a fairly complete history that includes dates of all purchases, items purchased, purchase dollar amounts, and a code indicating the source from which the name was originally acquired.

The cataloger would like to know if "new" customers buy more than "old" customers. Classifying new customers as anyone whose first purchase was made within the last 12 months and an old customer as anyone whose first purchase was made over a year ago, the mailer's analyst draws a sample of 100,000 names and calculates the following:

5,000 orders were received in the last month.
3,000 orders (60 percent) were from new customers.
2,000 orders (40 percent) were from old customers.

Even in this simple example, the analyst was involved in a fairly complicated and very structured process. First, observations of customer purchasing were encoded based on dates of first purchase, thereby creating the variable CUSTOMER TYPE with two values, new and old. Similarly, purchase data was encoded into the variable PURCHASE with two values, yes and no.

Finally, the resultant variables were analyzed by calculating the percentages of new and old customers among the total number of buyers in the period analyzed. The resulting information is that new customers accounted for 60 percent of sales volume and old customers represent 40 percent of sales volume.

Let's examine the process in more detail and discuss what else could have been done. The analyst transformed the observations into *categorical* data; that is, observations were classified into two distinct and nonoverlapping categories or groups. For CUSTOMER TYPE, a customer is either new or old; for PURCHASE, a customer either did purchase or did not purchase.

Data at this gross level of detail provides no discrimination among the customers within either group. For example, a customer whose first purchase is 11 months old is "equal" to a customer whose first purchase is 11 days old.

FIGURE 10–1

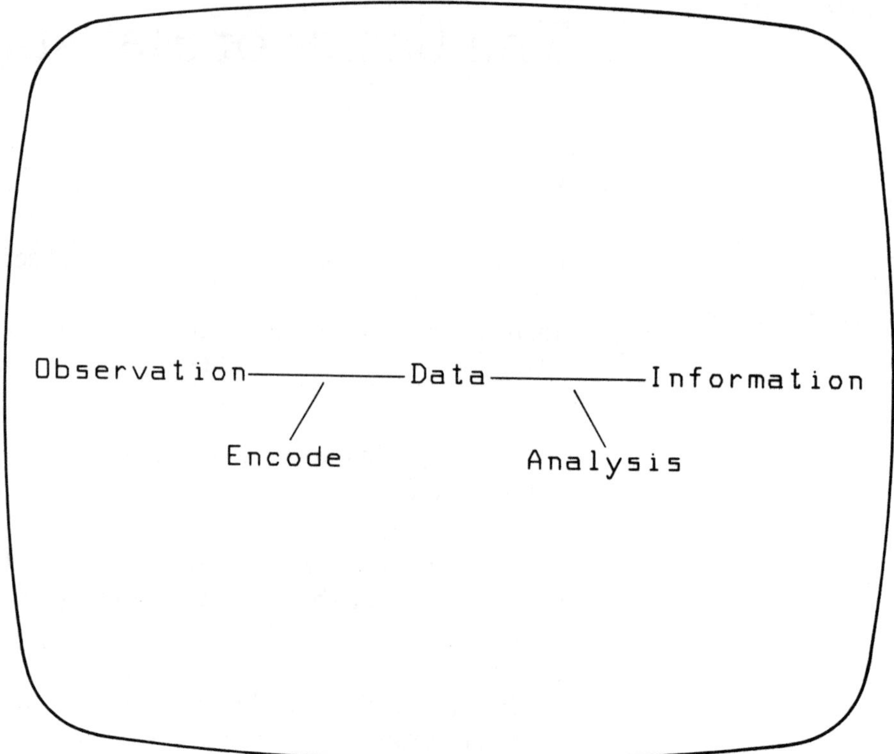

Similarly, customers who purchased any item, regardless of how many or their cost, are considered equal. Clearly, information is *lost* when using categorical data.

The analyst could just as easily have created *scalar* data or *continuous* data, which provide more information. The PURCHASE variable could use actual purchase amounts as its values. This new PURCHASE variable is scalar, by definition, because it satisfies the required condition: the four operations of arithmetic (+, –, ×, and /) can be meaningfully performed on the variable's values.

For example, the sum of two purchases may be added together—$5 and $2 equals $7—to produce a meaningful number. In contrast, if CUSTOMER TYPE, a categorical variable, is coded 1 for new customers and 0 for old customers, adding the two category numbers together results in a number that is obviously not meaningful.

If this scalar PURCHASE variable had been used, the analyst might have found that the average purchase amount among new customers was two or three times larger than the average among the old customers. This information adds to the understanding of the new-customer group. Not only do new customers purchase more, but also their purchases are worth more.

Hopefully, this short walk through the data process conveys the intended impression that the process of analyzing data requires a feeling for the data. However, because we never really know whether or not we have the right feeling, we need more tools to help us get that feeling, to help us better understand what we are about to analyze.

PICTURES OF DATA: STEM AND LEAF

Actually, we *can* see what the data looks like—in a picture statisticians call *stem and leaf*.

The stem-and-leaf picture is easy to draw, either by hand or computer, and easy to understand. Because it's easier to illustrate the method of construction than it is to describe it, let's go to an illustration.

EXAMPLE 2

Consider a small sample of a mailing consisting of 20 observations of purchase dollar amounts. Ranking the dollar amounts from low to high, we have:

5 6 7 8 10 12 14 15 17 18 20 30 40 45 47 50 50 50 66 90

Each number can be broken up into two parts: a stem and a leaf.

The stem is the first part of the number. In this case, because we are dealing with two-digit numbers, the stem is the digit representing the 10s position. The leaves are the unit digits.

Thus, the data can be first expressed as follows:

		Stem	+	*Leaf*
5	=	0	+	5
6	=	0	+	6
7	=	0	+	7
8	=	0	+	8
10	=	1	+	0
12	=	1	+	2
14	=	1	+	4
15	=	1	+	5
17	=	1	+	7
18	=	1	+	8
20	=	2	+	0
30	=	3	+	0
40	=	4	+	0
45	=	4	+	5
47	=	4	+	7
50	=	5	+	0
50	=	5	+	0
50	=	5	+	0
66	=	6	+	6
90	=	9	+	0

Accordingly, the stem-and-leaf picture of purchase amounts in dollar units looks like this:

Stem	*Leaf*
0	5678
1	024578
2	0
3	0
4	057
5	000
6	6
7	
8	
9	0

The stems are written vertically. The leaves are put on the stems horizontally in rank order, and if necessary they are repeated according to the actual number of occurrences (e.g., 50 occurs three times, resulting in stem 5 with three 0 leaves).[1]

At a glance, we can see the overall *shape* of the variable PURCHASE. The shape of the variable is dependent on *wild observations* (e.g., 90), *gaps* (70 through 89), and *clumps* (10 through 18) in the data.

Why this emphasis on the shape of the data? The answer is that traditional statistical techniques such as regression, which will be the focus of this section, work better if the shape of the data (or variables) conforms to a specific profile. If the data does not match this profile, then either certain techniques (like regression) should be used with caution, or the data must be "massaged" or reshaped to fit the desired profile.

The desired profile is the well-known bell-shaped curve, formally referred to as the *normal curve* or *distribution.* Figure 10–2 shows a stem-and-leaf display of normal data and Figure 10–3 shows a traditional graph of the normal curve.

The normal distribution is important to many traditional statistical methods. However, in order to understand its importance, we should understand two other basic concepts first. So let's present these basics and then discuss the role the normal distribution plays in data analysis and statistical model building.

NUMERICAL SUMMARIES

The two basic concepts are the *center* of a set of numbers of data, more commonly known as the *average,* with which everyone is familiar, and the *spread* or variation in the data set, a concept few of us who aren't statisticians think much about, if at all. There are three ways to find the center and several alternatives to measure spread.

Center of Data

EXAMPLE 3

Let's consider the following set of nine numbers, or observations:

1 2 3 5 5 5 7 8 9

The sum of these nine numbers is 45. The sum of the observations (45) divided by the number of observations (9) is called the *mean,* which is the everyday average. In this case, the mean is 5.

It is also true, in this case, that the mean is equal to the number in the center or middle of the set of numbers. The number in the center of a set of numbers ranked from high to low (or low to high) is called the *median.* Thus, in our example, the median equals the mean.

---

[1]When we are working with numbers having more than two digits, we must decide on the appropriate break for the stem and leaf. This depends on the data at hand and the objective of the analysis; therefore, rules of thumb for splitting the data cannot be made. However, let's consider the two possible breaks for data in the hundreds. One break is between the 100s and 10s positions, in which case we ignore the units digit. For example, 345 = 3 plus 4. This stem-and-leaf display implies the stem is multiplied by 100 and the leaf is multiplied by 10.

The second possible break is between the 10s and units' positions. For example, 345 = 34 plus 5. This implies the stem position is multiplied by 10 and the leaf is multiplied by 1.

FIGURE 10–2

0	13
1	009
2	3333
3	1111112
4	11112223346
5	112223334566
6	0003345699
7	444445
8	3333
9	5

FIGURE 10–3
Probability Distributions

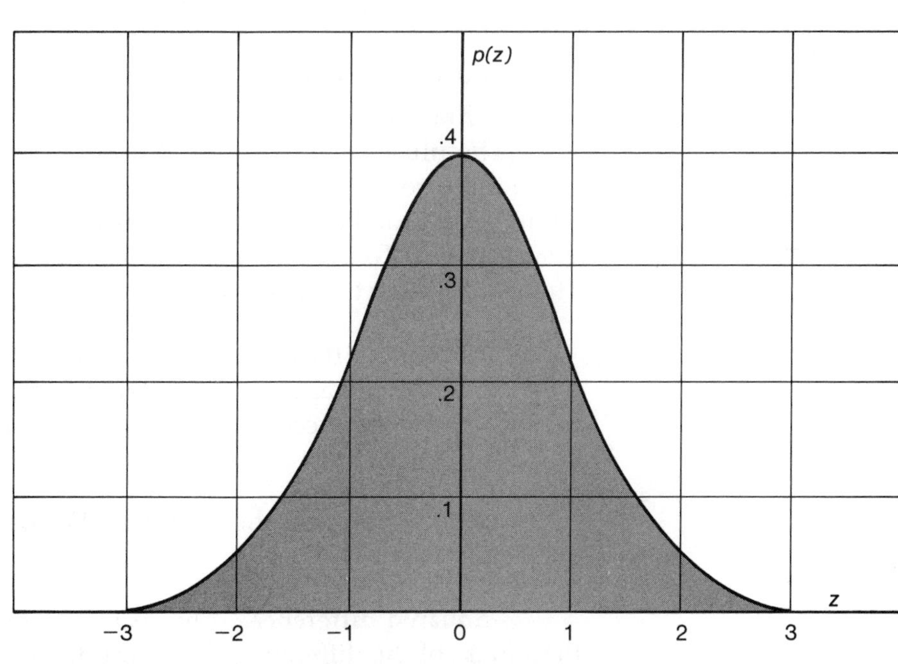

Source: T H Wonnacott and R J Wonnacott. *Introductory Statistics for Business and Economics,* 2nd ed. (Santa Barbara: John Wiley & Sons: 1977), p. 92.

If we look closely at our set of nine numbers, we will see that one number, the number 5, appears more frequently than any other number. The number that appears most frequently in a set of numbers is called the *mode.* Thus, in our example, all three measures of center are equal.

Variation within the Data

The notion of *variation* is more complicated but equally important. For example, three persons with incomes of $49,000, $50,000, and $51,000 could all be meaningfully described as coming from a fairly homogeneous group with a mean income of $50,000. But three persons with incomes of $25,000, $50,000, and $75,000 are clearly not alike even though their mean income is also $50,000.

To assess variation, we can use several summary measures.

Range. Going back to our simple example, we see that the numbers go from a high of 9 to a low of 1. We can measure the variation by the distance or difference between the high and low numbers. In this case, the difference or range is equal to 8.

Differences about the mean. We can measure variation by observing the differences of the numbers about their center, say, the mean. The set of differences about the mean of 5 are:

−4 −3 −2 0 0 0 2 3 4

Thus, we can summarize the differences by using the sum of the differences, or the mean of the differences. In either case, the value is zero.

Sum: $-4 + -3 + -2 + 0 + 0 + 0 + 2 + 3 + 4 = 0$

Mean: $\frac{-4 + -3 + -2 + 0 + 0 + 0 + 2 + 3 + 4}{9} = \frac{0}{9} = 0$

Intuitively, a numeric summary intended to represent variation should equal zero only when there is no variation, which is clearly not the case here. The pluses and minuses, in this case, cancel each other out and cause the zero. Although canceling out might not be a problem for a different set of numbers, we'd rather use a measure that is not sensitive to this problem. To avoid canceling out, we must eliminate the minuses. There are at least two ways to do this.

Absolute difference. The first way to eliminate minuses is to use only the absolute value of the difference; that is, to ignore the sign and use only the value. Accordingly, the set of absolute numbers is:

4 3 2 0 0 0 2 3 4

Using this approach, the sum and the mean of the differences are 18 and 2, respectively.

Squared difference. The second way to avoid minuses is to use the square of the difference, which produces a positive number. (Remember, a negative number times a negative number results in a positive number.) Accordingly, the squares of the differences are

16 9 4 0 0 0 4 9 16

The sum and mean of the squared differences are 58 and 6.4, respectively.

Thus, for summary measures of variation for the set of the nine numbers 1, 2, 3, 5, 5, 5, 7, 8, and 9, we have:

8.0 = Range.

0.0 = Either sum or mean of the difference about the center.

18.0 = Sum of the absolute difference.

2.0 = Mean of the absolute difference.

58.0 = Sum of the squared difference.

6.4 = Mean of the squared difference.

Aside from the effects of the canceling out issue, all the measures work the same way: the larger the value, the greater the variation.

To assess which of two or more sets of numbers has the greatest variation, we select *one* summary measure and calculate its value for all sets. The set with the largest numerical value has the greatest variation. Why have we taken you through all this? First, we want to demonstrate that the subjectivity or preference of the analyst can affect the objectivity of data analysis. Second, and more importantly, we want to give you a basic understanding of three very important measures that are used in a variety of statistical applications:

- **Total sum of squares**—the sum of the squared differences, used in all regression theory.
- **The variance**—the sum of the squared differences divided by the number of observations.
- **Standard deviation**—the square root of the variance.

The concept of variation, expressed in terms of the standard deviation, is integral to the understanding of *confidence intervals* and *tests of significance*—formal statistical procedures for determining the level of confidence with which we can assert that the findings of a study are real or due to chance (i.e., what the statisticians call *sample variation*). This is our next topic.

CONFIDENCE INTERVALS

EXAMPLE 4

Returning to our catalog example, let's assume our analyst is now interested in knowing the average purchase dollar amount of the customers on the house file. The analyst draws a sample of 75 customers and calculates the mean purchase amount, which turns out to be $68. This mean value seems small, so another sample of 75 is drawn and the mean turns out to be $122. Although the analyst knows that the means will vary from sample to sample due to the nature of randomly selecting different groups of customers, the analyst feels the two means are too far apart to provide an indication of the true mean purchase amount. Accordingly, the analyst draws another 38 samples of 75 customers and calculates the mean of each sample.

The analyst creates a stem-and-leaf display of the *sample means*. The shape of the distribution of sample means looks normal. (See Figure 10–4.) The variation and standard deviation of the 40 sample means can be calculated using the following formulas:[2]

$$\text{Variance of sample means} = \frac{\text{Sum (each sample mean} - \text{average of all sample means)}^2}{\text{Number of samples} - 1}$$

$$\text{Standard deviation of sample means} = \text{Square root of the variance of sample means}$$

Note that it is customary to refer to the standard deviation of sam
means as the standard error of the sample mean, and we will follow
custom from this point on.

[2]A statistical note: when working with a sample instead of the entire populati
always the case, the variance is calculated by dividing by the number of obser

FIGURE 10–4

Stem	*Leaf*
12	22
11	24
10	00222268888
9	0222444446688
8	00224466
7	048
6	8

Mean = 94.85
Median = 94.00
Variance = 166.75
Standard error = 12.91

In this case, the variance among the 40 sample means turns out to be 166.75 and the standard error is 12.91. The mean of the sample means is 94.85.

At this point, the analyst is prepared to consider $94.85 as the true mean purchase amount, that is, the average that would have been discovered if all customers on the database were included in the calculation. How confident should the analyst be in this mean of means? The analyst knows that the mean is affected by the variation of the data on which it is calculated. That is, if the variation is small, the mean is more representative of the true mean than if the variation is large. Thus, if the variation of the mean of the means is small, the analyst would have more confidence in the mean of means representing the true purchase amount. On the other hand, if the variation is large, then we would have less confidence.

Now, the analyst has three important pieces of information:

1. The shape of the data appears to be normal.
2. The mean of means is $94.85.
3. The standard error is $12.91.

To put the pieces together and establish a sense of confidence about the assertion of the true mean purchase, the analyst needs one of the fundamental rules (statisticians call them theorems) of statistics.

Theorem 1

95 percent of the time (95 out of every 100 sample means) the true mean purchase amount lies between plus or minus 1.96 standard errors from the mean of the sample means.

Thus, we can create a *95 percent confidence interval* around the mean of $94.85, which includes all values between the mean plus 1.96 standard er-
ınd the mean minus 1.96 standard errors.
our example, we get these figures:

$$1.96 \text{ times the SE} = \quad 1.96 \times \$12.91 = \$25.30$$

$$\text{The mean plus 1.96 times the SE} = \$94.85 + \$25.30 = \$120.15$$

$$\text{he mean minus 1.96 times the SE} = \$94.85 - \$25.30 = \$69.55$$

ple
that

on, which is almost
ations minus 1.

Thus, the 95 percent confidence interval includes all values between \$69.55 and \$120.15.

The theorem also allows for varying the levels of confidence, though 95 percent is a widely used standard. By increasing the confidence, the interval becomes wider; conversely, by decreasing the confidence, the interval becomes narrower. For example, the factor for a confidence interval that would include 99.7 percent of all observations is calculated by multiplying the standard error by 3.0 rather than 1.96. The factor for 90 percent confidence interval is 1.64.

Where do these factors—1.64, 1.96, and 3.0—come from? The normal distribution! When a variable is normally distributed or nearly normal, we have the following facts (see Figure 10–5):

90 percent of the observations or values fall between plus and minus 1.64 standard deviations.

95 percent of the observations fall between plus and minus 1.96 standard deviations.

99.73 percent of the observations fall between plus and minus 3.0 standard deviations.

The center or middle value is the mean of the variable.

In practice, we do not have to draw many samples to construct a *confidence interval for a mean.* We work with only one sample. However, to describe this one-sample approach, we need to have another way to calculate the standard error of the mean.

Standard error of the mean = Standard deviation from a single sample, divided by the square root of *n*, the number of observations.

We use the following example to illustrate the one-sample approach.

EXAMPLE 5

Let's say we want to know the mean age of all customers on a house file; that is, the true mean age. The file is too large to calculate the mean directly, so we pull a sample of 30 names from the house file and draw an inference from the data contained in the sample. (See Figure 10–6.)

We have the following pieces of information:

- The sample size, $n = 30$.
- The sample mean age, $\bar{x} = 44.03$.
- The sum of squared differences = 3,682.966.
- The variance equals the sum of squared difference divided by $n - 1$, which equals 126.9988.
- The standard deviation is the square root of the variance and the square root of 126,9988 = 11.26937.
- The standard error of the mean equals the standard deviation divided by the square root of *n*. The square root of 30 is 5.477. Therefore, the standard error is equal to 11.26937/5.477 = 2.0574.

We want to use the sample mean to estimate the true mean age, with 95 percent confidence. For this, we need another theorem, which is very similar to Theorem 1.

FIGURE 10–5

Areas under the Normal Curve for Various Standard Deviations from the Mean

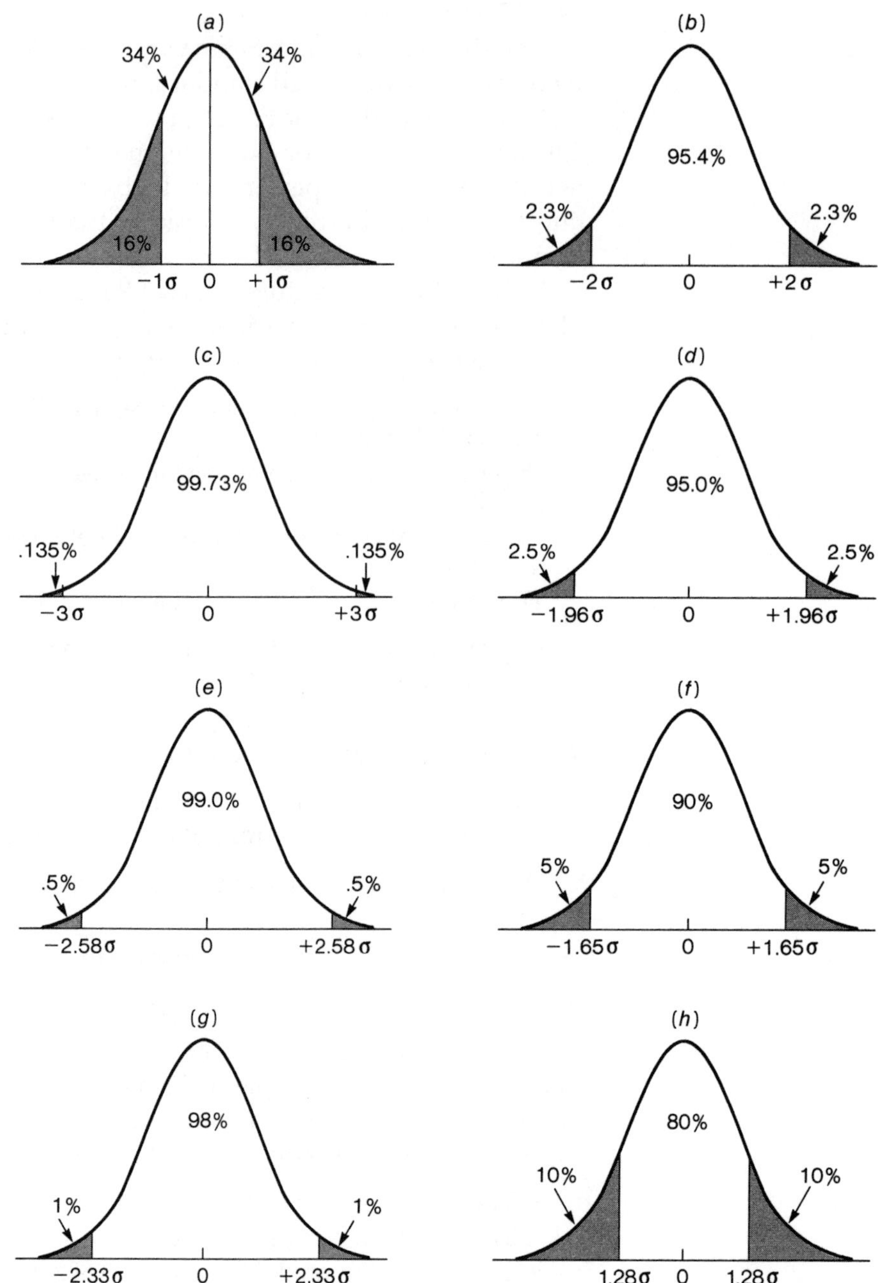

Source: S K Kachigan. *Statistical Analysis* (New York: Radius Press, 1986), p. 61.

FIGURE 10–6
Sample from House File

Observations	*Age*	$(x - \bar{x})$	$(x - \bar{x})^2$
1	45	0.967	0.934
2	45	0.967	0.934
3	45	0.967	0.934
4	65	20.967	439.601
5	45	0.967	0.934
6	36	–8.033	64.534
7	45	0.967	0.934
8	56	11.967	143.201
9	62	17.967	322.801
10	43	–1.033	1.068
11	34	–10.033	100.668
12	54	9.967	99.334
13	57	12.967	168.134
14	59	14.967	224.001
15	47	2.967	8.801
16	38	–6.033	36.401
17	38	–6.033	36.401
18	32	–12.033	144.801
19	23	–21.033	442.401
20	28	–16.033	257.068
21	47	2.967	8.801
22	49	4.967	24.668
23	58	13.967	195.068
24	61	16.967	287.868
25	26	–18.033	325.201
26	32	–12.033	144.801
27	34	–10.033	100.668
28	36	–8.033	64.534
29	38	–6.033	36.401
30	43	–1.033	1.068
Average	44.03		3,682.966
n	30		
$n - 1$	29		
Variance			126.9988
Standard deviation			11.26937
Standard error			2.057497
95% confidence			1.96
Range = + or –			4.032694
Range =			40.00063
			48.06602

Theorem 2

95 percent of the time (95 out of every 100 samples) the true mean lies between plus or minus 1.96 standard errors from the sample mean.

Accordingly, we can say that the sample mean age will differ from the true mean age by less than 4.03 (1.96 × 2.0574) years with 95 percent confidence. That is, we can assert with a confidence of 95 percent that the true mean age lies between

44.03 ± 4.03

or

40.00 and 48.07

Confidence intervals apply not only to means but also to percentages or, in case of direct marketing, to response rates.

CONFIDENCE INTERVALS AND TESTS OF SIGNIFICANCE FOR RESPONSE RATES

The theorem needed to calculate the 95 percent confidence interval for response rates is very similar to the theorem for means.

Theorem 3

95 percent of the time (95 out of every 100 samples) the true response rate lies between plus or minus 1.96 standard errors from the sample response rate,

where

p = Sample response rate

n = Sample size

Standard error = Square root of $p \times (1 - p)$ divided by n

Let's consider an example.

EXAMPLE 6

Our cataloger wants to test 1,000 names selected at random from a new list. However, to break even the list must be expected to have a response rate of 4.5 percent on a rollout mailing. The cataloger wants to be 95 percent certain that the list test will hold up on the rollout.

Prior to mailing the list, the cataloger could calculate a confidence interval based on the number of pieces mailed (1,000) and the desired level of confidence (95 percent). Using the formula,

Confidence interval = Expected response ± 1.96 × SE

or

$$\text{CI} = p \pm 1.96 \times \text{SE}$$
$$\text{CI} = .045 \pm 1.96 \times \sqrt{[(.045) \times (1 - .045)/1{,}000]}$$
$$\text{CI} = .045 \pm 1.96 \times \sqrt{(.04298/1{,}000)}$$
$$\text{CI} = .045 \pm 1.96 \times 0.00656$$
$$\text{CI} = .045 \pm 0.0128$$
$$\text{CI} = .0578 \text{ to } .0322 \text{ or } 3.22\% \text{ to } 5.78\%$$

Based on this confidence interval, a statistician would say that any response rate between 3.33 and 5.78 percent supports the hypothesis that the true response rate *is* 4.5 percent. However, this does not mean that the true response rate is definitely 4.5 percent. Therefore, the cataloger would say that any response rate within the confidence interval would support the conclusion that the true response rate *may be* 4.5 percent. If a response rate is achieved that is outside the interval, the cataloger is prepared to accept the conclusion that the true response rate is not 4.5 percent. The list is mailed and pulls a 3.5 percent response. Based on the confidence interval we just calculated, we can conclude that the true response rate is 4.5 percent.

On the other hand, we now have more information. We have an actual 3.5 percent response rate on a test mailing of 1,000 pieces. Therefore, we could calculate a confidence interval based on this information.

$p = .035$

$(1 - p) = 0.965$

$n = 1{,}000$

Standard error = Square root of $(.035 \times .965)/1{,}000 = .006$

$.035 - (1.96 \times .006) = .035 - .012 = .023$

$.035 + (1.96 \times .006) = .035 + .012 = .047$

Thus, we can be 95 percent certain that the true response rate lies in the interval between 2.3 to 4.7 percent. Of course, the confidence interval around 3.5 percent had to include the desired 4.5 percent response rate because the confidence interval around the 4.5 percent response rate included 3.5 percent.

How do we interpret this new information? Again, if 4.5 percent were *not* included in the interval, we could say with 95 percent confidence that the true response rate was not 4.5 percent. But, as we said before, and it bears repeating, the converse is not true. Even though 4.5 percent is included in the confidence interval, we cannot say with 95 percent confidence that the true response rate is 4.5 percent, but we can say that the true response rate may be 4.5 percent, and that the list should be tested again.

This phenomenon of a test result being different from the true result is often associated with the concept of *regression to the mean.* More often than not, regression to the mean is referred to in the context of a list that tests well but does not do as well when rolled out in larger quantities. What's happening here is that part of the high response is due to chance or sample variation. For example, a list with a true response rate of 4 percent on a test of 5,000 names might pull as high as 4.5 percent just due to chance. However, when rolled out in large quantity, in all likelihood the list will respond closer to its true mean of 4.0 percent. In statistical parlance, the performance of the list will regress back to its mean. Because direct marketers usually don't retest lists that fall below a cutoff rate, the reverse side of this phenomenon is seen less frequently. We don't often see lists that initially tested poorly do well on larger rollouts because we don't do larger rollouts on lists that initially don't test well. Hopefully, this discussion will cause marketers to give more thought to lists whose cutoff rate is within the confidence interval of the test result—and to be cautious when a test result is above the break-even point.

A clear implication of this analysis is that the size of the confidence interval is related to the number of pieces mailed. Remember, the confidence interval is equal to the response rate plus or minus 1.96 standard error. And the standard error is calculated using this equation:

$$SE = \sqrt{(p \times (1 - p))/n}$$

In the case where the response rate is 3.5 percent, $(p \times (1 - p))$ will always be equal to $(.035 \times .965)$ or 0.034, no matter what the size of the sample. Therefore, the larger the sample, the smaller the standard error. If $n = 1{,}000$, then the standard error is $\sqrt{.034/1{,}000}$ or .005811. If n were 10,000, then the standard error would be $\sqrt{.034/10{,}000}$ or .001837, and so on.

Following this example, it is clear that if we have some idea of how large an error we are prepared to tolerate, and if we have some idea of the expected response rate, we can use the above information to solve for the number of pieces to mail.

For example, if we think the true response rate is 3.5 percent, but we want to be 95 percent certain that our test mailing will tell us if the true response rate is between 3.3 and 3.7 percent, we are in effect saying that we want 1.96 times the standard error to be equal to .002 or 0.2 percent—because 3.5 percent plus or minus 0.2 percent is equal to 3.3 to 3.7 percent. Statisticians use the term *precision* to describe the amount of error we are willing to tolerate on either side of the expected response rate.

Therefore, in this example

$$\text{Precision} = .002 = 1.96 \times \text{SE (standard error)}$$

Then, solving for SE we get this result

$$SE = .002/1.96 = .001020$$

and

$$SE = \sqrt{(p \times (1 - p)/n)}$$

Thus,

$$.001020 = \sqrt{(p \times (1 - p)/n)}$$

and, substituting .035 for p and .965 for $(1 - p)$, we get

$$.001020 = \sqrt{(.033775/n)}$$

and, squaring both sides of the equation, we get

$$0.00000104 = .033775/n$$

$$n = .033775/.00000104 = 32{,}437$$

In general, then, the rule for determining the number of pieces to mail (at the 95 percent level of confidence) is equal to

$$n = \frac{(p) \times (1 - p) \times 1.96^2}{\text{Precision}^2}$$

where

p = Expected response rate

Precision = One half the length of the 95 percent confidence interval

EXAMPLE 7

Suppose the cataloger mailed not only one new list but two new lists, and suppose the second list consisted of 1,200 names and pulled 4.5 percent. Are the true response rates for the two lists unequal? Can we declare with 95 percent confidence that the true response rates are different?

What are we really asking? If we believe the two lists have the same true response rate, then we are in effect saying that we think the difference between the two true response rates is equal to zero, and the difference we observed is due to chance.[3]

In this case, the difference in response rates is equal to 1 percent (4.5 – 3.5 percent). So then we are really asking how likely it is to find a difference in sample response rates of 1 percent, when there is no difference in true response rates.

If this test of the two lists were repeated many times, there would always be differences between the lists, but statistical theory tells us that the differences would be approximately normally distributed—and if the two lists had the same true response rate, the average or mean difference would be zero.

Our discussion of the normal distribution told us that in any normally distributed population, 95 percent of all observations would fall within range equal to 1.96 standard errors, and that 90 percent of all observations would fall within a range of 1.64 standard errors. In the latter situation, 5 percent of the observations would be below 1.64 standard errors from the mean and 5 percent above 1.64 standard errors from the mean. In situations where we want to be 95 percent sure one number is greater than another, not just different but greater, we use 1.64 standard errors as our factor to determine statistical significance.

Now the question of whether 4.5 percent is different from 3.5 percent starts to come into sharper focus. The question can now be restated to read, "can we be 95 percent certain that an observed difference of 1 percent is more than 1.64 standard errors away from a mean value of zero?" Well, if 1.64 is the benchmark, all we have to do is divide 1 percent by the correct measure of the standard error and see if the result is more or less than 1.64. If it is more than 1.64, we will say that this difference couldn't be due to chance and we'll declare the difference to be statistically significant. If the result is less than 1.64, we'll say the difference may be due to chance and we will not declare the lists to be different.

It is algebraically cumbersome to calculate the standard error of a difference between two response rates. Because the concept is important we'll try the algebra anyway, but don't worry if you get lost.

First, we must estimate the true response rate, given the two results and the number of pieces mailed on both sides of the test. In effect, we calculate a weighted average response rate.

---

[3]In statistics, the argument that there is no difference between two percentages (two response rates in direct marketing language) is referred to as the *null hypothesis*. When a statistical test indicates that there is no difference between response rates, a statistician would say that we accept the null hypothesis; conversely, when we find a statistically significant difference, a statistician would say that we reject the null hypothesis.

Remember, the first list test was mailed to 1,000 persons and the response rate was 3.5 percent.

$p1 = .035$

$n1 = 1{,}000$

The second list test was mailed to 1,200 persons and the response rate was 4.5 percent.

$p2 = .045$

$n2 = 1{,}200$

The average value, called p, is equal to

$$p = \frac{p1 \times n1 + p2 \times n2}{n1 + n2}$$

$$p = \frac{.035 \times 1{,}000 + .045 \times 1{,}200}{1{,}000 + 1{,}200} = \frac{89}{2{,}200} = .04045$$

The standard error of p equals

$$SE = \sqrt{p \times (1 - p) \times \left(\frac{n1 + n2}{n1 \times n2}\right)}$$

$$SE = \sqrt{(.040450) \times (1 - .040450) \times \frac{1{,}000 + 1{,}200}{1{,}000 \times 1{,}200}}$$

$$SE = \sqrt{.03881379 \times \frac{2{,}200}{1{,}200{,}00}}$$

$$SE = \sqrt{.03881379 \times .001833}$$

$$SE = \sqrt{.00007159}$$

$$SE = .0084355$$

Now we divide the observed difference by the standard error of the difference:

$.01 / .0084355 = 1.185 < 1.64$

Because the observed difference divided by the standard error of the difference is less than 1.64, we can say that the difference is not statistically significant at the 95 percent level of confidence.

What if the same response rates were achieved but the quantity mailed on each side of the test were 5,000? Without going through all the arithmetic, the answer is that the observed difference of 1 percent would be divided by a standard error that would now equal 0.003919 and the result of 2.55 would be greater than 1.64, so we would say that there is a statistically significant difference in response rates. Again, the point is that the larger the sample size, the more confident we can be in the results. The result is no real surprise, but it is a factor that will come up again and again as we move into statistical modeling.

The questions of statistical significance and sample size can be answered through the formulas presented in this chapter; however, to make life a little easier for you, we've included in Appendix A three Lotus 1–2–3 programs that automatically calculate confidence intervals and sample size and test for statistical significance. We have included sample screens and the cell formulas supporting each screen.

TESTS OF SIGNIFICANCE—TWO TYPES OF ERRORS AND POWER

We hope the relationship between confidence interval and significance testing is apparent by now. In a test versus control situation, if the test result lies within the confidence interval of the control, then the finding is that the test is not different from the control. If the test result lies outside the confidence interval of the control, then we say the test result is significantly different from the control.

Implicitly related to both confidence intervals and significance tests are two kinds of errors. Recall that we state our findings with a confidence level of less than 100 percent but typically greater than 95 percent. Thus, if we are confident 95 percent of the time, what about the other 5 percent of the time? The other 5 percent of the time we make errors. Statisticians call them Type I and Type II errors.

To understand Type I and Type II errors, let's think about them in our test versus control situation and assume that the observed test result is greater than the observed control result.

A *Type I* error occurs when we

Reject the null hypothesis H when it is true.

The null hypothesis states that there is *no* difference between response rates. Therefore, when we reject the null hypothesis, we are in effect accepting the conclusion that the difference in observed rates is significant. So, if we make a Type I error—rejecting the null hypothesis when it is true—we therefore are also making the error of believing that (in our test/control situation) the test result is greater than the control result. We would therefore act to replace the control, when in fact the control should be maintained.

The probability of making this kind of error is defined by the alpha level you establish. The alpha level is equal to 1 minus the confidence level. A decision to work at the 95 percent confidence level means that you have established a 5 percent alpha level. Having established a 5 percent alpha level, you are in effect saying that 5 percent of the time you may be making this kind of error. If you want to be even more sure of not making this kind of error, reduce alpha to, say, 1 percent. This will have the effect of increasing the confidence interval of the control, thereby requiring an even higher test response before the observed response rate can be declared to be statistically different—in this case, greater.

A *Type II* error occurs when we

Accept the null hypothesis when it is false.

Again using the test versus control situation where the observed test result is greater than the control result, acceptance of the null hypothesis when it is false means not recognizing a test that really beat the control.

Now we would also like to make the chances of making a Type II error as small as possible. But here's the catch: the probability of making a Type II error, called beta, is mathematically related, in a complicated way, to alpha. As alpha decreases, beta increases. So if you want to make the probability of making a Type II error small, you have to make alpha, the probability of making a Type I error, large.

What do you want to do as a businessperson? Suppose you have a good solid business, with a control offer that makes money. You run a test of a new offer and it appears to beat the control. But what if this is one of the situations in which acting on the test results will result in implementing a Type I error? You never know when this is happening! Clearly, as a prudent businessperson, you don't want to roll out a test that is really not better than your control. One approach is to set a low alpha, between 1 percent and 5 percent, if the economics of the situation warrant such care, and not worry about making a Type II error.

To summarize, in most situations you want to be conservative—if you are going to make an error, you don't want to accept a difference as significant when it is not. In statistical terms, therefore, you want to minimize the probability of making a Type I error. Beyond lowering alpha, this can be accomplished by increasing sample size, not surprising because we know that confidence intervals decrease when sample size increases. It is even possible to state statistically how certain you are of not making a Type II error. This is called the *power* of the test. The mathematics are complicated but the point to remember is that the power of the test increases as sample size increases.

Chapter 11

Relationships between Variables

With some of the fundamentals of statistical analysis behind us, we can now begin to study the *relationship between variables*, which is the subject matter of statistical modeling. Simply stated, two variables are related if they move together in some way.

Variables can be related in varying degree from strong to weak, from a perfect relationship to no relationship at all. With a strong relationship, knowing the value of one variable will tell us a lot about the value of the other variable; knowing everything, we have a perfect relationship. With a weak relationship, knowing one variable will tell us little about the other variable; knowing nothing, we have no relationship at all.

EXAMPLE 8

Let's return to our cataloger, who just tested a mailing of two different catalogs (A and B) to both new and old customers. The mailer wants to know which customers, new or old, buy more from which catalog, A or B.

To address this query, our cataloger's analyst pulls a small sample of 100 names to see if there is a relationship between customer type and catalog received.

The sample results are in Table 11–1.

From Table 11–1, we see that all new customers buy only from Catalog A, and all old customers buy from only Catalog B. In terms of percentages, we have:

1. 100 percent of new customers buy from A and 0 percent from B.
2. 100 percent of old customers buy from B and 0 percent from A.

Apparently, there is a perfect relationship between the variables CUSTOMER TYPE and CATALOG.

It is interesting to plot the percentages of Table 11–1. Figure 11–1 plots the percentages with a vertical axis of percent of customers buying from Catalog A and a horizontal axis of CUSTOMER TYPE. We see a line with a steep slope, which tells us in some obscure way that the relationship is perfect.

Although the analysis seems convincing, the analyst wants to validate the finding with another somewhat larger sample. Table 11–2 shows the results of a second sample of names.

The findings of Table 11–2 look drastically different than the findings of Table 11–1.

1. 50 percent of new customers buy from A and 50 percent from B.
2. 50 percent of old customers buy from B and 50 percent from A.

TABLE 11–1

Catalog	New	Percent	Old	Percent	Total	Percent
	Customer Type					
A	50	100%	0	0%	50	50%
B	0	0%	50	100%	50	50%
	50	100%	50	100%	100	100%

TABLE 11–2

Catalog	New	Percent	Old	Percent	Total	Percent
	Customer Type					
A	500	50%	500	50%	1,000	50%
B	500	50%	500	50%	1,000	50%
	1,000	100%	1,000	100%	2,000	100%

FIGURE 11–1

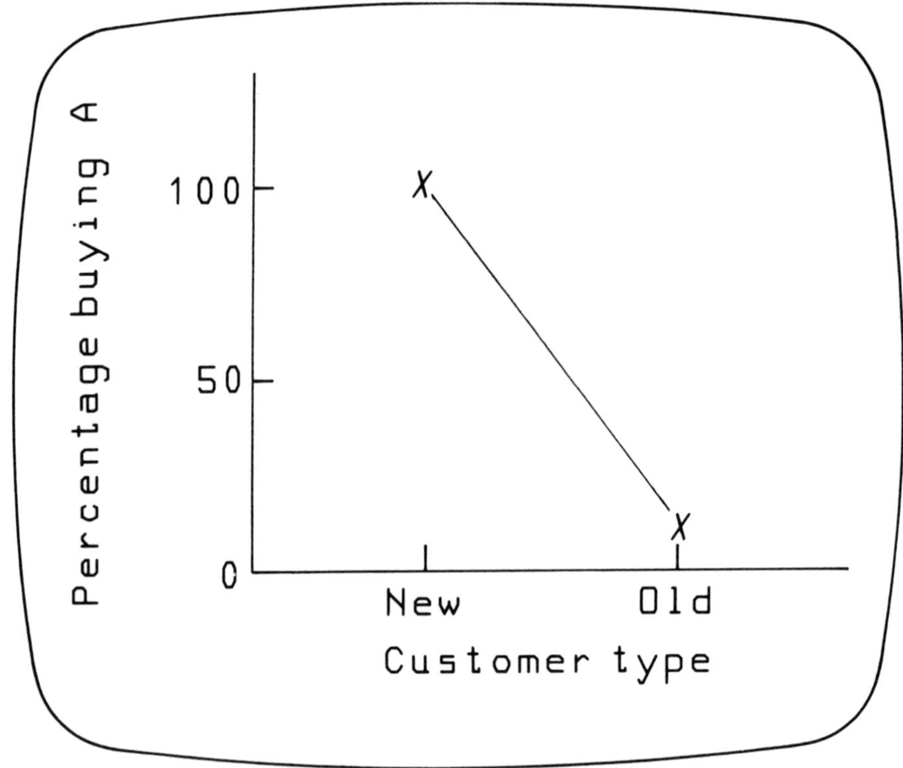

FIGURE 11–2

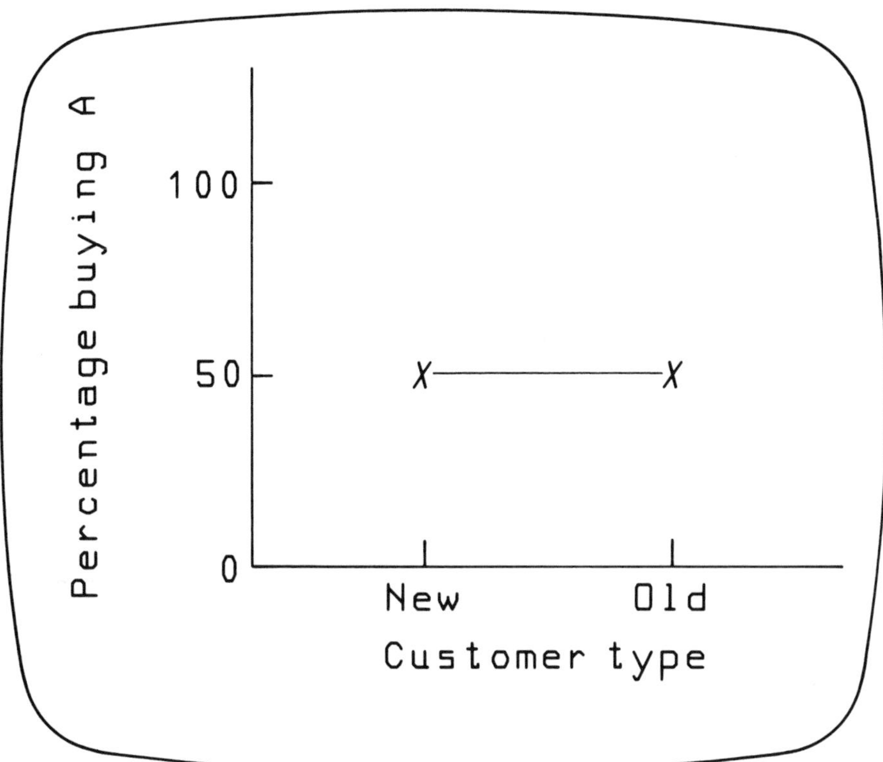

TABLE 11–3

Catalog	New	Percent	Old	Percent	Total	Percent
	Customer Type					
A	110,300	84%	11,500	13%	121,800	56%
B	20,700	16%	76,600	87%	97,300	44%
	131,000	100%	88,100	100%	219,100	100%

Clearly, there is no relationship between the CUSTOMER TYPE and CATALOG; for every new customer buying from B there is an old customer buying from A.

In Figure 11–2, the plot for the percentages of Table 11–2 shows us a horizontal line, or a line with no slope, which, following the logic of the plot in Figure 11–1, tells us there is no relationship.

The analyst, somewhat disturbed by the two conflicting sample results, pulls a third and much larger sample to obtain a truer picture of the house file. The sample results are in Table 11–3.

FIGURE 11–3

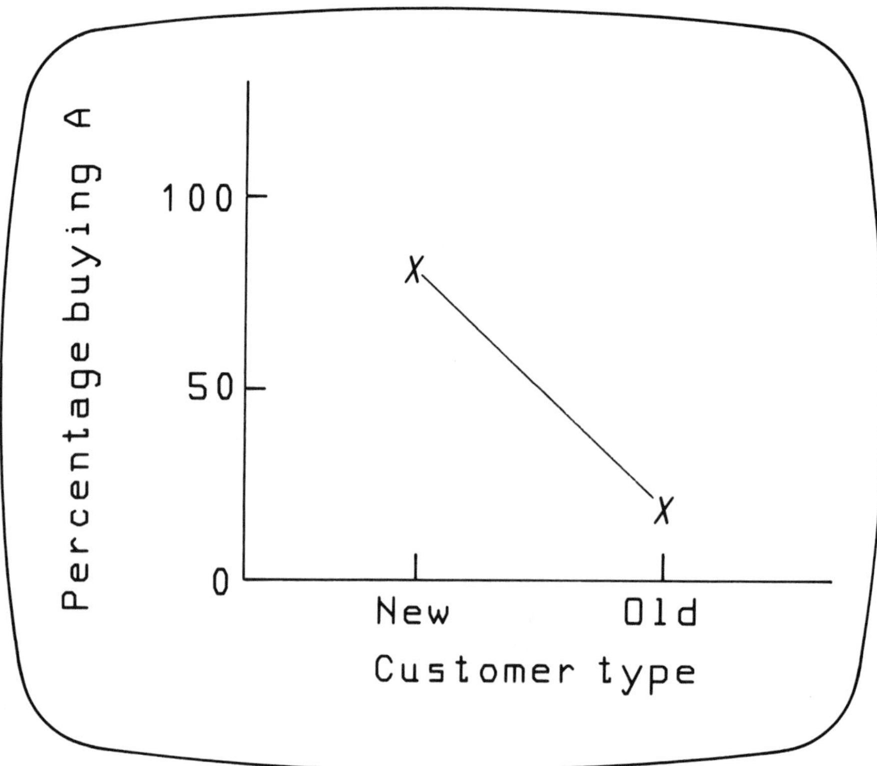

From Table 11–3, we have:

1. 84 percent of new customers come from A and 16 percent from B.
2. 13 percent of old customers come from A and 87 percent from B.

The corresponding plot is in Figure 11–3. The slope of this line is between the slopes of the perfect line (in Figure 11–1) and the no-relationship, horizontal line (Figure 11–2). It would seem that the closer this line's slope is to the perfect line's slope, the stronger the relationship; conversely, the more this line's slope conforms to the no-relationship line's slope, the weaker the relationship. How do we measure this relationship between CUSTOMER TYPE and CATALOG? Between any two variables?

CORRELATION COEFFICIENT

As you may suspect, there are statistical measures to indicate the degree of relationship between two variables. The most popular measure is the *correlation coefficient (r)*, which is the workhorse of many statistical theories, applications, and analyses. The correlation coefficient is used either directly or indirectly in statistical work ranging in complexity from 2 × 2 tables (like Tables 11–1 to 11–3), to simple regression models, to multiple regression models, factor and cluster analyses, and more.

For categorical variables, the correlation coefficient r takes on values ranging from 0 to 1, where

0 indicates no relationship.
1 indicates a perfect relationship.
Values between 0 and 1 indicate a weak to moderate to strong relationship.

These values are depicted in Figure 11–4.

FIGURE 11–4
Strength of Relationship as r Goes from 0 to 1

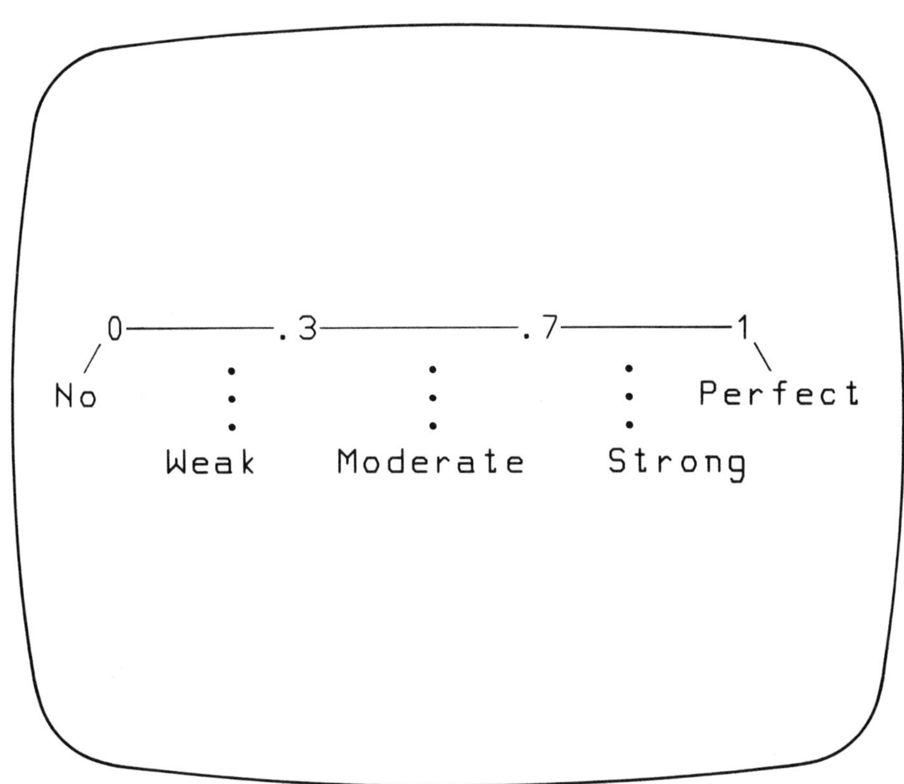

Returning to Table 11–3, our analyst calculates the correlation coefficient using a formula that applies to categorical variables and determines that r = .702. Accordingly, the relationship between CUSTOMER TYPE and CATALOG is strong.

Descriptively, we declare the relationship as strong; but is the relationship significant? Again, the analyst may choose to call the finding significant or not important based on experience. Or the analyst can defer to the objectivity of tests of significance, which address the issue of whether or not the finding of r = .702 is due to chance (sample variation) or is beyond chance. The former implies that the finding is not statistically significant, and the latter implies statistical significance. Fortunately, all computer programs you are likely to encounter calculate the correlation coefficient and a measure of the statistical significance of the correlation for you automatically, so we won't burden you with formulas for these calculations. The measure of statistical significance is, as you might imagine from Chapter 10, related to the concept of the normal distribution and confidence intervals. However, instead of declaring the coefficient of correlation to be statistically significant at the 95 percent confidence level, the programs produce a measure called the p-value. The p-value indicates the likelihood or probability of the sample correlation coefficient occurring given that there is no true relationship between the variables. If the p-value is less than .05 or 5 percent, then we conclude that the true coefficient is not zero and that there is a significant relationship. If the p-value is greater than 5 percent, then we conclude the true correlation coefficient is zero and that there is no significant relationship between the variables.

FIGURE 11–5
Scatter Plot

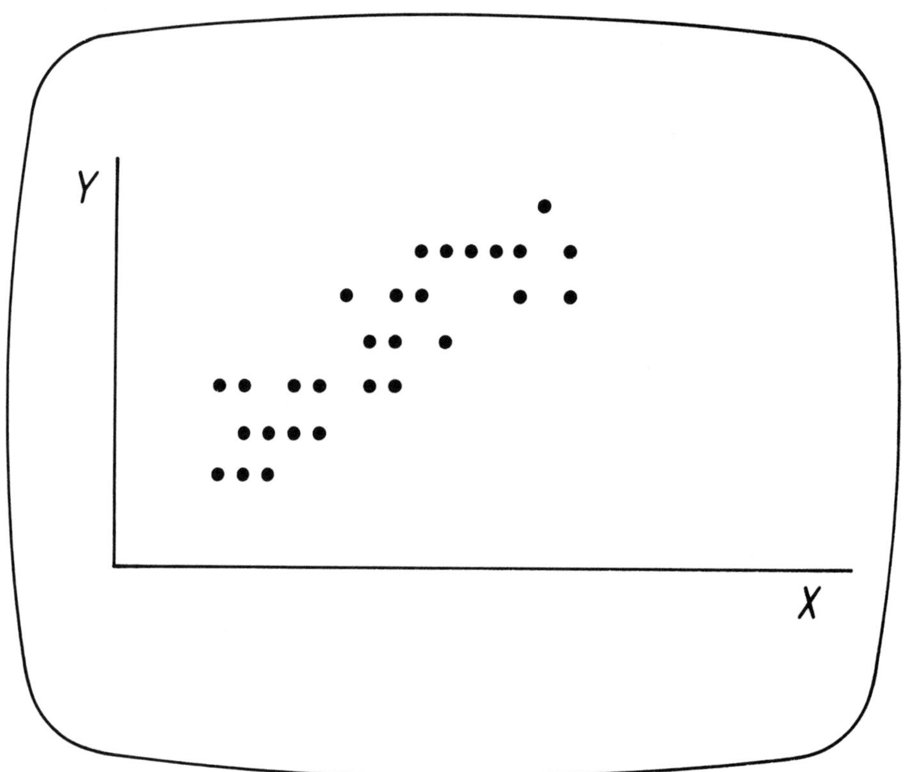

Correlation Coefficient for Scalar Variables

To the extent that scalar variables provide more information than categorical variables, the correlation coefficient for scalar variables gives more information about the relationship. Specifically, the correlation coefficient for scalar variables indicates both the *direction* and *degree* or strength of a *straight-line* relationship.

These concepts are best explained with an illustration.

EXAMPLE 9

Consider two scalar variables x and y, whose pairs of points are depicted in Figure 11–5. We see that large values of x correspond to large values of y, and that the reverse is also true—small values of x correspond to small values of y. The dots or points on the graph each represent a single observation of an x-y relationship. The entire set of points is called a *scatter plot* or *scatter diagram.* Finally, you can easily imagine drawing a straight line through the points, as in Figure 11–6.

The straight line has a positive slope, that is, as x increases in value, y also increases in value. So we say there is a positive straight-line relationship between x and y.

In Figure 11–7, we have an opposite pattern of scatter points: large values of x corresponding to small values of y. A straight line could still be drawn through the scatter points, but in this case the slope of the line would be negative. As x increases, y decreases. Therefore, we would say that a negative straight-line relationship exists between x and y.

FIGURE 11–6

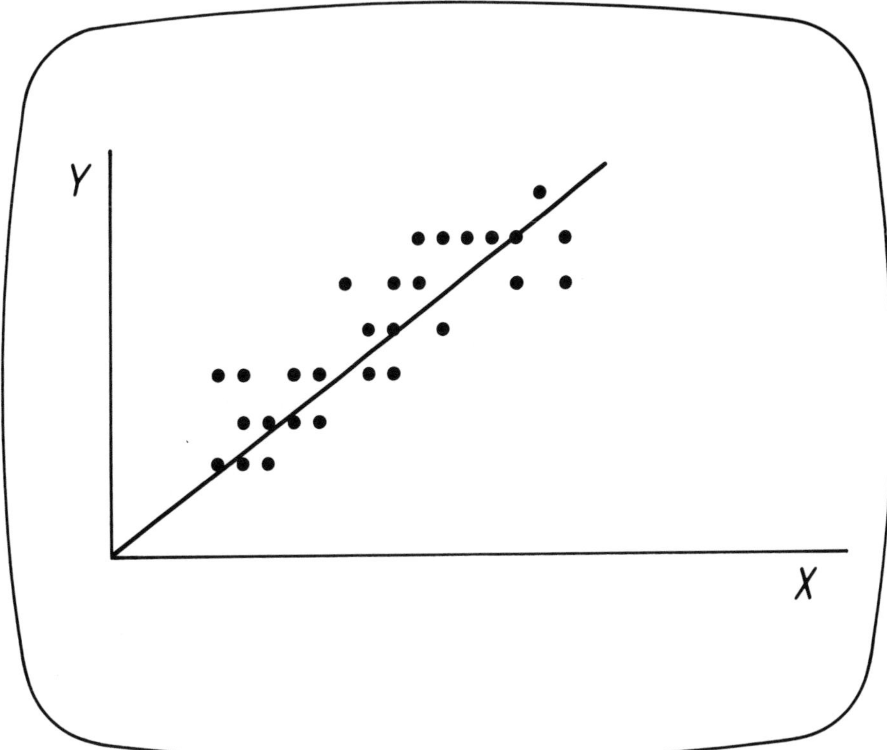

FIGURE 11–7

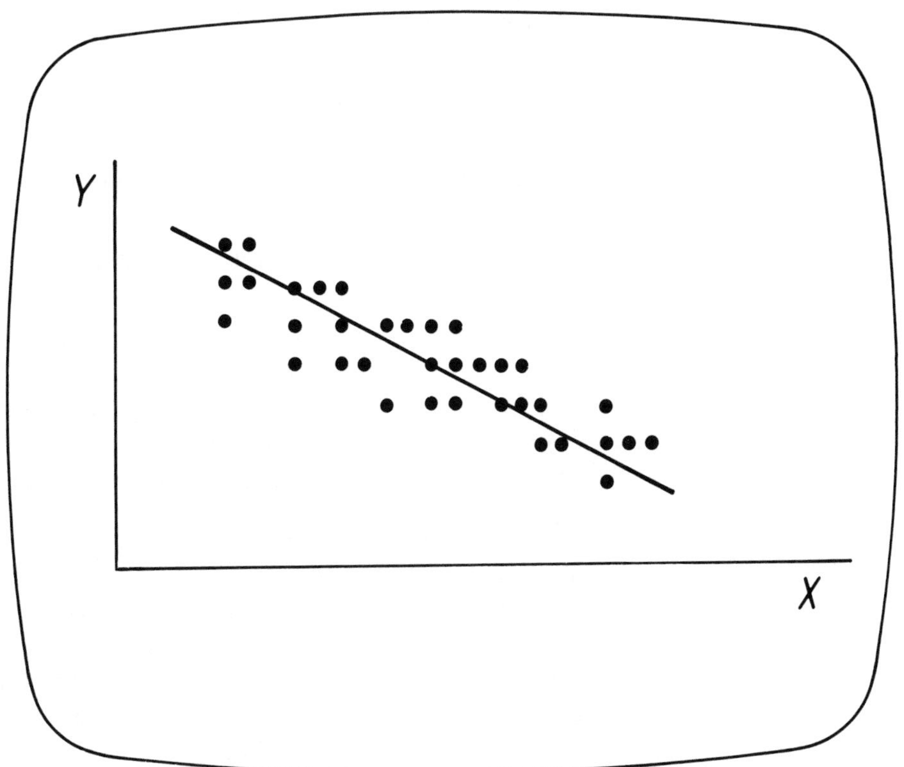

FIGURE 11–8

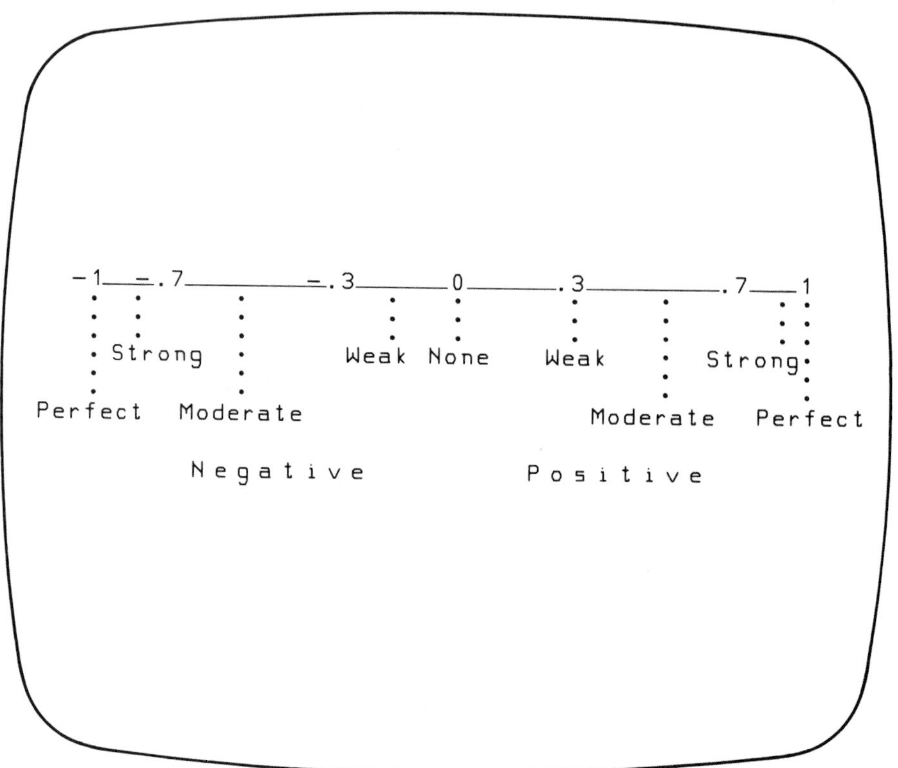

Accordingly, when working with scalar or continuous data, as opposed to categorical data, the correlation coefficient can range in values between –1 and +1 where

0 indicates no relationship.
+1 indicates a perfect positive relationship.
–1 indicates a perfect negative relationship.
Values between 0 and 1 or 0 to –1 indicate a weak to moderate to strong relationship.

Figure 11–8 depicts these relationships.

Correlation Coefficient in Practice

There are two basic issues when working with correlation coefficients in practice. First, are the data straight or linear? Pictorially, can the relationship between the x variable and the y variable be adequately expressed by a straight line? Second, as previously discussed, is the relationship between the two variables significant?

Are the data straight? The correlation coefficient for scalar variables should be used to measure the strength of a straight-line relationship. That is, the use of r is only valid when the data suggest a straight-line relationship. To the extent that the data do not support a straight-line or linear relationship, r can be misleading. In other words, an r of 1 does not guarantee that the data are straight, nor does an r of 0 indicate that the variables are not related. Accordingly, we use scatter plots to see what the data suggests. An illustration will make this point.

TABLE 11–4
Four Data Sets with Equal Descriptive Measures

	x1	*y1*	*x2*	*y2*	*x3*	*y3*	*x4*	*y4*
	10	8.04	10	9.14	10	7.46	8	6.58
	8	6.95	8	8.14	8	6.77	8	5.76
	13	7.58	13	8.74	13	12.74	8	7.71
	9	8.81	9	8.77	9	7.11	8	8.84
	11	8.33	11	9.26	11	7.81	8	8.47
	14	9.96	14	8.10	14	8.84	8	7.04
	6	7.24	6	6.13	6	6.08	8	5.25
	4	4.26	4	3.10	4	5.39	19	12.50
	12	10.84	12	9.13	12	8.15	8	5.56
	7	4.82	7	7.26	7	6.42	8	7.91
	5	5.65	5	4.74	5	5.73	8	6.89
Mean	9	7.50	9	7.50	9	7.50	9	7.50
Variance	10.96	4.12	10.96	4.12	10.96	4.12	10.96	4.12
r	.81		.81		.81		.81	

Source: S Chatterjee and B Price. *Regression Analysis by Example* (New York: John Wiley and Sons, 1977), p. 8.

EXAMPLE 10

Consider the four sets of data for *x* and *y* in Table 11–4. Although the sets have equal means, variances, and correlation coefficients, the scatter plots clearly show different relationships. (See Figures 11–9 through 11–12.)

In Figure 11–9, the relationship is straight; therefore, we can confidently use *r* to assess the straight-line relationship between *X*1 and *Y*1.

In Figure 11–10, the relationship is curved down and the use of *r* is not necessarily recommended; however, certain measures can be taken to salvage the relationship (more about this later).

In Figure 11–11, the relationship appears straight except for the wild point at (13, 12.74), which must be examined. If the point is a "typo-mistake," then *r* should be calculated after removing the point and the resultant *r* value can be used with confidence.

If the point is a valid but unusual observation, then either more data should be collected to firm up the shape of the relationship or the special situation in which it occurred should be investigated because the information surrounding the situation may be more helpful than *r* itself.

The relationship shown in Figure 11–12, which is really no relationship at all, is an example of how misleading statistics can be and why it is always important whenever possible to look at pictures of data, not just summary statistics.

SIMPLE REGRESSION

Now that we have a way of measuring the extent to which knowing one variable tells us something about the other variable, let's see how to extend this process to *predict* the value of one variable based on the value of the other variable, or from the value of many other variables. The technique is called *regression: simple* regression when there is only one other variable and *multiple* regression when there are many other variables.

FIGURE 11–9
Plot of Y1, X1

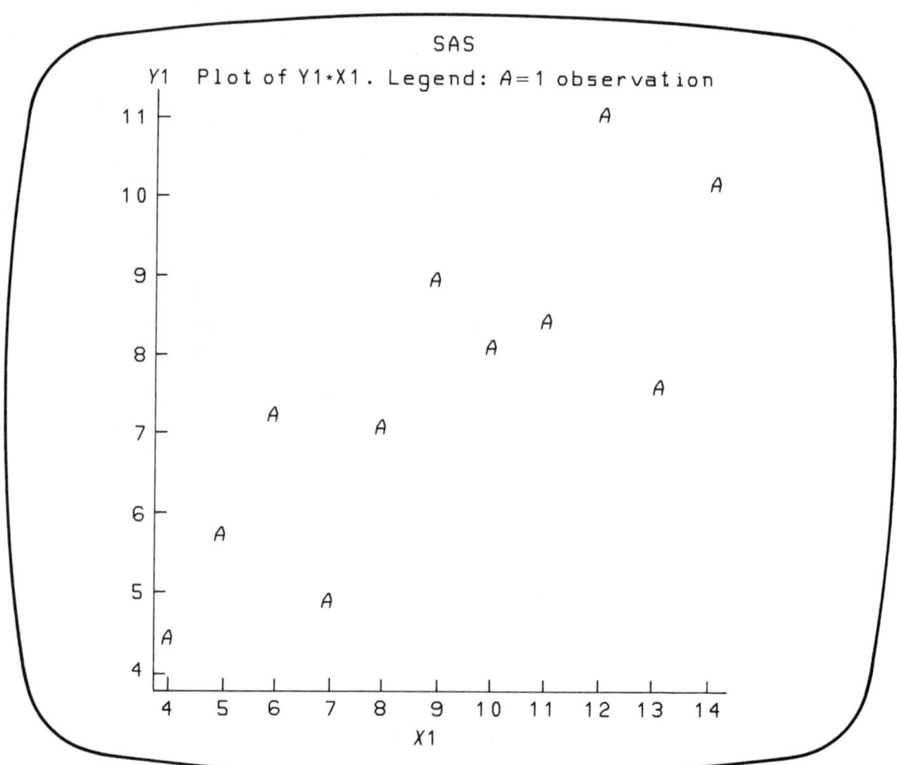

FIGURE 11–10
Plot of Y2, X2

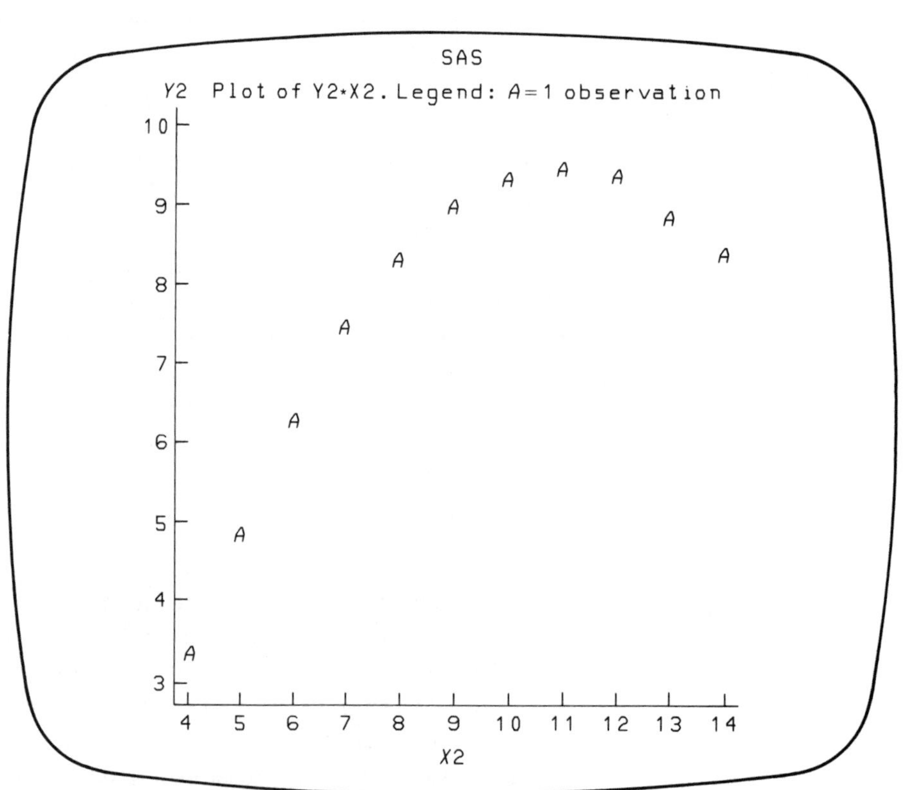

FIGURE 11–11
Plot of Y3, X3

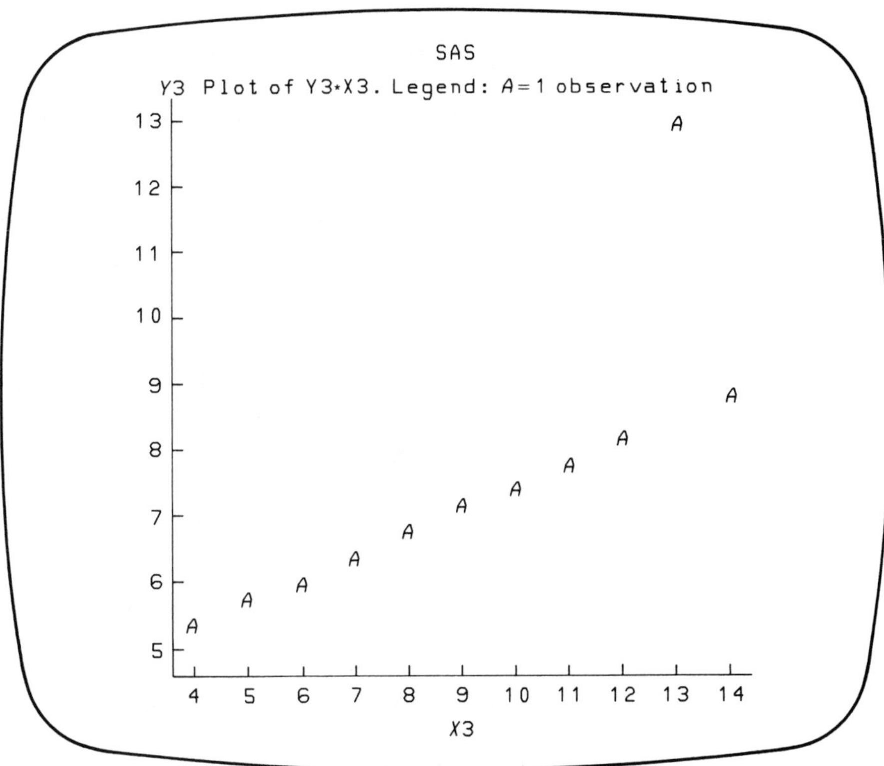

FIGURE 11–12
Plot of Y4, X4

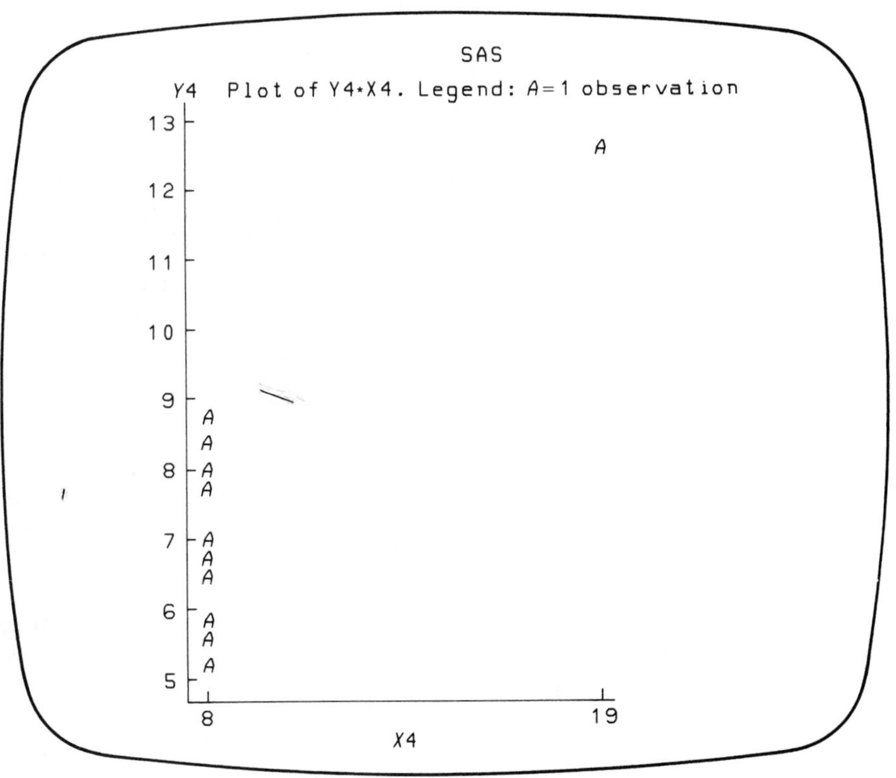

In statistics, the variable we want to be able to predict or forecast is called the *dependent* or *criterion variable.* The variable or variables used to make the prediction or forecast is called the *independent* or *predictor* variable(s).

The input for a simple regression is a table, where the first column consists of data for the independent variable (X) we always know, and the second column consists of data for the dependent variable (Y), the variable we are trying to predict. The output of the regression is an equation that permits us to

1. Explain why the values of Y vary as they do.
2. Predict Y based on the known values of X.

The equation is based on the relationship between X values and Y values for simple regression and on the relationship between each X and Y, and among the Xs themselves, for multiple regression.

The Regression Line

What makes regression tick?

EXAMPLE 11

Let's return to our catalog example, where we learned that there was a relationship between the length of time our customers have been on the file and sales. Remember, new customers purchased more orders and produced greater sales than old customers.

If we define length of time on file more specifically as the independent variable X, the number of months since the date of first purchase, and the dependent variable, the variable we would like to be able to predict (Y), as the dollar value of sales within the last month, we can build a model that will relate date of first purchase to sales.

Suppose our analyst draws a sample of 15 customer records from the house file and puts the data into a table format. (See Table 11–5.) Let's begin our analysis with a scatter plot of the observations, where Y (sales) is plotted on the vertical axis and X (months since date of first purchase) is the horizontal axis. (See Figure 11–13.)

We would like to draw a straight line using a ruler and our eye that passes through the middle of the cloud of points. Our objective should be to draw the line so a more or less equal number of points lie above and below the line. The reader will recall (we hope) from simple algebra that the equation of a straight line is

$$Y = mX + b$$

where

b = the point at which the line would cross the Y axis

m = the slope of the line, or the rate at which Y increases as X increases

We'll review this in more detail below.

In Figure 11–13, we draw such a line through the points and estimate that the line has a slope of 1.0 and intercept of 10.0. The "eye-fitted" regression line is therefore

$$Y = 10.0 + 1.0 \times X$$

TABLE 11–5

X *Months since First Purchase*	Y *Dollar Sales in Past Month*
3	10
3	9
3	12
5	15
5	13
5	11
7	14
9	18
9	17
9	15
13	23
13	21
13	16
15	26
15	23
15	20
19	30
19	27
19	23

FIGURE 11–13
Plot of Y, X

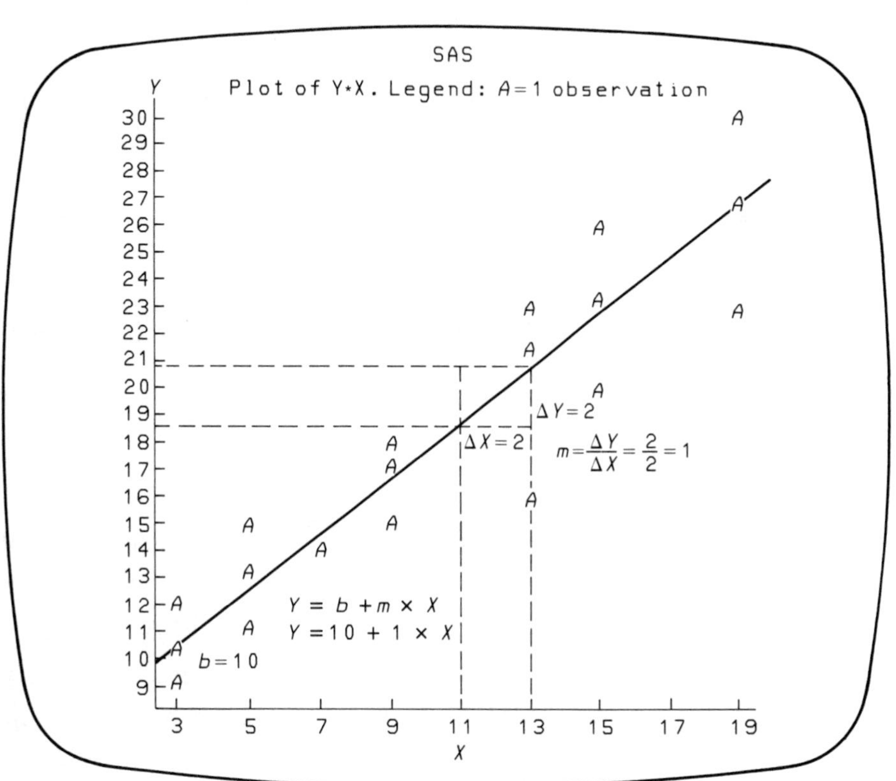

The goal of drawing a line with as many points above it as below it relates to the statistical objective of minimizing the difference between the actual observations and the estimated observations, referred to as the *fit*. The difference between an actual observation and a fitted point is called a *residual*. This leads to a very important identity:

An actual observation = A fitted observation + A residual

or more simply:

Residual = Actual – Fit

Recalling the canceling-out problem when measuring variation, a reasonable way to measure the *goodness-of-fit* of a line, fitted by eye or by formal statistical methods, would be to use the total sum of squares of residuals. Accordingly, the line or equation with the smallest total or mean *residual sum of squares* is said to have the best fit of the data.

It turns out that the most common fitting rule, referred to as *least-squares*, uses residual sum of squares as just described and produces the smallest residual sum of squares. Accordingly, the resultant equation, called the *ordinary least-squares regression equation*, produces the best fit of the data and is considered the best equation. The equation for the simple regression is:

$$Y = b0 + b1 \times X1$$

where

$b0$ = a constant called the Y intercept because it is the point on the Y axis through which the regression line passes when the value of X equals 0.

$b1$ = the slope of the regression line, referred to as the *regression coefficient*.

Most algebra texts use the letter m to represent the slope but statistics texts use b to represent this concept.

Simple Regression in Practice

Simple regression in practice is easy and fun because it takes only five steps to complete the regression analysis:

1. Turn observations into data (variables).
2. Assess whether the relationship between the X and Y variables is linear or straight.
3. Straighten out the relationship, if needed.
4. Perform the regression analysis using any one of a number of computer programs.
5. Interpret the findings.

We will illustrate the steps with a new example.

EXAMPLE 12

Let's build a regression model to support the argument that customers who purchase more frequently also buy bigger ticket items. Accordingly, we would like a model to predict largest-dollar-item (LDI) amounts based on frequency of prior purchases.

TABLE 11–6

X *Number of Purchases*	Y *LDI*
1	2
2	3
3	10
4	15
5	26
6	35
7	50
8	63
9	82

Again, the first step is to transform observations into data:

1. Define a period of time in which to measure frequency of purchase. Let's choose the past 12 months.
2. Find the LDI amount among customers who made only one purchase in the past year, among customers who made two purchases, and so on.

Based on a large random sample, the resulting data array consists of an independent variable X, the number of purchases in the past 12 months, and a dependent variable Y, the LDI amount. (The largest number of purchases in 12 months was 9, thus the X ranges from 1 to 9.) (See Table 11–6.)

To assess the relationship between X and Y, we review the scatter plot in Figure 11–14, which reveals that the relationship is more or less straight except for what looks like a curved relationship in the lower left corner. The curve is not too terrible, and we choose for now at least, not to attempt to straighten it out. Thus, we feel the assumption of straight-line relationship has been met, which enables us to confidently use the correlation coefficient.

A regression analysis on the data (using one of the standard statistical software packages, in this case SAS) resulted in the following output:

Variation of Y: Variance = 792.94
Total sum of squares: 6,343.55
Correlation coefficient: $r = +0.97254$
Intercept, $b0$: −18.22
Regression coefficient, $b1$: 10.00, with p value of .001

The regression equation is

$$Y = -18.22 + 10.00 \times X$$

The large positive value of r indicates there is a positive and strong straight-line relationship between X and Y, which is consistent with the hypothesis that large sales are associated with frequent purchase.

We can obtain a second and perhaps more useful interpretation of r by squaring its value and relating it to the amount of variation of Y that is accounted for by X.

The r-squared statistic is probably the most popular statistic associated with the output of a regression model. The name *coefficient of determination* has been given r squared, and it ranges in value from 0 to 1.

FIGURE 11–14
Plot of Y, X

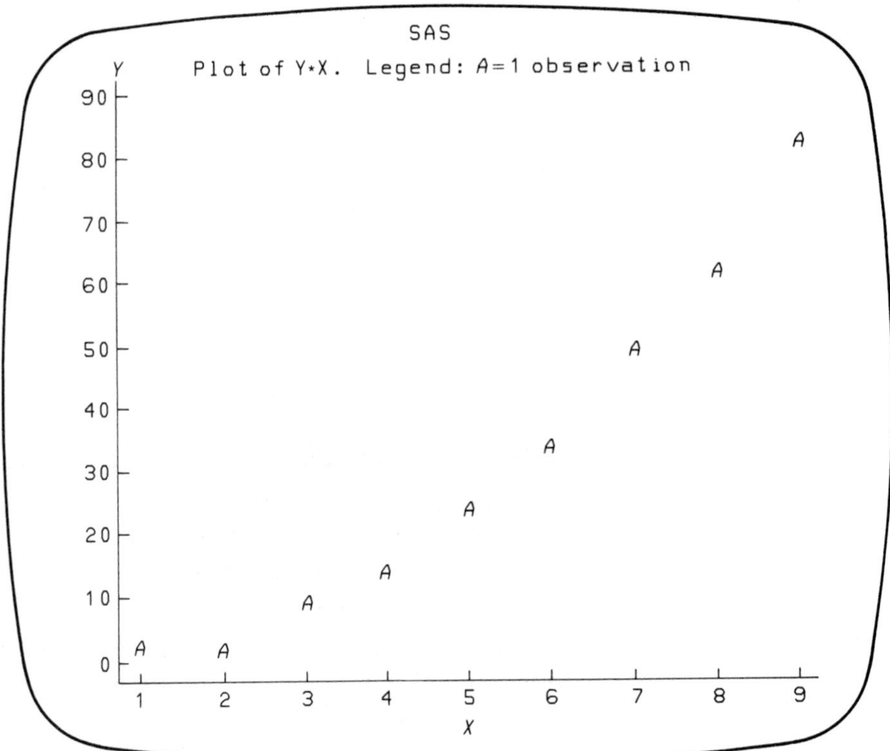

In this case, r squared is .946 or 94.6 percent. Therefore, we can say that 94.6 percent of the variation of Y can be accounted for by X. (Technically, of the variation [total sum of squares] of Y, 6,343, X accounts for 94.6 percent, or 6,000.)

The intercept has limited meaning and in most cases can be viewed as a "placeholder" in the equation. When the equation is built with X values that include zero, the intercept has meaning and the predicted value of Y when X equals zero can be used reliably. In the present example, the intercept must be treated as a placeholder because the predicted LDI amount is a nonsensical negative $18.22.

The regression coefficient $b1$ represents the change in Y for every change in X. That is, every additional purchase made (in the past 12 months) is associated with an increase in average LDI dollars (Y) of $10.

Is this $10 increase significant? Maybe it is due to the sample drawn, sample variation. The p value, the probability that a value of $b1$ will equal $10 by chance only, is .001. Because this is less than the usual .05 level, we conclude that the regression coefficient is statistically significant and the $10 increase for every additional purchase is meaningful.

The use of the regression equation as a predictive model is easy: To predict the expected largest-dollar-item amount from a customer who has made, say, three purchases in the past 12 months, simply plug in a value of 3 for X in the equation and calculate the Y.

$$Y = -18.22 + 10.00 \times 3$$
$$= 11.78$$

Thus, the expected dollar amount of the largest dollar item made by a customer with three purchases in the past 12 months is $11.78.

TABLE 11–7

X	Y	$\sqrt{Y}$
1	2	1.41
2	3	1.73
3	10	3.16
4	15	3.87
5	26	5.09
6	35	5.91
7	50	7.07
8	63	7.93
9	82	9.05

STRAIGHTENING OUT THE DATA

This just about wraps up the simple regression analysis of the data. However, what about that curve in the data? Since the analysis rests on the data being straight, *perhaps* the regression results will be better—in terms of explanatory and predictive powers—if we can straighten out the data to remove the curve. We say *perhaps* because straightening out the data may not necessarily make things better. Straightening out the data involves transforming or reexpressing the data (variables) by means of arithmetic operations, which include taking logs, squaring, and raising to powers. The choice of which operation or combination of operations to use may involve more art than science.

Accordingly, we use the reexpression that raises Y to the ½ power, more commonly termed as *taking the square root of* Y ($\sqrt{Y}$). The effect on Y values from the square root reexpression is in Table 11–7. The range of the new values is much smaller than the original values (9.05 – 1.41 = 7.64 compared to 82 – 2 = 80), and the new values are also much closer to one another than are the original values.[1]

The scatter plot of X and $\sqrt{Y}$ is in Figure 11–15. The curve is gone. The data look very straight. The new r is .99750, which is an improvement of 2.56 percent over the original r of .97254. Is this 2.56 percent improvement enough to make a difference, enough to bother with reexpressing?

Explanatory Power

An r of .99750 implies that virtually all, 99.5 percent, of the variation of the new reexpressed variable $\sqrt{Y}$ is explained by X. The 2.56 percent represents "topping the gas tank" and appears not to be a substantial improvement. Thus, reexpression here does not help in terms of explanatory power.

Predictive Power

The new (predictive) regression equation is:

$$\sqrt{Y} = .108845 + .984016 \times X$$

To assess the predictive gain of the new regression model over the original regression model, we look to see which model predicts better, that is, produces the smallest residual. (See Table 11–8.)

[1]The "magic" of reexpression, which is beyond the scope of this chapter, lies in the property that the reexpression preserves the order of the values. That is, the smallest original value is also the smallest new value, and the largest original value is the largest new value. The same holds true for all the values in between.

FIGURE 11–15
Plot of $\sqrt{Y}$, X

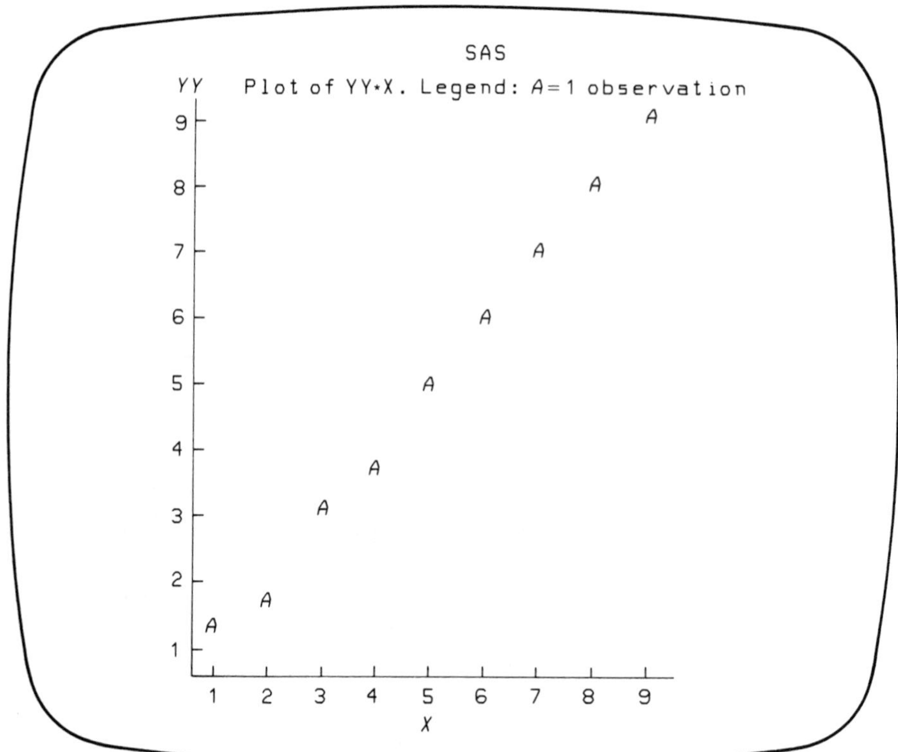

An examination of Table 11–8 shows that the errors or residuals resulting from the transformed data are clearly smaller than the residuals produced from the model built on the original data. In particular, the errors around the extreme values of *X* are smaller. When *X* equals 1 or 9, the errors are very large, which is characteristic of linear regression models applied to curved data.

In Table 11–9, we calculate the sum of the residuals squared to demonstrate that the straightened model produces a much smaller sum of squares. The sum of the errors or residuals squared using the original data is equal to 339.01. The sum of the residuals squared using the transformed data, the straightened model, is 10.79.

TABLE 11–8

Data			Estimated Y Original Model	Error	Estimated Value √Y	Estimated Value Y – sqrt Model	Error
X	Y	√Y					
1	2	1.41	–8.22	10.22	1.09	1.19	0.81
2	3	1.73	1.78	1.22	2.08	4.31	–1.31
3	10	3.16	11.78	–1.78	3.06	9.37	0.63
4	15	3.87	21.78	–6.78	4.05	16.36	–1.36
5	26	5.09	31.78	–5.78	5.03	25.29	0.71
6	35	5.92	41.78	–6.78	6.01	36.16	–1.16
7	50	7.07	51.78	–1.78	7.00	48.96	1.04
8	63	7.93	61.78	1.22	7.98	63.70	–0.70
9	82	9.05	71.78	10.22	8.97	80.38	1.63

TABLE 11–9

Data		Estimated Y Original Model	Error	Error Squared	Estimated Value Y – sqrt Model	Error	Error Squared
X	Y						
1	2	–8.22	10.22	104.04	1.19	0.81	0.64
2	3	1.78	1.22	1.44	4.31	–1.31	1.71
3	10	11.78	–1.78	2.89	9.37	0.63	0.39
4	15	21.78	–6.78	44.89	16.36	–1.36	1.84
5	26	31.78	–5.78	32.49	25.29	0.71	0.49
6	35	41.78	–6.78	44.89	36.16	–1.16	1.32
7	50	51.78	–1.78	2.89	48.96	1.04	1.08
8	63	61.78	1.22	1.44	63.70	–0.70	0.47
9	82	71.78	10.22	104.04	80.38	1.63	2.85
Total				339.01			10.79
Mean				37.06			1.19

Chapter 12

Multiple Regression

Multiple regression is used in situations where it is believed that more than one independent variable affects the dependent variable. Because in practice there is almost always more than one independent variable affecting the dependent variable, we almost always use multiple rather than simple regression.

The form of the multiple regression model is given by the following equation:

$$Y = b0 + b1 \times X1 + b2 \times X2 + b3 \times X3 + \ldots + bn \times Xn,$$

where

$X1, X2, X3, \ldots, Xn$ = Independent variables

Y = Dependent variable

$b0$ = A constant again, but this time it's impossible to visualize because the intercept is going through a multidimensional plane.

$b1, b2, b3, \ldots, bn$ = Regression coefficients associated with the n variables $X1, \ldots, Xn$.

Multiple regression is obviously much more complicated than simple regression. In simple (one-variable) linear regression, we always know what the two variables in the model are, and we simply decide which variable is the dependent variable and which is the independent variable. In a simple two-variable regression model, it is also fairly easy to look at a scatter plot of the relationship and determine if the relationship is linear or if the relationship needs to be straightened by the use of some transformation.

With multiple regression the tasks are more complicated in practice. Assuming for the moment that we know the dependent variable we want to predict (which is not always the case), we have to make the following decisions:

1. Which variables in our database should be included in the model and which should not? A direct marketing company may have literally hundreds of variables to choose from, making variable selection a difficult and time-consuming task.

2. Is the relationship between the dependent variable and each of the variables to be included in the model linear, or must transformation be performed?

3. Is the dependent variable normally distributed for all values of the independent variables? This is one of the basic assumptions of regression, needed for tests of significance. If nonnormality exists, transformations can be used to induce normality.

4. Without regard to their relationship with the dependent variable, are the independent variables each normally distributed? This condition is often overlooked in practice when building regression models. We'll talk about the consequence of this later in the chapter.

5. Are there variables that affect the dependent variables that we might have overlooked because they are not "natural" variables themselves but really contrived variables made from combinations of two or more independent variables? These are called *interaction variables* and we'll talk more about them later as well.

6. When we add many variables to our models, are the independent variables themselves highly correlated, causing a condition known as *multicollinearity.* If so, what effect will this have on the reliability of the models we produce?

Despite all these complexities, the procedures for performing multiple regression are a straightforward extension of simple regression. We'll illustrate these procedures and present solutions to all the issues raised above through a number of examples.

EXAMPLE 13

Let's return to our cataloger, who now believes that by knowing the age (AGE) and income (INCOME) of customers, a model can be built using these two variables to predict dollars spent in the last six months (DOLLSPENT). The analyst draws a sample from the house file, captures the three variables, and performs a multiple regression of DOLLSPENT on INCOME and AGE, which results in the output shown in Table 12–1.

The multiple regression equation is

$$\text{DOLLSPENT} = 351.29 - .65 \times \text{INCOME} + .86 \times \text{AGE}$$

MULTIPLE REGRESSION STATISTICS—HOW TO READ THEM

The first thing we notice about multiple regression statistics is that they look very much like the statistics associated with simple regression. We have variance and total sum of squares of the dependent variable (DOLLSPENT). We also have an *R*-square with the adjective *multiple* to indicate that multiple or many variables are being used.

The *R*-square for a multiple regression indicates the proportion of variation in DOLLSPENT "explained" by all the independent variables in the equation. In this example, *R*-square is .5480, indicating that INCOME and AGE together account for 54.8 percent of the variance in DOLLSPENT.

It is important to note that although it is desirable to have a regression model with high *R*-square values, a large *R*-square does not necessarily guarantee a better model. By a mathematical necessity of the regression calculations *R*-square can never get smaller and it typically increases on adding variables to the model, so we can arbitrarily increase *R*-square by just loading up the model with variables until we reach a comfortably large value of *R*-square.

Clearly, such a model built on a helter-skelter selection of variables will not assure good predictions and reasonable explanatory power despite its large *R*-square. Thus, the analyst must be guided by past experience

TABLE 12–1

Income (thousands)	*Age (years)*	*DOLLSPENT*
$35.6	52.5	$54.1
40.9	57.2	52.4
38.6	58.0	56.1
48.7	52.9	41.4
43.9	53.0	58.0
51.2	52.5	47.1
48.1	57.4	52.5
42.0	54.5	50.8
45.9	66.3	64.9
49.8	60.2	54.0
48.9	51.1	46.4
42.5	51.7	54.7
36.4	51.8	57.1
33.3	51.3	55.4
30.6	57.8	57.7
33.5	54.7	62.8
44.4	62.6	58.7
36.5	56.3	69.9
43.0	60.3	63.2
37.4	50.8	59.1

Variation of DOLLSPENT: Variance = 4,427.65
Total sum of squares: 84,126.55
Correlation coefficient: multiple R-square = .5480
Intercept, $b0$: 351.29
Regression coefficients:
$b1$ for INCOME: −0.65 with a p value of .0020
$b2$ for AGE: .86 with a p value of .0038

when building a regression model instead of striving for a model with a large R-square. Statistical search strategies can help the analyst systematically and logically add variables into a model. We'll discuss these in detail later.

The interpretation of the intercept, as in the simple regression model, must be treated as a placeholder in the regression equation because DOLLSPENT equals the intercept only when a customer has zero INCOME and is not born yet (AGE = 0), clearly a ridiculous condition.

The interpretation of the regression coefficients, however, requires careful explanation. Let's take the coefficient of AGE, .86.

.86 = the average change in DOLLSPENT associated with a unit change (i.e., every one year increase in AGE)

when INCOME *is held constant.*

By this means of control, we are able to separate the effects of AGE itself, free of any influence from INCOME.

Thus, for every one year increase in a customer's age, the predicted DOLLSPENT increases by $0.86, regardless of the customer's income. Or, in other words, if there are two customers one year apart in their ages, the older customer has an associated DOLLSPENT of $0.86 more than the younger one, regardless of their incomes.

Similarly, for the coefficient of INCOME, –.65, we can say that for every additional $100 in INCOME, there is an associated decrease in DOLLSPENT of $0.65, regardless of (controlling for) the influence of AGE.

Are these associated increases in the DOLLSPENT significant? Statistically speaking, the coefficients are statistically significant because the *p* values are less than the usual .05. However, if any one of the variables had a *p* value greater than .05, then it would be declared nonsignificant and would be deleted from the equation by redoing the regression analysis without that variable. If both variables were declared nonsignificant, there are two options:

1. Find new independent variables.
2. Use the mean value of DOLLSPENT based on the full sample of customers to predict DOLLSPENT. In other words, when good predictors cannot be found, the mean is the best predictor.

EXAMPLE 14

Let's go a little further with our catalog example. Our cataloger would now like to build a model to identify those customers who are most likely to buy from the catalog scheduled to be mailed next month. The cataloger wants to be sure to include the best customers in the mailing. By the same token, if those customers most unlikely to buy from the next catalog could be identified, the cataloger might exclude them from the next mailing.

In other words, the cataloger wants a model that predicts response so each customer can be assigned a score indicating the propensity to respond. After all customers on the file are scored, they can be ranked from most to least likely to respond. Assuming the cataloger does not wish to mail to all customers on the file, the cataloger can use the ranked file to mail to as many names as desired or as many as the budget allows.

Unfortunately, our cataloger has never tracked responses to individual catalog mailings and so isn't able to build a model based on the results of a similar prior mailing.

However, for the last year, while learning statistics, our cataloger started keeping extra data on a 10 percent sample of customers. Two of the statistics kept included the total number of pieces mailed (TOT__MAILED) and a record of the total number of orders received (TOT__ORDERS).

Our cataloger now hypothesizes that the ratio of total orders to total pieces mailed for an individual is a good measure of a person's likelihood of responding to the next planned mailing.

This seems to make sense. It may not be true, but it seems to make sense. Remember, we said the choice of a dependent variable is not always simple. Very often, the variable you want to use is not available and you have to improvise. This is an example of improvising.

In any event, the decision is made to make the ratio of TOT__ORDERS to TOT__MAILED the dependent variable. To make life simpler, we'll call this new variable RESP.

Our choice of independent variables must be sure to include only variables that appear on both the Sample file and the total Customer file so the model can be applied to all customers. For both files, we have the following variables that we will use as the independent variables:

TOT__DOLL—Total purchase dollars to date
AVG__ORDR—Average dollar order
LAST__BUY—Number of months (from today) since last purchase

We draw two samples of 100 customer records from the 10 percent Sample file that includes these three variables. One sample will be used to build the model and the other will be used to test or validate the model.

We always need to validate a model on a fresh sample because evaluating a model using the same data that produced the model would overestimate the model's predictive power. The data for building and validating the model are in Tables 12–2 and 12–3, respectively.

Quick and Dirty Regression

The cataloger is anxious for a model, so we perform a quick and dirty (Q&D) model regressing: RESP on TOT__DOLL, AVG__ORDR, and LAST__BUY. In other words, we expect to see a regression equation that has this form:

$$RESP = b0 + b1 \times TOT\_\_DOLL + b2 \times AVG\_\_ORDR + b3 \times LAST\_\_BUY$$

The SAS regression output is in Table 12–4.

We see a lot of output in Table 12–4, more than we previously discussed. We'll still focus on what we know: *R*-square, coefficient estimates and *p* values, but we will explain the rest of the printout as we go along. In SAS, *p* values are shown in the column labeled Prob > | T |.

TOT__DOLL and AVG__ORDR are very significant, with *p* values much less than .05. LAST__BUY is not significant, with a *p* value of .8204. Before deciding what to do about this nonsignificant variable, let's review the other new statistics and measures shown in Table 12–4.

Analysis of variance table. Table 12–4 reports how the total sum of squares are broken up into parts corresponding to the

Model—the sum of squares that can be accounted for or explained by the variables in the model.
Error—the sum of squares that are unexplained by the model.

Sum of squares (SS) has associated with it numbers called *degrees of freedom* (DF). DF for the model is the number of independent variables in the model; DF for the total SS is the number of observations minus 1; DF for the error is the difference between the total and model DFs.

We can obtain *R*-square from the ratio of sum of square explained by the model to the total sum of square:

$$\begin{aligned} R\text{-square} &= \text{Model SS/Total SS} \\ &= .50495/.90722 \\ &= .5427 \end{aligned}$$

The ratio of model SS divided by its DF to error SS divided by its DF is the *F* statistic, which is used to test the significance of all the independent variables in the model. If the *p* value of the *F* value is less than 5 percent, then the model is considered statistically significant with 95 percent confidence.

TABLE 12–2
Data for Building Regression Model

OBS	*TOT_DOLL*	*AVG_ORDR*	*LAST_BUY*	*RESP*
1	265.02	26.502	0.33333	0.05952
2	242.98	15.186	0.58333	0.09195
3	109.72	13.715	0.25000	0.06400
4	1990.12	73.708	0.16667	0.14286
5	307.82	11.839	0.25000	0.14525
6	416.04	32.003	0.16667	0.07647
7	534.89	7.429	0.16667	0.40449
8	773.58	17.990	0.16667	0.23118
9	285.65	20.404	0.08333	0.07865
10	579.76	23.190	0.08333	0.13812
11	370.43	24.695	0.41667	0.06818
12	143.26	6.822	0.91667	0.13816
13	479.35	8.410	0.08333	0.32571
14	555.40	29.232	2.58333	0.09314
15	427.35	11.550	0.91667	0.20670
16	256.63	12.220	0.83333	0.13208
17	1093.74	109.374	0.16667	0.05587
18	299.78	7.687	2.16667	0.19024
19	376.52	8.011	0.75000	0.26257
20	290.97	6.191	0.33333	0.21860
21	883.51	25.986	1.66667	0.19101
22	368.94	6.961	0.83333	0.28962
23	195.42	4.248	1.08333	0.28221
24	528.11	12.282	1.33333	0.24294
25	518.19	11.515	0.75000	0.24725
26	199.56	7.127	0.08333	0.18301
27	297.07	14.146	0.75000	0.12883
28	516.24	14.340	0.50000	0.18947
29	309.82	8.606	1.66667	0.20690
30	427.30	11.245	0.25000	0.21111
31	2722.85	42.545	0.00000	0.17827
32	1556.99	16.742	0.50000	0.52542
33	463.94	14.966	0.08333	0.16848
34	260.22	12.391	1.58333	0.12651
35	191.56	9.578	1.33333	0.12121
36	518.53	16.204	1.16667	0.18286
37	229.51	17.655	1.33333	0.07738
38	1033.03	19.130	0.50000	0.24000
39	382.97	8.510	0.41667	0.25568
40	430.83	21.541	0.41667	0.10929
41	843.90	21.097	0.50000	0.21277
42	965.85	16.370	0.91667	0.21533
43	276.14	4.315	1.91667	0.32323
44	1042.32	14.477	0.25000	0.37895
45	697.28	24.044	0.00000	0.14573
46	884.73	12.120	0.16667	0.38421
47	485.09	8.222	1.16667	0.34104
48	353.24	10.093	0.25000	0.20468
49	3092.58	44.820	0.00000	0.23549
50	1519.39	41.065	1.33333	0.16667

TABLE 12–2
Continued

OBS	*TOT_DOLL*	*AVG_ORDR*	*LAST_BUY*	*RESP*
51	640.34	14.553	0.83333	0.20091
52	1965.66	23.1254	0.08333	0.46703
53	514.83	9.7138	2.66667	0.31737
54	861.86	57.4573	0.25000	0.07979
55	260.32	18.5943	1.41667	0.10072
56	267.11	7.0292	0.41667	0.23457
57	207.75	20.7750	0.83333	0.06211
58	432.63	21.6315	0.75000	0.11173
59	583.20	25.3565	0.75000	0.12169
60	311.60	8.2000	0.50000	0.21229
61	1359.44	26.1431	1.16667	0.27513
62	456.68	11.7097	1.91667	0.20745
63	236.22	11.2486	0.00000	0.13816
64	476.55	12.8797	0.25000	0.20330
65	505.85	8.8746	0.58333	0.30978
66	845.57	31.3174	0.25000	0.14439
67	358.84	22.4275	0.75000	0.09581
68	103.93	3.8493	0.50000	0.18750
69	686.72	18.0716	0.50000	0.20430
70	586.02	10.6549	0.58333	0.25463
71	673.51	13.4702	1.25000	0.24272
72	364.15	17.3405	0.08333	0.12000
73	397.88	18.9467	0.33333	0.11351
74	2038.75	30.4291	0.16667	0.34359
75	322.07	12.8828	1.83333	0.14535
76	921.64	28.8013	1.08333	0.14545
77	686.71	16.7490	0.00000	0.20098
78	549.22	22.8842	0.33333	0.12698
79	724.27	38.1195	0.75000	0.10270
80	437.21	54.6512	0.58333	0.04848
81	256.18	8.5393	0.83333	0.18293
82	595.82	17.5241	1.25000	0.18085
83	792.00	34.4348	0.91667	0.12849
84	779.18	31.1672	0.50000	0.15625
85	859.21	13.4252	0.08333	0.28319
86	1716.75	30.1184	0.50000	0.31319
87	319.88	11.8474	0.50000	0.15882
88	627.58	14.2632	0.08333	0.24309
89	774.58	21.5161	0.16667	0.21429
90	559.81	27.9905	0.50000	0.10526
91	597.83	11.7222	0.25000	0.28492
92	691.70	20.3441	0.00000	0.20482
93	1964.13	22.5762	0.33333	0.46774
94	158.01	7.1823	0.08333	0.14103
95	420.93	15.5900	0.75000	0.14362
96	1061.77	16.0874	1.66667	0.31884
97	335.43	23.9593	0.75000	0.08383
98	768.71	23.2942	0.00000	0.18539
99	673.18	15.6553	0.58333	0.23118
100	453.98	15.1327	0.25000	0.15075

TABLE 12–3
Data for Validating Regression Model

OBS	*TOT_DOLL*	*AVG_ORDR*	*LAST_BUY*	*RESP*
1	1679.13	40.954	0.83333	0.18062
2	574.61	22.100	0.33333	0.13265
3	586.64	19.555	0.75000	0.17143
4	513.03	10.470	0.91667	0.28324
5	1561.91	53.859	0.25000	0.15591
6	274.26	13.713	0.75000	0.11765
7	477.19	22.723	0.08333	0.12209
8	232.09	8.596	0.41667	0.15976
9	879.43	39.974	0.08333	0.09692
10	432.25	36.021	0.08333	0.07643
11	350.53	21.908	0.16667	0.09249
12	311.95	12.998	0.83333	0.13953
13	236.54	14.784	1.08333	0.09357
14	440.33	17.613	0.75000	0.13298
15	1097.03	47.697	0.66667	0.12105
16	344.67	13.257	2.16667	0.15758
17	737.44	67.0404	2.00000	0.06748
18	319.66	9.133	1.00000	0.19774
19	1930.83	22.986	0.16667	0.44920
20	303.59	12.650	0.08333	0.12565
21	1009.29	59.370	0.08333	0.09140
22	1088.09	24.180	0.08333	0.24064
23	378.98	10.243	1.25000	0.22289
24	536.41	16.255	0.08333	0.19298
25	304.03	13.219	1.00000	0.12366
26	417.28	34.773	0.66667	0.06977
27	1080.00	30.000	0.25000	0.18947
28	501.70	23.890	0.66667	0.12000
29	376.15	34.195	1.00000	0.05612
30	817.06	28.174	0.08333	0.15676
31	1883.37	117.711	0.25000	0.07729
32	230.95	5.922	1.33333	0.24375
33	457.21	9.525	0.33333	0.24615
34	446.43	24.802	0.08333	0.10405
35	749.20	32.574	1.91667	0.10952
36	110.26	4.794	0.75000	0.14744
37	1664.19	46.228	0.00000	0.19149
38	183.75	12.250	0.25000	0.09934
39	249.64	7.801	0.50000	0.20126
40	196.55	16.379	1.41667	0.08955
41	852.11	23.030	0.08333	0.20330
42	914.48	35.172	0.16667	0.12322
43	892.33	21.764	0.41667	0.11549
44	2281.84	17.827	0.33333	0.47059
45	122.38	6.441	1.25000	0.11728
46	1800.32	47.377	0.41667	0.15323
47	752.08	19.792	1.16667	0.20879
48	448.52	12.122	1.25000	0.20670
49	756.85	42.047	0.00000	0.09677
50	536.83	16.776	0.00000	0.14884

TABLE 12–3
Continued

OBS	*TOT_DOLL*	*AVG_ORDR*	*LAST_BUY*	*RESP*
51	145.07	6.307	0.16667	0.15033
52	769.18	18.7605	1.00000	0.22043
53	1092.98	52.0467	0.50000	0.11538
54	547.62	19.5579	0.50000	0.11290
55	333.49	12.8265	0.00000	0.15205
56	859.70	26.8656	0.25000	0.17778
57	426.97	11.8603	0.08333	0.20225
58	288.86	11.1100	1.91667	0.15569
59	376.68	9.4170	0.08333	0.21978
60	511.88	15.9962	0.00000	0.18182
61	1766.24	47.7362	0.00000	0.19892
62	930.93	23.2732	0.66667	0.18957
63	690.51	36.3426	2.91667	0.11446
64	554.32	34.6450	1.41667	0.08889
65	1189.95	56.6643	0.00000	0.11351
66	805.75	73.2500	0.25000	0.05238
67	227.14	16.2243	0.33333	0.07143
68	556.49	20.6107	0.50000	0.13846
69	602.23	25.0929	0.58333	0.11111
70	1156.40	22.2385	0.50000	0.27660
71	349.65	13.4481	1.41667	0.15385
72	324.02	8.5268	0.08333	0.22353
73	515.43	13.5639	2.08333	0.21839
74	347.12	26.7015	0.66667	0.07429
75	227.91	9.1164	0.41667	0.15152
76	349.74	19.4300	0.41667	0.11043
77	320.61	14.5732	1.25000	0.12571
78	447.28	16.5659	0.00000	0.14211
79	2777.47	27.7747	0.16667	0.18975
80	501.86	33.4573	0.25000	0.08621
81	1130.55	32.3014	0.25000	0.17766
82	733.18	13.5774	0.58333	0.27411
83	295.82	10.2007	1.58333	0.12719
84	1115.04	38.4497	0.25000	0.15676
85	484.19	17.2925	0.16667	0.16000
86	255.10	28.3444	1.41667	0.05844
87	234.52	18.0400	0.66667	0.07602
88	991.80	70.8429	0.50000	0.06512
89	453.94	17.4592	0.33333	0.14943
90	426.52	25.0894	0.50000	0.09189
91	513.76	24.4648	0.25000	0.11538
92	345.89	15.7223	1.75000	0.09322
93	95.99	9.5990	1.25000	0.07937
94	854.35	32.8596	0.50000	0.13978
95	846.52	16.2792	2.08333	0.29050
96	1233.51	44.0539	0.33333	0.14973
97	1363.34	34.0835	0.08333	0.19048
98	1742.23	31.1113	0.16667	0.21374
99	389.75	16.9457	0.58333	0.12500
100	309.53	8.1455	0.08333	0.23313

TABLE 12–4

SAS

Model: MODEL1
Dependent Variable: RESP

Analysis of Variance

Source	DF	Sum of Squares	Mean Square	F Value	Prob>F
Model	3	0.50495	0.16832	40.168	0.0001
Error	96	0.40227	0.00419		
C Total	99	0.90722			

Root MSE	0.06473	R-square	0.5566
Dep Mean	0.19586	Adj R-sq	0.5427
C.V.	33.05019		

Parameter Estimates

Variable	DF	Parameter Estimate	Standard Error	T for H0: Parameter=0	Prob>|T|
INTERCEP	1	0.194386	0.01508134	12.889	0.0001
TOT_DOLL	1	0.000141	0.00001443	9.780	0.0001
AVG_ORDR	1	-0.004708	0.00051457	-9.150	0.0001
LAST_BUY	1	0.002589	0.01137582	0.228	0.8204

Variable	DF	Standardized Estimate
INTERCEP	1	0.00000000
TOT_DOLL	1	0.78196276
AVG_ORDR	1	-0.72689782
LAST_BUY	1	0.01589971

Another way to interpret the *F* statistic is to check to make sure the value of *F* is greater than 4; a value greater than 4 will correspond to a *p* of less than 5 percent. The reason for looking at the *F* statistic two ways is that when comparing two or more models to each other, each may have *p* values of less than .05, but an examination of the difference in the *F* statistic can provide a sense of which model is most significant, when all models are significant.

Also of note is the relationship between *R*-square and *F:*

$$F = \frac{R\text{-square}/(k-1)}{(1-R\text{-square})/(n-\text{k})}$$

where *k* equals the number of variables, including both the dependent and the independent variables included in the model. In a simple regression model *k* would be equal to 2. In a model with two independent variables *k* would be equal to 3, and so on.

From this definition of *F*, we see that when the number of variables increases without significantly increasing *R*-square, the *F* value becomes smaller, thus decreasing the statistical significance of the model. It is also clear for the formula that *F* increases as the number of observations increase.

Another way of considering the effects of adding variables to the model is as follows: As we mentioned, *R*-square typically increases when variables are added to the model even if they are not important; thus, to offset their unimportant contribution to *R*-square, we often consider adjusted *R*-square:

$$\text{adj } R = 1 - (1 - R\text{ sq}) \times \frac{(n-1)}{(n - \text{number of variables})}$$

Parameter estimates table. Table 12–4 reports the regression coefficients (called *parameter estimates*), their corresponding standard errors, *t* values (T for H0:), and *p*-values (Prob > | T |).

The *t* value is the ratio of parameter estimate to standard error. If the *t* value is less than –1.96 or greater than +1.96, then we conclude that the true parameter or regression coefficient is greater than zero and the variable in question is significantly related to the dependent variable, with 95 percent confidence. For a *t* value inside this interval, the true regression coefficient is zero and there is no relationship between the variable and the dependent variable.

Often it is useful to know which variables in the model are most important. The parameter estimates or regression coefficients cannot be used because the units are not comparable. In our example, we have dollars (for TOT__DOLL), number of orders (for AVG__ORDR), and number of months (for LAST__BUY) with a coefficient of .000141 for TOT__DOLL versus .002589 for LAST__BUY. We cannot say LAST__BUY contributes more than TOT__DOLL in predicting RESP on the basis of the apples-to-oranges comparison of the size of the coefficients.

One way around this problem is to use standard coefficients (standardized estimates), which are the regression coefficients converted into a common unit by multiplying the coefficient by the standard deviation of the independent variable divided by the standard deviation of the dependent variable. Thus, TOT__DOLL and LAST__BUY have standardized coefficients of .7819 and .0158, respectively, which indicate that the former is roughly 49 times more important than the latter.

More Quick and Dirty Regression

Now that our review of the regression output from an SAS program is complete, let's review the regression equation and decide what to do about that nonsignificant variable LAST__BUY.

The regression equation derived from Table 12–4 is

RESP = .19 + .00014 × TOT__DOLL – .0047 ×
AVG__ORDR + .0025 × LAST__BUY.

As we said before, the model includes TOT__DOLL and AVG__ORDR, and both variables are significant with *p*-values of .01 percent. But the LAST__BUY variable has a *t*-value of less than 2 and a *p*-value of .82. Clearly, the variable should not be used according to either of our rules: that *t* should be greater than 2, or that the *p*-value should be less than .05. However, before redoing the model with this variable removed, let's note that the model has an *R*-square of 55.66 percent and an *F* value of 40.1. We'll want to compare these values with the values produced from a new model with only two independent variables, TOT__DOLL and AVG__ORDR. Table 12–5 shows the results of running the model with the variable LAST__BUY removed.

The new model has this form:

RESP = .19 + .00014 × TOT__DOLL – .0047 × AVG__ORDR

In this case, the regression coefficients did not change with the removal of the nonsignificant variable LAST__BUY. We see that the two variables are still significant. Their *t* values are well above 2, and their *p*-values are below the .01 percent level. The *F* value has improved from 40.2 to 60.8,

TABLE 12–5

SAS

Model: MODEL1
Dependent Variable: RESP

Analysis of Variance

Source	DF	Sum of Squares	Mean Square	F Value	Prob>F
Model	2	0.50473	0.25237	60.820	0.0001
Error	97	0.40249	0.00415		
C Total	99	0.90722			

Root MSE	0.06442	R-square	0.5563
Dep Mean	0.19586	Adj R-sq	0.5472
C.V.	33.88825		

Parameter Estimates

Variable	DF	Parameter Estimate	Standard Error	T for H0: Parameter=0	Prob>|T|
INTERCEP	1	0.196591	0.01150215	17.092	0.0001
TOT_DOLL	1	0.000141	0.00001421	9.897	0.0001
AVG_ORDR	1	-0.004718	0.00051005	-9.251	0.0001

Variable	DF	Standardized Estimate
INTERCEP	1	0.00000000
TOT_DOLL	1	0.77937273
AVG_ORDR	1	-0.72849090

indicating that this model in total is stronger, in a statistical sense, than the prior model. The reason for this improvement is that the *R*-square value has not changed appreciably; its value is still 55.6 percent, but this *R*-square has been achieved by a model with one less variable, and you'll recall from our previous discussion that the *F* value tends to increase as the number of variables decreases.

So we have a good model, but should we stop here? Remember, this was a quick and dirty model; it was built with almost no examination of the data. We did not check to see if the independent variables were normally distributed. We did not check to see if the relationship between the independent variables and the dependent variables was linear or straight. We did not probe for interaction variables. We did not check for multicollinearity. We did a quick and dirty job—but we still got a pretty good model. Let's see what a better, more thorough, job would produce.

REGRESSION BUILT WITH CARE

Step 1—Examination of the Correlation Matrix

A thorough regression analysis often begins with an examination of a correlation matrix. A correlation matrix simply consists of correlation coefficients and *p*-values for each combination of all independent and dependent variables.

Table 12–6 shows a correlation matrix of the four variables in our example.

In practice, the analyst will scan the correlation matrix to get an idea of which independent variables appear to be related to the dependent variable. The reason for doing this is that in most real situations, there may be hundreds of potential independent variables, and it's literally impossible to deal with all of them thoroughly. So the analyst looks to include, for

TABLE 12–6

SAS
CORRELATION ANALYSIS
4 `VAR' Variables: RESP TOT_DOLL AVG_ORDR LAST_BUY

Pearson Correlation Coefficients/Prob > |R| under Ho: Rho=0/N = 100

	RESP	TOT_DOLL	AVG_ORDR	LAST_BUY
RESP	1.00000	0.39032	-0.32488	-0.09807
	0.0	0.0001	0.0010	0.3317
TOT_DOLL	0.39032	1.00000	0.57381	-0.29063
	0.0001	0.0	0.0001	0.0034
AVG_ORDR	-0.32488	0.57381	1.00000	-0.15539
	0.0010	0.0001	0.0	0.1226
LAST_BUY	-0.09807	-0.29063	-0.15539	1.00000
	0.3317	0.0034	0.1226	0.0

further analysis, only those variables that seem to have a good chance of being related to the dependent variable, that is, a good chance of entering a final regression model.

An examination of Table 12–6 indicates that the variables TOT__DOLL and AVG__ORDR both have relatively high correlation coefficients (.39032 and –.32488) with the dependent variable. The p-values of both are less than .05, indicating statistical significance.

On the other hand, LAST__BUY has a relatively low correlation coefficient (.09807) and its p-value is greater than .05.

At this point, the analyst looking at the correlation matrix may guess that LAST__BUY will fall out of the picture, but we'll try to salvage this variable. Maybe the variable is correlated with response, but the relationship is not linear, and this could account for the low correlation? We'll see.

Step 2—Normalization of All Variables

After deciding which variables are worthy of further consideration, the next step is to check to see if the variables in their raw form are more or less normally distributed. Does their shape correspond to the shape of the bell-shaped curve or normal distribution? If not, what can we do to make their shape appear normal?

In Figures 12–1 through 12–4, we see stem-and-leaf pictures of all four variables.

In each case, we see that the distributions are skewed toward the lower numbers in the stem. On the right-hand side of each figure we see something called a boxplot. The boxplot is simply an aid to answer the question, "Is the distribution normal or skewed?" When the bar with the stars on each end (*------*) is in the middle of the box, the distribution is normal. As you can see, these distributions are not normal.

So we'll normalize them. Distributions are normalized by transforming the original variable into some other variable. Often, this is done by replacing the original variable with its logarithm or by taking the square or the square root of the original variable. There are lots of ways to do this and these techniques are part of the statistician's bag of tricks. It really doesn't matter which method of transformation is used; what matters is that the final shape of the variable be as normal as possible before

FIGURE 12–1
SAS UNIVARIATE PROCEDURE

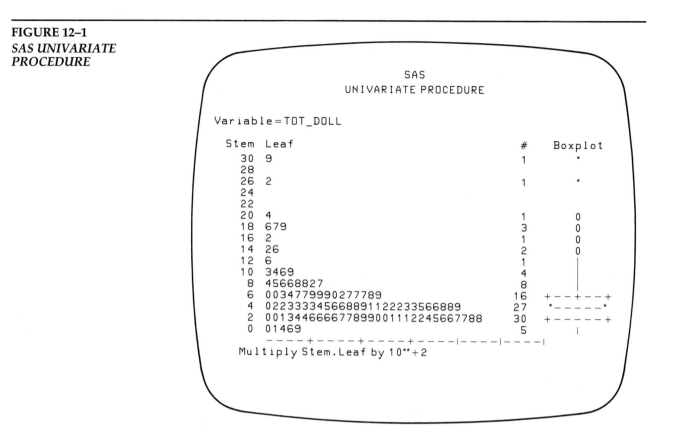

```
                              SAS
                      UNIVARIATE PROCEDURE

Variable=TOT_DOLL

 Stem Leaf                                  #    Boxplot
   30 9                                     1       *
   28
   26 2                                     1       *
   24
   22
   20 4                                     1       0
   18 679                                   3       0
   16 2                                     1       0
   14 26                                    2       0
   12 6                                     1       |
   10 3469                                  4       |
    8 45668827                              8       |
    6 0034779990277789                     16    +--+--+
    4 022333345668891122233566889          27    *-----*
    2 001344666677899001112245667788       30    +-----+
    0 01469                                 5       |
      ----+----+----+----|----|----|
   Multiply Stem.Leaf by 10**+2
```

FIGURE 12–2
SAS UNIVARIATE PROCEDURE

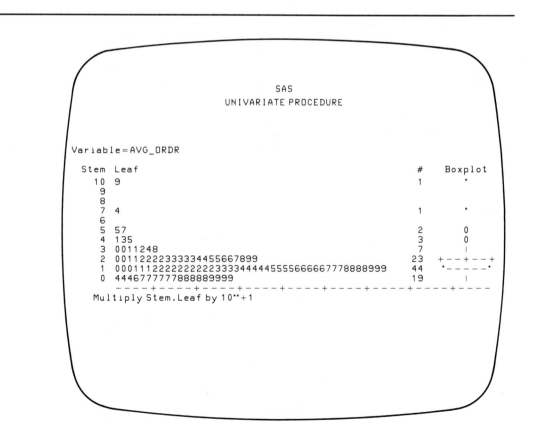

```
                              SAS
                      UNIVARIATE PROCEDURE

Variable=AVG_ORDR

 Stem Leaf                                              #    Boxplot
   10 9                                                 1       *
    9
    8
    7 4                                                 1       *
    6
    5 57                                                2       0
    4 135                                               3       0
    3 0011248                                           7       |
    2 00112222333334455667899                          23    +--+--+
    1 000111222222222233334444455555666667778888999    44    *-----*
    0 4446777777888889999                              19       |
      ----+----+----+----+----+----+----+----+----
   Multiply Stem.Leaf by 10**+1
```

FIGURE 12–3
SAS UNIVARIATE PROCEDURE

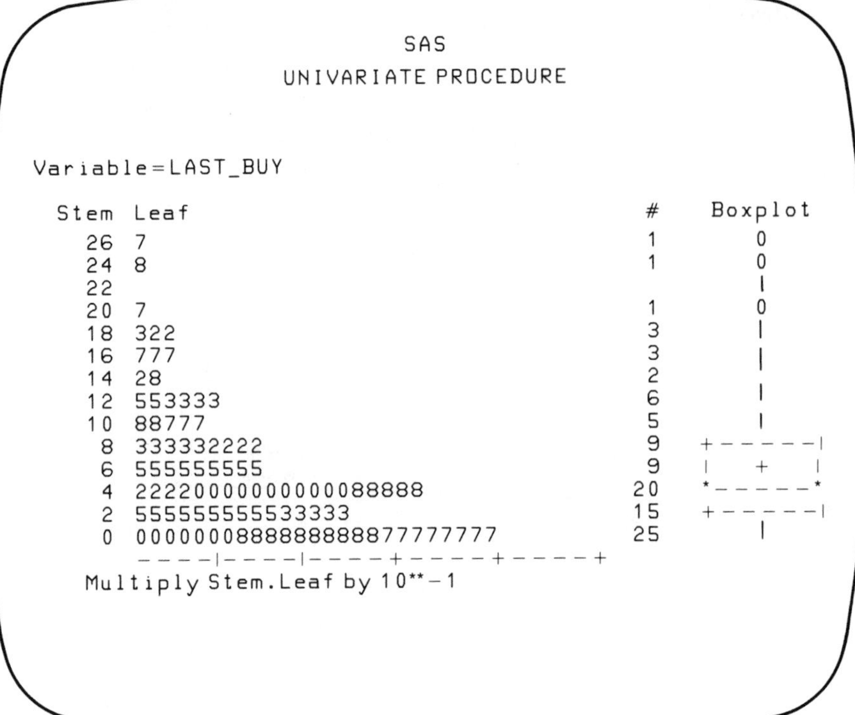

```
                         SAS
                 UNIVARIATE PROCEDURE

Variable=LAST_BUY

  Stem Leaf                                      #    Boxplot
    26 7                                         1       0
    24 8                                         1       0
    22                                                   |
    20 7                                         1       0
    18 322                                       3       |
    16 777                                       3       |
    14 28                                        2       |
    12 553333                                    6       |
    10 88777                                     5       |
     8 333332222                                 9    +-----|
     6 555555555                                 9    |  +  |
     4 22220000000000088888                     20    *-----*
     2 555555555533333                          15    +-----|
     0 0000000888888888877777777                25       |
       ----|----|----+----+----+
    Multiply Stem.Leaf by 10**-1
```

FIGURE 12–4
SAS UNIVARIATE PROCEDURE

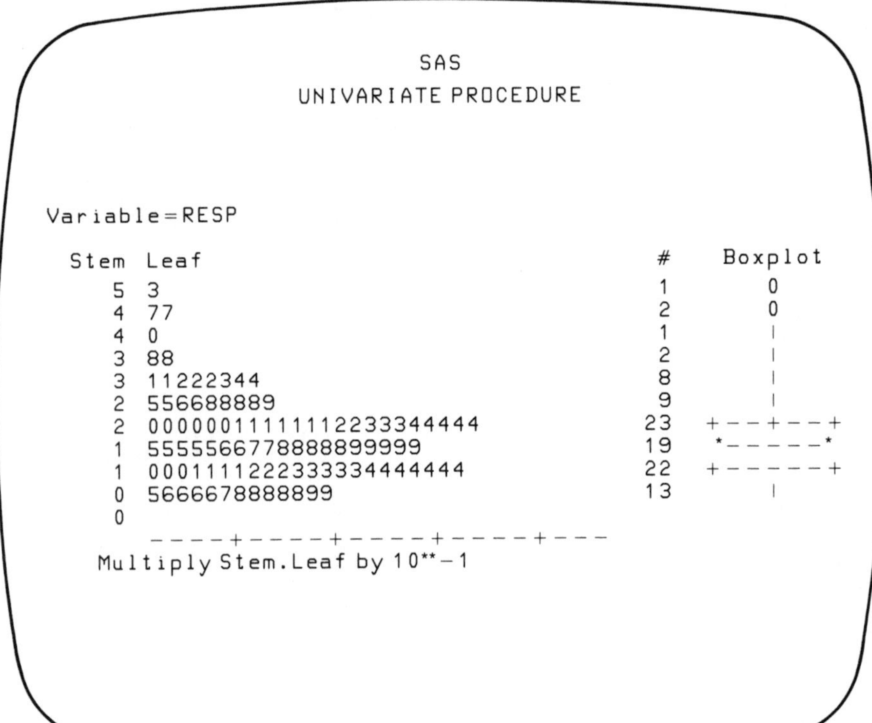

```
                         SAS
                 UNIVARIATE PROCEDURE

Variable=RESP

  Stem Leaf                                      #    Boxplot
     5 3                                         1       0
     4 77                                        2       0
     4 0                                         1       |
     3 88                                        2       |
     3 11222344                                  8       |
     2 556688889                                 9       |
     2 00000011111112233344444                  23    +--+--+
     1 5555566778888899999                      19    *-----*
     1 0001111222333334444444                   22    +-----+
     0 5666678888899                            13       |
     0
       ----+----+----+----+---
    Multiply Stem.Leaf by 10**-1
```

FIGURE 12–5
SAS UNIVARIATE PROCEDURE

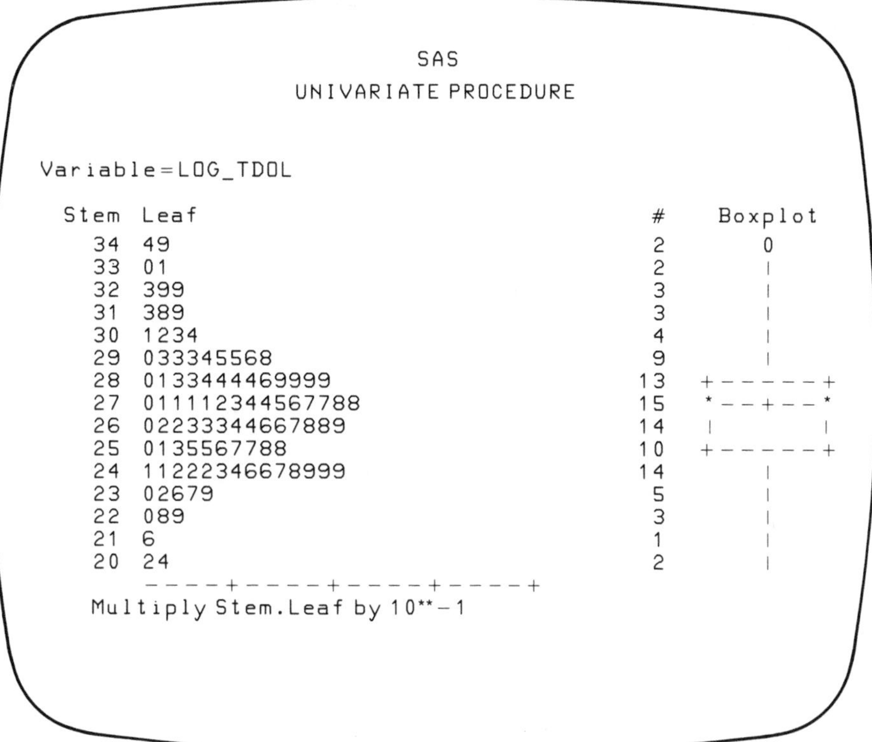

```
                         SAS
                 UNIVARIATE PROCEDURE

Variable=LOG_TDOL

  Stem Leaf                               #     Boxplot
    34 49                                 2        0
    33 01                                 2        |
    32 399                                3        |
    31 389                                3        |
    30 1234                               4        |
    29 033345568                          9        |
    28 0133444469999                     13     +------+
    27 011112344567788                   15     *--+--*
    26 02233344667889                    14     |      |
    25 0135567788                        10     +------+
    24 11222346678999                    14        |
    23 02679                              5        |
    22 089                                3        |
    21 6                                  1        |
    20 24                                 2        |
       ----+----+----+----+
  Multiply Stem.Leaf by 10**-1
```

entering the regression mode. Having said that, we should keep in mind the fact that a final regression model may have to be applied to a customer file of millions of names, and the more complicated the model, the more difficult it may be for programmers, who are not statisticians, and who may not have the programming tools required to deal with logs, to score the database. We'll come back to this point in later chapters.

In Figures 12–5 to 12–8 we see the effect of transforming each variable into its logarithm. (We used logs to the base 10, but natural logs would have accomplished the same objective.) The result is that the distribution of each variable comes closer to the shape of the normal distribution. The importance of this to the final regression model will become clearer in a few minutes.

Step 3—Checking for Linearity

To check for linearity or straight-line relationships, we ask the computer program (again we are using SAS) to produce scatter diagrams of the relationships between each independent variable and the dependent variable.

In Figure 12–9, we see the relationship between RESP and TOT_DOLL. The relationship isn't great but it seems to be linear and positive. In other words, an argument could be made that a straight line drawn through the points fits the points just as well as any curved line. To illustrate this observation, we've drawn a straight line through the scatter points.

FIGURE 12–6
SAS UNIVARIATE PROCEDURE

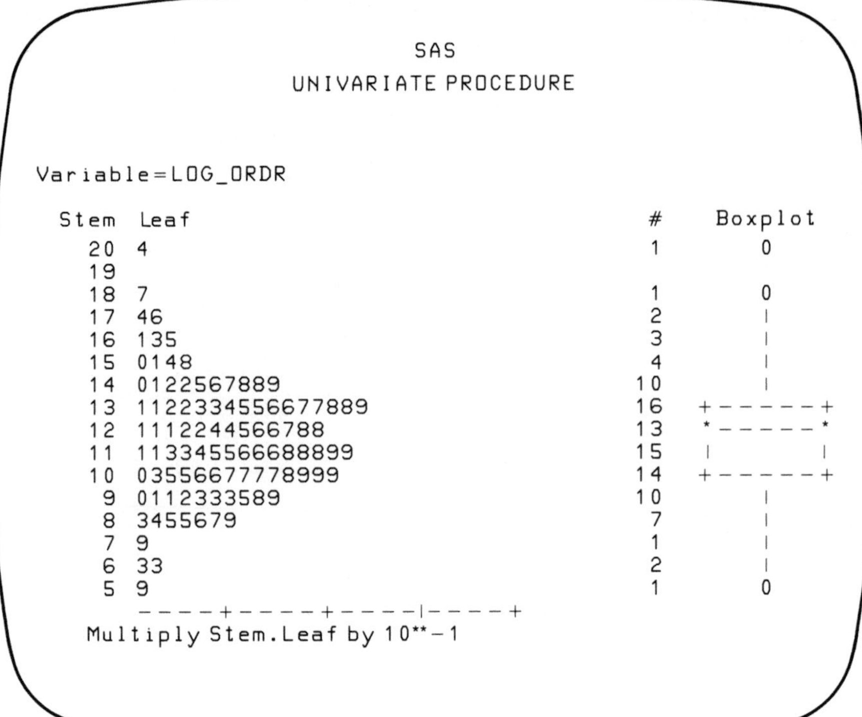

SAS
UNIVARIATE PROCEDURE
Variable=LOG_ORDR
Stem Leaf # Boxplot
20 4 1 0
19
18 7 1 0
17 46 2 |
16 135 3 |
15 0148 4 |
14 0122567889 10 |
13 1122334556677889 16 +-----+
12 1112244566788 13 *-----*
11 113345566688899 15 | |
10 03556677778999 14 +-----+
9 0112333589 10 |
8 3455679 7 |
7 9 1 |
6 33 2 |
5 9 1 0
----+----+----|----+
Multiply Stem.Leaf by 10**-1

FIGURE 12–7
SAS UNIVARIATE PROCEDURE

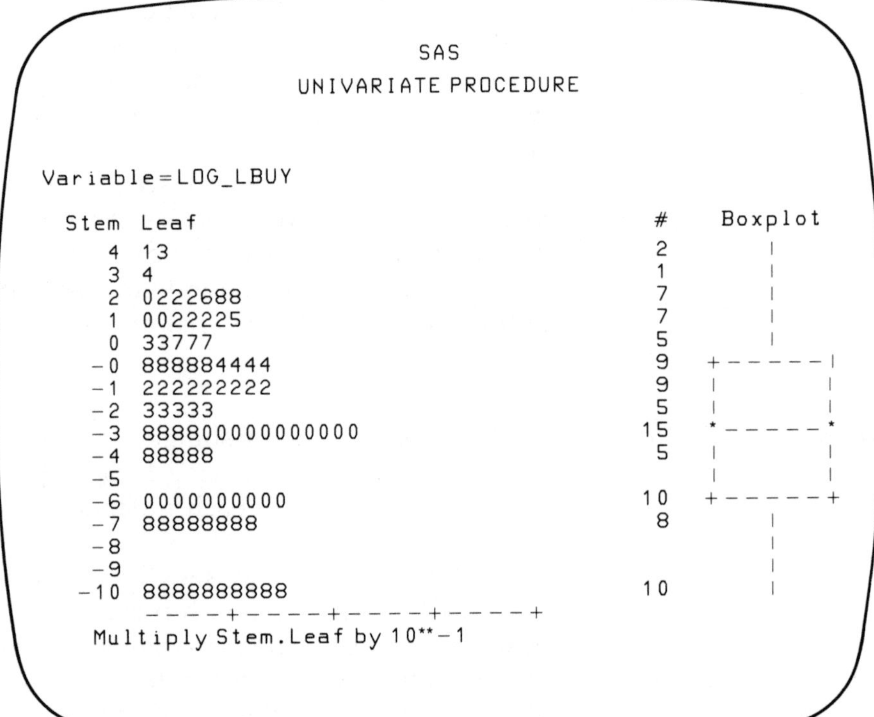

SAS
UNIVARIATE PROCEDURE
Variable=LOG_LBUY
Stem Leaf # Boxplot
4 13 2 |
3 4 1 |
2 0222688 7 |
1 0022225 7 |
0 33777 5 |
-0 888884444 9 +-----|
-1 222222222 9 | |
-2 33333 5 | |
-3 888800000000000 15 *-----*
-4 88888 5 | |
-5 | |
-6 0000000000 10 +-----+
-7 88888888 8 |
-8 |
-9 |
-10 8888888888 10 |
----+----+----+----+
Multiply Stem.Leaf by 10**-1

FIGURE 12–8
SAS UNIVARIATE PROCEDURE

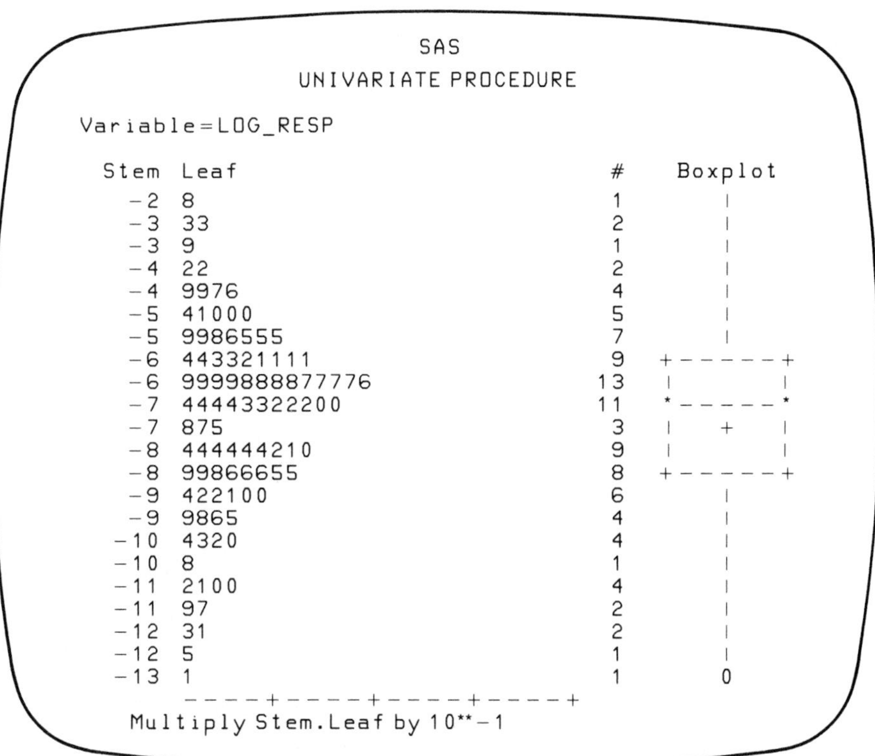

```
                     SAS
             UNIVARIATE PROCEDURE
Variable=LOG_RESP

  Stem Leaf                        #    Boxplot
    -2 8                           1       |
    -3 33                          2       |
    -3 9                           1       |
    -4 22                          2       |
    -4 9976                        4       |
    -5 41000                       5       |
    -5 9986555                     7       |
    -6 443321111                   9    +-----+
    -6 9999888877776              13    |     |
    -7 44443322200                11    *-----*
    -7 875                         3    |  +  |
    -8 444444210                   9    |     |
    -8 99866655                    8    +-----+
    -9 422100                      6       |
    -9 9865                        4       |
   -10 4320                        4       |
   -10 8                           1       |
   -11 2100                        4       |
   -11 97                          2       |
   -12 31                          2       |
   -12 5                           1       |
   -13 1                           1       0
       ----+----+----+----+
   Multiply Stem.Leaf by 10**-1
```

FIGURE 12–9
Plot of RESP, TOT_DOLL

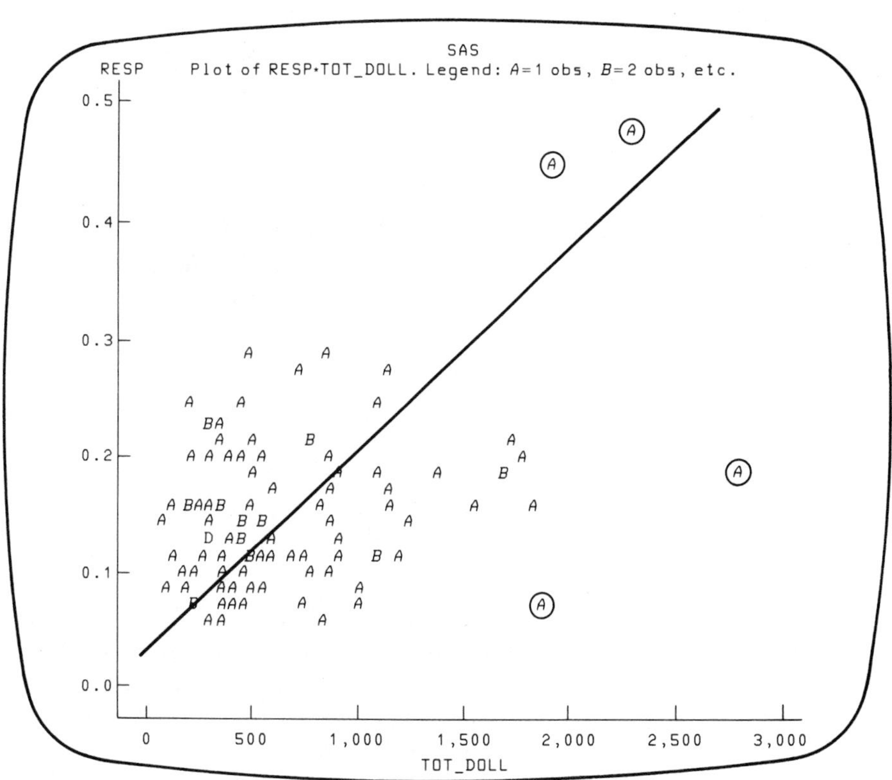

FIGURE 12–10
Plot of RESP, AVG_ORDR

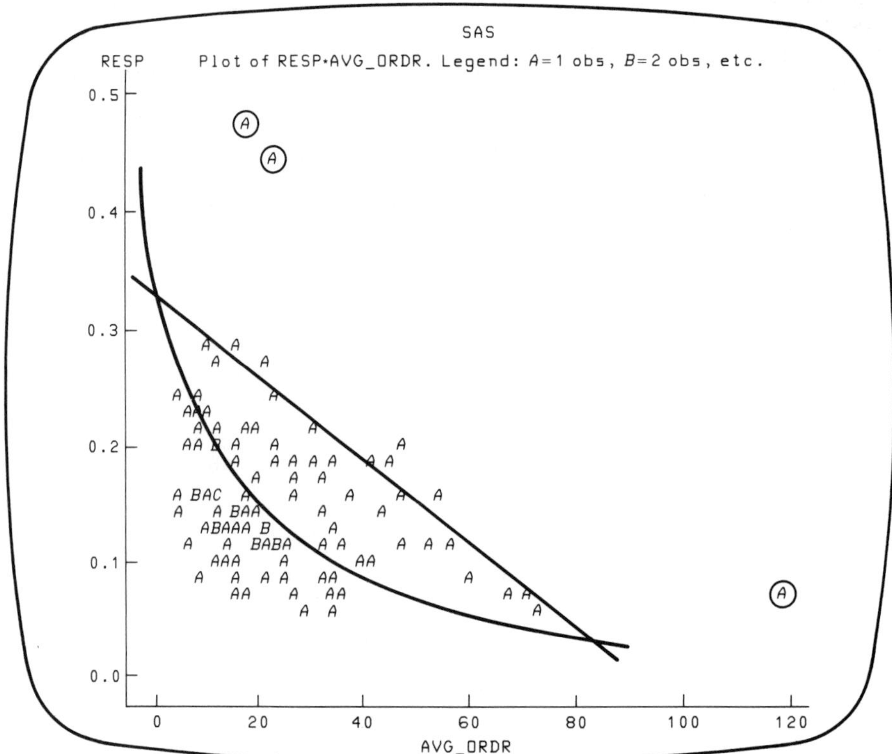

Figure 12–10 plots the relationship between AVG__ORDR and RESP. The relationship is clearly negative. The negative correlation sign told us this, and the scatter plot simply describes the relationship pictorially. If we assume for the moment that the three data points that stand apart from the rest of the data points are real, not errors, then we could argue that a curved line fits the points better than a straight line and some straightening is required.

Figure 12–11 simply reinforces the argument that there is no relationship between LAST__BUY and RESP.

At this point, you might be curious about what scatter plots of the transformed variables might look like and about what effect transforming the variables has on the question of linearity.

To assist in this analysis, we should also produce a new correlation matrix using the transformed variables. The new correlation matrix is shown in Table 12–7.

If we compare the results of Table 12–6 with Table 12–7 we note some interesting things:

- The correlation coefficient between RESP and TOT__DOLL decreased from .39032 to .30066.
- The correlation coefficient between RESP and AVG__ORDR increased from –.32488 to –.38477 (the direction sign can be ignored).
- The correlation coefficient between RESP and LAST__BUY also increased from –.09807 to –.16945.

FIGURE 12–11
Plot of RESP, LAST_BUY

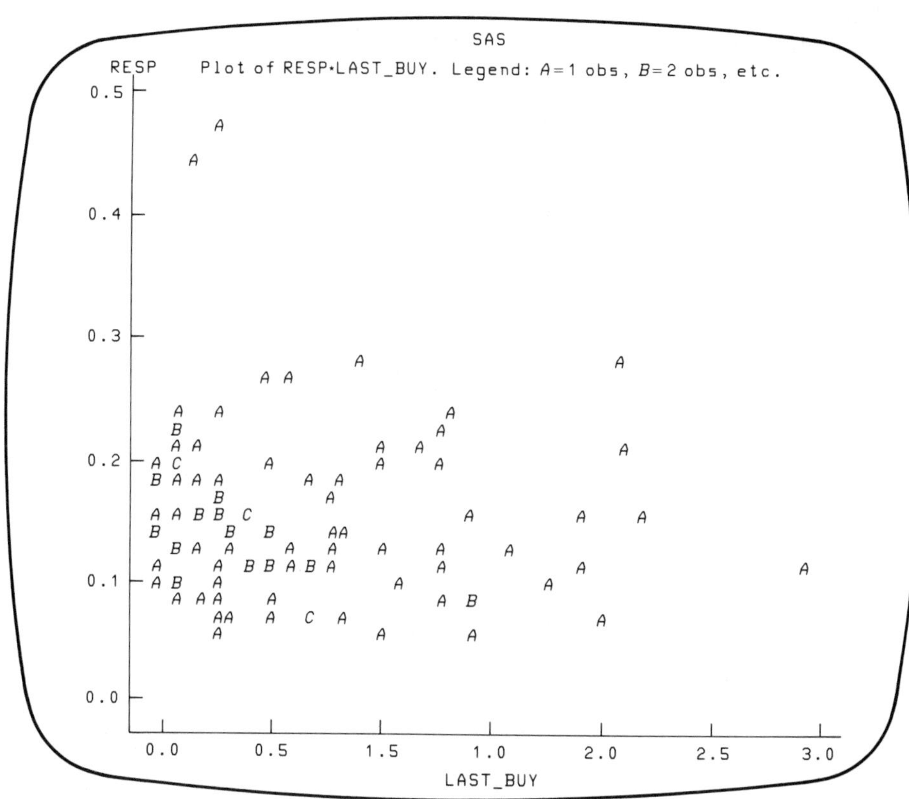

TABLE 12–7

SAS
CORRELATION ANALYSIS
4 `VAR' Variables: LOG_RESP LOG_TDOL LOG_ORDR LOG_LBUY

Pearson Correlation Coefficients / Prob > |R| under Ho: Rho = 0
/ Number of Observations

	LOG_RESP	LOG_TDOL	LOG_ORDR	LOG_LBUY
LOG_RESP	1.00000	0.30066	-0.38477	-0.16945
	0.0	0.0024	0.0001	0.1064
LOG_TDOL	0.30066	1.00000	0.73874	-0.28732
	0.0024	0.0	0.0001	0.0055
	100	100	100	92
LOG_ORDR	-0.38477	0.73874	1.00000	-0.14667
	0.0001	0.0001	0.0	0.1630
	100	100	100	92
LOG_LBUY	0.16945	-0.28732	-0.14667	1.00000
	0.1064	0.0055	0.1630	0.0
	92	92	92	92

FIGURE 12–12
Plot of LOG_RESP, LOG_TDOL

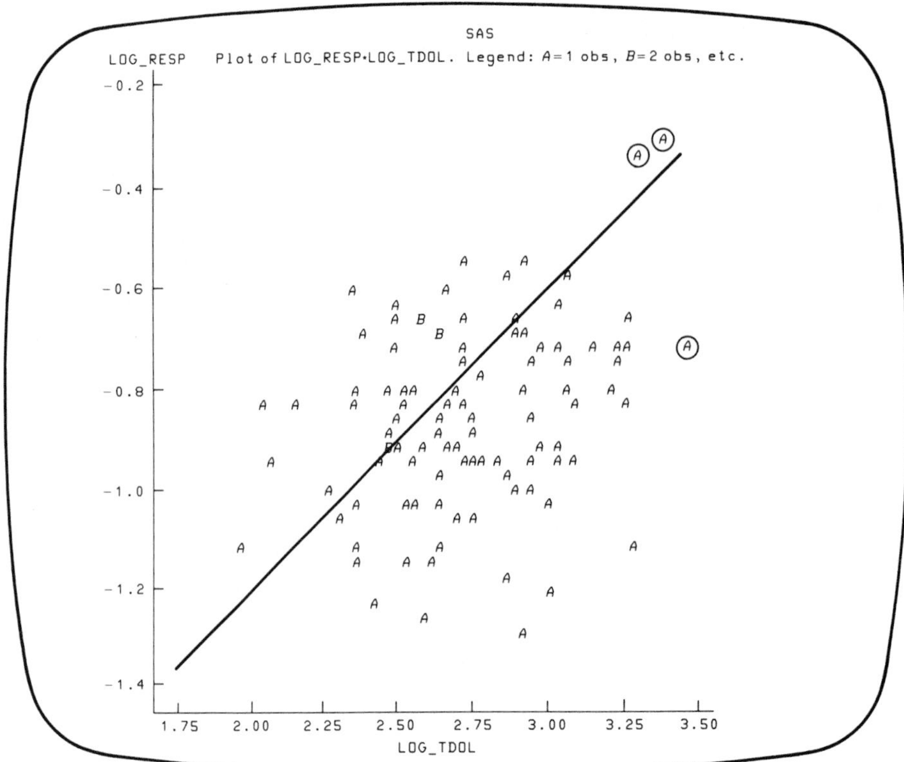

The decrease in correlation between RESP and TOT__DOLL suggests that we might have been better off by not transforming the data. However, even though we lost some "correlation" points from TOT__DOLL, we prefer to use relationships that are symmetrical or approximate the normal distribution because the underlying mathematics of regression analysis assumes linearity of all variables with the dependent variable, which is enhanced when the variables are as close to a normal distribution as possible. Also, models built on variables that do not violate these assumptions have a better chance of holding up in practice.

Another reason for sticking with variables that conform more closely to the normal distribution assumption is that, to the extent that the normality assumption is violated, the interpretation of the *t* and *F* statistics becomes difficult. In other words, the *t*s might not be as reliable estimates of significance as we assume them to be, and since variables are evaluated on the basis of their *t* scores, it's important that their interpretation be correct.

Now let's look at the scatter plots of the transformed variables.

In Figure 12–12, we see the relationship between LOG__TDOL and LOG__RESP. Compared to the raw data relationship shown in Figure 12–9, we see that the extreme values of response are somewhat closer to the rest of the data points, which is a function of the log transformation. To the naked eye it appears that the relationship is a bit more straight, but the difference does not appear to be significant.

FIGURE 12–13
Plot of LOG_RESP, LOG_ORDR

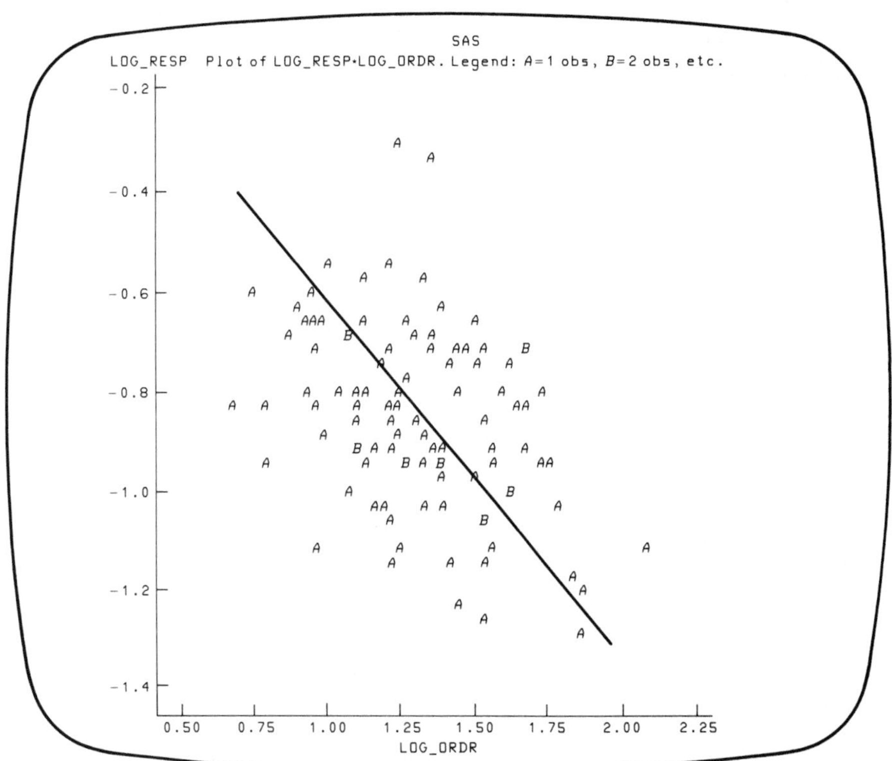

We see a bigger difference when we compare Figure 12–13 with Figure 12–10. Here the transformations have clearly resulted in a straighter relationship between LOG__ORDR and LOG__RESP. This example points to a very interesting and valuable conclusion: *Reexpressing most of the time normalizes and straightens the data simultaneously.* This means that by taking care of one problem, normality, most of the time you will take care of the second problem, the linear relationship assumption of regression.

Finally, the transformation of the LAST__BUY variable, Figure 12–14, doesn't make very much difference. It's getting close to the time when we should disregard this variable from further consideration.

RERUNNING THE MODEL

Now we're ready to build the model using the transformed variables. The first model we'll try will take the form:

$$\text{LOG\_\_RESP} = b0 + b1 \times \text{LOG\_\_TDOL} + b2 \times \text{LOG\_\_ORDR}, + b3 \times \text{LOG\_\_LBUY}$$

The regression printout (see Table 12–8) for this three-variable model shows a *t* value close to (but still less than) 2 for the variable LOG__LBUY, and a correspondingly large *p*-value. The *p*-value of the transformed variable is much smaller than before but is still greater than the .05 or 5 percent rule we established for entry into a model, so we'll drop this variable and run the model again with only two transformed variables.

FIGURE 12–14
Plot of LOG_RESP, LOG_LBUY

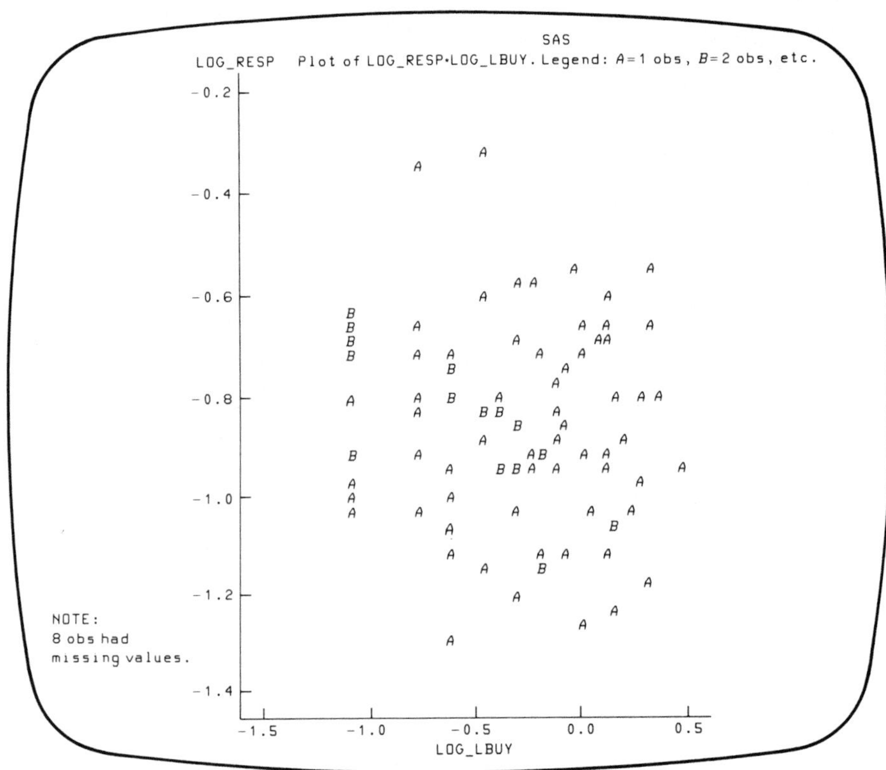

TABLE 12–8

SAS

Model: MODEL1
Dependent Variable: LOG_RESP

Analysis of Variance

Source	DF	Sum of Squares	Mean Square	F Value	Prob>F
Model	3	4.60627	1.53542	1052.486	0.0001
Error	89	0.12984	0.00146		
C Total	92	4.73610			

Root MSE	0.03819	R-square	0.9726
Dep Mean	-0.76149	Adj R-sq	0.9717
C.V.	-5.01583		

Parameter Estimates

Variable	DF	Parameter Estimate	Standard Error	T for H0: Parameter=0	Prob>|T|
INTERCEP	1	-1.973401	0.03939574	-50.092	0.0001
LOG_TDOL	1	0.875307	0.01787217	48.976	0.0001
LOG_ORDR	1	-0.961115	0.01887344	-50.924	0.0001
LOG_LBUY	1	0.015471	0.00991300	-1.561	0.1222

Variable	DF	Standardized Estimate
INTERCEP	1	0.00000000
LOG_TDOL	1	1.06809616
LOG_ORDR	1	-1.10992738
LOG_LBUY	1	-0.02768440

TABLE 12–9

SAS

Model: MODEL1
Dependent Variable: LOG_RESP

Analysis of Variance

Source	DF	Sum of Squares	Mean Square	F Value	Prob>F
Model	2	4.58193	2.29096	1124.797	0.0001
Error	97	0.19757	0.00204		
C Total	99	4.77949			

Root MSE	0.04513	R-square	0.9587
Dep Mean	-0.76009	Adj R-sq	0.9578
C.V.	-5.93756		

Parameter Estimates

Variable	DF	Parameter Estimate	Standard Error	T for H0: Parameter=0	Prob>|T|
INTERCEP	1	-1.890376	0.04300760	-43.954	0.0001
LOG_TDOL	1	0.844590	0.01995868	42.317	0.0001
LOG_ORDR	1	-0.959345	0.02220746	-43.199	0.0001

Variable	DF	Standardized Estimate
INTERCEP	1	0.00000000
LOG_TDOL	1	1.12039211
LOG_ORDR	1	-1.14375208

Rerunning the model without LOG_LBUY results in the following model (see Table 12–9):

LOG_RESP = –1.89 + .084 × LOG_TDOL – 0.959 × LOG_ORDR

Both transformed variables are very significant, with high *t*s and low *p*-values. The *R*-square for this model is 96 percent, which represents a large improvement over the Q&D model's *R*-square of 55 percent.

Based on *R*-square values, we may be tempted to say that the carefully built model is clearly better than the Q&D model because its *R*-square is larger. However, we cannot say this for two reasons.

First, a model with a larger *R*-square would be better than a competing model with a smaller *R*-square *provided* that the dependent variables were the same for both models. To compare models using different variables is, in effect, making the proverbial comparison of apples and oranges. And a transformed variable is equivalent to a different variable.

The second and more important reason for not using *R*-square as the ultimate measure in evaluating a model, as previously pointed out and to be repeated, is simply because it has been shown that models with large *R*-squares put to use under real situations or simulated conditions do not always perform better than their small *R*-square model counterparts.

To sum up, we have two models with the following equations:

The Q&D model:

RESP = .19 + .00014 × TOT_DOLL – .0047 × AVG_ORDR

The carefully built model:

LOG_RESP = –1.89 + .84 × LOG_TDOL – .95 × LOG_ORDR

TABLE 12–10
Decile Analysis—Mean Response Rate

	Careful Model		*Q&D Model*	
Decile	*Decile*	*Cum*	*Decile*	*Cum*
1	29.0%	29.0%	27.0%	27.0%
2	20.0	24.5	20.0	23.5
3	19.0	22.6	21.0	22.6
4	16.0	21.0	16.0	21.0
5	14.0	19.6	14.0	19.6
6	14.0	18.6	13.0	18.5
7	11.0	17.6	13.0	17.7
8	11.0	16.7	10.0	16.8
9	08.0	15.8	08.0	15.8
10	06.0	14.8	06.0	14.8
House file average response rate	14.8		14.8	

The model using log transformations has an *R*-square of 96 percent, the quick and dirty model has an *R*-square of 55 percent. It appears that the carefully built model is almost twice as good as the quick and dirty model. Is it?

VALIDATION—CHOOSING THE BEST MODEL

If we cannot rely solely on *R*-square, then how can we choose the best model? The answer lies in the validation of the candidate models under simulated conditions. That is, we apply the model to a file of names for which the dependent variable is known, and then evaluate the predicted values of the dependent variable with the actual values. The model that *performs best* in the validation test *is the best.*

For validating the cataloger's two models, we use the second sample of 100 fresh names for which the response rates are known. We score each name for each model and compare predicted and actual response rates by a decile analysis. A decile analysis starts by ranking the scored file from high to low score and dividing the ranked names into 10 equal groups or deciles. The mean value of the actual dependent variable for each decile is calculated. In this case, the model with the largest mean response rate for the top two or three deciles is declared the best model.

The decile analyses for the two models are in Table 12–10. We see that the carefully built model beats the Q&D model in the top decile with a mean response rate of 29 versus 27 percent, but performs the same in decile 2 with a mean response rate of 20 percent. Thirty percent into the file, both models perform the same. Depending on how deeply the cataloger plans to mail, the 2 percent difference could represent a significant gain in dollars per response, in which case the preferred model is the one built with care. However, if the cataloger plans to use the model to mail to 50 percent of the file, not just the top 10 percent, then either model will produce the same result.

This example was intentionally designed to produce a result in which two models produce very different *R*-squares, but have little difference in practical results, to convince you to pay less attention to the *R*-square statistic and more attention to the validation results.

In practice, users will discover that the R-squares associated with most models, particularly response models, where only a very small percent of the population responds are generally under 10 percent, very often under 5 percent. Nevertheless, these models can be used with confidence, provided (1) the individual variables are significant (*t*s greater than 2 and the corresponding *p*-values less than .05); (2) the *F* value for the entire relationship is greater than 4 or 5; and (3) most importantly, the model validates, that is, produces a meaningful difference in decile performance when applied to a fresh validation sample.

MULTIPLE REGRESSION—SOME ODDS AND ENDS

Through our illustrations, we hope that you've obtained some feel for how multiple regression works in practice. At this point, hands-on experience with regression models is the only way you will become proficient in the application of regression and your company will become efficient in its direct mail programs.

In Chapter 13, we will outline a how-to for building regression models. But before doing so, we would like to take care of three loose ends.

Interaction

We note that in the regression model, each independent variable is multiplied by a weight (its coefficient) and then all the weighted variables are added to obtain a score or predicted value of the dependent variable. In effect, we are saying that the regression model is an *additive* model—the independent variables in the models are said to have an additive effect on the dependent variable.

Let's recall the model in Example 13, where we predict DOLLSPENT based on income and age.

DOLLSPENT = 351.29 – .65 × INCOME + .86 × AGE

As the model stands, AGE and INCOME are in the model and contribute to the prediction of DOLLSPENT additively. That is, regardless of the age of a customer, the DOLLSPENT will decrease $0.65 for every thousand dollars of income. The equation tells us that if you hold age constant, there is a negative relationship between sales and income. In other words, the product line appeals more to lower income persons than to upper income persons. This may be true, but what if it's "really" true for younger people and only "a little" true for older persons?

What if the effect of income on sales is much greater than –$0.65 for younger people, but much less than –$0.65 for older people? If this is true, then the $0.65 regression coefficient is really an average that reflects the behavior of both older and younger people. Clearly, we would like to have a technique that would do better than simply average out the behavior of both older and younger people.

In regression analysis, there are a couple of ways to handle this problem. You could run two models, one for older people and one for younger people. You could create a categorical "dummy" variable to represent age and include this variable in the model. Or you could create what is called an interaction variable.

An interaction variable is needed when the additive effects of the independent variables do not adequately explain the relationship between the dependent variable and independent variables. An example we often use has to do with the sale of opera tickets. A statistical profile of opera ticket buyers would reveal that they are both highly educated and upper income. This observation could be used in building a model of opera ticket buyers. We would want both variables, education and income, to be included in the model as independent variables. However, as we all know, not all highly educated persons have high incomes, nor are all upper income persons highly educated. What we would like in the model, therefore, is a third variable that reflects the fact that a person is *both* highly educated and upper income. This third variable, which is the combination of the two original variables, is called an *interaction variable.*

If an analyst were building a regression model of opera ticket buyers and had correctly identified income and education as important independent variables but had failed to create the interaction variable, the regression model *would not* include the interaction variable. An analyst has to create interaction variables and include them in the set of variables to be considered by the regression program. Fortunately, interaction variables can easily be added into regression models.

Going back to our example where we believe there might be an interactive effect between AGE and INCOME, we create an interaction variable to take the suspected effect into account by simply defining a new interaction variable AGE__INCOME as the product of the AGE and INCOME: AGE__INCOME = AGE × INCOME.

Putting interaction variables into a model is easy because all we have to do mechanically is instruct the regression program to create a new variable by multiplying two old variables together. However, in practice, finding which two variables (or even three or four variables for higher order interaction effects) is not easy. Although a working knowledge of the variables is the best guide for creating interaction variables, a statistical method called Automatic Interaction Detection (AID/CHAID) has been expressly developed for finding interaction. (We'll discuss AID/CHAID in Chapter 13.)

Multicollinearity

For multiple regression to produce good and reliable coefficients for its independent variables, there must be the absence of perfect multicollinearity. That is, none of the independent variables has a correlation coefficient of 1 with any of the other independent variables or with any weighted sum of the other independent variables. When perfect multicollinearity exists, the regression coefficients cannot be calculated. In such cases, the problem is always identified—the program literally won't run.

The real problem arises when there is high multicollinearity; however, there are some practical rules for identifying multicollinearity:

1. Multiple *R*-square is high and all or most of the *p*-values are greater than 5 percent.
2. The magnitude of the regression coefficients changes greatly when independent variables are added or dropped from the equation.
3. There are unexpectedly large regression coefficients for variables thought to be relatively unimportant and/or small regression coefficients for variables thought to be relatively important.
4. There are unexpected signs of the coefficients.

Remedies for multicollinearity. OK, now that you know what multicollinearity is, what it does, and how to detect it, here's how to alleviate the problem:

1. Try to get more observations, more data. That's right, more data. Often, multicollinearity can be a data problem rather than a modeling problem and increasing the sample size will make the problem go away. Actually, although texts on statistics discuss multicollinearity extensively, in most direct marketing applications where we are dealing with thousands of observations, multicollinearity is generally not a problem.
2. If you cannot get more data, try to examine all correlation coefficients to spot those with *R*s greater than .90. Then, eliminate one of the two "culprit" variables.
3. Review all the independent variables to try to combine those that seem to measure the same content. For example, three variables capturing the number of hours spent listening to MTV, playing the stereo, and watching movies on the VCR can be summed or averaged to obtain a measure of passive media interest. Factor analysis, a technique we'll describe in Chapter 14, can be used for this purpose.

Selection of Variables

Perhaps the most important step in the building process is finding the right variables to include in the model. Without a relevant set of predictors, no amount of data manipulation can produce a good model.

There are three basic approaches to variable selection. The first one we recommend is by far the most important. It's not statistically elegant, but it satisfies the validity test of logic and reasonableness and, accordingly, will be accepted by all. It's the selection based on knowledge of the data. Nothing replaces the analyst's experience with the data in terms of what it measures, what it suggests, and how it behaves.

The second approach helps the analyst when her experience with the data is limited or she cannot distinguish among a subset of very good variables. The approach of (forward) stepwise selection starts off by finding the variable that produces the largest *R*-square with the dependent variable. Then, given that the "best" variable is in the model, it finds the next best variable in terms of adding to the *R*-square. This process of finding variables that add to *R*-square stops when variables can no longer add to *R*-square according to certain statistical criteria.

This approach is helpful in paring down a large number of variables; however, it is notorious for finding subsets of variables that do not "hang" together. That is, the selected variables are difficult to justify because they appear not to be related in any logical or reasonable way to the dependent variable.

Even if a subset of variables produced by the stepwise approach hangs together well, the fact that it is declared best because it has the largest *R*-square is no guarantee, as we pointed out, of it being the best. In sum, the stepwise selection is only a good first step in finding the right variables.

The third approach uses a relatively new measure of total prediction error, denoted by Mallow's C(p). Using this approach, which is produced automatically by one of the procedures in SAS, we obtain many subsets or combinations of independent variables to choose from. Each combination of variables is associated with a C(p) statistic. The rule of thumb for using C(p) is to work with sets of variables whose C(p) value is equal or less than 1 plus the number of variables in the subset. However, even though we favor this approach, selection based on C(p) is just like the first two approaches in that there's no guarantee of getting the best set of predictor variables.

If we've made variable selection into "mission impossible," that's because it sometimes seems that way. When the final model is not as strong as desired, we assume its' because we cannot find the right set of variables. This problem gets us back to the need to collect better data, which was the theme of Chapter 2 on primary research data.

Chapter 13

Response Analysis

In Example 14 in Chapter 12, we discussed building a regression model to predict response. The dependent variable was undoubtedly a response variable but not of the usual kind found in most DM response modeling projects. In most response analyses, the dependent variable is a categorical "dummy" variable. Each person mailed is given a score of 1 or 0 on the variable RESPONSE. A 1 means the person responded, and a 0 means the person did not respond. As we all know, the vast majority of recipients unfortunately do not respond; this is the problem.

INTRODUCTION

The technique of regression analysis was originally developed for scalar or continuous dependent and independent variables. When independent variables are categorical, there are ways (for example, using dummy variables, which will be discussed shortly) to include such variables in the analysis without violating the assumptions of the technique. Use and interpretation of a regression model with categorical variables is similar to that of a model with scalar independent variables.

When the dependent variable is a categorical response variable with two levels, response yes/response no, or 1/0, the regression model is formally called the *linear probability model* (LPM). This label is appropriate because the predicted value of the response variable is interpreted as the probability of response. However, this label gives a false sense of form (linear) and correctness (probability) of the model. It turns out that the presence of a yes/no response-dependent variable violates a number of the assumptions of the regression technique, which renders questionable the model and its utility. One assumption that is violated is that the dependent variable conforms to the shape of the normal distribution. A variable that can have only two values, 1 or 0, cannot be normally distributed. If the response rates to direct marketing offers were greater than 20 percent, this violation would have little practical consequence. However, because this is rarely the case, and many of our response rates hover around the 1 to 3 percent area, this violation of the normality assumption cannot simply be dismissed.

Without going too deeply into theoretical issues, the LPM suffers from *potentially* excluding important predictors from the final model. This can happen because the t and F statistics can give false signals, potentially causing the analyst to either include insignificant variables or exclude significant variables. In addition, the LPM often results in estimates with probabilities less than 0 or greater than 1.

Not all model builders consider these potential problems terribly serious. Knowing the subject matter, they feel it is easy to identify the important variables and put them into the model. As for the "outside" probabilities, if the number of occurrences is small (which is usually the case), they view the model as more than acceptable.

In practice if a marketer is only interested in ranking a file of customers from most to least likely to respond, then the LPM and alternative techniques (such as logistic regression and discriminant analysis, which will be described shortly) all produce essentially the same ordering of a customer file.

The following are more important issues: Does each technique have access to the correct set of variables? For example, are interaction variables available to all techniques? Is each technique being used properly? Are variables being transformed to approximate normality? Are linear relationships sought out, and so on?

However, for those analysts who just do not want to use a model that is flawed or who really need to go beyond ranking the names on a file to have reliable probabilities of response, there are alternative techniques.

Before getting into the mechanics of these techniques, it might be helpful to clarify some terms that are used almost interchangeably but in fact have slightly different meanings: (1) *log-linear models,* (2) *logit models,* (3) *logit regression,* (4) *logistic models,* and (5) *logistic regression.*

The terms *regression* and *models* in this context mean the same thing, so we have only to define the differences among log-linear models, logit models, and logistic models.

Logit models and *logistic models* are essentially the same thing. In both cases, the dependent variable is the categorical yes/no, or 1/0, or respond/did not respond variable we work with in direct marketing. However, some of the computer programs that perform these analyses distinguish between logistic models and logit models. In statistical packages such as SAS where there is a difference, logistic models or programs are run when the independent variables include one or more continuous variables; logit programs are run when all the independent variables are categorical. However, there are other statistical packages in which logit programs accept both continuous and categorical independent variables.

Log-linear models are used when all variables are categorical. Technically, log-linear models do not distinguish between independent and dependent variables. We can, however, take the results of a log-linear model and declare one variable as the dependent variable and run what is essentially a logit model.

Log-linear and logit models, as well as ordinary regression models, can accept interaction variables but cannot systematically identify them—the models can only test the variables for significance. However, the CHAID technique (which we will discuss in detail shortly) does identify significant interaction variables that can then be used as variables in any of the three techniques just mentioned.

With that as background, let's examine logistic regression in more detail. It should be pointed out that the following material is mathematically difficult and some readers may want to skip ahead to the sections on discriminant analysis and CHAID.

Just remember, for most direct marketers, the bottom line with regard to logistic or logit modeling is that they are perfectly appropriate techniques and should be used provided your statistician is familiar with

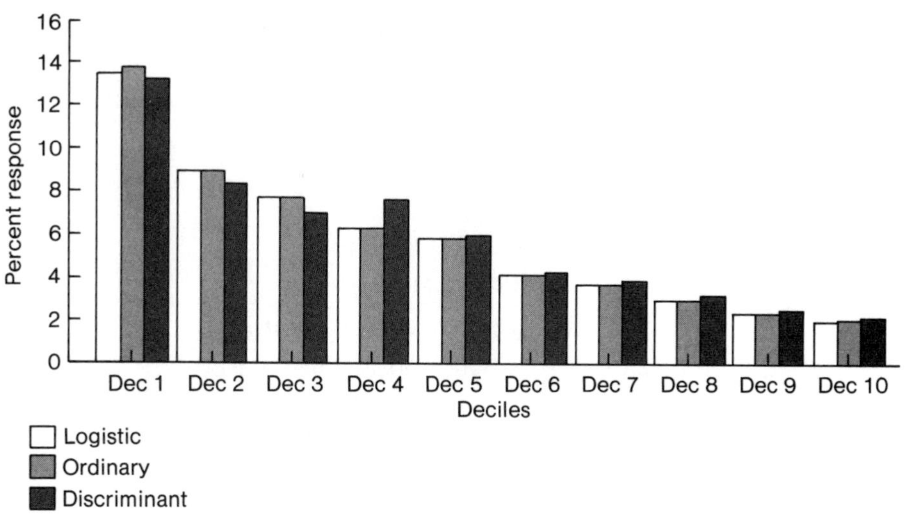

FIGURE 13–1
Comparison of Statistical Methods: OLS Regression, Logistic, and Discriminant

them. Not all statisticians are. On the other hand, if, as we said, you are using modeling to rank a large file in terms of each individual's probability of responding, the rankings developed with ordinary regression are likely to be equivalent to the rankings found using these more appropriate statistical techniques.

As a practical matter, most of the work involved in modeling projects has to do with understanding and massaging the available data. After all this preliminary work is done, it's a relatively simple matter to run the data through all three techniques: the LPM or ordinary least squares regression, discriminant analysis, or logit or logistic regression. Figure 13–1 shows the results of such a process. As you can see, from a ranking perspective the differences are not terribly different. More often than not we find this to be the case.

LOGISTIC REGRESSION

Concepts and Definition

The concepts that hold the logistic regression model together are these:

1. Probability
2. Odds
3. Logit
4. Odds ratio
5. Log odds

It takes a fair amount of algebra to transform raw yes/no data into a form that can be used in a logistic model. The algebra that follows is no more than a transformation, but the logic of the steps is not intuitively obvious. The reader who wishes to follow along is welcome but again, understanding how the transformation is accomplished is not necessary to understanding how to use the results.

To begin, let Y stand for the response to a mailing, where Y equals 1 for a yes response and 0 for a no response.

Let's define the probability of a response as p, and therefore the probability of a nonresponse is $(1 - p)$. (If the probability of a response is 5 percent, then the probability of a nonresponse is 95 percent.)

The next concept is the concept of *odds.* By definition, the odds of a yes response is the ratio of the probability of a response divided by the probability of a nonresponse.

$$\text{odds} = \frac{p}{(1-p)}$$

With a little algebra, the probability p can be expressed in terms of odds:

$$(1-p) \times \text{odds} = p$$
$$\text{odds} - p \times \text{odds} = p$$
$$\text{odds} = p + p \times \text{odds}$$
$$\text{odds} = p \times (1 + \text{odds})$$
$$p = \frac{\text{odds}}{(1 + \text{odds})}$$

We'll use this relationship later.

If the odds of a yes response are given by $p/(1-p)$, then the natural log of the odds of a yes response (log to the base e), denoted by *ln,* is

$$ln(\text{yes}) = ln(p/1-p) = ln(p) - ln(1-p)$$

This difference, the natural log of a yes response, is called the *logit* of yes.

Now, let's consider another variable X that takes on two values, a and b. Also, assume that Y depends on X, where

The probability of a yes response when $X = a$ is $p(a)$.
The probability of a no response when $X = a$ is $1 - p(a)$.
The probability of a yes response when $X = b$ is $p(b)$.
The probability of a no response when $X = b$ is $1 - p(b)$.

The odds of a yes response given $X = a$ is $p(a)/1 - p(a)$.
The log of a yes response given $X = a$ is

$$ln(\text{yes given } X = a) = ln\ p(a) - ln(1 - p(a))$$

This difference is called the *logit of yes given* $X = a$.
The odds of a yes response given $X = b$ is $p(b)/1 - p(b)$.
The log of a yes given $X = b$ is

$$ln(\text{yes given } X = b) = ln\ p(b) - ln(1 - p(b))$$

This difference is called the *logit of yes given* $X = b$.

The ratio of the odds of yes for $X = a$ to the odds of yes for $X = b$, called the *odds ratio,* is:

$$\frac{p(a)/1 - p(a)}{p(b)/1 - p(b)}$$

The log of odds ratio, called the *log odds* is:

$$ln\ (\text{odds ratio}) = (\text{Logit of yes given } X = a) - (\text{Logit of yes given } X = b)$$

Logistic Regression Model

All of the above algebra allows us to introduce the concept of a logistic regression model. The logistic regression model is a linear model in this form:

$$G = b0 + b1 \times X1 + b2 \times X2 + \ldots + bn \times Xn$$

TABLE 13–1

RESPONSE	*AGE*	*GENDER*
0	21	1
0	23	1
0	25	1
0	29	1
0	32	1
0	33	0
0	34	0
0	34	0
0	45	1
0	45	1
1	46	1
1	46	1
1	57	1
1	57	1
1	58	1
1	58	0
1	69	1
1	63	1
1	64	1
1	64	1

where

G = the logit of a yes response given specific values of $X1, X2, \ldots, Xn$. (Implicit in the phrase *yes response* is a categorical dependent variable with two values of yes and no)

$b0$ = the intercept, which, as in ordinary regression, can be viewed as a placeholder necessary to make the equation work well

$b1, \ldots, bn$ = logistic coefficients (to be discussed shortly)

EXAMPLE 15

Logistic Equation

Let's consider a sample of 20 customers from our cataloger's latest catalog mailing. The cataloger would like to build a model to predict response to this mailing for use in developing a list for future mailings of similar catalogs. The goal is to identify new customers on the file who have a high likelihood of responding to a similar program.

The 20 records consist of three variables: RESPONSE to the mailing (1 = yes/0 = no), AGE (in years), GENDER (0 = male/1 = female). (See Table 13–1.)

The variables of the model are the categorical dependent variable RESPONSE, the scalar independent variable AGE, and GENDER, a categorical independent variable.

Up to this point, all our independent variables were scalar. Can linear models, whether ordinary, logistic, or otherwise, handle categorical independent variables? Yes.

TABLE 13–2

SOURCE OF ORDER	*D1*	*D2*
Direct mail	1	0
Print	0	1
Other	0	0

Dummy Variables

The trick for putting categorical independent variables into any regression model is to create dummy variables. Suppose, for example, that the categorical variable is SOURCE OF ORDER, which has been coded as direct mail, print, and other. This case requires two dummy variables. The first dummy variable, *D*1, is coded 1 if the individual's source is direct mail, and 0 if the individual's source is print or other. The second dummy variable, *D*2, is coded 1 if the individual was acquired from a print source, and 0 if acquired from direct mail or other.

Accordingly, if an individual was acquired from a direct mail source, then for that person, *D*1 equals 1 and *D*2 equals 0; if an individual was acquired from a print source, then *D*1 equals 0 and *D*2 equals 1; and, if the source were neither direct mail nor print, that is, an other, then *D*1 and *D*2 are both equal to 0. Table 13–2 shows the dummy variables for SOURCE OF ORDER.

Thus, whenever a categorical independent variable is to be put into a model, we simply create a set of dummy variables (the number of variables in the set is equal to the number of category values minus 1).

Because the GENDER variable has only two values, which implies that only one dummy variable coded 1 if female and 0 otherwise (for male) is needed, GENDER is already a dummy variable. GENDER, as is, can go directly into the model.

Running the data through a logistic regression program produces the logistic equation shown below:

$$G = -10.83 + .28 \times \text{AGE} + 2.30 \times \text{GENDER}$$

G is the logit of a yes response to the mailing given specific values of AGE and GENDER.

Let's see what *G* is all about. Consider a male customer age 40 (GENDER = 0 and AGE = 40). His *G* or logit score is

$$\begin{aligned} G(0,40) &= -10.83 + .28 \times 40 + 2.30 \times 0 \\ &= -10.83 + 11.2 + 0 \\ &= .37 \text{ logits} \end{aligned}$$

A female customer of the same age would have a score of 2.67:

$$\begin{aligned} G(1,40) &= -10.83 + .28 \times 40 + 2.30 \times 1 \\ &= -10.83 + 11.2 + 2.30 \\ &= 2.67 \text{ logits} \end{aligned}$$

Logits, with the aid of tables, can be converted into odds, which can be converted into probabilities.

Accordingly, we have

Odds of yes response for a 40-year-old male = .37 logits = 1.44

Odds of yes response for a 40-year-old female = 2.67 logits = 14.44

recalling from above that

$$p = \frac{\text{odds}}{(1 + \text{odds})}$$

For the 40-year-old male

$$p = 1.44/(1 + 1.44)$$
$$p = .59$$

For the 40-year-old female

$$p = 14.44/(1 + 14.44)$$
$$p = .93$$

Thus, the 40-year-old male customer has a 59 percent probability of response. The female customer has a probability of 93 percent.

Logistic Coefficients

Because *G* is in logits, the coefficients are also in logits. Because we can unlog *G* logits to obtain odds, we can unlog the coefficients, too. Doing this will give us the meaning of the coefficients and add to our understanding of a logit.

Let's consider the coefficient of AGE, .28, that is, .28 logits. Unlogging the coefficient of .28, we have 1.32, that is, the odds of a yes response is 1.32. Thus, for every one-year increase in age, the odds of a yes response increase 1.32 times. Let's see.

The *G* logit score for a male 41-year-old is

$$\begin{aligned} G(0,41) &= -10.83 + .28 \times 41 + 2.30 \times 0 \\ &= -10.83 + 11.48 + 0 \\ &= .65 \text{ logits} \end{aligned}$$

The odds corresponding to .65 logits is 1.92 and the odds for a 40-year-old male corresponding to .37 logits is 1.44 (as calculated above); thus, the increase in the odds for a male when his age increases one year is 1.32 times (1.92/1.44 = 1.32).

Now that we have some idea of where logits come from, let's remind ourselves of how they are used. If everyone on a file is scored and the scores are in terms of logits, the scores, that is, the logits, can still be ranked from high to low and the traditional decile analysis can be performed. You recall that we, and others, argue that most of the time the ranking based on a logit analysis will be equivalent, from a practical decision-making perspective, to the rankings resulting from an ordinary regression analysis. On the other hand, each individual logit score can be transformed back into a specific probability of response, a probability that will always be between 0 and 1, which is not always the case in regression.

One last point. Although it is one thing to find a statistician who can build a logit model, it is another thing to find computer programmers who have the skills and tools available to translate logits back into probabilities. Scoring in logits and ranking in logits is simple because to the computer, a logit is just another number. This is a similar problem to the one of presenting a programmer with an ordinary regression equation that requires the use of logs or exponential functions. The point to be remembered is to always check with data processing to make sure any solution you come up with can be implemented.

DISCRIMINANT ANALYSIS

In the preceding discussion, we mentioned discriminant analysis as an alternative to regression when the dependent variable is a categorical yes/no or 1/0 response variable. The independent variables can be either scalar or categorical with the use of dummy variables, and interaction variables can also be included, just as in multiple regression.

Discriminant analysis is a statistical technique that was developed to identify variables that explain the differences between two or more groups (e.g., responders and nonresponders of a mailing) and that classify unknown observations (for example, customers) into the groups. The discriminant model looks like a multiple regression model where the categorical dependent variable is again expressed as a sum of weighted independent or discriminant variables.

$$Z = b0 + b1 \times X1 + b2 \times X2 + b3 \times X3 + \ldots + bn \times Xn$$

The weights (the *b*s), called *discriminant coefficients,* are derived such that the resultant discriminant model maximizes the statistical difference among the groups. It is interesting to note that in regression, the coefficients are derived to maximize *R*-square. Thus, both techniques are very similar in their maximizing derivation. In addition, both methods depend on certain assumptions about the normality of the variables that go into the model.

In a simple two-group discriminant analysis, if an individual's *Z* score is greater than some critical value determined by experience, the individual is placed in group 1; if the *Z* score is less than that value, the individual is placed in group 2. The evaluation of the model is based on whether or not the model places persons into groups more accurately than would occur by chance.

However, in practice discriminant analysis is more sensitive to violations of normality than regression. This is particularly true when the size of the two groups is very different, as is the case in response analysis when the yes group is generally below 10 percent. Although we try to reshape the data as best we can for those situations where the best we can do in reexpression is not enough, discriminant models will not perform as well as regression models. Therefore, a conservative approach is to stick with ordinary regression or logistic regression over discriminant analysis.

AUTOMATIC INTERACTION DETECTION—AID/CHAID

Thus far, we've described and illustrated two regression methods. If the dependent variable is scalar and the independent variables are scalar, categorical, or both then ordinary regression is the appropriate method to use. If the dependent variable is a categorical 0/1 response variable and the independent variables are scalar, categorical, or both, we can, in most circumstances, still use ordinary regression if the application is only to rank a file from most to least likely to respond. If good reliable estimates of probability of response are needed, then we must use the logistic regression method.

Now, we discuss two complementary methods to ordinary and logistic regression: Automatic Interaction Detection (AID) and CHAID. In an AID analysis, the dependent variable is scalar. In CHAID, the dependent variable is categorical, and the independent variables in either are categorical. If an independent variable is scalar, it must be transformed into a categorical variable. This is not hard to do—the analyst simply breaks the scalar variable into ranges. For example, Sales, which is a scalar variable, can be expressed in ranges of $0 to $9.99, $10 to $19.99, $20 to $49.99, and so on.

Notice the word *interaction.* This is the same interaction as previously discussed in the context of interaction variables. AID/CHAID was originally developed for the express purpose of finding interaction variables for inclusion into a regression, logit, or log-linear model.

As it turns out, today AID/CHAID is often used as an "end" analysis rather than as a "means" to provide insight for further model building. We'll discuss the use of AID/CHAID as both a complement to regression and as a stand-alone technique.

First, let's explain the differences between AID and CHAID. AID was developed in the 1960s at the University of Michigan as a method to identify segments of a market. It defines the segments in terms of *two-level* categorical independent variables. For example, an AID "model" with two independent variables (MARITAL STATUS and COLLEGE EDUCATED), each with two possibilities (MARRIED/NOT MARRIED, COLLEGE/NO COLLEGE), can divide a market into four segments:

1. Married, with college
2. Married, without college
3. Unmarried, with college
4. Unmarried, without college

Later, two significant improvements to the method were introduced. First, multiway splits of the independent variable were allowed—no longer was it necessary for the independent variables to be limited to two-way splits. Second, the differences between end-point cells in an AID analysis were not subject to a test of statistical significance. This deficiency was eliminated with the introduction of the chi-square test for statistical significance—thus, the addition of CH in CHAID, which stands for the chi-square test of statistical significance. Dr. Gordon V. Kass is credited with the development of the CHAID methodology.[1] Jay Magidson enhanced the basic CHAID program with a series of features that make CHAID more useful to direct marketers and produced a product called SI-CHAID™, which is now marketed by SPSS. (SI stands for Statistical Innovation, the name of Magidson's company.)

[1] G V Kass, "Significance Testing in, and Some Extensions of, Automatic Interaction Detection" (doctoral dissertation, University of Witwatersrand, Johannesburg, South Africa, 1976).

EXAMPLE 16

Let's illustrate the use of CHAID by making one last return to our cataloger, who now believes that it is possible to build a predictive response model based on knowledge of these basic factors:

1. How long a customer has been on the database (HOW__LONG).
2. What part of the country the customer lives in (REGION).
3. Whether or not the customer is married (MARITAL).

A random sample of approximately 40,000 customers who received a recent mailing was drawn. The data was coded as follows:

1. HOW__LONG
   a. Less than 1 year (coded 1)
   b. 1–2 years (coded 2)
   c. 2 years, plus (coded 3)
   d. Years unknown (coded 4)
2. REGION
   a. Northeast (coded 1)
   b. East (coded 2)
   c. Southeast (coded 3)
   d. Midwest (coded 4)
   e. Midsouth (coded 5)
   f. Northwest (coded 6)
   g. Southwest (coded 7)
3. MARITAL
   a. Divorced/separated (coded 1)
   b. Married (coded 2)
   c. Single (coded 3)
   d. Widowed (coded 4)
   e. Unknown (coded 5)
4. RESPONSE (to the last mailing)
   a. Yes (coded 1)
   b. No (coded 2)

The average response rate was 12.59 percent. Table 13–3 shows response rates by each level of the variables HOW__LONG, REGION, and MARITAL. In a regression model, each break will be treated as an independent variable. Not yet having heard of CHAID, the analyst runs an ordinary dummy variable regression analysis. Table 13–4 shows the results of that analysis.

Table 13–4 depicts a result that direct marketers are becoming accustomed to seeing: a significant model ($F = 58.295$), with significant independent variables (*t*s range from 4.2 to 9.0, and all *p*-values are less than .0001), and an almost nonexistent *R*-square of .0071 or .71 percent.

As we said, the real proof of the usefulness of a predictive model is in the analysis of a validation sample. In Table 13–5, we apply the model to a second sample of 40,000 names and look to see how well the model "spreads" the average response rate.

TABLE 13–3
Results by Segments of Individual Variables (in Percents)

HOW_LONG 1 = 13.98%	MARITAL 1 = 13.66
HOW_LONG 2 = 13.40	MARITAL 2 = 12.95
HOW_LONG 3 = 11.12	MARITAL 3 = 12.21
HOW_LONG 4 = 14.24	MARITAL 4 = 5.76
	MARITAL 5 = 12.25
REGION 1 = 9.44	
REGION 2 = 13.00	
REGION 3 = 15.53	
REGION 4 = 12.85	
REGION 5 = 14.93	
REGION 6 = 11.29	
REGION 7 = 13.20	

TABLE 13–4

```
Model: RESP_HAT
Dependent Variable: RESPONSE
                         Analysis of Variance
                           Sum of          Mean
Source          DF        Squares        Square       F Value      Prob>F
Model            5       33.00807       6.60161        58.295      0.0001
Error        40581     4595.56640       0.11324
C Total      40586     4628.57447
      Root MSE        0.33652     R-square      0.0071
      Dep Mean        0.13127     Adj R-sq      0.0070
      C. V.         256.34856
                          Parameter Estimates
                    Parameter      Standard       T for H0:
Variable     DF      Estimate         Error     Parameter=0     Prob>|T|
INTERCEP     1       0.149570    0.00270699          55.253       0.0000
MARITAL4     1      -0.070960    0.00784734          -9.042       0.0001
HOW_LNG3     1      -0.027374    0.00335740          -8.153       0.0001
REGION1      1      -0.034529    0.00434860          -7.940       0.0001
REGION3      1       0.028100    0.00564363           4.979       0.0001
REGION5      1       0.024340    0.00566267           4.298       0.0001
                 Standardized
Variable     DF      Estimate
INTERCEP     1     0.00000000
MARITAL4     1    -0.04497071
HOW_LNG3     1    -0.04052533
REGION1      1    -0.04058342
REGION3      1     0.02524823
REGION5      1     0.02181160
```

The model spreads the average response rate fairly well. The best 14.4 percent of the names mailed pulled 17.1 percent, the bottom 13.9 percent pulled 8 percent, and another 9.8 percent pulled 11 percent. The question is, "Can we do better?" and specifically, "Can CHAID identify important interactions between the independent variables that regression did not explicitly take into account?" Remember, regression has no provision to automatically look for interactions; it has to be told that interactions exist.

TABLE 13–5
Ordinary Dummy Variable Regression Model

Regression Segments	*Quantity*	*Number of Responses*	*Percent Mailing*	*Cumulative Percent Mailing*	*Percent Response*	*Cumulative Percent Response*
1	2,097	361	5.2%	5.2%	17.2%	6.8%
2	3,756	642	9.3	14.4	17.1	18.8
3	12,194	1,829	30.0	44.4	15.0	53.1
4	1,948	269	4.8	49.3	13.8	58.2
5	10,975	1,339	27.0	76.3	12.2	83.3
6	3,986	438	9.8	86.1	11.0	91.5
7	5,691	450	13.9	100.0	8.0	100.0
Total	40,587	5,223	100.0%		13.1%	

TABLE 13–6

Before Merging	*After Initial Merging*
HOW_LONG 1 = 13.98%	HOW_LONG 124 = 14.06
HOW_LONG 2 = 13.40	HOW_LONG 3 = 11.12
HOW_LONG 3 = 11.12	
HOW_LONG 4 = 14.24	
REGION 1 = 9.44	REGION 1 = 9.44
REGION 2 = 13.00	REGION 247 = 12.96
REGION 3 = 15.53	REGION 35 = 15.23
REGION 4 = 12.85	REGION 6 = 11.29
REGION 5 = 14.93	
REGION 6 = 11.29	
REGION 7 = 13.20	
MARITAL 1 = 13.66	MARITAL 1235 = 12.94
MARITAL 2 = 12.95	MARITAL 4 = 5.76
MARITAL 3 = 12.21	
MARITAL 4 = 5.76	
MARITAL 5 = 12.25	

THE SI-CHAID ANALYSIS OF THE SAME DATA

The SI-CHAID program begins by presenting the response rates for each segment of each variable, and then uses the chi-square test to combine segments that are not statistically different from each other. (See Table 13–6.)

Table 13–6 tells us that the SI-CHAID program has found no statistical difference among the HOW_LONG variables 1, 2, and 4, so it has combined them into HOW_LONG 124. Similarly, it has combined REGIONS 2, 4, and 7 and REGIONS 3 and 5 into two new variables: REGION 247 and REGION 35. The five original marital variables have been reduced to two variables.

The solution of the CHAID analysis is in the form of a tree diagram, found in Figure 13–2. There are seven end segments defined by the three independent variables HOW_LONG, REGION, and MARITAL, even though there were 105 possible segments (3 times 7 times 5) before the segments within variables were combined and 16 possible segments after the segments within variables were combined (2 times 4 times 2).

FIGURE 13–2

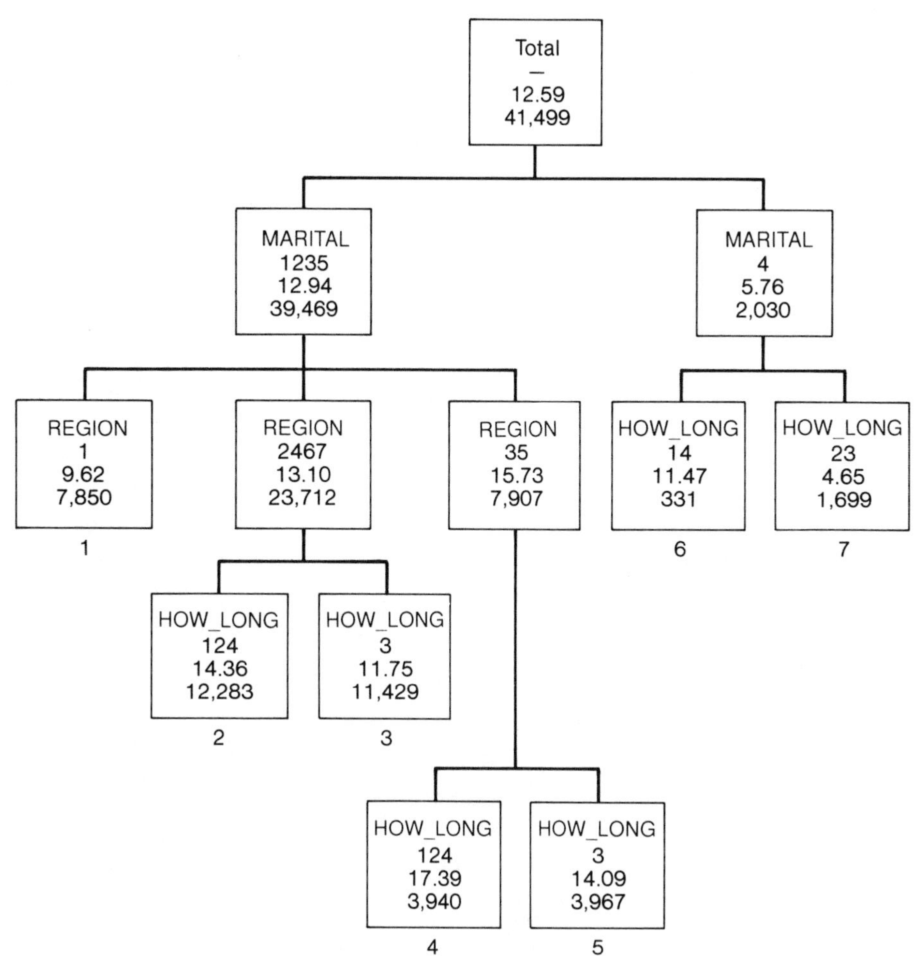

Notice that of the three "main effects" variables (MARITAL, HOW__LONG, and REGION), the CHAID program determined that MARITAL with the two new levels of 1, 2, 3, and 5 versus 4 was the single best predictor of response.

Next, CHAID treats the two segments of MARITAL as the starting point for two new analyses. CHAID now attempts to split the MARITAL cell (MARITAL 1235) by either REGION or HOW__LONG. CHAID determines that MARITAL 1235 is "best" (largest statistically significant difference) divided by REGION, resulting in three new levels (REGION 1 versus REGION 2467 and REGION 35). On the other hand, the cell identified as MARITAL 4, at this point, is "best" further divided by the variable HOW__LONG with two new levels HOW__LONG 14 and HOW__LONG 23.

Notice how REGION 6 has been combined with REGIONS 2, 4, and 7. Originally REGION 6 could not be combined with any of the other REGIONs, but after MARITAL 4 is removed from consideration, those persons in REGION 6 look statistically similar to those in REGIONs 2, 4, and 7. This is what we mean when we say that the process is repeated from the beginning at each new level in the tree.

TABLE 13–7
Model Based on CHAID Analysis

CHAID Segments	*Quantity*	*Number of Responses*	*Percent Mailing*	*Cumulative Percent Mailing*	*Percent Response*	*Cumulative Percent Response*
4	3,940	685	9.5%	9.5%	17.39%	13.1%
2	12,283	1,764	29.6	39.1	14.36	46.9
5	3,967	559	9.6	48.7	14.09	57.6
3	11,429	1,343	27.5	76.2	11.75	83.3
6	331	38	0.8	77.0	11.47	84.0
1	7,850	755	18.9	95.9	9.62	98.5
7	1,699	79	4.1	100.0	4.65	100.0
Total	41,499	5,223	100.0%			

The two HOW__LONG segments (segments 6 and 7 on the CHAID tree) are considered end or final segments because the remaining variable (REGION) does not provide any further predictive splitting power. The same holds true for segment 1, which cannot be split by HOW__LONG.

Thus, at this "depth" of the tree, there are three final segments defined as follows:

Segment 1—Customers who are either divorced/separated, married, single, or marital status unknown *and* live in the northeast region of the country. These customers have an average response rate of 9.62 percent, somewhat below the house file average of 12.59 percent, which is indicated in the top box of the tree.

Segment 6—Widowed customers who have been on the database less than one year or for an unknown number of years; these customers have an average response rate of 11.47 percent and consist of approximately 1 percent of the file (331/41,499).

Segment 7—Widowed customers who have been on the file two years or more. These customers have an average response rate of 4.65 percent.

The remaining two cells (defined by REGION 2467 and REGION 35) are both split by the HOW__LONG variables with the same combined levels (HOW__LONG 124 and HOW__LONG 3), resulting in four final segments. Segment 4 has the largest average response rate of 17.39 percent, significantly above the overall average 12.59 percent, and consists of a reasonable market size of 9.5 percent of the house file.

At this point, we could stop and use the results of the SI-CHAID analysis as the sole basis for segmenting the database, or we could use the results of the CHAID analysis as input to a regression model. If we were to stop here, we would have the model shown in Table 13–7.

As mentioned previously, many mailers will stop at this point and use the CHAID output to segment their file and mail accordingly. Others may use the CHAID output as input into a regression or a logit model, attempting to build a model with more predictive power than the CHAID model.

How does the CHAID solution compare to the dummy variable regression solution? Essentially, the results are the same. The CHAID solution appears to have identified a small, poor-performing segment of the file (4.1 percent of the names mailed that pulled only 4.65 percent) that the regression model missed, but we really can't be sure of that without looking much more closely at a ranking of the bottom 4.1 percent of the file scored with the regression model. And that's not easy to do. Another, easier way to see what CHAID has added to our understanding is to use the results of the CHAID analysis in a regression model.

USING CHAID IN REGRESSION ANALYSIS

There are lots of ways to use the information gained by CHAID in a regression model. One way is to take advantage of what the CHAID model tells us about the breaks within the main variables HOW__LONG, MARITAL, and REGION, as well as what CHAID tells us about the important interactions among the main variables.

For simplicity let's examine just the second level breaks shown in Figure 13–2. If we use a * to indicate the interaction between two main variables we see the following:

Second Level Breaks
MARITAL__1235 * REGION__1 = 9.62
MARITAL__1235 * REGION__2467 = 13.10
MARITAL__1235 * REGION__35 = 15.73
MARITAL__4 * HOW LONG__14 = 11.47
MARITAL__4 * HOW LONG__23 = 4.65

Given these five mutually exclusive categories we can create four dummy variables and use these dummy variables in a regression equation. Because the response rate to MARITAL 1235 * Region 2467 is closest to the average response rate of 12.59 we will use this category as the neutral or base case in setting up the dummy variables.

	Dummy Variables			
Conditions	*M1R1*	*M1R3*	*M4H1*	*M4H2*
MARITAL__1235 * REGION__1	1	0	0	0
MARITAL__1235 * REGION__35	0	1	0	0
MARITAL__4 * HOW LONG__14	0	0	1	0
MARITAL__4 * HOW LONG__23	0	0	0	1

The results of a regression model using all the dummy variables defined above is presented in Table 13–8. The significant variables turned out to be REGION 1, REGION 35, HOW__LONG 3, and the interaction variables: M4H2, M4H1, and M1R3.

Did the regression model provide the user with a better model? The answer to this question is in Table 13–9, which presents the validation results for the model built with the CHAID variables, and in Table 13–10, which compares the two regression models, the one built without the knowledge of interactions (Table 13–5) and the one just built with knowledge of interactions (Table 13–9).

As you can see from a comparison of the two models, the CHAID-enhanced model does the better job at the extremes. It identifies a small group (about 5 percent) that pulls 19.7 percent, compared to a similar-sized

TABLE 13–8

```
Model: RESP_HAT
Dependent Variable: RESPONSE
                          Analysis of Variance
                          Sum of          Mean
Source          DF       Squares         Square         F Value      Prob>F
Model            6      34.53475        5.75579          50.842      0.0001
Error        40580    4594.03972        0.11321
C Total      40586    4628.57447
     Root MSE       0.33647     R-square      0.0075
     Dep Mean       0.13127     Adj R-sq      0.0073
     C. V.        256.30914
                           Parameter Estimates
                     Parameter        Standard       T for H0:
Variable      DF      Estimate          Error       Parameter=0    Prob>|T|
INTERCEP       1      0.149459      0.00271559        55.037        0.0000
REGION1        1     -0.034585      0.00434798        -7.954        0.0001
REGION35       1      0.048844      0.00906417         5.389        0.0001
HOW_LONG3      1     -0.026411       0.0033888        -7.794        0.0001
M4H2           1     -0.084690      0.00883210        -9.589        0.0001
M4H1           1      0.044651      0.01928074        -2.316        0.0206
M1R3           1      0.028018      0.00980542         2.857        0.0043
                   Standardized
Variable      DF      Estimate
INTERCEP       1     0.00000000
REGION1        1    -0.04064964
REGION35       1     0.05834542
HOW_LONG3      1    -0.03910062
M4H2           1    -0.04918049
M4H1           1    -0.01165782
M1R3           1    -0.03087002
```

TABLE 13–9
Regression Model Using Information From CHAID

Regression Segments	*Quantity*	*Number of Responses*	*Percent Mailing*	*Cumulative Percent Mailing*	*Percent Response*	*Cumulative Percent Response*
1	1,976	379	4.6%	4.6%	19.7%	7.3%
2	3,554	608	8.6	13.2	17.1	18.9
3	12,202	1,830	29.4	42.7	15.0	53.9
4	3,302	466	8.0	50.6	14.1	62.8
5	10,975	1,218	26.5	77.1	11.1	86.1
6	4,034	403	9.7	86.8	50.0	93.8
7	5,456	322	13.2	100.0	5.9	100.0
Total	41,499	5,227	100.0%			

group that pulled only 17.2 percent, and on the bottom it identified a relatively large group that pulls only about 6 percent, as compared to a similar-sized group that pulled about 8 percent.

Are these results typical? That's a very hard question to answer. The results can be more (or less) dramatic than those shown in the example used. Certainly, when the effect of interaction does not work in the same direction for all combinations of variables, the results can be much more

TABLE 13–10
A Comparison of Regression Results

Regression Segments	Regression without Interaction Effects			Regression with Interaction Effects		
	Quantity	*Percent Mailing*	*Percent Response*	*Quantity*	*Percent Mailing*	*Percent Response*
1	2,097	5.2%	17.2%	1,976	4.6%	19.7%
2	3,756	9.3	17.1	3,554	8.6	17.1
3	12,194	30.0	15.0	12,202	29.4	15.0
4	1,948	4.8	13.8	3,302	8.0	14.1
5	10,975	27.0	12.2	10,975	26.5	11.1
6	3,986	9.8	11.0	4,034	9.7	50.0
7	5,691	13.9	8.0	5,456	13.2	5.9
Total	40,587	100.0%		41,499	100.0%	

TABLE 13–11
***The Effect of Interaction When the Effect of Variable* A *Depends on the Value of Variable* B**

Average response rate	= 4%
Response among men	= 3%
Response among women	= 5%
Response to COPY A among both groups	= 4%
Response to COPY B among both groups	= 4%
Response to COPY A among men	= 1%
Response to COPY B among men	= 5%
Response to COPY A among women	= 7%
Response to COPY B among women	= 3%

important. For example, take two variables—SEX and ADVERTISING COPY—each of which was split two ways—MALE/FEMALE and COPY A/COPY B. If COPY A had a positive effect on men and a negative effect on women, and COPY B worked in the reverse way, that is, a positive effect on females and negative on men, a model that took these two variables (SEX and COPY) into consideration but failed to look at the interactions of SEX and COPY would be incomplete and potentially misleading.

An examination of Table 13–11 indicates that a test of MALE versus FEMALE would conclude that females respond better than males. Without looking at the different effect COPY has on each SEX, one would also conclude that COPY had no effect on response when in fact COPY A increases response among women and decreases response among men. COPY B has the reverse effect; it increases response among men and decreases response among women. A regression model that had only two dummy variables, one for SEX and one for COPY, would not discover this interaction effect, and could in fact produce misleading results—an incorrect ranking of the four combinations of the variables. However, a regression analysis that included an interaction variable that was the product of the two dummy variables would take the interaction into account and produce a correct ranking of the four combinations of SEX and COPY.

The lesson to be learned is that interactions can be very important and a search for interactions should be one of the first steps in the modeling process. A summary of that process follows.

MULTIPLE REGRESSION: GUIDELINES FOR BUILDING A MODEL

The following are basic guidelines for building a multiple regression model:

1. Know your data, or work with someone who does. A data analyst without a working knowledge of your data is a data analyst who's going to get you in trouble.
2. Start with an examination of a correlation matrix to develop ideas about candidate variables and to check for two-variable multicollinearity.
3. Look at your data using stem-and-leaf displays. If the data is not normal, attempt to normalize it using the transformations we suggested.
4. Plot your original and transformed data two variables at a time, for all pairs of variables. Examine all the relationships to make sure they are straight.
5. Try some interaction variables, using your knowledge of the business or CHAID.
6. Select variables for inclusion into the model using all the approaches discussed: your choice of variables, stepwise selections, and models based on the C(p) statistic.
7. Validate the model on fresh data.

Chapter 14

Segmentation Analysis

In Chapters 11 through 13 of this section, we concentrated on predictive models. Predictive models are designed, as their name implies, to predict some outcome, for example, response to a mailing, returns, bad debts, sales volume, and so on.

In this chapter, we turn our attention to segmentation models. Segmentation models are designed to assign people or geographic areas to groups or clusters on the basis of the similarities in characteristics or attributes that describe them rather than on the basis of some specific action such as response to a mailing.[1]

In Chapter 2, we discussed the many segmentation products available to direct marketers: PRIZM, ClusterPlus, ACORN, MicroVision, and so on. All these products combine small geographic units, usually census block group, into larger units or clusters based on similarities among the block groups. The characteristics or attributes examined in making this decision include each area's values on the many census (and other) variables collected by the Census Bureau and other government and private agencies.

In this chapter, we will discuss the two primary statistical techniques used in building segmentation models: factor analysis and cluster analysis. These techniques can be used to build customized segmentation models of customers and prospects based on survey and customer or prospect performance information, as well as segmentation models based on census data.

One of direct marketing's unique strengths as a promotional medium is its potential ability to make customized promotional offers to individual customers through the use of available or inferred information about each customer. Unfortunately, all too often, this potential capability is still not adequately utilized. Most direct mail packages are still not customized for the recipient: The same package is usually sent to every name on the mailing. True, laser technology is often used to print the recipient's name in a dozen places in the package, and the recipient's address may be mentioned in the letter, but the guts of the offer are for the most part not customized. The product, the price, the terms, and the strategy are most often identical. And yet one would expect, intuitively, that just as different recipients have different buying preferences, a mailing would work better if its offer were tailored to each individual's specific needs.

Such targeting and customization of the offer is different in concept from the kind of list segmentation and decile analysis covered earlier in the discussions of predictive modeling. Predictive modeling is used to

[1]In Chapter 13, we treated CHAID as a tool to be used in predictive modeling. CHAID also may be used as a segmentation tool when the final step in the analysis is the CHAID model itself.

indicate *which* segment of a list should be mailed, or how often. It does not tell you *how* that segment of the list, or that individual name, should be mailed, in terms of the kind of offer that is most likely to be successful with that segment.

DATA NEEDED FOR SEGMENTATION MODELING

In customizing offers for each segment, the direct marketer uses the data on hand about the customer. At minimum, the direct marketer knows each customer by name, address, and ZIP code, and the list the customer's name came from. If this list is a response list of some kind, the mailer knows what kind of product or service the name responded to. It is sometimes possible to negotiate even more detailed information from the list owner, such as the amount of money spent, previous buying history, and so on. Even better, if promotion and sales history is maintained on a customer database, the direct marketer will know what this customer purchased in the past, how often he or she purchased, how purchases were paid for, and so forth. To this data could be added individual information from customer surveys on, for example, demographic characteristics, attitudes, and interests. Finally, actual or inferred demographic or lifestyle characteristics or both could be overlaid on the existing data; these could come from census, or survey sources (see Chapter 2 on sources of primary and secondary data).

The marketer's task now is to "beat the data till it confesses" on what kind of offer to mail each customer. Because it is usually impractical, infeasible, and financially ruinous to customize the offer to every individual mailing recipient, the best we can usually do is to assign names to a relatively small number of homogeneous groups, so we can send the people in each group the same mailing and different groups, clusters, or consumer segments (the three terms are used interchangeably) different mailings.

In discussing factor and cluster analysis, the techniques that make up segmentation analysis, our objective is to provide enough information to make you an *informed user* of these techniques—but definitely not an expert. To become an expert in these techniques usually requires several years of instruction and experience, and such expertise is more effectively "bought" than "made." After reading the following pages, you should know when to call for these kinds of analyses, how to conduct or manage a segmentation study yourself, how to understand the most important elements of the computer output that accompanies these procedures, and what questions to ask of an expert, if you decide to work with one.

FACTOR ANALYSIS: WHAT IT IS AND WHEN YOU SHOULD USE IT

Factor analysis is a technique used to reduce data to a workable form so it can then be used for some other analysis (like cluster analysis, discussed below, or response modeling using multiple regression, discussed earlier). Technically, the output of a factor analysis can be quite revealing in and of itself, and some researchers find it unnecessary to go further. However, we will treat the output of a factor analysis as input to another procedure.

Factor analysis is usually called for when there is too much data to deal with intuitively or statistically. It may seem paradoxical to marketers who are continually searching for more and better information about their customers to talk about situations where you have too much data, yet these situations can easily occur. Leaf through an information vendor's catalog and you will often find hundreds of pieces of information available. Look through what the Census Bureau has to offer, and you will find each ZIP code or census block described on more than 200 different variables. Conduct a customer survey on attitudes, lifestyles, opinions, interests, and values, and you will probably ask 200 different questions.

Two things happen when you get a huge amount of information. First, it just becomes too much to absorb and comprehend. (There is a well-known psychological principle that says humans cannot, at one time, hold more than seven pieces of information in working consciousness.) Second, it can become difficult to work with this mass of data, both statistically and operationally. Not only can it eat up huge amounts of computer memory, it can actually seriously distort the results of many statistical analyses, as we discussed earlier in Chapter 12 under multicollinearity. If you get, say, 150 pieces of information about a person or a ZIP code, it is very likely that some of those pieces of information will be highly related. For example, if you try to explain response rates to a mailing across different ZIP codes in terms of the average education and income levels of each ZIP code, your statistical coefficients for these two variables can get distorted because income and education are often highly related. This could threaten the validity of some statistical analyses.

In such situations, you need factor analysis. What factor analysis does is to take your 150 different pieces of information and reduce them to far fewer, say 20 (or 10 or 30). The reduced pieces of information are now called *factors* or *components.* The bulk (say, 75 percent) of the information contained in the 150 original pieces of information is now contained in the 20 factors. Factor analysis enables you to sacrifice some of the information you began with (in this example, 100 percent minus 75 percent, or 25 percent), for the benefit of greatly improved economy of processing and parsimony of description.

As an example: Suppose you buy Census Bureau data describing every ZIP code on 150 different variables such as percent male population, percent white, percent earning above $35,000, percent with two or more cars, median monthly mortgage, percent homeowner, percent with four or more years of college education, percent in white-collar occupations, and so on. These variables represent 100 percent of the raw information. You wish to use these census data to help you analyze statistically the results of a mailing. Having read this book, you know that (1) 150 raw variables are too many to work with and (2) factor analysis is the way to cope with this surfeit of data. After you or your statistical analyst factor analyze the data, you will be able to describe each ZIP code in terms of its scores on (perhaps) 20 factors, instead of the 150 original variables. In doing so, you will lose—willingly—some of the richness of the original data. Sacrificing perhaps 20 to 30 percent of the raw information you started out with is the price you pay for the benefit of a dramatic reduction in the number of ZIP code descriptors (from 150 variables to 20 factors) that you now have to work with.

HOW FACTOR ANALYSIS WORKS

There are actually many variation of factor analysis techniques. The one we are describing here is more accurately labeled *principal components analysis,* and what we are referring to as factors are what finicky statisticians would call *components.* But we will continue, for our purposes, to call them factors, for that is what nonstatisticians call them.

You need to understand essentially three key things about how factor analysis works. First, each factor is really a composite, or combination, of original raw variables. The score of each person or ZIP code on each factor is thus a weighted combination of the scores of each person or ZIP code on each of the original, raw variables. Factor analysis combines those raw variables that are highly related among themselves into composite factors, thereby allowing you to let this combination replace those original raw variables. Thus, if average income levels, average monthly mortgage payments, and the percent of households with two or more cars were highly correlated in the actual data, factor analysis would combine these three into a factor (which you might label "affluence"), and you could then create factor scores for each ZIP code for this factor. (In actual practice, the factor score would use information on all the raw variables, but these three would be the ones carrying the highest weights.)

If a ZIP code had average income of $40,000, average monthly mortgage payments of $1,500, and 30 percent of households owning two or more cars, the factor analysis computer output would tell you what weights to apply to these raw numbers to create the factor score (for example, .0035, .25, and 300.17). Thus, the factor score on this factor for this ZIP code would be (.0035 × 40,000) + (.25 × 1,500) + (300.17 × .30), which equals 605.0510. So in subsequent analyses you would not use those three original numbers ($40,000, $1,500, and 30 percent) but one composite factor score (605.0510). This is the data-reduction service of factor analysis.

Importantly, when factor analysis gives you these factor coefficients (similar to regression coefficients), called *loadings,* it does so in a manner that the factor scores you create (for the first, second, and third factor, and so on) have a zero correlation with each other. Thus, you can use them as independent (predictor) variables in a multiple regression without any danger of the problems of multicollinearity, which occurs when the independent variables are highly related to each other. These factor scores, as we just said, are not related to each other at all because of the way we do factor analysis. (A technical note: to get such uncorrelated factors, your analyst will have to ask the computer for *orthogonal* factors.)

The second key idea is that factor analysis "shifts" the information you feed to it for analysis. Suppose we give it 150 census variables to analyze. Let us say that each of these raw variables has a value, going in, of one *information unit* each. (Statisticians call this an *eigenvalue.*) So we are feeding the computer a total of 150 units of information, with each raw variable having exactly one unit. Factor analysis is a little like performing a centrifugal operation on milk to let the cream float to the top. If you think of the cream as being rich in information, factor analysis shifts the information when it creates the factors so that the first factor it creates is richest in information content, the next one a little less so, and so on, till the last one barely contains any—its information value (or eigenvalue) is close to zero.

In fact, the mathematics of factor analysis are such that if you feed it 150 raw variables (each with a raw information value of 1), the computer solution will initially give you 150 factors—as many as the number of variables you put in—but with this key difference: the first factors now contain most of the raw information that went in (the cream), whereas the rest are, from an information standpoint, trivial and unimportant. Therefore, the analyst tells the factor analysis program to retain only the first few (high–information value, or high-eigen value) factors, and to drop the rest from consideration.

Although there are many rules concerning which factors should be kept and which ones dropped, one frequently used rule is to drop those factors that have an eigen value of less than 1. The reasoning here is that if a raw variable starts out with an eigen value of 1, a final factor must, after the analysis, have at least that same amount of information if it is to be worth keeping.

There are many other ways to decide how many factors to keep, however, and you and your analyst should try several, ending with one that leaves you with a factor analysis output you can most easily and intuitively interpret and implement.

For example, you might decide to keep as many factors as are necessary to retain some fixed amount of information. This might be 70 percent, 80 percent, and so on. Alternatively, you might simply decide that 5 (or 6 or 10) are the number of factors you wish to keep. If you really want to be scientific, you could apply what is called a *scree test*. In this approach, you ask the computer to give you a graph of the eigen value of the first through last factors, and try to find the factor at which the curve bends sharply—what statisticians with anatomical bents call an *elbow.* This is very often the point where subsequent factors really add very little by way of extra information (i.e., where they begin to have small eigenvalues), and so it is reasonable to stop at the factor where the elbow occurs.

Before we get to interpretation, however, there is one last idea you need to grasp. Doing a factor analysis is a lot like taking a photograph with a camera. Just as you would focus the lens—by rotating it— to get a sharp (not blurred) picture on film of whatever it is that you are photographing, so also are you expected to "rotate" the factor analysis table of loadings (the output) to get a more focused interpretation of what is in the data. By focused, we mean a situation where you can look at the output table and read off unambiguously which raw variables are key to forming each factor. There are many ways to rotate the output, but one called *varimax rotation* is frequently used. Once again, you should try a few rotation alternatives to find one that yields an output table you find easiest to interpret.

RUNNING AND INTERPRETING FACTOR ANALYSIS

Let's walk through the steps you need to use factor analysis on your own and talk about how you would interpret what you get.

Let's suppose you are managing a negative option book club. You decide that instead of mailing the same negative option selection to all of your million-member file, you would like to customize the negative option to the reading preference of the member. You are thinking of dividing your file into perhaps five segments, or clusters, and featuring a different negative option selection in your monthly mailing to each segment. What you need is information to let you create these segments. So you mail a sample of 5,000 customers a 100-question survey on reading habits, lifestyle, demographics, attitude, and interests, and get 2,500 responses. Eventually, you will use cluster analysis to create these groupings of people, but first you want to use factor analysis to reduce these 100 questions into fewer factors so that you can later use these factor scores in your subsequent cluster analysis.

You first create a data file where the rows are the 2,500 people and the columns (or fields) are the answers to the 100 questions. A few things need to be quoted here. You can only use factor analysis on data that is continuous or scalar, such as age and income. Attitude questions answered on a 5- or 7-point agree/disagree scale also meet this requirement. You cannot legitimately use factor analysis on data where people are put into arbitrarily coded categories (such as male/female, coded 0/1). Note, also, that you should usually have many (e.g., 10 or more) times the number of rows (people or areas) than you have columns (questions or attributes). Since we have 25 times more people than we have questions to analyze, we have no cause for worry here.

Next, you pick Factor Analysis from your statistical software package's menu. In sub-menus, you pick Principal Components analysis. You tell the software package where your data file is and what the 100 raw variables are called, and you ask it to create *orthogonal* factors (those that have a zero correlation to each other) from those 100 variables.

In its first output solution, it will give you a table of the eigenvalues (remember, this was analogous to the amount of information) for each factor. There will be 100 factors because you used 100 raw variables. You notice from the table that, after the 20th factor, the eigenvalue drops below 1. You also note that the first 20 factors (of the 100) explain 80 percent of the variance, or raw information, that went in. You decide to ask the factor analysis program to rerun the output, but this time to keep only the first 20 factors (and retain 80 percent of the raw information). Though you are sacrificing 20 percent of the information, you are gaining the ability to work with just 20 factors instead of five times as many raw variables. (In later computer interactions, you can experiment with other cutoff rules.)

You also ask the software program to rotate the output table using varimax rotation (or another one from the menu). This time around, the output contains the key table of interest, called *rotated factor loadings.* The rows here, 100 in all, are the original question variables. The 20 columns correspond to your 20 retained important factors, with the first one being the most important (it has the highest eigenvalue). The numbers in the table, called *factor loadings,* represent the correlation relationship between each factor (column) and each variable (row), measured from –1.00 (strong negative relationship) through 0.00 (no relationship) to +1.00 (strong positive relationship). Mathematically, to create the first factor's score for each of the 2,500 people, you would multiply each person's score on each of the 100 raw variables by the loading for each variable on the first factor, and add up the results. Usually the computer program will do this automatically, if you ask it to, for each of the 20 factors. You can then create a new data file of 2,500 rows (people) and 20 columns (factors) and now use this second data file, instead of your first raw data file, in subsequent modeling (such as regression and cluster analysis).

To interpret the rotated loadings table, however, all you have to do is look down each column (factor) and see which variables have a high loading (e.g., 0.50 or above—use your judgment) on that factor. A positive and high loading means that a high factor score is created by a high score on that particular raw variable. A negative and high loading means that a high score on that raw variable *decreases* the factor score. Because the factor score is essentially based on those raw variables that have a high loading, you can now give the factor a name to summarize what those high-loading variables appear to have in common. For example, if the raw variables with a high loading on a factor all deal with aspects of religion and morality (such as attitudes toward sex on TV, prayer in public schools, and abortion), you might want to label that factor the "religious" factor. Giving names to factors is often the most enjoyable part of factor analysis, so savor this opportunity!

CLUSTER ANALYSIS: WHAT IT IS AND WHEN YOU SHOULD USE IT

Cluster analysis, as we said previously, is appropriate whenever you want to assign people or areas to groups so those people within a group are similar to each other and those in different groups are different from each other. After forming such groups (clusters) through cluster analysis, you can then tailor offers and packages to each group, thus (hopefully) increasing response and profitability. This is the promise and technique of market segmentation.

Not only can you assign people or areas to clusters, but also other things as well, for example, brands within a category. Any "thing" that is given a number for each of a reasonably large number of variables (such as ZIP codes rated on average age, average income, percent white population, and so on) is fair game for a cluster analysis. When we are dealing with consumers, we typically score each individual or household on demographic variables, previous purchases (what was purchased, when purchased, how much, how often, how paid), source of name, lifestyle and attitudinal data (perhaps from overlays), benefit preference data from surveys, and so on. This data is more easily handled in cluster analysis if it is of the continuous scalar type, but methods do exist for working with binary (yes/no) information as well. Thus, if your house file contains data on how each name responded in the past to different offers, that yes/no response history can also be used in certain kinds of cluster analysis to put your file into response segments.

The most common use of cluster analysis is with geo-demographic data—the kind discussed in Chapter 2 and marketed as ClusterPlus, PRIZM, Acorn, and so on. In essence, what these companies have done is to take census data on various variables by block group, update the data, add other data (such as auto registration statistics), and then use cluster analysis to create clusters of these block groups. Those block groups within a cluster are very similar to each other in terms of their scores on these variables (no matter where they happen to be geographically), and the clusters themselves are different from each other.

Thus, for example, Cluster S01 in the *ClusterPlus* scheme is described by the cluster concept of "Established Wealthy," which includes (among other things) the highest socioeconomic status indicators, highest median income ($75,000), homeowners living in prime real estate areas (73% in single family homes), high education levels (64% college graduates, 26% with graduate degrees), professionally employed people (58% so employed), and parents whose children go to private schools. Towns across the country having a large proportion of people in this cluster include Los Altos, California; Westport, Connecticut; Bethesda, Maryland; Scarsdale, New York; and Highland Park, Illinois. While forming only 1.4 percent of the nation's population, people in this cluster buy disproportionately large amounts of expensive clothes, financial products, imported wines, vacations, and expensive cars, and they fly more often. Not surprisingly, people in such a cluster respond more readily to high-priced offers, and packages sent to them most profitably appeal to upscale values. In contrast, people in the bottom clusters are not good targets for such offers and appeals.

These syndicated geo-demographic cluster assignments to ZIP codes or census block groups are used most often, and most easily, for name selection purposes in a mailing—to decide which names in a list you wish to mail to and which ones you wish to suppress. Yet the technology of cluster analysis is also used to classify customers or prospects, at an individual level, into benefit segments (people who value similar benefits in a product category, such as reading preference segments in a book club), or lifestyle and psychographic segments (people with similar attitudes, values, and interests).

HOW CLUSTER ANALYSIS WORKS

There are many different varieties of cluster analysis, so many that statisticians don't really know which ones are best or standard. In fact, these different varieties work in different ways and very often yield different cluster results. The practical consequence of this variety, and a very important one, is that you should often use more than one technique, and you should be satisfied only when two or more techniques yield outputs that look reasonably similar. Otherwise, you may be seeing clusters that exist only as figments of the computer's imagination. Always ask your analysts to try more than one technique and to demonstrate some convergence.

When you work with continuous, scalar data (such as income, years of education, age, and agree/disagree attitude scales), cluster analysis works much like the coordinate geometry that we all learned way back in high school. As we said earlier, the objective of cluster analysis is to put similar things together in a group. How do we know when things are similar? The computer calculates a statistical measure of similarity called *distance*—obviously, things that are similar are not distant, and things that have high distance (that are far apart) are not similar.

The distance between any two things is calculated much like we would calculate the distance between the two points A and B on a graph with two axes or dimensions (X and Y). If point A is located at ($X1$, $Y1$) on this map, and point B is located at ($X2$, $Y2$) on this map, coordinate geometry tells us that the distance between A and B is given by the square root of the squared total of ($X2 - X1$) and ($Y2 - Y1$). (If you don't remember, or don't care, that's OK; we are simply giving you an intuitive feel for what's inside the black box of cluster analysis.) Now, suppose we're dealing with ZIP codes instead of points. The same logic applies; the axes become the variables (such as average age, average income, or average education), and each ZIP code has a location (its score) on each axis. The computer first calculates a total distance between every pair of points (ZIP codes or people), and then uses some rule to put points that are closest to each other in the same cluster.

If you are working with binary (yes/no, bought/didn't buy) kinds of data, the methods of calculating similarity use a different approach. Suppose you market collectibles, and in the last year you mailed 10 offers to each of a million people. For each offer, some people bought, and most didn't buy. You had the good sense to record in your file how they responded (bought/didn't buy) to each of the 10 mailings. For such data, the computer will define similarity for every pair of names as the proportion of times they acted the same way (both bought, or both didn't buy) to the total number of offers mailed; if one name in the pair bought one offer while the other didn't, then that should count as dissimilar behavior.

The user has to tell the computer program which method it should use to calculate distance, which method it should use to bring close points together, and how many clusters it should create. Obviously, statisticians spend lifetimes studying which rules are best for making these methodological decisions. Although we will skip the details here, we will now give you some guidelines.

RUNNING AND INTERPRETING CLUSTER ANALYSIS

First, you have to create a data file in which each of the things you want to cluster (the rows) is scored on each of the variables you want it to be clustered on (the columns). These might be ZIP codes scored on various census variables. The columns might be factor scores, which (as we saw in the earlier section) are combinations of variables. (Some statisticians recommend that you *standardize* these column scores before using cluster analysis. Standardizing means mathematically converting each number to another equivalent one, with the new set of numbers having an average of 0 and a standard deviation of 1. Most computer programs do this painlessly, on request.)

When you pull up the cluster analysis portion of your statistical software, the menu will ask you (1) which kind of program you want to use, (2) how you want distance computed, (3) which method you want it to use to put points into clusters, based on their distances, and (4) how many clusters you want it to create. It may also ask you in what shape and form you want to see the output, that is, tables or trees (called *dendograms*).

The first decision—what kind of program—really depends on how large your data set is. Calculating and storing the distance between *every* pair of 35,000 residential ZIP codes, for example, is beyond the capacity of most computers and software. For really large data sets, therefore, you should pick a cluster analysis program that doesn't require these pairwise calculations and that works somewhat differently. Though the name may vary with the software package, such programs are often called *K-means* clustering programs (the software will usually tell you clearly that it is meant for large data sets). Smaller data sets are handled by most cluster analysis programs.

The second decision—what kind of distance measure to use—typically depends on your data as well. Binary (yes/no) data have their own types of distance measures (which not all software programs have, so check before you pick your software if you want to work with such data). If you are working with continuous, scalar data, you would normally pick Euclidean or squared Euclidean distance measures. (Your software might recommend which kinds of distance measures work best with different kinds of grouping methods, discussed next. The programs for larger data sets typically have a default measure and grouping method.)

The third decision—what kind of grouping rule you want to apply to the calculated distances—offers a big array of possibilities. Statisticians again have their preferences but one called *Ward's method* works well in many situations.

The fourth decision—how many clusters you want the program to form—is, unfortunately, the most judgmental. Although some statistical packages offer ways to help you here, most often how many clusters you want is simply a subjective question. It depends on your economics, the number of logical segmentation possibilities, and your production capabilities—how many customized offers or mailings you can profitably and feasibly handle.

After you indicate your choices to the computer, it will eventually give you (among a host of other output) a table in which each thing (person/ZIP code, and so on) you have clustered is given a cluster number. You can, optionally, get a tree diagram telling you the exact sequence of the clustering process; this will give you a visual idea of how the clusters and cluster members relate to each other in terms of overall similarity, and the sequence in which the method split up the total mass of things into a greater and greater number of clusters. Finally, the program may give you an average score for each cluster on each raw variable used for the clustering (if not, you can do this separately by computing the average scores on these variables for each of the things in that cluster); you use average scores to profile each cluster and to understand these clusters intuitively.

One final point on validation. We have already mentioned the need to repeat your analyses using different methods to see if you get similar solutions. Another method of checking the validity of your cluster solution is to first get a cluster output on a randomly selected half of your data, and then on the other half. Check to see that the clusters look similar—trust them only if they do.

USING SMALL-SAMPLE SURVEY DATA TO SEGMENT A MUCH BIGGER FILE

One of the practical issues that database marketers face is this: If I want to create cluster-based segments in my many-million name house file, using data on customers obtained through a questionnaire mailing, must I mail that survey questionnaire to every individual on my file? Since that is obviously an expensive and impractical undertaking, how can I feasibly use cluster analysis on my entire file, while still benefiting from consumer survey techniques?

Fortunately, there is indeed an answer to this problem. The steps you need to go through are as follows:

First, randomly select a small *N*th name sample from the huge file you want to create segments in. You could, for example, select 10,000 names to mail to. Mail each of these 10,000 people or households your questionnaire, which is probably quite long, with lots of questions on benefits sought in the product category, their attitudes and values, demographic data, product/brand usership, and so on. Consider (or test) giving them some incentive for responding to boost the response rate. You should develop this questionnaire through conventional marketing research techniques. It is very important to remember here that as many scales as possible in the questionnaire should be "continuous" (e.g., 5- or 7-point "agree-disagree" type scales).

The second step is to create segments among the responders (let's say 4,000 responded) through cluster analysis, using the data on this questionnaire (perhaps after you've reduced the data through factor analysis first). As suggested earlier, try to make sure you've got valid clusters by doing split-half replication, multimethod replication, and the like.

Let's say you end up with four clusters among these 4,000 people, and that these clusters make intuitive sense and also relate to differences in the customer performance data you earlier had on these customers from your file. Note that it is very important that you only accept clusters that differ meaningfully on some performance or response dimension relevant to your business.

The trick now is to take this information on these four clusters from these 4,000 people and use it to put each of your many-million house file people into the "most likely" cluster—even though only the 4,000 got the questionnaires.

This brings us to step three, which is to develop a predictive model for cluster membership, USING ONLY YOUR HOUSE FILE DATA AND NOT YOUR SURVEY DATA. You begin by taking your 4,000 responders, each of whom has been placed into one of these four new clusters. To the file that has the cluster membership scores for these 4,000 people, append all the house file information you already had without the survey (which is information you should also have for everybody else on your file).

Now, in step four, see if you can build a logistic regression or discriminant analysis to create a predictive model, for just these 4,000 people, using that "old and plentiful" house file data to predict which of the four "new" clusters each of them belongs to. Note that you already "know" this cluster membership from the cluster analysis you did earlier from the survey data. You are trying to see if you can come up with a model that would predict the cluster each of these 4,000 people belonged to IF ALL YOU KNEW was the standard house file data that you have on them—and on everyone else.

Hopefully, you should come up with a model that works reasonably well, though it will obviously misclassify some of these 4,000 people. In the final step, use the computer-estimated coefficients (weights) from this predictive model to score everyone else on your house file, using the house file data you have on everyone (which should be the same variables that you used in your predictive model in step four earlier). Use this score to place everyone in your file into a "predicted" cluster.

Then—and here's the payoff—use this predicted cluster membership to mail different offers or packages to the people you're mailing to. If you do the process right (and if you're lucky), response rates and performance should improve over a one-mailing-for-all strategy.

CONCLUDING EXAMPLE AND REVIEW

The example that follows came about as a result of what began as a simple use of one of the commercially available clustering products. An analysis of our client's mailing of an upscale product indicated that contrary to expectations, response was not coming from the very top socioeconomic clusters but from middle and lower socioeconomic clusters. The client questioned the reliability of the clustering product. To verify the analysis, we created our own clustering scheme for just New York state, based on available census data at the ZIP code level.

We selected forty census variables (of the more than 150 available) as the raw data for summarization through factor (principal components) analysis. Each of 2,000 New York state ZIP codes was rated on these 40 census variables; this formed the raw data file. Initial analysis showed that only the first 10 of the 40 factors extracted had an eigenvalue (amount of information) that exceeded 1, so only these 10 factors were retained in the next round. The table showed that these 10 factors retained 70 percent of the information (variance) that originally came in with the 40 raw variables, and we considered this an acceptable trade-off.

Table 14–1 shows abbreviated varimax-rotated factor loadings for the factor analysis of New York state ZIP code data. Figure 14–1 shows the scree diagram that suggested a 10-factor solution.

Table 14–1 describes the original census variables (the rows) and gives the loadings (the numbers relating each row to each of the factor columns). For brevity, we have reproduced only the first 26 rows and first 3 columns here. (The full table had 40 rows and 10 columns.) The computer would automatically create 10 factor scores for each ZIP code for use later. For interpretation, note that the first factor related highly negatively to the percentage of homeowners, percentage of households with two or more cars, percent white population, and percent born in the state where they now live. It related highly positively to the percentage of renter homes, percent homes with elevators, percent foreign born, percent Hispanic, and percent single-person households. This factor should paint an easily interpreted picture in your mind's eye. What the analysis suggests is that ZIP codes that will score high on this one factor will represent urban areas with large Hispanic populations.

As a contrast, the second factor is very different—almost the reverse image of the first but still urban. These ZIPs appear to represent educated, upper income professionals with children in nursery schools. Yuppies! Factor 3 scores high on two-income families, suggesting ZIP codes populated by hard-working, low- to middle-income families.

Factor scores were then derived for each of the 2,000 ZIP codes, for each of the 10 factors; this formed the new data file for later input into cluster analysis. We used a program suitable for large data sets and requested 50 clusters (to be consistent with the commercial product that was being questioned). The program output told us which of the 50 clusters each of the 2,000 ZIP codes belonged to, as well as how close each ZIP code was to the center of that cluster. For each cluster, we then selected the one ZIP code that was closest to that cluster's center and used that ZIP code's profile on the 10 factor scores as a proxy for the factor score profile of the entire ZIP code. Finally, we compared the resulting cluster profiles with that provided by the commercial product for these 16 center ZIP codes.

TABLE 14–1
Varimax-Rotated Factor Loadings for Census Variables (First Three Factors)*

Raw Census Data at ZIP Code Level	Factors		
	1	2	3
1. Percent homeowners	−.91	−.05	.00
2. Percent renters	.91	.05	.00
3. Percent two-car households	−.87	.14	.14
4. Percent households with elevators	.82	.06	.12
5. Percent born in foreign countries	.71	.29	.07
6. Percent Hispanic	.68	.02	−.14
7. Percent white	−.66	−.04	.18
8. Percent single-person households	.66	−.20	.12
9. Percent born in same U. S. state	−.62	−.17	−.04
10. Percent income of $25,000+	−.21	.80	.34
11. Median household income	−.30	.78	.30
12. Percent with central air conditioning	−.10	.70	.16
13. Median monthly mortgage	.03	.69	.18
14. Median monthly rent	.09	.67	.13
15. Percent in professional occupations	.10	.62	.18
16. Percent with four+ years college education	.17	.61	.42
17. Percent who work in a place different from where they live	.01	.60	−.03
18. Percent urban population	.54	.59	.08
19. Percent educated high school+	.03	.53	.47
20. Percent of children in nursery schools	−.02	.48	−.07
21. Percent in administrative occupations	.28	.47	.15
22. Percent of English origin	−.38	−.65	.10
23. Percent of population in total labor force	.06	.28	.90
24. Percent of females in labor force	−.11	.24	.78
25. Percent of males in labor force	.18	.24	.74
26. Percent of households with two or more workers	−.35	.13	.63

*Loadings have been sorted so that factor 1 has high (positive or negative) loadings on variables 1 through 9; factor 2, variables 10 through 22; and factor 3, variables 23 through 26. Factor 1 appears to be urban Hispanics; factor 2, affluent, white-collar, suburban commuters; and factor 3, level of employment in that ZIP code.

Table 14–2 shows the factor loadings for the three factors discussed above for three entirely different ZIP codes or neighborhoods.

As you can see, there is a strong relationship between the factor scores and the vendor's abbreviated description of the ZIP code. ZIP code 10504, described as Wealthy, scores highly negative on factor 1 and highly positive on factor 2. Center City ZIP code 10026 scores highly positive on factor 1 and highly negative on factor 2. ZIP code 14146, commercially described as Small Town, scores high on factor 3, which you will recall represented areas with large percentages of two-income families.

Thus, our analysis supported the integrity of the commercial product. But what about the conclusion that upscale ZIP codes were not responding as well to an upscale product as middle- and low-income ZIP codes were? Well, it turns out that we haven't been telling you the whole story. The key fact we omitted to tell you is that the upscale product was being promoted with the aid of a downscale premium, which did not appeal to an upscale market but did appeal to middle and lower level markets. The final result was that the premium offer was changed to an offer more attractive to the client's desired market.

FIGURE 14–1
SPSS Factor Analysis

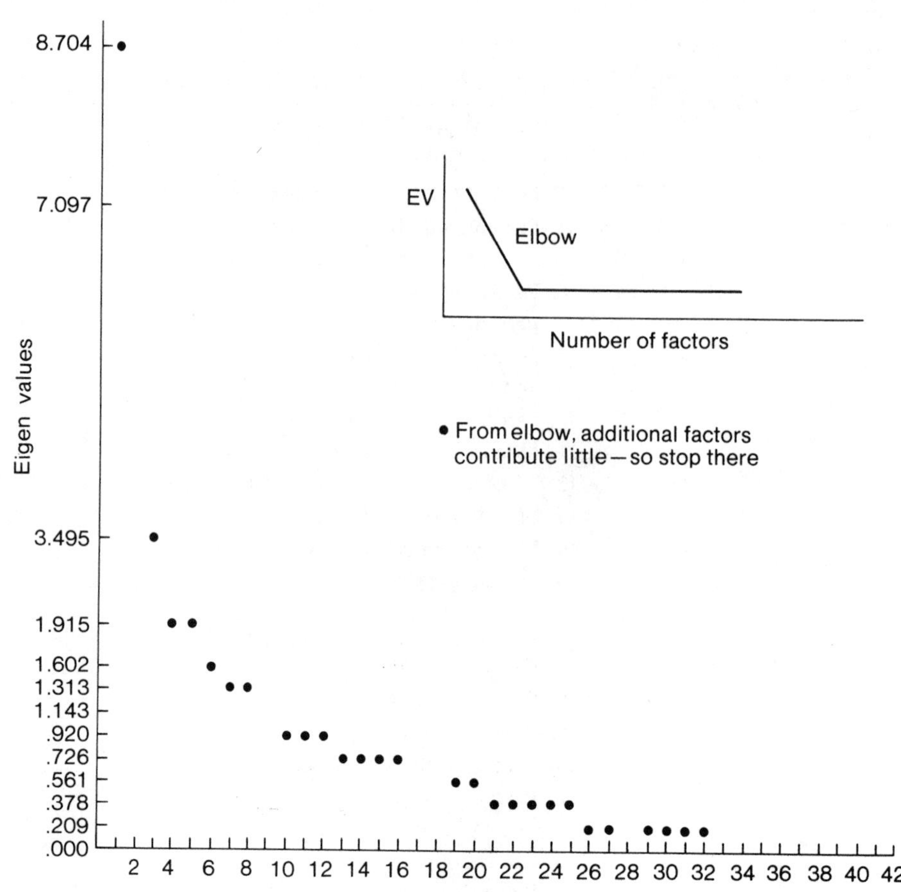

TABLE 14–2

ZIP Code	*Abbreviated Commercial Description*	*Factor 1*	*Factor 2*	*Factor 3*
10504	Wealthy	–1.04107	2.67803	.75684
10026	Center city	2.98245	–.92635	–1.88863
14146	Small town	.42019	–1.14470	3.36004

Chapter 15

A Closer Look Back

A note to our readers: Chapters 10 through 14 on statistical analysis, modeling, and segmentation were primarily intended to provide the users of models with enough information so that they could ask intelligent questions of those actually charged with responsibility for developing working models. The following chapter is intended to provide modelers with some additional insights and tools they may wish to incorporate into their modeling procedures. Nonstatisticians, users, are encouraged to follow along, but if the material gets a little too theoretical, just go on to the next chapter where we discuss the role of modeling in the New Direct Marketing and where the emphasis is on the issues associated with the use and implementation of models.

This chapter will further develop your understanding of some of the more important ideas introduced in the preceding chapters. From a practical perspective the material it covers will help you both develop new measures of the effectiveness of your models and improve the power of your models.

A CLOSER LOOK AT *r*, THE CORRELATION COEFFICIENT

In this section we'll discuss the key measure of most statistical analyses, *r*, the correlation coefficient first introduced in Chapter 11. After a brief review of the basics we'll introduce the concept of rematching, a technique that provides the analyst with a basis for evaluating the power of the models.

Review of r

The correlation coefficient *r* (Pearson's product-moment) measures the strength of the *linear* relationship between two variables.

In theory, *r* can range in value between +1 and –1 where

- 0 indicates no relationship
- +1 indicates a perfect positive relationship
- –1 indicates a perfect negative relationship

Values between 0 and 1 or 0 to –1 indicate a weak to moderate to strong relationship, as depicted in Figure 15–1.

Remember that *r* was originally built for two continuous variables, and it is expressed in the form of *standard scores* (each variable is reexpressed to have a mean of zero and a standard deviation of 1).

Let Z(X) and Z(Y) be standardized variables for X and Y, respectively,

$$Z(X) = \frac{X - \text{mean}(X)}{\text{std}(X)} \quad \text{and} \quad Z(Y) = \frac{Y - \text{mean}(Y)}{\text{std}(X)},$$

then *r* is defined as the average product of paired standardized scores:

$$r = \frac{\text{sum of } [Z\,(X) \times Z\,(Y)]}{n},$$

where n = the number of (x, y) pairs, and std = standard deviation. See Table 15–1 for a simple illustration.

FIGURE 15–1

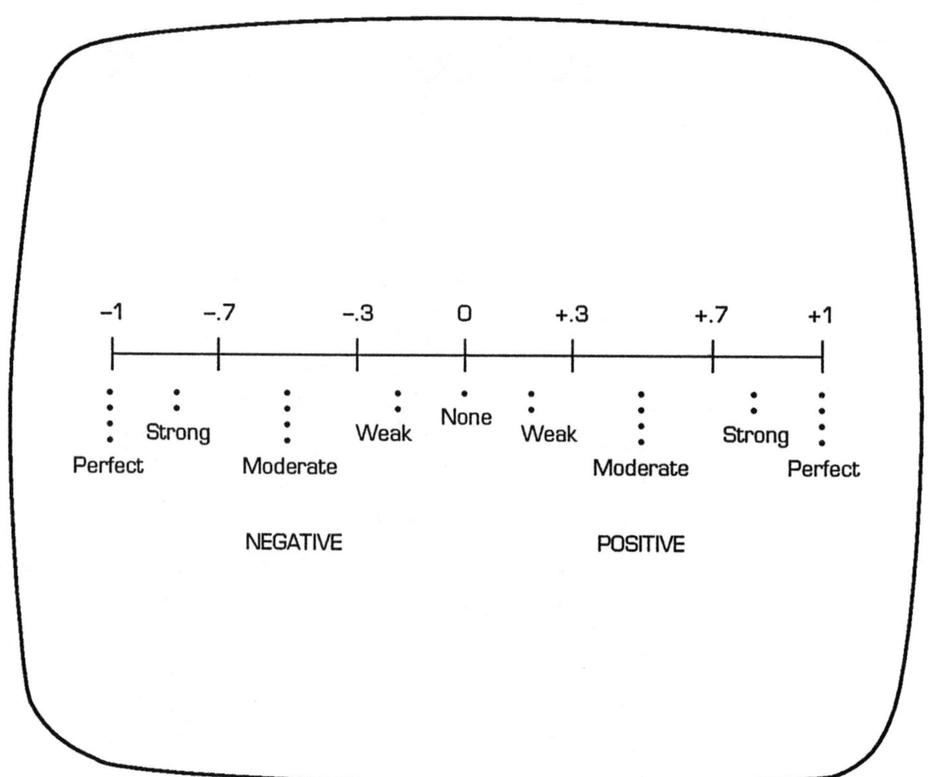

TABLE 15–1
Calculating the Correlation Coefficient
Data Set A– (X, Y)

	X	*Y*	*Z(X)*	*Z(X)*	*Z(X)* × *Z(Y)*
	124	779	−1.42313	−1.70114	2.42095
	153	988	−1.10020	1.04221	−1.14664
	170	759	−0.91090	−1.96366	1.78869
	192	933	−0.66591	0.32028	−0.21328
	235	922	−0.18708	0.17589	−0.03291
	267	891	0.16926	−0.23102	−0.03910
	292	942	0.44765	0.43841	0.19626
	316	924	0.71491	0.20214	0.14451
	347	946	1.06011	0.49092	0.52043
	422	1002	1.89529	1.22598	2.32357
mean	251.8	909.6		sum	5.96248
std	89.80	76.18		*r*	0.59625
n	10	10			

In the illustration in Table 15–1 *r* is equal to +.59625, so we would declare the relationship between *X* and *Y* as moderate using the schematic defined in Figure 15–1.

REMATCHING

The strength of a relationship as depicted in Figure 15–1 and as measured by the correlation coefficient is based on theoretical extreme values of plus and minus one. That is, if the data (*X* and *Y*) itself has the potential of a perfect correlation ($r = +1$ or $r = -1$) then the nominal

TABLE 15–2
Rematched Data Sets

A Original Pairing		*P* Rematched for Most Positive		*N* Rematched for Most Negative	
X	Y	X	Y	X	Y
124	779	124	759	124	1002
153	988	153	779	153	988
170	759	170	891	170	946
192	933	192	922	192	942
235	922	235	924	235	933
267	891	267	933	267	924
292	942	292	942	292	922
316	924	316	946	316	891
347	946	347	988	347	779
422	1002	422	1002	422	759
r = +.596		r = +.875		r = –.926	

weak/moderate/strong categories are valid. To the extent that *X* and *Y* cannot achieve the most positive value of $r = +1$ and the most negative value of $r = -1$, then the schematic in Figure 15–1 is not quite valid, and an adjusted *r* is needed.

We can realize the full potential of the data by using a technique called rematching. We know intuitively that for any set of *X*, *Y* values, the most positive relationship possible would come about when the highest *X* value was paired with the highest *Y* value, the second highest *X* value was paired with the second highest *Y* value, and so on until the lowest *X* is paired with the lowest *Y*. Equally intuitive, the most negative relationship would come about when the highest *X* value was paired with the lowest *Y* value, the second highest *X* was paired with the second lowest *Y*, and so on until the lowest *X* is paired with the highest *Y*.

Suppose that we took the data set we are working with and created positive and negative rematched data sets and then calculated the correlation coefficient for each rematched set. The result would be the largest positive *r* and the largest negative *r* possible.

Rematch Example

So, let's rematch *X* and *Y* to obtain the largest positive value and the largest negative value *r* for the data set A.

The data set named P (for positive) has *X* ordered from low to high and matched with *Y*, which is also ordered from low to high. Dataset N (for negative) has *X* ordered from low to high and matched with *Y* ordered the other way, from high to low. Table 15–2 shows the correlation coefficients for the rematched data sets and the original data set.

We see that, given this data set, the most positive value *r* can have is +.875 and not +1; and the most negative *r* is –.926 and not –1. Accordingly, we adjust *r* by simply dividing the original *r* of +.596 by its potential or actual (not theoretical) most positive value of +.875. Thus,

$$r_{\text{adj}} = +.596/+.875 = +.681$$

Now, referring to the schematic, we still must consider the relationship between *X* and *Y* as nominally moderate, but its numerical *r* has increased by 14.3 percent. We now have a more accurate numerical assessment of the relationship between X and Y. (Note: if r was negative, then we would have divided by the most negative r value.)

Rematching Phi

As we've seen, when two variables are continuous the calculations for r are messy. When the variables take on only two values (referred to as dichotomous or binary variables), the formula changes. Technically, the correlation coefficient r is now referred to as the *phi coefficient.*

Let X and Y take on values 0 and 1. This implies that there are only four possible combinations or pairs of X and Y.

$a = 1, 1$

$b = 1, 0$

$c = 0, 0$

$d = 0, 1$

Let a represent the number of times the pair (1, 1) occurs; b, c, and d are the number of times the pairs (1, 0), (0, 0) and (0, 1) occur, respectively. Accordingly, we can present the data in the table below, and *phi* is defined as follows:

		Y: 0	Y: 1	
X	1	a	b	$a + b$
	0	c	d	$c + d$
		$a + c$	$b + d$	

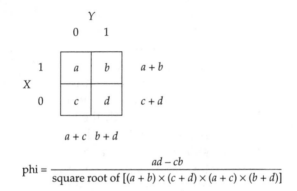

$$\text{phi} = \frac{ad - cb}{\text{square root of } [(a + b) \times (c + d) \times (a + c) \times (b + d)]}$$

Simple illustration.

Let X = Sex [(male, female) = (1, 0)]

Y = Response [(yes, no) = (1, 0)]

Suppose a sample of 100 names from a mailing with a 10 percent response from a list comprised of 70 males and 30 females produces the table below.

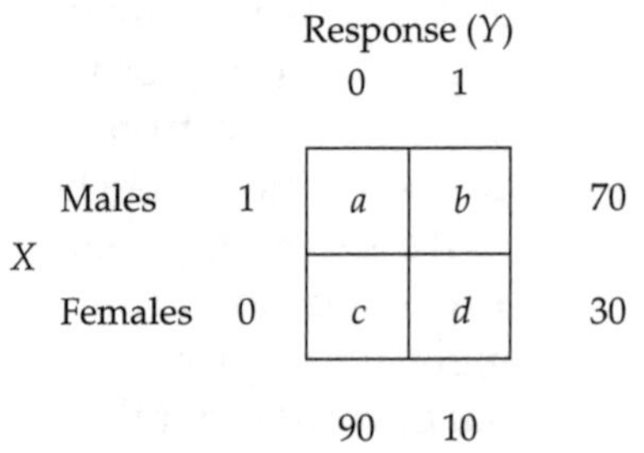

			Response (Y): 0	Response (Y): 1	
X	Males	1	a	b	70
	Females	0	c	d	30
			90	10	

The phi coefficient is calculated as follows:

$$\text{phi} = \frac{65 \times 5 - 25 \times 5}{\text{square root of } [(70) \times (30) \times (90) \times (10)]}$$
$$= +.145$$

The relationship between response and sex is declared weak if the most positive value phi could be is +1.

To determine the most positive value that phi can be, assume we must find the *a*, *b*, *c*, and *d* that make phi large with the restriction that the row and column totals (the marginals) remain fixed. In other words, we must fill in the empty cells in the table below to make the corresponding phi the most positive it can be.

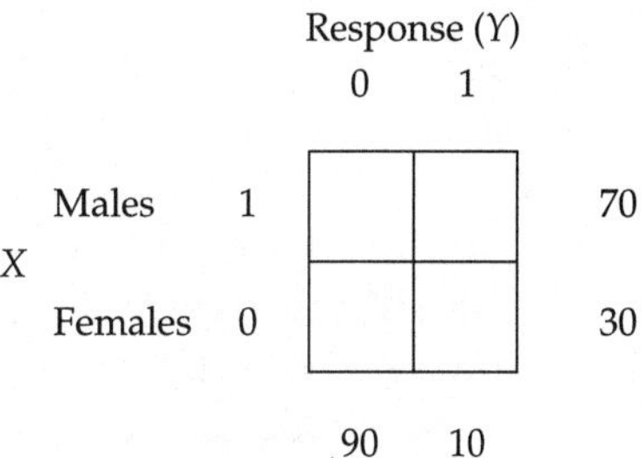

			Response (Y) 0	Response (Y) 1	
X	Males	1			70
	Females	0			30
			90	10	

The most positive phi occurs when the *a–c* diagonal is largest. This occurs when a = 70 and c = 10, which in turn forces b = 0 and d = 20. Thus, we have

			Response (Y) 0	Response (Y) 1	
X	Males	1	70	0	70
	Females	0	20	10	30
			90	10	

and phi = +.509.

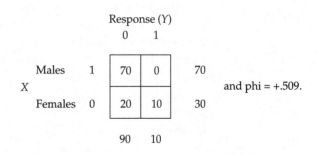

Similar to adjusting r by its extreme value, the adjusted phi is .285 (=.145/.509), still indicating a weak relationship but representing a numerical increase of 97 percent $((.285 - .145)/.145 \times 100)$ over the original and unadjusted r of +.145.

The "unadjusted" assessment of the effect of sex on response indicates that sex explains 2.1 percent (r squared = .145 × .145) of the response variation. In contrast, an "adjusted" assessment indicates that sex explains 8.1 percent of response variation and that it has promise as a candidate predictor in developing a response model. With the addition of a few more powerful predictors an excellent response model can be anticipated.

Although not needed here, the most negative value of phi is –.218 and occurs with the table below.

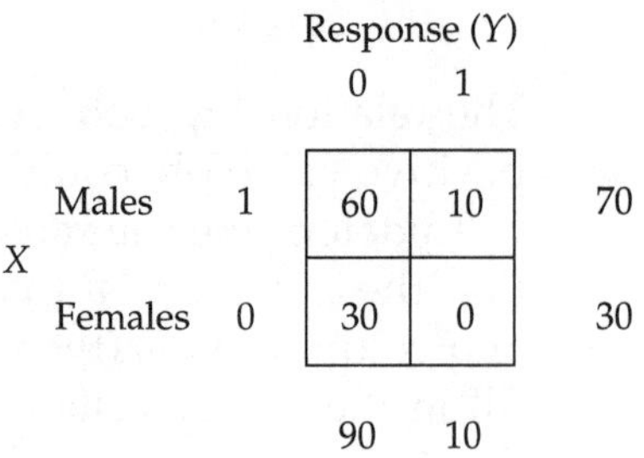

			Response (Y) 0	1	
X	Males	1	60	10	70
	Females	0	30	0	30
			90	10	

IMPLICATION OF REMATCHING

Rematching provides an accurate assessment of the relationships between variables by taking into account their "shapes." For a categorical variable, the shape refers to the marginals—the frequency distribution among the variables' categories or cells. The shape can be flat, indicating equal distribution among the cells, or skewed, indicating unequal distribution among the cells.

The shape of a continuous variable is the frequency curve as depicted by a stem-and-leaf, box-and-whisker plot, or a regular histogram. The shape can be symmetric or skewed. *To the extent that the shapes of variables are not the same, the rematching adjustment will improve the assessment of relationships between variables.*

Thus rematching is telling us that our variables should be in the same shape, the "best" shape being symmetry. However, as previously mentioned, symmetry and straightening go hand in hand. Accordingly, if we strive for the trio of symmetry, straightening, and rematching, our whole modeling results should be as close to optimal as possible.

Clearly, in direct marketing where a zero-one response is always very skewed (typical response rates are between 2 percent and 15 percent), rematching offers an effective way of performing more sensitive analyses and developing more precise predictive equations.

Consider a house file mailing with a known response rate and the usual key selection criteria. The analyst can properly assess the effects of the selection factors on response by taking into account both the level of the house file's response rate and the shape of the factors.

At a multivariate level of analysis, for example, response modeling, the analyst can adjust all the pair correlation coefficients of the correlation matrix and directly input the adjusted correlation matrix instead of the raw data into any regression routine. Model development will proceed as usual, but the results will reflect more accurate interrelationships among the predictor and response variables.

A CLOSER LOOK AT A MODEL'S POWER

In direct marketing a model's predictive power is typically assessed in terms of how well the model can identify the best customers, either the most responsive or the most profitable. The model's dependent variable, Y, is either a binary response variable (Y = yes or no) or a continuous performance variable (e.g., Y = sales dollars).

TABLE 15–3 *Assessing a Model's Power Using Rematching*

	Model			*Rematch*			*AID*		
Decile	*Decile Average Increased Total Net Sale*	*Cum Average Increased Total Net Sale*	*Cum Lift*	*Decile Average Increased Total Net Sale*	*Cum Average Increased Total Net Sale*	*Cum Lift*	*Decile Average Increased Total Net Sale*	*Cum Average Increased Total Net Sale*	*Cum Lift*
1	$150	$150	200	$337	$337	449	$170	$170	226
2	$112	$131	175	$172	$255	339	$134	$152	201
3	$94	$119	158	$117	$209	278	$119	$141	187
4	$80	$109	145	$82	$177	236	$85	$127	168
5	$89	$105	140	$57	$153	204	$67	$115	152
6	$73	$100	133	$33	$133	177	$63	$106	141
7	$62	$94	126	$12	$116	154	$62	$100	132
8	$65	$91	121	$0	$101	135	$52	$94	124
9	$25	$83	111	($17)	$88	117	$18	$86	113
10	$0	$75	100	($42)	$75	100	($15)	$75	100
Average	$75			$75			$75		

Models are used to predict Y, thus providing an estimate of Y, $\hat{Y}$ (pronounced *Y-hat*). The model scores a customer file to produce a score value, $\hat{Y}$. The scored file is ranked from highest to lowest value on $\hat{Y}$.

The ranked file is then divided into 10 groups or deciles, and the average (actual) Y (average response rate or average sales) is calculated for each decile. The results are typically displayed in a decile analysis, which provides the information needed to assess the model in terms of how well it finds the best groups of customers.

To make sense of all this, let's go to an example.

An Example

A regression model was built to predict increased total net sales within a specified period. The dependent variable Y was defined as *increased total net sales,* and because returns or credits were possible this variable could have had, and did have, negative values.

The final model consisted of five variables and produced the decile analysis shown in the first three columns in Table 15–3, under the heading *Model.*

The impact of the model. The actual average increase in the dependent, variable increased total net sales, was $75. The top decile consists of those customers predicted to be our best performing customers, and these customers had an actual average increase of $150.00.

The top decile shows a lift of 200, which indicates that the decile produced two times the file average of $75 in increased total net sales. That is, without a model any 10 percent of the file would have had an average increased total net sales of $75; but with this model the top 10 percent of the file produces an average of $150, or two times better than average.

The next best decile, decile 9, had a mean or average increased total net sales of $112. The top two deciles combined have a cumulative increased total net sales averaging 131 or a lift of 175. That is, without a model any 20 percent of the file would have an average increased total net sales of $75, but with the regression model the top 20 percent of the file produces an average of $131, or 1.75 times better than average.

The combined top four deciles had an average increase of $109 and a lift of 145.

The BIG question. How *good* is the regression model's predictive power?

The answer lies in how well the *model* decile analysis—reflecting the model's ranking of *Y*—compares to the best or *maximum* decile analysis—reflecting the full potential of the best ranking of *Y*, which is obtained by *rematching*.

To rematch to obtain the *maximum* decile analysis take these steps:

1. Rank the file on Y (not $\hat{Y}$) from high to low values.
2. Divide the ranked file into ten equal parts and produce a decile report.

The maximum decile analysis is shown in the next three columns of Table 15–3, under the heading *Rematch.*

Maximum decile analysis. The ranked file still, of course, shows an average increase of $75. Now rematched, the top "maximum" decile shows an average increase in increased total net sales of $337 and lift of 449.

The next best maximum decile, decile 9, has an average increased total net sales of $172. Combining the top two maximum deciles, there is a "maximum" average cumulative increased total net sales of $255, and a "maximum" lift of 339.

The combined top four maximum deciles show a maximum mean increase of $177 and maximum lift of 236.

Comparing the regression model and the true model. A maximum decile analysis reflects the results of the one and only true model—the model that has the correct variables in their optimal functional form. Accordingly, a comparison between a regression model's decile analysis and the true model's decile analysis is an indication of how good the regression model actually is.

Because model performance varies at different depths of file, comparisons are made at different "local" levels. At the level of 40 percent of the file, the comparison between the regression model and the true model's performance indicates that the regression model has a local efficiency of 62 percent (145 divided by 236). This means that the model captures 62 percent of the maximum cumulative increased total net sales. NOT BAD!?

Rematching with AID. The regression model with 62 percent of the maximum fares quite well, but is the comparison fair? The example compared the regression model based on available variables and the true model reflecting the correct variables, which are probably neither known nor available to the model builder. So, a more reasonable comparison is between the regression model with its set of selected variables and the best model possible using only the variables actually available to the modeler.

To calculate the best or maximum decile analysis *given* the known potential independent variables, we must rematch with the aid of an AID program.

To rematch an AID analysis to obtain a maximum decile spread based on model variables take these steps:

1. Perform an AID analysis on the dependent variable Y with the set of available variables.
2. Rank each of the resulting AID end-point cells from high to low with respect to the dependent variable.
3. Within each AID end-point cell rank the individuals (or geographic areas) within the segment from high to low with respect to the dependent variable.
4. Divide the resulting file into 10 equal parts.
5. Calculate the various columns of the decile report.

The result of the AID rematching is shown in the last three columns of Table 15–3. Under the heading AID we find the following:

The file, now rematched with the help of an AID program, shows the top decile with mean of $170 and a lift of 230.

The next best maximum-AID decile, decile 9, has a mean increased total sales of $134.

Combining the top two AID-maximum deciles, we arrive at an AID-maximum cumulative mean increased total net sales of $152, and an "AID-maximum" lift of 201.

The combined top four AID-maximum deciles account for 40 percent of the file with a mean increase of $127 and a lift of 168. As before, because model performance varies at different depths of file, comparisons are made at different "local" levels. At the usual level of 40 percent of the file, the comparison between the regression model and the AID-maximum model's deciles indicates that the regression model has a local (at the fourth decile) efficiency of 87 percent (a lift of 145 for the model divided by a lift of 168 for the AID-maximum model). This means that the model captures 87 percent of the AID-maximum cumulative increased total sales. Not bad? Very good!

You may now reasonably ask, "Why bother with a regression model if the AID analysis produces better results?" We are using the output of the AID analysis as a *maximum* benchmark of the potential predictive power of the variables available to the modeler. Our justification is as follows: AID is an optimal procedure (i.e., it finds the best splits of a variable such that the spread in the dependent variables is as large as possible), which unfortunately implies it capitalizes on the idiosyncrasies of the sample data at hand (even though there are explicit adjustments to minimize this capitalization). As such, AID finds predictive power that may or may not be real (also known as a positive bias). We assume the "extra" predictive power *is real* and use it to set a maximum benchmark for the dependent and set of independent variables under study.

A CLOSER LOOK AT STRAIGHTENING DATA

When we observe in an x-y plot that the relationship between two variables appears to bend or bulge, for example, as in Figure 15–3, every effort should be made to straighten the bulge. The importance of "straight" data bears repeating. Straight data is important, primarily for the sake of simplicity. Straight data, such as in Figure 15–5, clearly depicts the relationship between the two variables in question; the relationship is easy to see, understand, and interpret—as one variable increases so does the other variable.

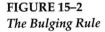

FIGURE 15–2
The Bulging Rule

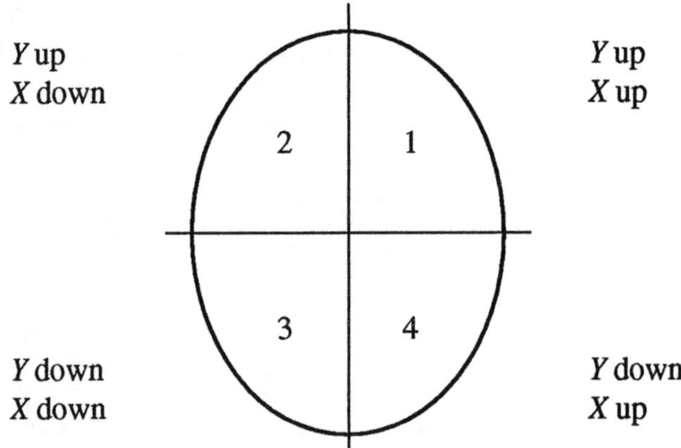

The second reason straight data is important is that most models, including the ones most often used in direct marketing, belong to the general class of linear models that assume the relationship between the dependent variable and each independent variable is linear or straight-line.

Bulges in the data can be generalized into four simple shapes, as depicted in Figure 15–2. When a curved relationship has a shape close to any one of the four, we can use the mnemonic plots, called the *Bulging Rule*,[1] along with the *Ladder of Powers* to guide us in choosing the appropriate reexpression of the variables to straighten the data.

LADDER OF POWERS

When we go up the Ladder of Powers we try reexpressions that raise the variable, either X or Y, to powers of p where p is greater than 1. The most common p values used are 2 and 3, but sometimes we may have to go farther up the ladder and use 4 and 5, or find in-between values and use mixed numbers like 1.333. Accordingly, the common "up-the-ladder" reexpressions are:

X is reexpressed to X^2 = X squared

X is reexpressed to X^3 = X cubed

Y is reexpressed to Y^2 = Y squared

Y is reexpressed to Y^3 = Y cubed

When we go down the ladder we try reexpressions that raise the variable, X or Y, to powers of p where p is less than 1. The most common p values used are 1/2, 0, –1/2 and –1, but sometimes we may have to go farther down the ladder or use in-between values. Some common down the ladder reexpressions are given below.

Note that the reexpression for $p = 0$ is not mathematically defined but conveniently defined as log to base 10. And, for negative power we again conveniently add a negative sign. The reasons for all this convenience are theoretical and beyond the scope of this chapter.

[1] John Tukey, *Exploratory Data Analysis* (Reading, MA: Addison Wesley, 1977).

TABLE 15–4
Sample Nonstraight Data

X	Y	X	Y
1	0.6	6	3.4
1	1.6	6	9.7
1	0.5	6	8.6
1	1.2	7	4.0
2	2.0	7	5.5
2	1.3	7	10.5
2	2.5	8	17.5
3	2.2	8	13.4
3	2.4	8	4.5
3	1.2	9	30.4
4	3.5	11	12.4
4	4.1	12	13.4
4	5.1	12	26.2
5	5.7	12	7.4

X is reexpressed to $X^{1/2}$ = square root X
X is reexpressed to X^0 = $\log_{10}X$
X is reexpressed to $X^{-1/2}$ = – 1/square root X
X is reexpressed to X^{-1} = – 1/X
Y is reexpressed to $Y^{1/2}$ = square root Y
Y is reexpressed to Y^0 = $\log_{10}Y$
Y is reexpressed to $Y^{-1/2}$ = – 1/square root Y
Y is reexpressed to Y^{-1} = – 1/Y

BULGING RULE

The Bulging Rule states that

If the data has a shape similar to that shown in the first quadrant, then we try to reexpress by going up the ladder for X, Y, or both.
If the data has a shape similar to that in the second quadrant, then we try to reexpress by going down the ladder for X and/or up the ladder for Y.
If the data has a shape similar to that in the third quadrant, then we try to reexpress by going down the ladder for Y, X, or both.
If the data has a shape similar to that in the fourth quadrant, then we try to reexpress by going up the ladder for X and/or down the ladder for Y.

Before we go to an example we must emphasize that the rule only offers hope that the data can be straightened—no guarantees and no one solution. The only way we fail in reexpressing is if we fail to reexpress.

An Example of the Bulging Rule

Let's consider the data set shown in Table 15–4:

The plot of X and Y in Figure 15–3 indicates that the relationship has a shape similar to the one in quadrant 4 of the Bulging Rule. Accordingly, to straighten out this bulge we must try reexpressing X, Y, or both by going up the ladder for X and/or down the ladder for Y.

Starting with X we reexpress it by creating X^2 and X^3. We can plot these new variables with Y, but instead we can just look at the correlation coefficients. Because the reexpressions straighten data we assume the new relationships with the new variable are as straight as possible; thus to find

FIGURE 15–3
Model Y = X—Plot of Y × X

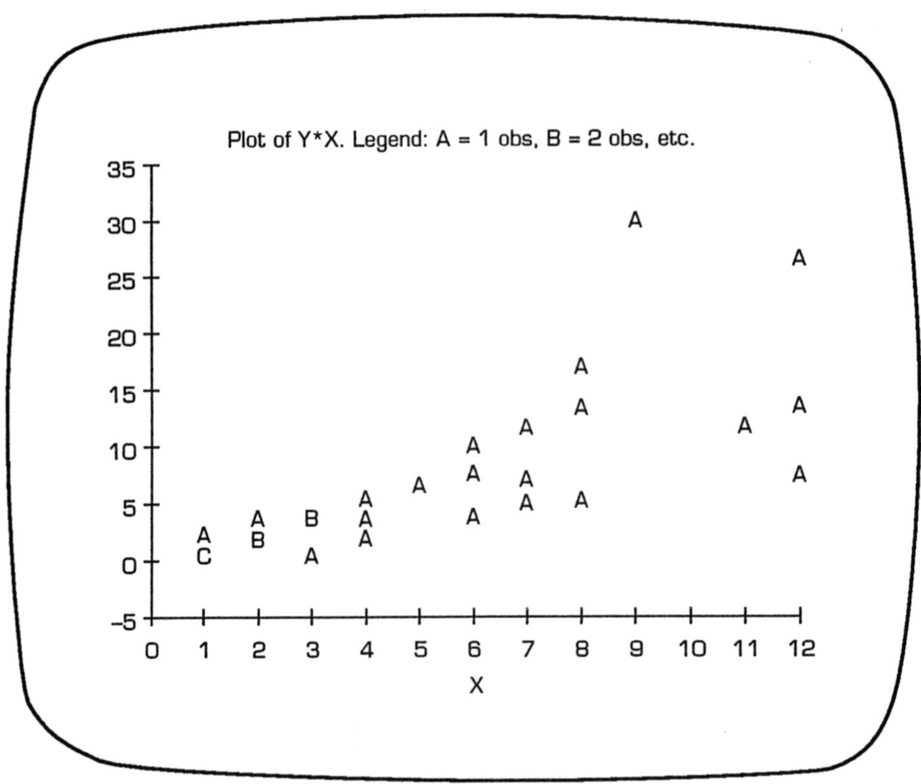

TABLE 15–5
Correlation Analysis: X up with Y

```
        1 'WITH' Variables: Y
        4 'VAR' Variables: X              SQUARD_X CUBED_X SQRT_X
Pearson Correlation Coefficients / Prob > |R| under Ho: Rho = 0 / N = 28
                              X              SQUARD_X            CUBED_X
           Y           0.73636               0.70770             0.65111
                       8.E-06                3.E-05              .00018
       power                 1                     2                   3
```

which reexpression works better, we just need to look at the correlation coefficient. The larger the value the better the reexpression.

The *r*s for *Y* and *X*, *X* squared, and *X* cubed are .736, .707 and .651 respectively. Clearly, the best reexpression for *X* is no reexpression, or *X* itself. Reexpressing *X* actually weakens the strength of the relationship as *r* decreases from .736 to .707 and .651. (See Table 15–5.)

So, we leave *X* alone, for the time being, and reexpress *Y* by going down the ladder, creating eight new variables corresponding to the powers of 1/2, 1/3, 1/4, 1/5, 1/6, 0, –1/2, and –1. The corresponding *r* value for each of these transformations is .825, .844, .850, .853, .854, .855, .794, and .678. (See Table 15–6.)

The best reexpression is Log *Y*.

Plotting Log *Y* and *X*, we see in Figure 15–3, that the bulge has changed direction; now, the shape is like that in quadrant 2 of the Bulging Rule.

TABLE 15–6
Correlation Analysis: Y down with X

```
1 'WITH' Variables: Y      SQRT_Y    CBRT_Y   F4_RT_Y   F5_RT_Y  S6_RT_Y
                     LOG_Y
1 'VAR'  Variables: X
Pearson Correlation Coefficients / Prob > |R| under Ho: Rho = 0 / N = 28
```

power		X
1	Y	0.73636 8.E-06
1/2	SQRT_Y	0.82501 7.E-08
1/3	CBRT_Y	0.84428 2.E-08
1/4	F4_RT_Y	0.85078 1.E-08
1/5	F5_RT_Y	0.85353 8.E-09
1/6	S6_RT-Y	0.85487 7.E-09
0	LOG_Y	0.85521 7.E-09
-1/2	RCPRT_Y	0.79410 5.E-07
-1	RECIP_Y	0.67875 7.E-05

FIGURE 15–4
Model Log_Y = X— Plot of LOG_Y × X

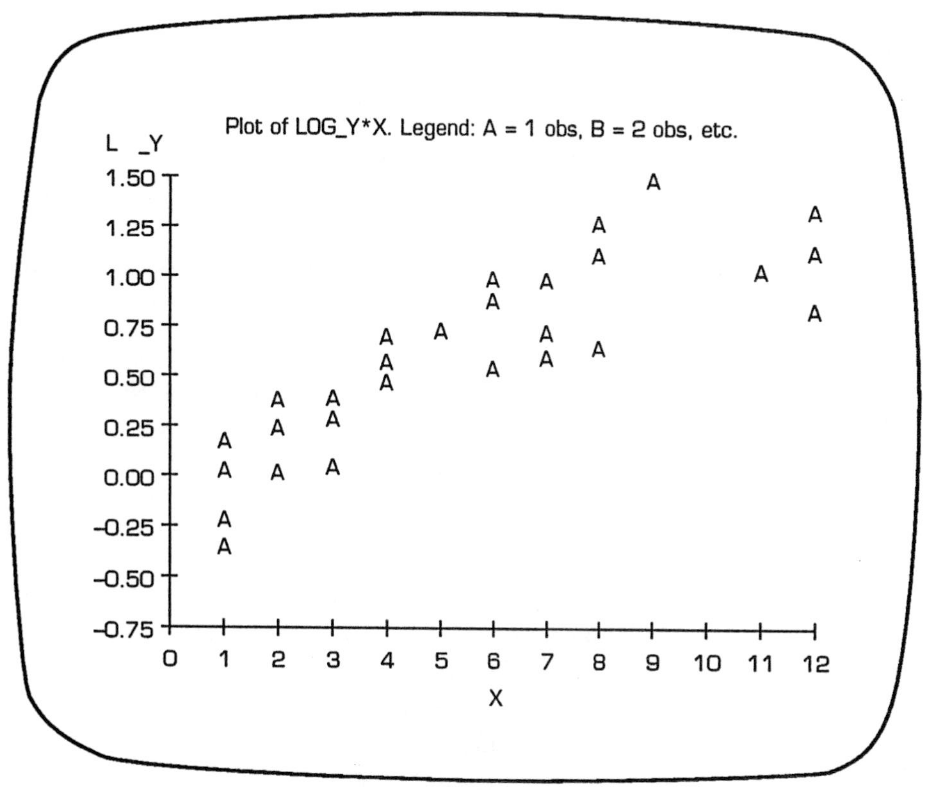

TABLE 15–7
Correlation Analysis: X down with Log_Y

'WITH' Variables: LOG_Y
7 'VAR' Variables: X SQRT_X CBRT_X F4_RT_X F5_RT_X S6_RT_X LOG_X

Pearson Correlation Coefficients / Prob > |R| under Ho: Rho = 0 / N = 28

	X	SQRT_X	CBRT_X	F4_RT_X	F5_RT_X	S6_RT_X	LOG_X
LOG_Y	0.85521 7.E-09	0.88663 3.E-10	0.89130 2.E-10	0.89233 2.E-10	0.89252 2.E-10	0.89246 2.E-10	0.88996 2.E-10
power	1	1/2	1/3	1/4	1/5	1/6	0

FIGURE 15–5
Model Log_Y = f5_rt_X—Plot of LOG_Y × F5_RT_X

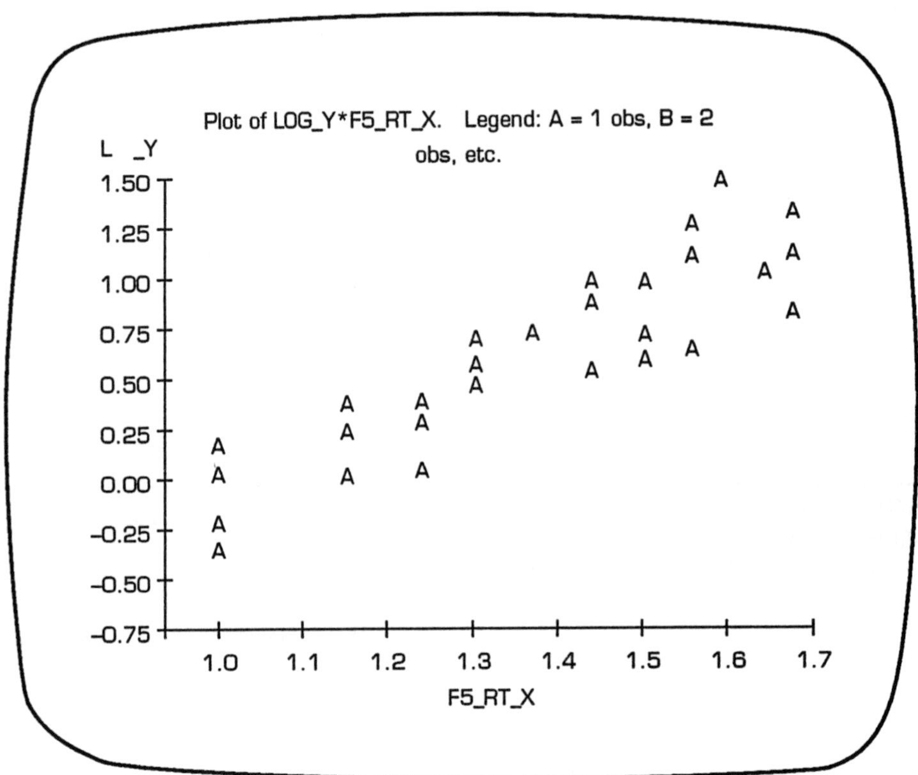

Thus, we must try to reexpress X by going down the ladder. We have already reexpressed Y variable in the plot, namely Log Y.

Going down the ladder for X we create six new variables corresponding to the powers of 1/2, 1/3, 1/4, 1/5, 1/6, and 0. The r values for Log Y with each of the six transformations of the X value are .886, .891, .892, .892, and .889. (See Table 15–7.) The best reexpression for X is the fifth root of X.

Hence the best pair of reexpressions is *F5_RT_X* and log Y. The plot for these two new reexpressed variables, given in Figure 15–5, reveals a very nice straight-line relationship. We obtained the equation for this relationship by running a simple linear regression program. Its output in Table 15–8 indicates

$$\text{Log } Y = -2.07 + \text{F5\_RT\_X} \times 2.00.$$

For those who are familiar with residuals, the residual plot, showing residual versus Y-hat, further indicates that this is the right reexpression.

TABLE 15–8
Model Log_Y = f5_rt_X

Model: MODEL1
Dependent Variable: LOG_Y

Analysis of Variance

Source	DF	Sum of Squares	Mean Square	F Value	Prob>F
Model	1	4.67556	4.67556	101.816	0.0001
Error	26	1.19396	0.04592		
C Total	27	5.86951			

Root MSE	0.21429	R-square	0.7966
Dep Mean	0.63665	Adj R-sq	0.7888
C. V.	33.65964		

Parameter Estimates

Variable	DF	Parameter Estimate	Standard Error	T for HO: Parameter=0	Prob > |T|
INTERCEP	1	-2.071624	0.27143839	-7.632	0.0001
F5_RT_X	1	2.001498	0.19835637	10.090	0.0001

FIGURE 15–6
Model Log_Y = f5_rt_X— Plot of RES_LOG5 × LOG5_HAT

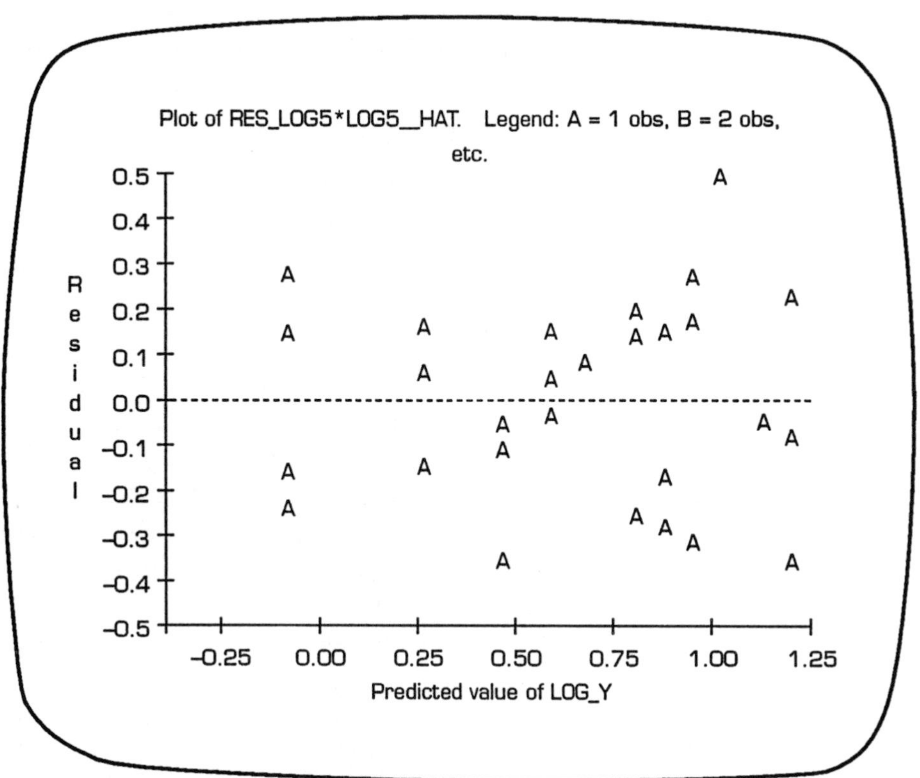

If the residual plot shows a random scatter of points above and below the zero line in the residual plot, then the model is a good fit and the correct representation of the data. Clearly, we have that situation, as depicted in Figure 15–6.

This example illustrates the value and the process of reexpressing variables. The approach is sometimes subjective (we could have started with

Y instead of X) and based on trial and error (how far up or down should we go), and, of course, there is no guarantee of success. But, as we mentioned when we began the example, we really only fail if we fail to try.

A CLOSER LOOK AT REEXPRESSIONS FOR MANY VARIABLES

In the prior chapter on segmentation we introduced the topic of factor analysis, specifically Principal Component Analysis (PCA). In this section we'll go into much more detail about the subject, emphasizing reexpression.

PCA is an exploratory technique that uncovers the interrelationships among *many* possibly correlated variables by reexpressing them into a smaller number of *new* variables such that *most* of the information or variation contained within the original set of variables is accounted for or retained by the smaller number of new and uncorrelated variables.

Formally, PCA reexpresses or transforms an original set of p variables $X1 \ldots Xp$ into a new set of p variables, called principal components (PCs), such that the newly created PCs are a weighted sum of the original variables. The weights are the coefficients of the principal components and are determined in somewhat the same way that we determine regression coefficients.

For convenience, let's assume we are working with the standardized versions of the original variables, or Xs. That is, the Xs have been replaced by their standardized counterparts, the Zs:

$$Zi = \frac{Xi - \text{mean of } Xi}{\text{standard deviation of } Xi}, \text{ for all } i$$

So, the principal components, PC1, PC2 . . . , PCp, look like this:

$$PC1 = a11 \times Z1 + a12 \times Z2 + \ldots + a1p \times Zp$$
$$PC2 = a21 \times Z1 + a22 \times Z2 + \ldots + a2p \times Zp$$
$$PCp = ap1 \times Z1 + ap2 \times Z2 + \ldots + app \times ZP$$

As we said before, the PCs are weighted sums of (standardized) variables. The number of PCs produced by the process is equal to the number of original variables, namely p. (In English, if we start with 36 variables we'll wind up with 36 PCs.) But, to reiterate the objective of PCA, we want to eventually come out at the end of the process with just a few PCs (much less than the number of original variables) that contain a large amount of the information (statisticians prefer the term *variation*) that was contained in the original set of variables.

These principal components have three important properties:

1. The variance of principal components, sometimes called *eigenvalues* or *latent roots,* will be presented in a sequence in which the first-named principal component contains the most information (the largest variance) and each successive principal component contains an amount of information, or a variance, equal to or less than the previous one.
2. The mean of a principal component is zero.
3. The correlation between any two principal components is zero.

Let's go to a simple example.

TABLE 15–9
Correlation Matrix for X1 to X4

	X1	*X2*	*X3*	*X4*
% Less than H.S.—X1	1.000	.2689	–.7532	–.8116
% Graduated H.S.—X2		1.000	–.3823	–.6200
% Some college—X3			1.000	.4311
% College or more—X4				1.000

TABLE 15–10
PCA OUTPUT: Latent Roots (Variances) and Latent Vectors (Coefficients) of Correlation Matrix

Standardized Variable	*Latent Vectors*			
	a1	*a2*	*a3*	*a4*
Z1	–.5514	–.4222	.2912	.6655
Z2	–.4042	.7779	–.3595	.3196
Z3	.4844	.4120	.6766	.3710
Z4	.5457	–.2162	–.5727	.5721
LRi	2.6620	.8238	.5141	.0000
Prop. Var %	66.55	20.59	12.85	.0000
Cum. Var %	66.55	87.14	100	100

A Simple PCA Example

Consider four variables X1, X2, X3, and X4, representing Education in a geographical unit, say a ZIP code.

X1 = Percentage of persons in a ZIP code with less than a high school education.
X2 = Percentage of persons in a ZIP code that graduated high school.
X3 = Percentage of persons in a ZIP code with some college education.
X4 = Percentage of persons in a ZIP code with college or more education.

Because PCA is performed on a correlation matrix (which is why we defined the principal components in terms of standardized variables), let's consider Table 15–9, the correlation matrix for X1 through X4.

Table 15–9 indicates that there is a positive correlation between *some college* and *college or more,* and a negative correlation between *less than high school* and *college or more.* This correlation table, then, reflects the observation that in a ZIP code that contains more than the average percentage of college graduates you will find more than the average percentage of persons with more than a college education and less than the average percentage of persons with just a high school degree—just as you would expect.

The standard output of a PCA also consists of variances and coefficients, or latent roots and latent vectors, respectively, as found in Table 15–10.

The variance of the principal component (LRi) corresponds to each latent root. The variance of the first principal component is 2.66, the largest. The variance of the second principal component is .8238; the third is .5141; and the fourth is zero! (A variance of zero indicates a special case, which we'll address later in this chapter.)

We can draw several conclusions from Table 15–10:

1. Because there are four variables, it is possible to extract four PCs from the correlation matrix.
2. The basic statistics of PCA are the four variances or *latent roots* (LR1, LR2, LR3, LR4), which are ordered by size, and the associated weight (i.e., coefficient) vectors, or *latent vectors* (*a*1, *a*2, *a*3, *a*4).
3. The total variance in the system or data set is four—the sum of the variances of the four (standardized) variables.
4. Each latent vector contains four elements, one corresponding to each variable. For latent vector *a*l we have

   –.5514, –.4041, .4844, .5457

   which are the four coefficients associated with the first and largest PC whose variance is 2.6620.
5. The first PC is the linear combination

   $$PC1 = -.5514 \times Z1 - .4042 \times Z2 + .4844 \times Z3 + .5457 \times Z4$$

6. PC1 explains that (100 × 2.6620/4) = 66.55 percent of the total variance of the four variables.
7. The second PC is the linear combination

   $$PC2 = -.4222 \times Z1 + .7779 \times Z2 + .4120 \times Z3 - .2162 \times Z4$$

8. PC2 with next-to-largest variance .8238 explains that (100 × .8238/4) = 20.59 percent of the total variance of the four variables.
9. Together the first two PCs account for 66.55 percent plus 20.55 percent or 87.14 percent of the variance in the four variables.
10. For the first PC, the first two coefficients are negative and the last two are positive; accordingly, PC1 is interpreted as a *contrast* between persons who at most graduated high school and persons who at least attended college.

    High positive scores on PC1 are associated with ZIP codes where the percentage of persons who at least attended college is *greater* than the percentage of persons who at most graduated high school.

    Low scores (high negative scores) on PC1 are associated with ZIP codes where the percentage of persons who at least attended college is *less* than the percentage of persons who at most graduated high school.

ALGEBRAIC PROPERTIES OF PCA

PCA has a lot of very appealing algebraic properties, some of which we list below. The previous example should provide you with "empirical" proof of these properties, and hopefully an appreciation of the value of the PCA method.

1. Almost always PCA is performed on a correlation matrix; that is, the analysis is done with standardized variables (means = zero and variances = 1).
2. Each principal component

   $$PCi = ai1 \times Z1 + ai2 \times Z2 + \ldots + aip \times Zp$$

has a variance also called a latent root or eigenvalue such that

a. Var(PC1) is maximum.
b. Var(PC1) > Var(PC2) > . . . > Var(PCp).
c. Equality can occur but it is rare.
d. Mean(PCi) = 0.

3. All PCs are uncorrelated.
4. Associated with each latent root i is a latent vector

   $(ai1, ai2, \ldots, aip)$

   that is the weight for the linear combination of the original variables forming PCi.

   $$PCi = ai1 \times Z1 + ai2 \times Z2 + \ldots aip \times Zp$$

5. The sum of the variances of the PCs (i.e., sum of the latent roots) is equal to the sum of the variances of the original variables. Since the variables are standardized, the sum of latent roots equals p.
6. The proportion of variance in the original p variables that k PCs account for is equal to the

   $$\frac{\text{sum of latent roots for first } k \text{ PCs}}{p}$$

7. Correlation between an original variable (Xi) and its principal component (PCj) equals

   $$aij \times \sqrt{[\text{Var(PC}j)]}$$

   This correlation is called a *PC loading.*
8. The sum of the squares of loadings across all the PCs for an original variable indicates how much variance for that variable is accounted for by the PCs (communality of the variable).
9. Var(PC) = 0 implies that a perfect collinear relationship exists.
10. Var(PC) = small (less than .001) implies high multicollinearity.

Properties 9 and 10 provide us with a way to identify whether the variables are highly correlated. Recalling our simple example in which the fourth PC has zero variance, the question we must address is how the four variables are perfectly correlated.

Actually, the answer is somewhat intuitive. The perfect relationship among the four variables is such that

$$X1 + X2 + X3 + X4 = 100\%$$

That is, the sum of the percentages of the four education variables or levels must sum to 100 percent. Thus, knowing any three of the education variables automatically provides us with the remaining variable's value. Such data, which add to 100 percent, are known as compositional data. Suffice it to say that census data frequently take this form and that modelers should be aware that compositional data can present difficulties not always associated with principal components analysis. However, the techniques needed to use this data correctly are well beyond the scope of this book.[2]

[2]Interested readers are referred to J. Aitchison, "The Statistical Analysis of Compositional Data," *J. R. Statistical Society B*, 44, 1982, pp. 137–77.

MODEL BUILDING WITH PCA—TWO CASE STUDIES

1. A Continuity Example

A continuity company wanted to develop a geography-based model that could be used against outside rented lists. The plan was to perform the usual merge-purge and then apply the scoring model to the resulting mail file. The decision was made to score the file at the block group level.

A principal components analysis was done on all the census categories. (There are about 300 census variables that can be collapsed into about 40 categories. Education, for example, as we discussed before, represents four variables, but one census category.) In this case study, a number of categories proved to be significant (i.e., correlated with response), but three categories were found to be exceptionally significant, and these three categories were the only categories to enter the model. One of the categories was household income, consisting of nine individual variables, and the other two categories will remain nameless for reasons of confidentiality.

Tables 15–11 and 15–12 describe PCA output having to do with the Household Income factor. In Table 15–11 we see that the analysis produced nine principal components, equal to the number of original variables shown in Table 15–12.

In Table 15–11 the first principal component contains 47 percent of the information or variance contained in all of the original nine variables. The second principal component contains 20 percent of the total variance. Thus, the first two PCs account for 67 percent of the total information in the entire data set.

In Table 15–12 we see the eigenvector or weights for the first principal component against which each ZIP code will be scored. Notice the contrast. The lower income variables have negative weights, and the higher income variables have positive weights.

In Table 15–13 we see the scores produced by a relatively low income block group that we'll label Case 1 and the scores produced by a relatively high income block group, labeled Case 2. Because a greater percentage of Case 1's population have lower incomes and because lower incomes are associated with negative weights in this data set, it's not surprising that this particular block group has a negative score with regard to income. The converse is true for Case 2, a block group with a relative upscale income distribution. Now let's use this principal component in a logistic regression model to see if it helps us predict response.

The top of Table 15–14 presents the logistic regression model. As we mentioned before, the actual model contained two other principal components that are not shown in this example. The coefficient of the income variable is a negative number (–0.7324). Because, as we have seen, block groups with relatively low income distributions have negative scores, or low positive scores, the model tells us that low income block groups will have higher scores than upper income block groups. (Remember a negative value times a negative coefficient yields a positive number, which will increase a block group's final score or probability of response.)

Note how the difference in the distribution of incomes between block groups changed the expected probability of response from 2.41 percent for the block group with the higher income to 3.07 percent for the block group with the lower income distribution.

TABLE 15–11
Household Income Principal Components Output—The Proportion of Total Variance Explained by Each Principal Component

Principal Component	*Eigenvalue*	*Proportion*	*Cumulative*
Principal component 1	4.213	47%	47%
Principal component 2	1.826	20	67
Principal component 3	0.837	9	76
Principal component 4	0.579	7	83
Principal component 5	0.497	5	88
Principal component 6	0.357	4	92
Principal component 7	0.300	4	96
Principal component 8	0.279	3	99
Principal component 9	0.109	1	100
Total	9.000	100%	

TABLE 15–12
Household Income First Principal Component Output—Eigenvector

Census	*Variable Description*	*Eigenvector/Weight*
1	%HH < $15	–0.342
2	%HH $15–$25	–0.370
3	%HH $25–$35	–0.261
4	%HH $35–$50	–0.003
5	%HH $50–$75	0.304
6	%HH $75–$100	0.404
7	%HH $100–$125	0.412
8	%HH $125–$50	0.376
9	%HH $150+	0.339

TABLE 15–13
Using Principal Components in Logistic Regression Models

		Case 1 Lower Income Block Group		*Case 2 Upper Income Block Group*	
Description	*Eigenvector*	*Distribution*	*Eigenvector Contribution*	*Distribution*	*Eigenvector Contribution*
% HH < $15	–0.342	25%	–0.0855	2%	–0.0068
% HH $15–$25	–0.370	10	–0.0370	3	–0.0111
% HH $25–$35	–0.261	10	–0.0261	6	–0.0157
% HH $35–$50	–0.003	30	–0.0009	4	–0.0001
% HH $50–$75	0.302	10	0.0302	10	0.0302
% HH $75–$100	0.402	4	0.0161	30	0.1206
% HH $100–$12	0.410	6	0.0246	10	0.0410
% HH $125–$15	0.374	3	0.0112	10	0.0374
% HH $150+	0.332	2	0.0066	25	0.0830
	Total Score	100%	–0.0608	100%	0.2785

TABLE 15–14
Scoring a Principal Components Logistic Regression Model

The Model	
The constant is equal to	–3.4964
The coefficient of HH INC 1 is equal to	–0.7324
Scoring Case 1	
Case 1's score for the HH INC 1 variable from Table 15–13	–0.0608
The product of Case 1's score × the coefficient of HH INC 1: –0.7324	0.0445
Adding the constant back to get Case 1's total score	–3.4519
Converting the score, which is a logit, to odds by exponentiating the logit	0.0317
Converting odds to probabilities using the formula Probability = Odds/(1 + Odds)	3.07%
Scoring Case 2	
Case 2's score for the HH INC 1 variable from Table 15–13	0.2785
The product of Case 1's score × the coefficient of HH INC 1: –0.7324	–0.2040
Adding the constant back to get Case 2's total score	–3.7004
Converting the score, which is a logit, to odds by exponentiating the logit	0.0247
Converting odds to probabilities using the formula Probability = Odds/(1 + Odds)	2.41%

Finally, we believe that census data—based models that use principal components turn out to be more stable over the long term than models that use individual census variables (percent of households with incomes between $100,000 and $125,000, for example) and we encourage their use. Too many companies have had the experience of developing models that validate but do not hold up over the long haul. We think this approach will help.

2. A Packaged Goods Example

A packaged goods manufacturer with a large database wanted to mail a promotion to customers on the database likely to buy Category A products. A significant percentage of customers on the database were known users of Category A products, but the promotion was budgeted to go to more than just these known category users.

A modeling file was created in which known users of Category A were coded 1 and customers on the database who were not known users were coded 0. We could now develop a logistic regression model on this data set, similar to a 0/1 response model. We are assuming that if we could identify users of Category A products through modeling (modeling data other than Category A usage) the model could be used to rank customers not known to be users on the database in terms of their probability of being a Category A user.

In this case the potential independent variables included the answers to 60 categorical (yes/no) lifestyle questions that a large majority of persons on the database (both users and nonusers of Category A products) had answered.

TABLE 15–15
A Comparison of Regression Models Using Dummy Variables versus Principal Components as Independent Variables

	Dummy Variables			*Principal Components*		
Decile	*Decile Usage Rate %*	*Cumulative Usage Rate %*	*Cum Lift*	*Decile Usage Rate %*	*Cumulative Usage Rate %*	*Cum Lift*
1	45%	45%	294	50%	50%	330
2	21	33	215	20	35	232
3	16	27	178	15	28	187
4	17	24	161	15	25	166
5	21	24	157	19	24	158
6	14	22	146	13	22	147
7	9	20	133	8	20	134
8	10	19	125	10	19	125
9	0	17	111	0	17	111
10	0	15	100	0	15	100

We analyzed the data two ways. First, we created 59 dummy variables and produced a model in the traditional way by coding each person in the data set a 0 or a 1 on each of the lifestyle questions. Next we completed a principal components analysis and ran the regression model on the resulting principal components. Five raw lifestyle variables entered the dummy variable regression model and two principal components (now used as independent variables) entered the principal components model. Table 15–15 compares the two models. Not only did the principal components model do somewhat better, but also the principal components model is expected to be more stable than the dummy variable model because it looks at all 60 lifestyle variables, not just the five that entered the model.

This concludes our discussion of principal components analysis, a tool we find to be increasingly useful in building stable regression models stemming from data sets that contain large numbers of potential independent variables such as retail SKUs or items within a mail order catalog.

Chapter 16

Artificial Neural Networks

INTRODUCTION

Unless you have been under a rock building statistical models, you must have heard something about neural networks. Most probably you heard something like the following: *"Neural networks outperform traditional regressions models by 20, 30, or even 1,000 percent."* Or, *"Neural network technology is so advanced it virtually builds models by itself, and very quickly too!"* Or, *"Neural networks find interaction variables automatically and also work especially well when the data are nonlinear. That's right, neural networks thrive on nonlinear data."* What more can we direct marketers ask for? Perhaps a clear-cut expository on neural networks, specifically Artificial Neural Networks (ANN).

The key word in ANN is *artificial.* Here, *artificial* does not mean fake, false, or sham. It means it's not the real thing. The Real Neural Network (RNN) is the human brain. However, ANNs are a serious effort at imitating or simulating the real thing. Otherwise, there is nothing artificial about ANNs. ANNs are based on rock-solid computational processing logic that is carried out by well-accepted mathematical algorithms.

The claims quoted above are made by sales people who either are good at selling by hyperbole or believe so much in the underlying concept of ANNs that they forget the A in ANN. They think they are selling a brain in a box. On the other hand, the die-hard ANN analysts, so absorbed in the theoretical beauty and mathematical elegance of ANNs, also get carried away and treat ANNs like RNNs. But that's only because they love their nets.

In this chapter we provide you with everything you need to know about ANNs, without a black belt in statistics. In discussing ANNs, we draw parallels to statistical modeling to set the stage for the final comparison of which technique is better; this is the real issue today in the direct marketing industry.

WHEN ARE ANNs USED

The two most popular applications of ANNs correspond to the two most popular applications of statistical modeling in the direct marketing industry: classification and prediction.

Classification

This type of application is the mainstay of direct marketing modeling: to find individuals in a population defined by distinct and separate classes. Specifically, the population is either a house file or an outside list, and the classes are customers/prospects that can be labeled as responders or non-responders. The classification problem is usually performed by developing a logistic regression response model.

FIGURE 16–1

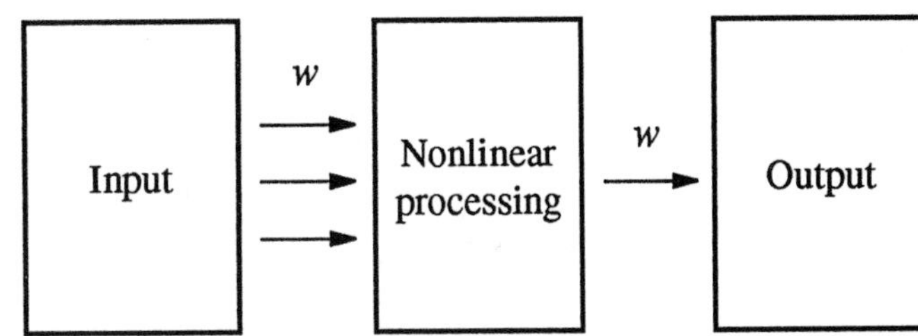

Prediction

Prediction in the direct marketing industry, and in every industry, focuses on finding customers or prospects most likely to generate significant dollar and/or volume sales. This task is typically performed by developing an ordinary least-squares regression model.

If ANNs and regression-based techniques do the same things, why bother with the newer and perhaps not-as-well-tested ANN? The answer lies not only from the emotional aspect of "something new is something better," but from a theoretical vantage point. ANNs are more complex than regression models by virtue of the fact that regression models are a special case of ANN. Accordingly, the potential gain of the more complex and encompassing ANN is real.

However, just because ANNs have more theoretical muscle does not imply that they can outperform regression techniques. In other words, the proof of the pudding is not how the pudding is made, but how the pudding tastes. Before we do a taste test comparison between ANNs and statistical modeling, let's formally discuss what ANNs are, and how ANNs are built.

WHAT ARE ANNs?

Definition

ANNs are multi-input nonlinear models with weighted interconnections between input and output layers, as depicted in Figure 16–1 above. The multi-input layer holds the information to be modeled, namely the independent/predictor variables. The independent variables are connected by weights to the middle layer, which is referred to as the hidden layer. A nonlinear function, called a *transfer* or *squashing function,* resides in the hidden layer. The hidden layer is also known as the black box of the ANN, because even the experts cannot figure out at all times how the nonlinear function treats the independent variables. Regardless, the independent variables are processed in such a way that when they reach the output layer the desired outcome is hopefully achieved.

This broad definition of ANN is provided to set the stage for a closer look at ANN—its basic structure.

Basic Structure

The basic structure of an ANN is

1. the weighted sum u of $n + 1$ inputs (variables) $X_0, X_1, X_2, \ldots, X_n$, where $X_0 \equiv 1$, $w_0 \equiv 0$,
2. which passes through a nonlinear function ψ,
3. thus producing output y.

$$y = \psi\ (\Sigma w_i X_i + \theta)$$

FIGURE 16–2
Basic Structure

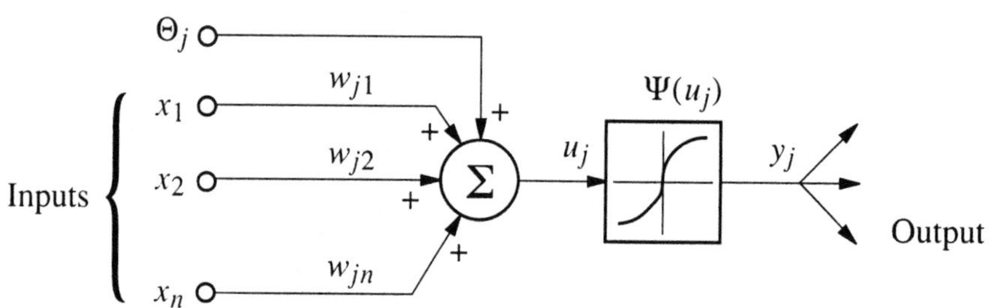

where

ψ is called the transfer or squashing function.

w_i are the interconnection strengths, or weights.

θ is called the bias, similar to the intercept term in a logistic regression equation in that it adjusts the weighted sum into a usable range.

Y is the output, whose values are called the activation levels produced by the (feedforward) relationship between input and output layers.

The basic structure of an ANN is depicted in Figure 16–2 above. We see that input elements, x_1, x_2,. . ., x_n, and the bias element are fully connected to the single hidden element, denoted by the encircled Σ. The weighted sum of these elements, u_j, passes through the transfer function, typically the *S*-curve.

Basic ANN

This basic structure is actually an ANN itself; however, the basic ANN consists of many basic structures, resulting in an input layer of many input elements, a hidden layer of many hidden elements, and lastly, an output layer of many output elements. The connections among the input elements to hidden elements, and hidden elements to output elements may be either fully or partially connected. See Figure 16–3 for the basic ANN structure or architecture.

Basic Architecture

With the basic structure of an ANN presented, we can characterize ANN in terms of how it is organized—its architecture. There are five components of the architecture; each one is briefly discussed below.

1. ***Number of Layers.*** With the necessity of input and output layers, the question of how many hidden layers are needed is very important, both from a theoretical and practical standpoint.
2. ***Number of Elements per Layer.*** This component relates to the issue of too many variables in a regression model. Too many variables is a good indication the model builder either had a problem developing an adequate model or did not know there was a problem. In other words, too many variables in regression and too many elements in a layer are signs of trouble, also known as *overfit.*
3. ***Type of Connections.*** Information within the ANN can flow in several directions. Although we have only described forward information flows, there are feedbackward and laterally connected ANNs.

FIGURE 16–3
Basic ANN

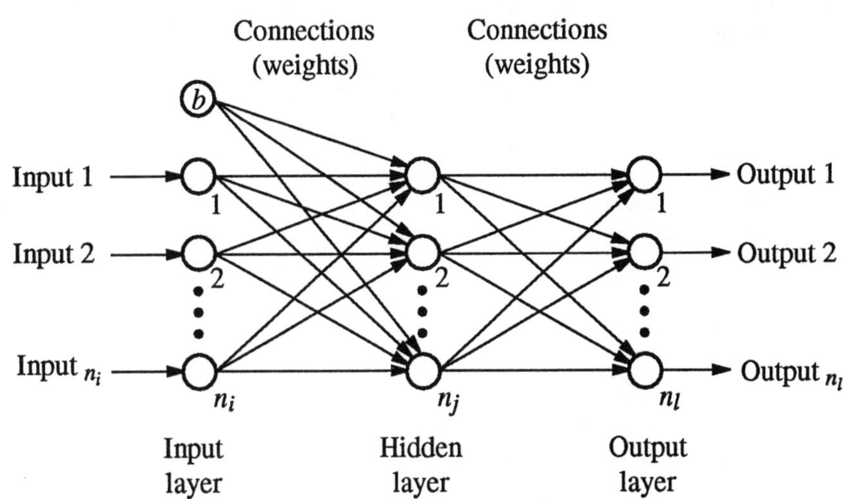

4. ***Degree of Connectivity.*** The elements within a layer can be connected to other layers either fully or partially connected. Partially connected layers minimize an overfitted ANN, but the trade-off is less predictive power.
5. ***Type of Transfer Function.*** The choice criterion for transfer function is simply the one that provides good performance with minimum training time. See Figure 16–4 for the types of transfer functions available.

As mentioned previously, the transfer function is also known as a squashing function because it takes u_j values, which can range from plus to negative infinity and "squashes" them into small output y_j ranges. This nonlinear structural component is what makes the ANN robust, or reliable. The squashing minimizes the effects' "far out" input values by replacing them with values restricted to a small range (e.g., values between plus and negative 1, or plus and negative 1/2, or between 0 and 1). See Figure 16–4.

HOW ANNs ARE TRAINED

When humans want to master a task, they practice or train themselves until the task is learned. ANNs do the same: train, train, and train until the task is learned. Humans sometimes need a teacher, and sometimes are self-taught. The same is true for ANNs. (A note on ANN terminology: where the statisticians say the regression model is estimated, the ANN analysts say the ANN undergoes learning or training.)

ANN learning/training can be either supervised by a teacher or unsupervised. Supervised learning is based on pairs of information: for every input there is a matched and known output. Specifically, for every input value, which is essentially a set of values for the independent variables $X_1, X_2, \ldots, X_n$, and for the corresponding output value, which is a set of values for the dependent variables $Y_1, Y_2, \ldots, Y_n$, the ANN learns the patterns within the X values that are associated with known Y values. The training is successful when the learned (i.e., observed or estimated) output agrees with known paired (i.e., desired or correct answer) output. The goal of supervised learning is to get correct answers.

FIGURE 16–4
Types of Transfer Function

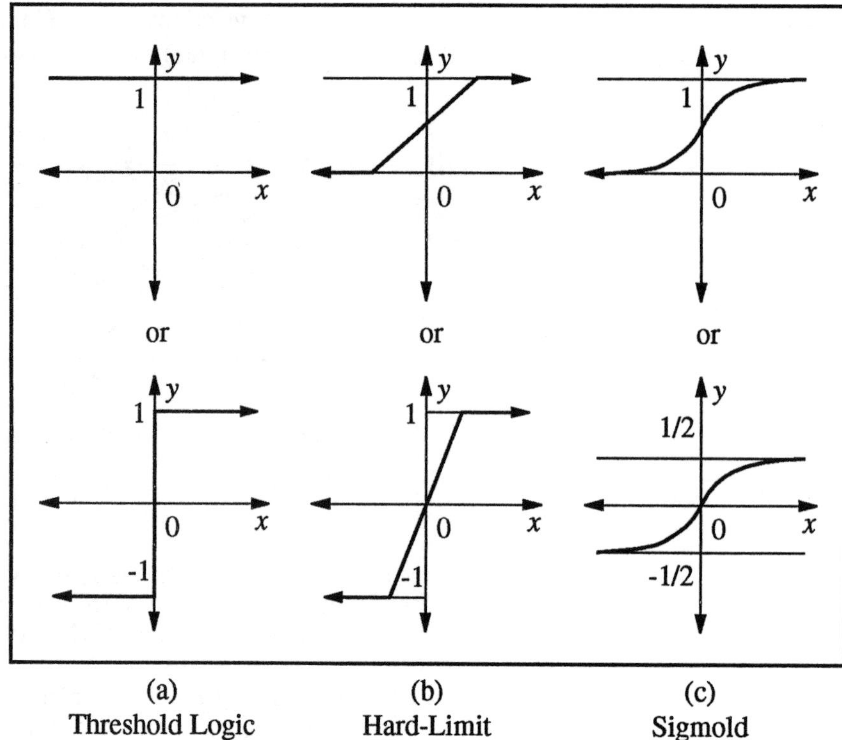

In contrast, unsupervised does *not* use pairs of information; it uses only input values. There are no direct comparisons between learned and known output; there are no correct answers. The goal is to discover patterns in the data using only the input itself and no external information. We will not discuss unsupervised ANNs, for they are second in application to their supervised counterpart, and offer no real potential in the direct marketing industry.

Supervised Training Method

Mathematically, learning means adjusting the weights so the desired outputs are produced by using an adaptive or optimization algorithm. Specifically, supervised learning involves adjusting the weights so the total error, *E*, defined below, is minimized.

- For a given training pair or single presentation, *p*, and for an output layer with *n* elements, the error is the mean-squared of *desired minus observed* outputs:

$$E_p = \frac{1}{n} \Sigma(d_{pj} - o_{pj})^2$$

- For *m* presentations (training sample/epoch size *m*), total error is the mean of all presentation errors:

$$E = \frac{1}{m} \Sigma E_p$$

The method of gradient steepest descent is the adaptive algorithm used in most ANN training. This method, which iteratively changes the weights to (hopefully) achieve an *absolute minimum* total error proceeds as follows:

1. Initial weights are random set to small values.
2. All training pairs, *p*, one at a time, are presented to the *ANN*.

3. The error E is calculated.
4. The weights are adjusted to minimize E.
5. Repeat steps 2 to 4 (called an epoch) until E converges.

It turns out that the algorithm is a "cruncher" requiring long training time, with no guarantee of convergence or convergence to an absolute minimum.

DESIGNING AN OPTIMAL MULTILAYER FEEDFORWARD ANN

Building an ANN is like cooking pudding; you need a well-tested recipe with quality ingredients and, of course, a good cook. Here we outline the best ingredients for the most popular and well-tested multilayer feedforward ANN.

1. ***Degree of Connectivity:*** fully connected between all layers.
2. ***Type of Transfer Function:*** the logistic function provides good performance with minimum training time.
3. ***Number of Hidden Layers:***
   a. Theoretically, it is sufficient to use no more than two.
   b. Practically, it is necessary to use only one.
4. ***Number of Elements per Layer.***
   a. Output layer—problem dependent.
   b. Hidden layer—$\sqrt{(\#inputs) \times (\#outputs)}$
      (1) Too few; network won't train/calibrate.
      (2) Too many; network won't validate/generalize.
      (3) Strategy—start with "too few" and end before "too many."
   c. Input layer—become an artist.
      (1) Less is "more":
         (a) Use PCA to reduce the number of input variables.
         (b) Use CHAID to combine input variables.
      (2) Linear scaling of input so values fall in [0, 1] interval.
         (a) Use $X = \frac{(x - x_{min})}{(x_{max} - x_{min})}$
      (3) Nonlinear transformations—use ladder of powers to symmetrize input.
5. ***Training Set:*** *Should include*
   a. Every input (covariate) pattern for a complete network.
   b. Some noise in every pattern for a robust network.
   c. Large number of pairs to minimize overfit tendency.
      (1) 16 inputs with 4 hidden and 1 output elements result in 72 weights/*free* parameters that will *cost* the network!
   d. Number of training pairs $\geq 10 \times$ *#weights.*
   e. Present many subsets of the training sets in random batches of increasing size.

THE BLACK BOX ANN

Theoretically, we now know how an ANN works. Practically, we will most probably never know how an ANN works, because, as previously mentioned, the hidden layer is considered the black box of the ANN. The hidden layer with all its weights coming in and going out is virtually impossible to interpret. But, perhaps its worth a try. Here are some approaches to better understand what's going on in the hidden layer.

1. To determine which variables are important, train in a forward, stepwise approach and check performance. Be careful. As in stepwise regression, the order of variable selection is dependent upon which variables are in and which variables are not.

2. Examine weights directly. Be careful. Also, as in regression, the coefficients are dependent upon which variables are in and which variables are not.
3. Perform cluster analysis on the training set based on the activation levels of all hidden elements. Be hopeful. Cluster analyze the activation levels; then, compute means on the original input variables for each cluster. Hopefully, the centriods make some sense. (Note: For each training input, there is a set of activation levels whose number equals the number of hidden elements.)

PROOF OF THE PUDDING

We conclude that at this stage in its development, ANN appears to not significantly outperform logistic regression. Interestingly, exploratory data analysis (EDA) appears to be *even* more important for the building of an ANN than for a logistic regression model (LRM).

The following two examples typify our experience with the two techniques.

Problem. 1. To identify financial investors most likely to purchase additional investment vehicles based on a current mailing to stimulate such activity.

Solution. Response rate of the mailing was 4.5 percent. The mail file was appended with over 50 internal and external variables.

EDA boiled down the variables to four candidate predictors:

1. RECENCY—number of months since last inquiries.
2. FREQUENCY—number of previous inquiries.
3. LIFE—number of months investor is active.
4. PRODUCTS—number of services an investor subscribes to.

ANN Model

The ANN optimally selected all four independent variables and decided on three hidden elements. The decile analysis shows a top decile with 7.9 percent response rate and lift of 174. However, the second decile has a higher response rate, 8.8 percent. Also, decile 3 has a higher response rate than decile 4, and decile 5 higher than decile 6. See Table 16–1.

Such "unsmooth" performance of any model (i.e., response rates not decreasing smoothly down through the deciles) is an indication the model was not given the "right" variables to train or estimate with. Whether we are modeling with ANN or LRM, we *never* know the right variables; and even if we do, they may not be available to us. Apparently, the ANN was not given the right set on input variables.

This ANN has three hidden elements, which may be one too many. Perhaps, in learning the training pairs and not having all the right variables, the ANN used an "extra" hidden element to find some pattern in the data to help the training and inadvertently modeled noise. This may result in a *negative-bias* overfit, which results in deterioration of performance, such as unsmooth response behavior. This kind of overfit is not as common as *positive-bias* overfit, in which the model's performance is spuriously enhanced by the inclusion of a redundant (highly correlated) variable.

TABLE 16–1
ANN Decile Analysis (4 variables/3 hidden elements)

Decile	Number of Customers	Number of Responses	Decile Response Rate	Cum Response Rate	Cum Lift
Top	2,410	190	7.9%	7.9%	174
2	2,410	212	8.8%	8.3%	184
3	2,410	106	4.4%	7.0%	155
4	2,410	114	4.7%	6.5%	143
5	2,410	88	3.7%	5.9%	130
6	2,410	91	3.8%	5.5%	122
7	2,410	88	3.7%	5.3%	117
8	2,410	74	3.1%	5.0%	110
9	2,410	69	2.9%	4.8%	105
Bottom	2,410	58	2.4%	4.5%	100
Total	24,100	1,090	4.5%		

LOGISTIC REGRESSION MODEL

We ran an LRM with all four candidate predictors and found that PRODUCTS should be dropped from the model because it is declared nonsignificant with a *p*-value of .36980.

(Note: Although our peddlers of ANN say that you can put all the variables you have in an ANN—the more the better—we have no way of knowing if a variable is really needed in an ANN, let alone that it may be hurting the ANN performance. The working assumption is that the weights from input to hidden layers will affect the importance of a variable. Is PRODUCTS hurting our ANN?)

Variable	DF	Parameter Estimate	Standard Error	Wald Chi-Square	Pr > Chi-Square
INTERCPT	1	–2.9531	0.0838	1242.3272	0.E+00
RECENCY	1	–0.00889	0.00177	25.1787	5.E-07
FREQUENCY	1	–0.1889	0.0337	31.3892	2.E-08
PRODUCTS	1	0.0285	0.0317	0.8043	.36980
LIFE	1	0.2839	0.0337	71.0918	3.E-17

We reran the LRM without PRODUCTS, and the model looks fine with *p*-values indicating all variables are statistically significant. We see that the coefficients do not significantly change from those in the first LRM, which indicates that PRODUCTS was providing noise.

The three-variable LRM decile analysis looks quite good with a top decile having a response rate of 8.1 percent, and the second decile having 6.7 percent. There is, however, as with the ANN, some unsmooth response behavior within the deciles 8 and 9. Again, this reflects that we do not know and/or have all the right variables; that is, we have a data problem, not a modeling issue. See Table 16–2.

Variable	DF	Parameter Estimate	Standard Error	Wald Chi-Square	PR > Chi-Square
INTERCPT	1	–2.9537	0.0838	1242.5492	0.E+00
RECENCY	1	–0.00882	0.00177	24.8038	6.E-07
FREQUENCY	1	–0.1870	0.0337	30.8287	3.E-08
LIFE	1	0.2942	0.0315	87.1062	0.E+00

TABLE 16–2
LRM Decile Analysis (3 variables)

Decile	*Number of Customers*	*Number of Responses*	*Decile Response Rate*	*Cum Response Rate*	*Cum Lift*
Top	2,410	196	8.1%	8.1%	180
2	2,410	162	6.7%	7.4%	164
3	2,410	135	5.6%	6.8%	151
4	2,410	122	5.1%	6.4%	141
5	2,410	102	4.2%	6.0%	132
6	2,410	89	3.7%	5.6%	123
7	2,410	65	2.7%	5.2%	114
8	2,410	78	3.2%	4.9%	109
9	2,410	85	3.5%	4.8%	105
Bottom	2,410	56	2.3%	4.5%	100
Total	24,100	1,090	4.5%		

TABLE 16–3
ANN Decile Analysis (3 variables without PRODUCTS/3 hidden elements)

Decile	*Number of Customers*	*Number of Responses*	*Decile Response Rate*	*Cum Response Rate*	*Cum Lift*
Top	2,410	203	8.4%	8.4%	186
2	2,410	179	7.4%	7.9%	175
3	2,410	123	5.1%	7.0%	154
4	2,410	121	5.0%	6.5%	144
5	2,410	83	3.4%	5.9%	130
6	2,410	94	3.9%	5.6%	123
7	2,410	72	3.0%	5.2%	115
8	2,410	86	3.6%	5.0%	110
9	2,410	80	3.3%	4.8%	106
Bottom	2,410	49	2.0%	4.5%	100
Total	24,100	1,090	4.5%		

ReRuns

Perhaps we should rerun the ANN without PRODUCTS. We do so and get an ANN with three hidden elements and a decile analysis, which looks much improved. Notwithstanding a possible positive-bias overfit as indicated by three hidden elements as opposed to the preferred two hidden elements, the top decile response rate is 8.4 percent (the first ANN top decile is 7.9 percent). The top five deciles have smooth response rates; however, there is still some unsmooth response behavior at deciles 6 and 8. See Table 16–3.

Apparently, PRODUCTS is hurting the performance of the first ANN. Since there is no *internal* ANN device to detect when a variable can deteriorate an ANN, EDA is very important to the building of a reliable ANN. Possibly, a more rigorous EDA assessment of PRODUCTS would have removed it from the initial training input set.

LRM has such devices. For a variable's overall contribution, we have the simple correlation coefficient; for a variable's unique contribution, taking into account the presence of other variables in the model, we have partial correlation coefficients.

TABLE 16–4
LRM Decile Analysis (4 variables with PRODUCTS

Decile	Number of Customers	Number of Responses	Decile Response Rate	Cum Response Rate	Cum Lift
Top	2,410	192	8.0%	8.0%	176
2	2,410	153	6.3%	7.2%	158
3	2,410	148	6.1%	6.8%	151
4	2,410	116	4.8%	6.3%	140
5	2,410	106	4.4%	5.9%	131
6	2,410	83	3.4%	5.5%	122
7	2,410	68	2.8%	5.1%	113
8	2,410	75	3.1%	4.9%	108
9	2,410	93	3.9%	4.8%	105
Bottom	2,410	56	2.3%	4.5%	100
Total	24,100	1,090	4.5%		

Just for the sake of completeness, let's look at the performance of LRM with the "noisy" PRODUCTS. The top decile has a response rate of 8.0 percent (the first LRM top decile is 8.1 percent). The second and third deciles have response rates of 6.3 percent and 6.1 percent, respectively (the first LRM second and third deciles are 6.7 percent and 5.3 percent, respectively). The response rates are still unsmooth in the same deciles as the first LRM, deciles 8 and 9.

The top three deciles have the same cum lift of 151, for the three- and four-variable LRM, respectively. The differences below 30 percent of the file are clearly nonsignificant but reflect the slight but nonetheless negative-bias overfit from the noise of PRODUCTS.

Discussion

We feel this example typifies two important implications. First, every attempt at the identification of unnecessary variables, either carrying redundant information or noise like that from PRODUCTS in the first ANN, must be made. Since ANNs do not have any internal devices for such analysis, EDA is important to ANN and should be part of the ANN building process. Interestingly, EDA may be more important to ANN than it is to LRM.

The second relates to modeling strategy. This example clearly suggests the modeling processing should be a partnership between the analyst and his/her tools. We should use both LRM with its EDA devices and ANN with its optimal components, not to pit one technique against the other but to gain predictive power in the synergy of using them together.

One question remains: Does ANN without PRODUCTS outperform LRM without PRODUCTS? We tested for significant differences in response rates between models for the top decile, and the top 20 percent and top 30 percent of the file.

Percent of File	Response Rate			p-value
	ANN	LRM	Difference	
Top decile	8.4%	8.1%	0.3%	35%
Top 20%	7.9%	7.4%	0.5%	18%
Top 30%	7.0%	6.8%	0.2%	32%

In all cases the differences were not statistically significant at any reasonable level. Thus, we must conclude that the ANN does not outperform the LRM.

The larger question for direct marketers is whether ANN models will hold up better than regression models over time. Given all that we have learned up to this point about ANNs, our conclusion is that if they are *used correctly,* as demonstrated by the work done in this case study, ANN models should not do any worse or any better than regression with regard to deterioration.

Of course, the reality is that if marketers think that they can blindly use ANN without the aid of an experienced statistician or an AI expert, they are making, in our opinion, a very serious mistake and may well find that ANN models, given their tendency to "overfit" the data, will deteriorate even faster than regression models. And it won't be the fault of ANN; it will be the fault of marketers looking for a quick, simple, and inexpensive alternative to solid analysis. With ANN, as is the case everywhere else, there's no free lunch.

Chapter 17

An Introduction to the Economics of the New Direct Marketing

What if this chapter were titled "The Economics of Direct Marketing?" Would the contents be any different? The answer is yes. The difference between the economics of the *new direct marketing,* or, to use the more conventional term, *database marketing,* and the economics of *direct marketing* is fundamentally the same as the difference between database marketing and what is generally thought of as *classical direct marketing.*

So before jumping into equations, formulas, and P&Ls, let's spend a few minutes on the differences we see between classical direct marketing and modern database marketing, the new direct marketing. Let's also take this time to define the important differences between a *traditional* direct marketing company, which may employ both classical direct marketing methods and database marketing methods, and companies that are not traditional direct marketing companies (*nontraditional* direct marketers) but who use classical direct marketing methods, database marketing methods or both, as just one part of their marketing mix. (See Figure 17–1.)

The differences are important and have much to do with the popularity of database marketing and the changes that are taking place within traditional direct marketing companies and within what is generally referred to as the direct marketing industry, as represented by the members of the Direct Marketing Association.

Traditional direct marketing companies or divisions of companies are operating units that depend entirely on acquiring and servicing customers through direct marketing methods. This definition would encompass all the business-to-business and consumer catalogers, fund raisers, continuity, club, and subscription businesses, as well as all financial service organizations that use only direct media to acquire and retain customers. If we include direct sales as part of direct media, this definition could also accommodate firms that may not consider themselves hard-core direct marketing companies, for example, all the direct door-to-door sales companies and cable TV firms.

Nontraditional direct marketers include all firms that use direct marketing methods, in combination with general advertising and nontraceable sales promotion techniques such as cents-off coupons, fulfillment offers, in-store price promotions, contests, refunds, sweepstakes, and the like to increase sales that are consummated either at retail or with the aid of a salesperson. This definition includes all retailers using classical direct marketing or database marketing methods to generate store traffic; all consumer products companies using targeted coupons or fulfillment offers to support retail sales; all car manufacturers, telecommunications companies, computer manufacturers, and office equipment dealers. The

FIGURE 17–1
A Framework for Understanding the Direct Marketing Industry

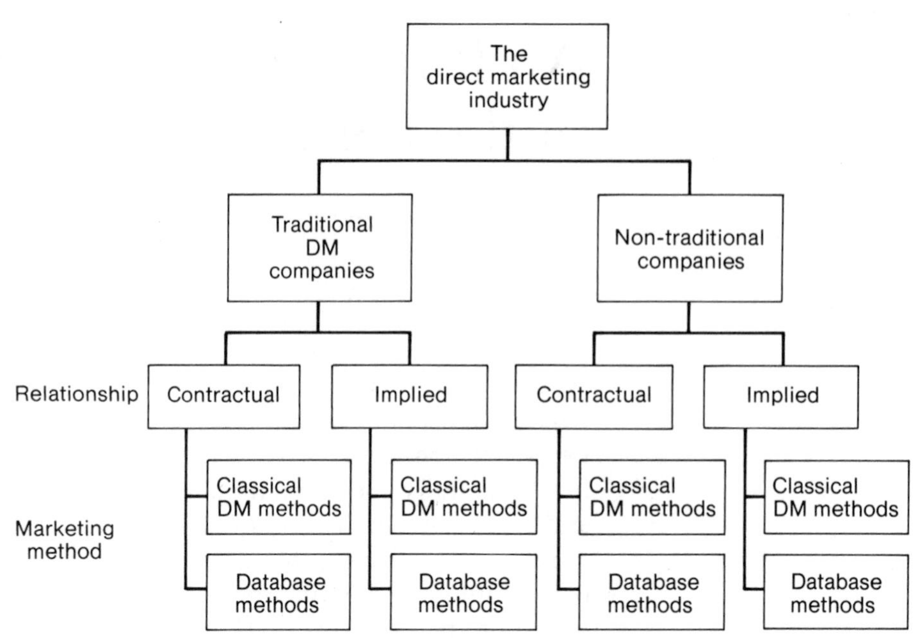

list goes on and on, and includes any organization using direct marketing as just one of a number of advertising, promotion, and marketing options.

IMPLIED VERSUS CONTRACTUAL RELATIONSHIPS

Traditional direct marketing organizations may, in turn, be divided into two groups: those that have contractual obligations with their customers or members and those whose relationships are only, at best, implied. As you'll see, organizations with contractual relationships have been among the slowest to employ database marketing techniques—even though these firms are at the heart of the direct marketing business. In fact, as we'll see later in this chapter and throughout this book, it has been the nontraditional direct marketing companies that have made the greatest contribution to database marketing.

Contractual relationships exist in all subscription programs, clubs, and continuities. A contractual obligation, as executed by a signed coupon or telephone call, means that both the customer and the company understand what is expected of the other. Subscribers expect to receive a year's worth of magazines and then to be renewed (even though there's no contractual obligation to be renewed or to renew); club members expect to receive offers every three or four weeks; continuity members expect to receive a shipment every four, six, or eight weeks, and so on. Contractual relationships also exist within nontraditional direct marketing companies. For example, customers who sign on with a frequent flyer (or any other frequent purchaser or user) program understand what is expected of them and what is expected from the organization sponsoring the program.

On the other hand, an implied relationship is one in which there is no obligation on either party's part to do anything in the future. For example, in a catalog situation, after the initial response on the part of a consumer to a cold solicitation, there is no obligation on the consumer's part to purchase again or even on the cataloger's part to mail another catalog.

However, most consumers will not be surprised when they receive another catalog in the mail. Some implied relationships are less obvious. For example, the flood of financial service offers that follow the establishment of a banking relationship, though not a complete shock to the knowledgeable consumer, might come as a surprise to the average person.

The extent to which relationships are contractual or implied is directly related to the decision-making discretion available to the direct marketer. In contractual obligations, there is less discretion, thus less obvious need for sophisticated decision-making tools. Conversely, when there is no contractual obligation, much more care needs to go into the decision of to whom to mail, what to mail, and how often to mail. Thus, don't be surprised to discover, later in this chapter, that database-driven decision making, or database marketing, is more likely in the absence of a contractual relationship or even a strong implied relationship.

CLASSICAL DIRECT MARKETING VERSUS DATABASE MARKETING

Having defined traditional and nontraditional direct marketing companies, we can begin to discuss in more detail how each of these types employs both classical direct marketing and database marketing methods. The principal difference between the two methods is that for all intents and purposes, classical direct marketing does not really deal with information about individuals; and database marketing, if it does nothing else, attempts to deal with information about individuals. Now that's a fairly broad generalization that requires some elaboration.

When we say that classical direct marketing does not really deal with individuals, what we mean is that the classical direct marketing methods used in traditional direct marketing companies focus attention on the behavior of groups of individuals. Traditional direct marketing companies include:

- Mail-order companies selling individual products or services.
- Negative option book or record clubs.
- Continuity programs.
- Catalog companies.
- Financial services, sold primarily through direct response media.
- Magazines, newsletters, and other subscription services.
- Fund raisers.

Anyone who has ever worked in a traditional direct marketing company knows that nearly all the analysis work is directed at groups of customers; all of the customers recruited from a particular list or a segment of a list, from a particular print ad, or from a particular TV spot. Even in firms using techniques generally associated with database marketing, such as *Prizm* clusters, the emphasis is on how well all the customers or the average customer from a particular cluster perform.

The way this is done, for those readers not familiar with the mechanics of the direct marketing business, is that each promotion vehicle, be it a rented list or ad in a magazine, is assigned a source code or key code (terminology changes from company to company) and all new customers acquired from that list or print ad are forever associated with that original source code.

The analysis task is then reduced to evaluating the cost of the promotion compared to the profit generated from the new customers acquired from the promotion. If the profit is sufficiently greater than the costs, then, all other things being equal, the direct marketer will probably decide to use that promotion vehicle, that is, that list or magazine, again in the future. We'll spend a lot of time on the mechanics of this decision-making process, but the basic point we want to stress is this focus on average or group behavior and how this information is used for decision-making purposes.

Later on we'll see that even within traditional direct marketing companies, more and more analysis work is being done at the individual level, thus affecting the way marketing decisions are made. In other words, classical direct marketers, too, are becoming database marketers.

So, classical direct marketing deals with groups or averages, and database marketing, in ways yet to be discussed, deals with individuals. That's only the beginning. Classical direct marketing tends to search for the perfect average solution to a variety of direct marketing business problems; database marketing searches for the perfect individual solution to the same set of problems. Both methods do a lot of compromising.

THE SEARCH FOR THE PERFECT CONTROL

A good example of the difference between classical direct marketing and database marketing is the way in which each method searches for the perfect new-customer acquisition strategy. Emotionally, the classical direct marketer would like to find one direct mail package that could be mailed to all prospects on all rented lists, regardless of the mix of lists that make up the total mailing and the composition of individuals within each list. The reasons for this are obvious and are perfectly valid. It's cheaper to create, produce, and mail one package to everybody than it is to create, develop, and mail multiple packages to different groups of individuals.

The database marketer, on the other hand, while understanding the economic impossibility of mailing a different package to each individual, intuitively prefers to move in this direction. Emotionally, the database marketer understands that there must be more than one market segment in a mailing going to a few million individuals. So, the database marketer reasons, doesn't it make economic sense to attempt to segment individuals on a mailing list or on a combination of mailing lists into at least a handful of different market segments and to create unique mailing packages that address the individual needs of the individual segments? Maybe, maybe not. Later, we'll see that the answer depends on the ability to implement a cost-effective segmentation strategy.

ONCE THE CUSTOMER IS ON THE FILE

New-customer acquisition is not the only area in which classical direct marketing differs from database marketing. In fact, new-customer acquisition is probably the one area in which classical direct marketers have moved closest to database marketing, without the aid of a marketing database. Once the direct marketing process moves beyond the new-customer acquisition phase, that is, after the new customer is acquired and is included on the customer file, there are even stronger reasons for treating all new customers in the same way.

Think about a book club or a continuity program or even a catalog operation for a moment. All these traditional direct marketing businesses are supported by computer systems (fulfillment systems, inventory systems, accounts receivable systems) that are infinitely easier to operate if all customers are treated in exactly the same way after they become part of the file. Remember, most computer support systems were originally designed to operate in only one way, and they have been fine-tuned over the years to handle larger and larger volumes with increasing efficiency.

Let's concentrate our attention again on the negative option book club, a business most readers will be familiar with as users or at least as readers of the *New York Times* Book Review section. It's obviously easier, and therefore, from a data processing perspective, more cost-efficient, to treat all new members the same way:

- Send the new member the four books they chose within 48 hours.
- Place the new member on the member file and send every member the same advance announcement every four weeks.
- Give every member 10 days to return or not return the same negative option refusal form.
- Send every member who does not return the form within 10 days the same "Featured Selection."
- Provide every member with the same credit limits, and so on.

Compare this procedure with a process that attempts to place members into even as few as three or four segments based on this information about the individual member:

- The books they selected when they joined.
- The books they purchased as members.
- Their buying and paying patterns.
- Individual household level demographics.
- Lifestyle data obtained from internal research or overlays, and so on.

Obviously, even if the data processing department could do it, implementation of a customized fulfillment system would cost considerably more, take more time, and so forth. Is it worth it? The answer depends on how much better individual members would respond to a more customized service.

The same argument, albeit to a lesser degree, applies to catalog marketers. You could argue that it's easier and therefore less expensive to send the same catalog to every catalog customer, with equal frequency, than it is to design special catalogs for individual market segments and to design customized mailing programs for customers based on individual performance data. And that's true—it is easier and less expensive. But catalog mailers, given their implied and therefore discretionary relationships with their customers, realized long before database marketing became fashionable that they could increase their profits by segmenting their file on three simple measures: recency of purchase, frequency of purchase, and some measure of the dollar volume of purchase. The shorthand for this methodology is *RFM*, which stands for recency, frequency, and monetary value. Based on relatively simple treatments of these three measures, catalogers determined whom to mail to and how often to mail. However, as we'll see shortly, one contribution of database marketing to this name selection process has been the introduction of more sophisticated analytical tools that introduce a broader set of predictive variables and make even better use of RFM data.

SOME ASSUMPTIONS ABOUT THE ECONOMICS OF MULTIDIVISIONAL DATABASES

A common occurrence among multidivisional firms is the attempt to combine data from a variety of business units into a single marketing database. For example, companies such as Sears and J C Penney not only run retail stores and catalog businesses, but also have financial services operations as well. Many insurance companies sell multiple forms of insurance: life, health, disability, home owners, automobile, and so on. Institutions such as the Smithsonian operate a number of different business units, from the magazine, to travel, to the museums. Companies such as Time-Warner and Reader's Digest operate magazines, clubs, and continuity programs. As often as not each business unit has its own operations systems and its own customer file or database.

In these situations cross promotions across business lines are common, and each business unit is likely to have a model, or at least a strategy, for marketing to customers on each of the other business unit files.

The intuitive strategy is to develop a common marketing database by merging all the individual business files, combining information at the person or household level, or both. When we do this we are implicitly making two fundamental assumptions:

1. That there is considerable duplication among files—otherwise there is no reason for a common database.
2. That decision making will improve because we will be able to develop models based on a more complete understanding of our relationship with our customer.

The first assumption is easy enough to prove—use merge-purge technology to see what the true duplication rate is. If it's significant, continue with the project; if the duplication rate is very small, discontinue the project.

The second assumption is a bit more difficult to prove, but it can and should be tested before or during the early stages of a database development project by building models to actual mailings based on all the information that would be contained in the combined marketing database, and then comparing the results of these models against models built on just the information contained in the files of the individual business units.

For example, the term insurance department of a very large bank may have one model to be used against the bank's checking customers, another model to be used against customers that maintain savings accounts, a third model to be used against customers with auto loans, and additional models to be used against other business units within the bank. If these business units pooled their data into a common marketing database, would the term insurance division and the other divisions within the bank be able to build more effective models and mailing systems than those already in place? Would these systems be so much more efficient that they could cost justify the investment in the common marketing database? These are the questions that need to be answered—it cannot just be assumed that a common database would be more effective and cost-efficient. These questions should be raised and answered during the early stages of a database development project.

Chapter 18

Back to Basics: The Economics of Classical Direct Marketing

This chapter deals entirely with the economics of traditional direct marketing.[1] We will begin with a review of the major business issues associated with these business forms:

- Solo promotions
- Multistep promotions
- Catalogs
- Continuities
- Clubs
- Newsletters
- Magazines

This review initially focuses on the economic trade-offs that direct marketers deal with daily. After a general discussion of each business form, we will analyze each business in terms of the relationship between acquiring new customers, which direct marketers refer to as *front-end analysis,* and the profitability that results from transactions that occur after the customer is acquired, called *back-end analysis.*

Long before databases were fashionable, direct marketers understood that long-term growth and profitability depended primarily on the direct marketer's ability to manage the equation that balances expenditures on new-customer acquisition with the flow of sales and profits that come back over the economic life of the acquired customer. Of course, it's a lot simpler to measure the immediate costs of acquiring a new customer than it is to measure the value of an acquired customer, particularly when that value may take years to fully materialize. And, as we'll see shortly, in an increasing number of direct marketing situations, the long-term value of an acquired customer is not simply a value waiting to be discovered; the long-term value of a customer is directly related to the way in which the customer is served by the direct marketing company. So we have a kind of chicken-and-egg problem that we'll try to solve after we've established some of the basic economic ground rules.

SOLO PROMOTIONS

The simplest form of direct marketing is the solo, or single-shot, promotion. Assume for the moment that the marketer has no other use for the name of the customer acquired. The only economic reason for the promotion is to make an immediate profit on this one mailing. In this situation,

[1]Portions of the following section first appeared in David Shepard, *Direct Marketing Handbook* (New York: McGraw-Hill, 1984).

the marketer must design, produce, and mail promotion pieces to enough potential buyers to generate a response that will cover the cost of the promotion and yield an acceptable level of profit.

Single-shot promotions are relatively simple but the seller must still answer many questions in the course of the promotion process. Should the promotion piece be a classical, direct response, full-mailing package, including an outer envelope, letter, brochure, business reply card, and return envelope? Or should the seller use a less expensive mailing piece? If the classical full-mailing package is used, should the letter be two pages or four pages, and should the flier be black and white or in full color? Should the seller offer credit or require cash with the order? Should credit cards be used? Should the seller offer an inexpensive premium to hype sales or as a reward for cash with order? Should the mailing use third-class postage or would the extra costs of first-class postage somehow result in extra sales and thereby pay for itself? Should an 800 telephone number be used? How strong should the guarantee be? Should the outer envelope contain copy and an illustration of the product, or just inviting copy, or no copy at all?

The list of legitimate questions that can be raised about even the simplest form of direct marketing is extensive, and answers to these questions affect the economics of the promotion. Many of these questions have to do with economic trade-offs. Does it pay to spend more on the promotion piece, to offer a premium, to offer credit, to mail first class, and so on? These questions with regard to a solo promotion apply to all types of direct response businesses and will be raised again and again throughout this chapter.

MULTISTEP PROMOTIONS LEADING TO A DIRECT SALE

Frequently, it is possible to identify the potential market for a product in terms of the circulation of one or more magazines while at the same time it is not profitable or legally possible to sell the product "off the page" in those magazines regardless of the unit of space employed. In some situations, the price of the product is exceptionally high, and closing the sale requires the power of a more expensive direct mail package with full-color illustrations and sufficient copy to define all the features and benefits of the product. Or, in the case of financial services, it may be neither economically feasible nor legally possible to attempt to directly consummate a sale. In these instances, magazine space often is used to generate leads or inquiries, which are followed up by one or a series of direct mail pieces. In some cases, the initial leads are followed up by a combination of mail and phone. Products sold in this fashion include, in addition to financial services, encyclopedias, expensive exercise equipment, office equipment, and many business-to-business services. The "bingo cards" found in trade magazines and airline magazines are prime examples of this kind of direct response marketing.

The economics of multistep marketing differs from the economics of single-shot promotions in that the total costs of both the initial effort and the costs of all of the follow-up efforts must be tracked carefully and balanced against the sales and gross margin resulting from the total effort.

CATALOG SALES

A catalog may be thought of as a very expensive solo mailing, selling anywhere from a few dozen to hundreds or even thousands of products. It is also possible, as in the case of the solo mailing, to compare the total gross margin resulting from a catalog mailing with the total costs of the mailing, but the analogy between a catalog business and a business based on solo mailings cannot be taken much further.

The success of a catalog business is related directly to a catalog manager's ability to efficiently develop and manage a company's database of past buyers, or its *house list,* as it is still referred to by many in the industry. In very general terms, the response of an outside rented list to a catalog mailing may range anywhere from .5 percent to 2 or 3 percent, depending on the quality of the rented names and their predisposition to the products being offered in the catalog. By way of comparison, the response of past buyers to another catalog offering may range from 5 to 20 percent or even higher.

Naturally, a new catalog company cannot open its doors with a list of past buyers. However, catalog operators have developed a number of techniques for developing house lists. One technique is to develop a relatively inexpensive "prospecting" catalog that can be mailed to names that have been rented from outside list owners. Respondents to these prospect mailings then are entered on the catalog company's prospect list. Of course, it is possible to mail a company's complete catalog to an outside rented list, and the limiting or deciding factor in this decision often is the catalog company's willingness and ability to sustain a large negative cash position while building its house file. Large companies wishing to enter the direct marketing business often are in a position to finance this development period, provided that they are convinced the eventual returns will justify the initial cash investment.

Smaller entrepreneurs generally attempt to exhaust all the other more conservative ways of building prospecting lists that can be converted eventually into buyers lists. Other techniques for building house lists include advertising the catalog free or for a token price in targeted-space media, using the same space to sell the most popular items in the catalog, and sending out solo mailings of individual popular products to names on rented lists. In general, regardless of the techniques used, it is common for a catalog operation to be in a net loss position with regard to new names added to the house list. As the mix between new names that result from cold prospect mailings, space advertising, and catalog buyer names changes in favor of the buyers, the profitability of the catalog operation increases.

However, even after the initial start-up period is behind the cataloger, this issue of allocating the amount spent on new-customer acquisition versus the amount spent on mailing catalogs to customers remains. In fact, this decision is one of the most crucial decisions a cataloger must make.

Ironically, advances in database marketing techniques have made this decision even more difficult. In predatabase days, most catalogers had a limited number of catalogs, which were mailed to all the customers on their buyers file. In many cases, the entire customer mailing strategy could be summed up in a sentence: "We mail four general catalogs a year to all customers on our file who have made a purchase within the last two years."

Now, given the ability to segment a file not only in terms of how frequently different customer segments should be mailed, but also in terms of which customers might respond better to specialized as opposed to general catalogs, the decision-making process has become infinitely more complex. Because of the importance of this subject, not only to catalogers but to all direct marketers that have implied as opposed to contractual relationships with their customers, let's spend some more time on the issue.

To the extent that a cataloger spends promotion dollars on acquiring new customers, the potential size of the business will grow. However, as we have seen, the response rate on new-customer acquisition mailings is significantly less than the response rate to mailings to the customer file. So in any one year, a dollar spent on new-customer acquisition, as opposed to customer mailings, will reduce both sales and profits. On the other hand, if year after year decreasing amounts are spent on new-customer acquisition, the potential of the business will diminish and eventually the actual size of the business will shrink as the customer file fatigues. Therefore, there has to be a strategy for managing both potential growth and annual profits.

In the simpler times referred to above, a cataloger could estimate the sales and profits expected from mailing a single catalog to the house file, say, three or four times a year. After allowing for overheads and desired profits, the cataloger could calculate the amount available for new-customer acquisition, and that would be that. The first complication was the discovery that not all customers need be or should be mailed the same number of catalogs each year. Relatively simple Recency, Frequency, Monetary Value (RFM) models were developed by catalogers that allowed them to segment a file into dozens of segments or cells based on recency of purchase, frequency of purchase, and the various measures of the dollar value of past purchases. The basic conclusion drawn from RFM cell segmentation was that individuals within the highest performing cells should be mailed more frequently than individuals within the poorest performing cells. So even if a cataloger still only produced four general catalogs a year, the best performing customers might receive those four catalogs 8 to 12 times a year (perhaps with a cover change), the poorest performing customers might receive only one catalog a year, and some customers would in fact be dropped from the file of active buyers.

The introduction of more sophisticated forms of predictive modeling (regression, logistic, discriminant analyses) did nothing to change the basic finding that some customers should be mailed more frequently than others. However, the introduction of these techniques and of models that predict falloff from mailing to mailing have improved the efficiency of the modeling process.

What made a fundamental difference for some catalogers was the not-surprising discovery that not all buyers bought the same mix of products, and that segmentation techniques could be extended to include the kinds of products purchased as well as the quantity of products purchased. Now the decision-making process also had to be extended to include consideration of the creation and distribution of specialty catalogs.

It is obviously a more difficult problem to decide who gets what mix of catalogs with what frequency than it is to simply decide how many general catalogs any one individual should receive.

Unfortunately, although predictive models are good at scoring customers in terms of their probability of responding to a promotion similar to one received in the past, the complications we just discussed do not lend themselves easily to statistical modeling solutions of the regression variety. To answer these kinds of economic trade-off questions we must rely on computer models that simulate an entire business structure and that are capable of answering "what if" questions. The good news is that such models are relatively easy to build using spreadsheet programs such as Lotus 1-2-3; the bad news is that the output of the models is only as good as the input assumptions. The model will tell you, for example, what the fiscal impact will be if you create a specialty catalog that will increase response for 30 percent of the file by 20 percent, but only old-fashioned direct marketing testing will tell you if the 20 percent number is correct.

Finally, no discussion of the catalog business would be complete without mention of the extraordinary problems of inventory control and fulfillment that are inherent in the catalog business. Success in mail order requires almost immediate fulfillment of orders as they are received and, the costs of carrying excess inventory can be as disastrous as the cost of being out of stock. Again, the ability of the catalog manager to perform advanced statistical analyses comes into play. Not only must catalog managers be able to forecast the expected level of overall response to a catalog mailing, but also they must be able to forecast the mix of products purchased so as to be in a position to manage inventories correctly.

CONTINUITY PROGRAMS

Continuity programs represent an important segment of the traditional direct marketing business. The continuity formula involves the periodic delivery of a product or service against periodic payments from the customer. The Time-Life Books series, the various Cooking Card programs, and the books and collectibles sold by the Franklin Mint are prime examples of products marketed this way. Because of the contractual nature of continuity programs, the management of a continuity operation is in many ways much less complicated than the management of a catalog operation. Given the product, such as a series of books, cards, or coins, the marketing problem is relatively straightforward. Options are severely limited relative to our catalog example.

New members or subscribers are acquired through the classical direct marketing channels: direct mail, magazine advertisements, newspaper preprints, broadcast (generally spot TV), and package inserts. In most cases, the first item in the continuity program is offered free or at a substantial discount. The subscriber then receives periodic shipments of the remaining items in the program until all the items have been shipped or until the subscriber notifies the seller to stop shipping the product.

From the subscriber's point of view, continuity programs are simple and easy to understand. From the seller's viewpoint, a number of key questions must be answered before the program can become operational.

How should the items in the series be priced? Should the items be priced relatively high and therefore targeted against the upper end of the potential market, or should a lower-price/higher-volume strategy be attempted? How generous should the initial offer be? Should the first item in the series be given away free, or for $1, or at no discount at all? Should the interval between shipments be four weeks, six weeks, or eight weeks? How much open credit should be granted? Does it make sense to ship the third item in a series if payment has not been received for the first item? How does the credit decision depend on the interval between shipments? Should the program be open ended with no limit on the number of items in the series, or should the series be limited to a fixed number of items, and if so, what is that number?

Clearly, the answers to these questions will have an important impact on the economics of the continuity program. Again, we are faced with a question of trade-offs. The more generous the offer and credit policy, the larger the program in terms of subscribers and sales volume. But what will be the effect on returns, bad debts, and profits?

Finally, let us briefly discuss the concept of a continuity load-up. The continuity programs we have described rely on periodic shipment of a product until cancellation or completion of the program. In continuity load-ups, the subscriber is informed that after he or she receives three or four single shipments, the balance of the items in the program will be shipped in a single load-up shipment. The load-up plan is an effective device for increasing the total number of items shipped to the average subscriber but, again, there are economic trade-offs to consider. Federal trade regulations require that the load-up provision be defined clearly in all promotional messages, and this can reduce the total number of respondents to any given promotion. Second, most load-up programs follow a policy of reminding subscribers that the load-up shipment is about to be mailed unless the subscriber notifies the company not to proceed with the shipment and to cancel membership in the program. This reminder will cause some subscribers to cancel their membership faster than they might have done in an open-ended continuity program. Finally, there is the problem of credit collections. A load-up program is based on the assumption that after the subscriber receives the full load-up shipment, he or she will pay for the shipment on a monthly or bimonthly basis. Of course, some percentage of the load-up shipment will not be paid for and eventually will have to be written off as bad debts.

On balance, only testing the load-up concept against the open-ended, or "till forbid," continuity plan will determine which plan is best for any given product.

NEGATIVE OPTION CLUBS

We have discussed negative option clubs before and they are indeed efficient vehicles for the distribution of books and records. The Book-of-the-Month Club and the Columbia Record Club are well-known examples of this type of direct marketing business. There are some similarities between continuity operations and negative option clubs. Most importantly, both employ contractual relationships with their members, thereby limiting service options. Both vehicles often are used as a means of distributing books, and both use the same media and direct marketing techniques for acquiring new members. But after the new member is acquired, the similarity from an operations or fulfillment point of view ends.

Negative option clubs constantly must ask their subscribers whether they wish to receive the coming selection, receive an alternative selection, or receive no product at all from the current catalog offering. If the member fails to respond, the shipment of the month is sent automatically. The fulfillment systems needed to handle a negative option club are much more complicated than those needed for a continuity program. In addition, the Federal Trade Commission has placed stringent restrictions on negative option clubs to ensure that members have sufficient time to return the negative option card should they not wish to receive the automatic shipment of the month.

Despite the differences in operating characteristics between negative option clubs and continuity programs, the economics of both types of businesses are remarkably similar. In both operations, new members are always acquired at a loss. The $1.00 or even the $4.95 that is often charged for the introductory shipment (the first book in a continuity series or the four books chosen from a book club's lead list) is never enough to cover the costs of promotion plus the cost of the introductory shipment. Therefore, continuity programs and negative option clubs are always in an investment position. The return on investment stems from future sales to the continuity subscriber or club member. In the case of continuity programs, future sales are simply a function of the price of the items in the program and the number of periods a subscriber chooses to stay in it. In a negative option club, the member need not buy from every catalog offering, and therefore sales are more dependent on the perceived quality of the merchandise offered and the effectiveness of the ongoing marketing effort. In both continuity and negative option, the final measure of profitability is the relationship between the cost of acquiring new members and the sales and payments those members yield over their economic life in the club or program. Later in this chapter we will develop the techniques used to measure and forecast these statistics.

As mentioned previously, up until quite recently, nearly all negative option clubs operated on the principle that all members would receive the same set of promotional materials. The notable exception was the record clubs, which have always asked their members to place themselves within listening preference segments. But within the book clubs, equality of treatment among all members was the general rule. Recently, the larger clubs have begun experimenting with customizing the negative option book selection to individuals based on the demonstrated reading preferences of the individuals. And, clearly in a major book club that offers both a wide range of fiction and nonfiction, it makes sense to do so. This is particularly true in data processing environments in which this kind of decision making can be handled efficiently. Of course, there are production costs to pay for not treating all members the same but these costs are offset by higher acceptance and lower returns of the negative option selection, increased purchase of alternate selections, and a longer member life as club members receive more and more selections that match their reading preferences.

NEWSLETTERS

Newsletters can be very profitable vehicles for distributing information to highly targeted markets. The most profitable newsletters often are aimed at small professional or business markets. Newsletters that are editorially able to provide critically needed information to a business audience that has both the need to know and the ability to pay (often referred to as "company money") have the greatest chance for success. This does not mean that more broadly based, lower-priced, mass-market newsletters can't be profitable, as witnessed by the continued success of the *Kiplinger Washington Newsletter* and the popularity of a number of consumer health newsletters such as the *Harvard Medical Letter* and the *Mayo Clinic Letter,* to name just two.

The economics of newsletters center on four key variables: pricing, new-order acquisition, conversion or pay rates, and renewal rates. Pricing is the most controllable of all the variables and perhaps the most important. Newsletters targeted at business markets can be priced anywhere from $9.95 to $495. Generally, it is not difficult to determine whether the value of the information is worth closer to $10 than to $500, but it is often next to impossible to tell without testing whether a given newsletter should be priced at $37, $49, or even $97.

Clearly, pricing can make an enormous difference in profitability. Price testing is therefore almost always a necessity when one starts out in the newsletter business, particularly if the newsletter has little or no perceived competition.

Newsletters are almost always marketed solely by direct mail; therefore, it is critical that, before starting out in the newsletter business, the publisher be assured of continued access to the target market. If access to the market depends on the cooperation of a trade association, provisions should be made with the association to guarantee a continuous supply of names.

Properly priced newsletters can be successful with a relatively small response to initial new-subscriber promotions. Profits can be achieved with initial response rates as low as 5 to 10 orders per thousand names mailed because renewal rates are usually high.

However, before a newsletter can be considered a proven success, it must demonstrate the merits of the editorial material. The first test of the quality of the editorial material is the pay rate or conversion rate on new orders. Most newsletter promotions allow for payment (and cancellation) after one or more issues have been sampled by the reader. A high pay rate (over 70 percent) will be indicative of a high future renewal rate. Products that demonstrate a high cancellation rate should not count on a high renewal rate to ensure the profits of the newsletter venture.

MAGAZINES

Magazines are, of course, much like newsletters in that they depend on direct mail for much of their new-subscriber marketing and are highly sensitive to fluctuations in pay rates and renewal rates. The obvious differences between newsletters and magazines are that magazines are much more costly to produce and have two additional revenue streams: newsstand sales and advertising revenues. But even in the subscription circulation area, where one finds the greatest similarity to newsletters, there are important differences.

Magazine subscriptions are sold in many more ways than newsletter subscriptions. There are door-to-door sales, telephone sales, and sweepstakes-sold subscriptions from companies such as Publishers Clearing House. In addition, a magazine company's direct mail efforts may be dependent on preview or premium offers to an extent not often found in newsletter circulation. Each of these promotional channels and devices runs the risk of producing subscriptions with relatively low pay and renewal rates. Therefore, the evaluation and management of a magazine's circulation list is considerably more complicated and subject to greater risk than the evaluation and management of a newsletter.

PERFORMANCE MEASUREMENT

Front-End versus Back-End Performance

Front-end performance and *front-end analysis* are terms used by direct marketers to describe the process of measuring the initial costs of and response to a direct marketing promotion. The economic analysis of the process that takes place after an initial response is received is referred to as *back-end analysis* or *back-end performance.*

FRONT-END PERFORMANCE

Measuring Promotion Expense

The first step in the process of measuring front-end performance is measuring the total expense attributable to a promotion. The only difficulty associated with this task is deciding which expenses will be included in the analysis and which expenses, if any, will be excluded.

Later we shall see how direct marketers generally approach this problem, but for now, let's assume we agree that it costs exactly $19,000 to mail 50,000 pieces of direct mail. The first statistic to be calculated is cost per thousand pieces mailed, more simply referred to as cost per thousand (CPM).

$$\text{CPM} = \frac{\text{Total promotion expense}}{\text{Number of pieces mailed}} \times 1{,}000$$

In our example

$$\text{CPM} = \frac{\$19{,}000}{50{,}000} \times 1{,}000$$

$$\text{CPM} = \$380$$

The CPM concept applies to space advertising as well as to direct mail. In space advertising, CPM is calculated by dividing total media costs plus the costs of printing any special insert material by the circulation of the magazine.

$$\text{Space CPM} = \frac{\text{Media costs} + \text{Insert costs}}{\text{Circulation}} \times 1{,}000$$

For example, consider a magazine with a circulation of 1 million and ad or media costs of $40,000 running an insert card that cost $20 per thousand to print.

$$\text{Space CPM} = \frac{\$40{,}000 + (20 \times 1{,}000)}{1{,}000{,}000} \times 1{,}000$$

$$\text{Space CPM} = \$60.00$$

In both direct mail and space advertising, the question always arises whether the fixed creative fees paid to an agency or a free-lancer and the fixed mechanical preparation and art expenses should be included in the calculation of CPM. Opinion is divided on this subject. Some direct response marketers insist on including all costs in the calculation of CPM to ensure that profitability analyses considers all costs associated with the promotion. Other direct marketers argue that creative material and mechanicals are intended for use in multiple promotions. These marketers either allocate a portion of the fixed creative expenses to each use of the material or maintain separate budgets and controls for creative expenses. They do not include fixed nonrecurring costs in the analysis of promotion results. This latter approach, which is more oriented to decision making, is favored by most large mailers who are concerned more with the decision to remail a promotion or repeat a space insertion than with the recording of historical costs. For decision-making purposes, the direct marketer wants to know the incremental costs of repeating a promotion that has been used in the past, regardless of such costs.

Calculating CPM for Different Direct Response Media

Direct mail. Direct marketers use three major types of direct mail promotion pieces, excluding catalogs, to generate new orders or new leads: the full-package solo mailing, the less expensive self-mailer, and the insert piece.

Full-package solo mailings. Table 18–1 shows the components of a standard direct mail package, including a four-page letter and color brochure. The CPM of the full package is shown at three mailing quantities: 50,000, 100,000, and 300,000. Printing costs per thousand are shown to vary with the quantity printed as the fixed printing preparation expenses (which must be incurred at each print run) are amortized over the number of pieces to be mailed. These fixed printing preparation expenses should not be confused with creative fees, art and production expenses, and other fixed fees such as agency or consultant's fees, which are truly one-time costs and do not vary with the quantity mailed or the size of the printing.

The example shown in Table 18–1 is typical of a consumer mailing of the kind used by book and record clubs, continuity programs, and magazines. These situations generally require a color brochure to display the product fully and almost always employ third-class postage.

On the other end of the direct-response spectrum, marketers for a high-priced newsletter aimed at top corporate management may decide against a full-color brochure but may mail first class to create a more businesslike impression, and hopefully avoid the secretary's wastebasket. In this case, the cost of the promotion will be reduced because the flier has been removed but increased because of the use of first-class postage.

Therefore, there is no hard and fast rule to determine the correct cost of direct mail promotion. Costs are a function of the components of the mailing package. Direct mail package costs can vary from $300 to $1,000 per thousand. The real question is what mailing package will be most profitable for the product or service being offered.

TABLE 18–1
Calculating CPM for a Typical Direct Mail Promotion at Three Mailing Quantities

	Quantity					
	50,000		*100,000*		*300,000*	
Printing costs						
Package element	CPM	%	CPM	%	CPM	%
Outer envelope	$18	4%	$16	4%	$15	3%
Four-page letter	33	7	23	5	22	5
Four-color brochure	28	6	25	6	21	5
Reply card	23	5	19	4	18	4
Return envelope	17	4	15	3	14	3
Total printing cost	119	26%	98	22%	90	21%
Mailing costs						
Mailing lists	95	21%	95	22%	95	22%
Letter shop	25	5	25	6	25	6
Computer processing	25	5	25	6	25	6
Postage	198	43	198	45	198	46
Total mailing costs	$343	74%	$343	78%	$343	79%
Total CPM	$462	100%	$441	100%	$433	100%
Dollar costs						
Total variable costs	$23,100	58%	$44,100	72%	$129,900	88%
Creative	5,000	12	5,000	8	5,000	3
Art and production	7,000	17	7,000	11	7,000	5
Contingency	5,000	12	5,000	8	5,000	3
Total costs	$40,100	100%	$61,100	100%	$146,900	100%
Total CPM	$802		$611		$490	

Self-mailers. One sure way to reduce mailing costs is to use a self-mailer, which is a promotion piece that does not contain multiple loose components. The self-mailer is a perforated form, one portion of which is a business reply card, and the respondent is instructed to tear off this card and return it to the mailer. The most common format is the two- or three-panel 8½- by 11-inch card stock format. A self-mailer eliminates the need for an outer envelope, reduces letter shop expense, and combines the selling message of the letter and the brochure in one format. There is also no need for a separate business reply card and business reply envelope. With the use of a self-mailer, promotion costs can be reduced significantly, but again the question arises as to what will happen to response. Will the self-mailer turn out to be more or less profitable than a full mailing package? As usual in direct response, only testing can provide the answer.

Inserts or enclosures. Another very inexpensive but cost-effective mailing format is the insert piece or enclosure promotion. An insert or enclosure is any promotion piece mailed at no additional postage expense inside an invoice, statement, merchandise shipment, or other primary mailing piece. Insert pieces mailed along with first-class mailings such as bills or statements must be small so that they do not increase postage expenses. Enclosures in third-class mailings and merchandise shipments are not weight restricted.

TABLE 18–2
Calculating Front-End Space Results

Total circulation	3,000,000
Cost per single black-and-white page	$24,000
Total response	1,500
CPM	$8
Percent response: (1,500/3 million) × 100	.05 %
Orders per thousand circulation (OPM): (1,500/3,000)	.50
Cost per response (CPR): CPM/OPM = $8.00/.50	$16.00

In general, insert pieces pull a much lower response than direct mail packages or self-mailers. However, because of the lower cost, which can be as low as $20 per thousand, response does not have to be very great to generate a profit.

Space advertising. The cost per thousand for space advertising is considerably lower than the CPM for direct mail. A typical magazine page may cost from $5 to $75 per thousand circulation, as compared with direct mail, which ranges between $300 and $1,000 per thousand pieces mailed. Of course, the response to a space advertisement will be less than the response to a direct mail promotion. In direct mail, a 3 percent response (30 orders per thousand) to a promotion costing $600 per thousand will result in a cost per response of $20, and is not atypical. In space advertising, a $20 cost per response is likely to be the result of a response rate of ⅒ of 1 percent in a medium with a CPM of $20.

As small as these numbers seem, they nevertheless result in very significant absolute numbers. For example, consider a mass-market magazine with a circulation of 3 million. The cost of a single black-and-white page is likely to be around $24,000 for a CPM of $8. If an ad in that magazine pulls at a rate of just .05 percent, or a rate of .5 order per thousand circulation, the ad will generate 1,500 responses at an average cost of $16 per response. (See Table 18–2.)

The actual CPM for an ad in any magazine will vary greatly, depending on a number of factors. For example, cover positions cost more than inside-the-book positions, color costs more than black and white, advertising in the direct mail section frequently costs less than advertising in the general editorial section, and discounts are available for multiple usage. Regional editions may be purchased, generally increasing the CPM but lowering the total dollar expenditure, and so on. The point is that buying space advertising is not simply a matter of placing an ad in a magazine. As always, the key decision is whether the more expensive ad format will result in a significantly greater response and increased profitability or, conversely, whether the less expensive format will result in fewer responses and lower profits.

Broadcast. Broadcast is an increasingly important direct response vehicle, and the emergence of cable TV with its highly targeted audiences has increased the significance of this medium.

TV broadcast advertising generally is purchased in one of two ways. In the first instance, an advertiser purchases a certain amount of time from a local station or national network at an agreed-on price. The exact times the commercial is to be aired and the number of spots or showings are agreed to in advance. This procedure is similar to placing an ad in a magazine. Before the ad is run or the commercial shown, the total investment in the medium is known. The cost per response will depend on the number of responses in the form of telephone calls to the local station or to an 800 number or on the number of responses received in the mail.

The second method of purchase is per inquiry (PI), also referred to as per order (PO). Very often, a broadcast station will agree with an advertiser to run a given commercial at times chosen by the station. In exchange for this airtime, the advertiser will pay the station an amount based on the number of responses received. In these situations, the initial response usually is directed to the local station and sent from there to the advertiser. PI or PO arrangements also are frequently available in space advertising.

When broadcast is used either to consummate a final sale or to generate leads, the key economic considerations are the length and frequency of the spot. Traditionally, direct response spots ran for 90 or 120 seconds, the argument for this length being the 20 seconds or so necessary for the tag line and the time it takes to establish the product and the offer in the viewer's mind. From the very outset, buying a two-minute spot on network TV was expensive and very often not available. Thus, direct marketers turned to local spot TV with its larger inventory of late night or non-prime time spots. The advent of cable TV opened up a whole new inventory of available times and the cable networks were more than happy to sell 90-second and two-minute spots to direct response advertisers. However, as cable's popularity grew, the inventory of two-minute spots decreased and direct marketers are once again trying to make 30- and 60-second spots pay for themselves. Closely aligned with the issue of the length of a direct response ad is the issue of frequency. How frequently should the spot appear in any one station? In any one market? Conceptually, there is a buildup period, a time in which response may be low but building, and then there is the falloff period after response has peaked. Obviously, the profits of a successful flight can be erased if airtime is purchased in significant quantity after the spot has peaked.

Thus, the economics of broadcast TV depend heavily on the marketer's ability to forecast response patterns and to tightly control spending decisions.

A second important use of broadcast is in support of a major direct mail, newspaper insert, or magazine promotion. It is intuitive that broadcast spots urging the viewer to look in the paper, mailbox, or TV guide will increase response, but the economic question is how much airtime is enough and how much is too much? Up to a certain point or media weight, the broadcast advertising will not be able to make a significant impact and the support money will be wasted; on the other hand, too many spots can be equally unproductive. The answer, of course, is testing to determine the appropriate mix of broadcast support.

Finally, on the subject of broadcast, TV is not the only broadcast medium; we shouldn't forget radio. Radio, particularly drive-time radio with its upscale commuting audience, has always been a great captive market. But until the advent of the cellular car phone it has not been a great direct response medium. Of course, all that is changing rapidly as car phones move from luxury to necessity status among the most desirable market segments. So we see a great future for direct response radio, and when that happens, the same issues of time and frequency that affect broadcast TV will have to be addressed for radio.

Telemarketing. Outbound telemarketing is apparently here to stay, certainly for magazine renewals as well as for cold solicitations offering a one-issue trial examination offer. The phone also is used with great success in business-to-business direct response, in which the goal is to generate a lead or qualify a lead generated from a space ad or a direct mail offer.

Independent telephone operations currently sell their services at rates of approximately $30 to $40 per hour. Within this time period, a qualified phone operator can make between 6 and 20 contacts. The contact rate will vary depending on the time of day, the day of the week, and whether the call is to a consumer at home or to a business executive or professional at the place of work. Because of its ability to generate low-cost trial subscriptions or leads, the telephone must be used with care. A low conversion rate can transform a very low cost per lead into a very high cost per order, as we'll see a little later on in this chapter.

MEASURING RESPONSE

One-Step Promotions

The response to a direct mail promotion is expressed as a percentage of the quantity mailed or stated in terms of the number of responses per thousand pieces mailed (RPM). If the response is an order, the term *orders per thousand* (OPM) is used.

$$\text{Percentage response} = \frac{\text{Total response}}{\text{Quantity mailed}} \times 100$$

$$\text{RPM} = \frac{\text{Total response}}{\text{Quantity mailed}/1{,}000}$$

$$\text{OPM} = \frac{\text{Total orders}}{\text{Quantity mailed}/1{,}000}$$

Because the response to a direct mail promotion often is less than 1 percent, many direct marketers prefer to use the RPM or OPM terminology rather than express results in terms of a fraction of a percent. This is particularly true with regard to space advertising, in which a response of one order per thousand or even less is not uncommon.

Two-Step Promotions

As discussed above, not all direct response promotions are one-step promotions. Often, the initial response to a direct response promotion is only the first step in a two-step or even a multistep promotion process. A magazine promoted by direct mail, using an offer that allows the potential subscriber to cancel after previewing one issue, is an example of a two-step promotion.

Consider a direct mail promotion of a magazine through a preview offer. Assume that 500,000 pieces are mailed and that 10,000 responses are received. The initial RPM is equal to

$$\frac{10{,}000}{500{,}000/1{,}000} = 20$$

If only 40 percent of the respondents to the preview offer convert to paid subscriptions, the final paid orders per thousand pieces mailed (OPM) will be equal to

$$20 \text{ RPM} \times 40\% = 8$$

CALCULATING COST PER RESPONSE

One-Step Promotions

In a one-step promotion the cost per response can be calculated by dividing the total number of responses into the total cost of the promotion. A quicker way preferred by many direct marketers is to divide the cost per thousand of the promotion by the number of responses per thousand to arrive at the cost per response (CPR):

$$\text{CPR} = \frac{\text{CPM}}{\text{RPM}}$$

Referring back to our magazine example, assume that the cost of the mailing was $350 per thousand. The initial cost per response would be

$$\frac{\$350}{20} = \$17.50$$

Two-Step Promotions

In two-step promotions, the promotion portion of the total cost per order is equal to the promotion cost per response divided by the conversion rate. In our magazine example, the cost per response is $17.50 and the conversion rate is 40 percent. Therefore, the promotion cost per order is equal to

$$\frac{\text{Initial CPR}}{\text{Conversion rate}} = \frac{\$17.50}{.40} = \$43.75$$

However, dividing the promotion cost per response by the conversion rate understates the cost of acquiring a new magazine subscriber.

Assume that in the process of converting preview subscribers into paid subscribers, those potential subscribers who eventually will cancel will receive three issues of the magazine and five invoices. Let's also assume that those who decide to subscribe will receive an average of three invoices before paying. The costs of this conversion process can be added legitimately to the cost of acquiring the average paid subscription.

The calculations would be as follows. If the cost of one issue of the magazine on an incremental basis is $.75, and the cost of one invoice, including first-class postage, computer expense, and printing, is $.55, the amount spent on each eventual nonsubscriber or "cancel" is equal to

$$\begin{aligned} &3 \text{ issues} \times \$.75 \text{ per issue} &= \$2.25 \\ +\ &5 \text{ invoices} \times \$.55 \text{ per invoice} &= \$2.75 \\ &\text{Total cost per cancel} &= \$5.00 \end{aligned}$$

Because only 40 percent of the initial respondents will subscribe, the cost of attempting to convert the eventual cancels or nonsubscribers must be allocated over those who do subscribe. The equation for this calculation is as follows:

$$\text{Conversion expense per subscriber because of cancellations} = \frac{\text{Cost per cancel} \times (1 - \text{Pay rate})}{\text{Pay rate}}$$

$$\text{Conversion expense per subscriber} = \frac{\$5.00 \times (1 - .40)}{.40}$$

$$\text{Conversion expense per subscriber} = \$7.50$$

In addition, the cost of billing the respondents who eventually will pay will be equal to 3 × \$.55, or \$1.65. Therefore, the total conversion expense is equal to \$7.50 plus \$1.65, or \$9.15 per paid order.

The total cost per new subscriber, including both promotion expense and conversion expense, is equal to the total new-subscriber acquisition expense:

Promotion expense	+	Conversion expense	=	Total acquisition expense
\$43.75	+	\$9.15	=	\$52.90

The lesson to be remembered from this example is that the initial CPR may be only a small part of the total cost per final order in a multistep promotion. The costs of converting initial responses or leads can be particularly expensive when the conversion process requires expensive sales literature or requires a sales call.

TRACKING BACK-END PERFORMANCE

In the section on front-end performance, we discussed the techniques used to measure the costs of acquiring leads, buyers, or subscribers. In each case, costs were expressed not in terms of the total dollars spent but rather in terms of the amount spent to acquire the average customer from a particular media investment. By defining costs in terms of the average cost per customer, it is possible for us to compare alternative media without regard to their size.

We will follow this same approach in discussing back-end performance. In general, *back-end performance* refers to the purchase behavior of a group of respondents from the time their names are entered on the customer file. More specifically, we shall define back-end performance as the sales, contribution, and profits resulting from a group of respondents acquired from a particular advertising medium.

To measure, or track, back-end performance, it is necessary to maintain a system in which each individual customer is identified as coming from a specific advertising medium: a list, a space insertion, or a broadcast spot. When this is done, it is possible to accumulate the behavior of all customers from the same initial source medium and calculate average sales, contribution, or profits.

For this reason, direct marketing advertisers include a key code on every coupon in every space ad and print a key code on the return card or label of every direct mail promotion. The key code identifies the advertising medium and becomes a permanent part of the responding customer's record, along with name, address, and purchase history.

Direct marketers have proved over and over that for a given order, back-end performance will vary significantly from one advertising medium to another. In general, direct marketers have discovered that buyers acquired from direct mail behave better than buyers acquired from space or magazine advertisements and that buyers acquired from direct mail or space will perform better than buyers acquired from broadcast promotions. However, there are wide variations in performance within the same media category. The best customers acquired from space media will perform better than the worst customers acquired from direct mail, and so on.

The critical concept to remember is that back-end performance varies from medium to medium and that the only way to operate a profitable direct response business is to be able to track the performance of customers in terms of the original source group so that the decision to reinvest promotion dollars can be made on the basis of proven performance.

At this point, it pays to remind you that we are describing classical direct marketing theory. Its concern is with the performance of the average customer, and what is being measured and about to be evaluated is the relationship between back-end performance and front-end or acquisition expense.

Back-end performance in this classical approach is assumed to be the same for every individual acquired from a given source code. In practice, when direct marketers set out to influence back-end performance, they do so using a natural extension of the source group concept. For example, if a classical direct marketer thought that it might be better in a continuity situation to ship books every six weeks instead of to use the usual four-week shipment cycle, the procedure most likely to be followed would be to run an A/B split in one or more important media sources disclosing the six-week shipment cycle to the A group and a four-week shipment cycle to the B group. The marketer could then measure if there was any immediate difference in up-front response and wait to see if back-end performance was better or worse for either group. More on influencing back-end response, through classical as well as database methods, later. First, let's finish the discussion of how back-end performance is measured.

Measuring Back-End Performance

Single-shot mailing. The measurement of back-end performance for a solo, or single-shot, mailing is simply the statement of profit or loss for the promotion. Table 18–3 lists the assumptions that would be typical of a solo mailing of a product with a sales price of $60. The profit and loss statement in Table 18–4 is based on the assumptions defined in Table 18–3.

Clubs and continuity programs. In clubs and continuity programs, the statistic that measures back-end performance is the contribution to promotion, overhead, and profit. If this contribution for a group of new orders or starters is greater than the cost of acquiring the starting group, the investment in the starting group can be considered to be at least marginally profitable.

This contribution statistic sometimes is referred to as the *order margin,* the *allowable,* or the *breakeven.* Each term implies a comparison to the cost per order expended to bring the starters into the business.

TABLE 18–3
Assumptions for a Single-Shot Promotion

Selling price	$65.00
Shipping and handling charge	$3.00
Return rate (percent of gross sales)	10.0%
Percentage of returns reusable	90.0%
Cost of product per unit	$15.00
Order processing:	
Reply postage per gross response	$.25
Order processing and setup per gross response	$2.00
Percentage of gross orders using:	
Credit cards	75.0%
Checks	25.0%
Credit card expense	3.0%
Percentage of charge orders with bad checks	5.0%
Shipping and handling per gross response	$3.00
Return processing:	
Return postage per return	$1.50
Handling per gross return	$.50
Refurbishing costs per usable return	$2.00
Premium expense per gross response	$6.00
Promotion CPM	$400.00
Quantity mailed	100,000
Percent response	2.0%
Overhead factor as a percent of net sales	10.0%

TABLE 18–4
Profit and Loss Statement for a Single-Shot Promotion

	Units	*Amount*	*Percent*
Gross sales	2,000	$130,000	
Shipping and handling	2,000	6,000	
Total revenue	2,000	136,000	111.1%
Returns	200	13,600	11.1
Net sales	1,800	$122,400	100.0%
Cost of sales:			
Product:			
Net shipments	1,800	$27,000	22.1%
Nonreusable units	20	300	.2
Order processing:			
Reply postage	2,000	500	.4
Setup costs	2,000	4,000	3.3
Credit card costs	1,500	3,060	2.5
Bad check expense	25	1,700	1.4
Shipping and handling	2,000	6,000	4.9
Return processing:			
Postage	200	300	.2
Handling	200	100	.1
Refurbishing	180	360	.3
Premium	2,000	12,000	9.8
Total cost of sales		$55,320	45.2%
Operating gross margin		$67,080	54.8%
Promotion expense		40,000	32.7
Contribution to overhead and profit		$32,080	22.1%
Overhead allocation		12,240	10.0
Profit		$14,840	12.1%

The contribution statistic excludes consideration of all fixed costs and overhead. Contribution is calculated by subtracting all direct expenses from the net sales of a group of starters and then dividing the result by the number of starters in the group.

In a club or continuity program, sales accumulate over the economic life of the starting group, and that life often can extend over a number of years. Therefore, in clubs or programs with an exceptionally long member life, the contribution from each monthly cycle should be discounted by some amount, generally the seller's cost of capital or opportunity cost, to take the time value of money into consideration.

The ability to forecast final sales and payments from individual starting groups on the basis of early performance data is critical in clubs and continuity programs. In these businesses, as in most direct response businesses, the key marketing decision is the decision to reinvest in media that have already been tested. Because of the long economic life of a club or continuity member, the decision to reinvest must be made on the basis of forecasted behavior. For example, if a new list is mailed in the winter and pulls as well as most other lists used by the club, the marketer may wish to remail the same names or test a larger segment of the list universe in the summer or fall campaign. However, by that time only a few cycles of actual data will be available for analysis. The decision, therefore, must be made on the basis of expected final contribution per starter. The forecast itself is based on the actual data accumulated to date.

In both clubs and continuity programs, one of the most important forecasting variables is the *attrition rate.* This is the term used to measure the rate at which members in a club or program either cancel their memberships or are cancelled because of failure to pay for previously shipped items.

In negative option clubs, the attrition pattern measures the percentage of original starters eligible to receive the periodic advance announcements that advertise the negative option selection of the cycle and the alternative selections. In addition to being able to forecast the attrition pattern, it is also necessary to be able to forecast the acceptance rate of the featured negative option selection and the acceptance of the alternative selections as well as the average price of each category of sale.

Table 18–5 shows a simplified negative option club model that forecasts and accumulates average gross sales per starting member. As we mentioned before, in an actual club operation, the forecast would include separate estimates for the negative option selection and the alternative selections.

According to the model shown in Table 18–5, the average sale per starter will be $52.81. Assuming that direct costs, excluding all promotion and premium costs, are equal to 35 percent of gross sales, the contribution to promotion, overhead, and profit from this group of starters would be $34.32. It is this number minus premium costs that would be compared with promotion costs to determine the profitability of the starting group.

In continuity programs, there are two attrition patterns to be concerned with. The first pattern measures the percentage of starters who initially receive each shipment level at the earliest possible date. This attrition pattern reflects the payment behavior of starters who pay for each shipment on time and continue in the program. The second pattern represents the

TABLE 18–5
Average Sales Accumulated over Time in a Negative Option Club

	Percent			Sales per Starting Member	
Cycle	*Still Active*	*Buying Product*	*Average Price*	*Incremental*	*Cumulative*
Actual Data					
1	97.0%	51%	$12	$5.94	$ 5.94
2	95.0	47	12	5.36	11.29
3	83.0	42	12	4.18	15.48
4	75.0	38	12	3.42	18.90
5	70.0	33	12	2.77	21.67
Forecast Data					
6	65.1	32	12	2.50	24.17
7	60.5	31	12	2.25	26.42
8	56.3	31	12	2.09	28.52
9	52.4	30	12	1.89	30.40
10	48.7	30	12	1.75	32.15
11	45.3	30	12	1.63	33.78
12	42.1	30	12	1.52	35.30
13	39.2	30	12	1.41	36.71
14	36.4	30	12	1.31	38.02
15	33.9	30	12	1.22	39.24
16	31.5	30	12	1.13	40.38
17	29.3	30	12	1.05	41.43
18	27.3	30	12	.98	42.41
19	25.3	30	12	.91	43.32
20	23.6	30	12	.85	44.17
21	21.9	30	12	.79	44.96
22	20.4	30	12	.73	45.70
23	19.0	30	12	.68	46.38
24	17.6	30	12	.63	47.01
25	16.4	30	12	.59	47.60
26	15.2	30	12	.55	48.15
27	14.2	30	12	.51	48.66
28	13.2	30	12	.47	49.14
29	12.3	30	12	.44	49.58
30	11.4	30	12	.41	49.99
31	10.6	30	12	.38	50.37
32	9.9	30	12	.36	50.73
33	9.2	30	12	.33	51.06
34	8.5	30	12	.31	51.36
35	7.9	30	12	.29	51.65
36	7.4	30	12	.27	51.92
37	6.9	30	12	.25	52.16
38	6.4	30	12	.23	52.39
39	5.9	30	12	.21	52.61
40	5.5	30	12	.20	52.81

percentage of original starters who eventually receive each shipment level by the end of the economic life of the starting group. The difference in the two patterns is due to starters who fall behind in their payments and are suspended temporarily from receiving further shipments. As these starters eventually pay, the percentage of starters receiving each shipment level gradually increases.

TABLE 18–6
Attrition Patterns in a Continuity Program

Shipment Number	*Attrition Pattern*		*By End of Cycle*	*Average Units Shipped*	*By End of Week*	*Average Units Shipped*
	Start	*End*				
1	100%	100%	1	1.00	40	5.09
2	92	92	2	1.00	41	5.23
3	85	85	3	1.00	42	5.25
4	50	60	4	1.00	43	5.26
5	35	45	5	1.92	44	5.27
6	30	40	6	1.92	45	5.39
7	20	28	7	1.92	46	5.40
8	18	25	8	1.92	47	5.41
9	16	23	9	2.77	48	5.42
10	15	20	10	2.77	49	5.54
11	13	18	11	2.77	50	5.55
12	12	17	12	2.77	51	5.56
13	11	15	13	3.29	52	5.56
14	10	13	14	3.30	53	5.67
15	9	12	15	3.32	54	5.68
Total	5.16	5.94	16	3.34	55	5.69
			17	3.70	56	5.69
			18	3.74	57	5.79
			19	3.75	58	5.80
			20	3.77	59	5.80
			21	4.10	60	5.81
			22	4.14	61	5.83
			23	4.17	62	5.83
			24	4.19	63	5.84
			25	4.40	64	5.85
			26	4.43	65	5.86
			27	4.45	66	5.86
			28	4.46	67	5.87
			29	4.65	68	5.88
			30	4.67	69	5.88
			31	4.69	70	5.89
			32	4.70	71	5.89
			33	4.88	72	5.90
			34	4.89	73	5.91
			35	4.90	74	5.91
			36	4.91	75	5.92
			37	5.00	76	5.92
			38	5.07	77	5.93
			39	5.08	78	5.94

To forecast sales properly, it is necessary to be able to forecast both attrition patterns. A forecast using only the first attrition pattern understates eventual sales. A forecast using just the second pattern forecasts final sales correctly but is unable to forecast when those sales will occur. Table 18–6 provides an example of continuity attrition and the growth of the average number of units shipped over time to a group of starters in a continuity program in which one item is shipped per month.

TABLE 18–7
The Economics of Newsletter Direct Mail Marketing

Event	*Unit Rate/Cost*	*Total Units/Dollars*
Quantity mailed		10,000
Response rate	2.00%	
Pay rate	70.00%	
Gross subscribers		200
Paid subscribers		140
Canceled subscribers		60
Price	$37.00	
Year One revenue		$5,180.00
Year One costs		
Fulfillment and renewal costs		
Costs of fulfilling a paid subscriber	$6.00	$840.00
Costs of fulfilling a canceling subscriber	$2.25	$135.00
Costs of renewing a subscriber per starting subscriber	$1.25	$175.00
Total Year One costs		$1,150.00
Total Year One contribution		$4,030.00
Promotion costs		$3,000.00
Year One profits		$1,030.00
Year Two		
Renewal rate and number of renewals	70.00%	98
Nonrenewal rate and number of nonrenewals	30.00%	42
Revenue from renewals	$37.00	$3,626.00
Costs of fulfilling renewals	$6.00	$588.00
Costs of renewing a subscriber	$1.25	$122.50
Costs of fulfilling nonrenewals	$2.50	$105.00
Total Year Two costs		$815.50
Total Year Two contribution		$2,810.50
Cumulative Year Two profits		$3,840.50

Decision Table—Cumulative Second Year Profits if Price = $37

	Initial Pay or Conversion Rates				
Renewal Rates	*30.00%*	*40.00%*	*50.00%*	*60.00%*	*70.00%*
40.00%	$(906)	$(58)	$ 790	$1,638	$2,486
50.00	(713)	200	1,113	2,025	2,938
60.00	(519)	458	1,435	2,412	3,389
70.00	(326)	716	1,758	2,799	3,841

Newsletters and magazines. The key economic variables that determine the profitability of a newsletter are (1) price, (2) the initial pay or conversion rate, (3) renewal rates, and (4) the response rate to direct mail promotions at different levels of promotion expense.

As we mentioned earlier in this chapter, many newsletters and magazines are successful in attracting trial subscribers through preview offers that allow the potential subscriber to cancel without paying after examining one or a few sample issues. In these situations, the initial pay rate or conversion rate is the single most important variable affecting the ultimate success of the venture. However, even a relatively high initial pay rate can be offset by a poor renewal rate. Only after both conversion rates and renewal rates have been tested can we be sure of the potential profits of a newsletter. Table 18–7 shows the range of profits after two years from

TABLE 18–8
Decision Table—Cumulative Second-Year Profits if Price is Reduced to $27

Renewal Rates	Initial Pay or Conversion Rate				
	30 Percent	*40 Percent*	*50 Percent*	*60 Percent*	*70 Percent*
40%	$(1,746)	$(1,178)	$(610)	$(42)	$ 526
50	(1,613)	(1,000)	(388)	225	838
60	(1,479)	(822)	(165)	492	1,149
70	(1,346)	(644)	58	759	1,460

TABLE 18–9
Decision Table—Cumulative Second-Year Profits if Price is Increased to $47

Renewal Rates	Initial Pay or Conversion Rate				
	30 Percent	*40 Percent*	*50 Percent*	*60 Percent*	*70 Percent*
40%	$ (66)	$1,062	$2,190	$3,318	$4,446
50	188	1,400	2,613	3,825	5,038
60	441	1,738	3,035	4,332	5,629
70	695	2,076	3,458	4,839	6,221

a direct mail investment of $3,000 that resulted in 200 gross subscriptions. The price of the subscription in this example is $37.00. In this situation the $3,000 investment is recovered at an initial conversion rate of a little more than 40 percent coupled with a renewal rate of 40 percent; or the initial conversion rate could be as low as 40 percent if the renewal rate were to go to about 45 percent.

The profits that can be generated from a newsletter are related directly to the price charged for the newsletter, since editorial costs and printing costs are not affected by the price of the service. Thus, it is very important that price testing be employed at the outset to determine the best and most profitable price for the service. Tables 18–8 and 18–9 show the effect of a $10 increase or decrease in price on the newsletter described in Table 18–7.

The economics of magazines are similar to the economics of newsletters but with a number of critical differences. First, magazines rely heavily on newsstand sales and advertising to supplement the revenue stream provided by subscription income. Second, because of competition and because magazines are targeted to reach circulation levels measured in the hundreds of thousands rather than just thousands, as is the case with most newsletters, magazines have much less price-setting flexibility. However, just as in newsletters, the response rate to direct mail, the conversion rate, and the renewal rates are the key economic variables that eventually determine the success or lack of success of the magazine venture.

Catalogs. The term *back-end analysis* in a catalog operation can have multiple meanings. We may use the term with regard to the analysis of past media selections in much the same way as we analyze media performance in a club or continuity situation. Or we may be concerned with the profitability of an individual catalog mailing, that is, whether the catalog made a profit, which items sold well, which didn't, and so on. Or we may be referring to the decision-making process in which we attempt to decide which customers should be mailed which catalogs and with what frequency in the future.

The first decision deals with evaluating individual media sources, and we act as if all customers acquired behave in exactly the same way by looking at the average performance of all customers acquired from the media source. Again, this is the classical direct marketing approach, as opposed to the database approach, which focuses its attention on the performance of individual customers across media sources. The reason we need two approaches is that two different decisions are involved. When evaluating a media source, we are asking, "is the media source profitable?" and "should we invest in it again?" What counts is the total or the average performance of all customers expected to be acquired from a future investment when compared to the cost of the investment. And we use past performance as a guide to future performance.

In a noncontractual relationship, after a customer is acquired from any media source, the decision to promote that customer is an independent decision. This decision should be based on the expected future performance of the individual, regardless of the source from which he or she was acquired, even though the original media source may be, as we'll see later, an important variable in making a prediction of future performance.

The mechanics of media source evaluation in a catalog or in any noncontractual relationship requires computer systems that track performance by original source code. Again, as always, the key question is, "will the eventual contribution from the customers acquired be greater than the cost of acquiring those customers, and if so, by how much?"

In practice, the same media source will have been used many times in the past, and an evaluation of each use reveals that profitability varies from use to use. Not only will the prediction of eventual contribution vary but also the cost of acquiring new customers, as measured by the cost per order, will vary from promotion to promotion. Therefore, the prediction of future performance, both front-end CPO and back-end contribution, must be based on a forecasting procedure that takes this variability into account. Time-series analysis, taking such factors as trend and seasonality into account, may be employed if the data is suitable, or the analyst may use simpler averaging techniques giving greater weight to more recent occurrences. In practice, this becomes much more of an art than a science, and to imply that there are highly reliable standard procedures for this process would be misleading.

Financial services. The provider of financial services is, in theory, in a nearly identical position to the traditional catalog marketer with respect to the noncontractual nature of the relationship between the company and the customer. However, in practice, we've found financial service providers to be more concerned with individual level database marketing decisions than with the classical direct marketing issue of relating back-end performance to initial cost per acquired customer. There are a variety of reasons for this and although none of them justify current practices they go a long way toward explaining why things are the way they are.

To begin with, many financial services providers using direct marketing methods are not traditional self-contained direct marketing companies whose only contact with the customer is through direct marketing media. Therefore, because it is difficult if not impossible to attribute response to a single ad or direct mail promotion, little attempt is made to do so. More significant, we suspect, is the fact that many direct marketing operations within financial services firms are developed in an ad hoc manner. Someone at a high level within the firm, perhaps because of exposure to competitive direct marketing offers, decided that direct mail or direct marketing should be done within the firm, and set out to do so using the existing computer support systems, which were not designed for direct marketing purposes but were, in all likelihood, designed to support a sales force network.

In an information or database environment, where decision making is based on knowledge about the individual customer, one might argue that knowledge about the average behavior of all customers acquired from the same media source is unimportant. This argument, although it seems reasonable, is wrong for two reasons: First, the original media source is an important piece of individual information, and second, this approach confuses the need to make decisions about customers with the need to make decisions about where to prospect for customers. Again and again, direct marketers must make trade-off decisions about how much to spend on current-customer marketing and how much to spend on new-customer marketing. This is true for any company using direct marketing methods, be they a traditional direct marketing firm or one of the newer nontraditional users of direct marketing.

The Return of the Chicken-or-the-Egg Problem

By now, the reader who has been paying close attention should have realized that we're back to the chicken-or-the-egg problem raised earlier in this chapter. The argument goes as follows. We wish to compare the lifetime performance or behavior of customers acquired from a media source to the cost of acquiring those customers. However, their performance will be a function of what we send them and how often we promote them. If our promotion decisions are faulty, if we mail too often or too infrequently, or if we mail the wrong products, the contribution of the group of customers will be less than it would have been if our decisions had been better. Fortunately, the only practical way to treat this problem is to ignore it, and that's OK if all media source groups have been treated in the same way, however good or bad that way was, and if all we're trying to do is rank media sources in terms of relative performance in order to decide how to allocate future media acquisition dollars. On the other hand, we always have to guard against self-fulfilling prophecies. If, for example, customers from a particular media source are always mailed less frequently because their performance is expected to be less than average, then we shouldn't be surprised to find that indeed sales from these customers always turn out to be less than sales from customers acquired from other sources. The solution to this problem, if the problem is thought to exist, is to create and track test groups across all media sources that are always treated in the same fashion.

We'll come back to the subject of how individuals should be evaluated for inclusion in future mailings in Chapter 19, where we discuss modeling and the relationship between modeling and RFM analyses. For now, let's assume that we can agree on an acceptable way to estimate the lifetime performance of customers acquired from individual media sources and that we can even agree on the expected CPO and the expected lifetime contribution of customers to be acquired in the future. How do we use this information in decision making?

MEASURING PROFITABILITY: COMBINING FRONT-END AND BACK-END STATISTICS

The previous discussion implied that if the contribution to promotion, overhead, and profit for a given media investment was greater than the cost per order, the investment could be considered to be at least marginally profitable. We shall now continue to develop the relationship between front-end and back-end statistics.

Many direct marketers, particularly those engaged in club and continuity programs, prefer to use the concept of return on promotion to measure the relationship between front-end and back-end performance. Return on promotion (ROP) is defined as the ratio of the contribution to promotion, overhead, and profit minus the cost per order divided by the cost per order.

$$\text{ROP} = \frac{[\text{Contribution} - \text{Cost per order}]}{\text{Cost per order}} \times 100$$

Conceptually, the ROP approach treats the decision to run a space ad or mail a list as an investment against which some financial return is expected. The return is measured by the difference between the contribution that results from all the purchases that occur after the order enters the house and the cost of acquiring the order.

For example, in the discussion on clubs and continuities, we showed how a group of starters with average sales of $52.81 might generate a contribution per starter of $34.21. Let's assume that the cost of acquiring this group of starters was $20 per starter. In this case, the ROP would be:

$$\text{ROP} = \frac{[\$34.32 - \$20.00]}{\$20.00} \times 100 = 71.6\%$$

The ROP statistic can be used in a variety of ways by direct marketers. One important use of this statistic is to evaluate alternative offers. The decision rule to be followed is that if the media investment required to implement both offers is the same, the offer with the highest ROP is the best offer.

Consider the example described in Table 18–10. In this example, the decision concerns whether to use a premium costing $6 per starter or a premium costing $9 per starter. The assumption is made that the average sales resulting from the use of either premium offer will be the same and will be equal to $70 per starter.

Naturally, increasing premium expense will reduce profits unless the premium offer results in an increased response. Thus, the question is, "what increase in response is necessary to justify the use of a $9 premium?" One way to answer this question is to assume a response rate to the $6 premium offer and then search by trial and error for a response rate to the $9 offer that would result in the same profit and loss as the profit and loss resulting from the $6 offer.

Under the Results column for Case 1 in Table 18–10, we see the profit and loss resulting from the $6 premium if a response rate of 20 OPM is

TABLE 18–10
Using Incremental ROP to Evaluate New Offers (from 20 to 25 OPM)

	Case 1	*Case 2*	*Incremental Results*
Assumptions			
Quantity mailed	50,000	50,000	
Orders per thousand	20	25	
Average revenue per starter	$70.00	$70.00	
Direct costs excluding premium expense	$30.00	$30.00	
Contribution	$40.00	$40.00	
Advertising CPM	$350.00	$350.00	
Advertising expense	$17,500.00	$17,500.00	
Advertising CPO	$17.50	$14.00	
Premium expense	$6.00	$9.00	
Results			
Orders	1,000	1,250	250
Sales	$70,000	$87,500	$17,500
Costs	$30,000	$37,500	$7,500
Contributions	$40,000	$50,000	$10,000
Advertising	$17,500	$17,500	$0
Premium	$6,000	$11,250	$5,250
Total contribution to overhead and profit	$16,500	$21,250	$4,750
Per starter	$16.50	$17.00	$.50
ROP	94.3%	121.4%	0

assumed. For Case 2, at a response rate of 25 OPM, which is assumed to result from the use of the $9 premium, contribution to overhead and profit would be increased by a total of $4,750. The ROP for each case is shown at the bottom of Table 18–10. The ROP for Case 2 is 121.4 percent, which is greater than the ROP of 94.3 percent for Case 1. As long as the media investment is the same—in this case, the $17,500 required to mail 50,000 pieces at a CPM of $350—the alternative with the higher ROP will be the most profitable.

Therefore, it is possible to use the ROP equation directly to determine the response rate that would cause the ROP on the $9 premium offer to equal the ROP on the $6 premium offer:

$$\text{ROP} = \frac{\text{Contribution} - \text{Premium} - \text{CPO}}{\text{CPO}}$$

$$\text{Old ROP} = \quad .943 \quad = \frac{\$40 - \$6 - \$17.50}{\$17.50}$$

$$\text{New ROP} = \quad .943 \quad = \frac{\$40 - \$9 - \text{New CPO}}{\text{New CPO}}$$

$$\text{New CPO} = \$15.95$$

$$\text{New OPM} = \frac{\text{CPM}}{\text{New CPO}} = \frac{\$350}{\$15.95} = 21.94$$

The required new response rate is 21.94 orders per thousand.

When the initial media investment is not the same, the ROP analysis must be applied to the incremental investment in order to reach the

TABLE 18–11
Using Incremental ROP to Evaluate New Offers (from 20 to 22 OPM)

	Case 1	*Case 2*	*Incremental Results*
Assumptions			
Quantity mailed	50,000	50,000	
Orders per thousand	20	22	
Average revenue per starter	$70.00	$70.00	
Direct costs excluding premium expense	$30.00	$30.00	
Contribution	$40.00	$40.00	
Advertising CPM	$350.00	$400.00	
Advertising expense	$17,500.00	$20,000.00	
Advertising CPO	$17.50	$18.18	
Premium expense	$5.00	$5.00	
Results			
Orders	1,000	1,100	100
Sales	$70,000	$77,000	$7,000
Costs	$30,000	$33,000	$3,000
Contributions	$40,000	$44,000	$4,000
Advertising	$17,500	$20,000	$2,500
Premium	$5,000	$5,000	$500
Total contribution to overhead and profit	$17,500	$18,500	$1,000
Per starter	$17.50	$16.82	$.68
ROP	100.0%	92.5%	0
Incremental ROP			40.0%

correct decision. In this situation, if the incremental ROP is greater than zero, there will be an increase in the contribution to overhead and profit.

Refer to Table 18–11. In this example, the decision is whether to increase the quality of the mailing package in order to increase response. Costs are expected to increase from $350 per thousand to $400 per thousand, and the response rate is expected to increase from 20 OPM to 22 OPM. In Table 18–11, we see that if the more expensive mailing package were chosen, the average ROP would decline from 100 to 92.5 percent, but the incremental ROP would be 40 percent and total dollar contribution would increase by $1,000.

However, if the response rate increased to only 21 OPM, as shown in Table 18–12, the incremental ROP would be negative, and contribution would decline.

The decision to invest funds up to the point at which the incremental ROP is zero is a management decision. Generally, the cutoff rate is substantially higher, around 30 percent, to reflect other factors such as risk, the company's cost of capital, and opportunity costs resulting from competing uses of funds from other investments.

Another important use of the return on promotion statistic is to rank alternative investment opportunities for budget allocations. We have already seen that if the size of the investment is held constant, the investment alternative with the highest ROP is the most profitable.

TABLE 18–12
Using Incremental ROP to Evaluate New Offers (from 20 to 21 OPM)

	Case 1	*Case 2*	*Incremental Results*
Assumptions			
Quantity mailed	50,000	50,000	
Orders per thousand	20	21	
Average revenue per starter	$70.00	$70.00	
Direct costs excluding premium expense	$30.00	$30.00	
Contribution	$40.00	$40.00	
Advertising CPM	$350.00	$400.00	
Advertising expense	$17,500.00	$20,000.00	
Advertising CPO	$17.50	$19.05	
Premium expense	$5.00	$5.00	
Results			
Orders	1,000	1,050	50
Sales	$70,000	$73,500	$3,500
Costs	$30,000	$31,500	$1,500
Contributions	$40,000	$42,000	$2,000
Advertising	$17,500	$20,000	$2,500
Premium	$5,000	$5,250	$250
Total contribution to overhead and profit	$17,500	$16,750	$(750)
Per starter	$17.50	$15.95	$(1.55)
ROP	100.0%	83.8%	0
Incremental ROP			–30.0%

In planning annual media budgets, a good first step is to begin by calculating the expected ROP for each independent media opportunity and then to rank all such opportunities in terms of descending order of ROP. Conceptually, as the size of the media budget increases, the average ROP generated by the budget decreases, but for any given budget total, a media budget constructed in such a fashion always yields the highest possible ROP.

One caution in the use of ROP in budget planning: The ROP statistic is an economic measure and does not take fiscal year profit and loss considerations into account. An investment with a 50 percent ROP and a first-of-the-year expense date is considered to be the same in an ROP ranking scheme as an investment with a 50 percent ROP with an end-of-the-fiscal-year expense date. From a financial accounting point of view, the investment made on the first of the year will result in sales from new members in that same fiscal year. The investment made at the end of the fiscal year will result only in expense; the corresponding sales will come in the next fiscal year.

This problem is alleviated to some extent by accounting procedures that allow new-member acquisition expense to be amortized over the economic life of the acquired new members or subscribers. For example, assuming an economic life of 12 months, only one-twelfth of the expense of a promotion that was released in the last fiscal month would be charged to the current fiscal year.

ROP AND THE INFAMOUS 2 PERCENT RESPONSE RATE

It is customary for direct marketers to be accused of settling for low response rates. The implicit assumption is that through better targeting, response rates will increase to a rate higher than 2 percent—2 percent in this case being used as a kind of shorthand for a break-even level of response. Of course, adoption of the ROP principle suggests that direct marketers should, if funds are available and fiscal budget restraints are not an issue, always continue investing promotion dollars until the marginal rate of return on promotion approaches the cost of capital, and if that happens at a 2 percent response level, so be it. The goal of targeting should therefore not be to increase the marginal cutoff rate from 2 percent to some higher number; the goal of targeting should be to find more names that can be mailed with a response rate of 2 percent (that is, the break-even level) or better, and in this way to increase the size of one's business. Of course, if promotion funds are limited, then the effect of targeting will be to increase the average response rate over its current level, in turn increasing the average return on promotion.

Chapter 19

The Role of Modeling in the New Direct Marketing

By the time this book gets to print, close to 3,000 direct marketing professionals will have attended the Direct Marketing Association's (DMA's) course in statistics and modeling. In an industry whose annual convention draws only between 8,000 and 10,000 delegates this number reflects a tremendous interest in the subject. The high level of interest in statistics is due directly to rising promotion costs and declining response rates. In light of shrinking margins many direct marketers can no longer rely on relatively simple recency, frequency, monetary value (RFM) methods to manage their house files. Nor can direct marketers afford to make their new customer acquisition decisions based solely on the limited name selection criteria list owners have historically made available to them.

In this chapter we focus on the role of modeling in managing a database-driven direct marketing company. We will emphasize the application and implementation of models, not the statistical techniques used to build them. Hopefully, you have found all you care to know about statistics in the previous chapters. Some readers may choose to start with this section and bypass all or some of the statistical theory found in earlier chapters. To accommodate them we necessarily have to repeat some points made earlier in the book.

THE DIFFERENCE BETWEEN SCORING MODELS AND FORECASTS

In earlier chapters of this book we focused on the regression techniques used to build scoring models. A number of critical points bear repeating:

1. These scoring models are sometimes referred to as *predictive models,* and the word *predictive* is used essentially to distinguish these models from *segmentation models.*
2. In segmentation models the objective is to divide persons or geographic areas into groups or clusters so the persons or areas within one cluster are similar to each other and different from persons or areas in other clusters. A characteristic of a segmentation model is the absence of a specific dependent variable—no response rate, no average order, no conversion rate, and so on. On the other hand, the presence of such a dependent variable is an essential characteristic of a predictive model.
3. The problem with the term *predictive model* is that it reasonably implies that the owner of such a model has the ability to forecast some future event, such as the *average or overall response rate* to an upcoming mailing. Unfortunately, predictive models, at least as the term is used in direct marketing circles, do not yield this kind of forecast. The modeling techniques that you would use to forecast the average response rate to an upcoming mailing are different from the techniques you use to score your entire file in terms of each *individual's expected response.* Sounds confusing? It is. But this is a critical point, and it's

necessary to clearly understand the difference between the predictive scoring models that are used to obtain estimates of *individual* response and the forecasting techniques that are used for estimating the overall response rate to an upcoming mailing. *In the former case we are saying that we think the probability of, say, Bill Smith responding is 4.5 percent; in the latter case we are saying that if we mail to all of our 2 million customers, we think the average response rate will be 2 percent.*

4. Another key concept to remember is that when you are building an *individual-level predictive model* you build it on the basis of some promotion that took place in the past. That promotion had some average response rate, let's say 2 percent. That 2 percent response rate was, in turn, a function of a host of factors that will never occur in exactly the same way again: seasonality, economic conditions, delivery conditions, competitive promotions, and the like. Therefore, it stands to reason that if you built a predictive model based on a mailing that pulled 2 percent, each individual's probability of response is in some way pegged or indexed to that average 2 percent response rate.

So, if Bill Smith's 4.5 percent probability of response stems from a mailing that pulled 2 percent, you would expect his probability of response to be higher than 4.5 percent when the overall average response is expected to be higher than 2 percent and vice versa. Because of the importance of this distinction between overall response rates and individual predictions of response we discuss in some detail in this chapter the techniques that you need to use when you apply a single response model to multiple mailings, all of which have different overall response rates.

The balance of this chapter, then, addresses a number of other practical modeling issues of concern to direct marketers, such as these:

- The relationship between RFM models and regression models.
- The relationship between CHAID models and both RFM and regression models.
- Typical modeling results.
- ZIP code models and how to evaluate them against household-level models.
- How modeling can be used in a lead conversion situation.
- The role of enhancement data in the model-building and profiling process.
- How to organize your marketing department around unique customer or prospect segments or both and model each segment.

But first let's return to the issue of how to apply *predictive* response models to mailings with different *forecasted* response rates.

Obtaining Forecasts of Response

As we said before, estimating the response rate to one or more future mailings is an exercise in *forecasting.* To make such estimates planners resort to techniques such as time series analysis, econometric forecasting models, expert opinion, and crystal ball gazing, anything but the kinds of models we have been discussing in this book. This is not to downplay the need for this kind of forecasting ability. In fact, the need to be able to forecast absolute levels of response is equally if not more important than the need to be able to rank individuals in terms of their relative response rate. Not only is forecasting absolute response level more important, but also a good estimate of total response—what would happen if the whole file or large segments of the file were mailed—is the first step in applying scoring models.

Applying Scoring Models to Forecasts

To illustrate this point, let's consider the following situation. A company has a total customer file of 2 million names. Using a simple recency, frequency, monetary value scheme (RFM), the company decides that only about 1 million names are worth mailing. In their most recent summer mailing the average response rate among these million names was 2.0 percent. The company decides to build a model based on this mailing.

Since the variable being modeled is a yes/no response variable, the proper modeling technique is logistic regression. The model is built, and each of the 1 million persons mailed is now scored such that individual estimated response rates range from 18 percent to 0.4 percent and the average predicted response is, as it should be, 2 percent. Now the company wants to use the model to plan its fall holiday mailing. The company would like to mail more than 1 million names, but it insists on mailing only to individuals whose predicted response rate is 1 percent or more.

To use the model in this situation the analyst would first have to obtain an independent estimate of what the response rate would be if all of the 1 million names included in the summer mailing were mailed again in the fall holiday season. Because the mailing season in question is the company's best season, we would expect the average response rate to be above 2 percent. But how much above? *Nothing in the modeling done to date answers this question.*

Let's assume that management supplies a forecast of 2.5 percent. That helps, but there are still more questions that have to be answered before the film can be scored for this mailing. What about the fact of seasonality itself? Can a model based on a mailing that took place in the slow summer months, be applied to a fall holiday mailing? Does this make sense? Are there customers on the file that only buy in the holiday season, which means that they would probably score low on a model built on a summer mailing? *Nothing in the modeling done to date answers this question.*

Let's also assume for the purpose of this exercise that we agree that the model can be used, but to be sure that we don't make any serious error we agree to mail to anyone who purchased in the last holiday season.

Incidentally, there's nothing wrong in mixing commonsense database selections with selections based on name-scoring models. On the contrary, this process is to be encouraged. In building mailing plans database-driven selections should be made first, and then mailings should be supplemented on the basis of scoring models, not the other way around.

The next issue to be addressed is what to do about the other million names that were not included in the model-building process. The assumption here is that these names would have done appreciably worse than 2.0 percent had they been mailed in the summer, and that they will do appreciably worse than 2.5 percent if mailed in the fall.

To use the second million names we have to ask at least two questions:

- What does management think the response rate would be if the second half of the file were sent the fall holiday mailing?
- Do the variables in the model suggest that the scoring equation would apply to names on the second half of the file as well as to names on the first half of the file?

We also have to make a couple of assumptions. Let's assume that the answer to the second question is a qualified yes, and that the expected

TABLE 19–1
Using Models to Score Files

	First Half of File			
Decile	*Summer Model*	*Index*	*Fall Mailing*	*Second Half of File*
1	5.00%	250	6.27%	2.50%
2	3.50	175	4.39	1.75
3	2.20	110	2.76	1.10
4	1.70	85	2.13	0.85
5	1.60	80	2.01	0.80
6	1.50	75	1.88	0.75
7	1.40	70	1.75	0.70
8	1.30	65	1.63	0.65
9	1.00	50	1.25	0.50
10	0.75	38	0.94	0.38
Average	2.00	100	2.50	1.00

The model and the index is based on the summer mailing. The index is applied to the fall mailing and to the second half of the file.

response rate to a holiday mailing among the second half of the file is 1 percent compared to the 2.5 percent response rate expected among the first half of the file.

Table 19–1 illustrates these assumptions.

The decile analysis of the summer mailing demonstrates our ability to divide the first half of the file into 10 segments of equal size so the best 10 percent of the file has an expected response rate of 5 percent and the worse 10 percent of the file has an expected response rate of .75 percent. The first critical assumption we must make is that these relative rankings will hold up in a fall holiday mailing, which will average 2.50 percent if the entire top half of the file is mailed. In this case the top 10 percent would now respond at the rate of 6.27 percent and the bottom 10 percent would respond at a rate of .94 percent. The requirement that names should not be mailed unless their expected response rate is greater than 1 percent means that at least some portion of the names in the tenth decile would not be mailed in the fall.

Now working on the assumption that names in the second half of the file can be legitimately scored with the model built on names from the top of the file, we see that about 30 percent of the names in the bottom half of the file (according to management's old selection criteria) are expected to have response rates above 1 percent. Therefore, this analysis suggests that we mail 90 percent of the originally defined top of the file and 30 percent of the originally defined bottom of the file, or a total of 1.2 million names, all of which meet the expectation of a response rate in excess of 1 percent.[1]

From this exercise it should be clear that building a response model is only one part of the final name selection process. To summarize, nearly all models are built on mailings neither to the entire file nor to random

[1]At this point you may question why any names defined by management as being in the second half of the file should be mailed before any name included in the top of the file. The assumption is that management's ability to rank names is based on some model or set of rules that is less efficient than the model we are building—that management's judgment regarding relative ranking is generally but not totally correct.

samples from the file. Therefore, the issue arises as how to score segments of the file that were not included in the model-building process. Then, as noted earlier, there is the issue of adjusting expected response rates for seasonality. A model built on a mailing that averaged a 3 percent response will yield individual probabilities of response that average 3 percent. If the mailing in question is expected to average some other rate of response, then the individual expected response rates must be adjusted to reflect this new average—if the individual estimates of response are to be used for decision-making purposes. On the other hand, if all the model is being used for is relative ranking, then this amount of care need not be taken. In this situation the marketer will have decided in advance how many names to mail and the only issue is to make sure that the most responsive names are selected.

RESPONSE MODELING: RFM VERSUS REGRESSION

Up to now we've referred to RFM models and implied that we believe that regression models will do at least as well as RFM models and that they have the potential to do considerably better. It's time to devote more attention to this issue and to spell out the advantages of regression models over RFM models.

Let's assume that we are managing a catalog company with 2 million customers that have been acquired and marketed to continuously over a five-year period. Our customer file contains the following information about each of our customers:

- Date the customer first came on the file.
- Original source code—both at the detail and major media level (direct mail, print, broadcast, etc.).
- Dates of all customer purchases.
- Dollar value of each purchase associated with each purchase date.
- Total number of purchases made.
- Total dollar value of purchases.
- Major product areas in which at least one purchase was made—assume there are a dozen possible product areas.
- Total dollars spent in each product area.
- Number of times the customer has been mailed.

Suppose we wished to mail the next catalog to only 1 million customers, rather than to the entire file of 2 million. Let's further assume that the last catalog mailing went to the entire file of 2 million and that we kept a copy of the file at the time of the mailing and have since updated that file with results from the mailing. What analysis could be done—with and without statistical modeling?

The experienced direct marketer will immediately recognize all the necessary ingredients for a traditional RFM (recency, frequency, monetary value) analysis, plus the data needed to extend RFM to include product information. So for starters, we could do an RFM model. Suppose we decided to create five recency periods:

1. **Period 1**—Includes all customers whose last purchase was within 6 months of the mailing date.
2. **Period 2**—Includes all customers whose last purchase was within 7 to 12 months of the mailing date.

3. **Period 3**—Includes all customers whose last purchase was within 13 to 24 months of the mailing date.
4. **Period 4**—Includes all customers whose last purchase was within 25 to 36 months of the mailing date.
5. **Period 5**—Includes all customers whose last purchase was more than 37 months ago.

Now our 2 million names would be divided into five groups, and undoubtedly we would find that the response rate to the promotion being studied would be highest among those that purchased most recently.

The next step in the RFM process is to decide how to treat frequency of purchase. The more times customers have purchased in the past, the more likely they are to purchase again. Therefore it would make sense to divide each of the five recency cells into two or more new cells, which would now reflect recency and frequency behavior. Let's arbitrarily decide that frequency should be represented by four categories:

1. One lifetime purchase.
2. Two or three lifetime purchases.
3. Four or five lifetime purchases.
4. Six or more lifetime purchases.

Note that not only is our choice of four categories arbitrary, but also the definition of each category is arbitrary. And not only are these decisions arbitrary—and therefore not necessarily optimal in any sense—but also they fail to consider such important factors related to frequency as length of time on the file or number of times mailed.

Leaving these considerations aside for the moment, let's go on with the RFM analysis. We now have 20 cells to work with (5 recency cells times 4 frequency cells). What about monetary value? It's intuitive that someone who purchased three times within any time period and whose total purchases equaled $300 is a better prospect for our next mailing than someone who also purchased three times within the same time period but whose purchases totaled only $30.

Therefore, to complete this simple RFM model (yes, RFM can be called a model) we need to decide on rules for dividing each of the 20 cells by some measure of monetary value. Assume we can agree that each cell should be split three ways, depending on the total dollars spent to date—again this rule is arbitrary. We would arrive at a final model with 60 cells, each cell of different size but averaging 33,333 customers.

Even a cursory review of the above procedure makes clear the totally arbitrary nature of RFM analysis. Why choose only five recency periods and why those five? What's more, it's clear on further reflection that a tremendous amount of data is lost in the RFM process. As mentioned above, times mailed never had a chance to enter the picture, nor did purchases per times mailed, or even the dollar value of purchases made within any time frame other than the customer's total economic life with the company. What's more, we haven't included any way to take into account the types of product(s) purchased. We could, of course, have continued dividing cells by other variables, but doing so would quickly result in a very large number of very small, difficult to manage, and statistically unusable cells.

Tree Analyses Compared to RFM Analyses

For all these reasons, direct marketers have adopted models or techniques other than RFM. One such technique is often referred to as a tree analysis. Technically, tree analyses are either AID or CHAID analyses. *AID* stands for Automatic Interaction Detector, and the *CH* in CHAID stands for the chi-square test for statistical significance. Both AID and CHAID analyses produce trees that physically resemble the tree-like structure found in a graphic presentation of an RFM model. Two popular products available to help direct marketers use AID and CHAID analyses are SI-CHAID and Knowledge Seeker, both of which were discussed in detail in the preceding chapters that dealt with the process of model building. In this chapter we treat AID and CHAID analyses more generally.

Essentially both SI-CHAID and Knowledge Seeker start off by trying to find the one single independent variable that does the best job of splitting an entire mailing population and its average response rate into two or more cells or market segments so the difference between response rates is as large as possible and is statistically significant according to the chi-square test of statistical significance. This best independent variable may be a recency, frequency, or monetary value variable, or it may be any other independent variable available for analysis.

After this first split is made the program treats each resulting cell as a brand-new analysis and the program attempts to split each cell derived from the first split into two or more cells. Again, the program searches all the available independent variables and finds the best variable to cause a split at this point. This process continues until no more splits are possible, given the condition that each split must meet the chi-square test of statistical significance. The analyst running the program can make the significance test more or less stringent by changing confidence levels.

Many direct marketers may find a CHAID program to be a perfectly acceptable replacement for an arbitrarily defined RFM methodology, and they may stop there. Others may choose to use the insights gained from such an analysis to improve their regression models and to use the output of the tree analysis as a benchmark to measure the success of their regression models. In the next section we first discuss trees as an aid to regression, and then as benchmarks against which to measure the results of a regression model.

A Quick Review of Interaction Variables

Previously, we discussed using a tree analysis to discover interactions among independent variables. Essentially, interactions occur when two variables combine to produce an effect that is significantly greater than the sum of the effects produced by each variable acting by itself. For example, we may know that all our customers are both highly educated and have high incomes. What's more, persons with high incomes but low levels of education are not our customers, and vice versa. A regression model that contained only income and education as independent variables would not capture this interaction effect. To capture it the analyst must create a third variable, an interaction variable, which is usually done by multiplying both independent variables together to create this third variable. For example, a model that includes only income and education would look like this:

$$Y = a + b1 \times \text{Income} + b2 \times \text{Education}$$

A model that includes both income and education plus their interaction, on the other hand, would look like this:

$$Y = a + b1 \times \text{Income} + b2 \times \text{Education} + b3 \times \text{Income} \times \text{Education}$$

If interaction were truly present, the latter model would be much more powerful than the model that excluded the interaction effect (a higher R^2, a better fit, etc.).

Trees as a Benchmark Against Regression Results

In previous chapters we have argued for models that contain fewer rather than more independent variables. We certainly want to examine as many potential variables as possible, but we want our models to contain only those variables that strongly influence the variable being predicted or modeled. Most importantly, we want the model to "hold up" for as long as possible and it's been our experience that models with a small number of relatively strong variables will hold up better than models with a larger number of relatively weak variables.

A tree analysis, particularly one in which the confidence level is reduced from the usual 95 percent to 90 percent or lower (a statistician would say the alpha level is raised from 5 percent to 10 percent or more) will produce a large number of cells or breaks and will include a relatively large number of independent variables. Some of the cells will be very small and may only contain a few individuals, all of whom can be described by some unique combination of independent variables and all or nearly all of whom have responded to the offer being measured. We can think of such a tree as an analysis that has "beaten the data to death" or, in less dramatic prose, an analysis that has taken full advantage of chance. In a sense, what such an analysis is saying is that given all the independent variables we have to work with, no finer subdivision of the data is possible at the significance level we have chosen.

Now, and this is the point of this section, if a regression model can be created that uses only a few of the variables contained in the tree, and if the regression model does nearly as well as the tree in modeling the variable under consideration, then we would feel much more confident in using the regression model than we would in using the tree analysis. In other words, we feel more confident in using a model with relatively few independent variables than we do in using a regression model with as many variables as contained in the tree or in using the tree analysis itself.

Table 19–2 shows the results of a tree analysis compared to a regression model that was created with only four independent variables. The tree contained twice as many variables as the regression model. Each row in Table 19–2 represents a segment produced by the tree analysis. The table shows that the first 32 segments defined by the tree accounted for 20 percent of the names mailed and 54 percent of the total responses. The last

TABLE 19–2
Tree Analysis Compared to a Regression Model Used to Benchmark Regression Results

	Number	*Cum*	*Cum %*	*Number*	*Cum*	*Cum %*	*Rsp*	*Regression Model*
Seg	*MLD*	*# Mld*	*MLG*	*Rsp*	*# Rsp*	*Rsp*	*Rate*	*Cum % Rsp*
46	2	2	0%	2	2	0%	100.00%	
49	2	4	0%	2	4	0%	100.00%	
1	270	274	0%	74	78	3%	27.42%	
41	52	326	0%	12	90	3%	22.93%	
3	273	599	0%	56	146	5%	20.48%	
53	72	671	0%	13	159	6%	18.04%	
16	132	803	0%	20	179	7%	15.11%	
24	88	891	0%	13	192	7%	14.79%	
35	182	1073	0%	14	206	8%	7.67%	
42	318	1391	0%	20	226	8%	6.29%	
13	230	1621	1%	13	239	9%	5.64%	
19	1256	2877	1%	66	305	11%	5.26%	
9	82	2959	1%	4	309	12%	4.89%	
38	634	3593	1%	29	338	13%	4.57%	
2	5598	9191	3%	239	577	22%	4.27%	
15	624	9815	3%	21	598	22%	3.36%	
28	2536	12351	4%	85	683	26%	3.35%	
4	1799	14150	5%	52	735	28%	2.89%	
5	5260	19410	6%	145	880	33%	2.76%	
8	803	20213	6%	18	898	34%	2.24%	
18	2834	23047	7%	63	961	36%	2.22%	
47	428	23475	8%	9	970	36%	2.10%	
31	1246	24721	8%	25	995	37%	2.01%	
29	840	25561	8%	16	1011	38%	1.91%	
43	1249	26810	9%	20	1031	39%	1.60%	
27	*1940*	*28750*	*9%*	*26*	*1057*	*40%*	*1.34%*	*34%*
17	7510	36260	12%	89	1146	43%	1.19%	
39	5325	41585	13%	58	1204	45%	1.09%	
14	6079	47664	15%	65	1269	48%	1.07%	
44	1352	49016	16%	14	1283	48%	1.04%	
26	7331	56347	18%	72	1355	51%	0.98%	
7	*7573*	*63920*	*20%*	*72*	*1427*	*54%*	*0.95%*	*48%*
10	10097	74017	24%	94	1521	57%	0.93%	
12	*17457*	*91474*	*29%*	*154*	*1675*	*63%*	*0.88%*	*58%*
21	10722	102196	33%	91	1766	66%	0.85%	
51	4714	106910	34%	36	1802	68%	0.76%	
22	*12917*	*119827*	*38%*	*96*	*1897*	*71%*	*0.74%*	*67%*
32	21321	141148	45%	128	2025	76%	0.60%	
36	15107	156255	50%	86	2111	79%	0.57%	
23	8801	165056	53%	45	2156	81%	0.51%	
6	16917	181973	58%	78	2234	84%	0.46%	
34	11185	193158	62%	51	2285	86%	0.46%	
25	4538	197696	63%	21	2306	87%	0.46%	
11	9531	207227	66%	39	2345	88%	0.41%	
20	8237	215464	69%	34	2379	89%	0.41%	
30	16447	231911	74%	66	2445	92%	0.40%	
50	11338	243249	78%	45	2490	94%	0.40%	

TABLE 19–2
Concluded

	Number	*Cum*	*Cum %*	*Number*	*Cum*	*Cum %*	*Rsp*	*Regression Model*
Seg	*MLD*	*# Mld*	*MLG*	*Rsp*	*# Rsp*	*Rsp*	*Rate*	*Cum % Rsp*
33	10444	253693	81%	36	2526	95%	0.34%	
37	4428	258121	83%	13	2539	95%	0.29%	
52	9939	268060	86%	26	2565	96%	0.26%	
45	36722	304782	98%	81	2645	99%	0.22%	
48	7055	311837	100%	14	2659	100%	0.20%	
54	202	312039	100%	0	2659	100%	0.00%	
40	81	312120	100%	0	2659	100%	0.00%	

column of this table shows the percent of responses accounted for by a regression model run on the same data, at approximately the same depth. The 48 percent figure in the last column represents the percent of responses accounted for by the top two deciles according to the regression model. In other words, according to the regression model 20 percent of the names mailed produced 48 percent of the responses. It could be argued that the tree did better, but our judgment is that the results are close and the regression model will hold up much better over time.

REGRESSION MODELS

Regression modeling begins at the exact same place as RFM modeling—with the available data. In regression modeling, the first decision is the selection of the dependent variable—what do we want to model or predict? In this example we of course want to predict response, and we will be in a position to predict response if the things we know about our customers, more formally referred to as the independent variables, are themselves good predictors of response.

The question is whether we believe that knowing past performance data, the same kinds of data that go into an RFM model, can help us predict who will and will not be likely to respond to a future mailing. Of course, because we know that RFM works, the real question is whether using all the information available to us in combination with the regression tool will produce a better result than using the same information in RFM analysis.

Let's review the list at the beginning of this chapter of the data we have to work with for each customer. Each element can be used to create a set of independent variables that will be considered for inclusion in a regression model. Generally, the data needs to be *massaged* before it can become useful for modeling. For example, the data types in the list could be turned into the set of independent variables in Table 19–3.

The list of independent variables that could be created from the data set is extensive, and it indicates the power of the modeling technique. It should be said immediately that the final model will contain only a few of the many possible variables. In fact, as we have repeatedly said, a sign of a good model is the presence of relatively few variables. The converse is also true; a model with a dozen or so variables is probably, despite its impressive appearance, a relatively poor model. (More about this subject is contained in Chapters 10 through 16 of this book.)

TABLE 19–3
Relating Original Data to Model Variables

VAR 1 =	Number of months on the file.
VAR 2 =	Number of months since last purchase.
VAR 3 =	Total dollars.
VAR 4 =	Total dollars divided by months on file.
VAR 5 =	Total dollars divided by number of times mailed.
VAR 6 =	Total dollars divided by number of purchases.
VAR 7 =	Number of times mailed.
VAR 8 =	Number of purchases.
VAR 9 . . . *n* =	Number of purchases within last (3, 6, 9, 12 . . .) months.
VAR 10 =	Number of purchases divided by times mailed.
VAR 11 =	Number of purchases divided by months on file.
VAR 12 . . . *n* =	Dollars per purchase within each product category.
VAR 13 =	Number of product categories with purchases.

Now let's assume you build a regression model based on the data from the recent mailing to the entire file. What will it look like, and what will it do for you? For simplicity of presentation and interpretation, let's agree to use ordinary least squares multiple regression as our modeling tool, even though in practice we would use logistic regression in a response model. Also, remember that we will be building the model on only half the names mailed, the calibration sample, and we will be validating the model on the other half of the names mailed, the validation sample.

What will the regression model look like? Which of the many possible independent variables will finally wind up in the model? To answer the second question first, the analyst using the statistical tools discussed in the earlier chapters will determine which independent variables are important in predicting response. Let's assume the following variables are important.

Variable Name	*Variable Description*
VAR 2	= Number of months since last purchase
VAR 10	= Number of purchases divided by times mailed
VAR 6	= Total dollars divided by number of purchases

In addition to identifying those variables that are significant predictors of response, the model will assign weights to each variable so the final regression equation or model might look something like this:

$$\text{Expected response} = 2.3 - .4 \times (\text{VAR } 2) + .8 \times (\text{VAR } 10) + .0012 \times (\text{VAR } 6)$$

Each customer on the file will be scored according to the above equation. For example, assume a customer with the following values for each of the performance variables:

VAR 2 = 6	Six months have elapsed since last purchase.
VAR 10 = .10	Customer buys once out of every 10 times mailed.
VAR 6 = 55.33	Average purchase equals $55.33.

The equation or the model (the model is simply the equation) makes intuitive sense. Each customer will start off with a score of 2.3 (the model provides this number, which could be positive or negative—in this case, it's positive). The weight of the variable VAR 2, number of months since last purchase, is negative and equal to –.4, so –2.4 (–.4 × 6) will be added to the score. Since adding a negative number decreases the score, the longer the time since the last purchase, the smaller the score, which makes sense. The higher the score, the greater the propensity to respond, and we know from experience that the likelihood of responding is greater among persons who have purchased from us in the recent past.

The second variable, VAR 10, represents the individual's average response to all prior in-house mailings; the larger this number, the higher the score. In this case, we will add .08 (.8 × .10) to the customer's score. The third variable, VAR 6, represents the individual's average sale from all prior purchases, and again we would expect a person's score to increase as this number increases. The value of the variable, its coefficient, is .0012; therefore, the person's score is increased by .0664 (.0012 × 55.33).

Adding up all of the above, we determine that this person's score is equal to 0.0464 (obtained from the equation 2.3 – 2.4 + .08 + .0664). This same procedure would be repeated for every customer on the validation file. Continuing our example, each customer would be scored and then all customers would be sorted or ranked, in descending sequence, in terms of their score. The last step in the procedure, for presentation purposes only, is to divide the entire validation file into 10 groups of equal size, called deciles. The persons in the top decile will have the highest scores and are expected to perform the best in an upcoming mailing.

A Reminder About Ordinary versus Logistic Regression Models

In practice, as we said before, we would use the logistic regression model rather than the ordinary least squares model for response models. One consequence of this difference would be that the scores assigned to each customer could be converted into probabilities of response, and the probabilities would range between 0 and 1.[2]

In the ordinary regression model, scores of less than 0 and greater than 1 are possible. This result may be acceptable if all you want to do is rank your customers in terms of their relative probability of responding, but it is not sufficient if you require an accurate measure of probability, as would be the case if you intended to stop mailing below some expected response rate.

TYPICAL RESPONSE MODEL RESULTS

The next question we have to ask ourselves is how response rates will vary among deciles. It's very important for anyone working with models to have some rules of thumb in mind. Most good models built on performance data show that the top two deciles behave much better than the bottom two deciles and the six deciles in the middle are somewhat flat, though below the top two and above the bottom two deciles. For example, if our mailing to our house file of 2 million names pulled 8 percent on average, it would be reasonable, given the quality of the data discussed above, to expect the decile result shown in Table 19–4.

[2]When logistic regression models are used, the scores produced by the logistic equation are logits. The logits in turn can be transformed into probabilities.

TABLE 19–4 ***Typical Regression Modeling Results***

	Modeling Internal Performance Data								*Modeling Census Data at the ZIP Code Level*					
	Example 1		*Example 2*		*Example 3*		*Example 4*		*Example 1*		*Example 2*		*Example 3*	
Decile	*Percent Response*	*Index*	*Percent Response*	*Index*	*Percent Response*	*Index*	*Percent Response*	*Index*	*Percent Response*	*Index*	*Percent Response*	*Index*	*Percent Response*	*Index*
1	26.0%	326	23.8%	298	18.3%	229	19.3%	241	3.2%	162	2.7%	137	2.3%	113
2	11.2	140	13.3	167	12.9	161	11.4	142	2.8	138	2.5	125	2.2	109
3	8.4	105	9.5	119	10.7	134	8.6	108	2.5	125	2.3	113	2.1	106
4	7.4	93	7.1	89	9.4	118	8.0	100	2.2	110	2.2	110	2.1	106
5	7.0	87	6.7	83	7.7	96	7.4	92	2.2	108	2.0	98	2.0	102
6	5.6	70	5.5	69	6.5	81	6.3	78	1.8	92	1.8	90	2.0	102
7	4.7	58	4.1	51	5.0	62	5.6	70	1.7	85	1.8	92	1.9	96
8	4.2	52	3.8	48	3.9	49	5.3	66	1.5	77	1.7	86	1.8	92
9	3.7	47	3.3	42	3.2	40	4.2	53	1.2	62	1.6	82	1.7	87
10	1.9	23	2.9	36	2.4	30	3.9	49	0.9	46	1.4	72	1.7	87
Average	8.0%	100	8.0%	100	8.0%	100	8.0%	100	2.0%	100	2.0%	100	2.0%	100
Best to worst		1400.0%		833.3%		767.1%		492.5%		350.0%		189.6%		130.4%
Best 20 percent to average		232.6%		232.1%		195.0%		191.8%		150.0%		130.8%		111.3%
Best 80 percent to average		116.3%		115.5%		116.3%		112.3%		112.1%		106.4%		103.3%

TABLE 19–5
Regression Modeling against a 2 Percent Response Rate

	Modeling Internal Performance Data							
	Example 1		*Example 2*		*Example 3*		*Example 4*	
Decile	*Percent Response*	*Index*	*Percent Response*	*Index*	*Percent Response*	*Index*	*Percent Response*	*Index*
1	6.5%	326	6.0%	298	4.6%	229	4.8%	241
2	2.8	140	3.3	167	3.2	161	2.8	142
3	2.1	105	2.4	119	2.7	134	2.2	108
4	1.9	93	1.8	89	2.4	118	2.0	100
5	1.7	87	1.7	83	1.9	96	1.8	92
6	1.4	70	1.4	69	1.6	81	1.6	78
7	1.2	58	1.0	51	1.2	62	1.4	70
8	1.0	52	1.0	48	1.0	49	1.3	66
9	.9	47	.8	42	.8	40	1.1	53
10	.5	23	.7	36	.6	30	1.0	49
Average	2.0%	100	2.0%	100	2.0%	100	2.0%	100

Each of the first four examples shown in Table 19–4 is based on a real case involving modeling response to a house file mailing. In each case, the independent variables were performance variables: when, what, and how much customers purchased in the past, how often were they promoted, and so on.

As the examples in the table show, models based on this kind of data allow users to divide a single house file into 10 distinct groups, each with its own expected response rate. We would describe Model 1 as a very powerful model. The best 10 percent of the file pulled 26.0 percent compared to the bottom decile, which pulled only 1.9 percent. Another way to look at the results is to compare the response rate of the top two deciles or the top eight deciles to the average. Again, referring to Model 1, the top two deciles (20 percent) did 2.3 times better than average [(26% + 11.2%)/2 = 17.1% and 17.1%/8% = 2.3)]; the sum of the top eight deciles did 1.16 times better than average.

Performance Models 2, 3, and 4 are not as powerful as Model 1, but they are still strong models, each capable of creating groups that perform significantly better or significantly worse than average.

It's important to understand just what you can expect from modeling for a variety of reasons, not the least of which is the fact that knowing what to expect can save you considerable time and money.

For example, suppose you are responsible for mailings at a financial services company. The market has turned down drastically, and your house list, which used to pull 5 percent, now only pulls 2 percent, and you need to pull 3 percent to break even. Can modeling help? Let's apply the indexes from Table 19–4 to a 2 percent average response rate and see what conclusions we can draw. The results are shown in Table 19–5.

As you can see from Table 19–5 any of the four models will allow you to mail the first decile and achieve a response rate well above 3 percent. All the models will also allow you to mail the second decile and receive a response rate close to 3 percent. But if your goal was to mail 50 percent of your file, modeling can't do that for you—at least the four models shown here can't.

TABLE 19–6
Regression Modeling against a .5 Percent Response Rate

	Modeling Internal Performance Data							
	Example 1		*Example 2*		*Example 3*		*Example 4*	
Decile	*Percent Response*	*Index*	*Percent Response*	*Index*	*Percent Response*	*Index*	*Percent Response*	*Index*
1	1.6%	326	1.5%	298	1.1%	229	1.2%	241
2	.7	140	.8	167	.8	161	.7	142
3	.5	105	.6	119	.7	134	.5	108
4	.5	93	.4	89	.6	118	.5	100
5	.4	87	.4	83	.5	96	.5	92
6	.3	70	.3	69	.4	81	.4	78
7	.3	58	.3	51	.3	62	.3	70
8	.3	52	.2	48	.2	49	.3	66
9	.2	47	.2	42	.2	40	.3	53
10	.1	23	.2	36	.1	30	.2	49
Average	.5%	100	.5%	100	.5%	100	.5%	100

What if you were pulling not 2 percent but only one-half of 1 percent? Table 19–6 shows that modeling can't help you, and you should look elsewhere for relief.

ZIP CODE MODELS

The last section referred to models based on internal performance data. What about response models that are based on mailings to outside rented lists? In this situation, there is no "hard" performance data. Generally, all you have to work with is ZIP code–based census data. There are a number of issues to consider, but first let's take a look at some typical ZIP-code-based census models. Referring back to Table 19–4, you'll see, not surprisingly, that the ZIP code–based census models are not nearly as strong as the models built on internal performance data. In the best case shown, Model 1, the best decile does only 3.5 times better than the worst decile, and mailing to 80 percent of the universe of names corresponding to this model will lift response by only 12 percent. The results are still less impressive for Models 2 and 3.

Despite the fact that ZIP code response models based on census data are not as strong as internal performance models, they may still be worthwhile. For example, suppose you were doing a mailing to 3 million outside names and were expecting a 2 percent response or 60,000 orders. A 10 percent improvement would mean another 6,000 orders and if each order were worth $30, this would mean another $180,000 in contribution. Of course, the larger the universe, the larger the potential profits.

Response models based on census data are complicated and involve a number of issues. First of all, a model of a mailing to a million or more names means that we will be mailing to a large number of individual lists, and much fewer but still a significant number of list categories. One of the underlying assumptions of ZIP code modeling is that the impact of the demographic characteristics associated with each ZIP code will work across all list categories and across all lists within a category. The report that accompanies a good ZIP code model shows you exactly how well the model does across categories and by list within a category.

TABLE 19–7
ZIP Code Regression Modeling

	Decile									
Category	*1*	*2*	*3*	*4*	*5*	*6*	*7*	*8*	*9*	*10*
Percent Response within Decile										
1	5.00%	3.90%	2.80%	2.60%	2.60%	1.60%	1.50%	1.10%	.40%	.01%
2	3.30	3.30	3.30	3.30	3.20	2.80	2.80	2.70	2.60	2.75
3	.50	.60	.70	.80	.90	1.10	1.20	1.30	1.40	1.50
4	3.80	3.20	3.00	2.20	2.20	1.70	1.50	1.00	.50	.00
Total	3.2%	2.8%	2.5%	2.2%	2.2%	1.8%	1.8%	1.5%	1.2%	1.1%
Indexed Response										
1	232	181	130	121	121	74	70	51	19	0
2	110	110	110	110	106	93	93	90	87	92
3	50	60	70	80	90	110	120	130	140	150
4	199	168	157	115	115	89	79	52	26	0
Total	156	136	121	110	110	89	87	76	61	53

It is not unusual to find that the model performs better within some list categories than others. In Table 19–7, the general model is represented by the row labeled "Total"; we see that the response rate in the best decile is about 3.2 percent and the response rate in the poorest performing decile is about 1.1 percent. Further, response rates decline as expected from decile 1 through decile 10. However, on closer inspection of the model's performance, among the four major list categories that make up the total universe of names mailed we see that the model works very well for list categories 1 and 4; the model doesn't work well for list category 2; and list category 3 behaves contrary to the model predictions. What should the user and the modeler do at this point?

One option is to eliminate list categories 2 and 3 from the analysis and build a new model based solely on the results of lists within categories 1 and 4. This would be a perfectly good solution if the mailing were very large and enough names were mailed in each list category. Generally, we try to build models in situations with 2,000 or more responders, using 1,000 responders and a representative sampling of nonresponders to build the model and validating the model by applying the results of the model to the remaining 1,000 responders and a corresponding sample of nonresponders.

However, suppose the mailing in question went to only 100,000 names and had a 2 percent response rate producing just 2,000 orders. Assuming that each category was equally represented would mean that a model built on just two list categories would include a total of only 1,000 responders. That would leave only 500 responders on which to build the model and 500 responders on which to validate the model. We could attempt to build a model on only 500 responders, but the odds of achieving a significant response model decrease as the number of responders decreases. Of course, there's no harm in trying, and the statistics that accompany the output of the model will tell the analyst whether the model is or is not significant.[3] What's more, if you are able to identify significant variables when the sample is small, the model you construct using these variables will also be strong.

Let's assume that a model based on list categories 2 and 3 proves not to be statistically significant. What's the alternative, and how could we use the model shown in Table 19–7? We could certainly employ the model when using lists in categories 1 and 4. We would not use the model against lists selected from category 3, and we would probably consider using the model to select ZIP codes from lists in category 2.

Another consideration in ZIP code models is the selection of the independent variables. As we discussed in Chapter 2, each ZIP code is associated with a string of census demographics. And although it is true that each ZIP code may therefore be described in terms of hundreds of census variables, it's also true that many of these variables are highly correlated with each other. Simply put, affluent people have high incomes, live in expensive homes, are better educated, have professional or managerial jobs, and so on. Therefore, a model that includes each, or many, of these variables is likely to suffer from multicollinearity. (See Chapters 10 through 15 for more details about multicollinearity.)

Analysts experienced with census data will be sure not to include variables that are highly correlated with each other, or they will perform a factor analysis prior to beginning a regression analysis to avoid this problem. In this case, factor analysis would combine the many variables that measure affluence into a single affluence factor that would be used as just one independent variable in a regression analysis. Another factor may measure the degree to which the ZIP code is an urban ZIP code, a third factor may be a measure of ethnicity, and so on.

Adjusting for ZIP Code Size

A third issue in ZIP code modeling is the small mailing quantity and the correspondingly small number of responses achieved within any one ZIP code. For example, even a mailing of 1 million pieces and 20,000 responses averages only 36 pieces per ZIP code and less than 1 response per ZIP code (based on 28,000 residential ZIP codes). To adjust for this condition, analysts experiment with different weighting schemes so the response rates from ZIP codes that receive relatively large numbers of pieces count for more in the regression model than ZIP codes that receive only a few pieces and whose response rates would distort the model if the number of pieces mailed were not taken into consideration.

Table 19–8 presents an example in which 2 percent and 4 percent response rates are achieved in mailings into ZIP codes of different sizes. Intuitively, the ZIP code receiving 10,240 pieces and producing 205 orders should receive more consideration or weight than the ZIP code into which only 80 pieces were mailed and only two responses were generated, even though the response rate (2 percent) is the same.

---

[3]It is interesting to note that models that do work—i.e., they pass all the tests for statistical significance—and that are based on a relatively small number of responders are probably particularly good models because their strength could be judged significant based on a small sample.

TABLE 19–8
ZIP Code Models—Adjusting for the Quantity Mailed and Response Rates

2% Response			*4% Response*		
Quantity Mailed	*Response Rate*	*Weight*	*Quantity Mailed*	*Response Rate*	*Weight*
10	2.0%	0.2	10	4.0%	0.4
20	2.0	0.4	20	4.0	0.8
40	2.0	0.8	40	4.0	1.5
80	2.0	1.6	80	4.0	3.1
160	2.0	3.1	160	4.0	6.1
320	2.0	6.3	320	4.0	12.3
640	2.0	12.5	640	4.0	24.6
1,280	2.0	25.1	1,280	4.0	49.2
2,560	2.0	50.2	2,560	4.0	98.3
5,120	2.0	100.4	5,120	4.0	196.6
10,240	2.0	200.7	10,240	4.0	393.2

Adjusting for ZIP code is accomplished by using a technique called *weighed least squares regression.* In this procedure each ZIP code receives a weight equal to the ZIP code's response rate (P) times one minus the response rate (Q) times the number of mailings (N) or ($N \times P \times Q$). In our example, the ZIP code with the larger mailing would receive a weight of 200.7 and the ZIP code that received only 80 pieces would receive a weight of 1.6.

You will notice that the $N \times P \times Q$ formula also assigns more weight to ZIP codes with higher response rates when the quantity mailed into each ZIP code is the same. Therefore, a ZIP code that received 10,240 pieces and produced a 2 percent response receives about half the weight of a ZIP code of similar size with a response rate of 4 percent.

Modeling Variables other than Response

The census data available for ZIP codes is also available for smaller geographic areas. Census data has always been available for block groups and census tracts, and it is now available at the ZIP-plus-four or nine-digit ZIP code level.

Naturally, models built at the block group or the ZIP-plus-four level should outperform models built with data associated with larger ZIP codes. For example, according to Equifax National Decision Systems, the composition of ZIP CODE 07712 is as follows:

Percent of Households in Each MicroVision Cluster*

Lap of Luxury	7.9%
Home Sweet Home	9.1
Great Beginnings	21.4
A Good Step Forward	11.3
Struggling Minority Mix	11.8
Difficult Times	10.9

*For a complete description of MicroVision and other segmentation or clustering products, please refer to Appendix B at the end of this book.

TABLE 19–9
Model Results Built on Block Group Data

	Response	*Cumulative*	
Decile	*Rate*	*Index*	*Lift*
1	4.16%	208	208
2	3.16	158	183
3	3.05	153	173
4	2.58	129	162
5	2.42	121	154
6	1.58	79	141
7	1.47	74	132
8	0.95	47	121
9	0.47	24	110
10	0.16	8	100
Average	2.00%		100

Clearly the census data that describe this ZIP code represents a fairly meaningless set of averages, and models based on block group or ZIP-plus-four data would deal better with persons living in this area and similar areas in which the ZIP code does not represent anything close to a homogeneous neighborhood.

Our experience working with block group data suggests that models can be developed that could spread a 2 percent response rate as indicated in Table 19–9.

As always, before deciding to model at the block group or ZIP-plus-four level, a decision has to be made regarding the extra costs associated with implementing the model at this level of detail as opposed to implementing the model at the simpler and always available ZIP code level. If block group codes or ZIP-plus-four codes are not readily available, your files will have to be geo-coded before the models can be applied.

However, there's no reason to think of modeling as being limited to response modeling. Performance models are similar to response models in the sense that the independent variables, the things we know about the customer or prospect, may be the same as those used in a response model. This may be area-related census data if we are modeling performance against outside lists, or internal performance behavior, overlay data, or other research data if we are modeling existing customers.

COMBINING MODELS—MODELING PROFIT

Long before modeling was a factor in direct marketing, direct marketers knew that response could be increased by softening or increasing the value of the offer. This is especially true for name acquisition models—mailings to rented lists. The rule of thumb is simple: increase the value of the offer, increase response—and watch out for poorer back-end performance. The same effect could be accomplished by extending payment terms, adding a trial offer, and so on. Direct marketers are good at increasing response, but they have always understood there is no such thing as a free lunch and would therefore expect back-end performance to be poorer.

The earlier ZIP code response modeling efforts sometimes missed this point, so models were built to identify those ZIP codes most likely to respond rather than those most likely to respond and produce profits. (We'll focus on ZIP code models in this section, but the same effect could be true for models dealing with persons.) Today, modelers understand that in situations in which the back-end is as important as the response itself—which is almost always the case unless you are selling a fixed-price product for cash with order—you must build two models, a response model and a performance model, and then combine the two models into a profit model.[4]

The response model provides you with an expected response rate or a probability of response, and the performance model provides you with a measure of expected lifetime profits. The product of expected response times expected profits is equal to expected profits per name mailed.

For example, a ZIP code with an expected response rate of 5 percent and an expected back-end profit of $15 has an overall expected value of $.75 ($15 × .05 = $.75); a ZIP code with a lower expected response rate of 3 percent but a higher expected back-end profit of $50 has an expected value of $1.50. Clearly, you would be better off mailing to the latter ZIP code with the lower expected response rate but the significantly higher expected back-end performance.

For ZIP code modeling we recommend the following procedure:

1. For each ZIP code determine the response rate, the number of pieces mailed, and some measure of back-end performance per starter or responder.
2. Append ZIP-code level demographics to each ZIP code record.
3. Divide the total mailing file into two parts, a calibration sample and a validation sample. Do this by placing half of the ZIP codes in the calibration sample and the other half in the validation sample. Check to make sure that both samples contain close to an equal number of mailings and responses.
4. From the calibration sample build a response model. For technical reasons having to do with the uneven distribution of response rates we recommend converting ZIP code response rates into logits and using weighted least squares regression as the modeling tool, the weights being assigned by the $N \times P \times Q$ formula defined above.
5. Apply the response model, the regression equation, to the ZIP codes on the validation sample.
6. Sort the validation file by predicted response score and create a decile analysis. When creating the decile analysis, each ZIP code should be represented by the quantity mailed into that ZIP code. In other words, each ZIP code does not always count as one unit.
7. Empirically determine the *actual response rate* within each decile. Check to see if the model spreads response rates as expected, and check to see if the predicted response rates are close to the actual response rates.
8. If the model is satisfactory, apply the model equation to each of the 28,000 residential ZIP codes.

---

[4]Sometimes it is possible to model a single performance variable such as payments per name mailed, a variable which takes both performance (sales, payments, profits, etc.) into account as well as response rates, but we prefer to model both back-end performance and front-end response separately, because we believe that more insights are gained into the *causal* effects of the independent variables by using this two-step procedure.

9. Each ZIP code, after it is scored, will then be assigned to a decile. This can be accomplished by sorting after the ZIP codes are scored or by the use of a table that relates ZIP code scores to decile levels.
10. Repeat the procedure, this time changing the dependent variable from a response rate to some measure of back-end performance, such as sales or payments.
11. Among the ZIP codes on the calibration sample, build a back-end performance model.
12. Apply the performance model to the validation sample.
13. Repeat steps 6 through 9 to score all 28,000 ZIP codes and to assign each ZIP code to a performance decile.
14. For each ZIP code on the validation file, multiply the expected ZIP code response rate by the expected back-end performance measure. The result is expected performance per name mailed (expected sales per name mailed or expected payments per name mailed depending on the back-end measure selected).
15. Sort the file in terms of expected performance per name mailed.
16. Check to see if the actual performance per name mailed is consistent with the predictions of the model.
17. If the cross-multiplication process works for the ZIPs in the validation sample, apply the same procedures to all 28,000 residential ZIPs—multiply each ZIP's expected response rate by its expected performance measure. Then sort all 28,000 ZIPs in deciles based on each ZIP's expected performance per name mailed score.
18. Now create one or more ZIP code tapes that will contain the ZIP code number and three decile rankings: a response decile, a performance decile, and a combined profit decile.
19. You can now use the ZIP code tapes when ordering outside lists. You may request only names from the best deciles, or you may use the ZIP code tape as a suppression file and not accept names selected from the lower deciles.

A Word of Caution Regarding Combined Models

Before leaving this subject we have a word of caution about combining front-end and back-end models. It is theoretically possible, and every once in a while it actually happens, that when you combine a front-end model with a back-end model the resulting combined model will be flat. An example of how this might happen is shown in Table 19–10 on page 292.

As you can see, when the front-end and back-end models are nearly mirror images of each other, the models tend to cancel each other out. When this happens the alternatives are to attempt to build a model that uses contribution per name mailed as the dependent variable, but in practice this doesn't work well with demographic models. The better solution may be to use the response model against lists that have a relatively strong back-end—eliminating the poorest performing areas from these lists. This procedure, though more tedious than simply using a combined model, has worked well in practice.

Lead Conversion Models

One of the frequently used applications of response models is in lead generation and fulfillment situations. Many companies generate leads through print advertising or broadcast advertising and attempt to convert the leads into sales through a series of direct mailings.

If we consider the conversion rate as being similar to a response rate in a response model, it's clear that it's possible to model conversions. In fact,

TABLE 19–10
Combining Front-End and Back-End Models

Typical Results: Combining Models Results in a Usable Combined Model

Decile	*Expected Response*	*Expected Contribution*	*Expected Contribution per Name Mailed*	*Response Index*	*Contribution Index*	*Combined Index*
1	5.00%	$35.00	$1.75	187	63	133
2	4.25	38.50	1.64	159	69	124
3	3.61	42.35	1.53	135	76	116
4	3.07	46.59	1.43	115	84	109
5	2.61	51.24	1.34	97	92	102
6	2.22	56.37	1.25	83	101	95
7	1.89	62.00	1.17	70	111	89
8	1.60	68.21	1.09	60	122	83
9	1.36	75.03	1.02	51	135	78
10	1.16	82.53	0.96	43	148	73
Average	2.68%	$55.78	$1.32	100	100	100

Possible Results: Front-End and Back-End Models "Wash Out" Combined Effect

Decile	*Expected Response*	*Expected Contribution*	*Expected Contribution per Name Mailed*	*Response Index*	*Contribution Index*	*Combined Index*
1	5.00%	$24.29%	$1.21	187	44	101
2	4.25	28.40	1.21	159	51	100
3	3.61	33.28	1.20	135	60	100
4	3.07	39.08	1.20	115	70	100
5	2.61	45.94	1.20	97	82	99
6	2.22	54.09	1.20	83	97	100
7	1.89	63.75	1.20	70	114	100
8	1.60	75.21	1.21	60	135	100
9	1.36	88.80	1.21	51	159	100
10	1.16	104.91	1.21	43	188	101
Average	2.68%	$55.77	$1.21	100	100	100

it's sometimes easier to model conversion than simple response, particularly if in the process of getting the lead one is able to capture additional information either on the coupon or in a telephone conversation.

In a conversion model, the objective is to divide all leads into deciles or some other scheme and assign a probability of conversion to each decile. The deciles with the highest probability of conversion should justify more follow-up mailings than the deciles in which the response rate is lower.

Table 19–11 shows a typical conversion sequence resulting in an overall conversion rate of 9.24 percent. The example describes a situation in which all leads receive a four-part follow-up series. The response rate to the first effort is 3.68 percent, the response rate to the second effort is 2.52 percent, and so on.

Table 19–11 also shows the effect of a regression analysis that results in a model with the response rate among those in the top decile to the first effort of 10 percent and the response rate among those in the last decile of 1.57 percent.

TABLE 19–11
Results of Traditional Four-Part Follow-Up Conversion Efforts

Falloff for deciles 1 to 5: 75 percent
Falloff for deciles 6 to 10: 50 percent

Decile	*Percent Falloff*	*Effort 1*	*Effort 2*	*Effort 3*	*Effort 4*
1		10.00%	7.50%	5.63%	4.22%
2	69.5%	6.95	5.21	3.91	2.93
3	43.8	4.38	3.28	2.46	1.85
4	34.6	3.46	2.60	1.95	1.46
5	24.9	2.49	1.86	1.40	1.05
6	21.0	2.10	1.05	.53	.26
7	19.8	1.98	.99	.50	.25
8	19.8	1.98	.99	.50	.25
9	18.6	1.86	.93	.47	.23
10	15.7	1.57	.78	.39	.20
Conversion rate		3.68%	2.52%	1.77%	1.27%
Cumulative rate			6.20%	7.97%	9.24%

Decile	*Percent Falloff*	*Effort 1*	*Effort 2*	*Effort 3*	*Effort 4*
1		5,000	3,750	2,813	2,109
2	69.5%	3,476	2,607	1,955	1,467
3	43.8	2,189	1,642	1,232	924
4	34.6	1,731	1,298	974	730
5	24.9	1,243	932	699	524
6	21.0	1,050	525	263	131
7	19.8	991	496	248	124
8	19.8	991	496	248	124
9	18.6	932	466	233	116
10	15.7	784	392	196	98
Conversions		18,388	12,604	8,859	6,348
Cumulative			30,991	39,850	46,198
Conversion rate		3.68%	2.52%	1.77%	1.27%
Cumulative rate			6.20%	7.97%	9.24%

The table is completed using the assumption of a 25 percent falloff rate among the top five deciles and a 50 percent falloff rate among the bottom five deciles. Continuing with these assumptions, the fourth effort to the top decile results in a 4.22 percent response, while the fourth effort to the bottom decile results in a conversion rate of only 0.20 percent. Clearly, it would appear that the money spent mailing the fourth effort to the bottom decile would have been better spent mailing a fifth effort to the persons in the top decile.

Table 19–12 completes this argument. Assuming that each person, regardless of decile assignment, must receive two efforts and further assuming that the total number of pieces mailed cannot be increased, Table 19–12 shows that it makes the most sense to send members of the top five deciles six efforts and members of the lower deciles only the two required mailings.

By following this strategy, the overall conversion rate is increased from 9.24 to 12.47 percent. Table 19–12 shows the economic impact of this.

TABLE 19–12
Results of Six-Part Database Conversion Effort

Falloff for deciles 1 to 5: 75 percent
Falloff for deciles 6 to 10: 50 percent

Decile	*Percent Falloff*	*Effort 1*	*Effort 2*	*Effort 3*	*Effort 4*	*Effort 5*	*Effort 6*
1		12.00%	9.00%	6.75%	5.06%	3.80%	2.85%
2	69.5%	8.34	6.26	4.69	3.52	2.64	1.98
3	43.8	5.25	3.94	2.96	2.22	1.66	1.25
4	34.6	4.15	3.12	2.34	1.75	1.31	.99
5	24.9	2.98	2.24	1.68	1.26	.94	.71
6	21.0	2.52	1.26			.00	.00
7	19.8	2.38	1.19			.00	.00
8	19.8	2.38	1.19			.00	.00
9	18.6	2.24	1.12			.00	.00
10	15.7	1.88	.94			.00	.00
Average		4.41%	3.02%	2.30%	2.76%	2.35%	2.02%

Decile	*Percent Falloff*	*Effort 1*	*Effort 2*	*Effort 3*	*Effort 4*	*Effort 5*	*Effort 6*
1		6,000	4,500	3,375	2,531	1,898	1,424
2	69.5%	4,172	3,129	2,347	1,760	1,320	990
3	43.8	2,627	1,970	1,478	1,108	831	623
4	34.6	2,077	1,558	1,168	876	657	493
5	24.9	1,491	1,118	839	629	472	354
6	21.0	1,260	630	0	0	0	0
7	19.8	1,189	595	0	0	0	0
8	19.8	1,189	595	0	0	0	0
9	18.6	1,118	559	0	0	0	0
10	15.7	941	470	0	0	0	0
Conversions		22,065	15,124	9,206	6,905	5,179	3,884
Cumulative average			37,189	46,396	53,300	58,479	62,363
Conversion rate		4.41%	3.02%	2.30%	2.76%	2.59%	2.59%
Cumulative rate			7.44%	9.28%	10.66%	11.70%	12.47%

From Table 19–13, we see that this company received 500,000 leads a year. Traditionally, each lead was mailed four efforts, or a total of 2 million pieces. (In practice, converters from early efforts would not be promoted again for the same offer.) Using the database marketing approach, which in this case evaluates an individual customer on the basis of a regression model score, the same number of total pieces are mailed but more mailings are directed at higher potential prospects, increasing the overall response rate to 12.47 percent and increasing the total number of converted prospects by 16,165. In our example, each converted prospect is worth $200, so this exercise is worth an additional $3,233,046 per year. Of course, if the margin were less, the overall increase in profits would be correspondingly reduced.

The example above assumed that the falloff between mailings was a constant 25 percent for the top deciles and a constant 50 percent for the bottom five deciles. Fortunately, there is a better way to estimate falloff rates between mailings that are equally spaced. In the Summer 1988 edition of the *Journal of Direct Marketing*, Professors Bruce Buchanan and

TABLE 19–13

	Traditional Marketing	*Database Marketing*	*Difference*
Annual number of leads	500,000	500,000	
Number of mailing efforts	4	4	
Total pieces mailed	2,000,000	2,000,000	
Overall response rate	9.24%	12.47%	
Number of conversions	46,198	62,363	16,165
Value of a customer	$200	$200	$0
Contribution to marketing and profits	$9,239,553	$12,472,598	$3,233,046
Mailing CPM	$450	$450	$0
Mailing costs	$900,000	$900,000	$0
Contribution to profits	$8,339,552	$11,572,598	$3,233,046
Decile	50,000		

Donald G. Morrison presented a model for estimating the falloff rates for a third, fourth, fifth, or higher level mailing based on the response rates to the first and second mailings, assuming a constant period between mailings.[5] This is nearly the perfect situation for a lead generation model. Table 19–14 presents a simple Lotus 1-2-3 model that was published along with the article itself to estimate falloff. The Lotus model can be easily recreated by any spreadsheet user.

Attrition Models

An increasingly popular modeling application is predicting attrition. Credit card companies want to know which customers are likely not to renew their credit cards, banks would like to know when customers are about to close their checking accounts, long distance telephone companies would like to know which customers are likely to switch and when, cable companies want to know about disconnects, and the list goes on and on.

Some situations don't require models. Basically, new customers are much more likely to leave than established customers, so all companies that use a "try it and see if you like it" approach should certainly have retention programs in place that are targeted against all new customers. But in other situations, such as bank card cancellations, not all customers need be, or should be, subjects of a retention program, because it's possible to build models that will accurately predict those customers who are likely to stay and those who are likely to cancel or not renew their credit card.

Table 19–15 shows the kind of results you could expect if you used a logistic regression model to predict cancels four months prior to the fee billing month, hopefully in time to execute an effective retention or antiattrition program.

Of course, before a credit card company decides to target potentially high cancel rate cardholders, the company has to decide whether someone with a very high probability of canceling is worth saving. This means

[5] B Buchanan and D G Morrison, "A Stochastic Model of List Falloff with Implications for Repeat Mailings," *Journal of Direct Marketing,* Summer 1988.

TABLE 19–14 *A Method for Estimating Falloff*

A1: [W31] 'DESCRIPTIONS READY

	A	B	C	D
1	DESCRIPTIONS		LOTUS 1-2-3 EQUATIONS	
2	Input: response to 1st mailing	5.00%	b2	
3	Input: response to 2nd mailing	3.00%	b3	
4	Calculate: Fall Off Factor	0.4000	1 – (b3/b2)	
5	Input: Unit Margin	$80.00		
6	Input: Cost Per M Pieces Mailed	$1,000		
7	Calculate: BE Response Rate	1.25%	b6/b5/1000	
8	General Equation		1 – ((1 + b4* (i – 2)/(1 + b4*(j – 2)))	
9	Fall off between 2nd & 3rd	28.57%	1 – ((1 + b4*(2 – 2)/(1 + b4*(3 – 2)))	
10	Fall off between 3rd & 4th	22.22%	1 – ((1 + b4*(3 – 2)(/(1 + b4*(4 – 2)))	
11	Fall off between 4th & 5th	18.18%	1 – ((1 + b4*(4 – 2))/(1 + b4*(5 – 2)))	
12	Fall off between 5th & 6th	15.38%	1 – ((1 + b4*(5 – 2))/(1 + b4*(6 – 2)))	
13	3rd Response	2.14%	b3 *(1 – b9)	
14	4th Response	1.67%	b13*(1 – b10)	
15	5th Response	1.36%	b14*(1 – b11)	
16	6th Response	1.15%	b15*(1 – b12)	
17	Cost Per Order on 3rd mlg	$46.67	b$6(b13*1000)	
18	Cost Per Order on 4th mlg	$60.00	b$6(b14*1000)	
19	Cost Per Order on 5th mlg	$73.33	b$6(b15*1000)	
20	Cost Per Order on 6th mlg	$86.67	b$6(b16*1000)	

TABLE 19–15
Modeling Attrition

Response		*Cumulative*	
Decile	*Rate*	*Index*	*Lift*
1	39.7%	307	307
2	25.7	199	253
3	19.6	152	219
4	12.7	98	189
5	8.1	63	164
6	6.1	47	144
7	5.9	46	130
8	4.3	33	118
9	4.0	31	108
10	3.2	25	100
Average	12.9%		100

estimating the expected profits that would result from saving customers with a high probability of canceling. In the case represented by the model shown above the company decided that decile 1 cardholders would not be targeted by the retention program, but rather the program should be targeted against cardholders predicted to fall into deciles 2 through 7. Cardholders in deciles 8 through 10 were excluded from the program given their low probability of canceling.

ADDING HOUSEHOLD LEVEL OVERLAY DATA TO PROSPECT MODELS

In Chapter 2, we paid a great deal of attention to the sources and uses of enhancement data. In this chapter, we will focus on the economics of enhancement data. As before, we first have to define whether we are concerned with new-customer acquisition through the use of rented lists or whether we are considering enhancing our customer database.

In the preceding sections of this chapter we discussed the procedures to follow in building a ZIP code or smaller area model. However, geographic models are not the only option for prospect promotions. It's theoretically possible to build stronger demographic-lifestyle models based on individual or household level data. The argument for considering this alternative is based on the fact that individual level data is more accurate than small-area data (when measuring the same variable) and that there is data available at the individual level that is not available at the ZIP code or lower level. Car ownership is one example.

There are two potential problems associated with this method:

1. To apply the method, a significantly larger number of names has to be ordered than mailed.
2. All names ordered have to be overlaid with data and scored so that only the better (to be defined) names are mailed.

Let's look at the first problem, that is, ordering more names than the number eventually mailed. How many more? Maybe 50 to 100 percent more, depending on the effectiveness of the model. Ordering more names than necessary is not the problem; the problem is getting the list owner's permission and paying for the right to screen the scored names and decide on just how many you wish to mail.

If a list owner insists on being paid the full rate for names not mailed, it will take an unusually good model to make the economics of this transaction pay for itself. If, on the other hand, the list owner is reasonable, understands what you are trying to accomplish, understands that this may be the only way you can use the lists, and finally is willing to accept some reduced rate on names ordered but not mailed, the first hurdle can be overcome.

The second issue is that all names ordered will have to be overlaid with data and scored. If only half the names are mailed, then the effective cost of the data overlay in terms of the names mailed is doubled. This too may be acceptable provided the model is sufficiently strong. And again, the data owner, understanding what you are trying to accomplish, may very well provide you with a favorable rate for data.

So these are the two key issues—the need to examine names that will not be mailed and the need to overlay all names with data so that scoring can take place. As you can see, both issues get down to a question of costs. Is all this trouble and expense justified? Shouldn't we just continue doing business as usual or maybe just use a simple ZIP code model? And again, it all depends, as we shall see, on the strength of the model.

However, before getting to the economics of the model, there are other difficulties associated with this method that should be addressed. The first is that this process obviously takes time and effort on the part of a number of persons and departments. The costs of starting the mailing analysis sooner (all of the work discussed must occur after the merge but before the actual mailing) and the cost of the data processing work

TABLE 19–16 *The Economics of Predictive Modeling*

CPM	$400
Profit per order	$30.00
Cost of data	$50.00
Cost of unused lists	$30.00
Extra lists	1,000,000
Pieces mailed	1,000,000
Average	3.21%

	Ratio of Response by Decile			
Decile	*Individual Segmentation*	*ZIP*	*1 Million Piece Mailing*	
1	240	150		
2	170	135	Contribution with individual segmentation	$770,084
3	138	125	Cost of data enhancement	100,000
4	112	120	Extra list rental costs	30,000
5	93	105	Profit with individual segmentation	$640,084
6	61	95		
7	55	89	Profit with ZIP code segmentation	$643,144
8	50	80	Difference	($3,060)
9	43	52	Profit without ZIP segmentation	$563,031
10	40	50	Difference	$80,113
Top/bottom	9.6	3.0		
Index	98	100		
Average response	3.91%	3.48%		

involved may be hard to quantify, but they are nevertheless real and must be evaluated as part of the decision to go ahead with the process.

Another issue is the fact that not all names will match against the overlay source. As we explained in Chapter 2, you can generally count on somewhere between 45 and 65 percent of your names matching against a national database such as Infobase, Polk, Donnelley, or Metromail. The exact match rate depends on the source and the quality of the names supplied to the outside party. Names that do not match also have to be scored, usually on the basis of block group or carrier route averages provided by the outside vendor.

Having said all this, let's get to the model itself and the decision making involved.

Table 19–16 presents the output of a model of a 1 million name mailing. The mailing is assumed to have a CPM of $400 and each order is worth $30. In the absence of modeling, the mailer is assumed to have selected the best lists so the mailing is expected to pull 3.21 percent. The profit from this mailing would be $563,031.

Table 19–17 defines the mailer's list universe of 2 million names and shows all the calculations leading to the $563,031 profit. For simplicity, we have grouped individual lists together in groups of 100,000. The best responding lists are shown to have an average response rate of 4.0 percent, the next best a response rate of 3.80 percent, and so on to the poorest

TABLE 19–17
Traditional List Selection Methods

List	*Cumulative Quantity*	*Percent Response*	*Cumulative Percent Response*	*Orders*	*Profit*	*Cumulative Profit*
100,000	100,000	4.00%	4.0%	4,000	$80,000	$80,000
100,000	200,000	3.80	3.9	3,800	74,000	154,000
100,000	300,000	3.61	3.8	3,610	68,300	222,300
100,000	400,000	3.43	3.7	3,430	62885	285,185
100,000	500,000	3.26	3.6	3,258	57,741	342,926
100,000	600,000	3.10	3.5	3,095	52,854	395,779
100,000	700,000	2.94	3.4	2,940	48,221	443,990
100,000	800,000	2.79	3.4	2,793	43,800	487,791
100,000	900,000	2.65	3.3	2,654	39,610	527,401
100,000	1,000,000	2.52	3.2	2,521	35,630	563,031
100,000	1,100,000	2.39	3.1	2,395	31,848	594,880
100,000	1,200,000	2.28	3.1	2,275	28,256	623,136
100,000	1,300,000	2.16	3.0	2,161	24,843	647,979
100,000	1,400,000	2.05	2.9	2,053	21,601	669,580
100,000	1,500,000	1.95	2.9	1,951	18,521	688,101
100,000	1,600,000	1.85	2.8	1,853	15,595	703,696
100,000	1,700,000	1.76	2.7	1,761	12,815	716,511
100,000	1,800,000	1.67	2.7	1,672	10,174	726,686
100,000	1,900,000	1.59	2.6	1,589	7,666	734,351
100,000	2,000,000	1.51	2.6	1,509	5,282	739,634

performing lists, whose average response rate is 1.51 percent. The traditional direct marketing procedure, if the objective were to mail 1 million names, would be to stop after the tenth list grouping. That group's response rate is estimated to be 2.52 percent, and the average expected response rate from the top 10 groups is shown to be 3.2 percent.

Now let's assume that a ZIP code model is available to the mailer, based on a prior mailing of the same offer to the same lists.

Table 19–16 shows the model under the heading ZIP. As you can see, this model shows the top decile performing at 150 percent of average and the bottom decile performing at 50 percent of average. This is an example of a typical three-to-one ZIP code model.

Table 19–18 shows the mailer would apply the ZIP code model to the list universe of 2 million names.

The first assumption is that the model would work equally well across all list segments. Thus, we would expect 10 percent of the best list segment, the segment that averages 4 percent, to pull at 150 percent of 4 percent or at 6 percent. Similarly, the bottom 10 percent of this list segment should pull 2 percent, that is, 50 percent of average.

Table 19–18 therefore creates a 20-by-10 matrix. Each of the 20 list segments is broken up into 10 smaller segments based on the model. Using the traditional method for selecting lists, no list in the eleventh segment (the segment that averages 2.4 percent) would have been mailed, whereas all names in the top 10 segments have been mailed. However, it's obvious that the top decile of lists in the eleventh segment (they pull 3.6 percent) perform better than the bottom decile of the first segment (they pull 2 percent).

TABLE 19–18
The ZIP Code Model (List Segments Split on the Basis of the ZIP Code Model)

Quantity	*List*	*D1*	*D2*	*D3*	*D4*	*D5*	*D6*	*D7*	*D8*	*D9*	*D10*
100,000	4.0%	6.0%	5.4%	5.0%	4.8%	4.2%	3.8%	3.6%	3.2%	2.1%	2.0%
100,000	3.8	5.7	5.1	4.8	4.6	4.0	3.6	3.4	3.0	2.0	1.9
100,000	3.6	5.4	4.9	4.5	4.3	3.8	3.4	3.2	2.9	1.9	1.8
100,000	3.4	5.1	4.6	4.3	4.1	3.6	3.3	3.1	2.7	1.8	1.7
100,000	3.3	4.9	4.4	4.1	3.9	3.4	3.1	2.9	2.6	1.7	1.6
100,000	3.1	4.6	4.2	3.9	3.7	3.2	2.9	2.8	2.5	1.6	1.5
100,000	2.9	4.4	4.0	3.7	3.5	3.1	2.8	2.6	2.4	1.5	1.5
100,000	2.8	4.2	3.8	3.5	3.4	2.9	2.7	2.5	2.2	1.5	1.4
100,000	2.7	4.0	3.6	3.3	3.2	2.8	2.5	2.4	2.1	1.4	1.3
100,000	2.5	3.8	3.4	3.2	3.0	2.6	2.4	2.2	2.0	1.3	1.3
100,000	2.4	3.6	3.2	3.0	2.9	2.5	2.3	2.1	1.9	1.2	1.2
100,000	2.3	3.4	3.1	2.8	2.7	2.4	2.2	2.0	1.8	1.2	1.1
100,000	2.2	3.2	2.9	2.7	2.6	2.3	2.1	1.9	1.7	1.1	1.1
100,000	2.1	3.1	2.8	2.6	2.5	2.2	2.0	1.8	1.6	1.1	1.0
100,000	2.0	2.9	2.6	2.4	2.3	2.0	1.9	1.7	1.6	1.0	1.0
100,000	1.9	2.8	2.5	2.3	2.2	1.9	1.8	1.6	1.5	1.0	.9
100,000	1.8	2.6	2.4	2.2	2.1	1.8	1.7	1.6	1.4	.9	.9
100,000	1.7	2.5	2.3	2.1	2.0	1.8	1.6	1.5	1.3	.9	.8
100,000	1.6	2.4	2.1	2.0	1.9	1.7	1.5	1.4	1.3	.8	.8
100,000	1.5	2.3	2.0	1.9	1.8	1.6	1.4	1.3	1.2	.8	.8
2,000,000											

In theory, what the mailer would like to do is obvious. The mailer would like to sort all of the 200 cells in descending order of expected response and mail only those segments that make up the top 1 million names. In practice, the mailer will not be able to perform with this degree of precision and he or she will approximate this procedure. For example, the mailer may mail all ZIPs where the expected average rate is above 3.5 percent, suppress the ZIPs represented by the bottom four deciles among lists expected to pull between 3 and 3.5 percent, suppress ZIPs from the bottom four deciles among lists expected to pull between 2 and 3 percent, and finally order only names from the top two deciles from among lists expected to pull between 1.5 and 1.99 percent.

Returning to Table 19–16, we see that the use of the ZIP code model would result in the average response rate going from 3.21 to 3.48 percent and profits going from $563,031 to $643,144, an increase of $80,113, or 14.2%.

Now let's consider the question of whether the mailer should attempt to build a more sophisticated model, built not on ZIP code census data but built instead on individual specific level data. These are the questions to ask:

- How good will this model be?
- What will it cost to overlay all of my 2 million names with data?
- What will I have to pay for names that are examined but not mailed?

The answer to the first question—how good will the model be—is shown in Table 19–16 under the heading Individual Segmentation. As you can see, the household model is much stronger than the ZIP code model. In statistical shorthand, it's a six-to-one model, whereas the ZIP

TABLE 19–19
The Household Model (List Segments Split on the Basis of Household Data)

Quantity	*List*	*D1*	*D2*	*D3*	*D4*	*D5*	*D6*	*D7*	*D8*	*D9*	*D10*
100,000	4.0%	9.6%	6.8%	5.5%	4.5%	3.7%	2.4%	2.2%	2.0%	1.7%	1.6%
100,000	3.8	9.1	6.4	5.2	4.2	3.5	2.3	2.1	1.9	1.6	1.5
100,000	3.6	8.6	6.1	5.0	4.0	3.4	2.2	2.0	1.8	1.5	1.4
100,000	3.4	8.2	5.8	4.7	3.8	3.2	2.1	1.9	1.7	1.5	1.4
100,000	3.3	7.8	5.5	4.5	3.6	3.0	2.0	1.8	1.6	1.4	1.3
100,000	3.1	7.4	5.3	4.3	3.5	2.9	1.9	1.7	1.5	1.3	1.2
100,000	2.9	7.0	5.0	4.0	3.3	2.7	1.8	1.6	1.5	1.3	1.2
100,000	2.8	6.7	4.7	3.8	3.1	2.6	1.7	1.5	1.4	1.2	1.1
100,000	2.7	6.4	4.5	3.7	3.0	2.5	1.6	1.5	1.3	1.1	1.1
100,000	2.5	6.0	4.3	3.5	2.8	2.3	1.5	1.4	1.3	1.1	1.0
100,000	2.4	5.7	4.1	3.3	2.7	2.2	1.5	1.3	1.2	1.0	1.0
100,000	2.3	5.4	3.9	3.1	2.5	2.1	1.4	1.2	1.1	1.0	0.9
100,000	2.2	5.2	3.7	3.0	2.4	2.0	1.3	1.2	1.1	0.9	0.9
100,000	2.1	4.9	3.5	2.8	2.3	1.9	1.3	1.1	1.0	0.9	0.8
100,000	2.0	4.7	3.3	2.7	2.2	1.8	1.2	1.1	1.0	0.8	0.8
100,000	1.9	4.4	3.1	2.6	2.1	1.7	1.1	1.0	0.9	0.8	0.7
100,000	1.8	4.2	3.0	2.4	2.0	1.6	1.1	1.0	0.9	0.8	0.7
100,000	1.7	4.0	2.8	2.3	1.9	1.6	1.0	0.9	0.8	0.7	0.7
100,000	1.6	3.8	2.7	2.2	1.8	1.5	1.0	0.9	0.8	0.7	0.6
100,000	1.5	3.6	2.6	2.1	1.7	1.4	0.9	0.8	0.8	0.6	0.6

code model was a three-to-one model. Further, the model assumes that overlay data and model scoring will cost $50 per thousand, and list owners have agreed to accept $30 per thousand for names not mailed.

If everything were to work as planned and the model could be applied with great precision across all lists, in theory response rates would increase to 3.91 percent, and contribution to profits would increase to $770,084 before data and extra list rental expense and would equal $640,084 after these expenses are taken into consideration. Table 19–19 shows how the decile segmentation would work in theory and Table 19–20 details how the individual cells would be sorted and how the 1 million piece mailing would be constructed.

This is a better statistical but less profitable model than the simpler and less expensive ZIP code model. Does this example mean that we should never try to use individual level data to build customer-acquisition models? Not at all; it just means that the models have to be significantly stronger to warrant their costs. Table 19–21 shows what would happen if the individual level model were not a 6-to-1 model but rather a 10-to-1 model. In this case, the additional profits after list and data expense would exceed the results of the ZIP code model by $60,535.

Is $60,535 enough extra profit to cover the additional costs not explicitly defined in the model? That's a difficult question to answer and different companies will answer it differently. However, the purpose of this exercise is primarily to provide mailers with a framework for evaluating model proposals. Armed with a framework in which to measure the likelihood of a model performing as promised, and knowing what cost questions to ask, mailers can make their own decisions about the value of new-customer acquisition modeling.

TABLE 19–20
Contribution by Sorted List Segments

Segment Quantity	*Cumulative Quantity*	*List Segment Ranked*	*Average*	*Orders*	*Before Enhancement Costs*	
					Contribution	*Cumulative*
10,000	10,000	9.58%	9.58%	958	24,743	24,743
10,000	20,000	9.10	9.34	910	23,305	48,048
10,000	30,000	8.65	9.11	865	21,940	69,988
10,000	40,000	8.21	8.89	821	20,643	90,631
10,000	50,000	7.80	8.67	780	19,411	110,042
10,000	60,000	7.41	8.46	741	18,240	128,283
10,000	70,000	7.04	8.26	704	17,128	145,411
10,000	80,000	6.79	8.07	679	16,359	161,770
10,000	90,000	6.69	7.92	669	16,072	177,842
10,000	100,000	6.45	7.77	645	15,341	193,183
10,000	110,000	6.36	7.64	636	15,068	208,252
10,000	120,000	6.12	7.52	612	14,374	222,626
10,000	130,000	6.04	7.40	604	14,115	236,741
10,000	140,000	5.82	7.29	582	13,456	250,197
10,000	150,000	5.74	7.19	574	13,209	263,406
10,000	160,000	5.53	7.08	553	12,583	275,989
10,000	170,000	5.51	6.99	551	12,527	288,515
10,000	180,000	5.45	6.90	545	12,349	300,864
10,000	190,000	5.25	6.82	525	11,754	312,618
10,000	200,000	5.23	6.74	523	11,701	324,318
10,000	210,000	5.18	6.66	518	11,531	335,850
10,000	220,000	4.99	6.59	499	10,966	346,816
10,000	230,000	4.97	6.52	497	10,916	357,731
10,000	240,000	4.92	6.45	492	10,755	368,486
10,000	250,000	4.74	6.38	474	10,218	378,704
10,000	260,000	4.72	6.32	472	10,170	388,873
10,000	270,000	4.67	6.26	467	10,017	398,890
10,000	280,000	4.50	6.20	450	9,507	408,397
10,000	290,000	4.49	6.14	449	9,461	417,859
10,000	300,000	4.47	6.08	447	9,413	427,272
10,000	310,000	4.44	6.03	444	9,316	436,588
10,000	320,000	4.28	5.97	428	8,831	445,419
10,000	330,000	4.26	5.92	426	8,788	454,208
10,000	340,000	4.25	5.87	425	8,743	462,950
10,000	350,000	4.22	5.82	422	8,650	471,600
10,000	360,000	4.06	5.78	406	8,190	479,790
10,000	370,000	4.05	5.73	405	8,149	487,939
10,000	380,000	4.04	5.68	404	8,105	496,044
10,000	390,000	4.01	5.64	401	8,018	504,062
10,000	400,000	3.86	5.60	386	7,580	511,643
10,000	410,000	3.85	5.55	385	7,541	519,184
10,000	420,000	3.83	5.51	383	7,500	526,684
10,000	430,000	3.81	5.47	381	7,417	534,101
10,000	440,000	3.71	5.43	371	7,138	541,239
10,000	450,000	3.67	5.39	367	7,001	548,240
10,000	460,000	3.65	5.36	365	6,964	555,204
10,000	470,000	3.64	5.32	364	6,925	562,130
10,000	480,000	3.62	5.28	362	6,846	568,976
10,000	490,000	3.53	5.25	353	6,581	575,557
10,000	500,000	3.48	5.21	348	6,451	582,008

TABLE 19–20
Continued

Segment Quantity	*Cumulative Quantity*	*List Segment Ranked*	*Average*	*Orders*	*Before Enhancement Costs* Contribution	*Before Enhancement Costs* Cumulative
10,000	510,000	3.47%	5.18%	347	6,416	588,424
10,000	520,000	3.46	5.15	346	6,379	594,803
10,000	530,000	3.35	5.11	335	6.052	600,855
10,000	540,000	3.31	5.08	331	5,929	606,783
10,000	550,000	3.30	5.05	330	5,895	612,679
10,000	560,000	3.29	5.02	329	5,860	618,538
10,000	570,000	3.18	4.98	318	5,549	624,088
10,000	580,000	3.14	4.95	314	5,432	629,520
10,000	590,000	3.13	4.92	313	5,401	634,920
10,000	600,000	3.12	4.89	312	5,367	640,287
10,000	610,000	3.02	4.86	302	5,072	645,359
10,000	620,000	2.99	4.83	299	4,961	650,320
10,000	630,000	2.98	4.80	298	4,931	655,250
10,000	640,000	2.97	4.77	297	4,899	660,149
10,000	650,000	2.87	4.74	287	4,618	664,767
10,000	660,000	2.84	4.71	284	4,513	669,280
10,000	670,000	2.83	4.69	283	4,484	673,764
10,000	680,000	2.82	4.66	282	4,454	678,217
10,000	690,000	2.73	4.63	273	4,187	682,405
10,000	700,000	2.70	4.60	270	4.087	686,492
10,000	710,000	2.69	4.58	269	4,060	690,551
10,000	720,000	2.68	4.55	268	4.031	694,582
10,000	730,000	2.59	4.52	259	3,778	698,360
10,000	740,000	2.56	4.50	256	3,683	702,043
10,000	750,000	2.55	4.47	255	3,657	705,700
10,000	760,000	2.54	4.44	254	3,629	709,329
10,000	770,000	2.46	4.42	246	3,389	712,718
10,000	780,000	2.44	4.39	244	3,305	716,023
10,000	790,000	2.42	4.37	242	3,274	719,297
10,000	800,000	2.42	4.34	242	3,248	722,545
10,000	810,000	2.34	4.32	234	3,020	725,565
10,000	820,000	2.31	4.29	231	2,940	728,505
10,000	830,000	2.30	4.27	230	2,910	731,415
10,000	840,000	2.30	4.25	230	2,886	734,301
10,000	850,000	2.22	4.22	222	2,669	736,969
10,000	860,000	2.20	4.20	220	2,593	739,562
10,000	870,000	2.20	4.18	220	2,587	742,149
10,000	880,000	2.19	4.15	219	2,565	744,714
10,000	890,000	2.18	4.13	218	2,541	747,255
10,000	900,000	2.11	4.11	211	2,335	749,590
10,000	910,000	2.09	4.09	209	2,263	751,854
10,000	920,000	2.09	4.07	209	2,257	754,111
10,000	930,000	2.08	4.04	208	2,237	756,348
10,000	940,000	2.07	4.02	207	2,214	758,562
10,000	950,000	2.01	4.00	201	2,018	760,580
10,000	960,000	2.00	3.98	200	1,988	762,568
10,000	970,000	1.98	3.96	198	1,950	764,519
10,000	980,000	1.98	3.94	198	1,945	766,463
10,000	990,000	1.97	3.92	197	1,903	768,367
10,000	1,000,000	1.91	3.90	191	1,717	770,084

TABLE 19–20
Continued

Segment Quantity	*Cumulative Quantity*	*List Segment Ranked*	*Average*	*Orders*	*Before Enhancement Costs*	
					Contribution	*Cumulative*
10,000	1,010,000	1.90%	3.88%	190	1,689	771,773
10,000	1,020,000	1.88	3.86	188	1,653	773,426
10,000	1,030,000	1.88	3.84	188	1,647	775,073
10,000	1,040,000	1.87	3.82	187	1,608	776,681
10,000	1,050,000	1.81	3.80	181	1,432	778,113
10,000	1,060,000	1.80	3.78	180	1,404	779,517
10,000	1,070,000	1.79	3.77	179	1,370	780,887
10,000	1,080,000	1.79	3.75	179	1,365	782,252
10,000	1,090,000	1.78	3.73	178	1,328	783,580
10,000	1,100,000	1.72	3.71	172	1,160	784,740
10,000	1,110,000	1.72	3.69	172	1,150	785,890
10,000	1,120,000	1.71	3.68	171	1,134	787,024
10,000	1,130,000	1.70	3.66	170	1,102	788,126
10,000	1,140,000	1.70	3.64	170	1,097	789,222
10,000	1,150,000	1.69	3.62	169	1,062	790,284
10,000	1,160,000	1.63	3.61	163	902	791,186
10,000	1,170,000	1.63	3.59	163	892	792,078
10,000	1,180,000	1.63	3.57	163	877	792,955
10,000	1,190,000	1.62	3.56	162	847	793,802
10,000	1,200,000	1.61	3.54	161	842	794,644
10,000	1,210,000	1.60	3.52	160	790	795,434
10,000	1,220,000	1.55	3.51	155	657	796,091
10,000	1,230,000	1.55	3.49	155	648	796,739
10,000	1,240,000	1.54	3.48	154	633	797,372
10,000	1,250,000	1.53	3.46	153	604	797,976
10,000	1,260,000	1.53	3.45	153	600	798,576
10,000	1,270,000	1.52	3.43	152	551	799,127
10,000	1,280,000	1.47	3.42	147	424	799,551
10,000	1,290,000	1.47	3.40	147	415	799,966
10,000	1,300,000	1.47	3.39	147	402	800,368
10,000	1,310,000	1.46	3.37	146	374	800,742
10,000	1,320,000	1.46	3.36	146	370	801,112
10,000	1,330,000	1.44	3.34	144	323	801,435
10,000	1,340,000	1.40	3.33	140	203	801,638
10,000	1,350,000	1.40	3.31	140	194	801,833
10,000	1,360,000	1.39	3.30	139	182	802,014
10,000	1,370,000	1.39	3.29	139	155	802,170
10,000	1,380,000	1.38	3.27	138	151	802,321
10,000	1,390,000	1.37	3.26	137	107	802,428
10,000	1,400,000	1.33	3.24	133	(15)	802,413
10,000	1,410,000	1.32	3.23	132	(27)	802,385
10,000	1,420,000	1.32	3.22	132	(52)	802,333
10,000	1,430,000	1.31	3.20	131	(56)	802,277
10,000	1,440,000	1.30	3.19	130	(98)	802,179
10,000	1,450,000	1.26	3.18	126	(214)	801,964
10,000	1,460,000	1.26	3.16	126	(226)	801,738
10,000	1,470,000	1.25	3.15	125	(250)	801,488
10,000	1,480,000	1.25	3.14	125	(253)	801,235
10,000	1,490,000	1.24	3.13	124	(293)	800,942
10,000	1,500,000	1.20	3.11	120	(404)	800,538

TABLE 19–20
Concluded

Segment Quantity	*Cumulative Quantity*	*List Segment Ranked*	*Average*	*Orders*	*Before Enhancement Costs*	
					Contribution	*Cumulative*
10,000	1,510,000	1.20%	3.10%	120	(415)	800,123
10,000	1,520,000	1.19	3.09	119	(437)	799,686
10,000	1,530,000	1.19	3.07	119	(441)	799,245
10,000	1,540,000	1.17	3.06	117	(479)	798,766
10,000	1,550,000	1.14	3.05	114	(584)	798,183
10,000	1,560,000	1.14	3.04	114	(594)	797,589
10,000	1,570,000	1.13	3.03	113	(615)	796,973
10,000	1,580,000	1.13	3.01	113	(619)	796,355
10,000	1,590,000	1.12	3.00	112	(655)	795,700
10,000	1,600,000	1.08	2.99	108	(754)	794,945
10,000	1,610,000	1.08	2.98	108	(764)	794,181
10,000	1,620,000	1.07	2.97	107	(785)	793,396
10,000	1,630,000	1.07	2.95	107	(788)	792,609
10,000	1,640,000	1.06	2.94	106	(822)	791,787
10,000	1,650,000	1.03	2.93	103	(917)	790,870
10,000	1,660,000	1.02	2.92	102	(926)	789,944
10,000	1,670,000	1.02	2.91	102	(945)	788,999
10,000	1,680,000	1.02	2.90	102	(948)	788,050
10,000	1,690,000	1.01	2.89	101	(981)	787,069
10,000	1,700,000	0.98	2.87	98	(1,071)	785,998
10,000	1,710,000	0.97	2.86	97	(1,080)	784,919
10,000	1,720,000	0.97	2.85	97	(1,098)	783,820
10,000	1,730,000	0.97	2.84	97	(1,101)	782,719
10,000	1,740,000	0.96	2.83	96	(1,132)	781,588
10,000	1,750,000	0.93	2.82	93	(1,217)	780,370
10,000	1,760,000	0.92	2.81	92	(1,226)	779,145
10,000	1,770,000	0.92	2.80	92	(1,243)	777,901
10,000	1,780,000	0.92	2.79	92	(1,246)	776,655
10,000	1,790,000	0.91	2.78	91	(1,275)	775,380
10,000	1,800,000	0.88	2.77	88	(1,356)	774,024
10,000	1,810,000	0.88	2.76	88	(1,365)	772,659
10,000	1,820,000	0.87	2.75	87	(1,384)	771,276
10,000	1,830,000	0.86	2.74	86	(1,411)	769,864
10,000	1,840,000	0.84	2.73	84	(1,489)	768,376
10,000	1,850,000	0.83	2.72	83	(1,496)	766,879
10,000	1,860,000	0.83	2.70	83	(1,514)	765,365
10,000	1,870,000	0.82	2.69	82	(1,541)	763,824
10,000	1,880,000	0.80	2.68	80	(1,614)	762,210
10,000	1,890,000	0.79	2.67	79	(1,621)	760,588
10,000	1,900,000	0.78	2.66	78	(1,664)	758,924
10,000	1,910,000	0.76	2.65	76	(1,733)	757,191
10,000	1,920,000	0.75	2.64	75	(1,740)	755,451
10,000	1,930,000	0.74	2.64	74	(1,781)	753,670
10,000	1,940,000	0.72	2.63	72	(1,847)	751,823
10,000	1,950,000	0.70	2.62	70	(1,892)	749,932
10,000	1,960,000	0.68	2.61	68	(1,954)	747,977
10,000	1,970,000	0.67	2.60	67	(1,997)	745,980
10,000	1,980,000	0.65	2.59	65	(2,057)	743,923
10,000	1,990,000	0.63	2.58	63	(2,097)	741,826
10,000	2,000,000	0.60	2.57	60	(2,192)	739,634

TABLE 19–21 *The Economics of Predictive Modeling*

CPM	$400.00
Profit per order	$30.00
Cost of data	$50.00
Cost of unused lists	$30.00
Extra lists	1,000,000
Pieces mailed	1,000,000
Average	3.21%

	Ratio of Response by Decile			
Decile	*Individual Segmentation*	*ZIP*	*One Million Piece Mailing*	
1	250	150		
2	200	135	Contribution with individual segmentation	$833,679
3	150	125	Cost of data enhancement	100,000
4	110	120	Extra list rental costs	30,000
5	80	105	Profit with individual segmentation	$703,679
6	61	95		
7	50	89	Profit with ZIP code segmentation	$643,144
8	40	80	Difference	$60,535
9	33	52	Profit without segmentation	$563,031
10	25	50	Difference	$80,113
Top/bottom	10.0	3.0		
Index	100	100		
Average response	4.11%	3.48%		

ADDING HOUSEHOLD LEVEL OVERLAY DATA TO INTERNAL CUSTOMER MODELS

Although new-customer acquisition models are totally dependent on ZIP code level data or individual level data appended from external sources, internal models of customer performance don't necessarily need to include enhancement data. In fact, the recommended procedure for building internal predictive models is to start with internal data and proceed to build the best model possible. Then, add external enhancement data to the set of independent data and see if the external data will enable you to build a more powerful model.

What are you likely to find? It depends on your business. If you are in the financial services business, selling expensive products or age-dependent products (and age and income are not normally captured internal variables on your prospect file), then there is a good likelihood that adding this kind of information will result in more powerful models. On the other hand, if the kinds of external demographic data, psychographic data, or both available to you are not as critical to the sale of your product or service, then the chances are less likely that the addition of external data will make a difference in your ability to develop predictive models.

So the answer is that you have to experiment and see if external data makes a difference. There are really two questions that need to be answered:

- First, will external data produce a better model in a statistical sense? That is, have the external variables entered the model and are they statistically significant?

TABLE 19–22
The Value of Enhancement Data to Predictive Customer Models

	ASSUMPTIONS	RESULTS
• TOTAL CUSTOMER DATABASE	2,000,000	
• PERCENT OF CUSTOMERS TO BE MAILED	50.00%	
• NUMBER OF NAMES TO BE MAILED		1,000,000
INTERNAL DATA MODEL		
• EXPECTED RESPONSE RATE USING INTERNAL DATA ONLY MODEL	8.00%	
• EXPECTED NUMBER OF RESPONSES		80,000
• VALUE OF AN ORDER	$20.00	
• VALUE OF ALL ORDERS		$1,600,000
INTERNAL PLUS ENHANCEMENT DATA MODEL		
• EXPECTED RESPONSE RATE USING ENHANCED DATA MODEL	8.80%	
• EXPECTED NUMBER OF RESPONSES		88,000
• VALUE OF AN ORDER	$20.00	
• VALUE OF ALL ORDERS		$1,760,000
INCREMENTAL RESULTS		
• INCREMENTAL RESPONSES		8,000
• INCREMENTAL VALUE FROM ENHANCED MODEL BEFORE DATA COSTS		$160,000
• COST OF ENHANCEMENT DATA M	$50.00	
• TOTAL COST OF ENHANCEMENT DATA		$100,000
• INCREMENTAL VALUE FROM ENHANCED MODEL AFTER DATA COSTS		$60,000

- Second, will the model account for more variation (have a higher R^2)? And, most importantly, will the validation study assign more customers to the top deciles than was the case based on the models that excluded external data?

If the answers to all of these questions are yes, the model is better from a statistical standpoint. The second issue is then one of costs. How much did it cost to overlay your entire file, and are the extra costs worth the added power they brought to your model? This kind of question can be answered quickly with a simple Lotus 1-2-3 model like the one shown in Table 19–22.

The example shown in Table 19–22 is that of a mailer with 2 million names on the customer database. Let's assume that the mailer has built a model based just on internal performance data, and that the model predicts that the response rate to the next mailing among the top half of the file will be 8 percent and will produce $1.6 million in profits.

Would this mailer have been better if the entire file had been overlaid with external data and a model that included both internal and external variables had been built? Let's assume that to build and implement such a model, the mailer would have had to overlay the entire file with data and that data costs $50 per thousand names, or $100,000. If a model built on this data could result in a 10 percent improvement in response (from 8 to 8.8 percent), profits before enhancement data from just this one mailing alone will increase by $160,000. Profits after enhancement data costs would be up by $60,000. So in this case, enhancing the file would have made sense. And it's important to point out that an enhanced file can

TABLE 19–23
The Value of Enhancement Data to Predictive Customer Models

	ASSUMPTIONS	RESULTS
• TOTAL CUSTOMER DATABASE	2,000,000	
• PERCENT OF CUSTOMERS TO BE MAILED	20.00%	
• NUMBER OF NAMES TO BE MAILED		400,000
INTERNAL DATA MODEL		
• EXPECTED RESPONSE RATE USING INTERNAL DATA ONLY MODEL	8.00%	
• EXPECTED NUMBER OF RESPONSES		32,000
• VALUE OF AN ORDER	$20.00	
• VALUE OF ALL ORDERS		$640,000
INTERNAL PLUS ENHANCEMENT DATA MODEL		
• EXPECTED RESPONSE RATE USING ENHANCED DATA MODEL	8.80%	
• EXPECTED NUMBER OF RESPONSES		35,200
• VALUE OF AN ORDER	$20.00	
• VALUE OF ALL ORDERS		$704,000
INCREMENTAL RESULTS		
• INCREMENTAL RESPONSES		3,200
• INCREMENTAL VALUE FROM ENHANCED MODEL BEFORE DATA COSTS		$64,000
• COST OF ENHANCEMENT DATA M	$50.00	
• TOTAL COST OF ENHANCEMENT DATA		$100,000
• INCREMENTAL VALUE FROM ENHANCED MODEL AFTER DATA COSTS		$(36,000)

support many mailings and many models and there is no need for enhanced data to pay for itself on the basis of just one mailing application.

Of course, if the mailer wished to mail less than 50 percent of the file, if the enhanced model were less powerful, or if data costs were more than $50 per thousand, the results would have been different. For example, Table 19–23 shows that if the mailing quantity were reduced to only 20 percent of the customer database, the result of this exercise would be $36,000 in reduced profits.

The point of this exercise is that each mailer will have to decide the likely benefits of enhancing the file. Of course, predictive modeling may not be the only reason to enhance a database with overlay information. It may not even be the best reason.

Let's assume for the moment that enhancement does not result in better, more cost-effective predictive models but that an examination of the customer file based on enhanced data shows that those customers in the best performing deciles have a different demographic profile than those customers in the poorer performing deciles. Let's assume that age and sex are the demographic variables in question, that younger males are performing better than older males, and that both male groups are performing worse than females of any age. Wouldn't it make sense to develop either different creative strategies for each market segment or to attempt to develop different products for males? It's important to remember that predictive modeling only forecasts what is likely to happen if you repeat the same offer to the same population. Predictive modeling won't necessarily tell you anything about the characteristics of your buyers and your nonbuyers. Profiling will, and profiling generally requires overlay data.

ENHANCING YOUR DATABASE WITH INTERNAL SURVEY DATA

Up to now we have dealt with only two kinds of data—internal performance data and external demographic or lifestyle overlay data. We expect that the next major source of data will be individual level research data based on internal customer surveys.

One of the interesting things about predictive models is that despite their ability to identify the best and poorest responding customers or prospects, even the best models, particularly response models, generally account for less than 5 or 10 percent of the variation we see in response. What's missing from our models is better, more relevant data. It's obvious that persons living within the same ZIP code, or even within the same block group, differ dramatically with regard to their product and service needs, and even individuals with identical demographic characteristics will differ significantly in their response to our promotions. So we need to know much more about the individual needs and wants of our customers and prospects, and this can only happen by creating a dialogue with the customer.

As mentioned in Chapter 1, Lester Wunderman observed that a customer has to be (1) able, (2) willing, and (3) ready to buy before a direct sale can be consummated. Overlay data is helpful in determining if a prospect has the economic ability to buy from us, but overlay data provides little or no information about the prospect's willingness or readiness to buy. So we have to ask.

The alternative to asking is to continue as usual, sending mailing pieces to lists and geographic areas within lists that work for our product or service. The problem with asking is that it is perceived to be difficult and expensive. Like everything else in this book, we eventually get back to the question of economic trade-offs.

Fortunately, we at least know how to ask questions if costs are of no concern. As we first mentioned in Chapter 2,[6] for years, market researchers have performed in-depth segmentation studies for traditional and nontraditional direct marketing companies. The process involves both survey design skills and statistical skills, and it goes as follows:

1. Select a random sample of from 500 to a few thousand customers or prospects.
2. Design an in-depth questionnaire. The total questionnaire may contain 100 or more questions. Frequently, the questionnaire is divided into three sections:
   a. Behavior information. Do you belong to a book club? Do you subscribe to magazines? Do you buy financial services through the mail? Do you have a stockbroker?
   b. Attitudes about the category. Do you read to relax or for information? Would you describe yourself as an intellectual? How important is it to you to be aware of best sellers? Would you describe yourself as a financial risk taker? Do you rely on others for financial advice? Do you think banks provide good investment advice?
   c. Demographic questions—the usual age, income, education, occupation, and family size questions.
3. Perform a factor and a cluster analysis on the results (see Chapter 14). If you are successful, you will probably discover that there are three to six different market segments within your prospect or customer file.

---

[6]Custom survey data and segmentation are also addressed in Chapter 2. In this chapter the intention is to show how classical segmentation results can be applied to an entire database.

Staying with our book club and financial services examples, the book club might discover that there is a segment of its market that consider *books* absolutely critical to their existence—to these people, books are the key to knowledge and information and without books they could not function. Conversely, the club is likely to find that there is another segment that reads a lot but entirely for escape. A third segment may consist of infrequent readers who feel guilty about not reading more, and so on.

On the financial services side there may be a segment of independent risk takers. These people do their own research, make up their own minds, and aren't afraid to invest by mail. On the other end of the spectrum may be the very conservative, who need the comfort of a personal representative to close a transaction. Nevertheless, this segment responds to mailings that promise financial rewards—they're great leads but very difficult to convert into customers.

The information and insights that this kind of segmentation analysis provides is clearly invaluable to direct marketers. If we knew to which segment an individual belonged, we could tailor our creative strategy and offers accordingly. However, the problem for direct marketers has been an inability to translate research results into actionable marketing information. Obviously, you can't send a 100-question survey to all your customers, much less to all of your prospects.

Database marketers committed to making this process work are experimenting with two solutions.

The first solution involves building a model in which the dependent variable is segment membership, and the independent variables are all those performance and overlay variables we know about the customer or prospect. This model scores each customer on the likelihood of belonging to any one segment according to values on the variables that were statistically determined to be linked with segment membership. In this case, each customer will have a probability of belonging to any of the market segments discovered by the survey.

If the model is successful, then every customer on the database can be scored and the database will maintain a record of each customer's probability of belonging to each market segment. The direct marketer will then be able to develop a targeted appeal to members of each segment and mail only to members whose probability of belonging to the particular segment exceeds some chosen level. Of course, it's possible that modeling will not be able to reliably link segment membership with the known performance and demographic variables.

In that case, there is a second method that can be tested. This method starts by using statistical methods to identify the smallest number of questions that can reliably define segment membership. The hope is that the analysis will discover a handful of questions that can be asked of everyone and that this information can economically be added to the database. This method offers particular promise to those companies that maintain large prospect files consisting of leads that have failed to respond to prior efforts but who may respond to more targeted appeals.

Table 19–24 provides a framework for examining the economics of this methodology. Table 19–24 begins by assuming a prospect file of 500,000 names to which a cumulative 14.32 percent response would be achieved if each person received up to six mailings. However, as shown, the response

TABLE 19–24 ***The Economics of Questionnaire Research***

Mailing Effort	*Percent Response*	*Mailed*	*Cost*	*Orders*	*Cost/ Order*	*Profit/ Order*	*Cumulative Orders*	*Cumulative Costs*	*Cumulative Profits*	*Cumulative Csts/Ord*
1	5.00%	500,000	$300,000	25,000	$12.00	$18.00	25,000	$300,000	$450,000	$12.00
2	3.00	500,000	300,000	15,000	20.00	10.00	40,000	600,000	600,000	15.00
3	2.14	475,000	285,000	10,165	28.04	1.96	50,165	885,000	619,950	17.64
4	1.67	460,750	276,540	7,695	35.93	(5.93)	57,860	1,161,450	574,336	20.07
5	1.36	450,890	270,534	6,132	44.12	(14.12)	63,992	1,431,984	487,765	22.38
6	1.15	443,360	266,016	5,099	52.17	(22.17)	69,090	1,698,000	374,708	24.58
Cumulative	14.32%									

Assumptions

Cost Per Piece	$0.60
Profit Per Order	$30.00
Mailing Universe	500,000

30% of universe answer questionnaire	30.00%
Number answering questionnaire	150,000
Percent wishing to be dropped	10.00%
Number wishing to be dropped	15,000
Number receiving six mailings	135,000
Number of mailings	810,000
Costs of promotion mailings	$486,000
Percent of total orders received	80.00%
Number of orders received	55,272
Contribution from orders	$1,658,166
Contribution to profits before questionnaire costs	$1,172,166

Questionnaire costs	
Mailing costs per questionnaire	$0.50
Total mailing costs	$250,000
Costs of processing completed questionnaires	$1.00
Total processing costs	$135,000
Costs of taking persons off file	$0.50
Total costs of taking persons off file	$7,500
Total questionnaire related costs	$392,500
Contribution after questionnaire costs	$779,666
Increased profits from questionnaire strategy	
Normal profits	$619,950
Questionnaire strategy	$779,666
Increase	$159,716

rates to the fourth, fifth, and sixth mailings are unprofitable. Therefore, this company would make only three mailings to the entire file.

What if, instead of mailing everyone on the file three times, we began by mailing everyone on the file a short questionnaire designed to determine if the prospect wished to receive more offers from the company, and, if so, to have the respondent supply us with the answers to a few attitude and demographic questions so that we could better serve his or her needs. We'll use this information to place the respondent in the correct market segment and send members of each segment the most appropriate mailing packages.

Can this process possibly pay for itself? As usual, the answer depends on the validity of some set of assumptions. Let's assume that 30 percent of the names receiving the questionnaire respond but that these 30 percent include 80 percent of the orders that would have resulted from a six-part mailing. Let's further assume that it costs $.50 to mail out the questionnaires to everyone, an additional $1.00 to process the respondents that complete the questionnaire and wish to receive more mailings, and $.50 to take a customer off the file, with 10% of the respondents asking to be taken off the file.

This means that a total of $392,500 will be spent before the first promotional mailing is made. Then, all of the respondents who wish to receive more information will stay on the database and receive six mailings at a cost of $0.60 per mailing. The nonrespondents will not receive additional mailings.

The result of all this work will be an additional $159,716 in bottom-line profits, after questionnaire costs.

How repeatable are these numbers? Again, it's very hard to say, and the results will vary from company to company. Once more, our primary objective is not to produce a set of rules but rather to provide a framework for thinking about the economics of database marketing.

IMPLEMENTING MODELS

The tendency among marketers new to modeling is to focus their attention on the statistical aspects of modeling—whether we should use logistic or ordinary regression, and so on. In fact, the more difficult problems have to do with the accuracy of the data available for modeling and the problems associated with integrating models into existing business systems.

For these reasons it is imperative to bring in data processing and operations personnel at the start of the modeling process. From the beginning they should be thinking about the systems that will have to be put in place if the modeling shows the results everyone is hoping for. In turn, the modeling effort should be tempered by the realities of the data that will be available for modeling on an ongoing basis.

For example, one common problem is that historical trend data is frequently useful in certain types of modeling applications, especially attrition models. Changes in behavior often signal an impending cancellation. But the problem is that historical data is frequently unavailable because files are updated each month with new data and cumulative fields recalculated. The need for historical information should be considered in advance—either existing systems will have to be changed if the models warrant this kind of expense, or the modeling will have to make do without historical data, as valuable as it might be.

The time to make all these decisions is at the start of the project. Before modeling begins, everyone involved should know what the consequences of a successful modeling project will be on existing operations.

MODELING, MANAGING, AND MARKETING TO UNIQUE CUSTOMER GROUPS

To a large extent this chapter has dealt with the issue of selecting customers or prospects for a single mailing or a series of mailings. The underlying premise has been that some mailing universe is about to become the target of a single mailing or mailing campaign; however, all available names will not be mailed either for budget or profitability reasons.

In the first instance the budget is not sufficient to mail all the names available, so a mechanism is needed to identify and mail to the most profitable segments within the mailing universe. In the second instance the budget may be sufficient, but not all names can be mailed profitably. That is, if everyone were mailed, the response rate would fall below the breakeven point so a process or a model is needed to identify segments of the mailing universe whose expected response rate is above breakeven, or some agreed-upon rate of return.

This scenario is useful for teaching purposes because it is simple and we can focus our attention on the statistical issues involved in building reliable models. But the real world is more complicated. Not all customers or prospects should necessarily be placed into the same mailing universe to which we will apply a single selection model.

For example, we all know of companies that produce only one monthly or one quarterly catalog. All customers selected for mailing receive the same promotion. In some cases the same promotion vehicle, especially if it is a catalog, is sent to prospects as well as to customers. (In this context *prospects* are defined as unconverted leads or inquirers, i.e., names on the database that have not yet made their first purchase, as opposed to rented names or compiled names.)

By now, everyone has figured out some strategy for deciding who gets mailed and how often. This contact strategy may be based on common sense, on simple or complex RFM models, or on regression models. For example, a company may choose to mail unconverted leads twice a year, and "model" the customer file so that one-third of the file receives 12 catalogs a year, another third of the file receives eight catalogs a year, and the bottom third of the file receives only four catalogs a year.

Although this approach to managing contact strategy is a step in the right direction, the problem is that the only marketing element that changes is frequency of contact. Anyone and everyone who is mailed is mailed the same thing. That's the problem we want to address in this section.

The hypothesis to be tested and hopefully proved is that not all leads and not all customers should receive the same promotion. To throw all customers and prospects into the same pool, develop a frequency strategy for individual groups, and then mail them all the same promotion is easy to do, and efficient from a cost perspective, but not necessarily the right thing to do.

One way to approach this problem is to first divide the potential mailing universe into customer or prospect groups or both to whom you would intuitively do different things. Some of the more obvious groups are these:

1. On-time inquiries or leads from cold catalog mailings or print or broadcast ads.
2. Leads that have responded more than once to your mailings or advertising but have never purchased.
3. Customers who have made only one purchase.
4. Customers who have made multiple purchases but from only one product line.
5. Customers who have purchased from multiple product lines.

To test the hypothesis that profitability can be increased by treating different customer segments differently you need to establish specific objectives and to develop different promotion strategies to test against your current control strategy. For example,

1. For one-time inquirers you might be looking for more information before attempting to close your first sale.
   Depending upon the characteristics of your product or service, different strategies for converting leads into buyers may be required. In the financial services area it is more cost-effective in some situations to use a two-step questionnaire and conversion strategy to reactivate dormant leads than it is to attempt to sell the leads directly.

2. For multiple inquiries or prospects who have responded to your request for more information your objective must be to close that first sale.
   A very targeted low-risk (to the customer) offer may be the way to achieve this objective.
3. For one-time purchasers you need to develop the buying habit, to turn a one-time sale into an ongoing relationship.
   One-time buyers are a major problem (or opportunity) for many mail order and catalog companies. All too often one-time buyers do not think of themselves as your customers—you just happened to be there at the right time with that right offer for a particular product that the customer needed right away.
4. For customers who have purchased in only one category you need to move them into the "other sections of your store."
   This phenomenon is common to all businesses but especially men's and women's clothing. "I like their shirts, but I buy my ties elsewhere" is the kind of comment frequently heard in focus groups. Why not just send a tie to your best shirt customers, or at least a coupon with a substantial discount for trying a tie?
5. For customers who have purchased from multiple categories your objective should be to understand the most common product affinities and then develop customized promotions that take advantage of these affinities.
   The concept is simple: if most people who buy product X also buy products A, B, and C, find people who have purchased A, B, and C but not X and offer them product X.

In situations where the number of customers, prospects, or both within each target group is large it often makes sense to organize marketing responsibility around each of the target groups. For example, one person may be assigned the responsibility for converting one-time buyers into repeat purchasers and another person the responsibility for reactivating dormant leads. Both are difficult but critical tasks.

Assigning specific management responsibility for individual customer or prospect segments ensures that each segment receives the attention it deserves. This approach of organizing around the customer prevents management from focusing its attention on easier and often more interesting things to do, such as generating more new leads from advertising.

Companies that fail to make this commitment may find that they are building a large database of unconverted leads or that their one-time buyers never make the commitment to become steady repeat customers.

Chapter 20

Financial Models

In this last chapter, we will attempt to tie everything we've been talking about together with the aid of financial business planning models. To begin this last group of chapters, in Chapter 17 we examined traditional direct marketers and the classical direct marketing they practice—marketing that focuses on groups of people linked together because they come from the same list or the same print media ad. We said that the emphasis in classical direct marketing is on the new-customer acquisition decision. To decide whether to use a particular medium again, or with what frequency, it is necessary to know how customers recruited from that medium behave—thus the emphasis on measuring and evaluating group performance. Then we switched gears and discussed the movement toward measuring and improving the performance of the individual, and we associated this development with the development of database marketing. Now, the source from which an individual is recruited is only one of many pieces of data that will influence our decision to promote or not to promote, and what to promote to the individual.

In both models, the traditional group behavior model and the individual database marketing model, we acted as if financial time constraints didn't exist. Maximizing lifetime profits and return on promotion were the tools on which economic decision making was based. But the reality is that all direct marketing operations exist within companies that are required to report on their financial performance on at least an annual, if not a quarterly, basis. So our decision-making apparatus must include provisions for the realities of the financial world. Investments cannot be made just because they make economic sense in the long run. Investments have to be funded and their effect on current period profits has to be taken into account.

We also stated in the beginning of this section that one of the most critical decisions a direct marketing manager has to make is the decision regarding how much to invest in new-customer acquisition promotion and how much to invest in current-customer promotions. Spending more on current customers tends to increase short-term profits at the expense of long-term customer growth, and vice versa.

The decision-making tool that allows direct marketers to make this decision is the financial planning model. The financial planning model lets the marketer experiment with the option of investing more or less in new-customer promotions, and it allows the marketer to see the effect of new-customer decisions on long-term fiscal profits immediately. What's more, the financial planning model starts with a model of lifetime value.

We will present the inputs and outputs of two Lotus 1-2-3 models and then show and discuss the effect on annual profits stemming from changing just a few critical assumptions.

TABLE 20–1 *Lifetime Value Assumptions*

CYCLE	ATTRITION	NEGATIVE OPTION ACCEPT RATE	NEGATIVE OPTION RTN RATE	NEGATIVE OPTION BD DBT RATE	OTHER ACCPT RATE	OTHER RTN RATE	OTHER BD DBT RATE	AVERAGE CLUB PRICE NEG OPT	AVERAGE CLUB PRICE ALT SEL
01	100	29%	20.0%	20.0%	5.0%	15.0%	3.0%	$22.00	$16.50
02	97	28%	20.0%	15.0%	6.0%	15.0%	3.0%	$22.00	$16.50
03	94	27%	20.0%	12.0%	7.0%	15.0%	3.0%	$22.00	$16.50
04	91	26%	20.0%	10.0%	8.0%	15.0%	3.0%	$22.00	$16.50
05	89	25%	20.0%	6.0%	9.0%	15.0%	3.0%	$22.00	$16.50
06	86	24%	20.0%	6.0%	10.0%	15.0%	3.0%	$22.00	$16.50
07	83	23%	20.0%	6.0%	11.0%	15.0%	3.0%	$22.00	$16.50
08	81	22%	20.0%	6.0%	12.0%	15.0%	3.0%	$22.00	$16.50
09	78	21%	20.0%	6.0%	13.0%	15.0%	3.0%	$22.00	$16.50
10	76	20%	20.0%	6.0%	13.0%	15.0%	3.0%	$22.00	$16.50
11	74	19%	20.0%	6.0%	13.0%	15.0%	3.0%	$22.00	$16.50
12	72	18%	20.0%	6.0%	13.0%	15.0%	3.0%	$22.00	$16.50
13	69	17%	20.0%	6.0%	13.0%	15.0%	3.0%	$22.00	$16.50
YR 2	67	16%	20.0%	6.0%	13.0%	15.0%	3.0%	$22.00	$16.50
02	65	15%	20.0%	6.0%	13.0%	15.0%	3.0%	$22.00	$16.50
03	63	14%	20.0%	6.0%	13.0%	15.0%	3.0%	$22.00	$16.50
04	61	13%	20.0%	6.0%	13.0%	15.0%	3.0%	$22.00	$16.50
05	60	13%	20.0%	6.0%	13.0%	15.0%	3.0%	$22.00	$16.50
06	58	13%	20.0%	6.0%	13.0%	15.0%	3.0%	$22.00	$16.50
07	56	13%	20.0%	6.0%	13.0%	15.0%	3.0%	$22.00	$16.50
08	54	13%	20.0%	6.0%	13.0%	15.0%	3.0%	$22.00	$16.50
09	53	13%	20.0%	6.0%	13.0%	15.0%	3.0%	$22.00	$16.50
10	51	13%	20.0%	6.0%	13.0%	15.0%	3.0%	$22.00	$16.50
11	50	13%	20.0%	6.0%	13.0%	15.0%	3.0%	$22.00	$16.50
12	48	13%	20.0%	6.0%	13.0%	15.0%	3.0%	$22.00	$16.50
13	47	13%	20.0%	6.0%	13.0%	15.0%	3.0%	$22.00	$16.50
YR 3+	45	13%	20.0%	6.0%	13.0%	15.0%	3.0%	$22.00	$16.50

A FINANCIAL MODEL OF A NEW BOOK CLUB BUSINESS

We'll begin with the inputs to a five-year book club model.

Lifetime Value

Table 20–1 assesses the lifetime value of the average customer. For simplicity, we will assume that all customers behave the same regardless of their source. In practice, we would create different models for each class of customer and then add all the models together to arrive at a model for the total club.

The key assumptions in a book club model regarding lifetime value are these:

- **Attrition rate.** In this example, we assume that 3 percent of the starting group drops out or is canceled each cycle. (This model assumes 13 shipping cycles a year and runs for five years. Only the first three years are shown in detail to save space.)
- **Negative option acceptance, return, and bad debt rates.** The rates shown are for the remaining members at each point in time, not the

TABLE 20–2

KEY ASSUMPTIONS DIRECT MAIL ADVERTISING

BASE RESPONSE RATE IN OPM'S:					35.0
RESPONSE RATE IN FOLLOWING YEARS				YEAR TWO	100.00%
INDEXED TO YEAR ONE				YEAR THREE	100.00%
				YEAR FOUR	100.00%
				YEAR FIVE	100.00%
				YEAR SIX	100.00%
QUANTITY MAILED		QUANTITY MAILED		YEAR 2-5 STANDARD DISTRIBUTION	
YEAR ONE		YEAR 2	2,000	CYCLE 1	50.00%
CYCLE 1	0	YEAR 3	6,000	CYCLE 2	0.00%
CYCLE 2	0	YEAR 4	8,000	CYCLE 3	0.00%
CYCLE 3	0	YEAR 5	10,000	CYCLE 4	0.00%
CYCLE 4	0	YEAR 6	0	CYCLE 5	0.00%
CYCLE 5	0			CYCLE 6	0.00%
CYCLE 6	0			CYCLE 7	0.00%
CYCLE 7	0			CYCLE 8	0.00%
CYCLE 8	0			CYCLE 9	50.00%
CYCLE 9	200			CYCLE 10	0.00%
CYCLE 10	0			CYCLE 11	0.00%
CYCLE 11	0			CYCLE 12	0.00%
CYCLE 12	0			CYCLE 13	0.00%
CYCLE 13	0			TOTAL	100.00%

averages for the starting group. Here, we have assumed that the negative option rate will decline over time as members become accustomed to the negative option procedure. Returns are assumed to be a constant 20 percent and bad debts are shown to decline as the remaining members become more sophisticated about the negative option.

- **Similar acceptance, return, and bad debt assumptions regarding alternate selections.** All alternates are treated as a group.
- **Average price of the negative option and alternate selections.** Adjustments for inflation are handled separately by an inflation multiplier so that the analyst can think in terms of constant dollars.

Combining all these assumptions together with other assumptions regarding product and fulfillment costs results in a fifth year margin per starter of 56.20. (See Year 5 in Table 20–7.)

Tables 20–2, 20–3, and 20–4 provide the other assumptions to the model. Table 20–2 provides the input assumptions regarding direct mail advertising. The key assumption, which we will change shortly, is a response rate of 35 OPM (3.5 percent), which in this first pass of the model is not shown to change even though the quantity mailed increases from 200,000 in the test year to 10 million pieces in Year 5. Table 20–3 provides the details of our print or space advertising plan. According to this first pass of the model, print orders will cost $20 per customer and will stay at that rate over five years as print media budgets go from $25,000 in the first year to $3 million in the fifth year.

TABLE 20–3

KEY ASSUMPTIONS PRINT OR SPACE ADVERTISING

BASE RESPONSE IN COST PER ORDER					$20.00
COST PER ORDER IN FOLLOWING YEARS				YEAR TWO	100.00%
INDEXED TO YEAR ONE				YEAR THREE	100.00%
				YEAR FOUR	100.00%
				YEAR FIVE	100.00%
				YEAR SIX	100.00%
PRINT MEDIA BUDGET		PRINT MEDIA BUDGET		YEAR 2-5 STANDARD DISTRIBUTION	
YEAR ONE		YEAR 2	$65,000	CYCLE 1	7.69%
CYCLE 1	$0	YEAR 3	$1,000,000	CYCLE 2	7.69%
CYCLE 2	$0	YEAR 4	$1,250,000	CYCLE 3	7.69%
CYCLE 3	$0	YEAR 5	$2,000,000	CYCLE 4	7.69%
CYCLE 4	$0	YEAR 6	$3,000,000	CYCLE 5	7.69%
CYCLE 5	$0			CYCLE 6	7.69%
CYCLE 6	$0	OTHER		CYCLE 7	7.69%
CYCLE 7	$0	ORDERS/CYCLE	50	CYCLE 8	7.69%
CYCLE 8	$0			CYCLE 9	7.69%
CYCLE 9	$5,000			CYCLE 10	7.69%
CYCLE 10	$5,000			CYCLE 11	7.69%
CYCLE 11	$5,000			CYCLE 12	7.69%
CYCLE 12	$5,000			CYCLE 13	7.69%
CYCLE 13	$5,000			TOTAL	100.00%

Table 20–4 provides the balance of the assumptions needed to complete the model:

- Direct mail cost per thousand.
- New-member premium expense.
- Provision for package insert orders.
- Product costs and revenue associated with new orders.
- Cost of the periodic catalog (advance announcement, or AA) that announces the featured negative option selection and the alternate selections.
- Provision for preparation expense defined as a percent of the total promotion budget.
- Product cost of sales rates.
- Bad debt and return rates for new customers.
- Fulfillment, warehousing, and customer service costs measured as a percentage of net sales.
- Summary provision for fixed overheads (which would be supported by detailed schedules and budgets).
- A vehicle for adjusting the model for inflation.

TABLE 20–4

KEY INPUT ASSUMPTIONS FOR P&L PROJECTIONS

NEW MEMBER PROMOTION ASSUMPTIONS--NOT ADJUSTED FOR INFLATION

	DIRECT MAIL AVERAGE CPM	PREMIUM EXPENSE	INSERT CPO	NEW ORDER PRODUCT COSTS INCLUDING SHIPPING		NEW ORDER REVENUE	
				SPACE	DM/INSRTS	SPACE	DM/INSRTS
YEAR 1	$375.00	$3.00	$5.00	$9.00	$9.00	$3.98	$3.98
YEAR 2	$375.00	$3.00	$5.00	$9.00	$9.00	$3.98	$3.98
YEAR 3	$375.00	$3.00	$5.00	$9.00	$9.00	$3.98	$3.98
YEAR 4	$375.00	$3.00	$5.00	$9.00	$9.00	$3.98	$3.98
YEAR 5	$375.00	$3.00	$5.00	$9.00	$9.00	$3.98	$3.98

OTHER NEW MEMBER EXPENSES, CURRENT MEMBER AND PRODUCT COST ASSUMPTIONS

	PREP EXP AS A % OF VAR PROMO	ANNOUNCEMENT EXPENSE PER MEMBER	COSTS AS A PERCENT OF NET SALES			
			PRODUCT NEG OPT	PRODUCT ALT SEL	INV W/O PERCENT	BD RATE NEW ORD
YEAR 1	5.00%	$0.35	71%	71%	3.00%	5.00%
YEAR 2	5.00%	$0.35	40%	40%	3.00%	5.00%
YEAR 3	5.00%	$0.35	28%	28%	3.00%	5.00%
YEAR 4	5.00%	$0.35	28%	28%	3.00%	5.00%
YEAR 5	5.00%	$0.35	28%	28%	3.00%	5.00%

OPERATING COSTS AS A PERCENTAGE OF NET SALES - OVERHEADS

	FULFILLMENT	WAREHOUSING	CUSTOMER SERVICE	OVERHEAD EXPENSE	INFLATION FACTORS	
					REVENUE/ PRODUCT COSTS	EXPENSES
YEAR 1	15.00%	4.00%	6.00%	160,000	100.0%	100.0%
YEAR 2	14.00%	3.00%	5.00%	100,000	100.0%	100.0%
YEAR 3	12.00%	2.00%	4.00%	100,000	100.0%	100.0%
YEAR 4	9.00%	2.00%	4.00%	100,000	100.0%	100.0%
YEAR 5	9.00%	2.00%	4.00%	100,000	100.0%	100.0%

OTHER COST ASSUMPTIONS

	% RETURNS REUSABLE	COST OF RETURNS	RETURN % GROSS NEW ORDS	NET DELIVERY EXPENSE/ GROSS BOOKS SHIPPED
YEAR 1	20.00%	$1.00	5.00%	$0.00
YEAR 2	20.00%	$1.00	5.00%	$0.00
YEAR 3	20.00%	$1.00	5.00%	$0.00
YEAR 4	20.00%	$1.00	5.00%	$0.00
YEAR 5	20.00%	$1.00	5.00%	$0.00

TABLE 20–5

FIVE YEAR P&L STATEMENT

	YEAR 1	YEAR 2	YEAR 3	YEAR 4	YEAR 5	TOTAL
GROSS SALES:						
NEGATIVE OPTION	$213	$3,251	$12,440	$22,853	$33,381	$72,138
ALTERNATE SALES	40	947	4,074	9,112	14,541	$28,714
TOTAL GROSS SALES	$253	$4,198	$16,514	$31,965	$47,922	$100,852
RETURNS:						
NEGATIVE OPTION	43	650	2,488	4,571	6,676	$14,428
ALTERNATE SALES	6	142	611	1,367	2,181	$4,307
TOTAL RETURNS	$49	$792	$3,099	$5,937	$8,857	$18,735
NET SALES:	$205	$3,406	$13,415	$26,027	$39,065	$82,117
COST OF SALES:						
PRODUCT COSTS	$145	$1,362	$3,756	$7,288	$10,938	$23,489
INVENTORY W/O	6	102	402	781	1,172	$2,464
PRODUCT DEVELOPMENT	0	0	0	0	0	$0
DELIVERY	0	0	0	0	0	$0
RETURN PROCESSING	0	8	30	58	87	$183
TOTAL COST OF SALES	$152	$1,472	$4,189	$8,127	$12,197	$26,136
GROSS MARGIN	$53	$1,934	$9,226	$17,901	$26,868	$55,981
CUSTOMER SERVICE	12	170	537	1,041	1,563	$3,323
FULFILLMENT/EDP	31	477	1,610	2,342	3,516	$7,976
WAREHOUSING	8	102	268	521	781	$1,680
OPERATIONS-BAD DEBT	30	368	1,370	2,318	3,320	$7,407
NEW ORDER-BAD DEBT	2	15	52	68	89	$226
TOTAL OPER COSTS	$83	$1,132	$3,837	$6,290	$9,269	$20,611
OPERATING MARGIN	($31)	$801	$5,390	$11,610	$17,599	$35,370
AMORTIZED						
PROMO/ACQUISITION	$49	$799	$2,999	$4,872	$6,448	$15,167
NEW ORDER REVENUE	35	294	1,030	1,364	1,788	$4,511
NEW ORDER RETURNS	$2	$15	$52	$68	$89	$226
NW ORDR CST OF SLS	79	665	2,330	3,084	4,043	$10,201
CURR MEMBER EXPENSE	$12	$215	$878	$1,788	$2,766	$5,661
FIXED AA EXPENSE	7	7	7	7	7	$33
TOTAL MARKETING	$114	$1,407	$5,235	$8,455	$11,565	$26,776
CONTRIBUTION TO						
OVERHEAD & PROFIT	($144)	($605)	$155	$3,155	$6,033	$8,594
OVERHEAD	$100	$100	$100	$100	$100	$500
CONTRIBUTION TO PROFIT	($244)	($705)	$55	$3,055	$5,933	$8,094
% NET SALES	-119.4%	-20.7%	0.4%	11.7%	15.2%	
CUMULATIVE	($244)	($949)	($895)	$2,160	$8,094	

"What If"

Table 20–5 shows the five-year profit-and-loss statement (P & L) resulting from combining all the assumptions. As you can see from inspecting the last two lines in Table 20–5, the assumptions provided have resulted in a very profitable business. Profit as a percentage of sales in Year 5 is 15.2 percent, the business breaks even on an annual basis in Year 3, and breaks even on a cumulative basis in Year 4. Tables 20–6, 20–7, and 20–8 present additional diagnostics.

Some skeptics might refer to this as a typically rosy consultant's projection. So let's change it—that's what models are for.

Let's see what effect a less optimistic set of assumptions would have on projected profits.

We can begin with a key assumption regarding lifetime value. Whereas the initial model assumed that customers would leave the club at the rate of 3 percent per cycle, let's make that 4 percent per cycle.

TABLE 20–6

	YEAR 1	YEAR 2	YEAR 3	YEAR 4	YEAR 5
BOOKS SHIPPED					
NEGATIVE OPTION	10	148	565	1,039	1,517
ALTERNATES	2	57	247	552	881
TOTAL BOOKS SHIPPED	12	205	812	1,591	2,399
BOOKS RETURNED					
NEGATIVE OPTION	2	30	113	208	303
ALTERNATE SALES	0	9	37	83	132
TOTAL BOOKS RETURN	2	38	150	291	436
AA'S MAILED TO MEMBERS	36	616	2510	5110	7904
YEAR END MEMBERS	7,943	65,093	254,706	449,940	668,584
AVERAGE MEMBERSHIP	2,744	47,346	193,070	393,041	608,010
NET BKS/MBR SERVICED	0.28	0.27	0.26	0.25	0.25
NET BKS/YEAR	3.6	3.5	3.4	3.3	3.0

TABLE 20–7

	YEAR 1	YEAR 2	YEAR 3	YEAR 4	YEAR 5
TOTAL NEW ORDERS	9	74	261	343	451
TOTAL CPO	$11.60	$11.07	$12.48	$12.39	$12.77
PIECES MAILED	200	2,000	6,000	8,000	10,000
DM ORDERS (000'S)	7	70	210	280	350
OPM	35.0	35.0	35.0	35.0	35.0
PROMOTION EXPENSE	103,250	818,250	3,253,250	4,253,250	5,753,250
DIRECT MAIL	75,000	750,000	2,250,000	3,000,000	3,750,000
SPACE	25,000	65,000	1,000,000	1,250,000	2,000,000
INSERTS	3,250	3,250	3,250	3,250	3,250
TOTAL PROMOTION	103,250	818,250	3,253,250	4,253,250	5,753,250
COST PER ORDER					
DIRECT MAIL	$10.71	$10.71	$10.71	$0.71	$10.71
SPACE	$20.00	$20.00	$20.00	$20.00	$20.00
INSERTS	$5.00	$5.00	$5.00	$5.00	$5.00
TOTAL PROMOTION	$11.60	$11.07	$12.48	$12.39	$12.77
SUBSCRIBER STATS					
START OF YEAR	50	7,943	65,093	254,706	449,940
ADDED	8,775	73,900	258,852	342,669	449,208
END OF YEAR	7,943	65,093	254,706	449,940	668,584
LOST	882	16,751	69,239	147,435	230,564
% AVE LOST	5.52%	11.47%	10.83%	10.46%	10.31%
GROSS SALES/STARTER	$164.12	$164.12	$164.12	$164.12	$164.12
RETURNS/STARTER	$30.02	$30.02	$30.02	$30.02	$30.02
NET SALES/STARTER	$134.10	$134.10	$134.10	$134.10	$134.10
PROD COSTS/STARTER	$95.21	$53.64	$37.55	$37.55	$37.55
VAR COSTS/STARTER	$43.15	$38.86	$33.74	$29.98	$30.22
BAD DEBTS/STARTER	$10.14	$10.14	$10.14	$10.14	$10.14
MARGIN/STARTER	($14.40)	$31.46	$52.68	$56.43	$56.20
GIFT REVENUE	$3.58	$3.58	$3.58	$3.58	$3.58
NEW ORDER EXPENSE	$9.00	$9.00	$9.00	$9.00	$9.00
PREMIUM EXPENSE	$3.00	$3.00	$3.00	$3.00	$3.00
NET GIFT EXPENSE	$8.42	$8.42	$8.42	$8.42	$8.42
CONTRIBUTION TO:					
OH, PROMO & PROFIT	($22.82)	$23.04	$44.26	$48.02	$47.78
OH & PROFIT	($34.42)	$11.97	$31.78	$35.62	$35.01
ROP	-151.6%	260.1%	389.5%	432.2%	406.1%
AVERAGE MEMBER LIFE		28.73			
# NO. OF AA'S/YR					
PERCENT RESPONSE	13	13	13	13	13

TABLE 20–8

	PERCENT OF NET SALES:				
	YEAR 1	YEAR 2	YEAR 3	YEAR 4	YEAR 5
GROSS SALES:					
NEGATIVE OPTION	84.1%	77.4%	75.3%	71.5%	69.7%
ALTERNATIVE SALES	15.9%	22.6%	24.7%	28.5%	30.3%
TOTAL GROSS SALES	100.0%	100.0%	100.0%	100.0%	100.0%
RETURNS:					
NEGATIVE OPTION	20.0%	20.0%	20.0%	20.0%	20.0%
ALTERNATE SALES	15.0%	15.0%	15.0%	15.0%	15.0%
TOTAL RETURNS	19.2%	18.9%	18.8%	18.6%	18.5%
NET SALES:	100.0%	100.0%	100.0%	100.0%	100.0%
COST OF SALES:					
PRODUCT COSTS	71.0%	40.0%	28.0%	28.0%	28.0%
INVENTORY W/O	3.0%	3.0%	3.0%	3.0%	3.0%
PROD DEVELOPMENT	0.0%	0.0%	0.0%	0.0%	0.0%
OPER DELIVERY	0.0%	0.0%	0.0%	0.0%	0.0%
RETURN PROCESSING	0.2%	0.2%	0.2%	0.2%	0.2%
TOTAL COST OF SALES	74.2%	43.2%	31.2%	31.2%	31.2%
GROSS MARGIN	25.8%	56.8%	68.8%	68.8%	68.8%
CUSTOMER SERVICE	6.9%	5.0%	4.0%	4.0%	4.0%
FULFILLMENT/EDP	15.0%	14.0%	12.0%	9.0%	9.0%
WAREHOUSING	4.0%	3.0%	2.0%	2.0%	2.0%
OPERATIONS-BAD DBT	14.9%	10.8%	10.2%	8.9%	8.5%
NEW ORDER-BAD DEBT	0.9%	0.4%	0.4%	0.3%	0.2%
TOTAL OPER COSTS	40.7%	33.2%	28.6%	24.2%	23.7%
OPERATING MARGIN	-15.0%	23.5%	40.2%	44.6%	45.1%
AMORTIZED					
PROMO/ACQUISITION	23.9%	23.5%	22.4%	18.7%	16.5%
NEW ORDER REVENUE	17.1%	8.6%	7.7%	5.2%	4.6%
NEW ORDER RETURNS	0.9%	0.4%	0.4%	0.3%	0.2%
NEW ORDR CST OF SLS	38.6%	19.5%	17.4%	11.8%	10.3%
CURR MEM EXPENSE	6.1%	6.3%	6.5%	6.9%	7.1%
FIXED AA EXPENSE	3.2%	0.2%	0.0%	0.0%	0.0%
TOTAL MARKETING	55.5%	41.3%	39.0%	32.5%	29.6%
OH EXPENSE	48.9%	2.9%	0.7%	0.4%	0.3%
CONTRIBUTN OH/PFT	-119.37%	-20.71%	0.41%	11.74%	15.19%

The results of this change can be seen in Table 20–9. This seemingly small change has the effect of reducing profits over five years from $8,094,000 to $5,147,000. Not such a small change. However, it is not surprising when you stop to consider that a change from 3 to 4 percent is a 33 percent change, and in fact profits dropped by exactly 36 percent.

Now let's examine the assumption that direct mail and print response rates will not change over time and in the face of rising expenditures. We agree that this set of assumptions is not realistic, so let's decrease direct mail OPMs and print cost per orders (CPOs) by 5 percent per year. The result is that the direct mail change reduced five-year profits by $1.8 million, and the print changes reduced five-year profits by another $441,000.

Now let's look at what would happen if we reduced the sales rate from 26 to 24 percent per cycle for all members that stayed past three years. The effect on five-year profits would be a decrease of less than $17,000 because, first, the change itself was small, and second, not many members stay for more than three years so the effect on total sales is therefore relatively small.

TABLE 20–9

BASE EXAMPLE						
TOTAL GROSS SALES	$253	$4,198	$16,514	$31,965	$47,922	$100,852
CNTRBTN TO PRFT	($244)	($705)	$55	$3,055	$5,933	$8,094
% NET SALES	-119.4%	-20.7%	0.4%	11.7%	15.2%	
CUMULATIVE	($244)	($949)	($895)	$2,160	$8,094	
THE EFFECT OF INCREASING ATTRITION FROM 3% TO 4% PER CYCLE						
TOTAL GROSS SALES	$249	$4,000	$15,507	$29,183	$42,707	$91,646
CNTRBTN TO PRFT	($244)	($739)	($249)	$2,147	$4,233	$5,147
% NET SALES	-121.3%	-22.8%	-2.0%	9.0%	12.2%	
CUMULATIVE	($244)	($983)	($1,232)	$914	$5,147	
THE EFFECT OF DECREASING DIRECT MAIL RESPONSE RATES 5% PER YEAR						
TOTAL GROSS SALES	249	$3,831	$14,372	$26,305	$37,371	$82,128
CNTRBTN TO PRFT	($244)	($736)	($402)	$1,589	$3,118	$3,324
% NET SALES	-121.3%	-23.7%	-3.4%	7.4%	10.2%	
CUMULATIVE	($244)	($980)	($1,382)	$207	$3,324	
THE EFFECT OF INCREASING PRINT CPO'S BY 5% PER YEAR						
TOTAL GROSS SALES	$249	$3,825	$14,183	$25,744	$36,156	$80,158
CNTRBTN TO PRFT	($244)	($736)	($420)	$1,484	$2,883	$2,968
% NET SALES	-121.3%	-23.7%	-3.6%	7.1%	9.8%	
CUMULATIVE	($244)	($980)	($1,400)	$85	$2,968	
THE EFFECT OF REDUCING BOOK ACCEPTANCE RATES FROM 26 PERCENT TO 24 PERCENT IN YEARS 4-5						
TOTAL GROSS SALES	$249	$3,825	$14,183	$25,742	$36,112	$80,111
CNTRBTN TO PRFT	($244)	($736)	($420)	$1,483	$2,866	$2,950
% NET SALES	-121.3%	-23.7%	-3.6%	7.1%	9.7%	
CUMULATIVE	($244)	($980)	($1,400)	$83	$2,950	
THE EFFECT OF INCREASING PRINT PROMOTION IN YEAR 4 TO $5,000,000 AND TO $9,000,000 IN YEAR FIVE						
TOTAL GROSS SALES	$249	$3,825	$14,183	$32,085	$55,170	$105,512
CNTRBTN TO PRFT	($244)	($736)	($420)	$34	$794	($572)
% NET SALES	-121.3%	-23.7%	-3.6%	0.1%	1.8%	
CUMULATIVE	($244)	($980)	($1,400)	($1,366)	($572)	

The point of the above "sensitivity" exercise is to demonstrate the usefulness (really the necessity) of a financial model in measuring the effect on profits based on changes in key variables.

Another use of the financial model, as discussed above, is to measure the effect on annual profits of major changes in new-customer spending. Let's start with the last set of assumptions, which produced a five-year cumulative profit of $2,950,000. (Please refer again to Table 20–9.)

Let's now increase print advertising expenditures in Year 4 from $1,250,000 to $5 million, and let's increase expenditures in Year 5 from $2 million to $9 million. Even if we assume no reduction in response rates (increases in print CPOs) or in the quality of the member acquired (both bad assumptions), annual profits will be reduced significantly. And remember that this model does not treat new-member acquisition expenditures as an expense taken in the month incurred. New-customer expenditures are written off over a 12-month period. However, if new-member expenses were written off over the full life of the member, the effect on profits would be reduced. On the other hand, if the company followed a practice of immediately writing off acquisition expenditures, the effect on annual profits would be significantly worse. The point is that accounting practices and the effect of new-member expenditures on reported profits must be carefully watched; direct marketing decisions cannot be made solely on the basis of long-term lifetime value and ROP considerations.

A CATALOG EXAMPLE

At the beginning of this section, we discussed the differences between traditional direct marketing companies that had contractual relationships and those that had implied relationships, and we said that book clubs were good examples of the former and catalogs were good examples of the latter.

In the five-year planning model discussed above, you will notice that the book club had relatively little discretion in terms of trading dollars between new-member acquisition and current-member marketing. More or less could be spent on new-customer acquisition but the money for new-customer marketing did not come at the expense of current-customer marketing.

In a catalog operation, the choices are more interesting because no contractual amount need be spent on current-customer marketing. As we said before, it's up to the cataloger to decide how much to spend on each.

Because catalog models are much more complicated than book club models, we won't attempt to reproduce all the assumptions that go into even a relatively simple model, but rather we'll focus on one use of the model—the economic trade-off between new-customer acquisition and current-customer marketing.

Our base case scenario starts with a new catalog operation. The initial business plan is developed on the assumption that the company will develop two catalogs a year. The catalogs will be mailed to the customer file a total of six times. Each catalog will be repeated with minimal changes three times. Table 20–10 shows a summary P&L taken from the budget model.

Lifetime Value

A key question to ask when reviewing this budget, and there are literally hundreds of assumptions to question, is what the assumed lifetime value of the average catalog acquired customer is and what assumptions are behind this estimate. Table 20–11 provides the answer.

Table 20–11 leads the marketing manager through a series of questions whose answers result in an estimate of lifetime value. The questions are relatively simple. (The answers that appear in Table 20–11 are repeated in parentheses below.) These are the questions:

- What percent of new customers will make at least one purchase within the next 12 months? (Assume an estimate of 40 percent; therefore 60 percent don't buy.)
- Among those that purchase in the first 12 months, what percent will purchase in the following 12 months? (Assume 60 percent; therefore 40 percent will not become repeat purchasers.)
- Among those who *failed to purchase* in the first 12 months, what percent, if mailed, will purchase within the following 12 months? (Assume that 25 percent buy and 75 percent continue not to buy.)

The answers to these questions will provide enough information to estimate Year 2 buy rates for the entire starting group. In addition, at the end of two years, all customers will be divided into four parts:

- The best customers, those that purchased in both years. They will represent 24 percent of the original group. (40% × 60% = 24%.)
- Customers who purchased in the most recent year but not in the first year or 15 percent of the file. (60% × 25% = 15%.)

TABLE 20–10

SUMMARY STATEMENT OF PROFIT AND LOSS ($000'S)

	YEAR 1	YEAR 2	YEAR 3	YEAR 4	YEAR 5
GROSS SALES ($000'S)					
REPEAT BUSINESS	$20	$476	$1,902	$4,104	$6,465
NEW CUSTOMERS	$310	$2,050	$4,850	$6,250	$7,650
TOTAL GROSS SALES	$331	$2,527	$6,752	$10,354	$14,116
RETURNS:					
REPEAT BUSINESS	$3	$73	$289	$621	$976
NEW CUSTOMERS	$62	$410	$970	$1,250	$1,530
TOTAL RETURNS	$65	$483	$1,259	$1,871	$2,506
NET SALES					
REPEAT BUSINESS	$17	$403	$1,613	$3,483	$5,489
NEW CUSTOMERS	$248	$1,640	$3,880	$5,000	$4
TOTAL NET SALES	$265	$2,043	$5,493	$8,483	$11,609
COST OF SALES	$126	$623	$1,677	$2,594	$3,552
% OF NET SALES	47.4%	30.5%	30.5%	30.6%	30.6%
GROSS MARGIN	$140	$1,420	$3,816	$5,889	$8,057
% OF NET SALES	52.6%	69.5%	69.5%	69.4%	69.4%
OPERATING COSTS	$77	$388	$1,097	$1,817	$2,588
% OF NET SALES	29.0%	19.0%	20.0%	21.4%	22.3%
OPERATING MARGIN	$62	$1,032	$2,719	$4,073	$5,470
% OF NET SALES	23.5%	50.5%	49.5%	48.0%	47.1%
MARKETING COSTS					
NEW CUSTOMERS	$133	$945	$2,659	$3,515	$4,371
REPEAT BUSINESS	$57	$138	$328	$609	$922
TOTAL MARKETING	$190	$1,083	$2,987	$4,124	$5,294
% OF NET SALES	71.4%	53.0%	54.4%	48.6%	45.6%
CONTRIBUTION	($127)	($51)	($268)	($51)	$176
% OF NET SALES	-48%	-2%	-5%	-1%	2%
OVERHEAD AND					
BUSINESS DEVELOPMNT	$103	$195	$250	$300	$350
LIST RENTAL INC	$7	$318	$767	$1,310	$1,997
PROFIT OR (LOSS)	($222)	$72	$249	$959	$1,823
% OF NET SALES	-83.7%	3.5%	4.5%	11.3%	15.7%
CUM P & (L)	($222)	($150)	$99	$1,058	$2,881

- Those that purchased in the first year but not in the second or 16 percent of the file. (40% × 40% = 16%.)
- Those that never purchased, your worst customers, or 45 percent of the file. (60% × 75% = 45%.)

It's relatively easy from this point on to estimate the purchase rate for each of the four groups in Year 3 and to apply a falloff rate to estimate purchase rates for subsequent years.

Needless to say, it's easy enough to complicate this argument even further by asking for estimates of multiple purchases as opposed to single purchases. But then you must ask, who is smart enough to answer more complicated questions more or less correctly?

When these assumptions are combined with other assumptions regarding attrition rates, prices, costs, and expenses, the model produces an estimate of the lifetime value of a catalog customer.

At the bottom of Table 20–11 we see that the lifetime sales corresponding to the above set of purchase assumptions is equal to $41.92. Other sections of the model (not shown) show that the average profit on sales

TABLE 20–11
Lifetime Value Assumptions

CATALOG SOLD CUSTOMERS: REPEAT PURCHASE RATE ASSUMPTIONS					
% NEW CUSTOMERS BUYING IN FIRST 12 MONTHS				40.00%	INPUT
% NOT BUYING IN FIRST 12 MONTHS				60.00%	
% YR 1 BUYERS BUYING IN YEAR 2				60.00%	INPUT
% YR 1 BUYERS NOT BUYING IN YEAR 2				40.00%	
% YR 1 NON-BUYERS BUYING IN YEAR 2				25.00%	INPUT
% YR 1 NON-BUYERS NOT BUYING IN YR 2				75.00%	
THE YEAR TWO BUY RATE IS THEREFORE:				39.00%	
COMPOSITION OF FILE AT END OF 24 MONTHS - ANY START GROUP					
PERCENT YEAR 1 ONLY BUYERS ON FILE				16.00%	GROUP 1
PERCENT YEAR 2 ONLY BUYERS ON FILE				15.00%	GROUP 2
PERCENT YEARS 1&2 BUYERS ON FILE				24.00%	GROUP 3
PERCENT OF NON-BUYERS ON FILE				45.00%	GROUP 4
TOTAL				100.00%	
YEAR 3 BUY RATE FOR GROUP 1				20.00%	INPUT
YEAR 3 BUY RATE FOR GROUP 2				44.00%	INPUT
YEAR 3 BUY RATE FOR GROUP 3				75.00%	INPUT
YEAR 3 BUY RATE FOR GROUP 4				10.00%	INPUT
THE YEAR 3 BUY RATE IS THEREFORE:				32.30%	
FALL-OFF RATE IN YEAR 4 AND 5				80.00%	
YEAR 4 BUY RATE				25.84%	
YEAR 5/6 BUY RATE				20.67%	
	# OF CATALOGS PRODUCED	% ACTIVE BUYERS	# of MAILING PERIODS	AVERAGE CAT RES RATE	AVE ANNUAL RESPONSE RATE
YEAR 1	2	40.00%	6	6.67%	40.00%
YEAR 2	2	39.00%	6	6.50%	39.00%
YEAR 3	2	32.30%	6	5.38%	32.30%
YEAR 4	2	25.84%	6	4.31%	25.84%
YEAR 5	2	20.67%	6	3.45%	20.67%
YEAR 6	2	20.67%	6	3.45%	20.67%
AVG LIFETIME SALES					$41.92
AVERAGE COST PER ORDER					$14.29
AVERAGE PROFIT ON SALES BEFORE PROMOTION COSTS					40.00%
CONTRIBUTION TO PROMOTION, OVERHEAD AND PROFIT					$16.77
RETURN ON PROMOTION/BEFORE LIST RENTAL					17.37%
NUMBER OF TIMES LIST RENTED					100
NET LIST RENTAL INCOME					$0.07
LIST RENTAL INCOME					$7.00
ADJUSTED RETURN ON PROMOTION AFTER LIST RENTAL					66.37%

before promotion expenses is 40 percent of sales, or $16.77. The average cost per new customer is shown to be $14.29, so that the difference (the contribution to overhead and profit) is only $2.48 and the return on promotion is only 17.37 percent ($2.48/14.20 = 17.37%).

Interestingly, the profit from this model comes from list rentals and the assumption that a single name will be rented 100 times over a five-year period, adding $7 to the value of a customer and increasing the after-list rental return on promotion rate to 66 percent.

"What If"

Now, assuming that we have satisfied ourselves with the assumptions of the basic model (a job we hardly began), let's play "what if." What if the business were built on the assumption of three catalogs a year, not two? Obviously, expenses would increase, but what if repeat purchase rates also increased by 20 percent each year? The results of this set of assumptions are shown (in summary form) in Table 20–12, under the heading Option One. Both sales and marketing costs increased, but unfortunately

TABLE 20–12

BASE CASE TWO CATALOGS PER YEAR MAILED AN AVERAGE OF SIX TIMES					
TOTAL GROSS SALES	$331	$2,527	$6,752	$10,354	$14,116
MARKETING COSTS					
NEW CUSTOMERS	$133	$945	$2,659	$3,515	$4,371
REPEAT BUSINESS	$57	$138	$328	$609	$922
TOTAL MARKETING	$190	$1,083	$2,987	$4,124	$5,294
CUSTOMERS	45,300	170,317	249,609	438,857	646,841
PROFIT OR (LOSS)	($222)	$72	$249	$959	$1,823
% OF NET SALES	-83.7%	3.5%	4.5%	11.3%	15.7%
CUM P & (L)	($222)	($150)	$99	$1,058	$2,881
OPTION ONE: THREE CATALOGS MAILED NINE TIMES SALES UP 20%					
TOTAL GROSS SALES	$326	$2,623	$7,177	$11,318	$15,690
MARKETING COSTS					
NEW CUSTOMERS	$133	$945	$2,659	$3,515	$4,371
REPEAT BUSINESS	$78	$198	$486	$910	$1,383
TOTAL MARKETING	$211	$1,143	$3,145	$4,425	$5,755
CUSTOMERS	45,300	170,317	249,609	438,857	646,841
PROFIT OR (LOSS)	($244)	$20	$158	$840	$1,676
% OF NET SALES	-93.3%	1.0%	2.7%	9.0%	12.9%
CUM P & (L)	($244)	($224)	($66)	$774	$2,450
OPTION TWO: PUT ADDITIONAL PROMOTION MONEY IN NEW CUSTOMER ACQUISITION					
TOTAL GROSS SALES	$382	$2,712	$7,262	$11,457	$15,844
MARKETING COSTS					
NEW CUSTOMERS	$165	$1,024	$2,868	$3,943	$4,971
REPEAT BUSINESS	$58	$144	$347	$655	$1,010
TOTAL MARKETING	$244	$1,168	$3,215	$4,599	$5,981
CUSTOMERS	49,538	182,951	267,581	479,870	717,284
PROFIT OR (LOSS)	($246)	$94	$297	$1,062	$2,055
% OF NET SALES	-80.0%	4.3%	5.0%	11.3%	15.8%
CUM P & (L)	($246)	($151)	$146	$1,207	$3,263

costs increased faster than sales, and the net effect is a reduction in profits over five years from $2,881,000 to $2,450,000. A good idea, but one not supported by the model. Of course, if we had assumed that sales would have increased by 50 percent or by 33 percent, we might have come to a different conclusion, which is a dangerous thing about "what if" models. You can make them support almost any answer you are trying to justify, so learn to live with your best estimates and resist the urge to change them when they don't support your objectives.

But let's not give up on making this model better. What if we took the extra dollars that would have gone into a third catalog and put them into customer acquisition? Option Two shows what would happen if we increased the acquisition budgets in each year by roughly the amount we would have spent on a third catalog. As you can see, cumulative profits are up from $2.89 million to $3.26 million, and the number of year-end customers has gone from 646,841 to 717,284.

CONCLUSION

We hope this last chapter on financial modeling has given you a better understanding of how all the elements of the economics or traditional direct marketing fit together. Front-end, back-end, lifetime value, and return on promotion all come together in the financial model. When this type of financial planning and analysis is combined with the database marketing methods discussed in the prior chapters of this book, the result is what we have called *the new direct marketing.*

Appendix A
LOTUS 1-2-3 PROGRAMS

SITUATION 1: Create a Confidence Interval (CI)

YOU HAVE COMPLETED A TEST MAILING AND OBTAINED A RESPONSE RATE. HOW CONFIDENT CAN YOU BE OF THIS RATE—WHAT IS THE CONFIDENCE INTERVAL?

TEST MAILING

PERCENT RESPONSE	2.00%
CONFIDENCE LEVEL: 80%, 85%, 90% OR 95%	95.00%
SAMPLE SIZE	10,000

THIS IS A TWO-SIDED TEST

THE EXPECTED RESPONSE RANGE IS BETWEEN	1.7256%	AND	2.2744%

WORK AREA

PERCENT RESPONSE	P =	2.00%	
SAMPLE SIZE =	N =	10,000	
STANDARD ERROR = SE = sqrt{P*(1–P)/N} =	SE =	0.14%	
CONFIDENCE LEVELS:	=	80.00%	1.282
TWO SIDED TEST		85.00%	1.440
		90.00%	1.645
		95.00%	1.960
LEVEL USED =	a =	1.96	
CONFIDENCE INTERVAL = P+/– a*SE;	a*SE=	0.27%	
P+a*SE =		2.27%	
P–a*SE =		1.73%	

```
C1: [W40] 'SITUATION 1: Create A Confidence Interval (CI)
C2: [W40] 'YOU HAVE COMPLETED A TEST MAILING AND OBTAINED A RESPONSE RATE.
C3: [W40] 'HOW CONFIDENT CAN YOU BE OF THIS RATE, WHAT IS THE CONFIDENCE
C4: [W40] 'INTERVAL?
C6: [W40] 'TEST MAILING
C7: [W40] 'PERCENT RESPONSE
F7: (P2) [W13] 0.02
C8: [W40] 'CONFIDENCE LEVEL: 80%, 85%, 90% OR 95%
F8: (P2) [W13] 0.95
C9: [W40] 'SAMPLE SIZE
F9: (,0) [W13] 10000
C11 [W40] 'THIS IS A TWO SIDED TEST
C12: [W40] 'THE EXPECTED RESPONSE RANGE IS BETWEEN
D12: (P3) [W7] +E31
E12: (P3) [W7] "AND
F12: (P3) [W13] +E30
C17: [W40] 'WORK AREA
C19: [W40] "PERCENT RESPONSE
D19: [W7] "P =
E19: (P2) [W7] +F7
C20: [W40] "SAMPLE SIZE=
D20: [W7] "N=
E20: (,0) [W7] +F9
C22: [W40] "STANDARD ERROR = SE = sqrt{P*(1-P)/N} =
D22: [W7] "SE =
E22: (P2) [W7] @SQRT (F7*(1-F7)/E20)
C23: [W40]
C24: [W40] "CONFIDENCE LEVELS:
D24: [W7] "=
E24: (P2) [W7] 0.8
F24: (F3) [W13] 1.282
C25: [W40] "TWO SIDED TEST
E25: (P2) [W7] 0.85
F25: (F3) [W13] 1.44
E26: (P2) [W7] 0.9
F26: (F3) [W13] 1.645
E27: (P2) [W7] 0.95
F27: (F3) [W13] 1.96
C28: [W40] "LEVEL USED =
D28: [W7] "a =
E28: [W7] @VLOOKUP (F8,E24..F27,1)
C29: [W40] "CONFIDENCE INTERVAL = P +/- a*SE;
D29: [W7] "a*SE =
E29: (P2) [W7] (E22*E28)
C30: [W40] "P+a*SE =
E30: (P2) [W7] +E19+E29
C31: [W40] "P-a*SE=
E31: (P2) [W7] +E19-E29
```

SITUATION 2: Solve For *N*–Two-Sided Test

YOU HAVE AN ESTIMATED RESPONSE RATE FOR AN UPCOMING MAILING.
HOW MANY PIECES SHOULD YOU MAIL GIVEN THAT YOU
WANT TO DEVELOP A CONFIDENCE INTERVAL OF PLUS OR MINUS SOME
PERCENT AROUND THAT EXPECTED RESPONSE RATE?

PERCENT RESPONSE	2.00%		
CONFIDENCE LEVEL: 80%, 85%, 90%, OR 95%	95.00%		
ALLOWABLE PERCENTAGE ERROR	0.2744%		
CONFIDENCE INTERVAL	1.73%	TO	2.2744%

THIS IS A TWO-SIDED TEST

ANSWER: THE QUANTITY MAILED SHOULD BE:	10,000

WORK AREA

PERCENT RESPONSE	P =	2.00%	
DESIRED PRECISION	D =	0.27%	
CONFIDENCE LEVELS:		80.00%	1.282
		85.00%	1.440
		90.00%	1.645
		95.00%	1.980
CONFIDENCE LEVEL USED	a =	1.96	
DESIRED PRECISION D=	(a*SE)	0.2744%	
If D = a*SE then D/a = SE =		0.140000%	
SE(SQUARED)= SE*SE =		0.0000020	
If SE = sqrt{(P*(1–P))/N}			
Then SE (squared) = P*(1–P)/N =			
And (P*(1–P+) =		0.0196	
SAMPLE SIZE = N = [P*(1–P)]/SE*SE	N =	10,000	

```
H1: [W37] 'SITUATION 2: Solve For N - Two Sided Test
H3: [W37] 'YOU HAVE AN ESTIMATED RESPONSE RATE FOR AN UPCOMING MAILING.
H4: [W37] 'HOW MANY PIECES SHOULD YOU MAIL GIVEN THAT YOU
H5; [W37] 'WANT TO DEVELOP A CONFIDENCE INTERVAL OF PLUS OR MINUS SOME
H6: [W37] 'PERCENT AROUND THAT EXPECTED RESPONSE RATE?
H8: [W37] 'PERCENT RESPONSE
J8: (P2) [W10] 0.02
H9: [W37] 'CONFIDENCE LEVEL: 80%, 85%, 90% OR 95%
J9: (P2) [W10] 0.95
H10: [W37] 'ALLOWABLE PERCENTAGE ERROR
J10: (P4) [W10] 0.002744
H11: [W37] 'CONFIDENCE INTERVAL
J11: (P3) [W10] +J8-J10
K11: (P2) [W6] ^TO
L11: (P3) [W7] +J8+J10
H13: [W37] 'THIS IS A TWO SIDED TEST
H14: [W37] 'ANSWER: THE QUANTITY MAILED SHOULD BE:
J14: (,0) [W10] +J32
H17: [W37] 'WORK AREA
H19: [W37] "PERCENT RESPONSE
I19: [W7] 'P =
J19: (P2) [W10] +J8
H20: [W37] "DESIRED PRECISION
I20: [W7] 'D =
J20: (P2) [W10] +J10
H21: [W37] "CONFIDENCE LEVELS:
J21: (P2) [W10] 0.8
L21: (F3) [W7] 1.282
J22: (P2) [W10] 0.85
L22: (F3) [W7] 1.44
J23: (P2) [W10] 0.9
L23: (F3) [W7] 1.645
J24: (P2) [W10] 0.95
L24: (F3) [W7] 1.96
H25: [W37] "CONFIDENCE LEVEL USED
I25: [W7] 'a =
J25: [W10] @VLOOKUP (J9, J21 .. L24, 2)
H26: [W37] "DESIRED PRECISION D=
I26: [W7] ' (a*SE)
J26: (P4) [W10] +J20
H27: [W37] "If D = a*SE then D/a = SE =
J27: (P6) [W10] +J26/J25
H28: [W37] "SE(SQUARED) = SE*SE =
J28: (F7) [W10] +J27*J27
H29: [W37] 'If SE =sqrt{(P*(1-P))/N}
H30: [W37] 'Then SE (squared) = P*(1-P)/N =
H31: [W37] "And (P*(1-P+) =
J31: [W10] (J19)*(1-J19)
H32: [W37] 'SAMPLE SIZE = N = [P*(1-P)]/SE*SE
I32:  [W7] 'N =
J32: (,0) [W10] +J31/J28
```

SITUATION 3: Solve for *N*–One-Sided Test

YOU HAVE AN ESTABLISHED CONTROL OR BREAK-EVEN RESPONSE RATE. YOU WON'T CHANGE THE CONTROL UNLESS YOU ARE SURE THAT THE NEW PACKAGE IS REALLY BETTER THAN THE CONTROL. HOW MANY PIECES SHOULD YOU MAIL OF THE NEW TEST PACKAGE?

(assumes certainty of control response, i.e., no sampling error on control side)	CONTROL RESPONSE	TEST PACKAGE
BREAK-EVEN RESPONSE RATE	2.00%	
CONFIDENCE LEVEL: 80%, 85%, 90% OR 95%	95.00%	
REQUIRED IMPROVEMENT IN RESPONSE		13.72%
THE NEW RESPONSE RATE MUST BE AT LEAST		2.2744%
ONE-SIDED TEST		
SAMPLE SIZE		7,988

WORK AREA

HISTORICAL CONTROL (BE) RESPONSE	P =	2.00%	
PERCENT RESPONSE FROM TEST	T =	2.27%	
DIFFERENCE	d =	0.27%	
CONFIDENCE LEVELS	CI =	80.00%	0.842
ONE-SIDED TEST		85.00%	1.036
		90.00%	1.282
		95.00%	1.645
SIGNIFICANCE LEVEL USED =	a =	1.645	
ANSWER		7,988	

LOGIC

If T –a*SE(of T) Must Be > P

T – P = d Must Be > a*SE(of T)

d Must BE > a*sqrt[T*(1–T)/N]

SQUARING BOTH SIDES

d*d > a*a{T*(1–T)/N}

n > [a*a{T*(1–T)}]/d*d

Exercise: Use Situation 1 to find CI for N = 7,988 and P = 2.2774%

```
N1: [W34] 'SITUATION 3: Solve For N - One Sided Test
N3: [W34] 'YOU HAVE AN ESTABLISHED CONTROL OR BREAKEVEN RESPONSE RATE. YOU
N4: [W34] 'WON'T CHANGE THE CONTROL UNLESS YOU ARE SURE THAT THE NEW PACKAGE
N5: [W34] 'IS REALLY BETTER THAN THE CONTROL. HOW MANY PIECES SHOULD
N6: [W34] 'YOU MAIL OF THE NEW TEST PACKAGE?
N8: [W34] '(assumes certainty of control response,
P8: [W12] "CONTROL
Q8: [W12] "TEST
N9: [W34] 'i.e. no sampling error on control side)
P9: [W12] "RESPONSE
Q9: [W12] "PACKAGE
N10: [W34] 'BREAKEVEN RESPONSE RATE
P10: (P2) [W12] 0.02
N11: [W34] 'CONFIDENCE LEVEL: 80%, 85%, 90% OR 95%
P11: (P2) [W12] 0.95
N12: [W34] 'REQUIRED IMPROVEMENT IN RESPONSE
Q12: (P2) [W12] (0.022744/0.02) -1
N13: [W34] 'THE NEW RESPONSE RATE MUST BE AT LEAST
Q13: (P4) [W12] +P10*(1+Q12)
N15: [W34] 'ONE SIDED TEST
N16: [W34] 'SAMPLE SIZE
P16: (,0) [W12] '
Q16: (,0) [W12] +P28
N19: [W34] 'WORK AREA
N20: [W34] "HISTORICAL CONTROL (BE) RESPONSE
O20: "P =
P20: (P2) [W12] +$P$10
N21: [W34] "PERCENT RESPONSE FROM TEST
O21: "T =
P21: (P2) [W12] +Q$13
N22: [W34] "DIFFERENCE
O22: "d =
P22: (P2) [W12] +P$21-P$20
N23: [W34] "CONFIDENCE LEVELS
O23: "CI =
P23: (P2) [W12] 0.8
Q23: [W12] 0.842
N24: [W34] "ONE SIDED TEST
P24: (P2) [W12] 0.85
Q24: (F3) [W12] 1.036
P25: (P2) [W12] 0.9
Q25: [W12] 1.282
P26: (P2) [W12] 0.95
Q26: [W12] 1.645
N27: [W34] "SIGNIFICANCE LEVEL USED =
O27: "a =
P27: [W12] @VLOOKUP(P$11,P$23..Q$26,1)
N28: [W34] "ANSWER
P28: (,0) [W12] (P$27*P$27)*(P$21*(1-P$21))/(P22*P22)
N29: [W34] "
P30: [W12] '
N31: [W34] "LOGIC
N32: [W34] "If T -a*SE (of T) Must Be > P
N33: [W34] "T - P = d Must Be > a*SE(of T)
N34: [W34] "d Must BE > a*sqrt[T*(1-T)/N]
N35: [W34] "SQUARING BOTH SIDES
N36: [W34] "d*d > a*a{T*(1-T)/N}
N37: [W34] "n > [a*a{T*(1-T)}]/d*d
N38: [W34] 'Exercise: Use Situation 1 to find CI for N = 7,988 and P = 2.277
```

SITUATION 4: Test for Significant Differences

IS THE RESPONSE TO THE TEST PACKAGE STATISTICALLY BETTER
(OR WORSE) THAN THE RESPONSE TO THE CONTROL PACKAGE?
(Better or worse implies a one-sided test.)

(When both test and control sides are mailed, sampling error applies to both mailings)	CONTROL PACKAGE	TEST PACKAGE
	2.00%	2.274%
CONFIDENCE LEVEL: 80%, 85%, 90% OR 95%	95.00%	
SAMPLE SIZE	15,000	15,000

ANSWER: IMPROVEMENT IN RESPONSE RATE IS . . . . . . **NOT SIGNIFICANT**

WORK AREA

CONTROL PROPORTION =	P	2.00%	
TEST PROPORTION =	T	2.27%	
ABSOLUTE DIFFERENCE =	d	0.27%	
CONFIDENCE LEVEL		80.00%	0.842
THIS IS A ONE-SIDED TEST		85.00%	1.036
		90.00%	1.282
		95.00%	1.645
LEVEL USED =	a =	1.645	
SAMPLE SIZE CONTROL =	N1 =	15,000	
SAMPLE SIZE TEST =	N2 =	15,000	
EST OF POPULATION VALUE OF % RSP = [{N1*P}+{N2*T}]/[N1+N2]	p* =	0.02137	
ESTIMATED STANDARD ERROR OF THE DIFFERENCE BETWEEN TWO SAMPLE PERCENTAGES–ESTIMATED FROM THE SAMPLES THEMSELVES: USING sqrt[{p*(1–p*)*(N1+N2)}/(N1*N2)]	E(of p*) =	0.001670	
DECISION PARAMETER			
(P–T)/SE(of p*) =	dp =	1.6431731783	
DECISION RULE:			
if @ABS(dp)>a then diff is significant		0	
TABLE =		0	NOT SIGNIFICANT
		1	SIGNIFICANT
ANSWER =		NOT SIGNIFICANT	

```
S1: [W34] 'SITUATION 4: Test for Significant Differences
S3: [W34] 'IS THE RESPONSE TO THE TEST PACKAGE STATISTICALLY BETTER (OR
S4: [W34] 'WORSE) THAN THE RESPONSE TO THE CONTROL PACKAGE?
S5: [W34] '(Better or worse implies a one-sided test.)
S7: [w34] '(When both test & control sides are mailed,
U7: [W12] "CONTROL
V7: [W16] "TEST
S8: [W34] 'sampling error applies to both mailings)
U8: [W12] "PACKAGE
V8: [W16] "PACKAGE
U9: (P2) [W12] 0.02
V9: (P3) [W16] 0.022744
S10: [W34] 'CONFIDENCE LEVEL: 80%, 85%, 90% OR 95%
U10: (P2) [W12] 0.95
S11: [W34] 'SAMPLE SIZE
U11: (,0) [W12] 15000
V11: (,0) [W16] 15000
S13: [W34] 'ANSWER: IMPROVEMENT IN RESPONSE RATE IS.........
U13: [W12] +U40
S15: [W34] 'WORK AREA
S16: [W34] "CONTROL PROPORTION =
T16: [W9] "P
U16: (P2) [W12] +U9
S17: [W34] "TEST PROPORTION =
T17: [W9] "T
U17: (P2) [W12] +V9
S18: [W34] "ABSOLUTE DIFFERENCE =
T18: [W9] "d
U18: (P2) [W12] +U17-U16
S19: [W34] 'CONFIDENCE LEVEL
U19: (P2) [W12] 0.8
V19: [W16] 0.842
S20: [W34] 'THIS IS A ONE SIDED TEST
U20: (P2) [W12] 0.85
V20: (F3) [W16] 1.036
U21: (P2) [W12] 0.9
V21: [W16] 1.282
U22: (P2) [W12] 0.95
V22: [W16] 1.645
S23: [W34] "LEVEL USED =
T23: [W9] "a =
U23: [W12] @VLOOKUP(U10,U19..V22,1)
S24: [W34] "SAMPLE SIZE CONTROL =
T24: [W9] "N1 =
U24: (,0) [W12] +U11
S25: [W34] "SAMPLE SIZE TEST =
T25: [W9] "N2 =
U25: (,0) [W12] +V11
S26: [W34] "EST OF POPULATION VALUE OF % RSP =
T26: [W9] "p* =
U26: (F5) [W12] ((U16*U24)+(U17*U25))/(U24+U25)
V26: [W16] '
S27: [W34] '[{N1*P}+{N2*T}]/[N1+N2]
S29: [W34] 'ESTIMATED STANDARD ERROR OF THE
S30: [W34] 'DIFFERENCE BETWEN TWO SAMPLE
```

```
S31: [W34] 'PERCENTAGES—ESTIMATED FROM THE
S32: [W34] 'SAMPLES THEMSELVES: USING
T32: [W9] "SE(of p*)=
U32: (F6) [W12] @SQRT(U26*(1-U26)*(U24+U25)/(U24*U25)
S33: [W34] 'sqrt[{p*(1-p*)*(N1+N2)}/(N1*N2)]
S34: [W34] 'DECISION PARAMETER
S35: [W34] "(P-T)/SE(of p*) =
T35: [W9] "dp =
U35: [W12] +U18/U32
S36: [W34] 'DECISION RULE:
S37: [W34] "if @ABS(dp)>a then diff is significant
U37: [W12] @IF(@ABS(U35)>=U23,1,0)
S38: [W34] "TABLE =
U38: [W12] 0
V38: [W16] 'NOT SIGNIFICANT
U39: [W12] 1
V39: [W16] 'SIGNIFICANT
S40: [W34] "ANSWER =
U40: [W12] @VLOOKUP(U37,U38..V39,1)
```

Appendix B
VENDORS OF DATA AND COMPUTER SERVICES

Direct marketers interested in enhancing their customer and prospect files with individual household level data; census data gathered at the block group, census tract, or ZIP code level; or with geography-based cluster codes can do so by obtaining such data from a number of data sources.

Some of the more popular sources are listed below, and selected samples of their promotional literature have been reproduced on the pages that follow.

The sources listed are by no means a directory of all available data sources, nor is the material presented for any of the listed sources meant to be a complete presentation of the data and services these companies provide. For a complete listing of data sources and computer service bureaus contact

The Direct Marketing Association
6 East 43rd Street
New York, NY 10017
Telephone: 212–768–7277

In addition to data sources, you may be interested in knowing more about database management software. To that end, Datapro Information Services Group, a McGraw-Hill company, has provided us with the copyrighted material you will find in Part 2 of this appendix (page 456). Again, this selection is not meant to be comprehensive. For more information contact Datapro directly by writing to

Datapro Information Services Group
600 Delran Parkway
Delran, NJ 08075
Telephone: 1–800–DATAPRO (1–800–328–2776)

In addition we have provided information regarding the database management system developed by one of this book's authors, Dr. Dhiraj Sharma, which is available through David Shepard Associates, Inc. and MegaPlex, Inc.

TABLE OF CONTENTS FOR DATA VENDOR EXHIBITS

PRIZM Market Segmentation

cluster snapshots

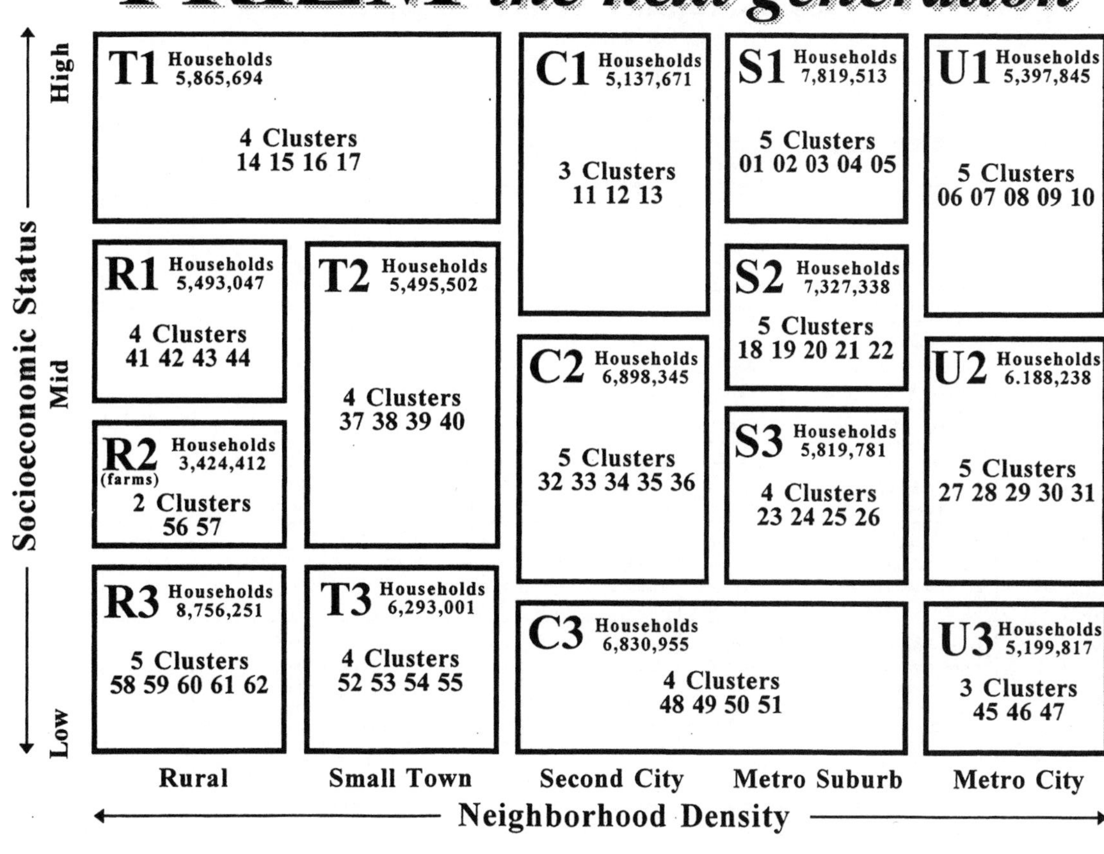
PRIZM the next generation
T1 Households 5,865,694
4 Clusters
14 15 16 17
C1 Households 5,137,671
3 Clusters
11 12 13
S1 Households 7,819,513
5 Clusters
01 02 03 04 05
U1 Households 5,397,845
5 Clusters
06 07 08 09 10
R1 Households 5,493,047
4 Clusters
41 42 43 44
T2 Households 5,495,502
4 Clusters
37 38 39 40
S2 Households 7,327,338
5 Clusters
18 19 20 21 22
C2 Households 6,898,345
5 Clusters
32 33 34 35 36
U2 Households 6.188,238
5 Clusters
27 28 29 30 31
R2 (farms) Households 3,424,412
2 Clusters
56 57
S3 Households 5,819,781
4 Clusters
23 24 25 26
R3 Households 8,756,251
5 Clusters
58 59 60 61 62
T3 Households 6,293,001
4 Clusters
52 53 54 55
C3 Households 6,830,955
4 Clusters
48 49 50 51
U3 Households 5,199,817
3 Clusters
45 46 47
Socioeconomic Status
High
Mid
Low
Rural
Small Town
Second City
Metro Suburb
Metro City
Neighborhood Density

PRIZM by Claritas
Demographic Reference Chart

Race/Ethnicity
W-White, B-Black, A-Asian
H-Hispanic, F-Foreign Born
□ Dominant • Above Avg

PREDOMINANT CHARACTERISTICS

Grp	Clstr	Nickname	Income Level	Family Type	Age	Education	Occup	Housing	W	B	A	H	F
S1	01	*Blue Blood Estates*	Wealthy	Family	35-54	College	Exec	Single	□		•		•
	02	*Cashmere & Country Clubs*	Wealthy	Family	35-54	College	Exec	Single	□		•		•
	03	*Executive Suites*	Affluent	Couples	25-34	College	WC/Exec	Single	□		•		•
	04	*Pools & Patios*	Affluent	Couples	55-64	College	Exec	Single	□		•		•
	05	*Kids & Cul-de-Sacs*	Affluent	Family	35-54	College	WC/Exec	Single	•		•		•
U1	06	*Urban Gold Coast*	Affluent	Singles	25-34	College	Exec	Hi-Rise	□		•		•
	07	*Money & Brains*	Affluent	Couples	55-64	College	Exec	Single	□		•		•
	08	*Young Literati*	Upper Mid	Sgl/Cpl	25-34	College	Exec	Hi-Rise	•		•		•
	09	*American Dreams*	Upper Mid	Family	35-54	College	WC	Single		•	•	•	•
	10	*Bohemian Mix*	Middle	Singles	< 24	College	WC	Hi-Rise		•	•	•	•
C1	11	*Second City Elite*	Affluent	Couples	35-64	College	WC/Exec	Single	□				
	12	*Upward Bound*	Upper Mid	Family	25-54	College	WC/Exec	Single	□		•		
	13	*Gray Power*	Middle	Sgl/Cpl	65+	College	WC	Single	□				•
T1	14	*Country Squires*	Wealthy	Fam/Cpl	35-64	College	Exec	Single	□				
	15	*God's Country*	Affluent	Family	35-54	College	WC	Single	□				
	16	*Big Fish Small Pond*	Upper Mid	Family	35-54	HS/College	WC	Single	□				
	17	*Greenbelt Families*	Upper Mid	Family	25-54	HS/College	WC	Single	□				
S2	18	*Young Influentials*	Upper Mid	Sgl/Cpl	< 35	College	WC/Exec	Multi	•		•		•
	19	*New Empty Nests*	Upper Mid	Couples	35-64	College	WC/Exec	Single	□				
	20	*Boomers & Babies*	Upper Mid	Family	25-54	College	WC/Exec	Single	•		•	•	
	21	*Suburban Sprawl*	Middle	Fam/Cpl	< 35	College	WC	Mixed		•	•	•	•
	22	*Blue-Chip Blues*	Middle	Family	35-54	HS/College	WC/BC	Single	□				
S3	23	*Upstarts & Seniors*	Middle	Cpl/Sgl	Mix	College	WC/Exec	Multi	□				
	24	*New Beginnings*	Middle	Sgl/Cpl	< 35	College	WC/Exec	Multi		•	•	•	•
	25	*Mobility Blues*	Middle	Fam/Cpl	< 35	HS/College	BC/Serv	Mixed		•	•	□	•
	26	*Gray Collars*	Middle	Couples	> 55	HS	BC/Serv	Single		•		•	
U2	27	*Urban Achievers*	Middle	Cpl/Sgl	Mix	College	WC/Exec	Hi-Rise	□		•	•	•
	28	*Big City Blend*	Middle	Family	35-54	HS	WC/BC	Single			•	□	•
	29	*Old Yankee Rows*	Middle	Couples	55+	HS	WC	Multi	•		•	•	•
	30	*Middle Minorities*	Middle	Fam/Cpl	35-54	HS/College	WC/Serv	Multi		□		•	•
	31	*Latino America*	Middle	Family	25-34	< HS	BC/Serv	Multi				□	•
C2	32	*Middleburg Managers*	Middle	Couples	> 55	College	WC/Exec	Single	□				
	33	*Boomtown Singles*	Middle	Sgl/Cpl	< 34	College	WC/Exec	Multi	□				
	34	*Starter Families*	Middle	Family	25-34	HS	BC	Mixed	•			•	
	35	*Sunset City Blues*	Lower Mid	Couples	> 55	HS	BC/Serv	Single	□				
	36	*Towns & Gowns*	Lower Mid	Singles	< 35	College	WC/Serv	Hi-Rise	•		•		•
T2	37	*New Homesteaders*	Middle	Family	35-54	College	WC	Single	□				
	38	*Middle America*	Middle	Family	25-44	HS	BC	Single	□				
	39	*Red, White & Blue*	Middle	Family	35-64	HS	BC	Single	□				
	40	*Military Quarters*	Lower Mid	Family	25-54	College	WC/Serv	Multi		•	•		

PRIZM by Claritas
Demographic Reference Chart

Race/Ethnicity
W-White, B-Black, A-Asian
H-Hispanic, F-Foreign Born
■ Dominant • Above Avg

PREDOMINANT CHARACTERISTICS

Grp	Clstr	Nickname	Income Level	Family Type	Age	Education	Occup	Housing	W	B	A	H	F
R1	41	*Big Sky Families*	Upper Mid	Family	35-44	HS/College	BC/Farm	Single	■				
	42	*New Ecotopia*	Middle	Fam/Cpl	35-54	College	WC/BC	Single	■				
	43	*River City, USA*	Middle	Family	35-64	HS	BC/Farm	Single	■				
	44	*Shotguns & Pickups*	Middle	Family	35-64	HS	BC/Farm	Single	■				
U3	45	*Single City Blues*	Lower Mid	Singles	Mix	Mix	WC/Serv	Multi		•	•	•	•
	46	*Hispanic Mix*	Poor	Family	< 35	< HS	BC	Hi-Rise			•	■	•
	47	*Inner Cities*	Poor	Sgl/Fam	Mix	< HS	BC/Serv	Multi		■		•	
C3	48	*Smalltown Downtown*	Lower Mid	Sgl/Fam	< 35	HS/College	BC/Serv	Multi		•		•	
	49	*Hometown Retired*	Lower Mid	Sgl/Cpl	65+	< HS	Service	Mixed	■				
	50	*Family Scramble*	Lower Mid	Family	< 35	< HS	BC	Mixed				■	•
	51	*Southside City*	Poor	Sgl/Fam	Mix	< HS	BC/Serv	Multi		■			
T3	52	*Golden Ponds*	Lower Mid	Couples	65+	HS	BC/Serv	Single	■				
	53	*Rural Industria*	Lower Mid	Family	< 35	HS	BC	Single	■			•	
	54	*Norma Rae-Ville*	Poor	Sgl/Fam	Mix	< HS	BC/Serv	Single		■			
	55	*Mines & Mills*	Poor	Sgl/Cpl	55+	< HS	BC/Serv	Single	■				
R2	56	*Agri-Business*	Middle	Family	35+	HS	Farm	Single	■			•	
	57	*Grain Belt*	Lower Mid	Family	55+	HS	Farm	Single	■			•	
R3	58	*Blue Highways*	Lower Mid	Family	35-54	HS	BC/Farm	Single	■				
	59	*Rustic Elders*	Lower Mid	Couples	55+	HS	BC/Serv	Single	■				
	60	*Back Country Folks*	Lower Mid	Couples	35+	HS	BC/Farm	Single	■				
	61	*Scrub Pine Flats*	Poor	Family	35+	< HS	BC/Farm	Single		■			
	62	*Hard Scrabble*	Poor	Family	35+	< HS	BC/Farm	Single	■				

Income Level	Avg Annual HH Income
Wealthy	$65,000 and over
Affluent	$50,000 - $64,500
Upper Mid	$37,000 - $49,500
Middle	$28,000 - $36,500
Lower Mid	$20,000 - $27,500
Poor	under $20,000

Education	
< HS	Grade School
HS	High School / Technical School
HS/College	High School / Some College
College	College Graduates

Family Type	
Family	Married Couples w/Children
	Single Parents w/Children
Couples	Married Couples (few children)
Singles	Singles / Unmarried Couples
Fam/Cpl	Mix of Married Couples with/without Children
Sgl/Cpl	Mix of Married Couples and Singles

Occupation	
Exec	Executives & Professionals
WC	Other White-Collar (Managers, Technical, Sales, etc)
BC	Blue-Collar (assembly workers, craftsmen, skilled trades, etc)
WC/BC	Mix of White-Collar & Upper-Level Blue Collar
Service	Clerical/Service (Hospitality, Bank Tellers, etc)
WC/Serv	Mix of Low-Level White-Collar & Service
BC/Serv	Mix of Blue-Collar & Service
Farm	Farming, Mining & Ranching
BC/Farm	Mix of Blue-Collar and Farming

Cluster 01

Blue Blood Estates

Short, one paragraph description of the demographic, lifestyle and/or behavior of the PRIZM Classic cluster.

PRIZM by Claritas **PRIZM by Claritas** **PRIZM by Claritas** **PRIZM by Claritas** **PRIZM by Claritas**

Predominant Characteristics

Households (%U.S.):	729,466 (0.8%)
Population (%U.S.):	2,181,437
Demographic Name:	**Elite, Super-Rich Families**
Ethnic Diversity:	Dominant White, High Asian
Family Type:	Married Couples w/ Children
Predominant Age Ranges:	35-54
Education:	College Graduates
Employment Level:	Professional
Housing Type:	Owners/Single Unit
Density Decile:	7 (1=Sparse, 9=Dense)
Social Group:	S1 - The Suburban Elite

Education

Education:	**U.S.**	**Cluster**	**Index**
4+ Years College	20.6	61.0	296
1-3 Years College	24.9	22.2	89
High School Graduate	29.9	12.0	41
Less than High School	24.6	4.8	20

Occupation

Occupation:	**U.S.**	**Cluster**	**Index**
Professional/Manager	25.8	57.0	221
Other White-Collar	31.4	31.0	99
Blue-Collar	26.6	5.8	22
Service	13.7	5.6	41
Farming/Mining/Ranching	2.5	0.6	24

Blue-Blood Estates - PRIZM Cluster 01

Family Composition

Family Type:	**U.S.**	**Cluster**	**Index**
Married Couples	55.2	77.5	140
Married Couples w/Children	26.7	35.3	132
Single Parents	9.3	3.3	35
Single Female HH Head	11.6	5.6	48

Household Size:	**U.S.**	**Cluster**	**Index**
1 Person	24.6	12.0	49
4+ Persons	26.0	33.1	127
HH w/ Children	36.0	38.6	107

Age of HH Head:	**U.S.**	**Cluster**	**Index**
Under 24	5.5	0.6	11
25-34	21.6	8.2	38
35-54	37.7	51.0	135
55-64	13.5	19.9	147
65+	21.7	20.3	94
Median Age	46.5	51.5	111

Ethnic Origin

Race/Ethnic Orgin:	**U.S.**	**Cluster**	**Index**
White	80.1	92.0	115
Black	10.6	1.1	10
Asian (API)	2.1	4.7	224
Hispanic	6.5	2.0	31
Foreign Born	7.7	12.2	158

Income

Household Income:	**U.S.**	**Cluster**	**Index**
Less than $15,000	24.3	4.2	17
$15,000 - $24,999	17.5	3.8	22
$25,000 - $34,999	15.9	4.9	31
$35,000 - $49,999	17.9	8.8	49
$50,000 - $74,999	15.0	17.0	113
$75,000 - $99,999	5.1	15.8	310
$100,000+	4.4	45.8	1041
Median HH Income	$31,900	$94,500	296

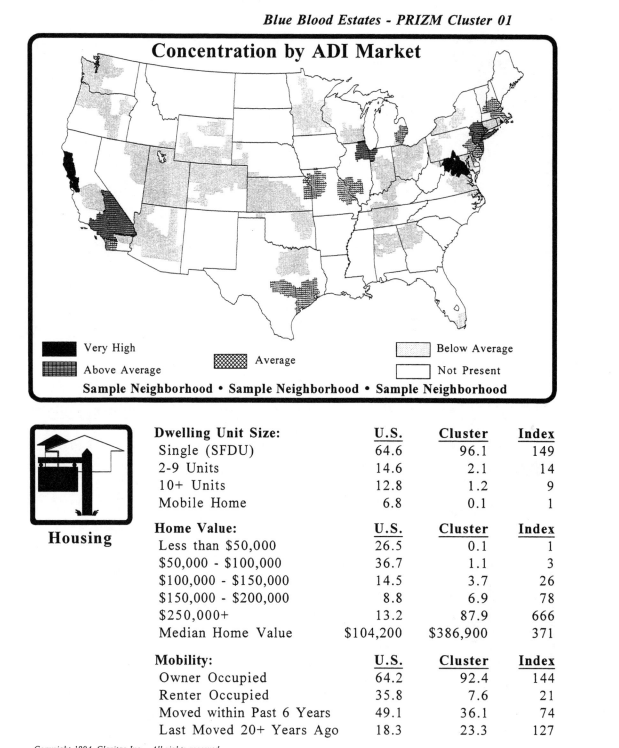

Blue Blood Estates - PRIZM Cluster 01

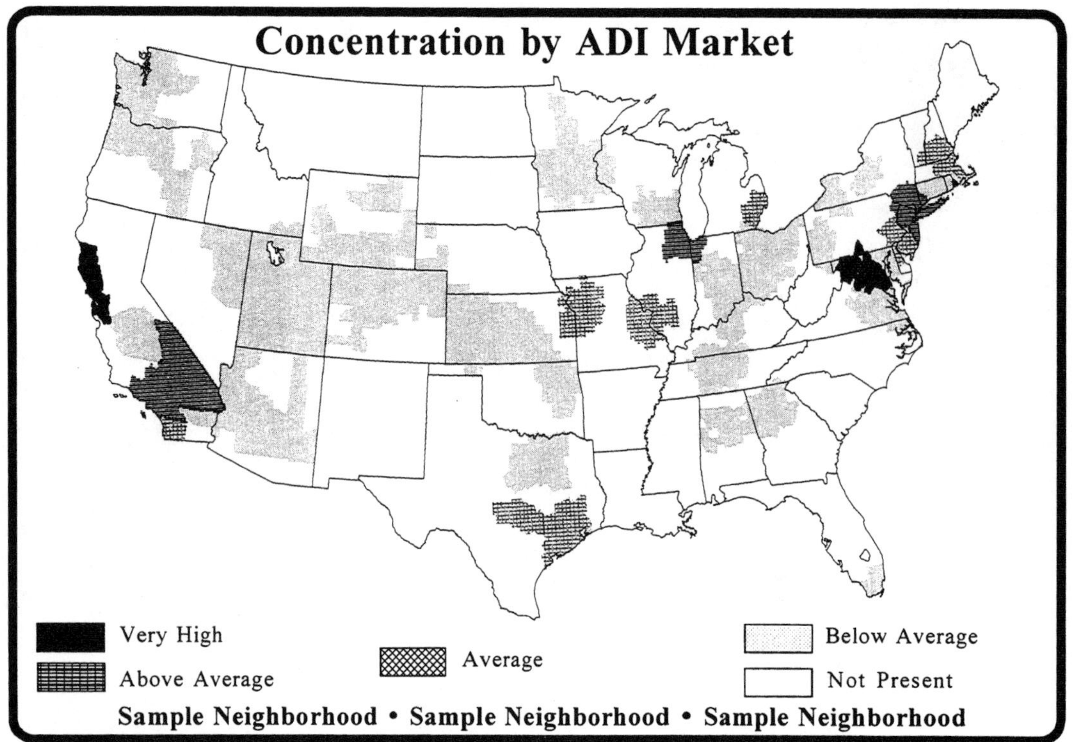

Housing

Dwelling Unit Size:	U.S.	Cluster	Index
Single (SFDU)	64.6	96.1	149
2-9 Units	14.6	2.1	14
10+ Units	12.8	1.2	9
Mobile Home	6.8	0.1	1

Home Value:	U.S.	Cluster	Index
Less than $50,000	26.5	0.1	1
$50,000 - $100,000	36.7	1.1	3
$100,000 - $150,000	14.5	3.7	26
$150,000 - $200,000	8.8	6.9	78
$250,000+	13.2	87.9	666
Median Home Value	$104,200	$386,900	371

Mobility:	U.S.	Cluster	Index
Owner Occupied	64.2	92.4	144
Renter Occupied	35.8	7.6	21
Moved within Past 6 Years	49.1	36.1	74
Last Moved 20+ Years Ago	18.3	23.3	127

Cluster 38

Middle America

Short, one paragraph description of the demographic, lifestyle and/or behavior of the PRIZM Classic cluster.

PRIZM by **Claritas** **PRIZM** by **Claritas** **PRIZM** by **Claritas** **PRIZM** by **Claritas** **PRIZM** by **Claritas**

Predominant Characteristics

Households (%U.S.):	1,118,537 (1.2%)
Population (%U.S.):	3,118,921
Demographic Name:	**Midsize Town, Middle-Class Families**
Ethnic Diversity:	Dominant White
Family Type:	Married Couples w/ Children
Predominant Age Ranges:	25-34, 35-44
Education:	High School
Employment Level:	Blue-Collar
Housing Type:	Owners/Single Unit
Density Decile:	3 (1=Sparse, 9=Dense)
Social Group:	T2 - Satellite Blues

Education

Education:	**U.S.**	**Cluster**	**Index**
4+ Years College	20.6	14.2	69
1-3 Years College	24.9	26.6	107
High School Graduate	29.9	36.6	122
Less than High School	24.6	22.7	92

Occupation

Occupation:	**U.S.**	**Cluster**	**Index**
Professional/Manager	25.8	21.2	82
Other White-Collar	31.4	32.3	103
Blue-Collar	26.6	32.5	122
Service	13.7	12.3	90
Farming/Mining/Ranching	2.5	1.7	68

Middle America - PRIZM Cluster 38

Family Composition

Family Type:	U.S.	Cluster	Index
Married Couples	55.2	65.2	118
Married Couples w/Children	26.7	33.3	124
Single Parents	9.3	8.1	85
Single Female HH Head	11.6	9.5	82

Household Size:	U.S.	Cluster	Index
1 Person	24.6	18.5	75
4+ Persons	26.0	29.1	112
HH w/ Children	36.0	41.4	115

Age of HH Head:	U.S.	Cluster	Index
Under 24	5.5	4.6	84
25-34	21.6	23.1	107
35-54	37.7	41.2	109
55-64	13.5	13.8	102
65+	21.7	17.4	80
Median Age	46.5	44.8	96

Ethnic Origin

Race/Ethnic Orgin:	U.S.	Cluster	Index
White	80.1	92.1	115
Black	10.6	4.3	41
Asian (API)	2.1	0.4	19
Hispanic	6.5	2.4	37
Foreign Born	7.7	2.2	29

Income

Household Income:	U.S.	Cluster	Index
Less than $15,000	24.3	17.8	73
$15,000 - $24,999	17.5	17.6	101
$25,000 - $34,999	15.9	19.0	119
$35,000 - $49,999	17.9	22.7	127
$50,000 - $74,999	15.0	16.7	111
$75,000 - $99,999	5.1	3.8	75
$100,000+	4.4	2.0	45
Median HH Income	$31,900	$32,700	103

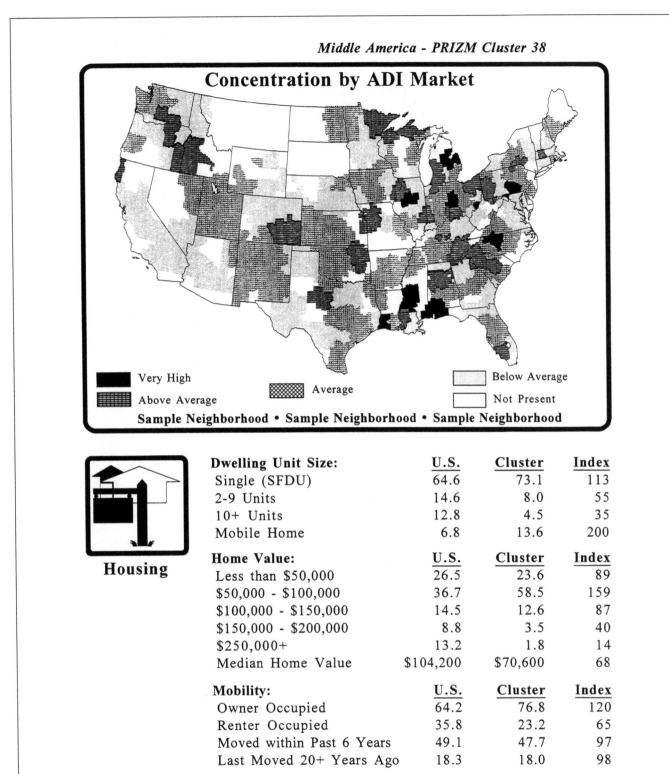

Middle America - PRIZM Cluster 38

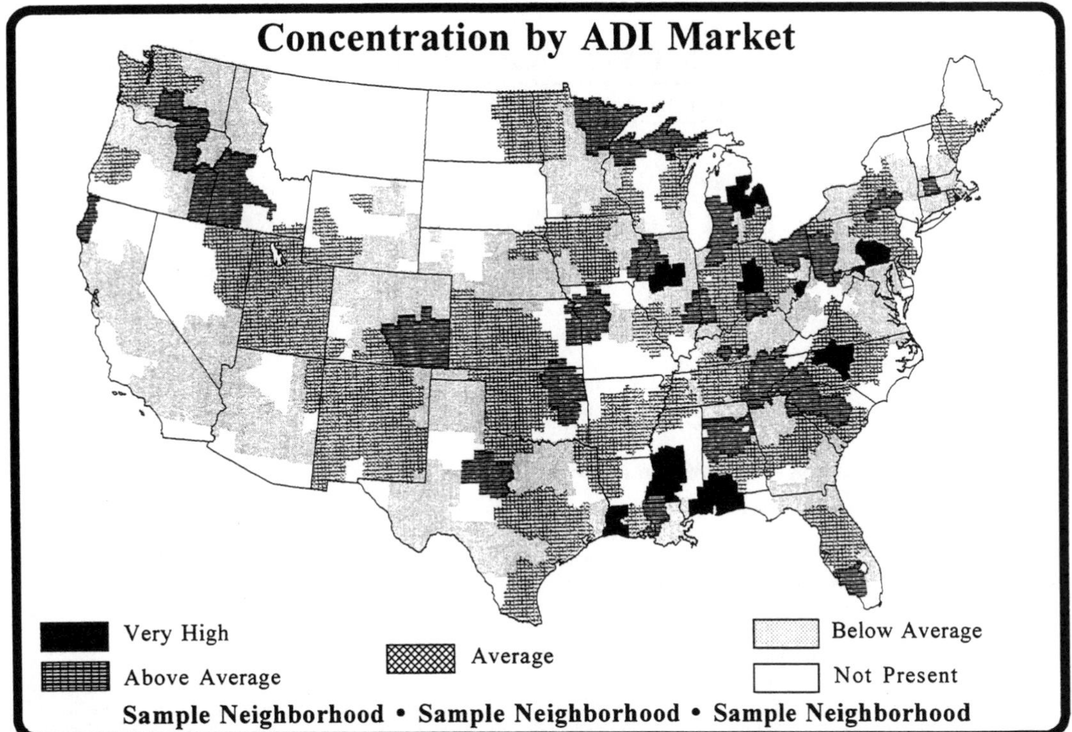

Housing

Dwelling Unit Size:	U.S.	Cluster	Index
Single (SFDU)	64.6	73.1	113
2-9 Units	14.6	8.0	55
10+ Units	12.8	4.5	35
Mobile Home	6.8	13.6	200

Home Value:	U.S.	Cluster	Index
Less than $50,000	26.5	23.6	89
$50,000 - $100,000	36.7	58.5	159
$100,000 - $150,000	14.5	12.6	87
$150,000 - $200,000	8.8	3.5	40
$250,000+	13.2	1.8	14
Median Home Value	$104,200	$70,600	68

Mobility:	U.S.	Cluster	Index
Owner Occupied	64.2	76.8	120
Renter Occupied	35.8	23.2	65
Moved within Past 6 Years	49.1	47.7	97
Last Moved 20+ Years Ago	18.3	18.0	98

Data Enhancement for Direct Marketers

DBA Information Systems Incorporated

INFO-ADD — The First Step in Database Marketing

INFO-ADD Supplies the Data that Lets You Get to Know Your Customers and Prospects

Info-Add is an easy way to get information about your customers and prospects - information that lets you make better decisions to:

- Identify and select the best potential from within prospect lists - and eliminate poor potential
- Get better, more detailed results from modeling programs
- Target your copy and offer to a known audience
- Strengthen any relationship marketing program

Give Each of Your Records an Identity of Its Own

INFO-ADD transfers data from our comprehensive database to your customer or prospect records.

Draw your data from our Consumer Database of over 130 million families and individuals. Or use our Business Database of over 9.2 million firms and organizations.

We match your file against our database. For every record matched, any or all of the following information is added to your customer or prospect name:

Consumer INFO-ADD

- Estimated Income
- Length of Residence
- Tenure (Own or Rent)
- Occupation Code
- Marital Status
- Presence of Children
- Number of People in the Household
- Number of Families/Surnames at This Address
- Age of Adults
- Telephone Number
- Dwelling Unit Size
- Dwelling Age/Year
- Credit Card Users
- Mail Order Responders
- Mail Order Buyers
- Number & Body Style of Cars
- Combined Market Value of All Vehicles Owned
- New Vehicle Purchaser Code
- Truck Owner
- Motorcycle Owner
- RV Owner
- County Coding (MSA, SMMA, ADI, SAMI, Nielsen ABCD)
- Census Tract/Block Group/Enumeration District Data
- Number of Data Sources That Contribute to the Record

Business INFO-ADD

- Telephone Number
- Contact Name
- Type of Business (SIC Code)
- Size of Business (by Sales or Number of Employees)
- New Business Code
- Sales Volume
- Advertising Code
- Carrier Route Code, ZIP+4 Code
- Trademark Identification
- County Code
- Population Size
- Headquarters/Branch Code

To find out how INFO-ADD can give an identity to your customers and prospects, contact us at:
Corporate Headquarters: Database America Companies • 100 Paragon Dr. • Montvale NJ 07645-0416
Phone: 201-476-2000 • Fax: 201-476-2152

Donnelley Marketing Inc.

SHARE FORCE℠

Pricing

SELECTIONS

Base Price $60.00/M
State $3.50/M
SCF $3.50/M
Nielsen County $3.50/M
Zip $5.00/M
Cluster Codes $10.00/M
Telephone $7.50/M
Bank Card $5.00/M
T&E Card $5.00/M
Key Coding $1.50/M
Any demographic or psychographic $5.00/M
Sex .... No Charge

ADDRESSING

4-up/5-up Cheshire .... No Charge
Pressure Sensitive $6.50/M
Magnetic Tape .... $15.00/L (non-refundable)
Diskette $15.00/L
Manuscript $2.75/M
Phone Manuscript $9.00/M

MINIMUM

5,000 Names

NET NAME

85% + $5.00/M running charges on 5,000+ names

- **Sample mailing piece required**
- **Inquire for additional selections and counts**

Now You Can Target Consumers by Product Preferences, Lifestyle Interests and Actual Buying Habits

1 WHAT IS SHARE FORCE?

The Share Force consumer database contains over 16 million mail responsive records generated from Donnelley Marketing's proprietary Share Force national survey. For over a decade, these surveys have reached households across America. Distributed primarily through the Carol Wright® Co-op to well over 50 million households, Share Force asks consumers specific questions about their product preferences, brand usage, buying habits, lifestyle interests and more.

The Share Force consumer database is also overlaid with information from Donnelley Marketing's DQI^2 consumer database, including age, income, children, type of dwelling, auto ownership and more.

2 WHAT SHARE FORCE CAN DO FOR YOU

The Share Force consumer database is designed to allow for effective list targeting. Selections include:

- Interests/Hobbies (cars, cooking, golf, tennis)
- Family/Home (age of child/adult, home value, pet ownership)
- Books/Magazines (home improvement, romance)
- Mail Order Buyers (apparel, contributors, gifts)
- Specific Categories (grocery items, HBA, beverages)*
- Survey Response
- Demographic Variables
- Geographic Area

Please turn over for a listing of lifestyle and demographic characteristics.

Call your local Donnelley Marketing representative for more information!

Donnelley Marketing Inc.

The Consumer Information Source

East: 800 333-6169 ■ 203 353-7000
70 Seaview Ave., Stamford, CT 06902

West: 800 223-2160 ■ 714 538-1122
1111 E. Katella Ave., Suite 140, Orange, CA 92667

Central: 800 323-3685 ■ 708 495-1211
1901 S. Meyers Rd., Oakbrook Terrace, IL 60181

Detroit: 313 746-6030
25800 Northwestern Hwy., Suite 875, Southfield, MI 48075

* *Call for category pricing and brand level information.*

Donnelley Marketing Inc.

Donnelley Marketing created PIC to meet the needs of direct marketers who want to focus on households with an investment potential profile.

The select group of consumers that PIC offers is on-target for many major marketers in financial services, insurance companies, estate planning, high-ticket collectibles and fund raising campaigns.

PIC is sourced from Donnelley Marketing's consumer database of 87 million unduplicated households. After establishing the universe of PIC qualifiers, Donnelley Marketing scores the household and ranks it high to low based on model performance.

The ability to "pick" these highly qualified consumers increases your potential for successful promotions. The accuracy of PIC provides more efficient use of promotion dollars. PIC's deeper market reach provides the most appropriate consumers for your marketing strategy.

POTENTIAL INVESTOR CONSUMER

A New, Accurate Way to Identify a Highly Desirable Market Segment

WHAT IS POTENTIAL INVESTOR CONSUMER (PIC)?

Selected from Donnelley Marketing's DQI^2 consumer database of 87 million households, a Potential Investor Consumer (PIC) is qualified by specific financial and consumer patterns that reflect high probability of investment activity and/or ability to participate in the investment marketplace.

Donnelley Marketing performs an extensive analysis using an annual survey of households, identifying those with IRAs, brokerage accounts or a record of recent investment purchases such as CDs, MMAs, stocks, bonds, mutual funds, MMFs, T-Bills, T-Notes and precious metals.

By building a multivariate model, Donnelley Marketing can predict a household's tendency to invest in one or more of the options listed above. As a result, Donnelley Marketing is able to accurately identify similar consumers who share the same characteristics. These "Potential Investor Consumers" are capable of high value buying in diverse markets from investments to hard goods.

WHAT PIC CAN DO FOR YOU

PIC provides you with direct access to highly qualified investment-potential consumers. With PIC you can:

- Select Potential Investor Consumers by rank and combine with any other Donnelley Marketing variable, such as age, length of residence, income, presence of children, availability of telephone numbers and more for your mailings or telemarketing campaigns.
- Add PIC ratings to your house file to "score" it against PIC and segment your file any way you want for targeted promotions.

Call your local Donnelley Marketing representative for more information!

Donnelley Marketing Inc.

The Consumer Information Source

East: 800 333-6169 ■ 203 353-7000
70 Seaview Ave., Stamford, CT 06902

West: 800 223-2160 ■ 714 538-1122
1111 E. Katella Ave., Suite 140, Orange, CA 92667

Central: 800 323-3685 ■ 708 495-1211 / 1279
1901 S. Meyers Rd., Oakbrook Terrace, IL 60181

Detroit: 313 746-6030
25800 Northwestern Hwy., Suite 875, Southfield, MI 48075

Stamford, CT 1 print 3/93 2500

Donnelley Marketing Inc.

Plus

Locate Better Prospects
Sharpen Your Targeting
Increase Your Sales

The DQI² Catalog Prospector *Plus* is a sophisticated method of identifying the most profitable new prospects for your catalog .

Donnelley Marketing will produce a statistical model based on your best customers. Then our entire Donnelley Quality Index² (DQI²) database of 86 million households and 140 million individuals is scored and ranked according to projected performance. This allows you to select only names with the highest rankings – your most qualified prospects.

Use DQI² Catalog Prospector *Plus* to mail with greater precision and maximize your revenues in the most effective way possible.

How the DQI² Catalog Prospector Plus Works:

- You supply Donnelley with a random sample of 10,000 of your current, best customers.
- These customer records are matched to our DQI² consumer database to add demographic, geographic and lifestyle information.
- Matched customer records are compared to a random sample of DQI² households.
- A regression model is developed which will identify your target audience.
- The entire DQI² database is ranked using a regression equation.
- Target segments are identified and prospects selected for your next catalog mailing.
- We recommend a verification mailing to evaluate the performance of the statistical model.

DQI² Catalog Prospector Plus PACKAGE

- $2,500.00 –
  Development of the Regression Model
- $45.00/M* –
  Rental of Modeled Names

*Broker Arrangements Available

Additional Costs:

- $10.00/M –
  Inclusion of DMIS ClusterPLUS℠ Codes
- $10.00/M –
  Inclusion of Claritas PRIZM® Codes

Donnelley Marketing Inc.

East: 800 433-5478
70 Seaview Ave., Stamford, CT 06902

Central: 800 323-3685
1901 S. Meyers Rd., Oakbrook Terrace, IL 60181

West: 800 223-2160
1111 E. Katella Ave., Suite 140, Orange, CA 92667

Detroit: 313 746-6030
25800 N. Western Hwy., Southfield, MI 48075

CONQUEST®
CONSUMER MARKETING INFORMATION SYSTEM
Total Information Power,
in One Powerful Source

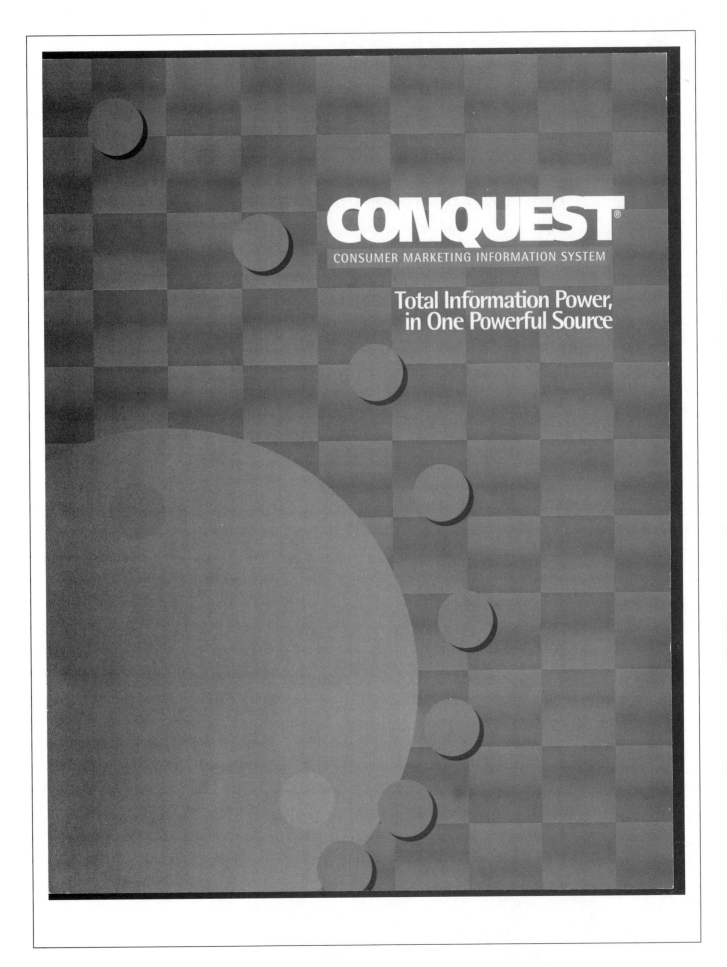

CONQUEST

The Power of Precise Information

Make the right decisions, right from the start

Getting enough information to make a decision used to be a problem; now the problem is information overload. How can you manage all of the available data in a manner which allows you to make accurate decisions? With CONQUEST. CONQUEST is more than a market research tool, more than a demographic retrieval system, more than a desktop mapping program. CONQUEST is a total marketing information solution.

The marketing power of CONQUEST

The power of CONQUEST is its ability to deliver, integrate, manipulate and analyze timely, accurate data in a way that helps you make better business decisions. Site selection. Market analysis. Customer profiling. Target marketing. Media planning. By putting the information you need right at your fingertips, in easy-to-interpret reports, maps, graphs and charts, CONQUEST puts your projects in a new perspective. It is an integrated, modular system for strategic problem solving.

Donnelley Marketing Information Services - The data powerhouse behind CONQUEST

The power behind CONQUEST is the power of information. Donnelley Marketing Information Services (DMIS) is the premier provider of demographic updates, geodemographic products and services, and marketing information services. With unique access to Dun & Bradstreet's powerful consumer and business databases and other leading information companies, DMIS can leverage an impressive array of data sources to build products that meet the ever changing needs of our customers.

The CONQUEST Advantage

Advertising Agencies/Media Companies

use CONQUEST to understand consumer purchasing and media behavior; provide account support and value-added market research services for client campaigns and new business development; design and implement strategic and tactical advertising and promotion plans; and to provide client accountability for promotion and ad spending.

Retail/Real Estate Industries

use CONQUEST for market and site analysis; identifying demographic trends; customer spotting and profiling; population projections; analyzing market potential; determining store mix; store clustering; competitive analysis; and strategic planning.

Financial Services Marketers

use CONQUEST to understand the demographics, lifestyles and financial behavior of existing and potential customers; identify cross-selling opportunities; target high prospect consumers for direct marketing campaigns; evaluate existing locations and select sites for new branch/ATM locations; track regulatory compliance (CRA, HMDA, etc.); conduct commercial prospecting; and help identify merger and acquisition opportunities.

Packaged/Consumer Goods Companies

use CONQUEST for understanding consumer behavior and demographic trends; profiling customers; promotion planning and evaluation; micro-marketing; category management; BDI/CDI analysis; market and distribution planning; merchandising strategies; and value-added sales support.

Utilities/Telecommunications Companies

use CONQUEST to analyze market demand for new and existing services; understand customer lifestyles, attitudes and behavior; map service areas; forecast future demand; determine, implement and evaluate marketing programs; perform economic analyses; conduct strategic planning and commercial development.

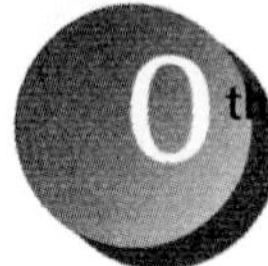

Other Industries

including cable TV, health care, insurance, direct marketing, business-to-business, manufacturing, transportation, consulting and government also use CONQUEST for various marketing, sales, advertising and strategic planning applications.

Accurate information, intelligently applied, equals success

It sounds very simple: accurate information, intelligently applied, equals success. Whether you're selecting the site for a new store, introducing a new brand of coffee or choosing where and how to spend your advertising dollars, the same questions apply: WHO are the customers, WHERE are they located, WHAT do they buy and HOW can they best be reached. CONQUEST gives you the answers, with applications and solutions for your specific industry.

CONQUEST System Features

- Proprietary block group-based current-year demographic estimates and five-year projections
- Precise data retrieval for geometric areas (i.e., circles, rings, bands, polygons, corridors, routes, etc.) using more than six million census blocks
- 2,000+ demographic variables at 14 levels of census, postal, marketing and media geography
- National geographic boundary file access for five-digit ZIP codes, 1990 block groups, census tracts, MCDs, counties, states, MSAs and CMSAs, Nielsen DMAs and SCANTRACK markets, Arbitron ADIs and IRI InfoScan markets
- Interactive trade area delineation and on-screen digitizing
- Enhanced TIGER-based street mapping
- Batch and individual point-coding and geocoding of addresses
- Standard and custom reports
- File Import/Export capabilities (i.e., dBASE, ASCII, DIF, Lotus, Atlas BNA, MapInfo MIF)
- Data linkages to popular geographic information systems (GIS) and desktop mapping programs including Atlas GIS
- Access to more than 40 industry-specific statistical and point-coded databases
- Utilizes CD-ROM technology for easy data storage and fast data retrieval
- Application software and databases are modular in design so you license only what you need
- System can be licensed at National, Regional and State levels with multi-year and multiple copy discounts available

The Power of CONQUEST at Work

Whatever your industry or application, CONQUEST's integrated, modular approach will provide strategic information upon which you can act with assurance.

Site Selection

Expand into profitable new markets. Analyze potential sites. Evaluate a competitive acquisition. Reassess existing locations. CONQUEST is <u>the</u> site selection tool for the '90s and beyond.

Whether you're targeting metropolitan areas, counties, census tracts, block groups or even street corners, CONQUEST's comprehensive databases provide the crucial information you need to select the right site: number of households, population projections, income, ethnicity, retail sales, daytime population, business activity, traffic counts, shopping centers, competitor locations, street networks and more. You can even integrate your own data and sales prediction models to rank your markets and sites.

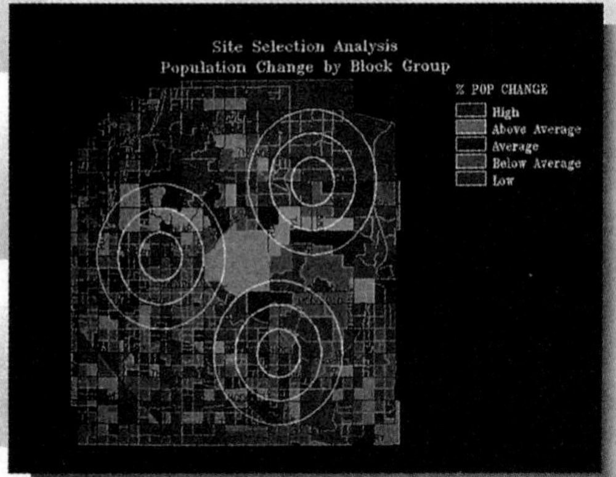

CONQUEST gives real estate and market analysts the competitive edge to succeed, at a very affordable price. It provides everything from data to boundaries to street maps to geocoding, not just market by market but for the entire U.S. And CONQUEST can now be integrated with popular desktop mapping programs, including Atlas GIS, to enhance your mapping performance and presentation.

Target Marketing

It used to be enough to know your customers' age and income. Now, in the era of target and micro-marketing, you need to know much, much more. Because your customer is getting more sophisticated and their needs more complex. CONQUEST answers the who, what, when, where and how of consumer demographics, so you can reach your customers effectively and expand your customer base.

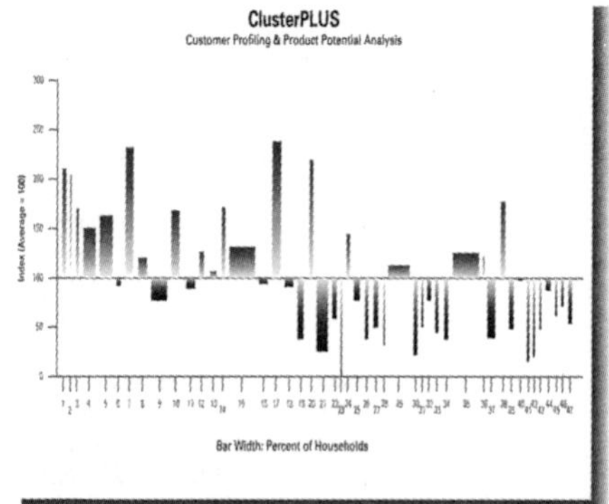

ClusterPLUS,® DMIS' lifestyle segmentation system gives you the edge by helping you identify the key market segments within your customer base. Whether you use your own information or turn to syndicated data sources, ClusterPLUS provides levels of detailed information about your customers—and potential customers—that will enhance your ability to penetrate new markets, successfully introduce new products, produce high impact advertising and more. You will communicate with your customers more effectively and efficiently, because you'll be speaking their language.

With CONQUEST and ClusterPLUS, target marketing, customer profiling and market segmentation applications can be handled quickly and productively. You'll spend more time strategizing and less time researching.

Market Analysis

CONQUEST is a powerful tool for analyzing markets and evaluating their potential. And CONQUEST provides the control, flexibility and information to base the analysis on, including demographics, consumer lifestyles, retail sales, product potential, business concentration or any combination of these factors.

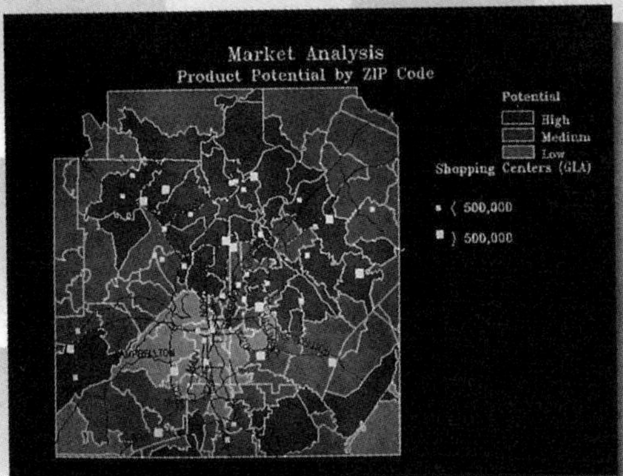

Want to know what markets have a high concentration of likely customers for your new product? Need to identify ZIP codes with incomes of $50,000 or more for a direct mail drop? How about identifying business concentrations for a new sales territory? When it comes to questions about macro and micro-market analysis, CONQUEST provides the answers quickly.

Once you define your target audience, CONQUEST's analytic capabilities allow you to scan the country to find and evaluate areas meeting your specific criteria. From ZIP codes, counties, cities and MSAs across the U.S. to block groups and census tracts within specific trade areas, CONQUEST lets you identify and map markets with high potential. With CONQUEST, you can analyze and display your target audience by number, penetration, index or however you want. And standard and custom reports will support your marketing, advertising, sales and strategic planning efforts.

Advertising & Media Planning

Advertising used to be pretty much a one medium, take it or leave it affair. Consumers didn't have much of a choice and neither did advertisers. Today, there are scores of options for both. CONQUEST can help you choose the best place to put your media dollars, from a mix which may include in-store, outdoor, print, network, spot and cable television, radio and direct response.

CONQUEST's key advantage is its ability to match buying behavior with media usage, helping you target specific or hard-to-reach audiences. By linking Simmons Market Research Bureau, Mediamark Research, Inc., Nielsen and Arbitron media databases with DMIS' ClusterPLUS lifestyles, CONQUEST becomes your most important media planning tool.

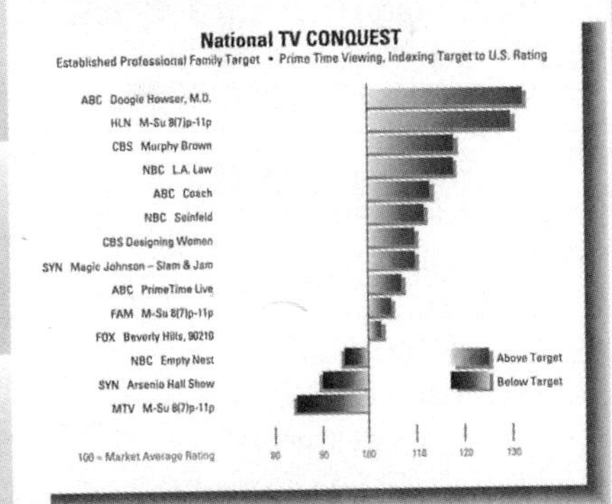

With TV CONQUEST,* you can analyze both national and local Nielsen ratings data against ClusterPLUS lifestyles to identify TV shows, dayparts and formats which match audience profiles for various products and services. Find programs which index higher than the national average for your products. At the local level, data can be profiled for specific DMAs or even individual trade areas. That's the power and flexibility of CONQUEST.

CONQUEST Databases

CONQUEST's modular design offers the ultimate in flexibility, allowing you to select exactly the databases you need.

Demographic Databases

- 1990 and Historical Census Data
- Current Year Demographic Estimates and Five-Year Projections
- Income By Age of Head of Household
- ClusterPLUS® Consumer Lifestyles
- Hispanic Portraits

Geographic Files

- 1990 Census Geographic Boundary Files
- 1990 Census Enhanced TIGER Files
- Metropolitan Street Files
- Interstates, U.S. & State Highways

Business and Financial Databases

- Affluence Model
- Dun's BusinessLine™ Registry (Business Locations)
- Dun's BusinessLine™ Basics (Summary Statistics)
- Financial Registry
- WealthWISE™ Financial Segmentation System

Retail Databases

- CAPCrime® Vulnerability Index
- Market Potential™ Retail Expenditures
- Progressive Grocer Trade Dimensions
- RE-COUNT Restaurants
- Shopping CenterProfile

Media Databases

- A.C. Nielsen National (NTI) TV Ratings Data
- A.C. Nielsen Local (NSI) TV Ratings Data
- Cable TV Franchise Boundaries
- NHI Cable On-Line Data Exchange (CODE)
- Yellow Page Directory Areas

Health Care Databases

- Ambulatory Demand
- Hospital Utilization
- ICD-9 Surgical Procedures
- MDC/DRG Forecasts
- Physician Specialty Counts
- Physician Reference File
- Provider of Services

Product Profiles

- Mediamark Research, Inc. (MRI)
- Nielsen Household Services (NHS)
- NPD CREST
- Simmons Market Research Bureau (SMRB)

Dun's Marketing Database

Your Richest Source of Business-to-Business Information

In today's competitive business environment, successful marketing programs are built upon the Dun's Marketing Database, a secure foundation of high-quality information.

The Dun's Marketing Database® helps you construct a solid framework for your sales and marketing efforts.

As the cornerstone of Dun's Marketing Services' vast array of products and services, our database gives you complete and essential building blocks to use in creating a results-oriented marketing program. You can choose your market from more than 9 million businesses and 10 million key executives ... and contact your highest-potential prospects through a wide array of selectivity options.

This powerful information base, combined with the expertise of your Dun's Marketing Services account executive, can provide you with real solutions to your sales and marketing needs. Just give us your current marketing challenge — then watch how we work with you to deliver results.

EMPLOYEES
SALES $740,000,000
TOTAL: 6,100
NUMBER OF
ACCOUNTS:
D-U-N-S N-U-M-B-E-R:
01-050-0108
SIC 1
SIC 2
SIC 3
STATUS:
MFG HQ SUB
DONALD C CONRAD, JR
MARTIN C GUNTHER
LAWRENCE CATHLESS
SECRETARY
CHAIRMAN

Dun's Marketing Database

Comprehensive coverage — for access to all your prospects

The vast size and scope of the Dun's Marketing Database assures that whether you define your market by geography, line of business, size, or other criteria, we'll deliver prospects. Our broad coverage also ensures that you will receive a complete and accurate representation of your overall market.

Because the Dun's Marketing Database captures more than 28,000 updates every day, it will also respond to your demands for quality, up-to-date information. As your priorities change or your markets shift, the dynamic information in the Dun's Marketing Database will keep you on top of your most important markets.

Quality that delivers results

The uncompromising quality, commitment, and expertise of Dun & Bradstreet is available to marketers only through the Dun's Marketing Database. Built with the extraordinary information resources of Dun & Bradstreet, the worldwide leading provider of business information, the Dun's Marketing Database is distinguished by the depth of information on each business in the file and its breadth of coverage in the marketplace. It's the kind of quality that will help generate a favorable return on your investment.

Our superior quality begins with the Dun & Bradstreet business analyst — the core of our information-gathering system. D&B business analysts are highly educated and skilled business professionals who are experts in evaluating businesses. More than 1,300 D&B business analysts worldwide use their expertise to conduct more than 2 million credit report revisions, backed by over 10 million face-to-face, telephone and mail interviews.

Once the information gathered by an analyst enters our system, it is supported by one of the most sophisticated and extensive information-gathering networks in the world. Numerous supplemental sources are used to enhance the business analyst's input, while an array of computerized cross-checks and data verification efforts assure you information that is timely, reliable, and useful.

Selectivity to find your most promising prospects

Give us the names and traits of your best customers, and we'll find more just like them. First, we match the characteristics of your customers against the more than 9 million businesses in the Dun's Marketing Database — to find your total prospect universe. Then, with Dun's Marketing Services' selectivity options, we'll further refine your prospect list to identify and target your highest-potential prospects. Our selectivity permits you to define your market by the parameters most important and most applicable to your business — by geography, industry, company sales or number of employees, executive name or functional title ... and, by many other criteria, some of which you won't find anywhere else. The flexibility of our database will help you find new prospects in existing markets, establish a prospect base for a specific market segment, or target unique markets that you define.

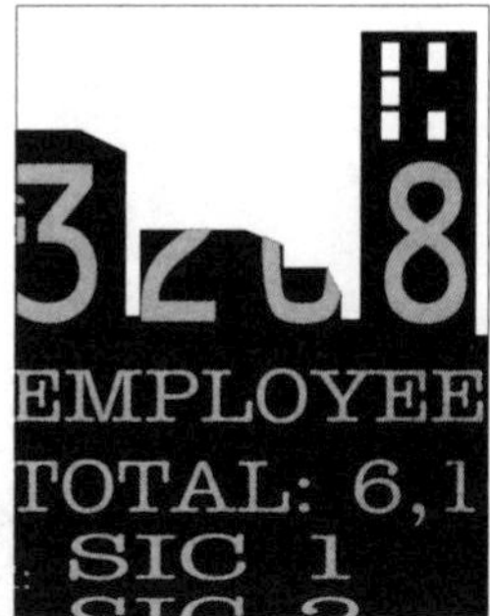

Define your market to the most precise level—with Standard Industrial Classification (SIC) 2+2

When you need to contact your particular niche markets, Dun's SIC 2+2[SM] will help locate them for you. Expanding the U.S.

Your richest source of business-to-business information

Government's four-digit Standard Industrial Classification system, Dun's SIC 2+2 gives you new power to segment your market into precisely defined activities. An additional two levels of business industry definition let you pinpoint areas of high specialization, base planning on a more finite level of detail, and develop markets for specialized products or services.

If you market to emerging or hi-tech industries, you'll find all the niches of today's advanced markets. Dun's SIC 2+2 will help you find prospects for computer manufacturers, computer graphics services, data verification services, optical scanning services — and a whole host of other related areas. Whatever your hi-tech specialization, Dun's SIC 2+2 can help you identify hard-to-locate prospects for your unique products.

Organized sales prospecting made easy

However you align your salesforce — by geographic territory, market segment or company size — the Dun's Marketing Database makes it easy to direct your people to their best prospects. Your order can be sequenced by ZIP code, sales volume, employee size, or other criteria, to help you easily divide prospect records into sales territories. Better organization means better control — and that produces results.

Corporate linkage information for targeted account planning

The Dun's Marketing Database offers you another vital component in selling to today's complex business environment — corporate family tree information. Our unique Data Universal Numbering System (D-U-N-S® Number) enables us to link the records of related corporate family members. Dun's Marketing Services' corporate family linkage capabilities give you the insight to identify which companies are related, the different levels within the corporate family, and who the highest decision-making authority is and where it is located. With this information, you can:

- Plan national account strategies more effectively.
- Develop centralized purchasing proposals that drive volume discounts.
- Tailor your offer to the needs of the entire corporate structure of your customer.

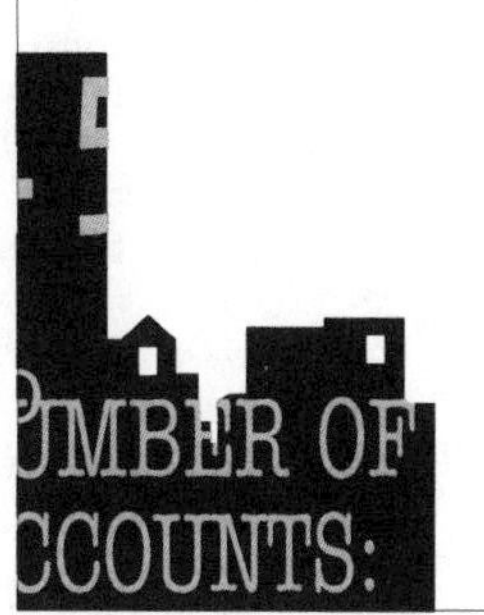

Depth of detail ... for improved selling

The more your salespeople know about a prospect, the better they can customize their presentation to that company's needs. Each record in the Dun's Marketing Database helps your salespeople leverage their skills by telling them vital facts about the prospect.

Just how many facts? *You* decide. The Dun's Marketing Database is available in a variety of formats developed to meet your specific information and budget requirements. If you need quick background information, our basic format gives you company name and address, sales volume, chief executive officer, number of employees, year started, and several other key bits of information about each prospect.

More in-depth information formats have been designed to meet the needs of companies with specialized selling techniques. Our enhanced formats provide you with valuable supplemental information, such as three- or five-year growth trends for sales and employment figures ... real estate information that includes square footage and an owns/rents indicator ... and important data about banking and accounting firm relationships.

Finally, if your marketing objectives require contacting a broad range of executives within the same company, you can obtain a list with the available names of a company's most influential decision-makers. Our most expanded record format puts "executive names" right at your fingertips.

Objective: Increase Your Sales Prospecting Power

Solution #1:
Dun's Telemarketing Lead Service – Ideal for organizing your telemarketing sales and prospecting programs.

Identify and reach prospects faster with 5" x 3" cards that include:

- Complete mailing or physical street address
- SIC Codes, up to 6 codes at the 8-digit level
- Manufacturing site indicator
- D-U-N-S® Number
- Tradestyle
- City, State & ZIP+4
- CEO name and title
- Line of business description
- Number of employees
- Magnetic tape and PC diskette formats.

You can order Dun's Telephone One Line Listings (T.O.L.L.) with company name, city, state and phone number on one line, on continuous form printout.

Solution #2:
Enhanced Dun's Market Identifiers Prospecting Cards – In-depth information to help plan your sales calls.

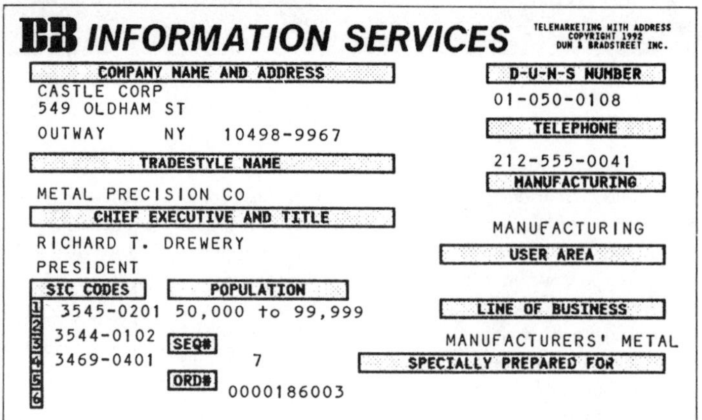

D&B INFORMATION SERVICES
TELEMARKETING WITH ADDRESS
COPYRIGHT 1992
DUN & BRADSTREET INC.

COMPANY NAME AND ADDRESS
CASTLE CORP
549 OLDHAM ST
OUTWAY NY 10498-9967

D-U-N-S NUMBER
01-050-0108

TELEPHONE
212-555-0041

TRADESTYLE NAME
METAL PRECISION CO

MANUFACTURING
MANUFACTURING

CHIEF EXECUTIVE AND TITLE
RICHARD T. DREWERY
PRESIDENT

USER AREA

SIC CODES
1 3545-0201
2 3544-0102
3 3469-0401
4
5
6

POPULATION
50,000 to 99,999

SEQ#
7

ORD#
0000186003

LINE OF BUSINESS
MANUFACTURERS' METAL

SPECIALLY PREPARED FOR

Each company record on Dun's Telemarketing Lead Service is provided on a 5" x 3" card to identify prospects quickly and easily.

REQUEST ITEM 1

Plan sales calls according to your prospects' business profiles with:

- Business name, street address, mailing address, telephone number and CEO name
- Activity by SIC Codes and lines of business
- Company size by sales volume and number of employees
- Organizational information such as parent/subsidiary, headquarters/branch and year started
- Executive names – in addition to the CEO, you can select up to three other executive contacts who influence buying decisions
- Expanded linkage – Enhanced Dun's Market Identifiers include the names of parent and ultimate corporate family members to make your national account planning easier and more effective
- Narrative descriptions of all numeric codes, including SICs and geographic codes.

REQUEST ITEM 2

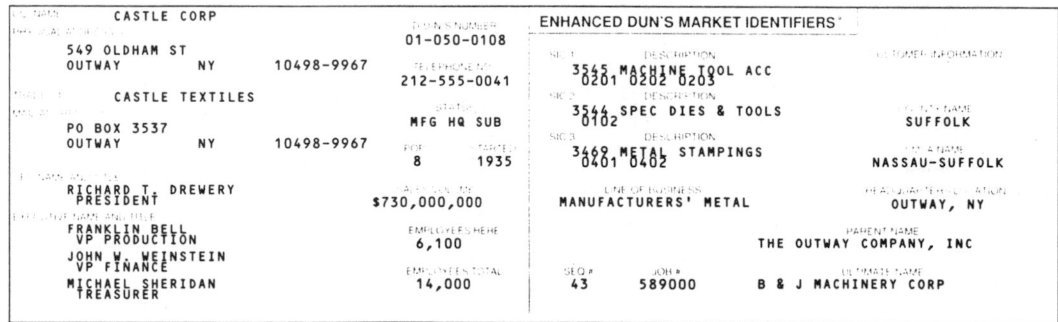

CASTLE CORP
549 OLDHAM ST
OUTWAY NY 10498-9967
CASTLE TEXTILES
PO BOX 3537
OUTWAY NY 10498-9967
RICHARD T. DREWERY
PRESIDENT
EXECUTIVE NAME AND TITLE
FRANKLIN BELL
VP PRODUCTION
JOHN W. WEINSTEIN
VP FINANCE
MICHAEL SHERIDAN
TREASURER

D-U-N-S NUMBER
01-050-0108
TELEPHONE NO
212-555-0041
STATUS
MFG HQ SUB
POP 8
STARTED 1935
SALES VOLUME
$730,000,000
EMPLOYEES HERE
6,100
EMPLOYEES TOTAL
14,000

ENHANCED DUN'S MARKET IDENTIFIERS
SIC 1 DESCRIPTION
3545 MACHINE TOOL ACC
0201 0202 0203
SIC 2 DESCRIPTION
3544 SPEC DIES & TOOLS
0102
SIC 3 DESCRIPTION
3469 METAL STAMPINGS
0401 0402
LINE OF BUSINESS
MANUFACTURERS' METAL
SEQ # 43
JOB # 589000

CUSTOMER INFORMATION
COUNTY NAME
SUFFOLK
MSA NAME
NASSAU-SUFFOLK
HEADQUARTERS LOCATION
OUTWAY, NY
PARENT NAME
THE OUTWAY COMPANY, INC
ULTIMATE NAME
B & J MACHINERY CORP

The 10" x 3" Enhanced Dun's Market Identifiers card provides a quick overview of a prospect to help salespeople evaluate potential and plan their approach.

38

Solution #3:
Enhanced Dun's Market Identifiers PLUS – Adds multiple executive contacts, banking and accounting firm affiliations and more.

Put even more prospect profile information in your hands with:

- Up to four executive contacts per company
- Banking and accounting firm affiliations
- Legal status
- Owns/rents indicator and square footage of floor space
- Territory served and number of accounts
- Three-year business trends including an analysis of the company's growth or decline of sales and employees.

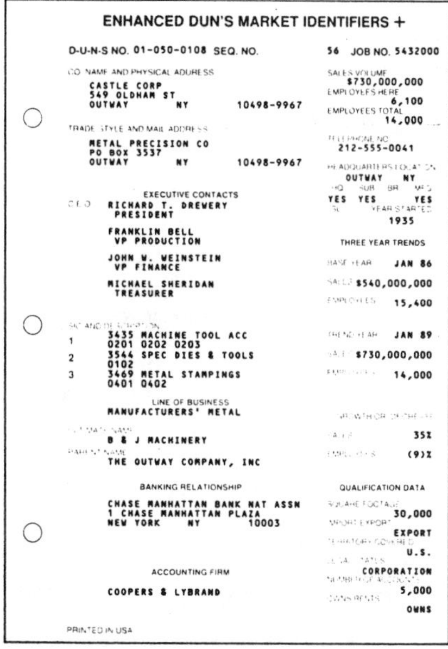

ENHANCED DUN'S MARKET IDENTIFIERS +

D-U-N-S NO. 01-050-0108 SEQ. NO. 56 JOB NO. 5432000

CO. NAME AND PHYSICAL ADDRESS
CASTLE CORP
549 OLDHAM ST
OUTWAY NY 10498-9967

TRADE STYLE AND MAIL ADDRESS
METAL PRECISION CO
PO BOX 3537
OUTWAY NY 10498-9967

EXECUTIVE CONTACTS
C.E.O. RICHARD T. DREWERY
PRESIDENT
FRANKLIN BELL
VP PRODUCTION
JOHN W. WEINSTEIN
VP FINANCE
MICHAEL SHERIDAN
TREASURER

SIC AND DESCRIPTION
1 3435 MACHINE TOOL ACC
0201 0202 0203
2 3544 SPEC DIES & TOOLS
0102
3 3469 METAL STAMPINGS
0401 0402

LINE OF BUSINESS
MANUFACTURERS' METAL

ULTIMATE NAME
B & J MACHINERY
PARENT NAME
THE OUTWAY COMPANY, INC

BANKING RELATIONSHIP
CHASE MANHATTAN BANK NAT ASSN
1 CHASE MANHATTAN PLAZA
NEW YORK NY 10003

ACCOUNTING FIRM
COOPERS & LYBRAND

SALES VOLUME
$730,000,000
EMPLOYEES HERE
6,100
EMPLOYEES TOTAL
14,000

TELEPHONE NO
212-555-0041

HEADQUARTERS LOCATION
OUTWAY NY
HQ SUB BR MFG
YES YES YES
YEAR STARTED
1935

THREE YEAR TRENDS
BASE YEAR JAN 86
SALES $540,000,000
EMPLOYEES 15,400
TREND YEAR JAN 89
SALES $730,000,000
EMPLOYEES 14,000

GROWTH OR DECREASE
SALES 35%
EMPLOYEES (9)%

QUALIFICATION DATA
SQUARE FOOTAGE
30,000
IMPORT EXPORT
EXPORT
TERRITORY COVERED
U.S.
LEGAL STATUS
CORPORATION
NUMBER OF ACCOUNTS
5,000
OWNS RENTS
OWNS

PRINTED IN USA

REQUEST ITEM 3

Enhanced Dun's Market Identifiers Plus information is provided on handy 6" x 8" cards, giving you in-depth information at your fingertips.

Solution #4:
Dun's Executive Marketing Summaries® – The ultimate sales prospecting tool.

Get all of the marketing information D&B has collected on the companies you are targeting on one easy-to-read form, including:

- Complete identification information (review of activities in descriptive form)
- Corporate linkages
- Banking and accounting firm relationships
- Square footage of floor space
- Growth or decline trends by sales and employees
- Names and titles of executives identified at that location.

REQUEST ITEM 4

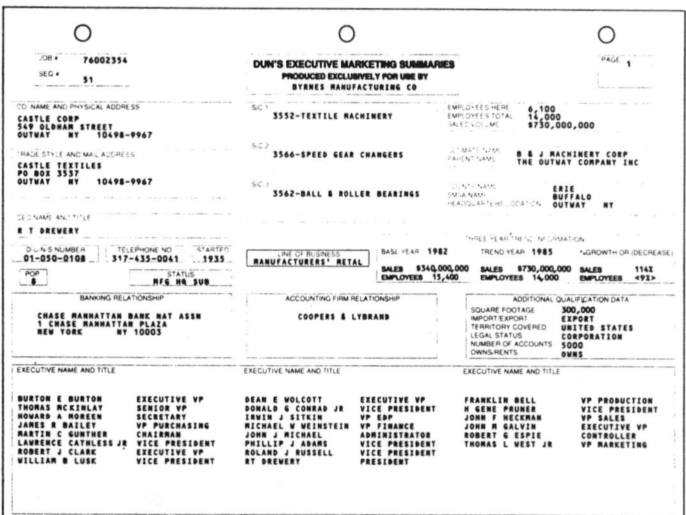

JOB # 76002354
SEQ # 51

DUN'S EXECUTIVE MARKETING SUMMARIES
PRODUCED EXCLUSIVELY FOR USE BY
BYRNES MANUFACTURING CO

PAGE 1

CO NAME AND PHYSICAL ADDRESS
CASTLE CORP
549 OLDHAM STREET
OUTWAY NY 10498-9967

TRADE STYLE AND MAIL ADDRESS
CASTLE TEXTILES
PO BOX 3537
OUTWAY NY 10498-9967

CEO NAME AND TITLE
R T DREWERY

D-U-N-S NUMBER 01-050-0108 | TELEPHONE NO 317-435-0041 | STARTED 1935
POP 8 | STATUS MFG HQ SUB

SIC 1 3552-TEXTILE MACHINERY
SIC 2 3566-SPEED GEAR CHANGERS
SIC 3 3562-BALL & ROLLER BEARINGS

EMPLOYEES HERE 6,100
EMPLOYEES TOTAL 14,000
SALES VOLUME $730,000,000

ULTIMATE NAME B & J MACHINERY CORP
PARENT NAME THE OUTWAY COMPANY INC

COUNTY NAME ERIE
SMSA NAME BUFFALO
HEADQUARTERS LOCATION OUTWAY NY

LINE OF BUSINESS
MANUFACTURERS' METAL

THREE YEAR TREND INFORMATION

BASE YEAR 1982	TREND YEAR 1985	%GROWTH OR (DECREASE)
SALES $340,000,000	SALES $730,000,000	SALES 114%
EMPLOYEES 15,400	EMPLOYEES 14,000	EMPLOYEES <9%>

BANKING RELATIONSHIP
CHASE MANHATTAN BANK NAT ASSN
1 CHASE MANHATTAN PLAZA
NEW YORK NY 10003

ACCOUNTING FIRM RELATIONSHIP
COOPERS & LYBRAND

ADDITIONAL QUALIFICATION DATA
SQUARE FOOTAGE 300,000
IMPORT/EXPORT EXPORT
TERRITORY COVERED UNITED STATES
LEGAL STATUS CORPORATION
NUMBER OF ACCOUNTS 5000
OWNS/RENTS OWNS

EXECUTIVE NAME AND TITLE		EXECUTIVE NAME AND TITLE		EXECUTIVE NAME AND TITLE	
BURTON E BURTON	EXECUTIVE VP	DEAN E WOLCOTT	EXECUTIVE VP	FRANKLIN BELL	VP PRODUCTION
THOMAS MCKINLAY	SENIOR VP	DONALD G CONRAD JR	VICE PRESIDENT	H GENE PRUNER	VICE PRESIDENT
HOWARD A MOREEN	SECRETARY	IRWIN J SITKIN	VP EDP	JOHN F HECKMAN	VP SALES
JAMES R BAILEY	VP PURCHASING	MICHAEL W WEINSTEIN	VP FINANCE	JOHN M GALVIN	EXECUTIVE VP
MARTIN C GUNTHER	CHAIRMAN	JOHN J MICHAEL	ADMINISTRATOR	ROBERT G ESPIE	CONTROLLER
LAWRENCE CATHLESS JR	VICE PRESIDENT	PHILLIP J ADAMS	VICE PRESIDENT	THOMAS L WEST JR	VP MARKETING
ROBERT J CLARK	EXECUTIVE VP	ROLAND J RUSSELL	VICE PRESIDENT		
WILLIAM B LUSK	VICE PRESIDENT	RT DREWERY	PRESIDENT		

With Dun's Executive Marketing Summaries all of the marketing information available on a company is provided for you on an 11" x 8 1/2" form.

Objective: *Reach Key Executives and Proven Responders . . . Personally, By Job Function*

Solution #1:
Dun's Decision Makers – 11 million executive names and titles when you need to reach people with clout.

Reach the key executives who make decisions about your products and services. Specify titles or areas of responsibility within each of your prospect companies by the following criteria:

- SIC Code
- Employee Size
- Sales Volume
- Title
- Responsibility Grouping
- Age Indicator
- Gender.

Executives by Title

Dun's Decision Makers identify over 11 million senior and middle management names and titles. So when you have to reach people with clout — you *do* reach people with clout.

The counts in the box below show the number of available executives.

Executives by Responsibility

Since, in many cases, an individual's title does not fully describe his or her complete responsibilities, D&B has identified each decision maker's full scope of responsibilities. As a result, you can target not only by titles, but, also by the responsibility for a given area. Listed to the right are counts of those executives:

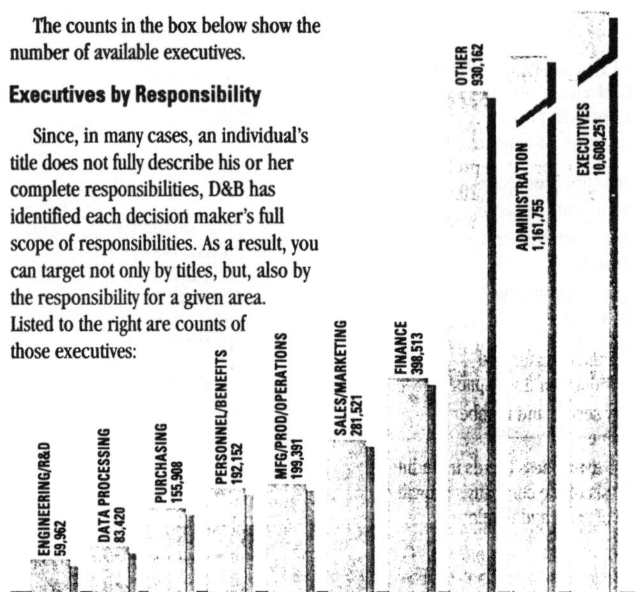

REQUEST ITEM 5
(Dun's Decision Makers)

At-A-Glance Counts

Group Selection	Group Counts
Owners	2,534,862
Partners	1,198,307
Chairman	141,435
Vice Chairman	11,508
Other Chairman	775
President	2,646,318
Vice President	1,342,070
Secretary	1,314,400
Treasurers	1,183,082
Managers	401,171
Trustees	12,734
Executives	1,103
Principals	245,063
Superintendents	17,262
Venturers	1,549
Counsels	5,616
Sales Executives	215,549
Marketing Executives	17,137
Operations Executives	21,627
Manufacturing Executives	146,210
Finance Executives	227,062
Controllers	99,288
Production Executives	7,974

Group Selection	Group Counts
Data Processing Executives	86,173
Engineering Executives	42,605
Research & Development Executives	4,299
Other Officers	13,281
Clerks	62,855
Purchasing Executives	140,490
Executive Vice Presidents	57,774
Senior Vice Presidents	41,258
Chief Executive Officers	91,255
Accounting Executives	28,817
Administrative Executives	148,397
Religious Executives	55,501
Government Executives	30,515
Transportation Executives	1,121
School Library Executives	2,952
Club/Lodge/ Organization Executives	5,839
Agents	13,180
Personnel/Human Resources/ Benefit Executives	223,258
Facilities/ Maintenance Executives	4,551

Group Selection	Group Counts
Publishing Executives	2,452
Public Relations Executives	1,003
Medical Executives	45,716
Dental Executives	16,481
Legal Executives	9,521
Banking/Credit Executives	2,757
Wholesale/Retail Executives	5,326
Training & Development Executives	423
Chief Operating Officers	11,038
Chief Financial Officers	34,134
Other Executives	26,179
Management Executives	207,976
Other Personnel	20,144
Sales & Marketing Vice Presidents	29,132
Manufacturing/Operations/ Production Vice Presidents	25,022
Finance Vice Presidents	39,219
Purchasing Vice Presidents	11,014
Engineering Vice Presidents	5,155
Geographic Responsibility Management	732,120

40

Solution #2:
Dun's American Executive Registry™ – Increase direct marketing results with proven responders.

Executives who have responded one or more times to direct response offers are HOT prospects. Dun's American Executive Registry can help increase the return on your direct marketing investment by providing names and titles of executives who have responded to previous direct response programs.

Here's what you get:

- Over 100 response lists matched with the D&B information base
- An unduplicated list of over 15 million executive names
- Names, titles, addresses and telephone numbers of senior and middle management executives who are proven direct mail responders
- Over 20 selectors for targeting
- Ability to select by multiple responses
- Ability to select subscribers, book buyers, seminar attendees and other types of direct mail responders
- Prospect selections by special interests, gender and age.

Top Management

Title:	Count:
Chairman	128,654
Board Member	15,348
Division President	404
Owner	2,631,789
President	2,598,996
Corporate Secretary	1,192,665
Senior Vice President	93,751
Vice Chairman	9,594
Chief Executive Officer	86,487
Chief Operating Officer	9,096
VP, Planning	52
VP, Corporate Development	6
VP, Mergers	2
Corporate Management	76,818
Executive Director	43,014
Secretary/Treasurer	7,949
Assistant Secretary	857
Partner	1,106,974
Other Top Executives, NEC	1,255
Total:	8,003,711

Administrative Executives

Title:	Count:
VP, Government Relations	8
VP, Administration	19,353
VP, Public Relations	134
VP, Stockholder Affairs	0
Office Manager	49,005
VP, Corporate Affairs	1
Manager, Planning	6,916
Manager, Security	310
Manager, Government Relations	14
Administrative Manager	12,501
Public Relations Manager	2,949
General Manager	139,326
Division Vice President	519
Government Official	3,725
Division Manager	8,253
Other Administrative Executives, NEC	354,354
Total:	597,368

Clerical

Title:	Count:
Secretary	19,917
Executive Secretary	2,596
Administrative Assistant	12,186
Clerk	1,426
Total:	36,125

Corporate/Legal Staff

Title:	Count:
VP, Legal	13
Counsel	3,490
Licensing Executive	17
Other Legal Executives, NEC	1,004
Total:	4,524

Data Processing Executives

Title:	Count:
VP, Information Systems	2,000
Programming Manager	2,324
System Support Manager	6,335
DP Operations Manager	16,612
Telecommunications Manager	19,402
DP Project Manager	15
Systems Analyst	4,707
Programmer/Analyst	8,653
Manager, Information Systems	10,532
System Engineer	4,015
Other DP Executives, NEC	119,998
Total:	194,593

Engineering Executives

Title:	Count:
Engineering Manager	17,224
VP, Engineering	4,357
VP, Research & Technology	330
VP, Product Development	114
Plant Engineering Manager	317
Production Engineering Manager	473
Design Engineering Manager	73,165
Industrial Engineering Manager	815
Draftsman	19,546
Packaging Engineering Manager	29
Research & Development Manager	3,521
Product Development Manager	0
Scientific Executive	37,223
Research & Technical Director	6,817
Engineer	285,113
Aeronautical Engineer	0
Chemical Engineer	431
Civil Engineer	2
Mechanical Engineer	7
Design Engineer	65
Manufacturing Engineer	8,243
Production Engineer	2,651
Industrial Engineer	44
Quality Control Engineer	1
Plastics Engineer	0
Computer Engineer	0
Plant Engineer	0
Technical/Engineering Manager	2,979
Other Engineering Executives, NEC	194,706
Total:	658,173

Financial Executives

Title:	Count:
Chief Financial Officer	24,696
Controller	94,219
Treasurer	1,080,356
VP, Finance	8,829
VP, Accounting	63
Senior Finance Executive	1,462
Auditing Manager	70
Tax Manager	22
Credit Manager	1,462
Accounting Manager	3,402
Investment Manager	188
Stockbroker	3
Banking Executive	7,976
Business Manager	11,391
Auditor	1,704
Assistant Treasurer	9,737
Senior Banking Executive	529
Finance Manager	4,979
Other Finance Executives, NEC	211,696
Total:	1,462,784

Human Resources/ Personnel Executives

Title:	Count:
VP, Personnel	1,701
Personnel Director	13,825
Director, Employee Affairs	712
Training Director	13,754
Compensation Manager	145
Benefits Manager	2,554
Safety Director	57
Human Resources Manager	6,054
Manager, Health Administration	23
Other Personnel Executives, NEC	197,956
Total:	236,781

International Executives

Title:	Count:
VP, International	52
International Director	72
Export Manager	123
Import Manager	13
Other International Executives, NEC	1,361
Total:	1,621

Manufacturing/Production/ Distribution Executives

Title:	Count:
Purchasing Director	52,999
Traffic Manager	3,553
Production Manager	71,960
VP, Purchasing	877
VP, Manufacturing	5,044
VP, Operations	5,133
VP, Production	1,159
Director of Traffic	26
Quality Control Manager	35,949
Foreman	17,849
Warehouse Manager	1,808
Inventory Manager	265
Materials Handling Manager	543
Facilities Manager	41,601
Distribution Manager	887
Manufacturing Manager	33,143
Operations Manager	40,795
Plant Manager	42,500
Purchasing Agent	26,388
Other Manufacturing Executives, NEC	251,447
Total:	633,926

Mid-Level Management Executives

Title:	Count:
Manager	653,321
Vice President	1,360,816
Director	258,496
Coordinator	19,769
Department Head	2,438
Supervisor	103,694
Branch Manager	651,754
Additional Top Management Executives	102,082
Total:	3,152,370

Professionals

Title:	Count:
Accountant	13,252
Attorney	7,792
Doctor	42,123
Dentist	15,145
Insurance Agent	38,107
Real Estate Agent	642
Architect	11,173
Clergyman	85
Nurse	472
Consultant	23,387
Librarian	3,768
Hospital Personnel	432
Total:	156,378

Sales–Marketing Executives

Title:	Count:
Advertising Manager	2,598
Sales Manager	32,938
Marketing Director	4,679
VP, Marketing	8,150
VP, Sales	11,776
VP, Merchandising	14
VP, Advertising	50
Sales Promotion Manager	280
Marketing Services Manager	13,752
Product Manager	2,713
Customer Services Manager	1,268
District Sales Manager	20
Account Executive	17,157
Buyer	28,777
Product Development Manager	641
Other Sales/ Marketing Executives, NEC	234,653
Total:	359,466

Services Executives

Title:	Count:
Food Service Executive	19
Air Transportation Executive	242
Service Executive	16,312
Hospitality Executive	3
Education Administrator	27,486
Communications Executive	5,266
Construction Executive	1,142
Publicity Executive	11,432
Total:	61,902

Executives by Number of Sources

The counts below show how many executives have responded to more than one business offer and appear on more than one list source.

Number of Sources	Count:
Two	1,534,567
Three	338,607
Four	131,360
Five	63,821
Six	34,634
Seven	21,039
Eight	13,249
Nine+	30,862

Recent Responders

Here are the hottest prospects! They need to be a part of your next direct mail plan. In the last year, over 1.5 million executive records have been noted on the file.

Year: 1992	Count:
1st Quarter	275,258
2nd Quarter	143,366
3rd Quarter	96,058
Year: 1991	**Count:**
4th Quarter	1,049,974

Executives by Interest

(Partial Listing of Key Interests)

Pinpoint your targets by selecting secondary interests of executives, based on past purchase and response information. Example: target CEOs with an interest in data processing. Listed below are some of the many different interests you can select by:

Interest	Count:
Finance	269,619
Banking	54,164
Business Administration	120,100
Self Improvement	67,755
Insurance	52,538
Real Estate	41,148
Investments	59,776
Manufacturing	1,062,278
Materials Handling	57,159
Quality Control	51,973
Packaging	138,813
Sales & Marketing	121,548
Retail Sales	128,203
Advertising	54,453
Conventions/Promotions	58,795
Microcomputers	107,120
Data Processing	260,424
Engineering	468,839
Design Engineering	147,034
Plant Engineering	108,257
Science	71,790
Electronics	134,316
Construction	147,072
Architecture	70,863
Petrochemicals/Fuel	46,920
Office Supply Management	79,741
Training & Management Development	69,229
Environment	83,884
Wholesale/Distribution	55,588
Traffic/Distribution	58,561
Auto Maintenance	112,989
Hospitality	146,848
Government	76,950
Human Resources	32,908
Corporate Travel	30,073
Communications	34,177
Energy	41,031

Source Type

(Gross counts based on multiple sources per executive; names appear on more than one type of list.)

Paid Subscribers	345,841
Controlled Circulation	4,839,680
Buyers	119,719
Book Buyers	416,424
Direct Response	79,430
Inquiriés	26,226
Seminar Attendees	72,857
Newsletters	3,357

Executives at Computer Sites

(Net counts without duplication among site selections)

IBM	46,644
DEC	24,996
Mainframes	44,934
Minicomputers	39,161
PC/Micro	24,657

Other Executive Selections

Female Executives	2,895,905

REQUEST ITEM 6

(Dun's American Executive Registry)

Objective: Improve Your Global Marketing Efforts

Solution:
The D&B Global File – Business information to help you compete worldwide.

When you need to know who your best international prospects are, D&B's Global File provides you with marketing and sales information on:

- 4 million businesses in 200 countries
- Linkage and family tree relationships on 1.7 million businesses.

With the Global File you get:

- Details on which companies are related
- Where a corporation has subsidiaries
- The highest decision making authority
- Corporate linkage starting with the parent company
- Subsidiaries around the world
- Ability to start with subsidiaries and trace back to owners or parent companies
- Other members of corporate families
- Information by number of employees, sales, primary line of business, corporate reporting level and countries.

Select your information by:

- D-U-N-S® Number of the business
- D-U-N-S® Number of parent company or owner
- Business name, address and phone number
- Line of business
- Number of employees
- Sales (in local currency)
- Standard Industrial Classification Code (SIC)
- CEO name
- Year started.

D&B will develop a personalized program to help you:

- Build a worldwide prospect database
- Uncover potential conflict of interest issues
- Identify risk exposures
- Pinpoint areas for business development
- Develop sales and planning analysis.

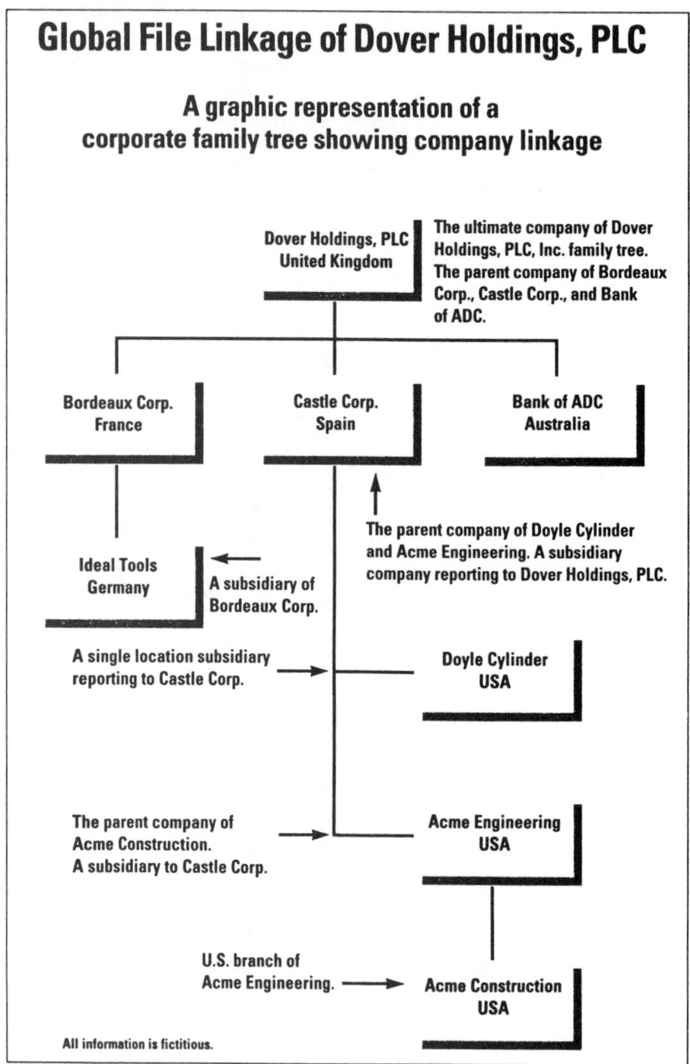
Global File Linkage of Dover Holdings, PLC
A graphic representation of a corporate family tree showing company linkage
Dover Holdings, PLC United Kingdom
The ultimate company of Dover Holdings, PLC, Inc. family tree. The parent company of Bordeaux Corp., Castle Corp., and Bank of ADC.
Bordeaux Corp. France
Castle Corp. Spain
Bank of ADC Australia
The parent company of Doyle Cylinder and Acme Engineering. A subsidiary company reporting to Dover Holdings, PLC.
Ideal Tools Germany
A subsidiary of Bordeaux Corp.
A single location subsidiary reporting to Castle Corp.
Doyle Cylinder USA
The parent company of Acme Construction. A subsidiary to Castle Corp.
Acme Engineering USA
U.S. branch of Acme Engineering.
Acme Construction USA
All information is fictitious.

Global File - Country Counts:

Country:	Count:	Country:	Count:	Country:	Count:	Country:	Count:
Algeria	135	Ecuador	2,353	Liechtenstein	2,092	San Marino	4
American Samoa	3	El Salvador	750	Lithuania	1	Sao Tome & Principe	1
Andorra	22	Ethiopia	69	Luxembourg	8,936	Saudi Arabia	602
Angola	68	Falkland Islands	2	Macao	31	Senegal	101
Anguilla	25	Fiji	94	Malagasy Republic	33	Seychelles	2
Antigua	48	Finland	2,011	Malawi	97	Sierra Leone	42
Arab Rep Of Egypt	225	French Guyana	90	Malaysia	3,586	Singapore	16,544
Argentina	12,532	France	249,973	Maldives	1	Solomon Islands	21
Aruba	451	French Polynesia	6	Mali	51	Somali Republic	16
Australia	96,949	Gabon Republic	121	Malta	109	South Africa	1,440
Austria	4,940	Gambia	8	Marshall Islands Rep.	3	Spain	153,111
Bahamas	1,083	Germany, Fed Rep Of	222,290	Martinique	272	Sri Lanka	203
Bahrain	108	Ghana	125	Mauritania	30	Sudan	59
Bangladesh	147	Gibraltar	118	Mauritius	121	Suriname	219
Barbados	1,004	Greece	1,996	Mexico	67,081	Swaziland	37
Belgium	138,320	Greenland	2	Micronesia Fed. St.	2	Sweden	9,992
Belize	147	Grenada	137	Monaco	646	Switzerland	117,802
Benin, Peoples Rep. Of	50	Guadaloupe	280	Montserrat	49	Syrian Arab Republic	55
Bermuda	1,448	Guam	447	Morocco	418	Taiwan (China, Rep. Of)	750
Bolivia	672	Guatemala	1,627	Mozambique	20	Tanzania	89
Botswana	58	Guinea, Republic Of	40	Namibia	23	Thailand	3,249
Brazil	90,627	Guinea-Bissau	9	Nepal	25	Togo	49
British Virgin Islands	203	Guyana	66	Netherlands	207,705	Tonga	6
Brunei	65	Haiti	592	Netherlands Antilles	1,882	Trinidad & Tobago	1,545
Bulgaria	6	Honduras	972	Nevis	11	Tunisia	209
Burkina Faso	47	Hong Kong	58,738	New Caledonia	40	Turkey	785
Burma (Myanmar)	24	Hungary	86	New Zealand	16,423	Turks & Caicos	44
Burundi	7	Iceland	1,671	Nicaragua	143	Uganda	98
Cameroon	189	India	983	Niger, Republic Of	33	UK-England	341,017
Canada	80,592	Indonesia	1,046	Nigeria	349	UK-Northern Ireland	6,072
Cape Verde	1	Iran	461	Northern Mariana Is.	6	UK-Scotland	20,899
Cayman Islands	617	Iraq	79	Norway	2,407	UK-Wales	10,894
Central African Republic	34	Ireland, Republic Of	16,370	Oman	157	United Arab Emirates	325
Chad	29	Israel	4,943	Pacific Islands	2	United Kingdom	6,619
Chile	12,798	Italy	501,290	Pakistan	344	United States	1,418,194
China, Peoples Republic	128	Ivory Coast Republic	241	Panama	2,567	Uruguay	556
China, Republic Of	5,718	Jamaica	1,111	Papua New Guinea	309	Vanuatu	42
Colombia	3,432	Japan	45,534	Paraguay	329	Venezuela	15,667
Comoro Islands	1	Jordan	109	Peru	15,526	Vietnam	1
Congo, Republic Of	71	Kampuchea	3	Philippines	2,042	Virgin Islands US	21
Cook Islands	59	Kenya	421	Poland	23	West Indies	16
Costa Rica	1,722	Khmer Republic	30	Portugal	85,163	Western Samoa	4
Croatia	1	Kirabati	1	Puerto Rico	19	Yemen Arab Republic	75
Cuba	9	Korea North	1	Qatar	73	Yemen Peoples Dem	1
Cyprus	216	Korea, Republic Of	5,102	Reunion Island	15	Yugoslavia	159
Czechoslovakia	21	Kuwait	260	Romania	1	Zaire	166
Denmark	5,289	Laos	1	Russian Federation	17	Zambia	214
Djibouti	8	Lebanon	57	Rwanda	7	Zimbabwe	440
Dominica	92	Lesotho	10	Saint Kitts	95	Total:	4,133,605
Dominican Republic	1,509	Liberia	758	Saint Lucia	232		
		Libyan Arab Republic	5	Saint Vincent	162		

REQUEST ITEM 7
(Global File)

MicroVision

Segment Summary Descriptions

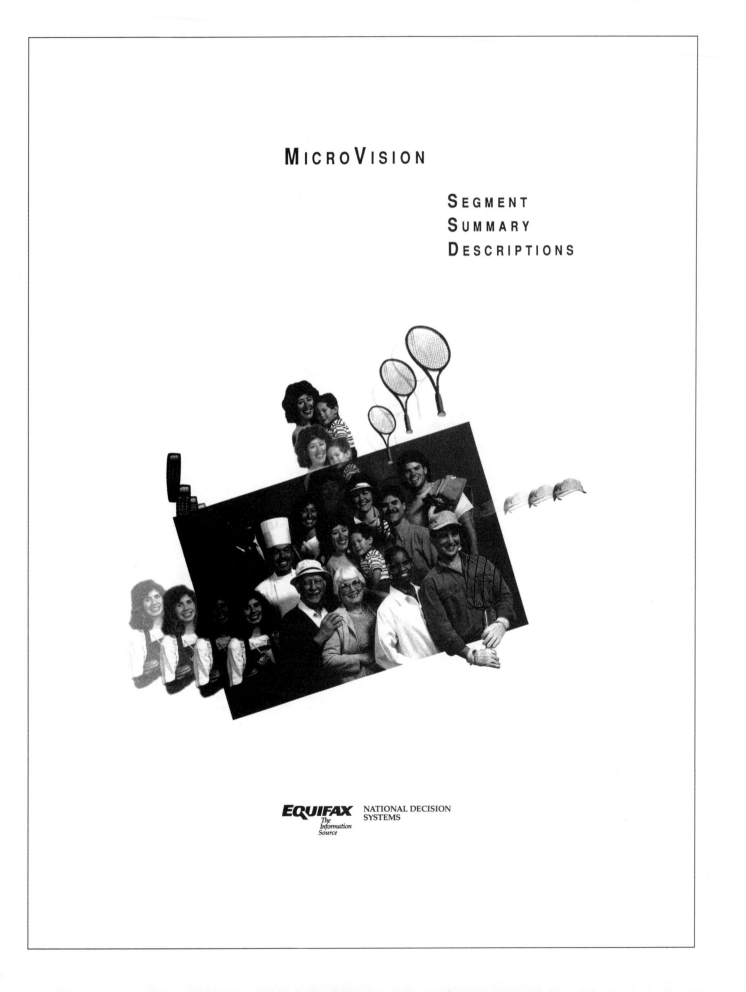

NATIONAL DECISION SYSTEMS

MicroVision

MicroVision™ is a revolutionary micro-geographic consumer targeting system created by National Decision Systems, a subsidiary of Equifax Marketing Decision Systems, Inc. It combines individual and census data, the ability to annually update market segment classifications, a lower level of geography (ZIP+4), and three distinct capabilities to create the most powerful customer segmentation tool available. This system was built with several objectives in mind:

- To take advantage of National Decision Systems' Equifax affiliation by incorporating individual consumer information from the Equifax Consumer Marketing Database (ECMD).
- To annually update the market segment classifications for 19 million ZIP+4s to account for population changes in geographic areas.
- To easily incorporate the 1990 Census data as soon as it is available.
- To use the smallest level of geography possible in order to more precisely target key market segments.
- To easily link other marketing information databases on consumer purchasing and consumption pattern information.
- To create homogeneous segments which display different lifestyle and purchasing behavior.
- To create a system that provides custom, industry-specific and general consumer segmentation capabilities.
- To improve address coding to segment coding by over 50 percent.

MicroVision™ -50 Segment Descriptions

SEG. #	NAME	DESCRIPTION
1	Upper Crust	Metropolitan families, very high income and education, manager/professionals; very high installment activity
2	Lap Of Luxury	Families, teens, very high income and education, managers/professionals; high installment accounts
3	Established Wealth	School-age families, high income and education, managers/professionals; medium-high installment activity, very low retail accounts
4	Mid-Life Success	Families, very high education, managers/professionals, technical/sales, high income; super high installment activity
5	Prosperous Ethnic Mix	Large families, metropolitan, high income and education, two workers, ethnic mix; medium-high installment accounts
6	Good Family Life	Large families, high income and education, two workers; medium-high installment, bankcard activity
7	Comfortable Times	Middle-age families, high income, medium-high education, technical/sales, managers/professionals; low-medium credit activity
8	Movers And Shakers	Singles, couples, students and recent graduates, high education and income, managers/professionals, technical/sales; average credit activity, medium-high installment activity
9	Building A Home Life	School-age families, new housing, medium-high income and education, technical/sales, managers/professionals; average credit activity, medium-high installment activity
10	Home Sweet Home	Families, medium-high income and education, managers/professionals, technical/sales; average credit activity
11	Family Ties	Large families, medium education, medium-high income, technical/sales, precision/crafts, two workers; average credit activity
12	A Good Step Forward	Mobile singles, high education, medium income, managers/professionals, technical/sales; average credit activity, medium-high retail accounts
13	Successful Singles	Young, single renters, older housing, ethnic mix, high education, medium income, managers/professionals; very high bankcard accounts, very high installment activity, very low retail activity
14	Middle Years	Mid-life couples, families, medium-high education, mixed jobs, medium income; very-high installment activity
15	Great Beginnings	Young, singles and couples, medium-high education, medium income, managers/professionals, technical/sales; average credit activity
16	Country Home Families	Large families, rural, medium education, medium income, precision/crafts; average to low credit activity
17	Stars And Stripes	Young, large school-age families, medium income and education, military, precision/craft; average credit activity
18	White Picket Fence	Young families, low to medium education, medium income, precision/crafts, laborers; average credit activity, very-low installment activity
19	Young And Carefree	Young, singles and couples, no kids, medium income, medium-high education, technical/sales, managers/professionals; new accounts, below average credit activity
20	Social Security	Mature/seniors, metro fringe, singles and couples, medium income and education, mixed jobs; very-low credit activity
21	Sunset Years	Seniors, suburban, singles and couples, medium income and education, mixed jobs; very low credit activity
22	Aging America	Seniors, low education, medium income, laborers, precision/crafts; very low credit activity
23	Settled In	Empty nester, medium education and income, technical/sales, services; low credit activity
24	Metro Minority Families	School-age families, medium income, low-medium education, services, laborers; high retail activity, very low installment activity
25	Bedrock America	School-age families, medium income, low-medium education, precision/crafts, military, laborers; very high retail, medium-high revolving, very low installment activity

SEG. #	NAME	DESCRIPTION
26	The Mature Years	Couples, small families, medium income, low-medium education, precision/crafts, laborers; low credit activity
27	Middle Of The Road	School-age families, mixed education, medium income, mixed jobs; very high revolving activity, very high bankcard accounts
28	Building A Family	School-age families, mixed jobs, medium income, medium-low education; very high retail activity, high revolving accounts, very low installment accounts
29	Establishing Roots	School-age families, medium income, low education, mixed jobs; very high retail activity, very high revolving activity
30	Retirement Age	Mature/seniors, singles and couples, medium-low income, mixed housing, medium education, technical/sales, managers/professionals; low credit activity
31	Golden Times	Seniors, medium-low income, low education, laborers; very low credit activity, low retail accounts
32	Metro Singles	Singles, renters, multi-unit housing, low education, medium-low income, technical/sales, laborers; average credit activity, medium-high bankcard accounts, medium-low installment accounts
33	Living Off The Land	School-age families, medium-low income, rural, low education, farming/fishing, laborers; very low credit activity, new credit accounts
34	Books And New Recruits	Young, students, managers/professionals, services, military, high education, medium-low income, renters; average credit activity
35	Late-Life Laborers	Empty nesters, medium-low income, laborers, low education; low credit activity, medium installment accounts
36	Metro Ethnic Mix	Young, seniors, singles, ethnic mix, medium-low income, renters, multi-unit housing; medium-high retail and revolving activity
37	Moving Ahead Minorities	Young, singles, ethnic mix, multi-unit housing, renters, medium-low income, high education, managers/professionals; average credit activity, medium-high installment activity
38	Back Country	Families, school-age kids, rural, low education, medium-low income, mobile homes, farming/fishing, laborers; average retail activity, very low installment activity
39	On Their Own	Young, seniors, singles, couples, medium-low income, medium-high education, managers/professionals, technical/sales, renters; average credit activity
40	Trying Metro Times	Young, seniors, ethnic mix, low income, older housing, low education, renters, mixed jobs; low credit activity, medium-high retail activity
41	South Of The Border	Hispanic, large families, low income, low education, precision/craft, laborers; high retail activity, very low installment activity
42	Hanging On	Black, large families, low income, low education, services, laborers; average credit activity, low installment activity
43	Low-Income Blues	Black, singles and families, older housing, low income and education, services, laborers; low credit activity, medium-high retail activity
44	Hard Years	Singles, couples, low income and education, older multi-unit housing, renters, services, laborers; average credit activity, very low installment accounts
45	Struggling Minority Mix	Young, singles, cultural mix, renters, low income, mixed education, older multi-unit housing; average credit activity, low installment accounts
46	Difficult Times	Black, school-age families, very low income, low education, laborers, services; low to average credit accounts; high retail activity
47	University USA	Students, singles, dorms/group quarters, very low income, medium-high education, technical/sales; low credit activity, high percent new accounts
48	Innercity Singles	Young, seniors, singles, renters, old multi-unit housing, very low income, mixed education, services, technical/sales; low to average credit activity
49	Anomalies	No homogeneity
50	Unclassified	P.O. Boxes, and unclassified population

Equifax Marketing Decision Systems (the new name for National Decision Systems)
Corporate Office: 539 Encinitas Blvd., Encinitas, CA 92024-9007 • (619) 942-7000
Regional Offices: New York, NY • Chicago, IL • Vienna, VA • Atlanta, GA ©10/1990

MicroVision® Plus Profile Data

The percent distribution shown represents the overall profile of each list.
Remember, you can select your specific profile from within all of these lists!

Name of List	Age			Buying Power Index / Income			Bankcard	Survey	Auto	Married	Home	LOR
	21-34	35-54	55+	High	Middle	Low	Holder	Respondent	Owner		Owner	0-5yrs
A Good Step Forward	38	44	18	39	46	15	70	8	58	35	40	56
American Classics	12	24	64	11	43	46	58	17	68	85	72	33
Bedrock America	28	47	25	3	41	56	47	11	74	75	63	44
Books and New Recruits	47	36	17	8	32	60	39	10	77	32	25	63
Building A Family	32	49	19	4	34	62	36	7	73	71	74	43
Building A Home Life	29	56	15	35	59	6	87	8	58	83	86	41
Buy American	26	45	29	1	25	74	33	12	73	78	89	41
City Ties	24	44	32	2	39	59	41	10	70	63	47	36
Close Knit Families	31	44	25	1	19	80	19	7	54	68	76	38
Comfortable Times	13	56	31	34	56	10	89	33	70	87	91	32
Country Classics	15	27	58	1	33	66	43	21	71	48	69	36
Country Home Families	24	48	28	3	68	29	43	16	75	79	86	43
Difficult Times	38	25	37	1	11	88	15	5	68	26	29	36
Domestic Duos	10	20	70	8	52	40	61	30	74	72	84	36
Established Wealth	20	48	32	55	40	5	90	26	74	82	87	46
Establishing Roots	31	48	21	4	64	32	41	5	72	79	85	40
Family Ties	25	50	25	9	80	11	57	23	76	87	90	50
Good Family Life	20	56	24	25	67	8	90	23	80	82	87	52
Great Beginnings	46	35	19	23	64	13	88	13	60	37	42	55
Hard Years	39	42	19	2	26	72	30	5	59	22	47	41
Home Sweet Home	23	46	31	24	67	9	89	24	68	79	86	45
Lap of Luxury	16	62	22	68	30	2	91	27	65	91	93	53
Living Off The Land	33	52	15	1	31	68	45	2	68	74	79	35
Manufacturing USA	17	28	55	1	17	82	19	10	65	54	61	29
Metro Mix	32	54	14	2	23	75	28	3	77	21	22	34
Metro Singles	33	44	23	5	37	58	49	10	68	31	41	40
Mid-Life Success	15	59	26	64	32	4	92	24	40	72	80	51
Middle Of The Road	31	50	19	11	39	50	56	7	65	63	69	41
Middle Years	15	59	26	28	55	17	84	15	69	68	73	46
Movers & Shakers	26	45	29	45	44	11	88	19	63	41	46	49
On Their Own	34	40	26	7	56	37	65	13	71	34	47	51
Prosperous Metro Mix	25	54	21	45	50	5	90	22	57	86	90	53
Rustic Homesteaders	26	48	26	1	23	76	25	8	72	86	82	37
Secure Adults	5	17	78	7	52	41	68	24	69	79	86	33
Settled In	12	28	60	5	57	38	65	22	73	77	86	41
Stars & Stripes	41	47	12	3	56	41	67	15	47	78	84	48
Struggling Metro Mix	36	47	17	4	36	60	48	5	58	21	28	43
Successful Singles	40	50	10	3	89	8	95	1	43	14	12	46
The Mature Years	5	15	80	1	39	60	43	7	61	86	83	40
Traditional Times	15	27	58	2	54	44	38	27	71	78	90	33
Trying Metro Times	40	25	35	1	30	69	41	13	67	63	55	43
Trying Rural Times	31	49	20	1	23	76	21	4	69	79	62	33
University USA	67	25	8	6	33	61	44	3	69	22	32	53
Upper Crust	13	46	41	90	9	1	92	28	57	91	93	37
Urban Singles	37	46	17	5	26	69	38	5	61	19	42	46
Urban Up & Comers	46	46	8	7	61	32	71	2	53	19	23	53
White Picket Fence	49	32	19	3	67	30	69	18	73	89	81	47
Young & Carefree	57	34	9	18	57	25	71	6	50	26	35	43

Numbers shown above represent percentages.

Page 6

High Income

Name of List	Total Names Available
A Good Step Forward	2,863,444
Building A Home Life	1,167,165
Comfortable Times	1,260,538
Established Wealth	4,699,784
Good Family Life	2,738,947
Home Sweet Home	10,753,480
Lap of Luxury	2,717,105
Middle Years	202,308
Mid-Life Success	1,742,966
Movers & Shakers	4,217,356
Prosperous Metro Mix	4,902,093
Upper Crust	1,330,568

Mid-Income

A Good Step Forward	2,863,444
American Classics	871,483
Bedrock America	4,061,734
Building A Home Life	1,167,165
Comfortable Times	1,260,538
Country Home Families	8,263,528
Domestic Duos	1,540,658
Established Wealth	4,699,784
Establishing Roots	560,239
Family Ties	7,545,667
Good Family Life	2,738,947
Great Beginnings	5,835,825
Home Sweet Home	10,753,480
Middle Of The Road	638,050
Middle Years	202,308
Movers & Shakers	4,217,356
On Their Own	4,295,167
Prosperous Metro Mix	4,902,093
Secure Adults	2,816,758
Settled In	7,345,358
Stars & Stripes	3,320,967
Successful Singles	700,299
The Mature Years	2,443,265
Traditional Times	4,139,545
Urban Up & Comers	778,110
White Picket Fence	10,597,585
Young & Carefree	902,607

Low Income

Name of List	Total Names Available
Books and New Recruits	1,727,404
Building A Family	1,914,150
Buy American	6,971,865
City Ties	2,754,509
Close Knit Families	964,856
Country Classics	882,376
Difficult Times	2,598,887
Hard Years	482,428
Living Off The Land	2,956,818
Manufacturing USA	373,492
Metro Mix	1,462,846
Metro Singles	2,843,213
Rustic Homesteaders	7,423,169
Struggling Metro Mix	1,626,250
The Mature Years	2,443,265
Trying Metro Times	3,890,550
Trying Rural Times	3,475,039
University USA	824,796
Urban Singles	1,078,460

Low Education

Bedrock America	4,061,734
Building A Family	1,914,150
Buy American	6,971,865
City Ties	2,754,509
Close Knit Families	964,856
Country Classics	882,376
Country Home Families	8,263,528
Difficult Times	2,598,887
Establishing Roots	560,239
Hard Years	482,428
Living Off The Land	2,956,818
Manufacturing USA	373,492
Metro Mix	1,462,846
Metro Singles	2,843,213
Middle Of The Road	638,050
Rustic Homesteaders	7,423,169
Stars & Stripes	3,320,967
Struggling Metro Mix	1,626,250
The Mature Years	2,443,265
Traditional Times	4,139,545
Trying Metro Times	3,890,550
Trying Rural Times	3,475,039
Urban Singles	1,078,460

High Education

Name of List	Total Names Available
A Good Step Forward	2,863,444
American Classics	871,483
Books and New Recruits	1,727,404
Building A Home Life	1,167,165
Comfortable Times	1,260,538
Country Home Families	8,263,528
Domestic Duos	1,540,658
Established Wealth	4,699,784
Family Ties	7,545,667
Good Family Life	2,738,947
Great Beginnings	5,835,825
Home Sweet Home	10,753,480
Lap of Luxury	2,717,105
Middle Years	202,308
Mid-Life Success	1,742,966
Movers & Shakers	4,217,356
On Their Own	4,295,167
Prosperous Metro Mix	4,902,093
Secure Adults	2,816,758
Settled In	7,345,358
Successful Singles	700,299
University USA	824,796
Upper Crust	1,330,568
Urban Singles	1,078,460
Urban Up & Comers	778,110
White Picket Fence	10,597,585
Young & Carefree	902,607

The mailing lists of MicroVision Plus have been ranked by percentile data. This data can be found on page 6. For you to easily reach your precise markets, we have also grouped the lists into categories.

In the Income categories, there are a few lists that overlap into two categories since the percentages for each are very close.

Page 7

SEGMENT 1 - UPPER CRUST
(MicroVision Group 1)

Metropolitan Families, Very High Income and Education, Manager/Professionals; Very High Installment Activity

UPPER CRUST is a middle-aged segment (ages 45 to 54), predominantly white, and almost half have college and/or graduate degrees. They primarily work in the managerial and professional fields, with the highest income in the nation. The majority of these families, with teenagers, own homes built in the 60s and early 70s. Their financial activity is high, with installment account balances much higher than the national average. City dwellers, they watch morning news programs, read *The Wall Street Journal*, attend live theater, and travel to foreign lands. Aerobics and jogging keep them fit and trim.

SEGMENT 2 - LAP OF LUXURY
(MicroVision Group 1)

Families, Teens, Very High Income and Education, Managers/Professionals; High Installment Accounts

This is a predominantly white, middle-aged, urbanite segment with an above average Asian population. College graduates, in the very high-income bracket, these individuals tend to be employed in the managerial/professional and technical/sales occupations. These parents have one or more teenage children. Homeowners, their installment and revolving accounts have high balances. Viewers of T.V. news magazine shows and morning news programs, news/talk radio enthusiasts, and foreign travelers, they also read *The Wall Street Journal* and sweat on the tennis courts.

SEGMENT 3 - ESTABLISHED WEALTH
(MicroVision Group 1)

School-Age Families, High Income and Education, Managers/Professionals; Medium-High Installment Activity, Very Low Retail Accounts

ESTABLISHED WEALTH individuals are between the ages of 35 and 55, and are predominantly white. Degree holders, they work in managerial/professional, and technical/sales occupations. High-income homeowners, their financial patterns are slightly above those of the nation, except for very low retail activity. They read *The Wall Street Journal*, attend live theater, and do aerobics. Families with school-aged children, they tend to live in metropolitan areas.

SEGMENT 18 - WHITE PICKET FENCE
(MicroVision Group 2)

Young Families, Low to Medium Education, Medium Income, Precision/Crafts, Laborers; Average Financial Activity, Very-Low Installment Activity

This segment is comprised of young parents in their late 20s and early 30s, with young children, mostly 0 to 4. The plurality are white, living on the borders of metropolitan areas. Their education level is low to medium, and income levels tend to be medium. The heads of household work in precision production, craft and repair occupations, as well as operators, fabricators and laborers. The majority own their single-family home, which was built between 1960 and 1974. The average household has three persons. WHITE PICKET FENCE households are frugal with their use of installment accounts, average on all others. Recreational enthusiasts, they enjoy billiards, bowling and golf. They primarily listen to rock and easy-listening music.

SEGMENT 19 - YOUNG AND CAREFREE
(MicroVision Group 3)

Young, Singles and Couples, No Kids, Medium Income, Medium-High Education, Technical/Sales, Managers/Professionals; New Accounts, Below Average Financial Activity

This segment is young (twenty-something), well-educated, with medium incomes, living on the periphery of urban areas. There are no children. They are predominantly white. They gravitate to managerial and professional specialty fields, such as management analysts and purchasing agents. One-third of them are still in school and are likely to rent apartments or live in dorms. They typically have just opened their first financial account. These individuals tend to listen to news/talk radio, and watch morning news programs and T.V. news magazine shows. *Newsweek* and *The Wall Street Journal* are standard reading fare.

SEGMENT 20 - SOCIAL SECURITY
(MicroVision Group 6)

Mature/Seniors, Metro Fringe, Singles and Couples, Medium Income and Education, Mixed Jobs; Very-Low Financial Activity

This over-50 segment is white. Their education and income levels are average. Employment includes precision production, craft and repair fields; or operators, fabricators and laborers. The majority own their home just outside the city limits, although a significant number live in retirement homes. The average household size is two, no children. These households have learned to develop a very cautious financial behavior, with balances 30% lower than the average American. As this segment ages, exercise is not their choice activity. However, they do exercise their minds by reading the daily paper and *Reader's Digest*, and watching morning news programs, T.V. news magazine shows, and prime time soap operas.

SEGMENT 21 - SUNSET YEARS
(MicroVision Group 6)

Seniors, Suburban, Singles and Couples, Medium Income and Education, Mixed Jobs; Very Low Financial Activity

This senior segment has a racial balance similar to that of the nation. With an average income and educational background, professions include precision, production, craft, and repair; operators, fabricators, and laborers; and services. Most own a home in the suburbs, although some live in retirement homes. They like to read newspapers, such as *The Wall Street Journal* and *USA Today*. Like the SOCIAL SECURITY segment, these individuals have a very low financial activity, and no children still at home.

SEGMENT 35 - LATE-LIFE LABORERS
(MicroVision Group 2)

Empty Nesters, Medium-Low Income, Laborers, Low Education; Low Financial Activity, Medium Installment Accounts

A suburban, mature/senior (50+ years of age), empty-nester group, this segment is mostly white, with an above average number of blacks and Native Americans. Almost half did not graduate from high school; most work as laborers (a few in farming/fishing) bringing home medium-low paychecks. Many own their homes, but their financial activity is below average. Owners of trucks and vans, they listen to country music and love to fresh water fish.

SEGMENT 36 - METRO ETHNIC MIX
(MicroVision Group 9)

Young, Seniors, Singles, Ethnic Mix, Medium-Low Income, Renters, Multi-Unit Housing; Medium-High Retail and Revolving Activity

Location, income, and marital status are what ties together the individuals of this segment. Single, childless and living in metropolitan areas, they come from diverse cultures. Ages range from 25 to 35 years to 60 years and older. While some have high educational backgrounds, others have not graduated from high school. With salaries in the medium-low income bracket, many are employed in the technical, sales and administrative support fields. Most rent multi-unit complexes. Their retail and revolving accounts are high on the activity scale. They listen to news/talk radio, attend live theater, and travel to foreign lands.

SEGMENT 37 - MOVING AHEAD MINORITIES
(MicroVision Group 9)

Young, Singles, Ethnic Mix, Multi-Unit Housing, Renters, Medium-Low Income, High Education, Managers/Professionals; Average Financial Activity, Medium-High Installment Activity

These medium-low income households are run by young (20s and 30s), childless singles of white, black, Asian, and Hispanic background. Some have graduated from college, and are in managerial and professional specialty occupations. The majority live alone in rented apartments in urban areas. Of those living with family members, two incomes are the norm. They exhibit average bankcard and revolving activity. This segment reads *TIME*, enjoys easy-listening music, travels abroad, and attends live theater.

CONSUMER INFOBASE

Spring/Summer 1993

Data Catalog

Order Form

INFOBASE™

Table of Contents

Consumer InfoBase Data Enhancement

InfoBase offers you the most sophisticated tool available to help you achieve increased profits and better response rates from your customer and prospect files.

This powerful tool — Consumer InfoBase — can help you:

- Define who your customers are.
- Cross sell existing customers more effectively.
- Target prospects who look most like your best customers to raise response rates.
- Enhance the value of your list rental file.
- Design new products and services matched to your customers' buying preferences.

All the Best Data Sources In One Database

With information on 95% of U.S. households, Consumer InfoBase is the largest database of its kind in the U.S. It is the only database that contains so much data from so many of the nation's acknowledged top data sources — R.L. Polk & Company, National Demographics & Lifestyles, TRW, TransMark, American Data Resources/Matrix, American Student List, and others.

The integration of all this data into one national consumer database is unique in the industry and gives you the maximum coverage and accuracy available. The graph below illustrates the additional coverage multi-sourcing provides. Consumer InfoBase gives you the most types of data and the flexibility to select the most specific data available from any data provider you choose. You can select demographic information such as age, income, occupation, marital status, and children's ages. You might choose such socio-economic data as car and home ownership, as well as lifestyle data on specific interests, hobbies, activities, and mail order purchase information. InfoBase data is put through rigorous screening to assure you get the highest quality information available in the industry, and it is kept current through regular updating.

InfoBase Premier — Your Best Value

Premier is a package of the key demographics and socio-economic data most frequently used by marketers. It provides the most recent, most specific, and most accurate data for each data element on each record appended.

A specific set of rules has been written for InfoBase Premier that selects the best information from all of InfoBase's sources. Pages 2 and 3 explain in detail what data is available in Premier and include an illustration of how the best data is selected.

Data Experts to Help You Maximize Results

InfoBase has a research department of statisticians and analysts with direct marketing experience. These professionals can help you achieve better response rates - or determine the long term value of your customers - by using advanced segmentation techniques such as CHAID, Logit and Regression Analysis. If you want a snapshot to gain more knowledge of your customers, InfoBase's research staff can prepare a Data Profile Analysis using all the key InfoBase data. Together, our research and account management teams can give meaning to the numbers and statistics that you receive. InfoBase provides more than data. We provide answers.

Put the Power of Consumer InfoBase to Work for You

Give us a call. An InfoBase sales representative will tailor a plan to meet your exact needs. And if you want to evaluate match rates, just provide us a test file of 50,000 to 100,000 records. We will give you a report illustrating the number of matches for each data element.

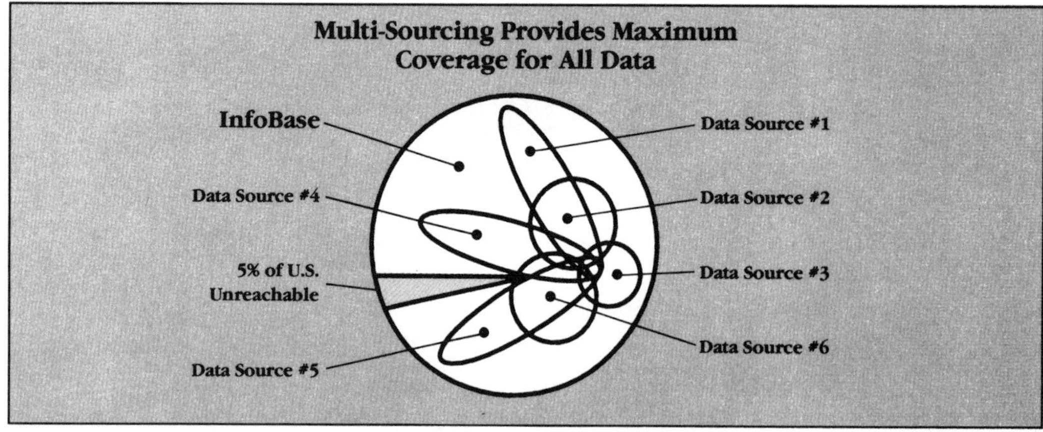

InfoBase Premier

Selected Consumer InfoBase Data . . . Accuracy, Coverage and Value

InfoBase Premier includes data from R.L. Polk, National Demographics & Lifestyles, American Data Resources/Matrix, TransMark, TRW, and American Student List to guarantee that the most recent, most specific and most accurate data is provided for each Premier data element for every individual record. In short, this sophisticated system architecture assures you the highest quality and maximum coverage for each data element. You simply specify the individual Premier data elements desired, or choose Bundled Premier to get all Premier demographic data on every matched record. The system does the rest.

Individual data elements may be selected at the indicated prices or all elements included in the shaded area below are available at a special bundled price. See element 635 for bundled pricing.

Data Element No.	Description	Price per M Matches
600	**Adult Age Ranges Present In Household** Includes an indication of male, female or unknown gender. • 18-24 • 35-44 • 55-64 • 75 + • 25-34 • 45-54 • 65-74	$10.00
616	**Age Range in Two Year Increments - Head of Household** Categories extend from under 18 to 100 plus.	$14.00
617	**Age Range in Two Year Increments - Spouse (2nd Individual)**	$14.00
626	**Age Range in Two Year Increments of Individual Name Appearing on Customer's File**	$14.00
627	**Age Range in Two Year Increments of Individual Name Appearing on Customer's File, with Default to Head of Household**	$14.00
610	**Head of Household - Name, Gender**	$ 3.00
612	**Second Individual - Name, Gender and Relationship to Head of Household**	$ 3.00
649	**Individual Name Appearing on Customer's File Household Status Indicator Reported as:** • Head of Household • Spouse • 2nd Individual (not spouse)	$ 3.00
628	**Number of Adults** Counts the number of adults in the household up to six or more.	$ 8.00
609	**Marital Status** • Married • Single	$ 3.00
622	**Presence of Children** Indicates the known and inferred presence of children age 0-18 in the household.	$ 5.00

Data Element No.	Description	Price per M Matches
601	**Children's Age Range** Children's age including indication of male, female or unknown gender, reported as: • 0-6 • 13-18 • 7-12 • 19-22	$15.00
604	**Occupation of Head of Household Expressed as:** • Professional/Technical • Housewife • Administrative/Managerial • Retired • Sales/Service • Farmer • Clerical/White collar • Military • Craftsman/Blue collar • Religious • Student	$10.00
605	**Occupation of the Spouse (2nd Individual) Expressed as:** • Professional/Technical • Housewife • Administrative/Managerial • Retired • Sales/Service • Farmer • Clerical/White collar • Military • Craftsman/Blue collar • Religious • Student	$10.00
619	**Working Woman** Working woman present in the household.	$ 5.00
641	**Estimated Income Code** Reported as one of the following: • Less than $ 15,000 • $ 50,000 - $ 74,999 • $ 15,000 - $ 19,999 • $ 75,000 - $ 99,999 • $ 20,000 - $ 29,999 • $100,000 - $124,999 • $ 30,000 - $ 39,999 • $125,000 Plus • $ 40,000 - $ 49,999	$10.00
625	**Address Confirmation** Confirms that your names and addresses exist on other outside lists. • Under 500M input $ 5.00 • 500M - 1,999M input 4.00 • 2,000M - 4,999M input 3.00 • More than 5,000M 2.00	
614	**Verification Date** (Year and quarter of most recent address verification) • Under 500M input $ 5.00 • 500M - 1,999M input 4.00 • 2,000M - 4,999M input 3.00 • 5,000M Plus 2.00	
160	**Apartment Number**	$ 2.00
647	**Number of Vehicles Owned**	$12.00
648	**Dominant Vehicle Lifestyle Indicator** This indicator distinguishes the classification of the primary vehicle registered to the household: • Personal Luxury Car, e.g. Corvette, Audi 100, Infiniti • Truck or Passenger Utility Vehicle, e.g., Jeep Cherokee, Toyota Previa, Lumina APV • Station Wagon, e.g. Buick Roadmaster, Taurus Station wagon • Import, (standard or economy car), e.g. Toyota Camry, Nissan Stanza, Volkswagen Passat • Regular, (mid-size or small car), e.g. Dodge Spirit • Specialty, (mid-size or luxury car), e.g. Grand Marquis, Eagle, Mustang, Accord, Corolla, Saab • Full Size, (standard or luxury car), e.g. Taurus, LeBaron, Continental, Cadillac	$ 8.00

Data Element No.	Description	Price per M Matches
194	**Aggregate Value of Vehicles Owned** The total value of all vehicles registered in the household based on blue book value.	$12.00
646	**New Car Buyer** Indicates a history of new car buying.	$12.00
165	**Truck/Motorcycle/RV Owners**	$10.00
615	**Mail Order Buyer**	$12.00
620	**Mail Responders**	$ 8.00
621	**Credit Card Indicator** Indication of possession of one or more of the following types of credit cards. • Retail/Other • Bank Card • Travel and Entertainment • Premium (Gold Cards) • Upscale Dept. Stores • Credit Card Buyer (Unspecified Type)	$15.00
606	**Home Owner/Renter**	$ 5.00
607	**Length of Residence Expressed in One Year Increments from Less than One to 15+ Years**	$ 3.00
608	**Dwelling Size (Single or Multi-Family)**	$ 5.00

Bundled Premier Prices

Data Element No.	Description	Price per M Matches
635	**Includes all InfoBase Premier Data Elements listed above. Does not include the Additional Premier Data listed below.**	
	• Under 1,000M input	$42.50
	• 1,000M - 1,999M input	36.75
	• 2,000M - 3,999M input	31.00
	• 4,000M - 4,999M input	25.50
	• More than 5,000M	21.25

Additional Premier Data

(Not included in the Bundled Premier Prices above)

Data Element No.	Description	Price per M Matches
623	**Date of Birth of Individual Name Appearing on Customer's File. Day and Month when Available**	$20.00
624	**Date of Birth of Individual Name Appearing on Customer's File with Default to Head of Household. Day and Month when Available**	$20.00
611	**Date of Birth of Head of Household. Day and Month when Available**	$20.00
618	**Date of Birth - Spouse (2nd Individual). Day and Month when Available**	$20.00

Sample InfoBase Premier™ Record

Data Element	Source A	Source B	Source C	Source D
Children	Yes	1 @ 7 to 12 1 @ under 6	Yes	X
Income	$25K to 30K	$25K to 30K	X	X
Home Owner	X	No	Yes	X
Occupation	X	Blue Collar	Blue Collar	Farmer
Age	28-29	27	X	28-29
Mail Order Buyer	Yes	X	X	High Ticket
Length of Residence	3 Years	X	<1 Year	X
Dwelling Type	SFDU	X	X	X
Telephone	213-473-9876	X	213-473-1234	X

Source A Mass compiled source, address verified 6 months ago
Source B Verified 12 months ago, source from questionnaires
Source C Phone survey, verified 4 months ago
Source D Multi-source compilation, data verification date varies by data element

The example above is a typical InfoBase Premier Data record—describing this individual as blue collar, age 28-29 with an income of $25,000-$30,000, living in a single family home for less than a year, two children (one at 7-12 years and one under six years) and a history of having bought by mail.

Data Element No.	Description	Price per M Matches
613	**Area Code, Telephone, Time Zone** Includes time zones and area codes.	
	• Under 1,000M input	$20.00
	• 1,000M - 1,999M input	18.00
	• 2,000M - 3,999M input	16.00
	• 4,000M - 4,999M input	14.00
	• 5,000M Plus	12.00
630	Element 613 purchased in conjunction with Bundled Premier for an additional $10.00/M overall Premier matches.	
642	**Home Market Value** • $ 1,000 - $ 24,999 • $ 25,000 - $ 49,999 • $ 50,000 - $ 74,999 • $ 75,000 - $ 99,999 • $100,000 - $124,999 • $125,000 - $149,999 • $150,000 - $174,999 • $175,000 - $199,999 • $200,000 - $224,999 • $225,000 - $249,999 • $ 250,000 - $274,999 • $ 275,000 - $299,999 • $ 300,000 - $349,999 • $ 350,000 - $399,999 • $ 400,000 - $449,999 • $ 450,000 - $499,999 • $ 500,000 - $774,999 • $ 775,000 - $999,999 • $1,000,000 Plus	$20.00
643	**Purchase Date of Home** Both year and month of purchase where available. Ranges from 1901 to 1991.	$10.00
644	**Year Home was Purchased** Years range from 1901 to 1991.	$ 5.00
645	**Month Home was Purchased** Ranges from 01 to 12.	$ 5.00
632	**Homeowner Data Package** Includes above elements: Home Market Value, Purchase Date, Year and Month. (642, 643, 644 and 645).	$25.00
633	Element 632 purchased in conjunction with Bundled Premier for an additional $10.00/M overall Premier matches.	

InfoBase Premier

You may also order demographic data from a specific InfoBase data source or a number of data sources, specifying which data you would like first. Your InfoBase sales representative will be happy to provide you with complete details.

3

Analysis Products

Data Element No.	Description
R1	**Match Rate Report** A report indicating the match rate of each data element from InfoBase for a sample of a customer file. Summary Page $150.00 Full Report 500.00
R2	**Data Profile Analysis** (includes Match Report) A univariate description of a customer file as compared nationally to the InfoBase file. National Reference File: $2,800
R3	**Data Profile Analysis** (includes Match Report) A univariate description of a customer file as compared to any special reference file other than the InfoBase National Reference file (e.g. Geographic area, other customer segments, etc.) Special Reference File: $3,300
R4	**CHAID** (Chi Square Automatic Interaction Detector) CHAID Analysis examines a customer list, separates the file into groups most likely to respond, and describes the key characteristics of each group. *Quote upon request*
R5	**Regression Analysis** A predictive modeling technique that ranks customers or non-customers as to their likelihood of responding to a specific promotion. *Quote upon request*
451	**All Data for Analysis** $50.00/M Input All catalog elements may be purchased for analysis purposes on sample files up to 100,000 records. Carrier Route or block group level optional.

Area Level Data

Data Element No.	Description	Price	Minimum
P5	**Geo-Coding Including Census Data - GeoPlus** GeoPlus is a software system developed by R.L. Polk & Co. which will attach the following census geo-data elements to a name and address record: • FIPS State Code • Census Tract Number • Confidence Code • FIPS MCD/CCD • FIPS Place/CDP Code • MSA Code • Census MCD/CCD • Census Place Code • FIPS County Code • Block Group Number • Small Area Characteristics (SMACS) **The GeoPlus System** contains information for all of the U.S. but not its territories or possessions.	$500.00	$2.50/M input
P7	**Carrier Route Marketing Information (CRMI)** Polk builds the CRMI file from over a billion data records each year. The TotaList file sources plus Ethnic and Religious lists are cross referenced with the U.S. Census information to create this dynamic source.	$750.00	$3.50/M input
P8	**The Neighborhood Selector** The TNS file is a carrier route based file developed by NDL. This file describes the demographic and lifestyle characteristics of U.S. Postal Service Carrier Routes. The information used to create this file is generated from NDL individual level data, which is then aggregated to the carrier route level.	$750.00	$4.50/M input

Market Segmentation Services

Household Level

Data Element No.	Description
459	**Lifestages Segmentation** $10.00/M input An easy-to-use segmentation system using all the features and multi-sourced power of individual household level InfoBase Premier Data. 42 major life segments and 252 subsegments. Based on the following six key data variables: • age • income • marital status • number of adults • presence of children • work status (Requires purchase of Bundled Premier Data. See Page 2.)
460	**Lifestages Segmentation Codes** $34.00/M input codes only Segmentation codes may be purchased without Bundled Premier data.

Area Level

Data Element No.	Description	Price	Minimum
P6	**Prizm Codes/Applications:** One-Time Mailing: $10.00/M Records Selected One-Time Analysis: $15.00/M Records Analyzed ($500 Minimum) Model: $5.00/M ($500 Minimum) Unlimited Annual Use: $45.00/M Records Coded Geo-demographic segmentation codes that classify all U.S. neighborhoods into 40 unique neighborhood types based on block group information. *File must be geo-coded before PRIZM codes can be applied. See P5 above.*		$2.50/M input
365	**MicroVision** Classifies households into market segments based on demographic, socio-economic, and housing characteristics at the Zip+4 level. (Please contact your InfoBase sales representative for more information if you don't have a MicroVision license.)	$500.00	$1.50/M input for MV licensee with Zip + 4 coded file. $3.50/M input without Zip + 4 coded file.

Financial Industry Product Propensity Codes

Data Element No.	Description	Price Minimum	Price per M
P14	**Premier Financial Profiles**	$3,000.00	$40.00/input

Identify customers or prospects likely to respond to specific financial product offers:

- Investment Funds
  - CD's, annuities/other term deposit accounts
- Liquid Funds
  - Checking, MMDA, money market, savings
- Consumer Credit
  - Credit card/other secured or unsecured credit products
- Home Equity Credit
  - Home equity loan/line of credit products

Easy-to-use yes/no product propensity codes are assigned to each record using a multivariate-based predictive modeling system. This system is especially developed for financial service organizations in conjunction with InfoBase Premier household-specific data.

Telephone Data

Data Element No.	Description	Price per M
P11	**Phone Confirmation Processing**	
	InfoBase format	$ 3.00/M input
	Customer format	$ 4.00/M input
	PLUS	
	Phones confirmed	$ 5.00/M matches
	and/or	
	New phones applied	$20.00/M matches

This service will update your file with new phone numbers and keep the phone numbers already on your file if they are the same as ours. Call your InfoBase sales representative for details.

P9 PhoneLink™

Identify those customers for whom you only have a phone number. For instance, a retailer may capture phones from point of sale registers and have their names and addresses applied. *(All orders must be pre-approved. Please call your InfoBase sales representative for assistance and scheduling.)

InfoBase Format	$500.00 Min.	$ 2.50/ M input
Customer Format	$500.00 Min.	$ 3.50/ M input
	$500.00 Minimum for Data	
• Under 1,000M input		$20.00/M
• 1,000M - 1,999M input		18.00/M
• 2,000M - 3,999M input		16.00/M
• 4,000M - 4,999M input		14.00/M
• 5,000M and over		12.00/M

List Cleaning

Data Element No.	Description	Price Minimum	Price per M
P3	**NCOA Address Standardization and Forwarding Address**	$750.00	$ 2.95/M input (Volume pricing is available)
	NCOA Nixie Matches		$15.00/M matches

NCOA is the U.S. Postal Service's National Change of Address service. It represents a timely and cost-efficient way to increase the accuracy of a file and reduce undeliverables. NCOA contains records for all the permanent change of address records filed with the U.S. Postal Service in the last 36 months - giving you access to the most current consumer and business addresses available. Besides providing a forwarding address, the NCOA process also corrects five-digit ZIP Codes, standardizes addresses and applies ZIP+4 Codes. The file is updated bi-monthly.

NCOA Nixie Matches indicate that a move has occurred or the address is no longer deliverable. A forwarding address is not included.

Data Element No.	Description	Price Minimum	Price per M
P4	**AddressAbility**	$500.00	$ 2.00/M input

- Verifies and corrects 5 digit ZIP codes.
- Overlays the correct ZIP+4 and associated carrier route codes to each output record.
- Passes and standardizes addresses according to postal service specifications.
- Standardizes city names and state abbreviations.

Data Element No.	Description	Price Minimum	Price per M
P12	**TransMark Deceased Suppression**		$50.00/M matches
	This service will suppress names of deceased and will return your file with those names deleted.		
	InfoBase format	$500.00	$ 2.50/M input
	Customer format	$500.00	$ 3.50/M input
P13	**TRW Deceased Suppression**		$50.00/M matches
	This service will suppress names of deceased and will return your file with those names deleted.		
	InfoBase format	$500.00	$ 2.50/M input
	Customer format	$500.00	$ 3.50/M input

ZIP + 4

Data Element No.	Description	Price Minimum	Price per M
P10	**ZIP+4 Coding**	$300.00	$2.00/M input

Prepares your file to take advantage of postal presort discount, and faster delivery.

Products & Services

AMERICAN DATA RESOURCES, INC.

American Data Resources data is derived from the city and county real estate property records of the following 29 states: AL, AK, AZ, CA, CO, DC, FL, GA, HI, ID, IL, MD, MO, NV, NJ, NM, NY, NC, OH, OK, OR, PA, SC, TN, TX, UT, VA, WA, WI. (Partial coverage available in some states. Contact your InfoBase sales representative for specific area coverage.)

Housing Information

Data Element No.	Description	Price per M Matches
753	**Home Owner** Indicates owner only, no renters available.	$ 5.00
754	**Home Owner and Purchase Date** Both year and month of purchase. Ranges from 1901 to 1991. Month and/or year may not be available in all cases.	$10.00
755	**Home Owner and Year of Purchase** Ranges from 1901 to 1991.	$ 8.00
769	**Dwelling Unit Size (Land Use Code)** • Condominium • Duplex • Tri-Plex • 5 Plus Units • Single Family Dwelling • Four-Plex • Mobile Home	$ 5.00
758	**Marital Status** Indicates married only, no singles, widows or divorced.	$ 3.00
759	**Length of Residence** Values range from 00 (less than 1 year) to 15 (fifteen or more years).	$ 3.00
766	**Home Market Value** • $ 1,000 - $ 24,999 • $ 25,000 - $ 49,999 • $ 50,000 - $ 74,999 • $ 75,000 - $ 99,999 • $ 100,000 - $124,999 • $ 125,000 - $149,999 • $ 150,000 - $174,999 • $ 175,000 - $199,999 • $ 200,000 - $224,999 • $ 225,000 - $249,999 • $ 250,000 - $274,999 • $ 275,000 - $299,999 • $ 300,000 - $349,999 • $ 350,000 - $399,999 • $ 400,000 - $449,999 • $ 450,000 - $499,999 • $ 500,000 - $774,999 • $ 775,000 - $999,999 • $1,000,000 Plus	$20.00
760	**Market Value Deciles** Values range from 1-9, with 1 meaning top 10% of market value at county level. The value of 9 represents the bottom 20% of market values.	$10.00
770	**Market Value/Market Value Decile** Package price for Elements 766 & 760.	$25.00
767	**Home Equity** This element expresses available home equity assuming an 80% loan-to-value ratio for the following equity ranges: • Less than $10,000 • $10,000 - $24,999 • $25,000 - $49,999 • $50,000 Plus	$20.00
756	**Month of Purchase**	$ 5.00
771	**Market Value/Market Value Decile/ Home Equity** Package price for Elements 766, 760 & 767.	$30.00
768	**Estimated Income** Specific-to-household income (home owners only). Based on minimum income to qualify for home financing at date of purchase. Adjusted forward each year using regional CPI. • Less than $ 20,000 • $ 20,000 - $ 29,999 • $ 30,000 - $ 39,999 • $ 40,000 - $ 49,999 • $ 50,000 - $ 59,999 • $ 60,000 - $ 69,999 • $ 70,000 - $ 79,999 • $ 80,000 - $ 89,999 • $ 90,000 - $ 99,999 • $100,000 Plus	$10.00
761	**Income Deciles** Values range by 10% ranked groupings at county level.	$ 5.00
772	**Household Income/Household Income Decile** Package price for elements 768 & 761.	$12.50
773	**All ADR/Matrix Elements** Package price for all household-specific data elements listed above.	$37.50

American Student List Company, Inc.

Data Element No.	Description	Price per M Matches
476	**Children's Age Ranges** Each range is coded by gender. • 2-6 years old • 13-18 • 7-12 • 19-22	$15.00

The National Demographics & Lifestyles data is provided by consumers who have filled out a questionnaire packaged with a consumer product and mailed it to NDL.

The NDL data is available for enhancement of customer files for a one year time period.

The NDL data may not be used to:
- enhance a customer file for list rental purposes;
- enhance compiled or credit files;
- enhance any list of names generated from warranty cards, etc.

The NDL data is available at the individual level and the neighborhood (carrier route) level. You may order just individual level data or use the option of ordering individual household level data with an automatic default to neighborhood level data when individual household data is unavailable.

Demographic Data

Data Element No.	Description	Price per M Matches
201	**Income Range** • Less than $15,000 • $15,000 - $19,999 • $20,000 - $24,999 • $25,000 - $29,999 • $30,000 - $34,999 • $35,000 - $39,999 • $40,000 - $44,999 • $45,000 - $49,999 • $50,000 - $74,999 • $75,000 Plus	$15.00
202	**Occupation of Head of Household** • Professional/Technical • Student • Management • Homemaker • Sales/Marketing • Retired • Clerical • Other • Blue Collar	$12.00
203	**Self-reported Credit Card Holder** Indication of possession of the following types of credit cards, alone or in combination. • Travel & Entertainment • Bank Card • Other (oil company, department store or specialty store)	$15.00
204	**Home Owner or Renter** Self-reported status as renter or owner of the home.	$12.00
280	**Age Range of Spouse** Range: 18-24 45-54 25-34 55-64 35-44 65+	$12.00
281	**Age Range of Head of Household** Range: 18-24 45-54 25-34 55-64 35-44 65+	$12.00
345	**2 Year Age of Head of Household**	$14.00
282	**Date of Birth, Head of Household** Year and month only.	$20.00
306	**Date of Birth of Individual Name Appearing on Customer's File**	$20.00
283	**Date of Birth of Spouse** Year and month only.	$20.00
346	**2 Year Age of Second Individual**	$14.00
307	**2 Year Age of Individual Name Appearing on Customer's File**	$12.00
348	**Individual Name Appearing on Customer's File Household Status Indicator** Reported as: • Head of Household • Spouse • 2nd Individual	$ 3.00
284	**Spouse Occupation** • Professional/Technical • Student • Management • Homemaker • Sales/Marketing • Retired • Clerical • Other • Blue Collar	$12.00
286	**Marital Status** • Married • Single	$12.00
287	**Children's Age** Available by One-Year Increments (No gender available)	$12.00
288	**Verification Date (By Quarter and Year)** Address verification date.	$12.00

Note: Much of the demographic data listed above can also be purchased as InfoBase Premier data. Please see pages 2-3 for more details.

Data Sources

How to Order

To Place an Order by Mail

1. Fill out the order form completely. (If you have any questions regarding this form, please feel free to call (501) 336-3600 and ask to speak with one of our customer service representatives.)

2. List the data element numbers of all data elements desired. (For example, if you wish to select "Estimated income data from InfoBase Premier," you would list #641.)

3. Make sure you fill out each section, so that we will have all the information we need to process your order.

4. Sign page 3 of the order form on the line titled Authorized Signature.

5. Be sure to also sign the "Data Use Agreement for InfoBase" that you will find on page 4 of the order form.

When you have completed the order form, send it with your magnetic tape, record layout and printout of 100 sample records to:

InfoBase
301 Industrial Boulevard
Conway, AR 72032
Attn: Sherri Hayes

If your order is more complex or if you would like to discuss special processing options, please phone us between 9:00 a.m. and 5:00 p.m., Central Time, at (501) 336-3600 and ask for a customer service representative or speak with your InfoBase sales representative. We'll be glad to discuss your needs with you.

Scheduling

Standard Consumer InfoBase processing takes place weekly. Tapes received by Noon Tuesday will be enhanced and shipped out the following week on Thursday (seven working days later) for household level data.

When Consumer InfoBase is used in conjunction with research or other list services, additional time is required. Your InfoBase sales representative can assist you in developing a schedule that meets your needs.

Optional Output

Additional processing charges for the optional forms of output listed below are $3.00/M records input. ($25 minimum/ZipString) plus materials charges as follows:

Cheshire Labels	**No Charge**
Galley Listing	**$2.00/M**
Pressure Sensitive Labels	**$3.00/M**
3x5 Cards	**$8.00/M**

 *Continued*

Lifestyle Data

Consumers fill out questionnaires indicating the hobbies, interests and activities they or their spouse participate in on a regular basis. Lifestyle data is available at both the individual and neighborhood level. The price for each data element listed below is:

Individual Level: $7.00/M matches
Carrier Route Level: $3.00/M input

Data Element No.	Description	Data Element No.	Description
205	Art/Antiques	233	Household Pets
207	Automotive Work	234	House Plants
208	Book Reading	235	Hunting/Shooting
209	Bible/Devotional Reading	312	Military Veteran
		236	Money Making Opportunities
210	Bicycling		
211	Boating/Sailing	237	Motorcycling
212	Bowling	238	Needlework/Knitting
213	Cable TV Viewing	239	Our Nation's Heritage
214	Camping/Hiking	240	Personal and Home Computers
308	Career Oriented Activities	241	Photography
309	Casino Gambling	242	Physical Fitness/ Exercise
216	Collectibles		
217	Community/Civic Activities	244	Real Estate Investments
		245	Recreational Vehicles
218	Crafts	246	Running/Jogging
219	Crossword Puzzles	247	Science Fiction
220	Cultural/Arts Events	248	Science/ New Technology
221	Current Affairs/ Politics	249	Self Improvement
310	Dieting/ Weight Control	250	Sewing
		251	Snow Skiing
311	Donate to Charities	252	Stamp/Coin Collecting
222	Electronics	253	Stereo/Records/ Tapes/CDs
223	Fashion Clothing		
224	Fishing	254	Stocks/Bond Investments
225	Foreign Travel		
226	Gardening	255	Sweepstakes/Contests
227	Grandchildren	256	Tennis
228	Golf	257	Watching Sports on TV
229	Gourmet Cooking/ Fine Foods	258	Video Games
		259	VCR Recording/ Home Video
230	Health/Natural Foods		
231	Home Furnishings/ Decorating	260	Walking for Health
		261	Wildlife/Environmental
232	Home Workshop	262	Wines

Lifestyle Dimensions

A lifestyle dimension is more tightly defined than a comparable Lifestyle Composite. It consists of respondents who checked off more than one of the interests from a logical group of interests (depending on the particular dimension). The price for each data element listed below is:

Individual Level: $7.00/M matches
Carrier Route Level: $3.00/M input

Data Element No.	Description
271	**Domestic** (Checked off three or more) • Crafts • Gourmet Cooking/Fine Foods • Home Workshop • Needlework/Knitting • Sewing • Gardening • House Plants • Book Reading
272	**Do-It-Yourself** (Checked off two or more with at least one being*) • Automotive Work* • Motorcycling • Recreational Vehicles • Electronics* • Home Workshop*
273	**Fitness** (Checked off two or more with at least one being*) • Bicycling • Running/Jogging • Health/Natural Foods • Self-Improvement • Physical Fitness/Exercise*
274	**Athletic** (Checked off two or more) • Bicycling • Running/Jogging • Golf • Snow Skiing • Tennis
275	**Outdoors** (Checked off three or more) • Boating/Sailing • Hunting/Shooting • Fishing, Camping/Hiking • Motorcycling • Recreational Vehicles • Fishing
276	**Good Life** (Checked off three or more) • Cultural/Arts Events • Health/Natural Foods • Fashion Clothing • Home Furnishings/ Decorating • Gourmet Cooking/ Fine Foods • Wines • Foreign Travel
277	**Cultural** (Checked off two or more with at least one being*) • Collectibles/Collections • Crafts • Foreign Travel • Art/Antiques/Collecting* • Cultural/Arts Events*
278	**Blue Chip** (Checked off two or more with at least one being*) • Real Estate Investments* • Community/Civic Activities • Self-Improvement • Stocks/Bonds Investments*
279	**Technology** (Checked off three or more) • Electronics • Stereo/Records/Tapes/CDs • Photography • Home Video Recording • Video Games • Science/New Technology • Personal Home Computers

 *Continued*

Lifestyle Composites

A lifestyle composite consists of the indication that at least two of the interests within the composite was checked as a positive response. A person is coded 'yes' on a composite if they have checked at least the minimum number of interests which comprise that composite. The price for each data element listed below is:

Individual Level: $7.00/M matches
Carrier Route Level: $3.00/M input

Data Element No.	Description
320	**Club Sports** (Checked off two or more) • Bicycling • Tennis • Snow Skiing
321	**Traditionalist** (Checked off two or more) • Bible/Devotional Reading • Grandchildren • Our Nation's Heritage • Sweepstakes/Contests • Health/Natural Foods • Stamps/Coin Collecting
322	**Professional** (Checked off two or more) • Career-Oriented Activities • Money Making Opportunities • Self Improvement
323	**Investor** (Checked off two or more) • Real Estate Investments • Money Making Opportunities • Stocks/Bonds Investments
324	**Audio/Visual** (Checked off two or more) • Cable TV Viewing • Stereo/Records/Tapes/CDs • Home Video Games • Photography • Home Video Recording
325	**Campgrounder** (Checked off two or more) • Boating/Sailing • Camping/Hiking • Motorcycling • Recreational Vehicles
326	**Intelligentsia** (Checked off three or more) • Cultural/Arts Events • Book Reading • Current Affairs/Politics • Art/Antique Collecting • Community/Civic Activities • Foreign Travel
327	**Mechanic** (Checked off two or more) • Electronics • Home Workshop • Automotive Work • Motorcycling
328	**Reader** (Checked off two or more) • Book Reading • Crossword Puzzles • Science Fiction
329	**Chiphead** (Checked off two or more) • Electronics • Science/New Technology • Home/Personal Computers • Home Video Games
330	**Home & Garden** (Checked off two or more) • Gardening • Home Furnishings/Decorating • Home Workshop • Household Pets • House Plants
331	**Triathlete** (Checked off two or more) • Bicycling • Physical Fitness/Exercise • Health/Natural Foods • Running/Jogging • Walking for Health
332	**Connoisseur** (Checked off two or more) • Cultural/Arts Events • Gourmet Cooking/Fine Foods • Foreign Travel • Wines
333	**Ecologist** (Checked off two or more) • Our Nation's Heritage • Wildlife/Environmental Issues • Science/New Technology
334	**TV Guide** (Checked off two or more) • Cable TV Viewing • Home Video Recording • Golf • Watching Sports on TV
263	**Collector** (Checked off two or more) • Art/Antique Collecting • Stamp/Coin Collecting • Collectibles/Collections
264	**Handicrafts** (Checked off two or more) • Crafts • Needlework/Knitting • Sewing
335	**Field & Stream** (Checked off two or more) • Boating/Sailing • Hunting/Shooting • Fishing

Price Structure for "Lifestyle Coding" Customer Files

Prices per thousand **input** records for household and neighborhood level data.

Input file In 1000's	All Lifestyles	20 Selected Lifestyles	10 Selected Lifestyles
Less than 1,000	$30.00/M	$20.00/M	$15.00/M
1,000 - 1,999	25.00/M	17.00/M	13.00/M
2,000 - 3,999	20.00/M	15.00/M	11.00/M
4,000 - 4,999	17.00/M	12.00/M	9.00/M
More than 5,000	15.00/M	10.00/M	7.00/M

Minimum order $1,500.00

- Additional $1.00/M input processing charge. See F5 on page 2 of the order form.

The R.L. Polk data is compiled from multiple sources. Information from motor vehicle registrations, Polk city directories and telephone directories is supplemented by numerous other sources.

Most of the Polk data is included in InfoBase Premier. The exceptions are registered vehicle model year, body size of newest registered car and the specific mail order data (#178-192).

Age and Household Composition

Data Element No.	Description	Price per M Matches
138	**Structure Age (Year)** Year in which this structure (house number) first appeared on some source list.	$ 5.00
136	**Household Census Retiree** Indicates a retiree is present in household. Information is gathered from door to door personal interviews.	$ 5.00
151	**Additional Name/Gender/Relationship** When the individual listed on the customer file matches a name and address on Consumer InfoBase, up to five additional names of householders can be overlaid. Included with each name are the gender and the position in the household (head of household, spouse or other). Price per each set of name, gender and relationship overlaid.	$ 3.00
152	**Individual Name Appearing on Customer's File Age in 2-Year Increments** Calculated from the exact date of birth, this element is delivered in the form of a 2-year age range. For example 38-39 years old, 40-41 years old. Provided for the individual whose first name is submitted for matching. Categories extend from under 18 to 100 plus.	$12.00
198	**Individual Name Appearing on Customer's File Household Status Indicator** Reported as: • Head of Household • Spouse • 2nd Individual • 3rd Individual • 4th Individual • 5th Individual	$ 3.00
153	**Household Member Age in 2-Year Increments** Two year increment age for each household member. No duplication occurs when selected in conjunction with element 152.	$12.00
154	**Adult Age Ranges** An inexpensive alternative to reporting age in 2-year increments, this segment categorizes ages in the following groups, including an indication of male, female or unknown gender. • 18-24 • 45-54 • 75+ • 25-34 • 55-64 • 35-44 • 65-74	$ 8.00
155	**Children's Age Ranges** Children's age, reported with gender (when known) as: • 0-2 • 6-10 • 16-17 • 3-5 • 11-15	$ 8.00
156	**Number of Adults in Household** This element reports the presence of up to nine and more adults as members of the household.	$ 5.00
168	**Presence of Children** Indicates the actual and inferred presence of children in the household.	$ 5.00
157	**Number of Children in Household** Counts the number of children in the household up to eight or more.	$ 5.00
197	**Estimated Income Range** An estimate of household income based on a variety of factors, including age, occupation, home ownership, median income for the local area, and more. Reported as one of the following: • Less than $15,000 • $ 50,000 - $ 74,999 • $15,000 - $19,999 • $ 75,000 - $ 99,999 • $20,000 - $29,999 • $100,000 - $124,999 • $30,000 - $39,999 • $125,000 Plus • $40,000 - $49,999	$10.00
170	**Verification Date (By Quarter and Year)** Address verification date.	$ 5.00
159	**Occupation** Coded for the following classifications: • Professional/Technical • Foreman • Doctors • Operatives • Lawyers • Farm • Teachers/Librarians • Unskilled • Administrative/Managerial • Service Workers • Management • Military • Proprietors • Student • Supervisors • Retired • Sales/Service • Homemaker • Clerical/White Collar	$10.00
169	**Marital Status** • Married • Single	$ 3.00

Housing

Data Element No.	Description	Price per M Matches
160	**Apartment Number**	$ 2.00
161	**Home Ownership** • Owner • Renter • Probable owner • Probable renter of a home	$ 5.00
162	**Dwelling Unit Size** Counts the number of known households at an address: 1 3 5 7 9 10-19 30-39 50-99 2 4 6 8 20-29 40-49 100+	$ 5.00
163	**Length of Residence** Approximated by the year that the household first appeared on TotaList.	$ 3.00

POLK. *Continued*

Mail Order Information

Data Element No.	Description	Price per M Matches
172	**Mail Order Buyer**	$10.00
173	**Mail Responder**	$ 5.00
174	**Credit Card Indicator** Indication of possession of the following types of credit cards, alone or in combination. • Bank Card • Bank & Retail Card • Retail Card • Other (unknown type)	$10.00
177	**Direct Mail Donors**	$12.00
178	**Mail Order Buyer by Dollar Amount** • Low (less than $15) • High (greater than $50) • Medium ($15 - $50)	$20.00
179	**Mail Order Responder by Dollar Amount** • Low (less than $15) • High (greater than $50) • Medium ($15 - $50)	$20.00
180	**Mail Order Donor by Dollar Amount** • Low (less than $50) • High (greater than $100) • Medium ($50 - $100)	$20.00
182	**Mail Order Responder by Type** • Catalog General Merchandise • Health/Fitness/Exercise • Bargain Seekers • Magazines • Books/Music • General Merchandise • Health Donor • Investments	$20.00
183	**Low Dollar Mail Order Buyer by Type (Less Than $15)**	$20.00
184	**Medium Dollar Mail Order Buyer by Type ($15 - $50)**	$20.00
185	**High Dollar Mail Order Buyer by Type (Greater Than $50)**	$20.00
186	**Low Dollar Mail Order Donor by Type (Less Than $50)** • Religious • Environmental, Humanitarian, Educational • Health Causes • Political	$20.00
187	**Medium Dollar Mail Order Donor by Type ($50 - $100)**	$20.00
188	**High Dollar Mail Order Donor by Type (Greater Than $100)**	$20.00

Motor Vehicle Information

Data Element No.	Description	Price per M Matches
164	**Registered Cars/Number of Cars Owned**	$12.00
165	**Truck/Motorcycle/RV Owners** Many of these specialty vehicle owners display a greater-than-average interest in outdoors and do-it-yourself activities.	$10.00
166	**Dominant Vehicle Lifestyle Indicator** This indicator distinguishes the classification of the primary vehicle registered to the household: • Personal Luxury Car, e.g. Corvette, Audi 100, Mazda 929, Infiniti, Lexus, Mercedes Benz • Truck or Passenger Utility Vehicle, e.g. Jeep Cherokee, Toyota Previa, Lumina APV • Station wagon, e.g. Buick Roadmaster, Taurus Station Wagon • Import, (standard or economy car), e.g. Toyota Camry, Nissan Stanza, Volkswagen Passat • Regular, (mid-size or small car), e.g. Dodge Spirit, Ford Tempo • Specialty, (mid-size or luxury car), e.g. Grand Marquis, Eagle, Mustang, Accord, Corolla, Saab • Full Size, (standard or luxury car), e.g. Taurus, LeBaron, Continental, Cadillac	$ 8.00
175	**Registered Vehicle Model Years** Up to three registered vehicles' model years.	Call for Quote
192	**Body Size of Newest Registered Car** • Standard, e.g. Buick Roadmaster, Caprice, Crown Victoria, Grand Marquis • Luxury, e.g. Cadillac De Ville, Chrysler New Yorker • Personal Luxury, e.g. Lincoln Continental, Corvette, Cadillac Seville, Dodge Viper • Intermediate Regular, e.g. Oldsmobile Cutlass Ciera, Chrysler LeBaron Sedan, Chevrolet Lumina, Ford Taurus • Intermediate Specialty, e.g. Cougar/XR7, Dodge 600 ES, Thunderbird • Compact Regular, e.g. Dodge Spirit, Skylark, Tempo, Topaz • Compact Specialty, e.g. Eagle, Grand Am, Mustang, Probe • Subcompact Regular, e.g. Escort, Saturn SC/SL1/SL2, Sundance • Subcompact Specialty, e.g. Eagle Talon, Plymouth Laser, Pontiac 2000 • Passenger Utility, e.g. Jeep Cherokee, GMC Suburban, Mazda MPV, Pontiac Trans Sport, Toyota Previa • Economy Import, e.g. Geo Metro, Volkswagen Golf, Hyundai Excel, Nissan Sentra, Toyota Tercel • Standard Size Import, e.g. Accord, Mazda 626, Mitsubishi Galant, Volkswagen Passat, Saab 900, Subaru Legacy • Sporty Import, e.g. Audi 80/Quattro, Volkswagen Corrado, Jaguar XJS, Mazda Miata, Porche • Luxury Import, e.g. Bentley, Infiniti, Lexus, Mercedes Benz, Rolls Royce	$12.00
194	**Aggregate Value of Vehicles Owned** The total value of all vehicles registered in the household based on blue book value.	$12.00
195	**New Car/Truck Buyer** An indication of a history of new car/truck buying.	$12.00

 *Continued*

Address Confirmation

Data Element No.	Description	Price per M Matches
167	**Positive Match Indicator** Help regenerate the lapsed, expired or inactive portion of your file by identifying matches against any TotaList record. Regularly recompiled and address-corrected, TotaList matches represent a strong likelihood that name and address records are still valid and deliverable.	
	• Under 500M input	$ 5.00
	• 500M - 1,999M input	4.00
	• 2,000M - 4,999M input	3.00
	• 5,000M Plus	2.00
171	**Telephone Number** The continuous compilation of telephone directories offers marketers an inexpensive alternative to directory assistance service and manual look-up charges. Each listing has been made market-ready with time zones and area codes.	
	• Under 1,000M input	$20.00
	• 1,000M - 1,999M input	18.00
	• 2,000M - 3,999M input	16.00
	• 4,000M - 4,999M input	14.00
	• 5,000M Plus	12.00
176	**Special Rate for R.L. Polk & Co. Data Elements 138-174, 194 Except Telephone Numbers**	
	• Under 1,000M input	$30.00
	• 1,000M - 1,999M input	26.00
	• 2,000M - 3,999M input	21.00
	• 4,000M - 4,999M input	17.00
	• 5,000M Plus	14.00
181	**Special Rate for R.L. Polk & Co. Data Elements 138-174, 194 Including Telephone Numbers**	
	• Under 1,000M input	$40.00
	• 1,000M - 1,999M input	36.00
	• 2,000M - 3,999M input	31.00
	• 4,000M - 4,999M input	27.00
	• 5,000M Plus	24.00

Miscellaneous

Data Element No.	Description	Price per M Matches
	Household Response Data by Type	$20.00 per category
801	Smokers	
802	Veterans	

Note: Most of the Polk data listed above can also be purchased in the InfoBase Premier data. Please see pages 2-3 for more details.

TRANSMARK LISTS

TransMark, the list marketing division of TransUnion, gathers data from credit grantors such as banks and chain/specialty department stores. The data is available at the individual level.

Age and Household Composition

Data Element No.	Description	Price per M Matches
875	**Verification Date** Address verification date by month and year.	$ 5.00
877	**2nd Individual Name, Gender And Relationship**	$ 3.00
878	**2 Year Age of Head of Household** Age represented in 2 year increments starting at under eighteen and ending with 100 plus.	$14.00
899	**2 Year Age of Individual Name Appearing on Customer's file**	$12.00
879	**Date of Birth of Head of Household** Year of birth and month when available.	$20.00
898	**Date of Birth of Individual Name Appearing on Customer's file**	$20.00
864	**Individual Name Appearing on Customer's File Household Status Indicator** Reported as: • Head of Household • Spouse • 2nd Individual • 4th Individual • 3rd Individual • 5th Individual	$ 3.00
876	**Head of Household Name, Gender and Relationship**	$ 3.00
880	**2 Year Age of 2nd Individual** Age represented in 2 year increments starting at under eighteen and ending with 100 plus.	$14.00
881	**Date of Birth of 2nd Individual** Year of birth and month when available.	$20.00
882	**10 Year Adult Age Ranges** (each range is coded by gender when available) • 18-24 • 45-54 • 75+ • 25-34 • 55-64 • 35-44 • 65-74	$10.00
888	**3rd Individual Name, Gender and Relationship**	$ 3.00
890	**2 Year Age of 3rd Individual** Age represented in 2 year increments starting at under eighteen and ending with 100 plus.	$14.00
891	**Date of Birth of 3rd Individual** Year of birth and month when available.	$20.00
892	**4th Individual Name, Gender and Relationship**	$ 3.00
893	**2 Year Age of 4th Individual** Age represented in 2 year increments starting at under eighteen and ending with 100 plus.	$14.00
894	**Date of Birth of 4th Individual** Year of birth and month when available.	$20.00
895	**5th Individual Name, Gender and Relationship**	$ 3.00
896	**2 Year Age of 5th Individual** Age represented in 2 year increments starting at under eighteen and ending with 100 plus.	$14.00
897	**Date of Birth of 5th Individual** Year of birth and month when available.	$20.00

Housing Information

Data Element No.	Description	Price per M Matches
870	**Home Market Value** • $ 1,000 - $ 24,999 • $ 250,000 - $274,999 • $ 25,000 - $ 49,999 • $ 275,000 - $299,999 • $ 50,000 - $ 74,999 • $ 300,000 - $349,999 • $ 75,000 - $ 99,999 • $ 350,000 - $399,999 • $ 100,000 - $124,999 • $ 400,000 - $449,999 • $ 125,000 - $149,999 • $ 450,000 - $499,999 • $ 150,000 - $174,999 • $ 500,000 - $774,999 • $ 175,000 - $199,999 • $ 775,000 - $999,999 • $ 200,000 - $224,999 • $1,000,000 Plus • $ 225,000 - $249,999	$20.00
871	**Month Home was Purchased** Ranges from 01 to 12	$ 5.00
872	**Year Home was Purchased** Years range from 1901 to 1992.	$ 5.00
873	**Purchase Date of Home** Both year and month of purchase. Ranges from 1901 to 1992. Month and/or year may not be available in all cases.	$10.00
874	**Home Owner Indicator**	$ 5.00
884	**Apartment Number**	$ 2.00

Motor Vehicle Information

Data Element No.	Description	Price per M Matches
866	**Personal Luxury Vehicle** Indicates the presence of a vehicle in a price range of $25,000 or more.	$ 8.00
867	**Vehicle Price Class** Low priced/used car buyers, medium and high priced car buyers. Low = $ 500 - $ 9,999 Med = $10,000 - $ 19,999 High = $20,000 - $100,000	$ 8.00
869	**New Car Buyer** A history of new car buying	$12.00
869	**Number of Cars** Numbers range from 1 to 3 or more cars.	$12.00

Miscellaneous

Data Element No.	Description	Price per M Matches
865	**Credit Card Indicator** Indicates presence of: • bank • premium • retail/department store • upscale retail/department store	$15.00

TRW data is derived from public records and consumer data.

Age and Household Composition

Data Element No.	Description	Price per M Matches
350	**Date of Birth of Head of Household** Year of birth, month and day when available.	$20.00
352	**2 Year Age of Head of Household** Age represented in 2 year increments starting at under eighteen and ending with 100 plus.	$14.00
394	**2 Year Age of Individual Name Appearing on Customer's File**	$12.00
353	**Verification Date** Address verification by quarter and year.	$ 5.00
354	**10 year Adult Age Ranges** • 18-24 • 45-54 • 75+ • 25-34 • 55-64 • 35-44 • 65-74 (each range is coded by gender when available)	$10.00
395	**Date of Birth of Individual Name Appearing on Customer's File**	$20.00
351	**Individual Name Appearing on Customer's File Household Status Indicator** Reported as: • Head of Household • Spouse • 2nd Individual • 4th Individual • 3rd Individual • 5th Individual	$ 3.00
355	**Date of Birth of Spouse or 2nd Individual** Year of birth, month and day when available.	$20.00
357	**Dwelling Unit Size** Single or multi-family dwelling.	$ 5.00
358	**Marital Status** Indicates married only, no singles, widows or divorced.	$ 3.00
359	**Estimated Income** • Less than $15,000 • $ 50,000 - $ 74,999 • $15,000 - $19,999 • $ 75,000 - $ 99,999 • $20,000 - $29,999 • $100,000 - $124,999 • $30,000 - $39,999 • $125,000 Plus • $40,000 - $49,999	$10.00
363	**Home Owner** Indicates owner only, no renters available.	$ 5.00

Data Element No.	Description	Price per M Matches
374	**Date of Birth of up to Seven Children** Coded by gender when available	$17.50
366	**Elderly Parent in Household** Indicates presence of a parent in household of offspring.	$ 2.00
377	**College Age Child in Household** Males, females, and unknown gender ages 18-24.	$ 5.00
380	**Presence of Children** Identifies household with child(ren) only.	$ 5.00
381	**Head of Household Name, Gender and Relationship**	$ 3.00
382	**2nd Individual Name, Gender and Relationship**	$ 3.00
383	**2nd Individual 2 Year Age** Age represented in 2 year increments starting at under eighteen and ending with 100 plus.	$14.00
384	**3rd Individual Name, Gender and Relationship**	$ 3.00
385	**3rd Individual 2 Year Age** Age represented in 2 year increments starting at under eighteen and ending with 100 plus.	$14.00
386	**3rd Individual Date of Birth** Year of birth, month and day when available.	$20.00
387	**4th Individual Name, Gender and Relationship**	$ 3.00
388	**4th Individual 2 Year Age** Age represented in 2 year increments starting at under eighteen and ending with 100 plus.	$14.00
389	**4th Individual Date of Birth** Year of birth, month and day when available.	$20.00
390	**Apartment Number**	$ 2.00
391	**5th Individual Name, Gender and Relationship**	$ 3.00
392	**5th Individual 2 Year Age** Age represented in 2 year increments starting at under eighteen and ending with 100 plus.	$14.00
393	**5th Individual Date of Birth** Year of birth, month and day when available.	$20.00
397	**Length of Residence** From less than one year to more than 15 years at the same address.	$ 3.00
398	**Number of Children** From one to six or more children ages 0-18.	$ 5.00

The InfoBase Service Guarantee

Orders for standard list enhancement received by Noon Tuesday with all information specified on the order form will be completed and shipped the following week on Thursday, seven business days later, or you pay only for the data applied and the processing is free.

This guarantee applies to files up to 4 million records that do not require special processing or priority selections.

May & Speh
DIRECT

DATABASE ENHANCEMENTS

Data enhancement is the addition of demographic and behavioral information to a customer or prospect file in order to identify the significant characteristics and traits of these individuals.

Enhancement data goes beyond basic purchase and payment history information and allows the user to develop detailed insights about specific individuals within the larger group of customers or prospects. It provides timely answers to key questions faced by the sales and marketing force such as:

- *What is the age of my customers?*
- *What is my customer's marital status?*
- *Does my customer have children?*
- *Does my customer own his/her home?*
- *Does my customer use credit cards?*
- *What is my customer's income?*
- *What is my customer's occupation?*

At May & Speh Direct, we maintain enhancement data on more than 90 million households and over 190 million individuals. It's compiled from in-depth consumer information to provide a lifestyle profile of your customers and prospects — thus increasing your marketing effectiveness. You'll also be able to identify the most profitable segments of your database — and eliminate unprofitable ones.

Our information is available in three categories of data:

Demographics
Information that describes the physical characteristics associated with an individual or household such as age, income, occupation, home ownership, etc.

Purchase Behavior
Information that describes the nature of how consumers spend their money, such as credit cards, automobiles and home ownership.

Geodemographic Targeting Systems
Geodemographic targeting is based upon the concept that people with similar cultural backgrounds, means and perspectives naturally gravitate toward one another. They choose to live among their peers in neighborhoods offering compatible lifestyles. They have similar social values, tastes and expectations. They share patterns of consumer behavior toward products, services, media and promotions.

Information Sources

R. L. Polk

The Polk TotaList database provides individual and household level demographics. It is the result of merging more than 456 million records annually from over 21 sources on more than 90 million households. The Polk data includes over 100 categories of information, such as:

- *Age, Income, Number of Adults/Children, Occupation*
- *Housing information such as home ownership, length of residence and multi/single family dwelling*
- *Mail order and consumer purchase information*

PRIZM/PRIZM + 4

PRIZM is a market segmentation system which partitions the U.S. into 40 clusters. The clusters are organized into 12 broad social groups. Through analysis of census demographic data and consumer activity, a cluster code is assigned to each of 540,000 neighborhood units.

PRIZM + 4 is an option used to target consumers by Zip + 4 areas which average less than 10 households in size.

Exact Age

May & Speh Direct provides exact age data on over 190 million consumers 18 years and older. This data is provided by a leading credit reporting source in the U.S.

MicroVision

Developed by Equifax Marketing Decision Systems, MicroVision is a market segmentation system that partitions the U.S. into 50 clusters. The clusters are organized into nine groups comprised of segments that have similar characteristics or habits. This system is based upon selected data elements from the U.S. Census and individual level data. MicroVision is available at the Zip + 4 level creating the ability to select groups as small as 10-15 households and fine-tuning your targeting efforts.

Deceased Screen

Through data provided by the U.S. government, we provide a list of 9 million recently deceased individuals. This data is available for screening purposes only.

Telephone Number Verification & Appending

We offer telephone numbers from the two leading national telephone sources. There are over 80 million records available with time-zone data to append to your file or verify your current data. Choose from either source, append both, or choose one as a priority and fill from the second.

May & Speh

DATA ENHANCEMENT SERVICES
Making A Good Product Better

Identify Who's Buying Your Products

A well built and maintained database provides a sophisticated marketing tool, however, that database is only as good as the information that is captured about customers and prospects.

Database enhancement allows a marketer to overlay externally compiled information on customer or prospect records already in the database. The result is an enhanced record with more information available for marketing purposes than a database marketer could compile on his or her own.

Learn More About Customers Or Prospects

A detailed picture can be built through single or multiple variate analysis techniques of the characteristics attributed to customers or prospects. This information can help identify customers as individuals, not aggregate statistics. These customer profiles can be used for research, new product development, media targeting, creative development and many more uses tailored to specific information needs.

Increase The Effectiveness Of Customer Programs

Database enhancement can help find the most profitable segments of a database (or eliminate unprofitable ones) and develop cross-selling opportunities. More effective data usage will create a true relationship with customers by communicating with them based on the detailed knowledge of their buying habits and product preferences.

Increase Response Rates For Prospecting Programs

The option to combine data enhancement with data modeling and analysis techniques helps to identify the key characteristics of your best customers and prospects. This process will identify consumers who have a propensity to respond like existing customers, thus increasing response rates.

May & Speh Direct - The Comprehensive Data Enhancement Resource

May & Speh's Data Enhancement Service provides data overlay and/or list rental services from the most comprehensive information warehouse available in the direct marketing industry. Our Enhancement System has immediate access to demographic, financial and behavioral information on more than 90 million U.S. households and over 125 million U.S. consumers.

The following is a brief synopsis of the enhancement products available at May & Speh.

TotaList

May & Speh's primary data enhancement file is based on R.L. Polk's TotaList data file. TotaList is the result of merging more than 456 million records annually from 21 different sources including: current motor vehicle registration, 1990 Census Data, telephone directories, birth date information, questionnaire data, new motor vehicle purchase and many other sources. The procedures used to compile the TotaList file capitalize on the strength of each source and allow May & Speh to quickly and effectively select and overlay customer files. TotaList contains individual information segments for each family member within a specific household.

Quantity: 109MM records

Maintenance/ Update Cycles: Quarterly

Age of Data: No record is older than 24 months. Any record that has not been verified within the last 18 months is dropped.

Usage Options: List Rental and/or File Enhancement

List Rental: Element: Name, Address, City, State, Zip.

Optional Elements:
Gender, Age, Income, Occupation, Marital Status, Dwelling, Children and expansions thereof.

Exact Age

May & Speh's Exact Age file is a timely and cost effective means to segment customer or prospect files. May & Speh's Exact Age file is compiled from over 195 million source records; 94% containing exact age.

Tel-Xpres

May & Speh's Tel-Xpres product is a timely and cost effective means to correct, append or validate customer telephone information. Tel-Xpres appends area code and telephone number and optionally time zone to customer files with guaranteed 48 hour turnaround. May & Speh's Tel-Xpres file is compiled from over 163 million source records that are updated on a quarterly basis.

Telephone-Name Conversion (Reverse Append)

May & Speh's Telephone Name Conversion product enhances raw telephone number lists with complete name and address information.

* *Some restrictions apply. See your Sales Representative for details.*

TOTALIST

ITEM	M&S OUTPUT POSITION	UNIV. COUNT (1,000's)	CATEGORY	DATA ELEMENT
1				X-1 Match Indicator
2	036-055			Last Name
3	056-069			First Name
4	070			Middle Initial
5	075-088	51,616.9		Secondary Given Name
6	090-129			Address
7	155-169	15,550.8	Dwelling	Apartment Number
8	170-184			City (Post Office)
9	185-186			State
10	008-011	97,716.1		Zip +4
11	032-035	96,995.2		Carrier Route Code
**12	012-014			Bar Code
13	074	103,768.0	Sex	Gender
14	187-189		Census	FIPS County Code
15	190-193		Census	Metropolitan Statistical Area - MSA
16	194-197		Census	Sales Management Metropolitan Area - SMMA
17	198-201		Census	Area of Dominant Influence - ADI
18	202-205		Census	Designated Marketing Area - DMA
19	210		Census	Nielsen County Size Code
20	211-220	60,416.5	Phone	Area Code and Phone 1,000M Input 1,000 - 2,000M Input 2,000 - 4,000M Input 4,000 - 5,000M Input 5,000 - 10,000M Input 10,000 - 15,000M Input 15,000 - 20,000M Input 20,000 - 40,000M Input 40,000M & Over
**21			Phone	Telephone Directory Publication Date
22	222	108,988.9	Mailing	Address Quality Code
23	223	108,988.9	Mailing	Address Type
24	225	108,988.9	Mailing	Record Status Code
25	226-228	98,077.0	Dwellling	Housing Size
26	229	82,410.6	Dwelling	SFDU/MFDU Dwelling Type
27	230	108,988.9	Mailing	Mail Code
28	231	108,981.3	Dwelling	City Delivery Service Code - CDS
29	232-233	108,988.9	Home	Length of Residence
30	234-235	103,581.3	Home	Structure Age Year
31	236-239		Recency	Polk Verification Date
32	240-241	108,309.3	Sources	# of X-1 Contributing Sources
33	242	44,283.0	Behavior	Mail Responder Buyer Code
34	243-245	108,954.4	Income	New Narrow Estimated Income Code
35	246	108,963.0	Income	New Income Code
36	247	45,776.2	Home	Home Ownership Code
37	248-249	37,014.2	Occupation	Occupation Code
38	250	6,009.3	Survey	HCL Retiree
39	251	40,205.0	Behavior	Credit Card User Code
40	254	108,442.8	Household	# of Persons in Household

42	255	107,590.8	Adults	# of Adults in Household
43	256	38,591.7	Adults	Presence of Adults - Unknown Age
44	257	6,428.2	Adults	Adults Age 75+ Specific
45	258	10,422.1	Adults	Adults Age 65-74 Specific
46	259	10,318.9	Adults	Adults Age 55-64 Specific
47	260	12,973.9	Adults	Adults Age 45-54 Specific
48	261	17,312.5	Adults	Adults Age 35-44 Specific
49	262	16,195.3	Adults	Adults Age 25-34 Specific
50	263	5,891.3	Adults	Adults Age 18-24 Specific
51	264	5,336.1	Adults	Adults Age 65+ Inferred
52	265	3,658.5	Adults	Adults Age 45-64 Inferred
53	266	19,112.1	Adults	Adults Age 35-44 Inferred
54	267	22,990.2	Adults	Adults Age < 35 Inferred
55	268	2,581.3	Children	Presence of Children 0-2
56	269	2,487.8	Children	Presence of Children 3-5
57	270	5,067.5	Children	Presence of Children 6-10
58	271	6,451.2	Children	Presence of Children 11-15
59	272	2,970.0	Children	Presence of Children 16-17
60	273	11,914.4	Children	Presence of Children Unknown Gender 0-17
61	274	22,504.0	Children	Number of Children
62	275-276	108,988.9	Home	Household Type (Family Composition)
63	277	53,758.7	Marital	Marital Status Code
64	278	108,988.9	Home	Household Age Indicator
65	279	108,988.9	Home	Household Age Code
66	280-281	108,988.9	Tri-Cell	Primary Tri-Cell
67	282-283	108,988.9	Tri-Cell	Secondary Tri-Cell
68	284-285	108,988.9	Tri-Cell	Tertiary Tri-Cell
69	286-289	44,271.6	Vehicle	Combined Market Value of all Vehicles
70	290	69,019.9	Vehicle	# of Cars Currently Owned and Registered
71	291-292	48,145.8	Vehicle	Body Size of Newest Car Owned
72	294	23,161.6	Vehicle	Truck Owner
73	295	21,348.2	Vehicle	New Vehicle Purchase Code
74	296	2,284.1	Vehicle	Motorcycle Owner
75	297	5,158.2	Vehicle	Recreational Vehicle Ownership Code
76	298	59,095.0	Household	Count of Age Elements
77	299-317		Household	Age Element 1
78	318-336		Household	Age Element 2
79	337-355		Household	Age Element 3
80	356-374		Household	Age Element 4
81	375-393		Household	Age Element 5
82	394	108,656.5	Phone	Time Zone
83	015	23,107.3	Move	Zip Mobility
84	016-020		Move	Move Distance (In Miles)

** Elements added in last update.

TOTALIST
TOP 19 ELEMENTS

ITEM	UNIVERSE COUNT (1,000's)	CATEGORY	DATA ELEMENT
1			X-1 Positive Match Indicator
2		Name	Secondary Given Name
3	15,550.8	Dwelling	Apartment
4	103,768.0	Sex	Gender
5	98,077.0	Dwelling	Housing Size
6	108,988.9	Home	Length of Residence
7		Recency	Polk Verification
8	108,954.4	Income	Income Code
9	45,776.2	Home	Home Ownership Code
10	37,014.2	Occupation	Occupation Code
11	108,442.8	Household	# of Persons in Household
12	107,590.8	Adults	# of Adults in Household
13	38,591.7	Adults	Presence of Adults - Unknown Age
	6,428.2		Adults Age 75+ Specific
	10,422.1		Adults Age 65-74 Specific
	10,318.9		Adults Age 55-64 Specific
	12,973.9		Adults Age 45-54 Specific
	17,312.5		Adults Age 35-44 Specific
	16,195.3		Adults Age 25-34 Specific
	5,891.3		Adults Age 18-24 Specific
	5,336.1		Adults Age 65+ Inferred
	3,658.5		Adults Age 45-64 Inferred
	19,112.1		Adults Age 35-44 Inferred
	22,990.2		Adults Age < 35 Inferred
14	2,581.3	Children	Presence of Children 0-2
	2,487.8		Presence of Children 3-5
	5,067.5		Presence of Children 6-10
	6,451.2		Presence of Children 11-15
	2,970.0		Presence of Children 16-17
15	11,914.4	Children	Presence of Children Unknown Gender 0-17
16	22,504.0	Children	Number of Children
17	53,758.7	Marital	Marital Status Code
18	108,988.9	Tri-Cell	Primary Tri-Cell
			Secondary Tri-Cell
			Tertiary Tri-Cell
19	44,271.6	Vehicle	Combined Market Value of All Vehicles

METROMAIL'S BEHAVIORBANK®

The BEHAVIORBANK DATABASE totals over 28 MILLION HOUSEHOLDS and is composed entirely of direct mail respondents who have shared their lifestyle and product usage information with us via detailed surveys. Our surveys are distributed in direct mail buyers' packages, direct mail co-ops, magazine and Sunday newspaper inserts.

SPECIAL CATEGORIES

Product Ownership	Master File	Last 6 Mos.
Compact Disc Player	2,614,328	307,216
Dishwasher	10,316,697	711,783
Exercise Bicycle	562,588	184,688
Microwave	13,421,755	988,088
Mobile Phone	665,587	197,554
Phone Answering Machine	2,895,980	453,348
Power Boat	871,708	31,257
Sailboat	298,508	18,944
Vacation Home	958,620	68,451
VCR	12,956,084	941,615
Video Camera	426,480	62,378
Video Games	379,991	69,159
Fundraising Contributors		
Animal Welfare	3,887,924	271,903
Child Welfare	3,910,016	268,455
Cultural Arts	1,191,646	75,377
Environmental	2,824,477	203,848
Health Related	7,398,962	500,698
Political	1,686,708	72,737
Religious	10,295,816	499,710
Pet Owners		
Birds	1,207,241	78,470
Cats	8,190,052	532,353
Dogs	10,763,501	699,627
Investors		
Annuities	394,588	24,228
Bonds	1,895,997	96,386
Certificates of Deposit	1,917,812	74,821
IRAs/401Ks	3,731,049	200,757
Money Market Funds	1,965,070	95,513
Mutual Funds	1,352,914	74,199
Savings Accounts	6,445,988	282,691
Stocks	2,706,156	135,155

Occupation	Master File	Last 6 Mos.
Blue Collar	4,185,624	346,840
Business Owner	1,946,534	127,658
Craftsman/Tradesman	2,745,109	194,746
Executive Upper Management	1,165,446	80,229
Homemaker	5,688,504	369,476
In-Home Business	411,844	66,442
Middle Management	2,542,228	175,334
Nurse	755,910	65,805
Office/Clerical	2,394,346	251,377
Professional	3,610,341	304,167
Retired	3,880,487	225,580
Teacher/Educator	901,195	69,321
Other Selections		
Cable TV Subscriber	3,905,683	127,180
Casino Gambler	971,924	66,112
Credit Union Member	1,642,465	221,358
Frequent Auto Renter	308,987	36,298
Frequent Flyer	1,466,101	116,146
Government Worker	1,504,687	103,585
Handicraft/Hobbyist	875,900	28,801
Hotel Club Member	566,731	40,182
Outdoor Sportsman	1,168,120	37,375
Veteran	5,122,764	309,156
Weight Watchers Member	220,388	36,284
Other Weight Loss Group	188,501	34,746
Personal Computer Owners		
Apple	801,244	55,312
Atari	150,222	13,852
Commodore	1,072,010	73,400
Computer Modem	1,702,704	20,301
IBM or Compatible	1,264,100	100,033
Macintosh	163,472	24,232
Other	1,135,662	81,330
Sweepstakes/Contests/Lotteries		
Entrants	16,670,328	1,061,411

Credit Cards	Master File	Last 6 Mos.
American Express	3,131,664	206,355
Diners Club/Carte Blanche	445,065	33,101
Dept. Store/Gas	9,269,118	696,181
Discover	2,950,106	179,168
Gold Mastercard/Visa	1,836,664	156,046
Mastercard/Visa	11,585,688	836,586
None	5,686,154	371,460
Mail Order Buyers		
Athletic Equipment	464,740	74,913
Books	6,051,884	569,419
Children's Products	3,079,088	255,215
Cosmetics/Jewelry	2,948,760	243,575
Crafts/Hobbies	3,095,395	364,604
Diet Aids	248,236	37,707
Electronics	773,556	32,813
Financial Services	50,172	22,269
Food/Sundries	1,631,805	112,625
Gardening Supplies	2,436,457	225,327
Gifts Below $50	4,682,431	359,527
Gifts Above $50	1,663,919	304,888
Housewares/Furniture	1,650,146	216,112
Insurance	1,481,344	113,089
Magazines	10,842,158	790,495
Men's Apparel/Shoes	2,368,598	169,380
Movie Videos	166,372	70,368
Records/Tapes/CDs	4,073,405	338,996
Stationery/Cards	281,104	110,213
Travel/Vacation	275,971	44,161
Vitamins/Health Products	503,822	71,268
Women's Clothes/Shoes	4,820,404	347,227
Other Merchandise	4,577,574	373,889
Residence Type		
Apartment	5,589,168	427,445
Single Family Dwelling Unit	16,000,140	912,990

LIFESTYLE INTERESTS

	Master File	Last 6 Mos.
Astrology/Occult	1,619,968	125,098
Automotive Work	5,541,788	434,629
Avid Book Reader	9,538,364	718,760
Bible/Devotional	1,922,815	207,323
Camping/Hiking	5,073,504	398,885
Collectibles	4,394,382	355,017
Crafts	8,170,948	611,349
Cultural/Arts Events	2,676,474	225,978
Cycling	2,187,975	173,987
Diet Conscious	4,168,597	210,021
Domestic Travel	4,702,356	377,149
Fishing	7,099,739	513,373
Fitness/Exercise	5,454,007	370,596
Foreign Travel	2,092,303	173,135
Gardening	8,957,740	611,710
Golf Frequently	2,620,138	216,091
Gourmet Foods/Cooking	5,830,324	483,456
Health Vitamins	4,415,404	357,666
Home Workshop/Do-it-Yourself	6,917,748	518,645
Hunting	4,096,109	134,636
Needlework	5,635,764	406,133
Photography	4,882,916	429,338
Racquetball	294,560	45,972
Records/Tapes/CDs	8,994,992	737,237
Self-improvement	628,976	2,639
Sewing	5,535,928	406,954
Snow Skiing	1,960,932	163,768
Stamp Collecting	1,040,038	89,233
Tennis	1,125,894	97,333
Vacation Cruises	2,070,449	159,178
Watching Sports on TV	143,700	161,398
Wines	1,834,429	259,156

Call now for the latest counts from any of our 150 demographic, lifestyle and behavioral selections.

METROMAIL'S NEW HOMEOWNERS

3,000,000 Annually

More than 4 million Americans buy homes each year and have no point of reference for locating available merchants and services in their new neighborhood. Yet, NEW HOMEOWNERS will spend more on home-related products and services within six months of moving than established residents will spend in two years! These new homeowners have above-average incomes and specific purchase needs, and are open to direct mail and telephone promotions for everything from **lawn and landscaping** services to **dentists.** And since they have just undergone exhaustive credit screening, they are ideal prospects for **major credit purchases,** as well as **mortgage insurance products... catalogs** (more than 75% of all new homeowners place catalog orders during the first year in their new home)... **fund raisers** (demographic characteristics of new homeowners closely match the prospect profile of many non-profits)... and **credit cards** (new homeowners are proven credit worthy as demonstrated by the extensive mortgage qualifying process)!

Metromail can put you in touch with these highly responsive prospects at the time they are establishing new buying patterns.

PRICING AND SELECTIONS

Minimum order: 10,000 Names

BASE PRICE

$75.00/M

GEOGRAPHIC SELECTIONS

State....................$3.00/M
County....................$4.00/M
SCF....................$4.00/M
ZIP Code....................$5.00/M

HOTLINE NAMES

Monthly....................$10.00/M
Last 3/Mo....................$8.00/M
Last 6/Mo....................$6.00/M

OTHER SELECTIONS

Mortgage Amount..........$10.00/M
Lender..................Upon Request
Down Payment Amount..$10.00/M
Purchase Price...............$10.00/M
Loan Type....................$10.00/M
Rate Type....................$10.00/M
Dwelling Type...............$4.00/M
Date of Sale....................N/C
Test (Nth Select).............$3.50/M
Telephone Number........$25.00/M
Key Coding....................N/C

AVAILABLE FORMATS

Cheshire Labels (4-up)...........N/C
Pressure Sensitive Labels..$5.50/M
Manuscript....................$5.00/M
3x5 Index Cards............$10.50/M
Magnetic Tape............$12.50/Reel

DELIVERY

10 working days. Sample mailing piece required.

SOURCE

Warranty and security deeds.

ST. LOUIS OFFICE
41 Kimler Drive
Maryland Heights, MO 63043
Phone: (314) 878-4212
TOLL FREE 1-800-829-5478
FAX: (314) 878-0751

ATLANTA OFFICE
1100 Johnson Ferry Road, N.E.
Suite 450
Atlanta, GA 30342-1779
TOLL FREE 1-800-523-7022
FAX: (404) 256-5836
Broker Direct Line
TOLL FREE 1-800-541-0524

LINCOLN OFFICE
901 West Bond Street
Lincoln, NE 68521
Phone: (402) 475-4591
TOLL FREE 1-800-426-8901
FAX: (402) 473-9796

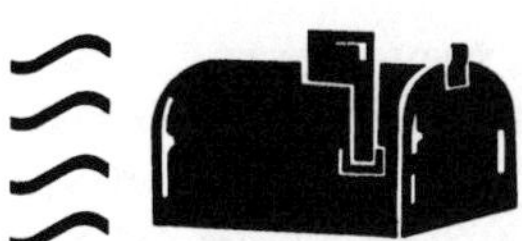

METROMAIL'S REALTY DATABASE

28,000,000 Names

Now you can reach **all** homeowners in a given area—established homeowners, homeowners with equity—with Metromail's REALTY DATABASE. Compiled entirely from legal documents and other public records, this file lets you select from a universe of more than 28 million homeowners nationwide. And since it is updated with our New Homeowner File each month, you can be assured of the most accurate, comprehensive and deliverable data on the market.

Our REALTY DATABASE entries have a classic preferred customer profile: above average income, greater buying needs, and more established credit than renters. They are excellent potential customers for **home improvement products and services** and, in fact, 85 percent are do-it-yourselfers—more interested in enhancing their existing property than in moving.

They are also ideal prospects for **additional real estate, mortgage refinancing, home equity loans** and other **high-level banking and investment products,** as well as for **luxury items** and **high-ticket collectibles.**

PRICING AND SELECTIONS

Minimum order: 10,000 Names

BASE PRICE

$45.00/M

GEOGRAPHIC SELECTIONS

State...............................$3.00/M
County...........................$4.00/M
SCF...............................$4.00/M
ZIP Code.......................$5.00/M

OTHER SELECTIONS

Dwelling Type.................$4.00/M
Purchase Price................$10.00/M
Purchase Date.................$5.00/M
Property Characteristics...$5.00/M (per characteristic)
Presence of Swimming Pool...........$10.00/M
Telephone Number.........$15.00/M

AVAILABLE FORMATS

Cheshire Labels (4-up)...........N/C
Pressure Sensitive Labels..$5.50/M
Manuscript.....................$5.00/M
3x5 Index Cards.............$10.50/M
Magnetic Tape............$12.50/Reel

DELIVERY

10 working days. Sample mailing piece required.

SOURCE

Publicly available county tax records.

ST. LOUIS OFFICE
41 Kimler Drive
Maryland Heights, MO 63043
Phone: (314) 878-4212
TOLL FREE 1-800-829-5478
FAX: (314) 878-0751

ATLANTA OFFICE
1100 Johnson Ferry Road, N.E.
Suite 450
Atlanta, GA 30342-1779
TOLL FREE 1-800-523-7022
FAX: (404) 256-5836
Broker Direct Line
TOLL FREE 1-800-541-0524

LINCOLN OFFICE
901 West Bond Street
Lincoln, NE 68521
Phone: (402) 475-4591
TOLL FREE 1-800-426-8901
FAX: (402) 473-9796

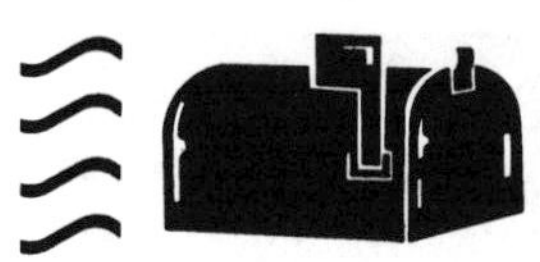

METROMAIL'S NEW MOVER FILE

800,000 New Names Monthly

How do you maintain the accuracy and value of customer or prospect data when nearly 20 percent of the U.S. population moves every year? With Metromail's NEW MOVER FILE! We have the quantities, the currency and the deliverability you need to efficiently update your house file or to pinpoint new prospects within this highly mobile population. With more than 800,000 records of nationwide nonbusiness moves available every four weeks, Metromail offers the largest and most "selectable" new mover resource on the market today.

The NEW MOVER FILE is generated as Metromail's National Consumer Data Base (NCDB)® is updated against the USPS National Change of Address File. (Metromail is a nonexclusive licensee of the USPS.) We then incorporate additional data, including our New Homeowner Hotline names.

All sources are merged/purged against the entire file every four weeks, and a rolling 12 months of information is maintained.

Metromail's NEW MOVERS are ideal prospects for **household furnishings and appliances, home improvement services, long distance telephone service,** and **banking/investment products,** including **credit cards.** They are also excellent candidates for **newspaper and magazine** subscriptions, and for **catalogers** seeking to combat list attrition.

PRICING AND SELECTIONS

Minimum order: 10,000 Names

BASE PRICE

$55.00/M

GEOGRAPHIC SELECTIONS

State..............................$3.00/M
County............................$4.00/M
SCF.................................$4.00/M
ZIP Code..........................$5.00/M

OTHER SELECTIONS

Move Date..............................N/C
Distance of Move.............$5.00/M
State of Previous Residence......$10.00/M
Dwelling Unit Type..........$2.50/M
Exact Age of Head of Household.......$5.00/M
Gender of Head of Household.......$2.50/M
Telephone Number.........$10.00/M
Homeowner *Flag*...........$10.00/M

AVAILABLE FORMATS

Cheshire Labels (4-up)...........N/C
Pressure Sensitive Labels..$5.50/M
Manuscript.....................$5.00/M
3x5 Index Cards.............$10.50/M
Magnetic Tape.............$12.50/Reel

DELIVERY

10 working days. Sample mailing piece required.

ST. LOUIS OFFICE
41 Kimler Drive
Maryland Heights, MO 63043
Phone: (314) 878-4212
TOLL FREE 1-800-829-5478
FAX: (314) 878-0751

ATLANTA OFFICE
1100 Johnson Ferry Road, N.E.
Suite 450
Atlanta, GA 30342-1779
TOLL FREE 1-800-523-7022
FAX: (404) 256-5836
Broker Direct Line
TOLL FREE 1-800-541-0524

LINCOLN OFFICE
901 West Bond Street
Lincoln, NE 68521
Phone: (402) 475-4591
TOLL FREE 1-800-426-8901
FAX: (402) 473-9796

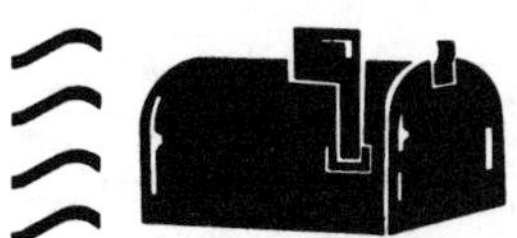

METROMAIL'S COLLEGE STUDENT INDEX

4,700,000 at School Address
3,900,000 at Home Address

A higher education means a higher income once you hit the workforce. It's something college students count on—**and spend on.** In fact, college students outspend the average American consumer by an eye-opening 40 percent! That's reason alone for you to look into Metromail's COLLEGE STUDENT INDEX.

College students represent one of the most ideal markets imaginable. Many are away from home for the first time and experiencing a life that invites inquiry. They enjoy sampling new products, following trends, establishing their own identity. They're big users of samples and coupons, and they love opening and reading their mail! Nothing delivers that mail more efficiently than our COLLEGE STUDENT INDEX. Recompiled every year (not merely rolled over) with verified addresses, the data is as current as the school year is long.

This compilation of 4.7 million students provides a number of identification and definition options designed for more cost-efficient marketing. Successful offers made to this student audience include **books** and **magazines; clothing; credit cards** and **banking services; computers; calculators; typewriters** and **cameras; automotive products** and **sports equipment; insurance; employment; vacations** and **luxury items.**

PRICING AND SELECTIONS

Minimum order: 10,000 Names

BASE PRICE

$37.50/M

GEOGRAPHIC SELECTIONS

State..............................$3.00/M
County...........................$4.00/M
SCF...............................$4.00/M
ZIP Code.......................$5.00/M

OTHER SELECTIONS

School............................$5.00/M
Gender of Student...........$1.00/M
Commuter Status............$1.00/M
Field of Study.................$5.00/M
Class Standing................$1.00/M
Tuition Range.................$5.00/M
School Type—private, public, religious......................$5.00/M

AVAILABLE FORMATS

Cheshire Labels (4- or 5-up)....N/C
Pressure Sensitive Labels..$5.50/M
Manuscript......................$5.00/M
3x5 Index Cards............$10.00/M
Magnetic Tape (Flat Fee).....$25.00
Key Coding....................$1.00/M

DELIVERY

10 working days. Sample mailing piece required.

SOURCE

Published college student directories.

ST. LOUIS OFFICE
41 Kimler Drive
Maryland Heights, MO 63043
Phone: (314) 878-4212
TOLL FREE 1-800-829-5478
FAX: (314) 878-0751

ATLANTA OFFICE
1100 Johnson Ferry Road, N.E.
Suite 450
Atlanta, GA 30342-1779
TOLL FREE 1-800-523-7022
FAX: (404) 256-5836
Broker Direct Line
TOLL FREE 1-800-541-0524

LINCOLN OFFICE
901 West Bond Street
Lincoln, NE 68521
Phone: (402) 475-4591
TOLL FREE 1-800-426-8901
FAX: (402) 473-9796

METROMAIL'S GOLDEN HOMEOWNERS

7,000,000+ Names

Americans over 50 are the fastest growing segment of the population, and one of the most sought-after by direct marketers. Now you can select from among more than 7 million of the country's most affluent seniors with Metromail's GOLDEN HOMEOWNERS file.

These are only the most prosperous of mature homeowners, 80 percent of whom own their own homes free and clear! They are the nation's wealthiest consumer group, accounting for 77 percent of the country's spending power, and a good one-half of its discretionary income. Their assets, together with their income, **and their willingness to spend it,** make them excellent targets for an entire spectrum of direct marketing efforts.

Our GOLDEN HOMEOWNERS are highly receptive to **home entertainment, home improvement** and **do-it-yourself** offers. (In fact, more than half of all do-it-yourselfers are over 50!) They are also prime prospects for **insurance, investment, tax** and **legal** services; **health care** products; and **books, magazines** and **newspapers.** Seniors also respond in greater numbers to **lotteries and sweepstakes,** and purchase 80 percent of all **luxury travel.**

PRICING AND SELECTIONS

Minimum order: 10,000 Names

BASE PRICE

$75.00/M

GEOGRAPHIC SELECTIONS

State	$3.00/M
County	$4.00/M
SCF	$4.00/M
ZIP Code	$5.00/M

OTHER SELECTIONS

Median Age	$5.00/M
Exact Age	$10.00/M
Purchase Price of Home	$10.00/M
Telephone Number	$15.00/M

AVAILABLE FORMATS

Cheshire Labels (4-up)	N/C
Pressure Sensitive Labels	$5.50/M
Manuscript	$5.00/M
3x5 Index Cards	$10.50/M
Magnetic Tape	$12.50/Reel

DELIVERY

10 working days. Sample mailing piece required.

ST. LOUIS OFFICE
41 Kimler Drive
Maryland Heights, MO 63043
Phone: (314) 878-4212
TOLL FREE 1-800-829-5478
FAX: (314) 878-0751

ATLANTA OFFICE
1100 Johnson Ferry Road, N.E.
Suite 450
Atlanta, GA 30342-1779
TOLL FREE 1-800-523-7022
FAX: (404) 256-5836
Broker Direct Line
TOLL FREE 1-800-541-0524

LINCOLN OFFICE
901 West Bond Street
Lincoln, NE 68521
Phone: (402) 475-4591
TOLL FREE 1-800-426-8901
FAX: (402) 473-9796

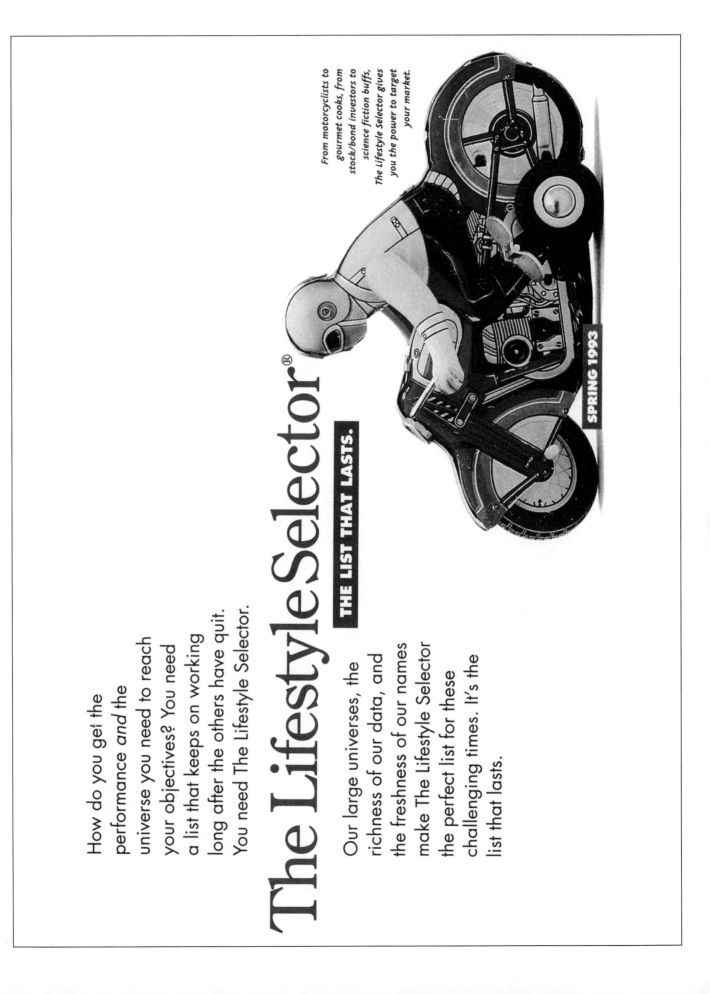

Expert help is just a call away.

Territory	Sales Director	Telephone
Financial Retail — East Coast	Brian McConnell	212-481-9200
Publishing	Beth Hurwitz	212-481-9200
Catalog — East Coast Fundraising	Sue Gloeckner	212-481-9200
Catalog — West Coast Communications Retail — West Coast Travel/Membership Packaged Goods	Sheri Paul	303-292-5000
West Coast Real Estate Insurance	Mary Reifsnyder	619-431-0300

NAME REMOVAL OPTION DATABASE

It has always been our policy to honor individuals' preferences regarding their inclusion on direct marketing mailing lists. Name removal requests are processed as quickly as possible.

The Lifestyle Selector®

The list that lasts.

1621 Eighteenth Street, Denver, Colorado 80202-1294
Phone 303-292-5000 Fax 303-294-9628
New York Phone 212-481-9200 Fax 212-213-2976
San Diego Phone 619-431-0300 Fax 619-431-5730
Customer Information Center 800-525-3533

MEMBER,
DIRECT MARKETING
ASSOCIATION, INC.

RENTAL RATES

BASE PRICE (Includes One Selection)	$65/M
◆ **Denotes premium selection**	$75/M
✈ **Denotes airline price**	$100/M
6 Month Hotline	+$5/M
60 Day Hotline	+$10/M
SELECTIONS:	
Each Additional Selection	$7/M
State/SCF	$3.50/M
ZIP Code	$5/M
Scoring Surcharge	$12/M
Keying	$1/M
Pressure Sensitive Labels	$5/M
Non-Returnable Tape Charge	$15
Cancellation Charge	$5/M
Minimum Order:	10,000
Net Name: (min: 100,000)	85% + $5/M
Delivery:	Three to Five Working Days
Tape Specs:	9 Track, 1600/6250 bpi, 38k bpi.

The Lifestyle Selector®

The Lifestyle Selector is a database of buyers of consumer goods who voluntarily complete and mail detailed customer questionnaires packed with the products. They provide information about their individual and household lifestyles, hobbies, and demographics.

The Lifestyle Selector works for a broad range of direct marketers, from travel to charities, from gardening to apparel, from insurance to publishing. Our 80% continuation rate attests to our effectiveness.

Here's a list with everything you want from a single source. It's a large, dynamic universe that allows you to extend your reach by targeting specific market segments. Our account reps, specialized by industry, are on hand to bring their experience to your selection process.

The Lifestyle Selector is rich in data supported by predictive scoring and comprehensive modeling for sophisticated targeting. Our performance group scores over 40% of the lists we sell. They'll build models to find the top-performing names for you.

Here's a list with a continuous flow of fresh names, so you're not going back to unresponsive prospects time after time. And you'll find superior back-end performance to make your business profitable over the long haul.

The Lifestyle Selector. The perfect list for these challenging times, with the performance, freshness, and data you need. It's the list that lasts.

SPRING 1993

Lifestyles Demographics

24 Month Count: 28,410,000

New names added twice a month. Inquire for details.

AFFLUENT/GOOD LIFE

Community/Civic Activities	1,594,000
Charities/Volunteer Activities	1,243,000
Cultural/Arts Events	3,348,000
Dining Out Frequently	125,000
Fine Art/Antiques	2,528,000
Gourmet Cooking	5,011,000
Own a Vacation Home/Property	75,000
◆ Real Estate Investments	1,636,000
Shop by Catalog/Mail Order	87,000
◆ Stock/Bond Investments	3,271,000
Travel	6,386,000
For Business	116,000
For Pleasure/Vacation	273,000
Foreign	3,281,000
◆ ✈ Frequent Flyers	3,200,000
USA	4,079,000
Wines	2,652,000

When you put together book reading with the children at home select you'll make the best seller list.

COMMUNITY/CIVIC

Charities/Volunteer Activities	1,243,000
Community/Civic Activities	1,594,000
Cultural/Arts Events	3,348,000
Current Affairs/Politics	1,709,000
◆ Donate to Charitable Causes	2,752,000
Military Veteran	3,430,000
Our Nation's Heritage	1,106,000
Veteran's Benefits/Programs	462,000
Wildlife/Environmental Issues	4,047,000
Wildlife/Animal Protection	463,000
Environmental Issues	434,000

DOMESTIC

Automotive Work	4,061,000
Bible/Devotional Reading	4,378,000
Book Reading	10,420,000
Fashion Clothing (Sizes Available)	3,444,000
Gourmet Cooking	3,975,000
Grandchildren	5,375,000
Home Furnishing/Decorating	2,619,000
Household Pets	10,442,000
Own a Cat	3,478,000
Own a Dog	4,749,000
Own a Microwave Oven	10,182,000
◆ Shop by Catalog/Mail Order	5,847,000

ENTERTAINMENT

◆ Buy Pre-Recorded Videos	1,337,000
Cable TV Subscriber	12,610,000
◆ Casino Gambling	1,129,000
Home Video Games	1,575,000
◆ Home Video Recording	15,537,000
◆ Own a VCR	10,524,000
Stereo/Records/Tapes/CDs	13,628,000
◆ Own a CD Player	4,822,000
Watching Sports on TV	10,156,000

Our nearly five million dog owners are an exclusive breed.

◆ Denotes premium selection ✈ Denotes airline price

HIGH TECH

Electronics	2,240,00
◆ Have a Camcorder	168,000
◆ Own a Cellular Phone	86,000
◆ Personal/Home Computers	6,387,000
◆ Use an IBM PC Compatible	549,000
◆ Use an Apple/Macintosh	182,000
Photography	5,170,000
Science Fiction	1,708,000
Science/New Technology	1,838,000

HOBBIES

Automotive Work	4,061,000
Camping/Hiking	5,898,000
Collectibles/Collections	3,192,000
Coin/Stamp Collecting	1,947,000
Crafts	7,986,000
Crossword Puzzles	2,263,000
Fine Art/Antiques	2,528,000
Fishing	6,583,000
Gardening	10,100,000
Flower	4,252,000
Houseplants	6,826,000
Outdoor	3,027,000
Vegetable	3,210,000
Gourmet Cooking	5,011,000
Home Workshop/Do It Yourself	7,096,000
Needlework/Knitting	5,471,000
Photography	5,170,000
Sewing	5,509,000

MONEY

Career Oriented Activities	1,214,000
Money Making Opportunities	1,250,000
◆ Real Estate Investments	1,636,000
◆ Stock/Bond Investments	3,271,000
Sweepstakes/Contests	4,398,000

OUTDOOR

Boating/Sailing	3,047,000
Power Boating	1,931,000
Sailing	887,000
Camping/Hiking	5,898,000
Fishing	6,583,000
Hunting/Shooting	4,512,000
Motorcycling	1,010,000
Recreational Vehicles	2,146,000
Snow Skiing	2,000,000
Wildlife/Environmental Issues	4,047,000

SELF IMPROVEMENT

Career Oriented Activities	1,214,000
Dieting/Weight Control	3,089,000
Health/Natural Foods	3,295,000
Improving Your Health	171,000
Physical Fitness/Exercise	8,867,000
Self Improvement	3,739,000
Walking for Health	7,885,000

SPORTS

Bicycling	4,063,000
Boating/Sailing	3,047,000
Power Boating	1,931,000
Sailing	887,000
Hunting/Shooting	4,512,000
Fishing	6,583,000
Golf	5,329,000
Motorcycling	1,010,000
Physical Fitness/Exercise	8,867,000
Running/Jogging	2,814,000
Snow Skiing	2,000,000
Tennis	1,714,000
Walking for Health	7,885,000

Gender

Male	13,744,000
Female (Mrs., Ms., or Miss Available)	14,190,000

Location

State, County, DMA, SCF, or ZIP Selection

Age

18-24	1,855,000
25-34	5,311,000
35-44	5,896,000
45-54	4,763,000
55-64	4,070,000
65 and Over	5,718,000

Year of Birth Available

Home

Own	20,241,000
Rent	6,355,000
◆ New Movers	669,000

Marital Status

Married	19,167,000
Unmarried	8,346,000

Household Income

Under $15,000	2,739,000
$15,000 - $19,999	2,270,000
$20,000 - $24,999	2,216,000
$25,000 - $29,999	2,190,000
$30,000 - $34,999	2,120,000
$35,000 - $39,999	2,102,000
$40,000 - $44,999	1,945,000
$45,000 - $49,999	1,567,000
$50,000 - $59,999	2,296,000
$60,000 - $74,999	2,324,000
◆ $75,000 - $99,999	1,376,000
◆ $100,000+	1,339,000

Our occupation selects help you round up the right audience.

Occupation

Professional/Technical	6,102,000
Upper Mgt./Administrative	1,302,000
Middle Management	1,617,000
Sales/Marketing	1,388,000
Clerical	1,959,000
Craftsman/Blue Collar	2,248,000
Student	1,312,000
Homemaker	4,067,000
Retired	4,717,000
Self-Employed/ Business Owners	1,606,000
Working Women	6,228,000

Spouse's Occupation Also Available

Credit Cards Used

Travel/Entertainment	4,073,000
Bank	18,340,000
Gas, Dept. Store, Etc.	9,041,000

Children at Home

Exact Ages of Children

Select From Infant to 18	13,407,000

Gender of Children Also Available

Religion/Ethnicity

Asian	191,000
Catholic	2,352,000
Hispanic	689,000
Jewish	587,000
Protestant	21,633,000

Education

◆ Some High School	782,000
◆ Completed High School	3,061,000
◆ Vocational/Technical School	833,000
◆ Some College	3,071,000
◆ Completed College	2,172,000
◆ Some Graduate School	587,000
◆ Completed Graduate School	1,174,000

POLK
DIRECT

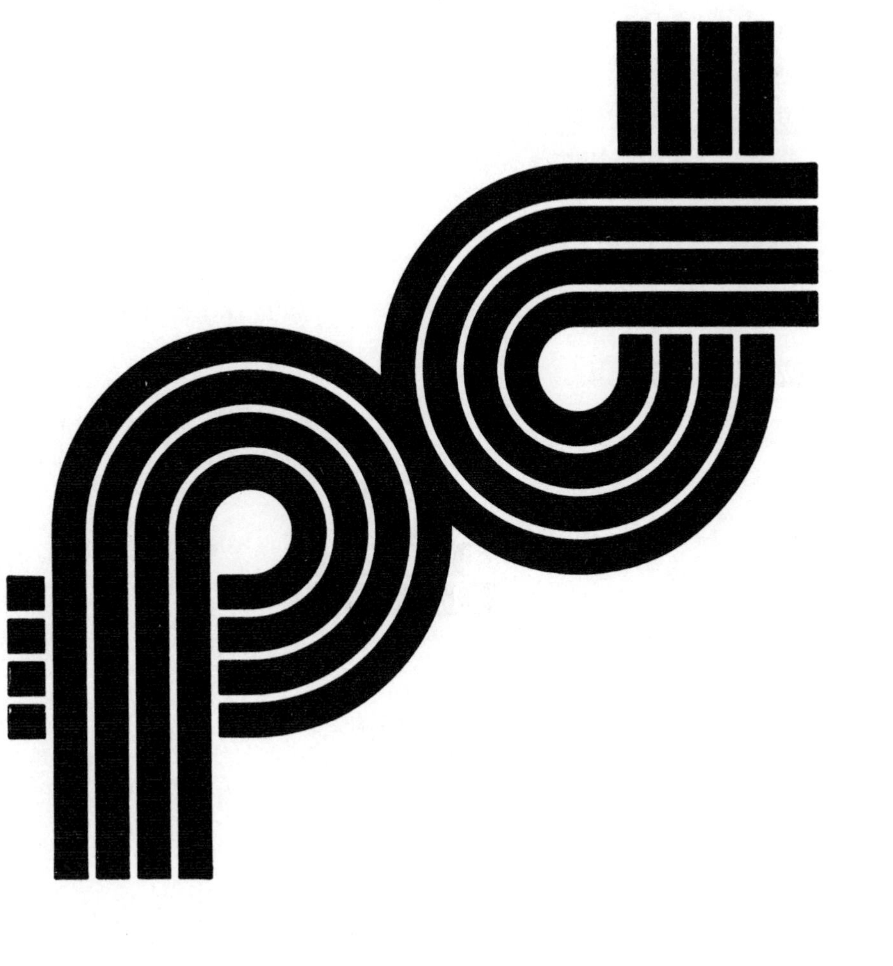

TOTALIST

1993

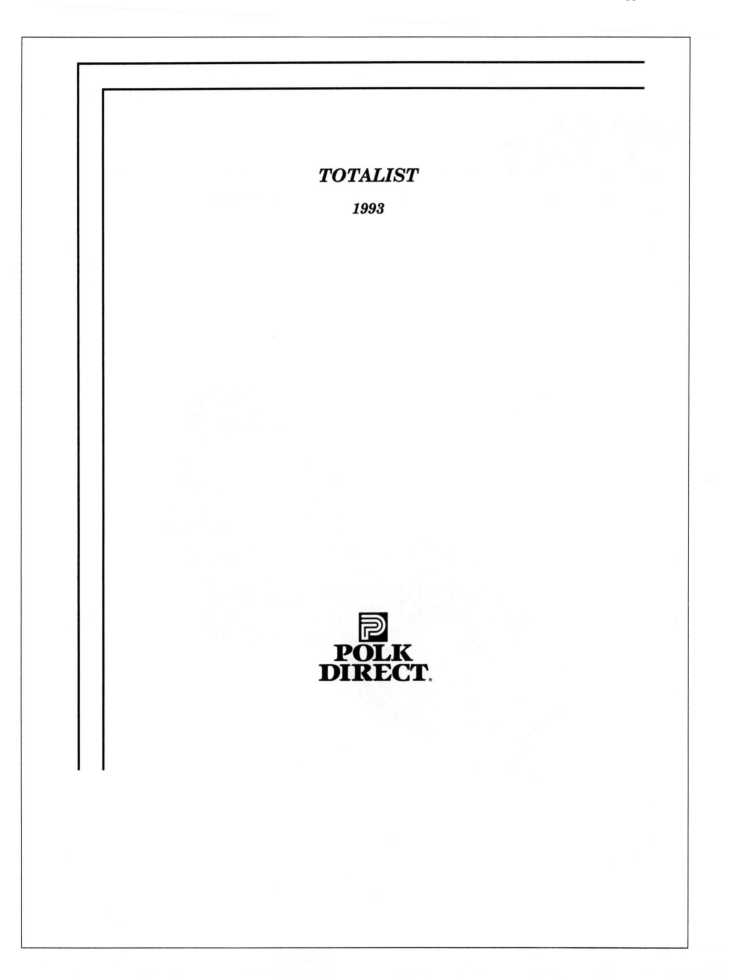

CONTENTS

INTRODUCTION

This presentation describes what we believe, taken as a whole, is the most accurat deliverable, selective and largest consumer compiled list: *TotaList.*

TotaList combines the vast data resources of R. L. Polk & Co. into a single multi source relational database and supports this product with inquiry and analysi capability, as well as selection flexibility. The database combines Polk consumer dat for each family within a household into a single record, with information segment for individual household members. This database, combined with the capability fo fast and flexible counting, analysis and list selection creates a powerful audienc delivery system for you.

DATABASE STRUCTURE

The diagram below helps illustrate the database structure. In this example, the Smith household resides at 104 Beechwood. The household has several characteristics associated with it--address, ownership, and several characteristics about the neighborhood. Within this household are three individuals: John, Mary, and Nathan. Each of these individuals has a variety of characteristics associated with them.

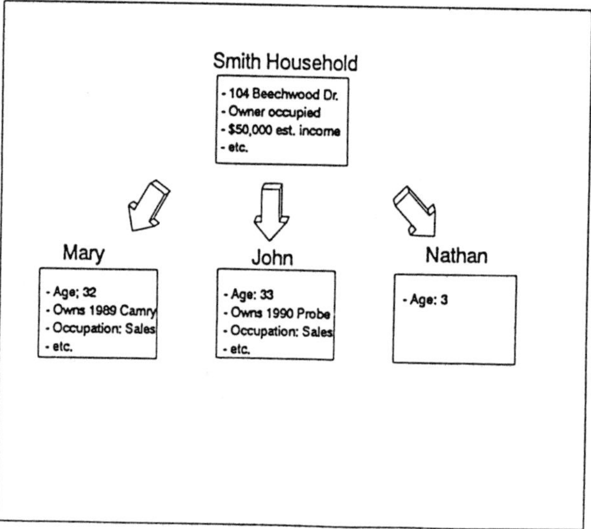

DATABASE STRUCTURE (Cont'd)

What are the advantages of this database structure? First, it means that specific individuals can be targeted for direct marketing promotions. Second, because TotaList is a relational database, each individual may be updated with information independently from the household record. This helps ensure that every family member in the database is as up-to-date as possible.

TOTALIST FEATURES

TotaList has many features including . . .

- **Enhanced Deliverability**, through its accurate names & addresses.
- **Comprehensive Coverage**, with over 91 million families available.
- **Zip Code and Carrier Route Radiating**, to define your trade areas.
- **Detailed Selectivity**, because of the many selection factors in the system.
- **Up-To-Date Information**, as a result of bi-monthly updates.
- **Faster Counts**, through the available on-line count system.
- **Faster Output**, from the automated order and delivery system.

TotaList is a **complete system** that provides an aggregated, relational database and the tools to quickly and effectively **analyze, count, select** and **order**. The system includes a flexible **automated output delivery** capability with built-in mail qualification capabilities, as well as the ability to easily and quickly produce various forms of output.

TOTALIST DATA

From the beginning, TotaList was designed to be a growing, highly dynamic consumer information database. Our objectives for maximum coverage, accuracy, deliverability, and selectivity are met by merging a list of addresses to which are added:

- The name of the family head.
- The names of other family members.
- Other facts known or inferred about each family and its members within a household.
- Facts about the neighborhood area in which the household is located.

Some facts, known or inferred, about TotaList households are obtained from more than one source. Occupation data, for example, is supplied by three sources. To simplify the counting and selection of households with this data, the information from each source, in addition to being stored in its own place in the family record is examined and summarized into a separate and distinct place called "Common List Data."

TOTALIST ACCURACY

The most important of our objectives in maintaining TotaList is to make it the most accurate mass list compiled. Accuracy refers to all of the elements of the name and address, the selection factors available, and especially the deliverability of the list.

To ensure accuracy, TotaList is created with a matchkey whose component is based on surname spelling, or SOUNDEX codes, that group similar names to a household. In terms of correct addressing, TotaList favors Zip+4 standardized elements over non-standardized sources.

TotaList chooses those elements from each list that will make the record more complete and accurate. Thus if a recent Polk derived list source's input to TotaList shows Robert S. Farmer at 132 Brookside and an older non-Polk derived source shows R. S. Farmen at 132 Brookside, we will use the Polk derived list sources spelling. In addition, if we examine the United States Postal Service's (USPS) Zip+4 file and find that the address is 132 Brookside Drive, Apt. C, the address will be corrected since the Zip+4 source is more likely to be accurate on that element.

TOTALIST ACCURACY (Cont'd)

The change in given name identification permits us to determine that Robert Farmer is a male householder rather than of unknown sex as was the case when only the first initial was known. We have also added a more complete address by including "Drive" and "Apt. C" on the record by matching to the USPS' Zip+4 system. Due to the completeness of the address elements found within the Zip+4 system, we can more accurately target our mail in urban and rural areas.

In addition to accuracy and completeness, the inclusion of other list input permits the development of a more deliverable list since each input record is dated according to the month the data was known to be accurate.

Another extremely important point with respect to deliverability is the number of lists on which a name appears. Our vast number of list sources provides you with the most up-to-date, accurate information available. Here are five case histories bearing on that subject:

TotaList

	Cards To USPS For Correction		"Address Correction Requested"	Response Rates To Mailings		
	1	2	3	4	5	Overall Average
Total List	100	100	100	100	100	100
1 Source	78	82	90	77	70	79
2 Sources	104	102	102	103	99	102
3 Sources	112	113	107	123	129	117
4 Sources	124	119	109	117	135	121

Column 1 is read as follows: 1-source names were only 78% as correct as the entire list; 2-source names were 4% better; 3-source names, 12% better; and 4-source names, 24% better than the entire list.

Column 5 is read as follows: 1-source names pulled only 70% as many orders as the entire list; 2-source names pulled 99% as many; 3-source names, 29% more orders; and 4-source names, 35% more orders than the entire list.

TOTALIST ACCURACY (Cont'd)

In considering why the one source names were relatively so poor, one must understand that, by the very nature of the compilation process, the unique names and addresses from each source list survive in TotaList. TotaList has over 64 million names sourced by two or more lists.

Thus, a name from a 20-month old directory unconfirmed by another list will be found in TotaList with a 20-month validation date. However, all names not validated within 24 months of updating are automatically suspended from any TotaList selection. TotaList has over 79 million households verified by at least one source list within the last 16 months.

The way to improve the deliverability of one source names is to specify a validation date beyond which a name is not to be selected or to address those households on a "Resident" basis (mainly for CDS addresses). This date can vary based on the mobility of the class selected.

For example:

> Because the mobility rate of retired people is quite low and that of laborers is quite high, one might specify that all retired persons be selected with a validation date of 24 months or less and all laborers be selected with a validation date of 9 months or less.

Deliverability of TotaList is further improved by applying to it the NCOA[1] (National Change of Address) system. Being an NCOA licensee, Polk receives all the moves and address changes reported to the U.S. Postal Service. This file is enhanced twice a month by new moves and address changes. Each month the entire file is passed against TotaList and where the new address for a moved family or individual is known, the TotaList record is updated accordingly. In cases where a move has been reported but the new address is not known, the record is removed from the list. At this time over 30 characteristics (date and distance of last move are two examples) involved in a move are maintained on file. We keep track of a maximum of five moves per family.

These are but a few examples of the way TotaList operates to make a more complete, accurate, and deliverable list.

[1] Polk is a non-exclusive licensee of the USPS' National Change of Address System

SOURCES

More sources of information are input to TotaList (26) than to any other mass compiled list. The sources include:

1. Current Automobile Registrations
2. Current Truck Registrations
3. Current Recreational Vehicles
4. Current Motorcycle Owners
5. Current Monthly New Car Buyers*
6. Current Monthly New Truck Buyers*
7. Household Census List*
8. Telephone List
9. Last Available Automobile Registrations
10. Last Available Truck Registrations
11. Last Available Recreational Vehicles
12. Last Available Motorcycle Owners
13. New Car Buyers (Back to 1964)*
14. New Truck Buyers (Back to 1968)*
15. New Birth, High School, College Information
16. Mail Response Coding
17. Adult Birthdate Information
18. Questionnaire Data
19. Credit Card Holders
20. Homeowner Information
21. Product Registration Data
22. Mail Order Buyer Data
23. United States Census Bureau Statistics
24. United States Postal Service Information
25. Children's Age Data
26. County Assessor Information

Almost 2 billion records are input to TotaList each year in order to keep the information current. Sources 1-8 supply both name/address and selection demographics while the other sources provide selection data only, as well as confirmation of continued residence for those households already on the list.

* Exclusive to R. L. Polk & Co.

TOTALIST FAMILIES AS OF NOVEMBER, 1992

Motor Vehicle List

State	Usable For Non-Auto Related Purposes: Yes	No	Family Count
Alabama		X	1,169,957
Alaska	X		253,197
Arizona	X		1,537,836
Arkansas		X	637,572
California		X	7,066,083
Colorado	X		1,524,871
Connecticut		X	920,024
Delaware	X		294,013
D.C.	X		202,433
Florida	X		6,286,486
Georgia		X	1,713,852
Hawaii		X	240,258
Idaho	X		508,864
Illinois	X		4,760,003
Indiana		X	1,647,536
Iowa	X		1,368,563
Kansas		X	791,162
Kentucky	X		1,678,881
Louisiana	X		1,721,230
Maine	X		658,619
Maryland	X		1,914,109
Massachusetts	X		2,552,285
Michigan	X		3,927,667
Minnesota	X		1,916,055
Mississippi	X		1,138,655
Missouri	X		2,447,046
Montana	X		416,597
Nebraska	X		704,180
Nevada	X		235,154
New Hampshire	X		639,670
New Jersey		X	1,685,806
New Mexico		X	324,931
New York	X		6,726,926
North Carolina	X		2,925,846
North Dakota	X		309,020
Ohio	X		4,647,221
Oklahoma		X	832,181
Oregon	X		722,435
Pennsylvania		X	3,194,205
Rhode Island		X	301,344
South Carolina	X		1,616,723
South Dakota	X		325,749
Tennessee	X		2,477,816
Texas	X		7,238,185
Utah	X		757,808
Vermont	X		299,347
Virginia		X	1,647,482
Washington		X	1,330,863
West Virginia	X		792,032
Wisconsin	X		2,296,841
Wyoming		X	148,243
	U.S. Total--name addressable		91,473,862

TOTALIST 7

TOTALIST SELECTIVITY

There are three types of selectivity in TotaList:

A. Inherent

B. Geographic

C. Individual

A. Inherent

This refers to the selectivity inherent by virtue of merely being on a certain list. If you are selling automobile insurance, the Automobile List inherently "selects" your market. The Phone or Household Census Lists do not because they both include non-car owners.

The Phone, New Car Buyer, and Auto Lists have important inherent selectivity. For all practical purposes, the HCL has none for this application since it covers everyone in the directory canvass area.

B. Geographical

TotaList is subject to selection by:

1. State
2. Postal Sectional Center
3. County
4. Zip Code (Basic + Zip+4)
5. 1990 and 1980 Census Tracts (where they exist)
6. 1990 and 1980 Census Block Groups (where they exist)
7. 1990 and 1980 Census Enumeration Districts (in many places)
8. USPS Carrier Routes
9. Area Code and Exchange
10. ADI
11. MSA
12. DMA
13. Nielsen County Size Code

TOTALIST SELECTIVITY (Cont'd)

C. Individual

TotaList combines the individual selection factors available on each source list.

Although TotaList is, by far, the most selective mass list ever compiled, the full range of selectivity is not present for each name. This is so because not all names are present on all input lists. Several of the principal factors are listed on the next page.

22 OF THE MOST IMPORTANT INDIVIDUAL HOUSEHOLD SELECTION FACTORS IN TOTALIST

	DERIVED FROM THESE LISTS:				
	HCL	Vehicle	Phone	New Vehicle	Other
1. Household income estimate	X	X		X	X
2. Sex of head of household	X	X	X	X	X
3. Type of dwelling unit (single or multiple)	X	X	X		
4. Month/Year of birth					X
5. Marital status	X				X
6. Home owner	X				X
7. Number of children under 18	X				X
8. Number of persons employed	X				
9. Number of persons in household	X				X
10. Occupation of head of household	X				X
11. Spouse's name	X	X			X
12. Birth, high school, college information					X
13. Mail responsive household					X
14. Length of residence	X	X	X		
15. Possession of telephone; telephone number	X		X		
16. Credit card user					X
17. Year model, make, body style of up to 3 cars owned, plus number of cars owned up to 6		X			
18. Year model, make, body style of up to 2 trucks or RV's and motorcycles owned, plus number of motorcycles owned up to 4		X			
19. Current market value of vehicles owned (CMVI)		X		X	
20. Number of cars purchased new since 1964 with detail on most recent 4				X	
21. Number of new trucks or RV's purchased since 1968 with detail on most recent 4				X	
22. Move data					X

TOTALIST 10

Welcome
To The Story of Niches...

Each of us has a Niche, a station in life, and that's what this book is all about...people and their lives.

Our Niches, our stations, our stopovers are usually temporary. It's because we're so often driven between stops by the lasting urge to find something better, to find some fun in life, to find something new. This book is about that too.

Our Niches are powerful **individual** and family stories — not neighborhood stereotypes — and so it is with this book, which you'll find as easy to read as our Niches are easy to use. It's a story of people that needs to be told; not of their blurring neighborhood similarities, but of the **differences** that make them real — their relative wealth, lifestage and product interests. It's all in this guide to Niches, and it covers your market from A to Z.

So say hello to the best of both worlds — the power of custom segmentation and the convenience of cluster systems. Welcome to Niches, for your reading pleasure...**and profit!**

Niche	Average Household Incomes	Average Age of Head	Approximate % of Niches Households	
A. ALREADY AFFLUENT		30		0.8
B. BIG SPENDER PARENTS		44		4.5
C. CASH-TO-CARRY	Over $75,000	50	15	4.1
D. DIAMONDS-TO-GO		52		3.3
E. EASY STREET		65		2.0
F. FEATHERING-THE-NEST		34		2.3
G. GO-GO FAMILIES		44		1.1
H. HOME HOPPERS	$50,000–75,000	47	13	5.7
I. IRA SPENDERS		69		4.1
J. JUST SAILING ALONG		33		4.6
K. KIDDIE KASTLES		42		6.2
L. LOOSE CHANGE	$30,000–49,999	44	20	1.9
M. MID-LIFE MUNCHKINS		53		3.6
N. NOMADIC GRANDPARENTS		69		4.1
O. OODLES OF OFFSPRING		28		3.2
P. PARENTUS SINGULARIS		38		4.3
Q. QUIET HOMEBODIES	$20,000–29,999	44	20	5.3
R. ROCKY ROAD		45		5.8
S. STILL GOING STRONG		65		1.3
T. TOTEBAGGERS		29		2.3
U. UNDER-THE-CAR		33		1.5
V. VERY SPARTAN		37		9.6
W. WORKING HARD	Under $20,000	49	32	2.4
X X-TRA NEEDY		69		5.2
Y. YOUNG-AT-HEART		70		3.2
Z. ZERO MOBILITY		71		7.6

Demographic Profile	Product Interests
White collar, few kids, high home value	Stocks, home improvements, import cars, extensive travel, multiple credit cards
Traditional families with kids, white collar	Video cameras, home computers, camping equipment, home improvements
High home ownership, 2 or more adults, no kids, high education	Stocks/bonds, apparel, home remodeling
Two or more adults, 1 or more kids, highly mail responsive	Multiple new car buyers, catalog by phone, frequent flyers
High home ownership, white collar, 2+ adults	Home computers, high credit card spending
High presence of kids, white collar, high mobility	Kid and baby items, video cameras, catalog buyers, multiple credit cards, import car loyalty
High presence of kids, high mobility	Home computers, camping equipment, kids' items, multicar owners, jogging apparel
Low home ownership, low presence of kids, high mobility	Racquetball, home furnishings
High home ownership, 2+ adults	Catalog by phone, stocks/bonds, multiple credit cards
Low presence of kids, high mobility, renters, college education	Camping equipment, domestic business travel, beer
Large households, 2+ adults/2+ children, high home ownership	Multiple new car buyers, video cameras, kids' clothing, computers, multiple credit cards
High home ownership, low presence of kids, 2-person households	Import loyal new car buyers, stocks, domestic business travel, video cameras
High home ownership, high presence of kids	Home improvements, tapes and records, children's items, multiple credit cards
Two persons, grandchildren, mail responsive	Bonds, gardening, foreign travel
High mobility, very high presence of children	Import car loyalty, kids' clothing, baby items, tape rentals
Single parents, not mail responsive	Automotive tools, kids' clothing, food extenders/helpers
High home ownership, low home value	Camping equipment, home improvements, tapes and records
Blue collar, low home value, low presence of kids	Used car buyers, camping equipment, food extenders/helpers
Highly mail responsive, grandchildren	Luggage, camping equipment, baby items, domestic vacations, multiple credit cards
Mostly singles, female headed, high mobility	Men's and women's apparel, biking gear, sporting goods, high credit card ownership
High mobility, high home ownership	Automotive tools, jewelry
Renters, low presence of children, blue collar	Low credit card and car ownership, beer, cigarettes/cigars
Blue collar, low education, mostly female heads	Kids' clothing, cigarettes/cigars, domestic car loyalty
Low home ownership, female heads, low education, grandchildren	Food extenders/helpers, low credit card and car ownership
Two or more adults, highly mail responsive, low mobility	Luggage, travel, own only one car but bought new
Two adults, low mobility, low education	Single car owners, auto service centers, diet control

MAJOR APPLICATIONS OF NICHES

The marketing applications of Niches are virtually unlimited. Here are some key ones:

- Customer Profiles (as shown below)
- Direct Marketing
- Mail and Telemarketing Audiences
- Print and Broadcast Selection
- Creative Targeting
- Product Positioning
- Analysis of Market Potential
- Customer & Other Databases
- Cross-Selling
- Survey Analysis
- New Product Development
- Site Location
- Research Sampling
- Strategic Planning

(SAMPLE)

NICHES CUSTOMER PROFILE REPORT

Rank	Niche	Number of Hhlds	Percent of Hhlds	Number of Customers	Percent of Customers	Niche Penetration	Index
1	G. Go-Go Families	880,000	1.1	5,500	5.5	0.625%	500
•	•	•	•	•	•	•	•
•	•	•	•	•	•	•	•
12	E. Easy Street	1,600,000	2.0	2,400	2.4	0.150	120
•	•	•	•	•	•	•	•
•	•	•	•	•	•	•	•
26	Z. Zero Mobility	6,080,000	7.6	800	0.8	0.013	10
	Totals	80,000,000	100.0	100,000	100.0	0.125%	100

This year on my 30th birthday, my wife and I took a trip to California. You know, it's tough for both of us to be out of the office at the same time, especially when the market's active, but somehow we did it.

The limo was packed so full, the golf clubs barely fit for the drive to the airport. The same thing happens every time we travel though. My wife, Judy, always has to bring a supply of books to read and I always sneak in a little work from my briefcase. Plus, there's all our clothes, and, well, I could go on and on.

With all those credit cards, you always head back home with more than you started with. Sometimes I think we keep expanding the house just to accommodate the souvenirs!

Avg. Income Over $75,000  Average Age 30

BIG SPENDER PARENTS

My dad is the best dad in the whole wide world. He buys me all sorts of stuff all the time, because he's got lots of money. That's why I have my own computer and why I get all the video games I want.

Sometimes we even go camping. That's when dad likes to bring the video camera along. You know, he's pretty good at taking movies, even though he's kinda old. He's 44 already. It's no wonder he pays other people to come and fix up the house. Last year we had this really neat playroom added on. It's like me and my brother and sister's own little house!

And when dad gets home from a business trip, it's the best, 'cause he brings us all presents. He's the only dad on our whole cul-de-sac but even if he wasn't, he'd still be the best.

Avg. Income Over $75,000	B	Average Age 44

CASH-TO-CARRY

Allow me to introduce myself. My name is Regina, and at the risk of sounding pompous, I must say that I have done quite well for myself. Both Charles and I married well. After graduating from college he went on to law school, and he's now, at age 50, a prominent attorney.

Our stocks, bonds and other well-placed holdings are the talk of the Club. Charles even made money on his polo ponies last year! In short, we live comfortably. Of course, with all the socializing we do, one must dress appropriately and constantly shop. But being on the board of a major clothier *does* help.

All this leaves us little time to spend at Thousand Oaks, our glorious estate. Pity that we aren't there more often to enjoy it. Our maid, Maria, complains of being lonely. She misses the children. But she'll be caring for a new generation soon enough.

Avg. Income Over $75,000	C	Average Age 50

My grandma told me she's 69 years old. I really think she's pretty neat. When I grow up, I want to be just like her. She says that's fine with her except that I should go to college. She says that way, I won't have to clip coupons, and that someday I could even make enough money to *own* a house instead of renting one like she does.

I like going to visit grandma on Saturdays best of all. She lets me help her with her sewing, and then I get to go with her to the flea market and pick out stuff to decorate her house. I asked grandma how come she doesn't like to use her credit cards like mom always does when she buys things. She said it's because she doesn't want to get any more bills to pay.

The last thing we do is make dinner for ourselves. Usually it's spaghetti or meat loaf. And that's our Saturday. Pretty fun, huh?

Avg. Income Under $20,000  **Average Age 69**

My wife Gladys and I are retired now. We're 70 years old after all, so we figure it's time we enjoyed ourselves. We always wanted to travel, seeing as how we've lived in the same place since we were married. It's just that we never had the time. Now we have all the time in the world, so we just pack up our suitcases and go! We just have the one car, but we bought it new. We thought it would be a good idea to make sure and get a dependable car since we're going to be traveling so much.

While we're gone, the lady next door takes in the mail for us. Gladys buys a lot of things through the mail, and we both enter a lot of those sweepstakes.

When we're home, we usually just relax around the house and go to church on Sundays. All in all, I'd say the retired life definitely agrees with us.

Avg. Income Under $20,000  Average Age 70

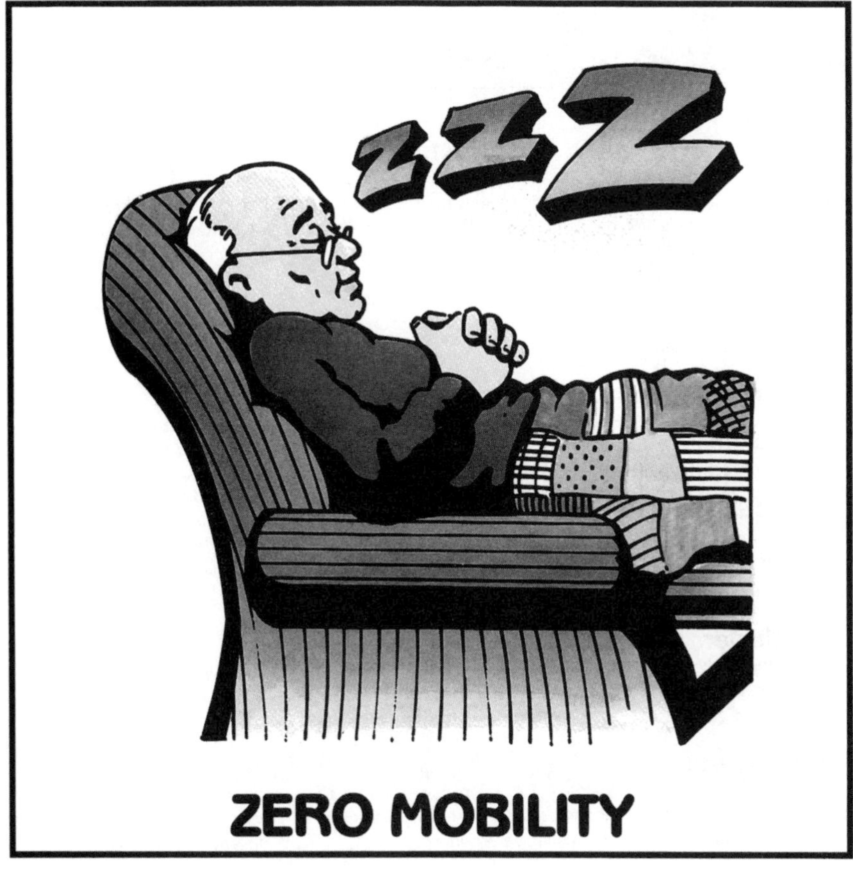

I'm over 70 now and since I've been retired, I've followed a strict schedule. Almost every day I wake up at seven o'clock sharp, then I watch TV, eat, and watch some more TV until it's time to go to sleep again.

If it wasn't for my wife watching my diet, I'd be doing alright. I know she means well, but I'll let you in on a little secret. Whenever she goes out to one of her craft shows, or sits in the other room running that noisy sewing machine of hers, I sneak a cookie. That satisfies my sweet tooth, and besides, then I have something to confess when we go to church.

But, like I said, most days I just kick back in my lounger here and watch whatever program comes on TV, except for those quiz shows. That's a little too much exercise for me. So I usually nap until the soap operas come on.

Avg. Income Under $20,000	Z	Average Age 71

ClusterPLUS 2000 Enhanced Cluster Description Guide

Introduction

This Enhanced Cluster Description Guide provides marketers with detailed information regarding the brand new 60 lifestyle segments which make up ClusterPLUS 2000, the revolutionary new marketing segmentation system from Strategic Mapping, Inc. (SMI).

By incorporating concepts such as "urbanicity", "predictive clusters" and "atomic segmentation," ClusterPLUS 2000 provides marketers with greater precision and accuracy in lifestyle clustering and market segmentation than has ever before been possible.

Urbanicity Concept

In re-clustering America, we developed and integrated six urbanicity groupings into our cluster classification system. Urbanicity is a geographic measure created by SMI to include a geography's proximity to an urban center, population density, housing type and structure characteristics. Our six neighborhood geographic settings – *Center City, Urban, Suburban, Small Town, Rural and Group Quarters* – go beyond the census urban and rural geographic definitions. *Group Quarters* was added to the urbanicity definitions to segment colleges, military bases and other institutions such as hospitals, nursing homes and prisons. Urbanicity takes into account the differences in lifestyle and purchasing behaviors which often exist between urban, suburban, small town and rural areas.

Predictive Clusters Concept

To add more predictive capabilities to our ClusterPLUS 2000 product, we incorporated new and innovative methodology in our clustering algorithms to transcend traditional descriptive clustering systems. ***The result: more precision and greater dimension in predicting consumer product consumption.***

Atomic Segmentation

Another key advantage to our ClusterPLUS 2000 product is its linkage to more than 450 atomic clusters. These minute, homogeneous clusters – derived from our 60 cluster classification system – serve as the building blocks for future industry specific segmentation products as well as **custom segmentation** products for our clients.

ClusterPLUS 2000 Classifications

ClusterPLUS 2000 classifies U.S. neighborhoods (blocks and block groups) and postal areas (ZIP codes and ZIP+4s) into 60 new unique lifestyle segments. Each cluster represents a neighborhood geographic setting (reflecting *urbanicity* groups) with distinct product consumption, service usage patterns and psychographic profiles. These 60 clusters are further segmented into 11 Multi-Factor Groupings. The Multi-Factor groupings combine individual clusters which share similar demographic characteristics. This enables you to work within the cluster framework in situations where sample size may preclude analysis by 60 clusters.

The first 57 clusters in our ClusterPLUS 2000 product are classified by the five urbanicity groupings: C = Center City, U = Urban, S = Suburban, T = Small Town, and R = Rural – and are ranked by SMI's proprietary *Socio-Economic Measure (SEM)*. G = Group Quarters for clusters 58, 59 and 60.

SEM is a new proprietary classification system from SMI that describes neighborhoods on the basis of their relative prosperity. SEM blends the socio-economic quality of the immediate neighborhood – using demographics such as education, occupation, housing and income – with local environment information, including crime statistics, access to health care, arts and entertainment, cost of living and climate. The result is a unique quality of life index for each neighborhood. SEM scores range in value from 0 - 100, where the highest scores identify areas of highest socio-economic status and prosperity.

By combining urbanicity and a socio-economic measure into the individual cluster descriptions, we give marketers maximum flexibility in their analyses and applications with our ClusterPLUS 2000 product.

ClusterPLUS 2000 Enhanced Cluster Description Guide

ClusterPLUS 2000 Linkages

Since consumers, audiences and subscribers are multi-dimensional, ClusterPLUS 2000 offers linkages to the databases of other specialty research firms, such as Nielsen Marketing Research, Simmons Market Research Bureau, Mediamark Research, Inc., Nielsen Media Research, and NPD/Crest, so that the media habits, purchasing patterns, behavior, attitudes and opinions can be related to each ClusterPLUS 2000 lifestyle segment.

With ClusterPLUS 2000, survey and panel data can be applied to every neighborhood in the country, providing a powerful means of precisely analyzing your marketplace. Any database coded with ClusterPLUS 2000 can be analyzed using the ClusterPLUS 2000 Workstation in CONQUEST®, our geodemographic, CD-ROM based system. This linkage capability allows marketers to profile customers, key prospects and identify and locate prospects geographically.

Enhancement Guide Information

In this Enhanced Cluster Description Guide, the 60 lifestyle clusters are arranged according to their Multi-Factor Cluster Group listing *(See Table of Contents)*. The 60 clusters are arranged in this order to help you interpret and implement cluster results and to provide further flexibility in marketing applications. *A quick reference guide listing the 60 clusters in numerical order and their page numbers within this Guidebook is provided on page iii for your convenience.*

Each Multi-Factor Cluster Group Section contains detailed descriptions of the cluster segments with two pages per cluster reporting selected demographic and lifestyle behavior data. A thematic map representing cluster concentration throughout the U.S. is also included.

Demographic Data

The demographic information reported in this Guidebook uses 1990 Census data to focus on such areas as Occupation, Household Composition, and Education as well as SMI's current year estimates in the areas of Income, Age Distribution and Current Year Population Estimates.

Lifestyle Behavior

Lifestyle behavior indications are taken from examinations of the product preferences exhibited by the clusters. Based upon data from Simmons Market Research Bureau's 1992 Study of Media and Markets, usage patterns have been identified by cluster, for hundreds of products and services. The product preferences listed in this document were selected from an analysis of these usage patterns, identifying products and services at least 20 percent more likely than average to appeal to a given cluster.

Cluster Concentration Maps

Maps of the United States by DMA (Designated Market Area) illustrate the relative concentration of each cluster across these markets. Although not regionally based, many of our clusters are frequently found in specific geographic areas - a fact which is highlighted through the DMA maps.

Appendix Section

Background information on the ClusterPLUS 2000 framework is listed in the Appendix Section and includes standard descriptions of the ClusterPLUS 2000 clusters, as well as a glossary of definitions for demographic variables used in the development of this Enhanced Cluster Description Guide.

ClusterPLUS 2000 ENHANCED CLUSTER DESCRIPTION GUIDE

Classification by Urbanicity Group

G01: CENTER CITY

C11: Settled, affluent with few kids, prestige older homes
C15: Highly educated, singles, professionals, apartment dwellers, high rent
C17: Middle-age professionals, retirees, fewer kids, apartments & condos
C25: Young singles, white collar apartment dwellers, very mobile
C27: Younger, ethnic mix, Hispanic, apartment dwellers, mobile, average income
C29: Average age, below average income, few kids, older homes & apartments
C33: Black singles, high unemployment, average age & income
C34: Younger, Hispanic & Asian, mobile, average income, high value homes
C40: Younger, very mobile, singles, average education, low income
C49: Less educated, Black female head of household, low income, old apartments
C52: Middle-age, low income, fewer kids, old housing, female head of household
C54: Younger, Black female head of household with young kids
C55: Younger, low income, mobile, Hispanic families
C57: Younger, lowest income, mobile, Black female head of household

G02: URBAN

U04: Married, affluent, homeowners, highly educated, white collar
U08: Well educated, high income, professionals, large older homes
U10: New families, white collar, high income, new homes
U14: White collar, high value apartments & condos, mobile, high income
U18: Younger homeowners, Hispanics & Asians, high income
U20: Retirees, professional and white collar workers, apartment dwellers
U23: Younger homeowners, low value homes, married with kids
U24: Average income, apartment dwellers, middle age, fewer kids
U30: Average age homeowners, low value older homes
U31: Young, very mobile, below average income, older apartments
U36: Ethnic mix, Hispanic, younger, average income, high rent, mobile
U44: Average age Black families, low income, female head of household
U46: Average age, low income, low rents, few kids
U48: Younger Hispanics, large families, blue collar laborers

G03: SUBURBAN

S01: Established wealthy, highly educated, professionals, prestige homes
S02: Middle-age, affluent, high incidence of teens, highest educated, professionals, new homes
S03: Well educated, affluent married professionals, prime real estate areas
S05: Average age, affluent, professionals, high incidence of kids
S07: Younger couples, highest incidence of kids, very high income
S09: Older couples, high income, professionals, high value homes
S12: High income, settled couples & families, homeowners
S13: Average age white collar workers, above average education, high value homes
S21: Married couples, middle age, low mobility, homeowners
S22: Younger working couples, high incidence of kids, new homes
S35: Average age and income, less educated, blue collar workers
S38: Retirees, homeowners, below average income, less educated
S45: Average age, low income, less educated, Black, female head of household
S50: Younger, Hispanic families, blue collar laborers
S51: Unskilled, less educated, older housing, low income

vi ■

ClusterPLUS 2000 ENHANCED CLUSTER DESCRIPTION GUIDE

G04: SMALL TOWN

T19: White collar, average age & income, average value homes
T37: Below average income, less educated, blue collar and unskilled
T39: Low income, retirees, low rent apartments, female head of household
T53: Low income, ethnic mix, unskilled workers

G05: RURAL

R06: Well educated, affluent couples, settled, new homes
R16: Average age working couples with kids, white collar, new homes
R26: Settled blue collar families with kids
R28: Settled couples, low value homes, below average income
R32: Retirees, below average income, settled, homeowners, newer homes
R41: Settled, families with teens, below average income, some farmers
R42: Hispanic families with kids, low income, settled, some farmers
R43: Blue collar & unskilled, below average income, less educated, retirees
R47: Below average income, working couples, blue collar & unskilled
R56: Black families, low value newer homes, settled

G06: GROUP QUARTERS

G58: Group Quarters: Colleges
G59: Group Quarters: Military
G60: Group Quarters: Other Institutions

ClusterPLUS® 2000 Enhanced Cluster Description Guide *Source: SMI, SMRB 1994*

Multi-Factor
CLUSTER GROUP 01

Affluent, Older Professionals, Prime Real Estate

Cluster Members S01, S02, S03, U04, S09, C11 and C17

Cluster S01: Suburban, middle age, wealthiest, very high percentage of professionals and white collar workers, many married couples, highest percentage of college educated, very high percentage of single family homes, prestige homes, established neighborhoods, very high rent, larger and older homes

Cluster S02: Suburban, middle age, wealthy, many married couples with children, especially teenagers, very high percentage of professionals and white collar workers, highest percentage of college graduates, very high percentage of single family homes, prime real estate, very high rent, new homes

Cluster S03: Suburban, middle age, affluent, very high percentage of professionals and white collar workers, married couples, very high percentage of college educated, prime real estate, very high rent, settled neighborhoods

Cluster U04: Urban, middle age, affluent, very high percentage of professionals and white collar workers, married couples, very high percentage of college educated, prime real estate, very high rent, settled neighborhoods, very high percentage of owner occupied housing

Cluster S09: Suburban, older, married couples, high percentage of retirees, high income, very high percentage of professionals and white collar workers, high percentage of college educated, average home value, high rent

Cluster C11: Center City, middle age, affluent, high percentage of professionals and white collar workers, prime real estate and high rent, older homes

Cluster C17: Center City, middle age, average income, high percent of female head of household, high presence of one person households, high percent of apartments, high home value, very high percent of professionals and white collar workers, high percent of college educated

2 ■

Multi-Factor
CLUSTER GROUP 01

Affluent, Older Professionals, Prime Real Estate

DETAILED DEMOGRAPHICS

	CLUSTER AVERAGE	U.S. AVERAGE	INDEX
Occupation			
Professional	43.85	25.79	170
White Collar	63.08	41.15	153
Blue Collar	12.31	26.61	46
Unskilled	1.79	4.05	44
Unemployed	3.49	6.57	53
Females in Work Force	55.88	57.30	98
Neighborhood Composition			
Female Head of Household	22.81	28.00	81
Married Couples Households	65.02	55.43	117
One Person Households	20.53	24.39	84
Households with Kids	31.79	36.17	88
Householder Age 65+	24.98	21.53	116
Caucasian HHs	92.41	83.86	110
African American HHs	2.53	10.60	24
Native Indian HHs	0.21	0.65	32
Asian or Pacific Islander HHs	4.01	2.19	183
Other Races - HHs	0.84	2.70	31
Hispanic HHs	3.29	6.52	50
Socio-Economic Measure	87.58	50.78	172
Education			
No High School Diploma	10.53	24.45	43
High School Graduate	21.45	29.85	72
Some College Education	26.73	25.09	107
Bachelors Degree	24.26	13.32	182
Graduate Degree	17.02	7.30	233

	CLUSTER AVERAGE	U.S. AVERAGE	INDEX
Age Distribution			
Children 0-5	6.84	8.68	79
Children 6-11	6.97	8.39	83
Children 12-17	7.11	7.79	91
Adults 18-24	8.00	10.19	78
Adults 25-34	13.55	17.62	77
Adults 35-49	23.65	20.73	114
Adults 50-64	17.13	13.27	129
Adults 65+	16.75	13.33	126
Median Age Adult	46.72	42.00	111
Housing			
Single Family	74.37	67.41	110
Multi-Family (2-9)	9.61	14.07	68
Apartments (10+)	8.43	12.32	68
Median HomeValue ($)	222,995.25	103,070.44	216
Median Rent ($)	689.53	409.23	168
Length of Residence 1-5 yrs.	36.36	43.18	84
Income			
Income $0-$14,999	8.93	21.80	41
Income $15,000-$29,999	13.45	23.90	56
Income $30,000-$44,999	15.00	20.17	74
Income $45,000-$59,999	14.34	13.89	103
Income $60,000-$99,999	26.04	14.19	184
Income $100,000+	22.24	6.05	368
Income $150,000+	9.04	1.97	460
Median HH Income ($)	62,014.81	35,503.22	175

ClusterPLUS® 2000 Enhanced Cluster Description Guide

Source: SMI, SMRB 1994

4 ■

CLUSTER S01 Suburban Established Wealthy

Detailed Demographics

	CLUSTER AVERAGE	U.S. AVERAGE	INDEX
Occupation			
Professional	56.87	25.79	220
White Collar	76.85	41.15	187
Blue Collar	6.07	26.61	23
Unskilled	0.93	4.05	23
Unemployed	2.66	6.57	41
Females in Work Force	52.10	57.30	91
Neighborhood Composition			
Female Head of Household	14.90	28.00	53
Married Couples Households	76.02	55.43	137
One Person Households	12.79	24.39	52
Households with Kids	35.69	36.17	99
Householder Age 65+	22.50	21.53	104
Caucasian HHs	92.14	83.86	110
African American HHs	1.07	10.60	10
Native Indian HHs	0.13	0.65	19
Asian or Pacific Islander HHs	6.26	2.19	285
Other Races - HHs	0.41	2.70	15
Hispanic HHs	2.44	6.52	37
Socio-Economic Measure	98.78	50.78	195
Education			
No High School Diploma	5.16	24.45	21
High School Graduate	11.98	29.85	40
Some College Education	23.64	25.09	94
Bachelors Degree	31.39	13.32	236
Graduate Degree	27.83	7.30	381

	CLUSTER AVERAGE	U.S. AVERAGE	INDEX
Age Distribution			
Children 0-5	6.58	8.68	76
Children 6-11	7.57	8.39	90
Children 12-17	8.33	7.79	107
Adults 18-24	7.38	10.19	72
Adults 25-34	9.29	17.62	53
Adults 35-49	26.66	20.73	129
Adults 50-64	20.41	13.27	154
Adults 65+	13.77	13.33	103
Median Age Adult	47.85	42.00	114
Housing			
Single Family	93.62	67.41	139
Multi-Family (2-9)	1.70	14.07	12
Apartments (10+)	1.51	12.32	12
Median HomeValue ($)	458,227.25	103,070.44	445
Median Rent ($)	926.14	409.23	226
Length of Residence 1-5 yrs.	29.78	43.18	69
Income			
Income $0-$14,999	4.04	21.80	19
Income $15,000-$29,999	5.37	23.90	22
Income $30,000-$44,999	7.25	20.17	36
Income $45,000-$59,999	8.33	13.89	60
Income $60,000-$99,999	22.38	14.19	158
Income $100,000+	52.63	6.05	870
Income $150,000+	31.40	1.97	1597
Median Household Income ($)	107,905.43	35,503.22	304

ClusterPLUS® 2000 Enhanced Cluster Description Guide

Source: *SMI, SMRB 1994*

6 ■

CLUSTER S02 Suburban Middle-Age Affluent with Kids

DETAILED DEMOGRAPHICS

	CLUSTER AVERAGE	U.S. AVERAGE	INDEX
Occupation			
Professional	56.03	25.79	217
White Collar	77.07	41.15	187
Blue Collar	6.19	26.61	23
Unskilled	1.05	4.05	26
Unemployed	2.54	6.57	39
Females in Work Force	54.29	57.30	95
Neighborhood Composition			
Female Head of Household	12.36	28.00	44
Married Couples Households	80.87	55.43	146
One Person Households	10.37	24.39	43
Households with Kids	43.08	36.17	119
Householder Age 65+	16.76	21.53	78
Caucasian HHs	95.42	83.86	114
African American HHs	1.46	10.60	14
Native Indian HHs	0.12	0.65	18
Asian or Pacific Islander HHs	2.76	2.19	126
Other Races - HHs	0.23	2.70	9
Hispanic HHs	1.61	6.52	25
Socio-Economic Measure	98.36	50.78	194
Education			
No High School Diploma	4.13	24.45	17
High School Graduate	12.50	29.85	42
Some College Education	23.30	25.09	93
Bachelors Degree	33.80	13.32	254
Graduate Degree	26.27	7.30	360

	CLUSTER AVERAGE	U.S. AVERAGE	INDEX
Age Distribution			
Children 0-5	7.62	8.68	88
Children 6-11	9.20	8.39	110
Children 12-17	9.73	7.79	125
Adults 18-24	7.05	10.19	69
Adults 25-34	9.25	17.62	53
Adults 35-49	28.93	20.73	140
Adults 50-64	17.91	13.27	135
Adults 65+	10.30	13.33	77
Median Age Adult	46.03	42.00	110
Housing			
Single Family	93.86	67.41	139
Multi-Family (2-9)	1.50	14.07	11
Apartments (10+)	0.90	12.32	7
Median HomeValue ($)	248,164.72	103,070.44	241
Median Rent ($)	796.42	409.23	195
Length of Residence 1-5 yrs.	36.92	43.18	86
Income			
Income $0-$14,999	3.31	21.80	15
Income $15,000-$29,999	5.55	23.90	23
Income $30,000-$44,999	7.96	20.17	39
Income $45,000-$59,999	10.06	13.89	72
Income $60,000-$99,999	29.50	14.19	208
Income $100,000+	43.62	6.05	721
Income $150,000+	20.71	1.97	1054
Median Household Income ($)	91,850.51	35,503.22	259

ClusterPLUS® 2000 Enhanced Cluster Description Guide

Source: SMI, SMRB 1994

CLUSTER S03 Suburban Well Educated Professionals

Detailed Demographics

	CLUSTER AVERAGE	U.S. AVERAGE	INDEX
Occupation			
Professional	42.36	25.79	164
White Collar	61.34	41.15	149
Blue Collar	13.96	26.61	52
Unskilled	1.97	4.05	49
Unemployed	3.35	6.57	51
Females in Work Force	61.27	57.30	107
Neighborhood Composition			
Female Head of Household	17.14	28.00	61
Married Couples Households	72.75	55.43	131
One Person Households	13.54	24.39	56
Households with Kids	38.93	36.17	108
Householder Age 65+	18.45	21.53	86
Caucasian HHs	92.17	83.86	110
African American HHs	2.20	10.60	21
Native Indian HHs	0.20	0.65	30
Asian or Pacific Islander HHs	4.58	2.19	209
Other Races - HHs	0.85	2.70	32
Hispanic HHs	3.38	6.52	52
Socio-Economic Measure	94.12	50.78	185
Education			
No High School Diploma	9.43	24.45	39
High School Graduate	22.36	29.85	75
Some College Education	28.07	25.09	112
Bachelors Degree	24.20	13.32	182
Graduate Degree	15.94	7.30	218

	CLUSTER AVERAGE	U.S. AVERAGE	INDEX
Age Distribution			
Children 0-5	7.72	8.68	89
Children 6-11	8.14	8.39	97
Children 12-17	8.29	7.79	107
Adults 18-24	8.37	10.19	82
Adults 25-34	13.42	17.62	76
Adults 35-49	25.95	20.73	125
Adults 50-64	16.81	13.27	127
Adults 65+	11.30	13.33	85
Median Age Adult	44.29	42.00	105
Housing			
Single Family	89.38	67.41	133
Multi-Family (2-9)	3.95	14.07	28
Apartments (10+)	2.47	12.32	20
Median HomeValue ($)	232,658.86	103,070.44	226
Median Rent ($)	756.26	409.23	185
Length of Residence 1-5 yrs.	33.55	43.18	78
Income			
Income $0-$14,999	5.73	21.80	26
Income $15,000-$29,999	9.76	23.90	41
Income $30,000-$44,999	13.35	20.17	66
Income $45,000-$59,999	15.58	13.89	112
Income $60,000-$99,999	32.71	14.19	231
Income $100,000+	22.86	6.05	378
Income $150,000+	7.33	1.97	373
Median Household Income ($)	65,719.26	35,503.22	185

ClusterPLUS® 2000 Enhanced Cluster Description Guide

Source: SMI, SMRB 1994

10 ■

CLUSTER U04 Upscale Urban Couples

DETAILED DEMOGRAPHICS

	CLUSTER AVERAGE	U.S. AVERAGE	INDEX
Occupation			
Professional	43.66	25.79	169
White Collar	62.57	41.15	152
Blue Collar	12.72	26.61	48
Unskilled	1.75	4.05	43
Unemployed	3.30	6.57	50
Females in Work Force	59.78	57.30	104
Neighborhood Composition			
Female Head of Household	21.08	28.00	75
Married Couples Households	67.37	55.43	122
One Person Households	16.82	24.39	69
Households with Kids	34.56	36.17	96
Householder Age 65+	22.21	21.53	103
Caucasian HHs	90.95	83.86	108
African American HHs	2.32	10.60	22
Native Indian HHs	0.20	0.65	30
Asian or Pacific Islander HHs	5.60	2.19	255
Other Races - HHs	0.93	2.70	35
Hispanic HHs	3.93	6.52	60
Socio-Economic Measure	93.27	50.78	184
Education			
No High School Diploma	9.59	24.45	39
High School Graduate	21.63	29.85	72
Some College Education	27.70	25.09	110
Bachelors Degree	24.19	13.32	182
Graduate Degree	16.89	7.30	231

	CLUSTER AVERAGE	U.S. AVERAGE	INDEX
Age Distribution			
Children 0-5	7.34	8.68	85
Children 6-11	7.25	8.39	86
Children 12-17	7.41	7.79	95
Adults 18-24	8.24	10.19	81
Adults 25-34	14.39	17.62	82
Adults 35-49	24.70	20.73	119
Adults 50-64	16.99	13.27	128
Adults 65+	13.68	13.33	103
Median Age Adult	44.87	42.00	107
Housing			
Single Family	80.02	67.41	119
Multi-Family (2-9)	7.17	14.07	51
Apartments (10+)	4.76	12.32	39
Median HomeValue ($)	270,138.69	103,070.44	262
Median Rent ($)	824.18	409.23	201
Length of Residence 1-5 yrs.	31.82	43.18	74
Income			
Income $0-$14,999	6.29	21.80	29
Income $15,000-$29,999	10.30	23.90	43
Income $30,000-$44,999	13.54	20.17	67
Income $45,000-$59,999	15.04	13.89	108
Income $60,000-$99,999	30.59	14.19	216
Income $100,000+	24.23	6.05	401
Income $150,000+	8.63	1.97	439
Median Household Income ($)	67,043.83	35,503.22	189

ClusterPLUS® 2000 Enhanced Cluster Description Guide

Source: SMI, SMRB 1994

12 ■

CLUSTER S09 Suburban Older Couples, Professionals

Detailed Demographics

	CLUSTER AVERAGE	U.S. AVERAGE	INDEX
Occupation			
Professional	42.16	25.79	163
White Collar	62.48	41.15	152
Blue Collar	12.49	26.61	47
Unskilled	1.88	4.05	46
Unemployed	3.50	6.57	53
Females in Work Force	45.45	57.30	79
Neighborhood Composition			
Female Head of Household	23.88	28.00	85
Married Couples Households	66.26	55.43	120
One Person Households	22.57	24.39	93
Households with Kids	23.24	36.17	64
Householder Age 65+	38.88	21.53	181
Caucasian HHs	96.98	83.86	116
African American HHs	1.70	10.60	16
Native Indian HHs	0.18	0.65	29
Asian or Pacific Islander HHs	0.80	2.19	37
Other Races - HHs	0.33	2.70	12
Hispanic HHs	1.61	6.52	25
Socio-Economic Measure	85.51	50.78	168
Education			
No High School Diploma	11.78	24.45	48
High School Graduate	24.70	29.85	83
Some College Education	27.37	25.09	109
Bachelors Degree	21.98	13.32	165
Graduate Degree	14.17	7.30	194

	CLUSTER AVERAGE	U.S. AVERAGE	INDEX
Age Distribution			
Children 0-5	5.46	8.68	63
Children 6-11	5.69	8.39	68
Children 12-17	5.76	7.79	74
Adults 18-24	5.68	10.19	56
Adults 25-34	10.48	17.62	59
Adults 35-49	19.20	20.73	93
Adults 50-64	19.75	13.27	149
Adults 65+	27.99	13.33	210
Median Age Adult	54.24	42.00	129
Housing			
Single Family	88.88	67.41	132
Multi-Family (2-9)	4.19	14.07	30
Apartments (10+)	3.25	12.32	26
Median HomeValue ($)	118,234.81	103,070.44	115
Median Rent ($)	521.06	409.23	127
Length of Residence 1-5 yrs.	35.01	43.18	81
Income			
Income $0-$14,999	11.21	21.80	51
Income $15,000-$29,999	18.95	23.90	79
Income $30,000-$44,999	19.72	20.17	98
Income $45,000-$59,999	16.13	13.89	116
Income $60,000-$99,999	21.65	14.19	153
Income $100,000+	12.34	6.05	204
Income $150,000+	4.38	1.97	223
Median Household Income ($)	46,506.82	35,503.22	131

ClusterPLUS® 2000 Enhanced Cluster Description Guide

Source: SMI, SMRB 1994

CLUSTER C11 Center City Affluent, Few Kids

Detailed Demographics

	CLUSTER AVERAGE	U.S. AVERAGE	INDEX
Occupation			
Professional	35.61	25.79	138
White Collar	52.37	41.15	127
Blue Collar	17.18	26.61	65
Unskilled	2.39	4.05	59
Unemployed	4.67	6.57	71
Females in Work Force	55.96	57.30	98
Neighborhood Composition			
Female Head of Household	27.86	28.00	99
Married Couples Households	56.42	55.43	102
One Person Households	24.27	24.39	100
Households with Kids	29.62	36.17	82
Householder Age 65+	26.07	21.53	121
Caucasian HHs	86.87	83.86	104
African American HHs	3.09	10.60	29
Native Indian HHs	0.22	0.65	34
Asian or Pacific Islander HHs	7.88	2.19	359
Other Races - HHs	1.94	2.70	72
Hispanic HHs	6.33	6.52	97
Socio-Economic Measure	76.24	50.78	150
Education			
No High School Diploma	18.33	24.45	75
High School Graduate	26.89	29.85	90
Some College Education	25.26	25.09	101
Bachelors Degree	17.54	13.32	132
Graduate Degree	11.98	7.30	164

	CLUSTER AVERAGE	U.S. AVERAGE	INDEX
Age Distribution			
Children 0-5	7.02	8.68	81
Children 6-11	6.34	8.39	76
Children 12-17	6.33	7.79	81
Adults 18-24	9.05	10.19	89
Adults 25-34	16.89	17.62	96
Adults 35-49	21.79	20.73	105
Adults 50-64	15.68	13.27	118
Adults 65+	16.91	13.33	127
Median Age Adult	44.64	42.00	106
Housing			
Single Family	41.88	67.41	62
Multi-Family (2-9)	28.03	14.07	199
Apartments (10+)	12.47	12.32	101
Median HomeValue ($)	252,733.44	103,070.44	245
Median Rent ($)	668.46	409.23	163
Length of Residence 1-5 yrs.	35.86	43.18	83
Income			
Income $0-$14,999	11.97	21.80	55
Income $15,000-$29,999	15.56	23.90	65
Income $30,000-$44,999	17.50	20.17	87
Income $45,000-$59,999	15.87	13.89	114
Income $60,000-$99,999	24.26	14.19	171
Income $100,000+	14.84	6.05	245
Income $150,000+	4.97	1.97	253
Median Household Income ($)	51,573.67	35,503.22	145

ClusterPLUS® 2000 Enhanced Cluster Description Guide

Source: SMI, SMRB 1994

CLUSTER C17 Center City Professionals & Retirees, Apartments & Condos

Detailed Demographics

	CLUSTER AVERAGE	U.S. AVERAGE	INDEX
Occupation			
Professional	41.48	25.79	161
White Collar	60.87	41.15	148
Blue Collar	11.97	26.61	45
Unskilled	1.87	4.05	46
Unemployed	3.96	6.57	60
Females in Work Force	55.36	57.30	97
Neighborhood Composition			
Female Head of Household	36.39	28.00	130
Married Couples Households	44.43	55.43	80
One Person Households	37.84	24.39	155
Households with Kids	20.67	36.17	57
Householder Age 65+	29.42	21.53	137
Caucasian HHs	92.59	83.86	110
African American HHs	4.67	10.60	44
Native Indian HHs	0.31	0.65	48
Asian or Pacific Islander HHs	1.52	2.19	69
Other Races - HHs	0.91	2.70	34
Hispanic HHs	3.11	6.52	48
Socio-Economic Measure	71.79	50.78	141
Education			
No High School Diploma	12.35	24.45	51
High School Graduate	22.05	29.85	74
Some College Education	27.21	25.09	108
Bachelors Degree	23.02	13.32	173
Graduate Degree	15.37	7.30	211

	CLUSTER AVERAGE	U.S. AVERAGE	INDEX
Age Distribution			
Children 0-5	5.88	8.68	68
Children 6-11	5.22	8.39	62
Children 12-17	5.04	7.79	65
Adults 18-24	9.24	10.19	91
Adults 25-34	17.06	17.62	97
Adults 35-49	20.56	20.73	99
Adults 50-64	14.77	13.27	111
Adults 65+	22.23	13.33	167
Median Age Adult	46.93	42.00	112
Housing			
Single Family	39.55	67.41	59
Multi-Family (2-9)	19.78	14.07	141
Apartments (10+)	28.60	12.32	232
Median HomeValue ($)	124,257.13	103,070.44	121
Median Rent ($)	460.38	409.23	112
Length of Residence 1-5 yrs.	48.80	43.18	113
Income			
Income $0-$14,999	16.96	21.80	78
Income $15,000-$29,999	22.96	23.90	96
Income $30,000-$44,999	19.79	20.17	98
Income $45,000-$59,999	13.92	13.89	100
Income $60,000-$99,999	16.59	14.19	117
Income $100,000+	9.78	6.05	162
Income $150,000+	3.80	1.97	193
Median Household Income ($)	38,514.08	35,503.22	108

ClusterPLUS® 2000 Enhanced Cluster Description Guide

Source: SMI, SMRB 1994

TABLE OF CONTENTS FOR DATABASE MANAGEMENT SYSTEMS

Product : adabas

Software Directory

Product Name:	Adabas
Vendor:	Software AG of North America, Inc.
Address:	11190 Sunrise Valley Dr. Reston VA 22091 (703) 860-5050; (800) 843-9534; Fax (703) 391-6614 USA
System Class:	Mid-Range/Mainframe
Product Category:	Data Base Management Systems
Function:	Relational database management system (RDBMS) with functionally integrated set of application development and end-user tools, and distributed database functions.
Pricing:	1500 -$450,000
GSA:	yes
Discount:	education; multi-copy
Hardware:	Digital VAX; Hewlett-Packard; IBM RISC System/6000; IBM System/370/390 architecture; NCR; UNIX; Wang VS
O/S:	DOS/VSE; MVS; MVS/ESA; MVS/SP; UNIX; Ultrix; VM; VM/ESA; VM/SP; VMS; VS; various UNIX platforms
Min. Memory:	450K
Source Language:	ALC; C
Source Listing:	no
Options:	Adabas is available on platforms ranging from PCs to large mainframe environments.
Customizing:	yes
Maintenance:	90 days included; annual fee of 15% charged thereafter
Documentation:	included
Training:	contact vendor
Current Users:	45000 -worldwide
Description:	Adabas (Adaptable Data Base System) is used in environments varying from high-volume, batch, on-line transaction processing (OLTP) applications to ad hoc end-user queries. It provides support for multiple data models including relational, entity-relational, and non-first normal form. It includes a comprehensive security system (data encryption and file, field, and field value level security), automatic restart/recovery capabilities, and advanced data compression techniques, and it permits additions and modifications to data fields and indices without reloading or reorganizing the database.
Page Number:	D30-100-001

Product : CA-Datacom/DB

Software Directory

Product Name: CA-DATACOM/DB
Vendor: Computer Associates International, Inc.
Address: One Computer Associates Plaza
Islandia NY 11788
(516) 342-5224; (800) 225-5224; Fax (516) 342-5329
USA
System Class: Mid-Range/Mainframe
Product Category: Data Base Management Systems
Function: Database management.
Pricing: contact vendor Available on GSA schedule
Hardware: IBM System/370/390 architecture
O/S: MVS; VM; VSE
Min. Memory: 250K
Source Language: Assembler; C
Source Listing: Not available
Maintenance: available
Documentation: included
Training: contact vendor
First Installed: 1974
Description: RDMS which stores data in tables; provides relational index system, query system, accounting facilities, data access, and security; provides program development, maintenance, and information center supprt; includes data dictionary for definition, design, reporting, auditing, and control.
Page Number: D30-100-001

Software Directory

Product Name:	DB2 (Database2)
Vendor:	IBM
Address:	Old Orchard Road Armonk NY 10504 (800) 426-3333 USA
System Class:	Mid-Range/Mainframe
Product Category:	Data Base Management Systems
Function:	Relational data base management.
Pricing:	contact vendor
Hardware:	IBM System/370 architecture
O/S:	MVS; MVS/SP; MVS/XA
Min. Memory:	2.5M
Peripherals:	CICS, IMS/VS DC, and TSO
Maintenance:	contact vendor
Documentation:	available
Training:	available
First Installed:	June 1987
Description:	DB2 (5740-XYR) is a large-system relational DBMS. It can be installed with the IMS/VS/DB hierarchical system or configured as a standalone DBMS. The DB2 system employs the SQL (Structured Query Language) as its host data base language, and is compatible, to some degree, with the SQL/DS relational system designed for use with the DOS/VS environment. It has IBM's SAA data base interface. SQL enhancements include date/time and single, precision-floating, point data types and operations and extended ANSI SQL compatibility. Operational and performance enhancements include DL/1 batch support; and SQL optimization, utility improvements, and MVS/XA storage usage improvements. DB2 provides relational file structure, views, table space, SQL, data space management, user interface, monitoring and accounting, security and authorization, and data set protection. The product features an integrated data base dictionary. All data in a DB2 data base is stored in VSAM entry sequenced data sets (ESDS), which can be defined and maintained by the user or by DB2. DB2 supports a relational data model. The data in DB2's data base is defined in terms of tables and accessed through operations on tables. Data definition, retrieval, manipulation, and control operations are supported by the SQL. SQL is a high-level data language available to users through an interactive terminal and through application programs written in APL2, Cobol, Fortran, PL/1, Basic, or Assembler language. DB2 is independent of both DASD and tape device type. Its architecture provides for data bases with up to 64 billion bytes per table. DB2 is supported by a set of data base utilities that operate on-line , including the Data Extract (DXT) and DB2 Performance Monitor.
Page Number:	D30-100-003

Product : Image/3000

Software Directory

Product Name: Image/3000
Vendor: Hewlett-Packard Co.
Address: Inquiries, 19319 Pruneridge Ave.
Cupertino CA 95014
USA
System Class: Mid-Range/Mainframe
Product Category: Data Base Management Systems
Function: Data base management.
Pricing: contact vendor
Hardware: Hewlett-Packard HP 3000
O/S: MPE
Source Language: Cobol; Fortran; SPL
Source Listing: available
Peripherals: Disk, console, magnetic tape or tape cartridge
Maintenance: available
Documentation: included
Training: 5 days at $725/day
Current Users: 20,000+
First Installed: June 1973
Description: Image is a Codasyl-like, general-purpose data base management system. It uses a network data structure as its data base organization. Data entry selection is made using one of four access methods: Serial, Chained, Directed, and Calculated. Image allows information to be related logically between data sets, minimizing data redundancy and facilitating information retrieval. Image operates concurrently in both terminal and batch environments and consists of four components: Data Base Definition Language: to describe data items (fields), data sets, data set relationships, security, and storage requirements. Data Base Management Subsystems: to access and maintain data, a set of Image library routines is provided. The routines can be called from user-written programs to open, close, get, update, put, delete, find, lock, unlock, log, and return information about the data base being currently accessed. Data Base Utilities: can be used to create, maintain, and restructure a data base, and back up data. Data Base Enquiry Facility: designed for nonprogrammers to easily locate, report, and update data values within an Image data base through English-like commands. Security is provided at several levels. Up to 63 classes of users can be defined. A password is associated with each class. Sets of user classes can then be permitted ``read'' or ``read-and-write'' access to any or all data items and/or data sets, independent of the elements accessible to other user classes. Concurrency control is provided by Image 3000 at the data base, data set, and record level. The system also offers a logging and recovery system which is designed to restore data bases to a consistent state, both logically and structurally.
Page Number: D30-100-003

```
Product      :   Ingres

                         Software Directory

                    COPYRIGHT (c) DATAPRO 1993

Product Name:      INGRES
Vendor:            Ingres
Address:           An ASK Company
                   1080 Marina Village Parkway
                   Alameda CA 94501-1041
                   (510) 769-1400; (800) 446-4737; Fax (510) 748-2514
                   USA
System Class:      Mid-Range/Mainframe
Product Category:  Data Base Management Systems
Function:          Distributed relational data base management system
                   application development tools.
Pricing:           950 -$160,000
GSA:               yes
Discount:          multi-copy
Hardware:          AT&T 3B Systems; Alliant FX Series; Apollo Domain; CCI
                   Power Series; Data General MV Family; Digital VAX;
                   Gould PowerNode; Hewlett-Packard HP 3000; Honeywell
                   Bull; IBM RISC System/6000; IBM System/370
                   architecture; NCR; NCR Tower 32; Pyramid x; Sequent
                   Balance; Unisys U Series
O/S:               Domain/IX; HP-UX; MPE/XL; MVS; OSx; UNIX; Ultrix;
                   VM/CMS; VMS
Min. Memory:       1M
Source Language:   C
Options:           Micro versions available.
Customizing:       available
Maintenance:       included
Documentation:     included
Training:          contact vendor
Current Users:     11000
First Installed:   June 1981
Description:       Ingres is a full-function, relational data base
                   management system combined with a visual programming
                   applications development system along with
                   knowledge-management and object-management extensions.
                   It includes SQL, an English-like query language for
                   interactive definition, protection, and manipulation
                   of data through simple tables. The system features
                   automatic optimization algorithms that provide access
                   to on-line data bases. Routines for data validation,
                   concurrency control, security, recovery, and
                   transaction processing are also included. Ingres
                   automatically stores and maintains all information
                   about a data base and related applications in an
                   integrated data dictionary. Ingres' knowledge
                   management and object management extensions allow
                   organizations to model their data upon their business
                   model.
Page Number:       D30-100-003
```

Product : Mapper

Software Directory

Product Name: MAPPER System
Vendor: Unisys Corp.
Address: Township Line and Jolly Roads
P.O. Box 500
Blue Bell PA 19424-0001
(215) 986-3111
USA
System Class: Mid-Range/Mainframe
Product Category: Data Base Management Systems
Function: End-user computing facility providing a foundation for executive information systems (EIS).
Pricing: contact vendor
Hardware: AT&T 3B2 Systems; NCR Tower and Tower XT; Sun Microsystems SPARCstation Series; Unisys 1100/2200; Unisys A Series; Unisys CTOS; Unisys U Series
O/S: Platform dependent
Maintenance: available
Documentation: included
Current Users: 14,000
Description: The MAPPER System is an open, responsive user-driven computing environment with powerful ad hoc processing and reporting capabilities, and a high productivity interactive application development facility. The MAPPER System provides an easy-to-use, nonprocedural way to make the problem- solving power of the computer available to everyone in an enterprise. The product was designed to allow nonprogrammers to shape solutions around their personal working style and requirements. The MAPPER System provides the following features in one product: programmerless computing using a large selection of generic macro functions; a comprehensive, interactive language with on-line documentation; large-scale database capability which supports high-volume real-time updating and information processing; and a full set of security, service coordination, accounting, recovery, audit trail, and monitoring capabilities.
Page Number: D30-100-004

Product : Mapper

Software Directory

Product Name: MAPPER System PC Version
Vendor: Unisys Corp.
Address: Township Line and Jolly Roads
P.O. Box 500
Blue Bell PA 19424-0001
(215) 986-3111
USA
System Class: Mid-Range/Mainframe
Product Category: Data Base Management Aids
Function: End-user database development facility providing a foundation for executive information systems (EIS).
Pricing: contact vendor
Hardware: AT&T 3B2 Systems; NCR Tower; Sun Microsystems SPARCstation Series; Unisys
Peripherals: printer
Maintenance: available
Documentation: included
Current Users: 14,000
Description: The MAPPER System is an open, responsive, user-driven computing environment with ad hoc processing/reporting capabilities and a high-productivity interactive database application development facility. It provides a user-friendly, nonprocedural way to make the problem-solving power of the computer available to everyone in an enterprise. It allows nonprogrammers to shape solutions around their personal working style and requirements. The following features are included: programmerless computing using a large selection of generic macro functions; a comprehensive, interactive language with on-line documentation; large-scale database capability which supports high-volume real-time updating and information processing; and a full set of security, service coordination, accounting, recovery, audit trail, and monitoring capabilities.
Page Number: D30-150-008

Product : Oracle

Software Directory

Product Name: ORACLE
Vendor: Oracle Corp.
Address: 500 Oracle Parkway
Redwood Shores CA 94065
(415) 506-7000; Fax (415) 506-7809
USA
System Class: Mid-Range/Mainframe
Product Category: Data Base Management Systems
Function: Relational database management systems (RDBMSs) and services.
Pricing: Contact vendor
Hardware: AT&T 3B Systems; Apollo Domain; CCI Power Series; CDC Cyber Series; Concurrent Series 3200; Data General MV Family; Datapoint All; Digital VAX; Elxsi 6400; Encore; Gould NPL; Gould PowerNode; Harris H Series; Hewlett-Packard HP 3000; Honeywell Bull; IBM System/370 architecture; IBM System/88; Intergraph; Motorola Computer Systems; NCR; Prime 50 Series; Pyramid x; Sequent Balance; Stratus/32; Unisys; Wang All
O/S: A/UX; AIX; AOS; DOS/VSE; Finder; HP-UX; MPE XL; MVS; NOS/VE; OS/2; Primos; UNIX; UTS; VM/CMS; VMS; VS
Min. Memory: 2M
Source Language: C
Source Listing: no
Options: Micro versions available.
Customizing: yes
Maintenance: available
Documentation: included
Training: Day and week-long sessions available
First Installed: 1979
Timesharing: no
Description: ORACLE is relational database management system software based on SQL. It provides data definition, data manipulation, and data control facilities. ORACLE is compatible with IBM's DB2 and SQL/DS. ORACLE provides a common software platform to develop complete systems across a variety of computers and operating systems. Applications do not need to be rewritten to take advantage of newer processors or be moved to smaller computers. The ORACLE kernel is a component of the SQL*Star distributed architecture, which provides distributed data base processing and the database. The database includes an interactive data dictionary that gives database administrators complete control over access and resources within the database. Security audit features detect and log all unauthorized access or misuse of selected data within the system. ORACLE can both roll forward and roll back transaction recovery. Users realize continuous operations with a fault-tolerant enterprise-wide

database. Oracle's Application Tools include SQL*Plus, an ad hoc query processor capable of producing standard business reports; SQL*Forms, which allows development and running of online , screen-based applications; SQL*ReportWriter, a productivity tool geared to assist the application builder in specifying a wide range of report styles; and SQL*Menu, an application tool that controls any Oracle application. A common front end to both ORACLE and non-ORACLE applications is provided. SQL*ReportWriter, SQL*Forms, or any other application can be tied into one common interface. Oracle has a complete set of tools that allow Cobol, Fortran, C Pascal, PL/1, Ada, Hypercard, and BASIC programs to directly manipulate the data base. The PRO products allow the extension of SQL*Forms to do special processing. PL/SQL is a language for specifying the flow of control of SQL statements within one or more transactions being processed. PL/SQL is also a universal portable language allowing applications as diverse as SQL*Plus, SQL*Forms, and Pro*C or Pro*COBOL to invoke a common language. Logic written in PL/SQL will automatically be portable to every computer on which ORACLE runs.

Page Number: D30-100-005

Product : Oracle

Software Directory

Product Name: Oracle 3.1
Vendor: Oracle Corp.
Address: 500 Oracle Parkway
Redwood Shores CA 94065
(415) 506-7000; Fax (415) 506-7809
USA
System Class: Microcomputer
Product Category: Database Management Systems
Function: A relational database management system for micros, minis, and mainframes.
Pricing: contact vendor
Hardware: AT&T 3B 20A; AT&T 3B 20D; AT&T 3B 20S; AT&T 3B5; DEC PDP 11; DEC VAX 11; Data General Eclipse MV-4000; Data General Eclipse MV-6000; Data General Eclipse MV-8000; Data General Eclipse Series; FORTUNE 32:16; HARRIS COMPU; HP 9000 SRS 500 520; IBM 3081; IBM 308X; IBM 30XX; IBM 370; IBM 4331; IBM 4341; IBM 4381; PYRAMID TECH 90
O/S: Data General AOS/VS; Digital RSTS; Digital RSX-11 M; Digital RSX-11 M+; Digital VAX-VMS; Harris Vulcan; MS-DOS 3.0+; UNIX
Source Listing: not available
Maintenance: updates available
First Installed: July 1, 1979
Description: ORACLE's SQL PLUS data language provides Dynamic Data Definition, Data Manipulation and Data Control facilities. SQL PLUS is a compatible superset of IBM's SQL for SQL/DS and DB 2 and offers the end user an English-like interface language for all database inquiry, update and reporting tasks. An Integrated Data Dictionary centrally defines all information that is stored in the database. ORACLE's Interactive Application Facility (IAF) allows end-users to generate on-line data entry and maintenance applications without the need for conventional programming.
Page Number: MS20-300-018

Category : "DATABASE MANAGEMENT SYSTEMS"

Software Directory

Product Name: Supra 2.2
Vendor: Cincom Systems, Inc.
Address: 2300 Montana Avenue
Cincinnati OH 45211-3899
(513) 662-2300; (800) 543-3010; Fax (513) 481-8332
USA
System Class: Microcomputer
Product Category: Database Management Systems
Function: Relational database management system.
Pricing: 1500 and up
GSA: yes
Discount: contact vendor
Lease: available
Hardware: Compaq Deskpro 286; Compaq Deskpro 386; Digital MicroVAX; Hewlett-Packard HP 9000; IBM PC/XT/AT and compatibles; IBM PS/2 or compatible; Sun Microsystems SPARCstation Series; Sun Microsystems Sun-3 Family; Sun Microsystems Sun-4 Family
O/S: MS-DOS; OS/2; PC-DOS; SCO Xenix; SunOS; UNIX; VMS
Min. Memory: 2M
Source Language: C; source not available
Source Listing: not available
Network Support: Ethernet; IBM LAN Manager; Novell NetWare; TCP/IP; Token Ring
Peripherals: Hard disk; printer
Options: Also available for IBM RS/6000, Amdahl, Nixdorf, Fujitsu, Pyramid, Sequent, and Sequoia.
Customizing: available
Maintenance: Hot line included; contact vendor for other options
Documentation: included
Training: included
Current Users: 1,400+
First Installed: 1985
Description: Supra is a multi-server solution built for production application development; desktop to data center. The advanced multi-server design provides transparent open access to multiple servers across a network. Based on the ANSI-SPARC Three Schema Architecture, SUPRA delivers on the promise of distributed processing across a widening multi-vendor environment. Automated facilities insure complete accuracy and integrity of the users data while providing the user with a single system image of the application regardless of where the data and application reside. A variety of tools are supported so that users have the right tool for the job regardless of the level of complexity.
Page Number: MS20-300-025

Product : SQL/DS

Software Directory

Product Name: Structured Query Language/Data System (SQL/DS)
Vendor: IBM
Address: Old Orchard Road
Armonk NY 10504
(800) 426-3333
USA
System Class: Mid-Range/Mainframe
Product Category: File Management/Data Management
Function: Relational data management.
Pricing: contact vendor
Hardware: IBM System/370 architecture
O/S: DOS/VS(E); VM/SP
Min. Memory: 2M
Peripherals: 3480 magnetic tape unit; 9-track tape drive
Maintenance: contact vendor
First Installed: December 1988
Description: SQL/DS (5688-004) provides on-line query, a report writer, and end-user relational database facilities. Features include database backup and archive operations, database recovery, and error diagnosis; diagnostics for isolating database failures; and options for handling database recovery from system or user errors. Remote Relational Access Support (RRAS), when used with VM/SP Transparent Services Access Facility (TSAF), allows users on one CPU to access an SQL/DS database on another locally or remotely connected CPU. Other features include logical optimization; multiple language help text support and archive tape blocking support for VM; allowing users to query, manipulate, and define their data; American National Standards (ANS) compatibility; VARCHAR 254 data definition support; and Fortran preprocessor capabilities. SQL requests can be entered through CICS/VS- or ICCF-supported terminals as input to the SQL/DS Database Services utility, or can be embedded in application programs written in Cobol, PL/1, or Assembler. SQL/DS supports multiple, concurrent access from batch partitions, on-line environments, and interactive program execution environments. Other features include restart and recovery, in-line catalog capabilities, a DL/1 extract facility, and relational productivity family and access generator technology. VSE Guest Sharing allows VSE users and programs running within a VSE Guest machine to access an SQL/DS database running under VM/SP. An SQL Application Interface for VSAM allows the execution of CICS/VM transactions against the same VM/SP-SQL/DS or remote database containing migrated MVS or VSE VSAM data sets.
Page Number: D30-200-005

Product : sybase

Software Directory

Product Name: SYBASE
Vendor: Sybase, Inc.
Address: 6475 Christie Avenue
Emeryville CA 94608
(510) 596-3500; (800) 879-2273; Fax (510) 658-9441
USA
System Class: Mid-Range/Mainframe
Product Category: Data Base Management Systems
Function: Relational data base management system.
Pricing: 3750 -$250,000
GSA: yes
Hardware: AT&T computers; Apple Macintosh; Data General; Digital VAX; Hewlett-Packard; NCR; NeXT; Pyramid; Sequent; Silicon Graphics; Stratus; Sun Microsystems
O/S: OS/2; PC-DOS; UNIX; VAX/VMS; VOS
Min. Memory: 4M
Source Language: C
Source Listing: no
Customizing: no
Maintenance: annual fee - 15% of primary license
Documentation: included
Training: Included in price of support
Current Users: 2,000
First Installed: October 1986
Description: SYBASE is a leading portable relational data base management system providing the capabilities required by on-line applications. SYBASE consists of two components--SQL Server and SQL Toolset. The SYBASE SQL Server is built on an advanced client/server architecture where application functions are separable from the data base management functions provided by the SQL Server. The SQL Server runs as a multithreaded, single process that handles data request from all users. The SYBASE SQL Toolset is a comprehensive set of tools for developing and deploying on-line applications as well as for end-user computing. It offers developers an integrated suite of window-based tools for designing, prototyping, building, and maintaining forms-based, on-line applications. It offers end users decision support tools to access data from the SYBASE SQL Server using a visual interface for queries, reports, and simple applications. The SQL Toolset's integration with SQL Server guarantees data integrity, security, and recovery.
Page Number: D30-100-005

Software Directory


```
Product Name:      Informix-SQL
Vendor:            Informix Software, Inc.
Address:           16011 College Blvd.
                   Lenexa KS 66219-9943
                   (913) 599-7330; Fax (913) 599-7350; Telex 209542
                   USA
System Class:      Microcomputer
Product Category:  Database Management Systems
Function:          File management/data management.
Pricing:           Contact vendor
Hardware:          MS-DOS Operating System; PC-DOS Operating System; Unix
Min. Memory:       128K
Options:           Also available for Digital Equipment Corporation
                   VAX/VMS environments.
Maintenance:       available; starting at $220
Training:          Available, contact vendor
First Installed:   April 1985
Description:       Informix-SQL combines the Informix relational database
                   system with the industry standard query language, SQL.
                   It includes a powerful set of development tools to
                   assist the programmer in developing relational
                   database applications quickly, and in customizing
                   screen and report formats.
Page Number:       MS20-300-013
```

Software Directory

Product Name:	Informix-4GL
Vendor:	Informix Software, Inc.
Address:	16011 College Blvd. Lenexa KS 66219-9943 (913) 599-7330; Fax (913) 599-7350; Telex 209542 USA
System Class:	Microcomputer
Product Category:	Database Management Systems
Function:	Database application development language.
Pricing:	Contact vendor
Hardware:	MS-DOS Operating System; PC-DOS Operating System; UNIX
Options:	Also available for Digital Equipment Corporation VAX/VMS environments.
Maintenance:	available; prices start at $275
Documentation:	included
First Installed:	February 1986
Description:	Informix-4GL is a fourth-generation language designed specifically for database applications. The product allows the database developer to build even the most sophisticated application, and to customize that application to meet the needs of any end-user. In addition, the simplicity inherent in Informix-4GL speeds the process of building and maintaining applications.
Page Number:	MS20-300-013

Category : "DATABASE MANAGEMENT SYSTEMS"

Software Directory

Product Name: dBASE IV
Vendor: Borland International Inc.
Address: 1800 Green Hills Road, P.O. Box 660001
Scotts Valley CA 95067-0001
(408) 438-5300; Fax (408) 438-0389; Telex 172373
USA
System Class: Microcomputer
Product Category: Database Management Systems
Function: Database management.
Pricing: Contact vendor
Hardware: IBM PC/XT/AT and compatibles; IBM PS/2
Min. Memory: 640K
Maintenance: 90 days free support
Documentation: included
First Installed: 1988
Description: dBASE IV is a database management package that provides improved relational capabilities and SQL compatibility. It includes a redesigned menu system called the Control Center, which provides a menuing system for creation and maintenance of records. Most features are accessible from the Control Center. The user does not have to leave the menu at any time during the creation process. The transition from record creation to data entry is accomplished with a few keystrokes. Reports and queries can be generated from the Control Center or from the dot prompt. A file skeleton displays the fields and files available. A view skeleton shows the fields that have been selected for the query. The calculated field skeleton shows any temporary variables. It supports character, numeric, floating-point, binary coded decimal, date, logical, and memo fields. Modifying a field definition and data transfer are supported. The import facility permits direct import of files in the RapidFile, dBASE II, FrameWork II, Lotus 1-2-3, and PFS:File formats. The protect command provides the system administrator with three types of security control. Login security and user passwords can be assigned. The relational capabilities allow a user to define multiple relations per file, and to link multiple files. The menu-driven applications generator allows the user to build and save modifiable and executable dBASE programs without actually writing the code. It does not support EMS or expanded memory.
Page Number: MS20-300-009

Category : "DATABASE MANAGEMENT SYSTEMS"

Software Directory

Product Name: KnowledgeMan 3.0
Vendor: Micro Data Base Systems, Inc.
Address: P.O. Box 6089
Lafayette IN 47903
(317) 447-1122; (800) 445-MDBS; Fax (317) 448-6428
USA
System Class: Microcomputer
Product Category: Database Management Systems
Function: Database management system.
Pricing: 995 and up
GSA: no
Discount: education
Lease: not available
Hardware: Digital MicroVAX; IBM PC/XT/AT and compatibles; IBM PS/2 or compatible; SUN SPARCstation Series
O/S: Digital microVMS; MS-DOS; OS/2; Sun OS; UNIX
Min. Memory: 640K
Source Language: C
Source Listing: not available
Peripherals: Hard disk
Customizing: available
Maintenance: 90 days included; contact vendor thereafter; updates available
Documentation: included
Training: contact vendor
First Installed: August 1991
Description: KnowledgeMan combines a relational database management system and a fourth-generation programming language with a set of decision support tools. Information processing tools include: a spreadsheet, business graphics, text processing, report generation, communications, a natural language interface, and more. KGL, an object-based fourth-generation programming language, and a KGL compiler are also included. Binary Large Objects (BLOBs) enable the user to store any type of information (even sounds and images) in variable-length records that can be accessed with standard SQL queries.
Page Number: MS20-300-014

Category : "DATABASE MANAGEMENT SYSTEMS"

Software Directory

Product Name: MDBS IV 4.3
Vendor: Micro Data Base Systems, Inc.
Address: P.O. Box 6089
Lafayette IN 47903
(317) 447-1122; (800) 445-MDBS; Fax (317) 448-6428
USA
System Class: Microcomputer
Product Category: Database Management Systems
Function: Database management system.
Pricing: 3900 and up
GSA: no
Discount: education
Lease: not available
Hardware: AT&T 3B2/300; Digital MicroVAX; Hewlett-Packard HP 9000; IBM PC/XT/AT and compatibles; IBM PS/2 or compatible; NCR Tower; SUN SPARCstation Series
O/S: Digital microVMS; MS-DOS; MS-Windows; OS/2; SCO Xenix; Sun OS; UNIX
Min. Memory: 512K
Source Language: Basic; C; C++; Cobol; Fortran; Object/1; Pascal; SmallTalk; Visual Basic
Source Listing: available
Customizing: available
Maintenance: contact vendor thereafter; first year included; updates available
Documentation: included
Training: contact vendor
Description: The MDBS IV database management system is for applications involving complex data relationships and massive amounts of data. The client/server technology supports a wide variety of networking environments. This system provides the flexibility to directly represent numerous data relationships while providing access to databases as large as 4 gigabytes. Features include: transaction processing, fault tolerance, abortable transactions, and transaction logging capabilities.
Page Number: MS20-300-015

Software Directory

Product Name:	Paradox 4.0
Vendor:	Borland International Inc.
Address:	1800 Green Hills Road, P.O. Box 660001 Scotts Valley CA 95067-0001 (408) 438-5300; Fax (408) 438-0389; Telex 172373 USA
System Class:	Microcomputer
Product Category:	Computer Training
Function:	Database management.
Pricing:	795 -S.R.P.
GSA:	yes
Lease:	not available
Hardware:	IBM PC/XT/AT and compatibles; IBM PS/2 or compatible
O/S:	MS-DOS 1.2 or higher
Min. Memory:	1M
Source Language:	Turbo C and assembly
Source Listing:	not available
Network Support:	IBM PC - NET; StarLAN; Ungerman Bass
Options:	Mainframe or Midrange Version have several SQL Links available. Additional Maintenance Details have several Tech. Support options available free and Subcribed.
Customizing:	available
Maintenance:	90 days included
Documentation:	included
Training:	contact vendor
Description:	Paradox is a user-friendly database management product. It supports full multiuser capability whether installed on 286 or higher PC's or the network file server.
Page Number:	MS22-300-016

Category : "DATABASE MANAGEMENT SYSTEMS"

Software Directory

Product Name: FoxPRO 2.02
Vendor: Fox Software, Inc.
Address: 134 W. South Boundary
Perrysburg OH 43551
(419) 874-0162; Fax (419) 874-8678
USA
System Class: Microcomputer
Product Category: Database Management Systems
Function: Relational database management.
Pricing: $1,095 - multiuser; $795 - single user
Hardware: IBM PC/XT/AT and compatibles
O/S: MS-DOS
Min. Memory: 512K
Source Language: Watcom C; source code not available
Network Support: 3 Com 3+; ARCnet; Ethernet; IBM PC-NET; Novell; StarLAN; Token-Ring
Peripherals: 8086/8088 or 80286/80386 microprocessor required; Hard disk; mouse and expanded memory are optional
Maintenance: hot line
Documentation: included
Training: Contact vendor
First Installed: November 1989
Description: FoxPRO 2.0 is a DBMS that provides a user-friendly Graphic User Interface on a character-based DOS PC. Current dBASE applications run without change and custom applications are made easy with screen and menu builders that automatically generate their own code. The Relational Query-by-Example allows the immediate use of SQL in any application. Features include: memory management, compound indexes, automatic project management and open architecture for C and Assembly programming. A Local Area Network version is available.
Page Number: MS20-300-011

Product : Model 204

Software Directory

Product Name: Model 204
Vendor: Computer Corp. of America
Address: 4 Cambridge Center
Cambridge MA 02142
(617) 492-8860; Fax (617) 497-1072; Telex 7103206479
USA
System Class: Mid-Range/Mainframe
Product Category: Data Base Management Systems
Function: Data base management.
Pricing: 40000 - $300,000--purchase
Hardware: IBM System/370 architecture
O/S: MVS/ESA; MVS/XA; VM/ESA; VM/SP
Min. Memory: 670K
Source Language: Assembler
Source Listing: no
Documentation: included
Training: Additional training available
Current Users: 400+
First Installed: November 1969
Timesharing: no
Description: Model 204 is a data base management system that provides data manipulation and independence. It provides extensions to the relational model that allow the application developer flexibility in data base design. The Model 204 fourth-generation language, User Language, is a powerful developer and end-user application development tool used for query reporting and data base updates. The host language SQL interface allows access to Model 504 data from embedded SQL in COBOL, CICS/COBOL, and a C call level interface. It is a true multithread system that supports thousands of users. Comprehensive data administration facilities include a data dictionary, nine levels of security, an audit trail, an on-line monitoring system, and complete restart/recovery utilities to ensure data base integrity. The system is highly modular, enabling users to select the most appropriate configurations to meet their needs.
Page Number: D30-100-004

FAST-COUNT™ DBMS
David Shepard Associates, Inc.
and
MegaPlex Software, Inc.

OVERVIEW

What is Fast-Count DBMS?

Fast-Count™ DBMS is a very high-speed database management system that has been especially designed to support:

- Executive information systems.
- Decision support systems.
- Back-end data processing applications that involve data merging, matching, sorting, and other bulk data operations.

It offers state-of-the-art software technology on Unix platforms to build:

- Analysis and reporting applications.
- Batch data processing -- including data update, extraction, and transformation.

Benefits of Using Fast-Count DBMS

Potential benefits of using Fast-Count DBMS are:

- **Productivity Improvements:** Very high processing speeds boost productivity for decision makers and analysts alike.
- **Ease of Data Access:** Its point-and-click interface allows decision makers to easily access all the data.
- **Unlimited Variety of Data Exploration:** Unlike systems with precomputed results, all data is accessible for processing at all times. No restrictions, period!
- **Cost Savings:** Due to high processing speeds and data compression, Fast-Count DBMS can perform the same tasks on smaller, less-expensive computers.

Fast-Count is a trademark of MegaPlex Software, Inc. *Unix* is a trademark of AT&T.

POSSIBLE USES

Fast-Count DBMS can be used to efficiently perform the following tasks:

- Perform *ad-hoc* count queries using Boolean conditions of any complexity.
- Create *ad-hoc* reports consisting of one-, two-, and three-dimensional profiles of customers selected by a previous query.
- Create multi-column, customized reports involving elementary statistical operations.
- Reports can be exported to a variety of PC programs, including spreadsheets, graphics packages, word processors, and databases; for example, Lotus 123, Improv, Excel, Quattro, Harvard Graphics, Freelance, Word, Word Perfect, Paradox, and DBase.
- Segment Customer and Prospects Files using *ad-hoc* or custom procedures.
- Allocate marketing codes to segments.
- Incorporate response analysis data in the decision support databases.
- Perform elementary statistical analysis on groups of products, customers, prospects, and households.
- Extract selected samples from the decision support database to be exported for modelling purposes, and format them for the statistical analysis systems such as SAS, S, SYSTAT, Sigma-Stat, Knowledge-Seeker, and others.
- Implement a variety of scoring equations, which are created by statistical modelling.
- Export selected data to an operations system for incorporation in the fulfillment stream. This data is sorted and pre-formatted so that it can be imported into the operations system with minimal additional processing.
- Process operations data to create the decision support data through a combination of data extraction, linking, matching, consolidation, and summarization operations. Such processing could involve the following steps:
    a. Summarize Transactions File.
    b. Link Customers File with Transactions File.
    c. Link Prospects File with Customers File.
    d. Link Promotion History and Responses with Customers and Prospects Files.

CAPABILITIES

Speed and Compression

Fast-Count DBMS achieves its high speed, usually 100's of times faster than the Relational DBMSs, through built-in data compression and efficient algorithms. Data compression of 2 to 4 times is achieved in most practical applications.

Since it does not use any type of indexing or pre-calculated results to achieve the high speed, it can be used to perform virtually limitless types of query, reporting, and processing functions. It can process household, person, and transaction level data with equal ease. Moreover, data can be quickly updated and refreshed because loading is not slowed down by creation of indexes or calculation of pre-stored results.

Operations that would otherwise take hours to complete can be done literally in minutes by Fast-Count DBMS. This not only boosts productivity, but also greatly shrinks the hardware costs by allowing the use of less expensive computer models and fewer disks. Alternatively, much more comprehensive analysis and reporting could be performed for the same hardware cost.

Ease-Of-Use

All the speed and power of this DBMS is brought out to the end-users through a user-interface that runs under Windows 3.1 in a client-servers architecture.

The user-interface program paints the screen, accepts user's point-and-click selections, and formulates the requests that are sent to the server. The server carries out the requests and sends the results back to the user-interface program which displays them in a window.

For presentation quality output, the results obtained from the DBMS can be imported into the popular PC programs, for example, Lotus 123, Improv, Excel, and FrameMaker, running under Windows 3.1.

Data Import and Export

Fast-Count DBMS can accept customer, transactions and any other data from the mainframe or mini-based operations support systems. It can also accept practically any kind of enhancement and overlay data from other data sources.

It has comprehensive data export capabilities to support a variety of formats required by the operations support systems or PC-based analysis systems.

Support of Statistical Modelling

In addition to performing simple statistical calculations, Fast-Count DBMS can be used to draw samples for statistical modelling. The samples could be downloaded to a modelling platform, e.g., SAS, where statistical models would be built. Fast-Count DBMS could then be used to score the full database and to validate the models on the Unix host.

□ Page 3 □

SUCCESSFUL APPLICATIONS

Bench Mark Figures

In a Transactions table of 1 million rows, a relational DBMS running on Sun 4/490 took 30 minutes to count the number of customers who bought one product and not another. Fast-Count DBMS does the same task in under 5 seconds on a comparable hardware platform.

Timely Scoring of Customer Records

This application required scoring customers based upon their recent purchasing behavior using a scoring equation. All the customers had to be scored within a time interval of 2 days and results had to be uploaded to the mainframe fulfillment system for further processing. The Fast-Count DBMS was able to perform this task in under 3 hours, leaving ample time to schedule jobs on the fulfillment system. This task was not considered suitable for the mainframe due to a long expected run time and high expected cost of programming.

Attribution of Sales to Reps

This application required attributing sales dollars and number of units sold from 4 millions transactions to 10,000 reps. This task took over 10 hours on a large mainframe. It could be done in under 5 minutes on a desk-top Sun computer.

Assignment of Geo-Demographic Codes

This application required assigning geo-demographic codes to customers in a Customers table of 3 million rows. Some customers had 5 digit zip code while the others had 9 digit zip codes, and the cluster codes table has 16 million rows. This task was programmed in approximately 1 hour and took under 1 hour on a high-end IBM RS-6000 computer to run. It could have been done on the mainframe, but would have taken so long that it could not be allocated a processing window and would have required a couple of days of programming time.

A Report-Intensive Application

This application required reporting the number of current and dormant customers, number of units sold, and revenue for each product, for groups of products, and for all products. These reports also compare year-to-date figures of last and this year and percentage changes from last to this year.

This set of over 50 reports is done on a low-end Sun computer in under 4 hours by using the Fast-Count DBMS in batch mode. Before the introduction of Fast-Count DBMS, about 200 of these reports were done on an AS-400 in more than 8 days.

* * *

□ Page 4 □

FAST-COUNT™ DBMS
David Shepard Associates, Inc.
and
MegaPlex Software, Inc.

TECHNICAL DESCRIPTION

Ease-Of-Programming

Fast-Count DBMS is programmed in Fast-Count Language (FCL), a 4GL which is specially designed to support analysis, reporting, and batch applications. Its English-like syntax makes it easy to learn and use and thereby enhances programmer productivity and reduces application development costs.

FCL's capabilities include:

- A complete set of data definition, access, and manipulation facilities, including arbitrarily complex arithmetic expressions and logical conditions, creation of temporary, user-defined fields, and ability to handle transactions-level data.
- Comprehensive report generation facilities to generate a wide variety of reports, including built-in support for one-, two-, and three-dimensional profiles and crosstabs.
- Programming facilities that are suitable to build large, multi-module applications as well as small, *ad-hoc* applications.

By including the above capabilities in one systems, FCL provides one seemless environment to build complete applications -- large or small. This makes the design, creation, and maintenance of application easier and less costly than using multiple programming environments (which is the case in several popular DBMSs).

Flexible Data Storage

- Fast-Count DBMS can store a large number of tables with hundreds of fields each, limited by the available disk space.
- Data tables can be *linked* in a one-to-one, one-to-many, or many-to-many fashion.
- Records can have repeating fields. For example, in a database of households, children's names and ages would be repeating fields -- one household may have only 1 name and age, while another may have 2 or 3.
- Fields can be of the following types: *alpha*, *label*, *unsigned*, *signed*, *float*, and *date*.
- Several *data-systems* can be setup, each with its own tables.

  This facility can be used to keep multiple versions of the decision-support data wherein the current download can be processed to create the *new* version while the end-users continue using the *current* version. After a successful processing run, the *new* data would be made *current.*

- Several simultaneous users can access shared data for reading and their own private data for reading and writing.
- Data is stored in the standard Unix file systems -- the use of raw disk partitions is not required.

Speed

Fast-Count DBMS can perform most *ad-hoc* queries 100's of times faster than the conventional relational DBMSs.

For example, it would *count* the number of records that satisfy a single condition in a table at the rate of 1 million records per second for a one-field query on a computer equivalent to the IBM RS-6000 Model 950. This speed is independent of the number of fields in the table.

The *join* operation on sorted tables takes approximately twice as long as the above-described *count* operation, and *sort* proceeds at the rate of 1 million records per minute.

Data Analysis

Data analysis capabilities include, but are not limited to, the following:

- Identify records that satisfy any arbitrary Boolean expression. The Boolean expression could contain constants and fields both.
- Aggregation operations: sum, average, minimum, and maximum of a field over a selected set of records.
- Determine the distribution of records over a 1, 2, or 3 dimensional grid of fields. For example, number of customers by state by income range.
- Determine the distribution of aggregates (sum, average, minimum, and maximum) of a field over a 1, 2, or 3 dimensional grid of fields. For example, average age by state by income range.
- *Ad-hoc* RFM analyses.
- Draw contiguous batches or uniformly spaced samples of records.
- Calculate break-points in the distributions of records, e.g., deciles and quartiles.

Data Transformation

Data transformation capabilities include, but are not limited to, the following:

- Create number, date, and alpha fields using arbitrarily nested expressions involving other fields and constants.

- Create fields using conditional assignment of values drawn from other fields.
- Create and delete temporary tables and fields.
- Create label fields, that is, those with categorical values, such as income range.
- Convert fields from one type to another; for example, from *unsigned* to *alpha*.
- Sort a field in the order of another field.
- Remove duplicates in a field.
- Combine data from multiple tables using *join* and *group-join* operations. The latter can perform group counts, sums, averages, minimums, and maximums.
- Match data using a combination of *join* and *sort* operations.

Report Generation

- Reports are 2-dimensional grid of cells of sizes that are limited only by the available disk space. Report-related commands can be used to navigate in the grid and paste information in it.
- Cell values can be left aligned, right aligned, or centered.
- Distributions (of one, two, or three dimensions) can be pasted on the grid using crosstabs. For example, in a distribution of customers by state by income level, the state names would be placed along the rows on the left and income levels would be placed along the columns at the top.
- Row and column sums can be calculated from the distributions and placed on the report.
- Existing reports, fields from tables, and Unix files can also be pasted to make complex reports.
- Reports can be output in the ASCII form suitable for printing directly or in the quoted form suitable for importing into other programs such as Lotus 123.

Data Import and Export

Fast-Count DBMS accepts ASCII data in a variety of data formats including fixed or variable length records, with or without record terminator, with or with out repeating fields, etc. It also accepts binary data compatible with the Unix host.

It can export data in a variety of ASCII formats, including the database formats listed above and quoted and comma delimited formats.

In addition to ASCII data, Fast-Count DBMS can also import and export binary data compatible with the Unix host. This facility can be used to pass the required data to specialized processing algorithms outside the database and to import the results back into the database.

Programming Constructs

FCL provides the following programming constructs, which can be combined with other FCL commands to build complete applications or custom operations that can be invoked from the graphical user-interface.

- String macros.
- Global and local variables.
- If-then-else construct.
- While-do construct.
- Internal and external procedures, which are called in a stack-based execution environment.
- Access Shell variables.
- Invoke standard Unix utilities or other special-purpose programs.

* * *

□ Page 4 □

Index

E

F

G

H

I

J

K

L